TO THE STUDENT: A Study Guide for this textbook is available through your college bookstore under the title *Study Guide for Management Accounting* by Donna Ulmer. The *Study Guide* can help you with course material by acting as a tutorial, review, and study aid. If the *Study Guide* is not in stock, ask the bookstore manager to order a copy for you.

Management Accounting
Planning and Control

Harry I. Wolk
Drake University

Quentin N. Gerber
Drake University

Gary A. Porter
Loyola University of Chicago

PWS-Kent Publishing Company
Boston, Massachusetts

PWS-KENT
Publishing Company

Publisher—Accounting: John B. McHugh
Production Editor: Pamela Rockwell
Designer: Catherine Dorin
Cover Design: Lindgren Design Associates, Inc.
Production Coordinator: Marcia Locke

PWS-Kent Publishing Company is a division of Wadsworth, Inc.

Printed in the United States of America
1 2 3 4 5 6 7 8 9—92 91 90 89 88

Library of Congress Cataloging-in-Publication Data

Wolk, Harry I.
  Management accounting.

  Includes index.

  1. Managerial accounting.   I. Gerber, Quentin N., 1930–
II. Porter, Gary A., 1950–   III. Title
HF5657.4.W64   1988   658.1′511   87-7348
ISBN 0-534-050-7

Management Accounting
Planning and Control

Harry I. Wolk
Drake University

Quentin N. Gerber
Drake University

Gary A. Porter
Loyola University of Chicago

PWS-Kent Publishing Company

Boston, Massachusetts

PWS-KENT
Publishing Company

Publisher—Accounting: John B. McHugh
Production Editor: Pamela Rockwell
Designer: Catherine Dorin
Cover Design: Lindgren Design Associates, Inc.
Production Coordinator: Marcia Locke

PWS-Kent Publishing Company is a division of Wadsworth, Inc.

Printed in the United States of America
1 2 3 4 5 6 7 8 9—92 91 90 89 88

Library of Congress Cataloging-in-Publication Data

Wolk, Harry I.
    Management accounting.

    Includes index.

    1. Managerial accounting.   I. Gerber, Quentin N., 1930–
II. Porter, Gary A., 1950–   III. Title
HF5657.4.W64   1988   658.1'511   87-7348
ISBN 0-534-050-7

Contents

CHAPTER 6

Cost Accumulation and Allocation   161

CHAPTER 7

Job Order Costing   198

CHAPTER 13

Capital Budgeting   462

CHAPTER 14

Advanced Topics in Capital Budgeting   506

CHAPTER 15   Controlling Decentralized Operations   539

CHAPTER 16   Transfer Pricing in Decentralized Operations   584

CHAPTER 17   Quantitative Techniques for Decision Making   617

CHAPTER 18 Funds Flow Statements: Cash and Working Capital   650

CHAPTER 19 Financial Statement Analysis   692

Index   743

Preface

While there are many management accounting books that are on the market, it is our belief that a particular niche has not as yet been filled. Our specific objectives in writing this book have been threefold:

1. To present the role of management accounting in the organization and the relatively complex and sophisticated concepts of management accounting in an understandable and down-to-earth manner with numerous illustrations;

2. To have an excellent group of questions, exercises, and problems, including the most varied and challenging selection of problems on the market from CMA and CPA examinations;

3. To present the elements of cost accounting, which form an important part of the underlying structure of management accounting, in a manner that will allow this subject matter to be appropriately integrated with the material of management accounting proper.

In terms of the third objective, the cost accounting chapters appear fairly early in the text (Chapters 6–10). We realize, of course, that many instructors will prefer to cover this material later in the course. Therefore, several alternative chapter sequences are suggested in the Instructor's Manual.

Teaching Aids

The Instructor's Manual also contains important information relative to the ancillaries accompanying this text. Included among the ancillary materials are templates utilizing Lotus 1-2-3 (series 3.0) spreadsheets that can be used for solving problems in many chapters throughout the book. These problems are designated in the text with the following symbol:

Other ancillaries accompanying this book, in addition to the Instructor's Manual and the template for solving problems with Lotus 1-2-3, are:

Solutions Manual

Student Study Guide

Test Bank

Transparencies for all exercises and problems as well as selected key exhibits in the text

Check Figures

The User

There are two primary audiences for whom this book is intended. The first group is comprised primarily of sophomores in undergraduate programs in business administration and economics. The business administration students consist of both nonaccounting majors and accounting majors, although the former generally predominate in terms of sheer numbers. Typically, these students take a course in management accounting in the second semester of the sophomore year after a three-hour course in financial accounting. The second group consists of students in "generalist" types of MBA programs. One MBA approach often consists of a single required accounting course. The prerequisite is often six hours of accounting with the bulk of that generally being financial accounting. A second variation in MBA programs is a two-sequence accounting requirement with the second course being one devoted to management accounting. There is certainly much diversity within each of these two groups, not to mention differences between them. Nevertheless, we believe that both of these audiences of primarily nonaccounting majors can be well served by this book. The text itself has been made extremely flexible by the use of several appendixes containing more advanced material that can be included or excluded at the instructor's behest based upon student needs and abilities. Suffice it to say that whether sophomore or MBA, the student should gain a very significant understanding and appreciation of the importance of management accounting and its role and place in the organization of the enterprise.

Acknowledgments

We have found that many debts are accumulated along the way to completing an enterprise of this sort. Our reviewers provided many excellent insights and useful suggestions for both the book and the ancillaries. The reviewers and their present affiliations included Jack Bailes, Oregon State University; Jim Brown, University of Nebraska-Lincoln; Frank Daroca, Loyola Marymount University; Laverne Gebhard, University of Wisconsin-Milwaukee; Bob Koehler, The Pennsylvania State University; Linda Marquis, Northern Kentucky University; Diane Pattison, University of San Diego; Lynn Rans, California State University of Los Angeles; William Ryan, California State Polytechnic University at Pomona; and Jack Truitt, Washington State University. Special thanks go to Donna Ulmer of Southern Illinois University-Edwardsville for her work on the student study guide and Mick Watterson of Drake University for developing the templates.

We would also like to thank the many individuals at PWS-Kent Publishing Company for their work in helping to bring this project to its fruition, in particular Jack McHugh, Pam Rockwell, and Marcia Cole. We found them to be very knowledgeable professionals as well as fun to work with.

Our typists, Sue Hart and Ginger Wheeler deserve a very special commendation. They did an outstanding job of turning our often illegible pages into finished manuscript form. In addition, they showed a suprising mastery of high-tech accoutrements such as word processing programs and laser printers, which are absolutely indispensible to book writing in the age of the computer.

We would also like to thank the American Institute of Certified Public Accountants for its generosity in allowing us to use questions and problems from the CPA examinations. Permission has also been received from the Institute of Certified Management Accountants of the National Association of Accountants to use questions from past CMA examinations. In addition, special thanks go to The Quaker Oats Company and Meredith Corporation. Quaker Oats kindly allowed us to use their annual report, and Meredith provided us with several of their organization charts.

Finally, we dedicate this book to our wives: Barbara, Muriel, and Melissa. Without their patience and encouragement this project would have been more difficult to complete.

Kent Series in Accounting

CHAPTER 1

An Introduction to Management Accounting

Learning Objectives

After reading this chapter you should be able to:

1. Understand what management accounting involves.

2. Know how management accounting differs from financial accounting.

3. Understand the relationship between management accounting and cost accounting.

4. Understand what the planning process is.

5. Comprehend the types of decisions that comprise short-run planning.

6. Be aware of long-run planning issues.

7. Understand what control is and how it ties together with the planning function.

Organizations need information to make decisions. One very important source of information for management is its accounting system. The information provided to management from its accounting system, as well as additional related analyses, forms the subject matter of management accounting.

It is probably obvious that information is needed by management in order to facilitate decision making. Without appropriate information, we cannot expect correct decisions to be made. Decision making is actually part of the broader managerial function of planning. Management accounting also facilitates the function of control (comparing actual results against plan). Both of these functions and how they relate to management accounting will be discussed shortly.

In order to put management accounting into perspective, let us first see — in very simple terms — how an accounting system works. A simple portrayal of an accounting system is shown in Exhibit 1–1.

To summarize Exhibit 1–1, we can say that an accounting system captures data, represented by the transactions of a firm, and converts the raw data into useful types of information. Among the useful reports prepared by the firm's accounting system are the three types of financial statements that you are familiar with: the balance sheet (also called the statement of financial position), the income statement, and the statement of changes in financial position (formerly called the funds flow statement). However, not all the information coming from the enterprise's accounting system falls under the scope of managerial accounting. Much of it goes to users outside the particular entity.

Financial Accounting and Management Accounting

Financial accounting is concerned with information provided by a firm's accounting system for users external to the firm. Some examples of financial accounting information include the following:

Financial statements to prospective lenders such as banks or other financial institutions;

Tax returns provided to the Internal Revenue Service (IRS) or state taxation agencies;

Filings with the Securities and Exchange Commission (SEC), a regulatory agency of the United States government, for firms whose securities are traded on stock exchanges such as the New York Stock Exchange or the American Stock Exchange;

Annual reports for stockholders of enterprises whose securities are publicly owned: registered for trading (buying and selling) on security exchanges.

EXHIBIT 1–1

The Accounting System

Transactions →	Recorded in books →	Information processed →	Information arranged in the form of meaningful output →	Financial statements go to management, owners, and other interested parties
	(Raw data inputs enter the accounting system)	(Transferred to appropriate accounts in ledger from journals)	(Financial statements are the end product)	(Evaluate the firm's position and its operations)

All the above examples of financial accounting uses require extensive information provided by the firm's accounting system, much of it in the form of the three financial statements and additional related analyses. There is one extremely important difference between financial accounting information, such as the types listed above, and management accounting information. Financial accounting information must be prepared in accordance with prescribed rules, whereas in the case of management accounting, the enterprise is free to prepare whatever information it desires in accordance with whatever methods it finds to be beneficial.

In the case of financial accounting, there are several regulatory authorities. The Tax Code of the United States government provides the precise rules under which tax returns must be prepared. The SEC provides the rules under which SEC filings must be made. That agency was also empowered by the Securities and Exchange Act of 1934 to set the rules under which the financial statements for stockholders must be prepared. In the latter case, the SEC has shared its rule-making authority with an organization in the private sector called the Financial Accounting Standards Board (FASB).

In all these cases, it is quite clear why financial accounting is regulated. The public interest requires that financial information must be disclosed and prepared by a similar set of rules to enable the financial statements of different firms to be comparable with each other. Similarly, in the case of the Tax Code and its collection and enforcement agency, the IRS, the tax laws should be as fair and equitable as possible.

The relationship between the enterprise and outside parties is not present in management accounting as it is in financial accounting. Nevertheless, business enterprises have similar needs in terms of managerial accounting information. To understand why there is a significant harmony of management accounting needs by firms, we must return again to the common enterprise functions of planning and control.

Management accounting, which is concerned with providing management with information and analysis to facilitate planning and control, is a relatively new academic subject. Many of the concepts presented in management accounting come from related disciplines such as managerial economics, managerial finance, and statistics (decision theory). However, management accounting is very closely related to (and actually stemmed from) the important branch of accounting known as cost accounting. **Cost accounting** is that branch of accounting that is concerned with valuing inventories and measuring cost of goods sold in manufacturing situations and determining the cost of various functions within an enterprise. Much of the subject matter of managerial accounting was originally developed within cost accounting. Later it was recognized that management accounting was a separate, though closely related, area.

Several cost accounting topics likewise form an important underpinning of management accounting. Included here are the elements of the three components of manufacturing cost: direct materials, direct labor, and manufacturing overhead (discussed in depth in Chapter 6 but introduced in Chapter 2). In addition, costing in the two generalized types of cost accounting systems—job order costing and process costing—is discussed in Chapters 7 and 8. Standard costs, covered in Chapters 9 and 10, are also an important cornerstone of cost accounting as well as a vital aspect of control. The remaining chapters in the book deal more explicitly with the management accounting emphasis of management's need for information and analysis pertaining to planning and control.

Management Accounting and the Planning and Control Functions

Planning is a *process* involving members of management. The process of **planning** consists of the following general steps:

1. Defining the problems faced by management,
2. Identifying the alternatives,
3. Gathering information relative to the alternatives, and
4. Making decisions.

In order to come to grips with the planning process, it is first necessary to divide it into two categories: short run and long-run planning. A somewhat arbitrary but widely used guide is that the **short run** involves a year or less and the **long run** is concerned with periods beyond a year. The key difference between the short run and the long run is that the firm has much less flexibility in the short run. For periods of less than a year, the enterprise cannot easily change its products or its markets. Thus, in short-run planning fewer options are open to management. Let us examine the short run more closely.

Short-Run Planning

The types of decisions that can be made in the short run generally fall into the following categories:

1. Pricing of products,
2. Marketing efforts,
3. Production decisions,
4. Production processes,
5. Special production and marketing decisions, and
6. Changing personnel.

Pricing of Products

A basic tenet of pricing is that prices must cover all costs plus a fair return on investment. The (management) accountant should be the individual charged with determining costs.

Pricing of product lines is usually reviewed annually in accordance with the budgetary process. Further changes are often made during the year as needed in response to unforeseen economic events or to fine tune the original decision. Pricing policies are basically the result of marketing decisions and are briefly touched on in Chapter 12.

Marketing Efforts

Short-run marketing decisions involve determining amounts of money to commit to advertising and other functions as well as allocating the total pie among the firm's product lines. Marketing issues are addressed in Chapter 4.

Production decisions involve the quantities of the various products to be manufactured and the timing of that production. The question of how much of the various products to produce stems directly from the marketing policies concerning pricing, advertising expenditures, and other marketing efforts. The timing of production concerns the question of whether production should be done evenly throughout the year or (where applicable) seasonally in anticipation of sales. Production decisions and timing decisions are discussed in Chapters 9 and 12.

Production Processes

Production processes are the technology of converting inputs into outputs: the combination of labor, materials, and capital (machinery, equipment, and buildings) that are used to produce enterprise goods and services. Very frequently, the question involved here is whether new machinery and equipment should be acquired to either increase output or replace obsolete technology. These questions have important long-run ramifications but often can be implemented fairly quickly in a short-run time setting. Decisions of this type are called capital budgeting decisions and are extensively examined in Chapters 13 and 14.

Special Production and Marketing Decisions

There are many production and marketing decisions of a nonroutine nature that frequently occur for most firms. For example, a potential customer may want a special order of a product that the enterprise could produce. The buyer may thus desire a price quote. Numerous special marketing and production decisions are discussed in Chapter 12.

Changing Personnel

This area involves issues such as hiring and replacing individuals. It therefore falls mainly in the area of personnel management. Management accounting information and reports, however, often provide useful insights into making these decisions. Most of the chapters in this book discuss management accounting information, analyses, and reports that can influence personnel decisions.

Short-Run Planning and the Budgetary Process

Of the six areas of short-run planning discussed above, the first four (pricing of products, marketing efforts, production decisions, and production processes) are formally brought into focus by means of the annual budgetary process. The budgetary process, discussed in Chapter 5, is therefore an extremely important managerial tool. The special decisions involving production and marketing are by their nature outside the regular and recurring budgetary process. The involvement of management accounting with personnel decisions mainly involves reports stemming from the control function. As such, it shows the linkage between planning and control, a subject that will be discussed later in this chapter.

Long-Run Planning

In the long run, more alternatives are open to management because it has time to make the various adjustments that are deemed necessary to carry out its policies. Some of the issues that are therefore considered in long-term planning include the following:

1. Assessing new products and markets to which the enterprise should adapt, and
2. Assessing new physical capital acquisitions such as buildings, machinery, and equipment.

Assessing New Products and New Markets

The evaluation of new products and markets should be the responsibility of the top level of management. Because the highest order of policy issues comes under the scope of this long-run planning function, it is necessary for management to closely monitor political, social, economic, and technological conditions.

For example, a baby food manufacturer could have foreseen the decline in the birth rate that occurred in the mid-1960s due to, among other things, changing lifestyles and other social factors. These changing social factors, however, have led to new demands in the food area, such as fast foods, gourmet foods, and other special food markets that baby food producers could have been monitoring and possibly entering.

This planning function may lead to diversification out of the firm's present industry. Thus, cigarette manufacturers have acquired firms that produce totally different products because of the health issue surrounding tobacco.

Assessing new products and markets is beyond the scope of this book. Generally, however, this type of planning is done by a higher level of management than is short-run planning, and top management therefore should coordinate between the two levels of planning.

Assessing New Physical Capital Acquisitions

If a firm is going into new product lines, new capital acquisitions will be handled in accordance with these needs. New capital acquisitions, such as factories and buildings, require extensive planning. Often they cannot be in place and ready to operate for several years. Part of the planning for these acquisitions also entails extensive questions of financing — that is, how large amounts of additional capital should be raised.

We previously discussed how some capital acquisitions of machinery and equipment can be implemented in the short run. The planning for these projects should nevertheless take into account the long-run benefits and costs of potential capital acquisitions. The discussion of capital budgeting techniques and approaches in Chapters 13 and 14 is the only place in the text where long-run planning is examined.

Control

Control is the managerial process whereby actual results are compared against plan. If results of operations do not materialize according to plan, management wants to know why this occurred. Several possible reasons might account for the differences between plan and fact:

1. The planning process went awry with unrealistic or unattainable targets;
2. Events beyond the control of management occurred that were not foreseen in the planning process;
3. Poor performance stemmed from factors that can be changed or corrected.

The Planning Process Went Awry

Business, like many other activities, is one in which the control process is used in conjunction with planning. If a shortstop on a baseball team sets a target batting average for himself of .350 when he has never hit above .220, comparing actual results against the target goal may be meaningless. The same reasoning applies in a business situation. If top management sets goals that are unattainable or if those engaged in the planning process forecast inaccurately, then the control process will break down; correction should be made as rapidly as possible. Correction may consist of top management's ceasing to impose unattainable goals on lower levels of the firm. It also may consist of replacing personnel who are involved with the technical process of forecasting, the first step in the budgetary process.

Events Beyond the Control of Management

Very often unforeseen (and possibly unforeseeable) events may arise that cause plans to be unattainable. For example, a new firm may enter a market and cut into another enterprise's share of that market. The entry of the new firm in the market may have been a well-kept secret that was not known publicly. Another example of an uncontrollable occurrence would be a fire or other natural disaster that interferes with a firm's meeting its production schedules.

When it meets with uncontrollable elements and events, the firm should correct, as rapidly as possible, its plans. Adjustment or adaptation to the unforeseen event itself is also part of the adjustment process.

Poor Performance from Factors That Can Be Corrected

The essence of the control function is its link to planning. Without control, planning itself would become meaningless. An essential element of control is feedback. **Feedback** refers specifically to the receipt of reports comparing actual results against plan by those responsible for performance.

Control also is linked to planning because future planning is influenced by the control process. Consider an example of how control and feedback influence planning. A petroleum company finds that its sales are well below expectations. As a result, management conducts market research that reveals that consumers do not like bulky steel cans. The company introduces a new, trigger-shaped plastic container to recapture its share of the market. Thus, the original approach and product are changed when it becomes clear that the steel can needed to be modified by a new container that meets consumer needs.

Many of the reports that are part of the control process are thoroughly discussed in this text. Chapter 2 introduces basic cost and managerial accounting performance reports as well as basic terminology. This same theme is continued in Chapter 6. Standard costing is discussed in Chapters 9 and 10. This topic is concerned with developing basic benchmarks in production situations against which actual results can be compared. Chapter 11 intro-

EXHIBIT 1–2
Orientation of Chapters in This Text

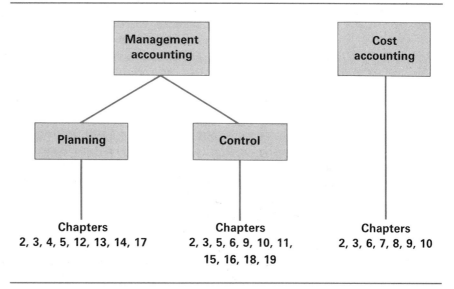

duces an important method of measuring income that eliminates some inconsistencies in the traditional income reporting model. Chapters 15 and 16 are concerned with how the performance of segments of a firm can be evaluated. Chapter 18 presents the statement of changes in financial position (funds statement). Finally, Chapter 19 discusses the many financial and operating ratios which can be derived from financial statements. Exhibit 1–2 presents a diagram of planning and control and where the chapters in this book fit into these functions.

The Role of Management Accounting in the Organization

The preparation and interpretation of both financial and management accounting reports are staff functions in virtually all firms. **Staff functions** are those activities of a firm that are advisory or service oriented in nature. The staff function can be contrasted with line activities and functions. **Line functions** are those activities of a firm concerned with carrying out its basic purposes and objectives. The chief executive officer (CEO) of a firm is its principal line officer. The various production and marketing activities are the principal line functions.

The various staff functions in the Meredith Corporation, a major publishing and communication firm, are shown in Exhibit 1–3. As shown in Exhibit 1–3, these activities are under the control of the executive vice-president of corporate services. Of particular interest is corporate planning. This group works very closely with the corporate manager of budget and financial analysis and division heads of Meredith's operating groups in publishing, broadcasting, printing, and real estate.

The vice-president of finance at Meredith is responsible for accounting, finance, and internal auditing functions. The organization of these functions at Meredith is shown in Exhibit 1–4. The internal auditor has primary responsibility for ensuring that transactions of the firm have been appropriately authorized by the responsible individual, safeguarding the firm's assets, and maintaining the accuracy of the firm's accounting records. At the corporate level, the treasurer's department is responsible for preparing tax returns and reports (and the minimization thereof) and the management of corporate cash. In this capacity the corporate cash manager is responsible for short-term investment of excess funds and making sure that lines of credit are available for any short-term borrowing needs.

Preparation and interpretation of corporate management accounting reports is carried out by the controller and his staff. The corporate manager of budgets and financial analysis is largely responsible for the preparation and interpretation of corporate planning and control activities. This individual works closely with corporate planning (as mentioned previously) and people within Meredith's operating groups who are responsible for reporting on planning and control activities.

Financial accounting activities, including payroll accounting, is another responsibility of the corporate controller. These functions are carried out under the auspices of the director of accounting.

The importance of the function of the corporate controller's staff is well appreciated by other members of top management. This reflects the importance of management accounting information relative to carrying out the planning and control functions of the enterprise.

Management Accounting and the Student

The Meredith Corporation, of course, is not unusual in terms of the importance accorded to the management accounting function. An additional point likewise requires emphasis. Although management accounting is an essential course for accounting majors, it is of virtually equal importance even for those who do not plan to be accounting majors: (1) It provides an excellent framework for understanding and participating in managerial decision making in both the public and private sectors; and (2) a basic understanding of management accounting makes it easier to communicate with persons who specialize in the discipline.

EXHIBIT 1–3

Organization of Staff Functions in the Meredith Corporation

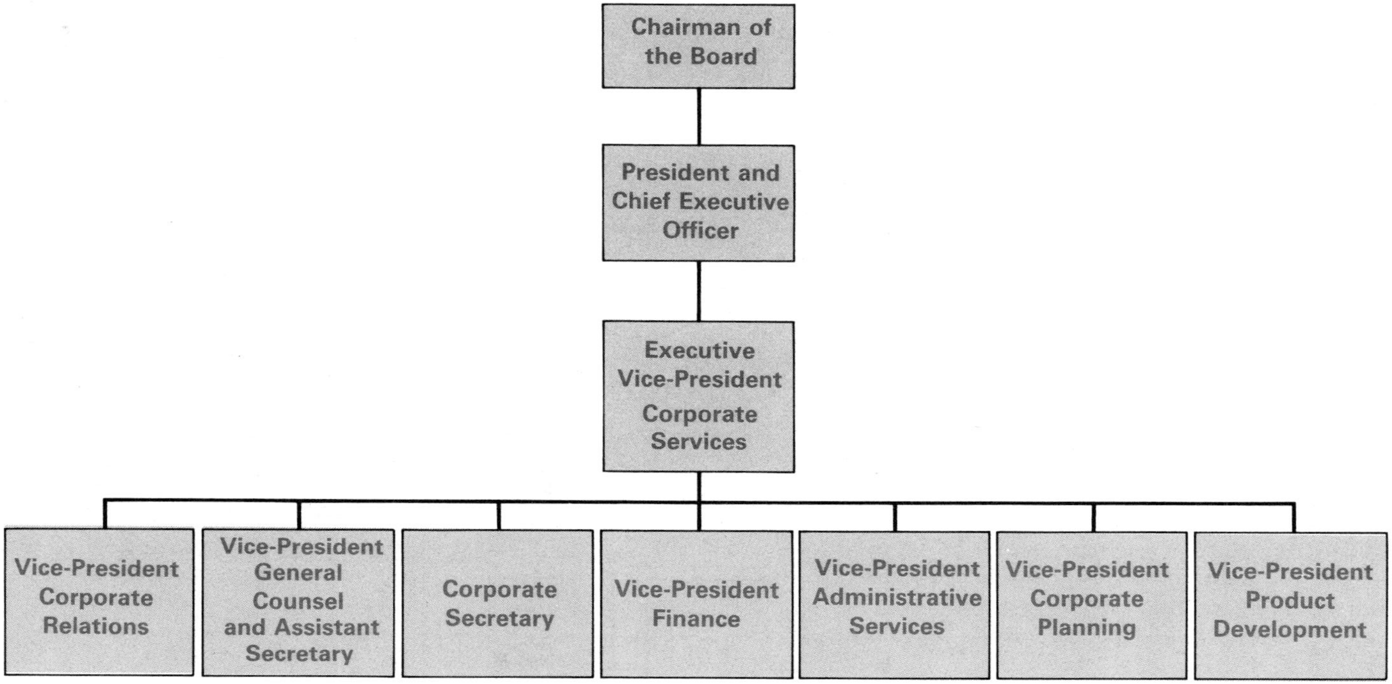

EXHIBIT 1—4
Organization of Accounting and Finance Functions at Meredith Corporation

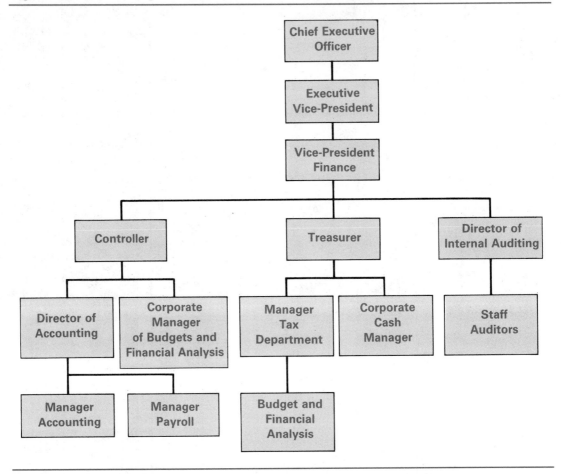

Professional Designation

Those who plan to major in accounting and may be planning careers in management accounting should note that the National Association of Accountants (NAA), an important accounting organization, sponsors a professional examination in management accounting. The examination and program are administered by the Institute of Certified Management Accountants. Those who pass the examination become Certified Management Accountants (CMA).

Although the program has been in operation for a relatively short time, the professional designation of CMA already carries a high status. The CMA program requires candidates to pass a series of uniform examinations as well as meet specific educational and professional standards to qualify for and maintain the certificate.

Summary

Management accounting is that branch of accounting that involves the presentation of information to management for planning and control purposes. Unlike financial accounting, rules for management accounting are not prescribed by regulatory agencies and organizations. Instead, management accounting is an outgrowth from cost accounting. Many of the methods and techniques used in management accounting have been adopted from managerial economics, managerial finance, and statistics.

Planning is a process that involves defining the problems that face management, identifying the alternatives, gathering information relative to the alternatives, and making decisions. Long-range planning involves factors beyond a year, and short-run planning concerns alternatives that can be acted on and implemented in less than a year. Long-run decisions involve basic questions relative to what the firm's products and markets should be in the future. Short-run planning is more constrained by the firm's given products and markets because periods of less than a year do not allow enough time to adapt to possible basic and extensive changes in the firm's products and markets. The essence of short-run planning is embodied in the process of budgeting.

Control involves comparing actual results against plan. As a result of this process, those who are responsible for carrying out the various plans of the firm receive feedback on how well they are doing. In turn, the feedback element provides an input into future planning as correction and improvement result from the feedback process.

Management accounting reports and analyses are generally prepared by the controller's department, which is generally within the financial area of the firm. The controller performs a staff function for the line management of the firm. The controller and his staff provide important information to management. As a result, the controller is considered to be an important member of enterprise management.

Key Terms

Control   is the managerial process in which actual results are compared against plan. If results of operations are significantly different from the plan, management wants to know why this occurred and should take steps to change the situation if poor performance stemmed from factors that can be corrected.

Cost accounting   is that branch of accounting that is concerned with valuing inventories and measuring cost of goods sold in manufacturing situations and determining the cost of various functions within an enterprise.

Feedback   refers to the receipt of reports comparing actual results against plan by those responsible for performance.

Financial accounting   is concerned with information provided by a firm's accounting system for users external to the firm.

Line functions are those activities of a firm concerned with carrying out its basic purposes and objectives, such as production and marketing activities.

Long run concerns decisions involving periods beyond one year.

Management accounting is concerned with providing management with information to facilitate the planning and control functions.

Planning consists of defining problems, identifying the alternatives, gathering information relative to the alternatives, and making decisions.

Short run concerns decisions involving periods of less than a year.

Staff functions are those activities of a firm that are advisory or service oriented relative to the line functions.

Questions

Q1–1   How do management accounting and financial accounting differ?

Q1–2   Why does accounting information prepared for outside users need to be regulated?

Q1–3   Why do you think that management accounting evolved from cost accounting?

Q1–4   Many individuals see decision making as being a separate function from planning. Why do you think it was included as part of the planning function in this text?

Q1–5   Give some examples of short-run planning decisions.

Q1–6   How do short-run planning decisions differ from long-run planning decisions?

Q1–7   How does management accounting information benefit short-run planning decisions?

Q1–8   Why do some physical capital acquisition decisions resemble short-run planning decisions even though they are long-run planning decisions?

Q1–9   What is control?

Q1–10   Of the three possible reasons cited for actual performance not being in accordance with plan, two might be termed noncontrollable and the third might be called controllable. Which of the three is controllable and why?

Q1–11   What is the linkage between planning and control?

Q1–12   What is feedback?

Q1–13   How do line and staff functions differ?

Q1–14   Why do both financial and management accounting activities fall under the category of staff activities?

Q1–15   Name some other examples of staff activities.

Q1–16   Give some examples of line activities.

Basic Cost and Management Accounting Concepts

Learning Objectives

After reading this chapter you should be able to:

1. Comprehend the components of manufactured inventories.

2. Understand how cost of goods manufactured and cost of goods sold in manufacturing firms are determined.

3. Be able to distinguish between the income statements of manufacturing and nonmanufacturing firms.

4. Comprehend the difference between fixed and variable costs.

5. Understand the basic planning and control concepts.

Planning and control are the basic functions underlying management accounting information systems. A proper understanding of management accounting requires a grasp of the conceptual elements underlying the discipline. In this chapter we examine three fundamental areas: basic cost components, cost behavior, and planning and control concepts.

The basic cost components are the building blocks of cost and management accounting information systems because they are the elements that comprise these systems. After these concepts are introduced, they will be examined in an important management accounting context: the income statement of the manufacturing enterprise. Income statements of manufacturing firms will be contrasted with those of a simpler form: retailing and wholesaling types of operations.

The next major topic is how costs behave. Cost behavior pertains to how costs change either over time or in relation to factors such as production or sales. The question of how costs are expected to behave pervades virtually every aspect of management accounting.

Once the basic cost concepts and how costs behave are introduced, some fundamental cost terminology of planning and control is then examined. An understanding of these terms is essential for all managers.

Basic Cost Components

Basic cost components refer to the cost of product to the firm. In service types of establishments there is no tangible product sold by the enterprise. In retailing and wholesaling companies merchandise inventory is acquired and sold to other customers who are further down the distribution chain. Merchandise accounting in these situations is relatively simple. Acquisitions of inventory, including transportation-in costs, are charged to either a merchandise inventory or a purchases account. As inventories are used up, cost flows are measured by accepted inventory costing methods such as first-in-first-out (FIFO), last-in-first-out (LIFO), or weighted average in order to determine the ending inventory and cost of goods sold for the period.

The situation is more complex in manufacturing enterprises. Raw materials and component parts are transformed into new products by means of applying labor in conjunction with sophisticated industrial technology in the form of buildings, machinery, and equipment. These costs of manufactured inventories are classified as direct materials, direct labor, and manufacturing overhead.

Manufactured Inventories

Let us examine each of the three components of inventories in manufacturing firms.

Direct Materials

Direct materials are those material inputs that become a measurable part of the manufactured product. Some examples are fabric and wood or steel in furniture, paper in printing firms, and cloth for clothing manufacturers. In complex firms such as automobile makers, hundreds of items fall under the category of direct materials. An automobile battery would qualify as a direct material for the automobile company but from the viewpoint of the battery manufacturer it would be a product containing its own direct materials, direct labor, and manufacturing overhead.

Several other points relative to direct materials are worth noting. Records are kept relatively easily on either a manual or computerized basis for the quantity of direct materials (and also direct labor) going into production. Direct material costs of production are determined by the usual inventory costing methods mentioned previously. Direct material inventory accounting can be viewed as a subset of production cost accounting. Direct materials that are minerals such as coal, sulphur, or iron ore are frequently called **raw materials.** Finally, it should be noted that materials that go directly into product but are relatively insignificant are classified as manufacturing overhead. Some examples are glue, nails, and tacks used in the furniture industry.

Direct Labor

Direct labor consists of the major work effort going into a product that helps to transform it from direct materials into final output. Examples of direct labor include assemblyline workers in smokestack industries such as automobile production, riveters and welders in metal fabricating industries, assemblers of high-tech products such as personal computers, linotype operators in printing plants, and violin makers. Direct labor covers a wide range of possibilities from situations requiring a minimum of skills to those requiring a high amount of craftsmanship (as in the case of violin making).

Several other points also should be made about direct labor. The relative amount of direct labor in our economy is decreasing as a result of two factors. The first is the continued increase of automation of manufacturing, which has resulted in the use of more capital (machinery and equipment) and less direct labor. Direct labor is thus becoming more involved with operating and controlling equipment rather than immediately transforming direct materials by means of manually operated tools. Direct materials and direct labor together are known as **prime costs.**

The second factor is the rise of service industries. Much labor in service industries performs a function that is analogous to that occurring in manufacturing industries: contributing to the final product (service) that the firm markets. An example would be a travel agent who plans and books trips for clients. Unfortunately it is sometimes difficult to determine the direct labor function in many service industries. One of the emerging managerial problems in the service industry sector, therefore, is a need for precise identification of direct labor relative to performance of the enterprise's service.

Direct labor cannot be separately inventoried as can direct materials. However, direct labor is a component of product inventory costs in manufacturing firms. Inventories of goods that are in an incomplete state are called either **work-in-process** or **goods-in-process.** Product that is complete is called **finished goods.** Finally, labor that is only indirectly involved with the transformation of raw materials to finished output is designated as part of manufacturing overhead, our next topic.

Although direct materials and direct labor are conceptually precise and well defined, manufacturing overhead is a much broader concept. **Manufacturing overhead** consists of all other costs that are defined as part of the manufacturing process although they usually cannot be specifically identified with particular units of output. In complex industries, manufacturing overhead may consist of literally hundreds of items. A representative listing is shown in Exhibit 2–1.

Depreciation of factory buildings and machinery and equipment are the capital costs of production. **Indirect materials** are relatively minor and difficult to trace directly to product. Supplies include lubricants, oil, and greases that are used by personnel in production departments (departments in which manufacturing operations occur) for the purpose of keeping machinery and equipment in running order. **Indirect labor** includes salaries and wages of personnel in production departments who are not directly engaged in manufacturing operations. An example would be janitorial wages in production departments. Occasionally some production is defective and requires additional work comprising direct materials, direct labor, and manufacturing overhead to make the product acceptable. This situation comes under the category of spoilage and rework costs. Overtime premium arises when the labor rate exceeds the regular rate due to overtime. If the overtime premium is not attributable to any particular order but arises due to general production scheduling problems, the overtime premium portion of direct labor costs is classified as manufacturing overhead. **Service departments** perform func-

EXHIBIT 2–1

Examples of Manufacturing Overhead

> Depreciation of factory buildings
> Depreciation of machinery and equipment
> Indirect materials and supplies
> Indirect labor
> Spoilage and rework costs
> Overtime premium
> Service department costs
> Insurance on factory buildings and machinery and equipment
> Property taxes on factory buildings and machinery and equipment

tions that are auxiliary to the manufacturing process. Some examples would be production planning and control, materials storage and control, and equipment maintenance and repair. These are some of the more common examples of manufacturing overhead.

The most important thing to note about manufacturing overhead is the fact that unlike direct materials and direct labor, it is not easily traceable to specific units of output. Hence indirect or roundabout means must be used to assign manufacturing overhead to product. Another important point to bear in mind is that many manufacturing overhead costs do not change as output changes. For example, depreciation of factory buildings is unaffected by the amount of productivity occurring during any particular time period. How costs behave or vary as productivity changes is an important management accounting issue and is discussed shortly. Also, it should be mentioned that direct labor and manufacturing overhead together are called **conversion costs.**

Overhead certainly occurs in service-type enterprises. Due to the rather primitive state of associating costs with output in service firms, however, breakdowns are usually not made between overhead related to producing the service and other types of overhead in these organizations.

Product Costs and Period Costs

These two categories are considered together because they are complementary. **Product costs** are those costs that are chargeable to inventory in manufacturing situations. They thus include the categories previously discussed: direct materials, direct labor, and manufacturing overhead. Manufacturing costs that are a function of time, such as depreciation and property taxes, are defined as product costs. Product costs become expenses when goods are sold. Thus costs of finished goods inventories are incurred in one period but are not expensed until the following period (or whenever they are sold).

Period costs are not inventoried. They become expenses in the time period when incurred. Period costs include administrative, marketing, and finance costs. Their handling is in accordance with the precepts of basic financial accounting.

Income Statements of Manufacturing Firms

Comparative income statements for service, merchandising (retailer or wholesaler), and manufacturing enterprises are shown in Exhibit 2–2. Notice that the cost of goods manufactured substitutes for purchases in the merchandising statement. Cost of goods manufactured, however, is a fairly complex element. It is illustrated in Exhibit 2–3 (page 21).

The sum of the direct materials, direct labor, and manufacturing overhead incurred during the period are designated as **total manufacturing costs.** In practice, manufacturing overhead costs are generally charged to

EXHIBIT 2–2

Comparative Income Statements for Service, Merchandising, and Manufacturing Firms

Service Firm

Revenues		$4,000,000
Operating expenses		2,200,000
Net income		$1,800,000

Merchandising Firm

Revenues		$5,000,000
Cost of goods sold		
Beginning inventory	$ 800,000	
Add: Purchases	2,000,000	
Cost of goods available for sale	2,800,000	
Less: Ending inventory	400,000	2,400,000
Gross profit		2,600,000
Operating expenses		1,500,000
Net income		$1,100,000

Manufacturing Firm

Revenues		$7,500,000
Cost of goods sold		
Beginning finished goods inventory	$ 600,000	
Add: Cost of goods manufactured	3,000,000	
Cost of goods available for sale	3,600,000	
Less: Ending finished goods inventory	200,000	3,400,000
Gross profit		4,100,000
Operating expenses		2,400,000
Net income		$1,700,000

production on an estimated basis, rather than as illustrated in Exhibit 2–3 (this is discussed in Chapter 6). It should be clear that the total manufacturing costs end up in one of the following three categories:

1. Added to beginning work in process inventory to complete these goods;

2. Applicable to units of product that were started and completed during the period;

3. Applicable to units of product that were started but *not* completed prior to the end of the period.

The costs in category 3 would, of course, be the ending work-in-process inventory. Similarly, it would be the case that the beginning work-in-process inventory plus the first two categories would equal the cost of goods manufactured during the period. The same result is determined in Exhibit 2–3 by

EXHIBIT 2–3
Cost of Goods Manufactured

Direct materials		
Beginning inventory of raw materials	$ 300,000	
Add: Purchases of raw materials	1,000,000	
Cost of raw materials available for usage	1,300,000	
Less: Ending inventory of raw materials	400,000	
Direct materials used		$ 900,000
Direct labor		1,400,000
Manufacturing overhead		
Indirect materials	30,000	
Indirect labor	40,000	
Depreciation of machinery and equipment	300,000	
Depreciation of factory buildings	200,000	
Insurance, property taxes, etc. pertaining to manufacturing	30,000	600,000
Total manufacturing costs		2,900,000
Add: Beginning work-in-process inventory		300,000
		3,200,000
Less: Ending work-in-process inventory		200,000
Cost of goods manufactured (to Exhibit 2–2)		$3,000,000

taking the total manufacturing costs for the period, adding to it the beginning work-in-process inventory, and deducting the ending work-in-process inventory. These relationships are summarized in Exhibit 2–4.

With the cost of goods manufactured transferred to Exhibit 2–2, it should be clear that the beginning finished goods inventory plus the cost of

EXHIBIT 2–4
Where Total Manufacturing Costs Go

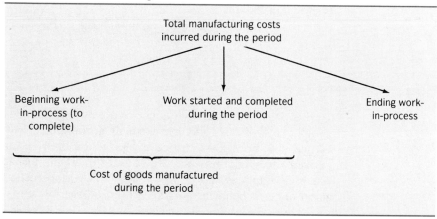

EXHIBIT 2–5
Overview of Manufacturing Cost Relationships

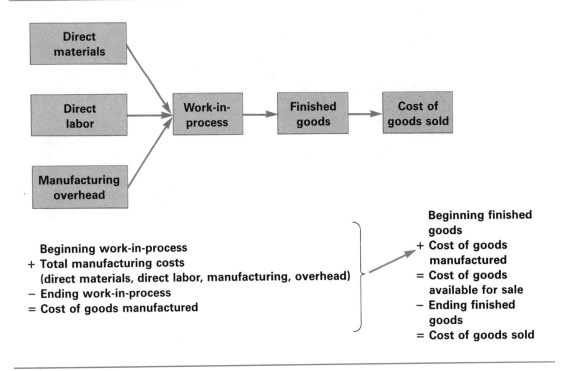

goods manufactured less the ending finished goods inventory equals the cost of goods sold. Beginning finished goods plus the cost of goods manufactured equals the cost of goods available for sale. An overview of these relationships is shown in Exhibit 2–5.

Cost Behavior

To this point we have been concerned with the classification of the various components of cost and management accounting. **Cost behavior** is concerned with how costs change as production or sales vary. Cost behavior is perhaps the single most important idea underlying management accounting. The idea is applicable to both product and period costs. The two classic examples of cost behavior are fixed costs and variable costs.

Fixed Costs

Fixed costs remain the same within a given time period even though output or sales may change, provided that output or sales remain within a relevant range (defined shortly). Some classic examples would be building rents, depreciation of buildings, depreciation of machinery and equipment, and salaries of administrative and production personnel.

Illustration

Assume that a washing machine manufacturer rents a factory building and owns the machinery and equipment inside. The rental contract is for $10,000 per month. Depreciation of machinery and equipment is $75,000 per month. Washing machine production has been between 10,000 and 15,000 per month for several years. Assume that with the present amount of machinery and equipment, the factory has a productive capacity of up to 20,000 washers per month. If monthly production were to drop below 8,000 units per month, some machinery and equipment would be sold. Similarly, assume that with the present building, up to 30,000 washers per month could be produced. The plant would be uneconomic to operate—and would thus be closed down—below 5,000 units per month.

Costs are fixed—that is, they do not change in total during the period—for depreciation of machinery and equipment between 8,000 and 20,000 units per month and for factory rent between 5,000 and 30,000 units. For an item to be classified as fixed, it must have a relatively wide span of output where costs are expected to remain constant, as in the case being discussed here of factory rent and depreciation of factory equipment. These spans are called the **relevant range** for each type of fixed cost.

If washing machine production were to begin exceeding 20,000 units per month, additional machinery and equipment would have to be acquired, raising the relevant range. Similarly, if productivity were cut back below 8,000 units per month, the firm would dispose of some machinery and equipment, lowering the monthly fixed costs.

The same considerations apply in the case of factory rent, which has a wider relevant range. Above 30,000 units per month, more space would have to be rented. On the other hand, it appears that if productivity were to drop below 5,000 units per month on a regular basis, the lease would not be renewed.

Graphs depicting fixed costs for factory rent and depreciation of factory equipment are shown in Exhibits 2–6 and 2–7. The dotted lines indicate the end of the relevant range areas. Notice that the costs are in terms of totals per month.

Very often fixed cost per unit of output is determined by dividing the total fixed costs by the production for the period. Thus, if production were 10,000 units during October and 15,000 units during November, depreciation of factory equipment cost per unit of output would be

EXHIBIT 2–6

Fixed Costs (Depreciation of Factory Equipment)

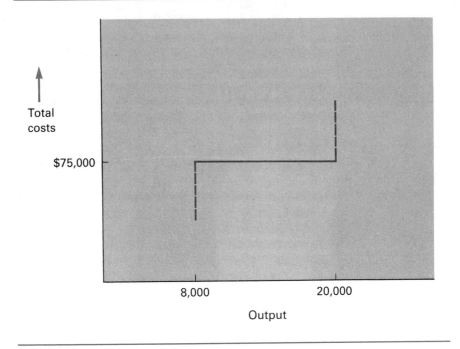

	October		November	
$\dfrac{\text{Costs}}{\text{Output}}$	$\dfrac{\$75,000}{10,000}$ = $7.50		$\dfrac{\$75,000}{15,000}$ = $5.00	

The spreading effect can be seen relative to fixed costs as long as production remains within the relevant range: the higher the output, the lower the cost per unit of output. However, inclusion of fixed costs can be misleading in many management decision situations because fixed costs are not responsive to changes in output in the short run. For example, as long as production remains between 8,000 and 20,000 units per month, machinery and equipment are kept in good running order, and drastic technological changes do not occur, no change in monthly depreciation of factory equipment costs will arise.

Variable Costs

Variable costs change when production or sales change. A pure variable cost will increase or decrease proportionately with production or sales. Examples are direct materials as a function of production and sales commissions as a function of sales. Variable cost behavior is illustrated in Exhibit 2–8 (page 26).

EXHIBIT 2–7

Fixed Costs (Factory Rent)

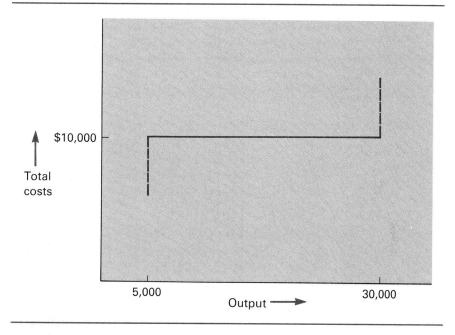

Certain elements of manufacturing overhead exhibit a variable cost behavior. These include maintenance of machinery and equipment affected by the amount of usage, power costs for running machinery and equipment, and indirect materials used in the product that are too minor to be accounted for as direct materials. However, most of the components of manufacturing overhead have a fixed cost behavior. As a result, manufacturing overhead is often broken down into **fixed manufacturing overhead** and **variable manufacturing overhead** for planning and control purposes. This is a useful distinction for management accounting purposes.

In our washing machine example mentioned previously, assume that a particular model has a variable manufacturing cost (direct materials, direct labor, and variable manufacturing overhead) of $125 per unit. Total variable manufacturing costs for October and November would be

October
10,000 units × $125 = $1,250,000
November
15,000 units × $125 = $1,875,000

Notice that fixed costs are the same in total per time period but vary *per unit;* the higher the output, the lower the cost per unit. Variable costs, on the other hand, are constant per unit but vary in total as factors such as productivity or sales change. The fixed–variable cost distinction is important in many planning and control operations that are of vital concern to management. These relationships are summarized in Exhibit 2–9. Many of these uses are discussed and illustrated throughout this text.

EXHIBIT 2–8
Variable Costs

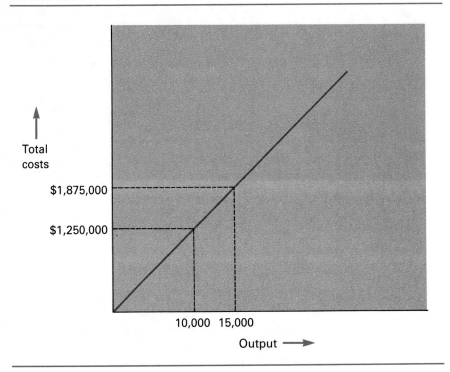

EXHIBIT 2–9
Summary of Fixed and Variable Cost Relationships

		Behavior	
Type of Cost	Per Unit	In Total
Fixed	Decreases per unit as production increases	Total remains constant per time period
Variable	Remains the same per unit	Varies in total in proportion to changes in output or sales

Planning and Control Concepts

Given the basic cost components and the fact that most costs behave in either a fixed or variable fashion, certain concepts are fundamental to the planning and control functions. We begin with those applicable to planning.

Planning Concepts

The essence of planning is that it involves an analysis of future courses of action available to the enterprise. In evaluating these choices, it is important to estimate the costs and revenues associated with them. The terminology presented in this section is concerned with appropriately defining these costs and revenues in order to enable management to make correct decision choices.

Differential Costs and Revenues

Differential costs and revenues are those costs and revenues that differ between alternatives. The alternatives may involve a choice between producing more or fewer units of a particular product or even producing an entirely different product. Differential costs for producing 25,000 washing machines per month rather than 15,000, using the figures from our previous example, are shown in Exhibit 2–10.

In Exhibit 2–10, the variable costs per washing machine are $125 in total consisting of $50 of direct materials, $65 of direct labor, and $10 of variable manufacturing overhead. Depreciation of machinery and equipment increased by $25,000 per month due to the acquisition of additional equipment, but all other items of manufacturing overhead remained within their relevant ranges.

A key point to remember is that differential costs will almost always include variable costs but fixed costs are affected only if the decision involves

EXHIBIT 2–10
Differential Costs of Washing Machines

	15,000 Units per Month	25,000 Units per Month	Differential Costs
Direct materials ($50 per unit)	$ 750,000	$1,250,000	$ 500,000
Direct labor ($65 per unit)	975,000	1,625,000	650,000
Variable manufacturing overhead ($10 per unit)	150,000	250,000	100,000
Fixed manufacturing overhead:			
Depreciation of machinery and equipment	75,000	100,000	25,000
All others	150,000	150,000	—
	$2,100,000	$3,375,000	$1,275,000

going outside of the relevant range. The term ***incremental costs*** is virtually synonymous with differential costs; it should be used in alternatives involving *increasing* differential costs. Should an alternative involve lower differential costs, the appropriate synonymous term is ***decremental costs.*** Another frequently used term that is similar to differential costs is *avoidable costs.* A term that is close in meaning to differential costs is ***out-of-pocket costs.*** As the name implies, it refers to outlays of funds attributable to a given alternative. **Avoidable costs,** as the name implies, can be escaped under at least one of the decision choices open to the firm by not adopting a particular alternative.

Sunk Costs

Sunk costs are the result of past decisions. As such, they cannot affect current or future decisions. If an asset were acquired a short time ago for $100,000 and a newer, more efficient model came on the market at a cost of $150,000, the original purchase price of $100,000 should not affect a decision of whether to acquire the more expensive technology. Management undoubtedly wishes that it did not buy the cheaper machine but its regret is irrelevant and should not affect the new decision. Sunk costs are frequently called ***unavoidable costs*** in situations involving choice among alternatives.

An item which would be relevant to the decision, however, would be the trade-in value of the old equipment or its selling price in the used equipment market, say $70,000 in our example. This is an amount that would be received (or reduced from the cost of the new equipment) if — and only if — the old technology is disposed of by trade-in or sale. The $70,000 affects the two alternatives under consideration: keep the old equipment or acquire the new, but the $100,000 of acquisition cost cannot be changed.

Opportunity Costs

Opportunity costs are defined as the sacrifice of forgoing the next best alternative. If, for example, an individual decides that he must immediately see the latest blood-and-guts war movie, he may have to give up seeing (live) a World Series game. This example, though frivolous, illustrates the idea that opportunity costs may not involve dollars (assuming one owns a television set) although they certainly will involve time.

From the standpoint of management, opportunity costs should be quantified in dollar terms to facilitate the decision-making process. Assume that a firm is evaluating two potential orders whose differential revenues and costs are as follows:

	Order 1	Order 2
Differential revenues	$2,000,000	$1,500,000
Differential costs	1,200,000	1,000,000
Differential income	$800,000	$ 500,000

If it were the case that the firm had the available productive capacity to accept only one of the two jobs, Order 1 would be more desirable. The opportunity cost of taking on Order 1 is the differential income of $500,000 given up by rejecting Order 2. If there were adequate capacity to take on both jobs, and no other order is given up, then neither order would have an opportunity cost.

Notice the opposite nature of sunk costs and opportunity costs. Opportunity costs must be considered when evaluating alternative decisions but they do not affect the accounting: if Order 1 is taken, the $1,200,000 of differential costs will be entered on the books but not the $500,000 opportunity cost of the differential income given up by not taking Order 2. A sunk cost, on the other hand, is a cost that is on the books but that does not directly affect a managerial decision. Traditional accounting systems often provide the wrong information and exclude relevant information for managerial decisions.

The opportunity cost notion is often of great importance at the level of personal decision making. If an individual makes a decision to pursue a master's degree on a full-time basis, the income lost from not taking a job is an opportunity cost. Similarly, if an individual is in business for himself or herself, the opportunity cost is the income forgone by not working for someone else.

Imputed Costs

Imputed costs are a special type of opportunity cost: they are the interest earnings lost on money tied up in particular assets. For example, most firms sell goods on a credit basis. As a result, money is tied up in accounts receivable that is unavailable for investment elsewhere. The imputed cost is equal to the average balance of accounts receivable times the interest rate. Thus, a firm having an average balance of accounts receivable during a year of $100,000, which could earn 15% in an alternate investment, would have an imputed cost of $15,000. Of course, selling on credit is an absolute necessity for most business enterprises, and so the imputed costs of accounts receivable can generally be ignored. However, there can be considerable costs to a firm if its collection procedures slow down with a resulting increase in average accounts receivable outstanding. Hence, an accounting ratio such as turnover of accounts receivable can be exceedingly important for management to monitor.

Imputed costs also have applicability in the managerial decision context when evaluating different projects. Assume that a firm is evaluating a particular capital project in which average inventories are $75,000 and average accounts receivable are $50,000 during a particular year. Again, assuming that the appropriate interest rate is 15%, the imputed cost of money tied up in inventories and receivables on the project is $18,750 ($125,000 × .15). Imputed costs are an important opportunity cost but, unfortunately, are often overlooked in important managerial decisions.

Control Concepts

Control of costs involves comparing actual costs against an estimate of what they should be. In addition to gauging what costs should be, two other properties are required. Costs (or revenues) must be both direct to, and controllable by, a particular organizational unit.

Direct Costs

Direct costs are incurred as a result of or for the benefit of operations within an organizational unit of a firm such as an assembly department in a plant making electronic equipment. Whether a cost is direct to a particular organizational unit is extremely important in terms of determining whether or not it is controllable by that unit. Some examples of direct costs at the individual department level include depreciation of machinery and equipment used exclusively by that department, salary of the departmental foreman, and direct labor performed within the department. Notice that these examples include both fixed and variable elements.

The concept of direct costs also can be applied to production. Direct materials and direct labor, as their names imply, are direct costs that are easily traceable to individual products or orders. Manufacturing overhead is always indirect relative to production except in the very restricted example of a one-product firm. However, depreciation costs are somewhat arbitrary among accounting periods because they depend on factors such as depreciation method, number of years of estimated life, and expected salvage value. It can be said that depreciation costs are indirect to the various accounting periods comprising its economic life.

Indirect Costs

Indirect costs cannot be traced specifically to individual organizational units or production elements. Some costs are charged to production departments on a "fair and equitable" basis for the purpose of assigning them to product for inventory valuation and income measurement purposes. An example would be salaries of the plant manager and his staff. These costs are an element of manufacturing overhead and must be assigned to production departments on a reasonable basis so that they may be charged to product.

There is a relative aspect to the question of whether a cost is direct or indirect. In the example above, salaries of the plant manager and his staff were indirect when viewed from the perspective of the production departments constituting the plant. However, when viewed from the standpoint of the entire factory, these salaries are a direct cost. The higher the organizational perspective, the more costs that become direct. All costs are direct to General Motors.

Controllable Costs

A **controllable cost** is one that can be influenced by a particular manager. For a cost to be controllable, (1) it must be a direct cost of the particular department being analyzed, and (2) the amount incurred during a period must be capable of being held in line by good management. Virtually all direct and variable costs are controllable by a particular manager.

Some direct fixed costs are controllable whereas others are not. If depreciation of machinery located within a particular department is calculated by formula and cannot be changed in the short run by managerial efforts, it would not be controllable. Research and development (R&D) costs are generally fixed per year by budget. However, the budget may be exceeded for several reasons:

1. Costs of materials used in the R&D process may be greater than were anticipated in the budget;

2. Quantities of materials actually used may have exceeded budgeted quantities due to carelessness on the part of personnel;

3. The budget may be deliberately exceeded because research has led to an unexpected breakthrough promising important new results.

In the first case, although budget was exceeded, material prices are generally beyond the control of top R&D management. In the second case the cost was controllable because good management should have been able to prevent material waste. In the third case the budget was intentionally broken to take advantage of the situation. The R&D manager might have received approval from a higher echelon in this case. If approval was not sought, the R&D manager should be ready to justify his actions. Controllability refers to accountability by a manager having both the authority over and responsibility for administering a particular function. Even though a cost may be fixed, it is still controllable if managerial actions are capable of influencing how much those costs will be.

Noncontrollable Costs

A manager should not be held responsible for costs that are noncontrollable at his or her level of the organization. **Noncontrollable costs** either are indirect to the particular organizational unit being analyzed or cannot be changed or influenced by management in the short run.

Ideally, all costs are controllable by some manager at some point in time. As mentioned above, depreciation costs are noncontrollable even when direct. The point of controllability of fixed assets would be when acquisition occurs. Controllability would not involve depreciation costs, which are determined by formula, but rather a comparison of actual acquisition cost against budget. After acquisition, controllability would involve production-related costs and statistics such as maintenance and productivity costs.

Summary

This chapter developed basic concepts and terminology that are applicable to management and used throughout this text. Product costs in manufacturing situations were examined first. Direct materials and direct labor, as their names imply, are major components that can be traced directly to the product. Manufacturing overhead is comprised of all other costs of a manufacturing nature that are considered to be product costs. Product costs are expensed as goods are sold. They can be contrasted with period costs that are expensed as incurred. Period costs include general and administrative, marketing, and financial costs. Income statements of manufacturing firms are more complex than are those of merchandising firms. Beginning work in process plus total manufacturing costs (direct materials, direct labor, and manufacturing overhead) less ending work in process equals the cost of goods manufactured during the period. In turn, beginning finished goods plus cost of goods manufactured minus ending finished goods equals the cost of goods sold.

The two principal types of cost behavior are fixed and variable. Fixed costs are fixed in total during the period as long as production (or sales) is within the relevant range. The higher production is during the period, the lower will be the fixed cost per unit of output. Variable costs are constant per unit and vary with total production.

Important planning terminology includes differential costs, sunk costs, opportunity costs, and imputed costs. Differential costs—as the name implies—are the differences in costs or revenues for different levels of output or for other alternatives. Sunk costs are unaffected by decisions. They are, in fact, the results of past decisions that cannot be undone. Opportunity costs are the sacrifice resulting from taking one alternative and forgoing another one. Imputed costs are a special type of opportunity cost involving interest costs applicable to funds that are tied up in particular investment alternatives.

Important control concepts include direct costs, indirect costs, controllable, and noncontrollable costs. Direct costs are traceable to a particular organizational unit such as a production department or a specific order of goods. Indirect costs cannot be easily identified with specific organizational units or particular orders of goods. The difference between direct and indirect costs is a relative one. All costs are direct to some organizational unit at some point in time. For costs to be controllable for a particular organizational unit, they must be direct relative to that unit, and the costs must be capable of being influenced or changed by managerial action. If a cost is controllable, management should be held responsible for it. If a cost is noncontrollable, it is either indirect or cannot be changed in the short run by managerial action.

Key Terms

Avoidable costs   are costs that can be eliminated under at least one of the decision choices open to the firm.

Controllable costs   can be influenced by a particular manager. To be controllable, the cost must be a direct cost of the unit in question and capable of being held in line by good management.

Conversion costs   consist of direct labor and manufacturing overhead.

Cost behavior   is concerned with how costs change as production or sales vary.

Decremental costs   are lower differential costs resulting from a potential or actual decision alternative.

Differential costs (and revenues)   are those costs and revenues that differ between alternatives.

Direct costs   are incurred as a result of or for the benefit of operations within a particular organizational unit of an enterprise.

Direct labor   consists of the major work effort going into a product that helps to transform it from direct materials into final output.

Direct materials   are those material inputs that become a measurable part of the manufactured product.

Finished goods   are completed units of product.

Fixed costs   remain the same within a given time period even though output (or sales) may change as long as the particular cost stays within the relevant range.

Fixed manufacturing overhead   is that part of manufacturing overhead whose cost behavior is fixed.

Imputed costs   are the interest earnings lost on money tied up in particular assets.

Incremental costs   are higher differential costs resulting from a potential or actual decision alternative.

Indirect costs   cannot be traced to individual organizational units or production elements.

Indirect labor   includes salaries and wages of personnel in production departments who are not directly engaged in manufacturing operations.

Indirect materials   are relatively minor and difficult to trace directly to product.

Manufacturing overhead   are those product costs that cannot be specifically identified with particular units of product.

Noncontrollable costs   either are indirect to the particular organizational unit being analyzed or cannot be changed or influenced by management in the short run.

Opportunity costs   are the sacrifice of forgoing the next best alternative.

Out-of-pocket costs   refers to outlays of funds attributable to a given alternative.

Period costs   are not inventoried. They became expenses in the time period when incurred.

Prime costs   consist of direct materials and direct labor.

Product costs   are inventoriable costs. They include direct materials, direct labor, and manufacturing overhead.

Raw materials   are direct materials consisting of minerals such as coal, sulphur, and iron ore.

Relevant range   is the span of input or output where fixed costs remain constant.

Service departments   perform functions that are auxiliary to the manufacturing process.

Sunk costs   are the result of past decisions. As such they cannot affect current or future decisions.

Total manufacturing costs   are the sum of direct materials, direct labor, and manufacturing overhead incurred during the period.

Unavoidable costs   cannot be avoided in situations involving choice among alternatives. The term is synonymous with sunk costs.

Variable costs   change as a result of production or sales changing. The change will be proportional resulting in the same cost per unit.

Variable manufacturing overhead is that part of manufacturing overhead whose cost behavior is variable.

Work in process (goods in process) are inventories of product that are in an incomplete state.

Questions

Q2–1   What are the components of manufactured inventories?

Q2–2   Are all materials that go into manufactured products categorized as direct materials?

Q2–3   What is the difference between direct labor and indirect labor?

Q2–4   What are prime costs?

Q2–5   What is the principal difference between manufacturing overhead and the other components of manufactured costs?

Q2–6   What are conversion costs?

Q2–7   How do product costs and period costs differ from the accounting standpoint?

Q2–8   What are total manufacturing costs for any period?

Q2–9   Where do total manufacturing costs go?

Q2–10 How does cost behavior (fixed and variable) relate to product costs and period costs?

Q2–11 What does the term *relevant range* refer to?

Q2–12 What happens to cost per unit as production increases for fixed cost elements?

Q2–13 What happens to cost per unit as production increases for variable cost elements?

Q2–14 How do fixed and variable costs relate to differential costs?

Q2–15 How do sunk costs and incremental costs relate to each other?

Q2–16 How do sunk costs and opportunity costs relate to each other?

Q2–17 Why is there a relative aspect to the question of whether costs are direct or indirect?

Q2–18 Are direct costs synonymous with controllable costs?

Exercises

E2–1   **Period costs and product costs.** Identify which of the following transactions and events are product costs and which are period costs:

   a. Lubricants for machinery and equipment used in production departments
   b. Gain or loss on disposal of factory equipment
   c. Social security taxes paid by the employer for employees in the Assembly Department
   d. Storage and handling costs for raw materials

e. Depreciation of a factory building

f. Social security taxes paid by the employer for employees in the Production Planning and Control Department

g. Depreciation of a building containing both manufacturing and administrative operations

h. Social security taxes paid by the employer for sales personnel

i. Depreciation of an administrative building

j. Social security taxes withheld from the pay of employees in the Assembly Department

k. Leasehold costs for land on which factory buildings stand

l. Inspection costs of finished goods

E2–2   **Fixed costs and variable costs.** Identify which of the following costs are fixed and which are variable:

a. Direct labor

b. Property taxes on factory building

c. Property taxes on administration building

d. Sales commissions

e. Base salaries paid to sales personnel regardless of their level of sales

f. Royalty on a patent based on the number of units produced

g. Factory fire insurance

h. Regular maintenance on machinery and equipment

i. Electricity for machinery and equipment in the plant

j. Heat for the plant in winter

k. Maintenance on machinery and equipment based on the amount of usage

E2–3   **Computing cost of goods manufactured and sold.** Buffet Company had the following beginning and ending inventories for the year 19X8:

	Beginning	*Ending*
Raw materials	$200,000	$260,000
Work-in-process	160,000	143,000
Finished goods	120,000	135,000

During 19X8, the following costs were incurred:

Purchase of raw materials	$1,300,000
Direct labor cost	1,600,000
Manufacturing overhead	2,100,000

Required: Present a statement of cost of goods manufactured and sold.

E2–4   **Classification of costs.** Shown below are some representative costs incurred by a furniture manufacturer. You are to fill out the following classification table in terms of whether the cost is a product or period cost, whether it is direct to product or indirect (manufacturing overhead), and whether it is fixed or variable.

1. Labor responsible for cutting and shaping the wood

2. Factory manager's salary

3. Commissions to the sales force

4. Glue, tacks, and staples used on the furniture

5. Cloth and other fabric going into the product

6. Rent on the factory building

7. Salaries of individuals in Production Planning and Control
8. Lubricants for machinery and equipment that are affected by machine hours of production
9. Insurance on factory building
10. Insurance on corporate headquarters building

Required:　Set up the following table and write in each of the ten items above, checking the appropriate categories.

Cost Item	Product or Period Cost		Direct or Indirect to Product		Cost Behavior	
	Product	Period	Direct	Indirect	Fixed	Variable

E2–5　**Identifying cost concepts.** Identify the cost concept that is being described in each of the following situations:

1. Costs that remain constant per unit of output
2. Costs that are expensed as incurred rather than charged to product
3. Product costs that are indirect to the product
4. Total manufacturing costs for the period plus (or minus) the change in work-in-process inventories
5. The area, outside of which, fixed costs can be expected to change during a period
6. Total maximum dollar value of goods that theoretically could be sold during any given period
7. No further work has to be done on these even though the costs are on the books at the beginning of the period
8. Costs per unit that decrease as more units are produced during the period
9. Costs of goods manufactured during the period plus (or minus) the change in finished goods inventories
10. Total manufacturing costs incurred during the period minus both the costs necessary to complete beginning work-in-process inventory and ending work-in-process inventory

E2–6　**Identifying planning and control concepts.** Identify the planning or control concept that is being described in each of the following situations:

1. The income from a project that is given up if another alternative is accepted in its place
2. A cost that should be ignored when making a decision
3. The change in costs when going from a lower to a higher output level
4. A cost that is easily traceable to a particular organizational unit
5. A cost for which a supervisor can be held accountable
6. Interest lost by not putting money into a savings account
7. Comparison of actual results against plan that is received by the manager responsible for results

E2–7　**Determining certain costs.** Shown below are some cost categories of the Joshua Haydn Corporation for the year 19X8:

Total prime costs	$68,000
Total conversion costs	84,000
Fixed manufacturing overhead	29,000

Required:
1. By what amount does the total manufacturing overhead exceed the direct materials?
2. What is the total variable manufacturing costs if direct labor is $20,000?
3. Assume that direct labor is 150% of variable manufacturing overhead. Determine the amount of the direct materials.

E2–8   **Identifying planning and control concepts.** Name the planning or control concept that is being described in each of the following situations:

1. A college student has gone over her monthly lunch budget.
2. Instead of investing in a stereo system, an individual could put his money in the bank.
3. A person has bought a very expensive automobile that is performing poorly, but she does not want to trade it until she "recovers" more of the cost.
4. Ivy University and State College have different tuitions.
5. A salary is given up when a person works full time on an MBA rather than works for a public accounting firm with a bachelor's degree.
6. A college education includes costs for room, board, tuition, and books.
7. In assessing the costs of your first year at college, your father includes the cost of a ticket that he got while driving you to school at the start of the year.

E2–9   **Determining unit costs.** Listed below are the costs of Joel Alan Enterprises for two different levels for the year 19X8:

Output level (units)	10,000	20,000
Direct materials	$ 200,000	$ 400,000
Depreciation of factory building	50,000	50,000
Depreciation of machinery and equipment	40,000	40,000
Sales commissions	80,000	160,000
Direct labor	120,000	240,000
Administrative salaries	300,000	300,000
Indirect labor	15,000	15,000
Service department costs	170,000	170,000
Electricity costs for machinery and equipment	12,000	24,000
	$ 987,000	$1,399,000

Required:
1. What is the variable production cost per unit for each level of output?
2. What is the fixed production cost per unit for each level of output?
3. From the standpoint of setting a selling price for your product, which costs are you concerned with for each level of output?
4. What would you have concluded if indirect labor costs were $25,000 at the 20,000-unit level of output (instead of the $15,000)?

E2–10   **Effect on income of inventorying fixed manufacturing overhead.** Sorter Company manufactures one product. It has no beginning inventories. Selling price of Sorter's product is $25 per unit. Total variable manufacturing costs are $10 per unit. Total fixed manufacturing overhead is $4,000 per year (fixed and variable selling and administrative costs are inconsequential).

Required:
1. Determine Sorter's income if 300 units are produced and sold.
2. Determine Sorter's income if 400 units are produced and only 200 units are sold. You are to assign one-half of the fixed manufacturing overhead to ending inventory.

3. Do the results seem strange when you compare the incomes in the first two parts? Discuss.

Problems

P2–11   **Determining missing amounts.** The following situations are independent. In each case, determine the missing amounts.

	A	B
Sales	$1,000,000	?
Manufacturing costs:		
Direct materials	300,000	600,000
Direct labor	100,000	300,000
Manufacturing overhead	120,000	200,000
Gross profit	455,000	720,000
General, selling, and administrative costs	270,000	?
Cost of goods manufactured	550,000	?
Cost of goods available for sale	?	?
Cost of goods sold	?	1,190,000
Work in process		
January 1, 19X2	?	240,000
December 31, 19X2	34,000	120,000
Finished goods		
January 1, 19X2	54,000	140,000
December 31, 19X2	?	170,000
Net income	?	410,000

P2–12   **Cost behavior and incremental costs.** Gulseth Company is a small appliance manufacturer. Its toaster line is capable of producing 20,000 toasters per year. During 19X8 it expects to be able to sell 10,000 toasters. Total manufacturing cost of the toasters is

Direct materials	$ 60,000
Direct labor	40,000
Variable manufacturing cost	15,000
Fixed manufacturing cost	50,000
	$165,000

Toasters sell regularly for $25 apiece. The Cornwell Company wants to buy a large order of 3,000 units and would like Gulseth to quote a special price to them. Selling costs of the order would be $3 per unit for Gulseth. Fixed manufacturing costs will not increase if Gulseth accepts the order. The three requirements are independent of each other.

Required: 1. What is the full product cost per unit without considering the Cornwell order?
2. What is the cost per unit that would allow Gulseth to break even on the order (have a zero profit)?
3. If the Cornwell order is accepted, Gulseth would have to add one more supervisory individual in the assembling department. The salary of the individual would be $8,000 (supervisory costs are classified as fixed manufacturing overhead). What is the cost per unit that would allow Gulseth to break even on the order?

P2–13   **Unit and total cost concepts.** Francis Company manufactures one product. Costs for the year 19X9 for output levels of 500 and 1,000 units are as follows:

Units	500	1,000
Direct materials	$10,000	$20,000
Direct labor	15,000	30,000
Variable manufacturing overhead	6,000	12,000
Fixed manufacturing overhead	18,000	18,000
Variable selling, general, and administrative costs	2,500	5,000
Fixed selling, general, and administrative costs	11,000	11,000
	$62,500	$96,000

Required:

1. What are the *total* manufacturing costs at each level of output?
2. What are the manufacturing costs *per unit* at each level of output?
3. What are the *total* variable costs at each level of output?
4. What are the total variable costs *per unit* at each level of output?
5. What are the *total* costs that have to be covered at each level of output if the firm is to make a profit?

P2–14   **Pricing of product.** Refer to the data in P2–13. This problem attempts to show the role of costs in pricing.

Required:

1. What would the selling price per unit be at each level of output if Francis attempts to recover all costs and desires a profit equal to 10% of the selling price?
2. How do the role of fixed and variable costs differ in the setting of prices?
3. What other factors besides costs should be taken into account in setting selling prices? Discuss.

P2–15   **Planning concepts.** Cinnamon Company manufactures a specialized industrial pump. It expects to manufacture and sell 15,000 pumps in 19X9. It can manufacture an additional 5,000 pumps without going out of the relevant range on its fixed costs. Its projected total costs for the 15,000 units are as follows:

Direct materials	$ 75,000
Direct labor	150,000
Variable manufacturing overhead	52,500
Fixed manufacturing overhead	90,000
Fixed selling and administrative costs	65,000
Variable selling and administrative costs	
Sales commissions	60,000
Delivery cost	97,500

Regular selling price is $75. Sklar Company desires to buy up to 5,000 pumps on a special purchase basis. If Sklar buys the pumps, there would be no sales commission because of the direct nature of the sale. In addition, the delivery cost per unit would be equal to one-half the regular delivery cost per unit.

Required:

1. What is the total manufacturing cost per unit if 15,000 pumps are produced?
2. What is the total manufacturing cost per unit if 20,000 pumps are produced?
3. What is the lowest acceptable price (break-even price) on the pumps to Sklar (zero profit on the transaction)?
4. Assume that the Sostik Company also wants 5,000 pumps. It would be willing to pay $50 per pump (there would be no sales commissions, and delivery price

would also be cut in half per unit). What is the lowest acceptable price now on the pumps for Sklar? What concept does this illustrate? Explain.

P2–16   **Determining unknowns in manufacturing income statements.** Determine the missing numbers in each of the cases shown below:

	A	B	C
Direct labor	$14,000	$23,500	$ 40,200
Raw materials inventory, 12/31	4,000	9,000	12,300
Sales	90,000	?	150,000
Manufacturing overhead	16,000	?	24,000
Work in process, 12/31	?	16,300	27,300
Raw materials purchases	15,000	20,000	30,000
Finished goods inventory, 1/1	8,300	21,000	?
Cost of goods manufactured	45,500	61,800	93,900
Raw materials inventory, 1/1	6,000	8,000	?
Work in process, 1/1	12,000	18,000	?
Cost of goods sold	41,300	?	88,900
Finished goods, 12/31	?	12,300	21,000
Cost of goods available for sale	53,800	82,800	109,900
Gross profit	48,700	49,500	61,100
Total manufacturing costs	?	60,100	97,200

P2–17   **Income statement for manufacturing firm.** Prepare an income statement in good form for the Mayman Company for the year ending December 31, 19X8, from the following information:

Sales	$1,200,000
Purchases of raw materials	320,000
Indirect labor	22,000
Indirect materials	14,000
Depreciation of factory equipment	68,000
Depreciation of factory buildings	41,000
Depreciation of administrative building	20,000
Marketing costs	180,000
Direct labor	162,000
Raw materials inventory, 12/31/X8	31,000
Work in process, 1/1/X8	76,000
Sales returns and allowances	24,000
Raw materials inventory, 1/1/X8	46,000
Work in process, 12/31/X8	64,000
Sales discounts	18,000
Finished goods inventory, 1/1/X8	176,000
Finished goods inventory, 12/31/X8	163,000

P2–18   **Analyzing product costs.** The following information pertains to unit production and cost information for the Wolozin Company for 19X0:

	Units	Cost
Beginning work in process inventory	200	$ 60,000
Currently incurred (units of product started)	1,000	
Direct materials		84,000
Direct labor		120,000
Manufacturing overhead		116,000
Ending work in process inventory	120	30,000
Beginning finished goods inventory	220	70,400
Ending finished goods inventory	240	81,600

Required:
1. How many units were sold during the year?
2. How many units were completed during the year?
3. Of the units completed during the year, how many were *started* during 19X0?
4. What is the average unit cost of goods completed during 19X0?
5. Would you say that costs appear to be increasing or decreasing from 19X9 to 19X0 (assume FIFO inventory costing)? Explain.
6. If the costs to *complete* the beginning inventory were $4,400, what is the *average* cost of units started and completed during 19X0?

P2–19 **Comprehensive problem on product costs, unit costs, variable and fixed costs.** Young Company manufactures a single product. Costs are designated as variable (V) or fixed (F). The year 19X9 was the company's first year of operations. Costs incurred were as follows:

Direct labor	$2,400,000 V
Depreciation of factory machinery	240,000 F
Depreciation of factory building	380,000 F
Depreciation of administrative and marketing facilities	160,000 F
Selling expenses	925,000 V
Selling expenses	650,000 F
Administrative salaries	720,000 F
Indirect labor	600,000 V
Direct materials purchased	3,120,000
Finished goods inventory, 12/31/X9	496,500
Direct materials inventory, 12/31/X9	120,000

Total dollar sales of product were $11,100,000. Each unit of product requires 3 pounds of direct materials. Direct material costs were constant at $5 per unit throughout the year. Total costs per unit are the same for all units produced.

Required:
1. How many units were produced during the year?
2. What is the total product cost per unit?
3. How many units were in the ending finished goods inventory?
4. What is the selling price per unit?
5. Determine the net income for the year.

P2–20 **Continuation of previous problem.** Prepare a budgeted income statement for the year 19X0. Assume that the selling price and variable costs per unit remain the same as they were in 19X9 as shown in P2–19. All fixed costs are expected to remain the same in total. Sales in units are expected to be 250,000 units, and the ending inventory is projected to be 9,000 units.

Required: Prepare a budgeted income statement for 19X0. First-in first-out (FIFO) is used so that the ending inventory will be carried at average 19X0 costs. (Remember that the change in productivity will change the fixed manufacturing overhead per unit in 19X0.)

CHAPTER 3

Cost Behavior – Types and Measurement

Learning Objectives

After reading this chapter you should be able to:

1. Differentiate between and give examples of variable costs, fixed costs, step costs, and mixed costs.

2. Illustrate and explain the effect of a change in activity on total variable costs and unit variable costs.

3. Illustrate and explain the effect of a change in activity on total fixed costs and fixed costs expressed on a unit basis.

4. Explain the difference between discretionary and committed fixed costs.

5. Understand the relationship of the relevant range to the analysis of cost behavior.

6. Identify the fixed and variable elements of a mixed cost using the high-low points method and understand the strengths and weaknesses of this technique.

7. Analyze a mixed cost using a scattergraph and appreciate why a scattergraph is particularly useful in doing cost analysis.

8. Perform an analysis of a mixed cost using simple linear regression and appreciate the additional precision and other statistical information obtainable by using this technique.

9. Develop a cost function and appreciate how the analysis techniques explained in the chapter help in the choice of better activity bases for explaining cost changes.

10. Understand that careful judgment needs to be exercised in extending the results of analyzing past costs to cost estimates for the future.

A t some point in your career you will undoubtedly be called on to develop a budget, to approve a budget, to be expected to control costs for which you are responsible, to make proposals for price quotations for selling products or for bidding on jobs (manufacturing or service), or to evaluate the performance of those under your span of control. Elements of these different tasks are present in the operation of simple households, positions in churches, clubs, schools, or other nonprofit organizations, and in small, medium, and large companies in the private sector.

These tasks all deal directly or indirectly with planning and/or controlling costs. One of the first requirements in order to be able to plan and control costs is to know how costs change in relation to activity. In other words, how do costs behave or change as the level of activity changes? It was suggested in Chapter 2 that some costs change in direct proportion to changes in activity whereas others don't change at all.

The purpose of this chapter is to build a basic conceptual and practical foundation for cost behavior analysis, which is the study of how costs react to the changes in the level of activity. Analytical techniques will be explored that will help in the identification of the various costs according to their behavior in changing activity environments. Once costs are analyzed by behavior, cost functions can be developed for cost estimation or prediction.

The point should be stressed that this is one of the most important concepts in management accounting. It is basic to many of the topics that will be explored throughout this text and, as mentioned above, has innumerable applications in the real world. To avoid frustration, we suggest that you feel confident with the material before going on to other topics.

Cost Behavior Patterns

In the discussion of cost behavior in the preceding chapter, two types of costs were identified — variable and fixed. In this chapter we will review and expand on that discussion and also identify and discuss two additional cost behavior classifications known as step costs and mixed costs.

Variable Costs

In Chapter 2 we saw that a variable cost is a cost that changes in direct proportion to the change in activity level. Another way of saying this is to state that it is the uniform incremental cost of each additional unit of activity. The first statement says that if the activity level increases 20%, the total variable costs will increase by 20%. The second statement relates to the first in that if the total variable cost is to increase in *direct proportion* to the change in activity level, the cost added per activity unit must be constant. For example, let us consider the case of a bicycle manufacturer who installs a wheel-powered generator on its bicycles to power lighting equipment that is added to the unit. If the generators cost $20 each, the following total and unit costs would be incurred:

Bicycles Produced	Generator Cost per Bicycle	Total Generator Cost
0	$20	$ —0—
100	20	2,000
200	20	4,000
300	20	6,000
400	20	8,000
500	20	10,000

The cost schedule above illustrates two important points regarding variable costs. First, the cost *per unit* remains constant. In other words, there is no saving per unit of activity because more or less units are produced; it still costs $20 per bicycle for a generator. Second, and stemming from the first, the total cost increases in direct proportion to the change in the level of activity. When production is doubled (going from 10 units to 20 units), the total cost doubles ($200 to $400). When production increases 50% (going from 20 units to 30 units), the total cost increases 50% ($400 to $600), and so forth. These important concepts are graphically illustrated in Exhibit 3–1. Note that the constant cost per generator for each bicycle produced causes the total cost to increase a constant amount for each bicycle produced. This means that the slope of the total variable cost line is constant and thus the total variable cost line is linear. This phenomenon will be emphasized again in the discussion of mixed costs.

The nature of an organization will determine the variety and amount of variable costs. If the firm is highly capital intensive, such as an oil refinery or a public utility engaged in the production of electricity, there may be few variable costs. Many service-type organizations with a rather stable number of staff on fixed salaries, such as a counseling service, will also tend to have relatively few variable costs. Such an organization may find that their variable costs are little more than clerical supplies and costs associated with psychological tests purchased. A merchandising firm, on the other hand, would have variable costs such as cost of goods sold, commissions, delivery expense, and perhaps clerical costs. A manufacturing firm would most likely also have variable elements like commissions, delivery, and some administrative costs. Rather than cost of goods sold we would expect to see variable manufacturing costs such as direct materials, direct labor, and variable manufacturing overhead items including power, supplies, lubricants, and indirect materials (remember that cost of goods sold for a manufacturing firm includes fixed manufacturing overhead).

Fixed Costs

Fixed costs are those costs that do not change in total during a period regardless of the change in the level of activity. We must hasten to add two caveats here. First, we refer to a *period of time* when stating that the total costs will

EXHIBIT 3–1

Total and Unit Variable Costs

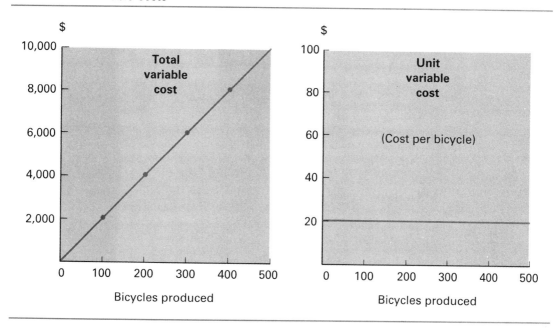

not change in relation to changes in the level of activity. This time period is a short-run time span of usually no longer than one year. Second, as referred to in Chapter 2, there is the consideration of a *relevant range*. The relevant range refers to an activity span within which our cost relationships are valid. It is possible, for example, that we are a warehousing firm with certain warehouse space available. To increase our activity level (goods warehoused) beyond a certain point, it may be necessary to acquire additional warehouse space (through leasing or buying), thus increasing the total fixed cost. This idea will be discussed again in relation to step costs.

We will again refer to the bicycle manufacturer to illustrate total fixed cost behavior and the effect of activity on unit fixed costs. If the building used for the manufacturing process is leased for $20,000 per year, the amount of the rent expense does not change because of the number of bicycles manufactured per year. A cost schedule symmetrical with the variable cost schedule shown previously is presented below to emphasize this particular cost behavior.

Bicycles Produced	Rental Cost per Bicycle	Total Rental Cost
0	$ 0	$20,000
100	200.00	20,000
200	100.00	20,000
300	66.67	20,000
400	50.00	20,000
500	40.00	20,000

In contrast to variable costs, the above schedule emphasizes that the *total* fixed costs remain constant, but the *unit* fixed cost varies depending on the number of bicycles produced. This is why management is interested in utilizing the full capacity of their plant—the fixed costs are spread over the *maximum* number of units resulting in the *minimum* amount of cost per unit produced. Exhibit 3–2 graphically illustrates these relationships.

Note in Exhibit 3–2 that a relevant range has been indicated on the graphs. It is possible that if production were to fall below 250 bicycles per year management might consider moving to smaller quarters, negotiating a lower lease cost for only part of the premises, or subleasing part of the premises if their lease has that flexibility. The fixed cost line from the lower point on the relevant range to the y-axis (horizontal axis) intercept on the graph is shown as a dotted line to indicate that the fixed cost *may* be adjusted if production activity falls below the relevant range. The upper limit on the relevant range may suggest that management suspects that to increase production beyond 450 bicycles per year they may need to rent additional space.

Also note on the unit fixed cost graph that the unit fixed cost line has not been extended to the y-intercept. If production is zero, then there can be no fixed cost per unit because there is no production to absorb the cost. If there is only one bicycle produced, we are faced with the strange situation of the unit cost for rent being $20,000. This, first of all, would be an unten-

EXHIBIT 3–2
Total and Unit Fixed Costs

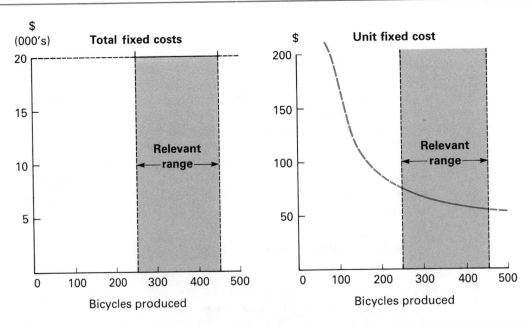

able position for management, and second, would not be allowed from an inventory valuation standpoint. Most of this rent expense would then need to be charged off to expense (a period cost) rather than being allocated to the cost of the bicycle (a product cost). The main point to grasp from the graphs is that the fixed costs remain constant in total over the relevant range, but the *unit* fixed costs vary depending on the amount of activity. The graph shows clearly that the variation in the unit fixed cost is *not* linear, that is, the unit fixed costs do not decrease by a constant amount as more units are produced.

Fixed costs can be further classified according to the time frame over which they may be influenced or managed. We refer to this fixed cost classification as discretionary (or managed) fixed costs and committed fixed costs.

Discretionary Fixed Costs

Discretionary (or managed) fixed costs are costs that are set at some fixed amount each year at the discretion of management. Examples of this type cost would be advertising, research and development, employee training programs, preventive maintenance, and contributions. During the budget planning period management is able, at its *discretion*, to decide how much will be spent in each of these areas. From a control standpoint, management is usually not able to exert much influence on these costs once the budget is adopted and, perhaps, contracts signed, but they do have the opportunity on a yearly basis, at least, to influence or manage the amount of these costs. The costs become fixed each year because management has chosen the level of spending.

Because the amount spent in this area is at the discretion of management and can be influenced at least annually, it is frequently regarded as an area where cutbacks can be made during periods of hard times. Conversely, considerable expenditures may be budgeted during periods of well-being. Management needs to exercise careful judgment in administering these costs: they should be viewed from a cost-benefit standpoint like any expenditure. A reduction in the advertising budget during a time when sales are decreasing may be the wrong strategy entirely. Reduction in the amount spent on research and development may cause the company to fall behind their competitors in a few years (not to mention the difficulty of reassembling a research and development staff). Reduction of amounts spent on preventive maintenance may be offset in the future with excessive costs for major overhauls or production down-time. In other words, these expenditures are made with expected future returns, and indiscriminate increases or decreases in the amounts may result in unhappy consequences.

Committed Fixed Costs

Committed fixed costs are costs that arise from having property, plant, equipment, and a basic organization. In other words, these are costs resulting from the decision to maintain some current service or production capacity. The costs result from long-term *commitments* made in the form of purchasing property, plant, and equipment. Examples of committed fixed costs would be depreciation, property taxes, insurance, and key management and operating personnel. We would normally view these costs as irrevocable even though production is cut to near zero—the costs are necessary in order to stand ready to produce.

These committed fixed costs are the result of management positioning itself to achieve its long-range goals. As such, once the firm has committed itself to these costs there is little that can be done to influence them in the short run without changing the overall capacity or long-range thrust of the firm. Once committed, management is able to manage or control these costs only by effective and efficient use of the facilities and people involved.

The classification of fixed costs may vary somewhat between firms because of basic management philosophy. The authors are aware of one medium-size successful company that regards its personnel—from president to clerks—as committed fixed costs: they feel that there is a long-term commitment to any person hired. As you would expect, this has an effect on the policies regarding hiring and release of employees. Hiring decisions are made very carefully, and employees are reluctantly released. Other firms may view personnel costs for everyone other than a few key employees as variable or discretionary fixed at best.

Step Costs

Step costs are constant *within* a range of activity but change *between* ranges of activity. This suggests that the total cost increases or decreases in a step-like fashion as the level of activity changes. An example could be a university offering a CPA or CMA review course. The policy might be that if 40 or fewer students sign up for the course, one section or class is offered. If 41 to 80 sign up, two sections are offered. If instructors for the course are paid $3,000 for each section taught, the instructional costs for the course would appear graphically as shown in Exhibit 3–3.

As the example of the university offering a CPA or CMA class shows, the step cost is a fixed cost with a relatively narrow relevant range. From period to period, there is a much greater probability that the firm will operate at different levels or steps for the typical step cost than is the case for true fixed-cost elements.

Another example of a step cost is the case of the manufacturer who has signed a union contract that stipulates that a worker is paid a full hour of wages for any part of an hour worked over five minutes. If a worker is paid $10 per hour, the earning of a day's wages would appear as shown graphically in Exhibit 3–4 (page 50).

A number of costs in the real world fall in the category illustrated in Exhibits 3–3 and 3–4. In the case of Exhibit 3–3, the cost of the instructors' salaries might be referred to as *step fixed.* In the case of Exhibit 3–4, the wages of the hourly worker might be referred to as *step variable.* There are,

EXHIBIT 3–3

Step Costs – Instructor Salaries

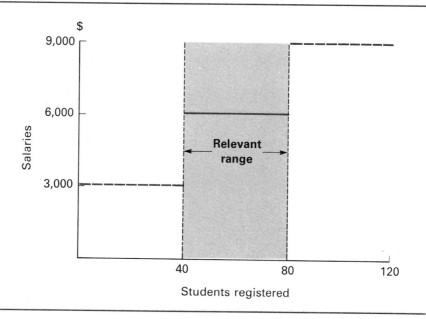

of course, shades of gray concerning the size of the steps making it difficult to choose between the two.

The discontinuity between the steps in step costs makes them very difficult to deal with in terms of analysis, development of cost functions, or graphic representation. The solution to the problem is to adopt some substitute approach that will represent the costs accurately for planning and control purposes. The substitute used will depend on the length and height of each step, that is, how large an activity range the step covers and how much the cost jumps at each step. If the steps cover very small ranges and the cost does not change a great deal from step to step, the cost can most likely be treated as a regular variable cost. This would be true for the situation of the hourly worker referred to above. As the cost of all hourly workers is aggregated, there is little or no distortion by treating the cost as variable. The diagonal line in Exhibit 3–4 suggests such treatment.

If the steps are somewhat larger but not as large as in Exhibit 3–3, a different alternative may be necessary. Exhibit 3–5 (page 51) illustrates the addition of a production supervisor for each 200 hours of direct labor hours generated.

The dotted line in Exhibit 3–5 intercepts the y-axis at $250. This suggests that we should treat this as a mixed (semivariable) cost—it has both fixed and variable cost elements. The next section discusses mixed costs and

EXHiBIT 3—4
Step Costs — Hourly Worker

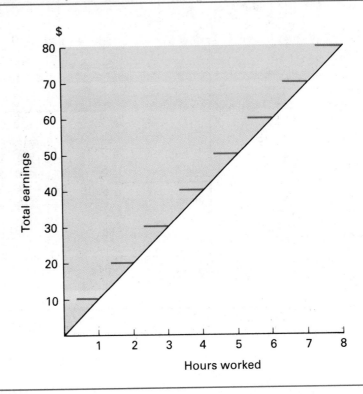

explores techniques for identifying the fixed and variable cost elements involved.

In the case where the steps cover a wide range of activity and the cost steps up or down a significant amount at each step, the best we can hope for is that the relevant range encompasses only one step, as suggested in Exhibit 3–3. If the relevant range includes part of two or more steps, it will be necessary to analyze the cost as a step cost to obtain any degree of accuracy. This would mean, for instance, that cost functions for total costs would need to be designated by the range covered by each of the functions (a separate cost function within each step). For purposes of our discussion, we will treat this type of cost as either a regular variable cost or as a mixed (semivariable) cost.

Mixed Costs

As the name implies, **mixed costs** contain elements of both fixed and variable costs and are often referred to as semivariable costs. Total mixed costs

EXHIBIT 3–5

Step Costs — Addition of Production Supervisors

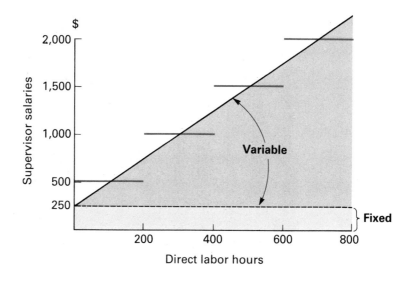

are positive when the activity level is zero (like fixed costs), and they increase in a linear fashion as the activity level increases (similar to variable costs). Examples of mixed costs could be maintenance, leases of many types of equipment or buildings, power, and sales commissions coupled with a base guaranteed salary.

Mixed costs are illustrated by assuming a company enters into a lease for a computer, agreeing to pay $3,000 per month plus $20 per hour of run time. A schedule of the possible costs for a month follows:

Hours of Run Time	Fixed Cost	Variable Cost	Total Cost
0	$3,000	$ 0	$3,000
50	3,000	1,000	4,000
100	3,000	2,000	5,000
150	3,000	3,000	6,000
200	3,000	4,000	7,000

Note that when the level of activity (run time) increases from 50 to 100 hours (100% increase), that the total cost increases $1,000 (25%). And when the level of activity increases from 100 to 150 hours (50% increase), the total cost increases another $1,000 (but now only a 20% increase). In other words, the mixed cost total increases but not in direct proportion to changes in the level of activity. The above schedule is shown graphically in Exhibit 3–6.

EXHIBIT 3—6
Computer Rental as a Mixed Cost

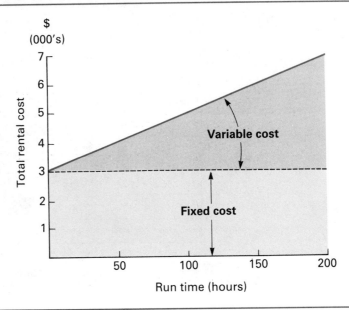

The preceding schedule and Exhibit 3—6 illustrate that the computer rental cost is made up of a combination of $3,000 of fixed cost and variable cost equal to $20 times the number of hours of run time. We could express this in a cost function as follows:

Total mixed cost = $3,000 + $20(X)

where X equals the hours of run time. We would then have a cost function that would be useful for estimating the computer rental costs for any level of activity (number of hours of run time).

Determining Cost Behavior

A major goal of cost behavior analysis is to develop cost functions for the various costs incurred so that we can estimate individual costs for various projected levels of activity or aggregate the individual cost functions into an overall cost estimation model. To do this, we need to be able to identify all costs as either fixed or variable. We run into difficulty in the case of mixed costs that have elements of both. In order to identify cost behavior and to determine the amount of fixed and/or variable cost associated with each cost item, four analysis techniques will be explored. They are the industrial engineering approach, high-low points, scattergraph, and statistical regression analysis. These techniques are not mutually exclusive. A firm may use one or a combination of these techniques over time or as different degrees of accuracy are desired.

Industrial Engineering Approach

If a company has installed a standard costing system (covered in Chapters 9 and 10), it is possible that they might use the **industrial engineering or work measurement approach** to analyze costs and determine cost functions. In this approach, the engineer studies relationships between inputs and outputs to determine how much input is required to produce a certain amount of output. For example, the engineer could conduct a study to ascertain the exact number of pounds of material or the number of minutes of direct labor required to produce a unit of output. These physical measures can then be translated into standard or budgeted costs. In the process the engineer should discover how costs react to changes in level of activity and could develop a cost function (which describes the cost behavior) from his or her study.

There are two problems with this approach. First, the technique is expensive and therefore will not be available to most small firms and many medium-size firms. In the case of direct labor, for example, time and motion studies are often involved, which can be very costly. Second, the input/output relationships may be practically nonexistent in the case of manufacturing or selling and administrative overhead. Therefore, the application of this technique may be limited. The procedure should be accurate in identifying certain variable cost functions but would have little value in identifying the fixed and variable cost elements in mixed costs. Because of its limited applicability, we will not discuss this method further.

High-Low Points Method

Perhaps the most straightforward approach to analyzing cost behavior is the **high-low points method.** As its name suggests, the method utilizes data from two time periods—a representative high volume with its associated cost and a representative low volume with its associated cost. If we assume that fixed costs remain constant in both periods, the only reason for a change in the total cost is the variable cost component. The variable cost per unit of activity can be found by dividing the difference in total costs between the high and low levels of activity by the difference in the levels of activity. The formula for the variable cost per unit of activity would be:

$$\text{Variable cost per unit of activity} = \frac{\text{Difference in total costs}}{\text{Difference in high and low levels of activity}}$$

Once the variable cost per unit of activity is determined, the fixed costs are computed by estimating the total variable costs at either the high or low levels of activity and subtracting them from the total costs at the chosen level of activity.

An example will illustrate the simplicity of the approach. The following information is available for Rupert Company regarding their monthly repairs and maintenance expense for 19X6:

Month	Direct Labor Hours	Cost of Repairs and Maintenance
January	2,000	$1,500
February	2,500	1,600
March	3,500	2,000
April	3,200	1,800
May	3,700	2,250
June	4,000	2,150
July	4,500	2,500
August	5,000	3,000
September	4,200	2,500
October	4,700	2,750
November	4,400	2,400
December	3,900	2,100

Rupert feels there is a close relationship between direct labor hours (DLH) worked and the amount of repairs and maintenance cost incurred. They feel that 2,000 to 5,000 direct labor hours is the relevant range and would like to be able to develop a cost function to predict future repairs and maintenance costs. A quick glance at the data tells us that the cost is not fixed. We can see that the cost increases as the level of activity (DLH) increases, but it does not appear that it increases in direct proportion to changes in the level of activity. Using the high-low points method, we first determine the variable cost per direct labor hour:

$$\text{Variable cost per DLH} = \frac{\text{Difference in total costs}}{\text{Difference in high and low levels of activity}}$$

$$= \frac{\$3,000 - \$1,500}{5,000 \text{ DLH} - 2,000 \text{ DLH}}$$

$$= \frac{\$1,500}{3,000} = \$.50/\text{DLH}$$

We can now estimate the variable cost element for either the high or low level of activity (it does not matter which is chosen). Next, we subtract the variable from the total cost at the corresponding level of activity to estimate the fixed cost. For illustrative purposes the low level of activity is used:

Total variable cost at 2,000 DLH = 2,000 × $.50 = $1,000

Fixed cost = Total cost at (2,000 DLH) − Variable cost at (2,000 DLH)

= $1,500 − $1,000

= $500

You might wish to check to see that you get the same answer if the high level of activity is used in solving for the amount of fixed cost. The fixed and variable cost elements have now been isolated. Our suspicions were correct; the cost is a mixed cost and the cost function or formula for monthly repairs and maintenance cost can be expressed as

Total monthly repair and maintenance
costs (over the relevant range of
2,000 to 5,000 DLH)   = \$500 + \$.50 (DLH)

The high-low points method is a simple technique that is easy to understand and apply. It does, however, have some serious weaknesses. You should have noted that even though we had data from twelve different levels of activity, we used only two. That is one of the reasons that at the beginning of the discussion we made a point of stating that the high and low levels of activity should be *representative* of normal operations. It is possible that at either of the obvious high or low points of activity there could have been a serious machine breakdown, a strike, material shortages, or some other abnormal event. In these situations, professional judgment would be required in choosing a suitable alternative level of activity(ies).

Without further analysis, there is also the danger that the cost behavior is definitely curvilinear rather than linear. This is very difficult to determine by merely looking at an array of numbers. Because of the inherent risk of arriving at a cost function that incorrectly describes the actual cost behavior, it is recommended that a scattergraph always be prepared to help decide whether the high-low points method is acceptable.

Scattergraph

If a cost is being analyzed by looking at past costs and their associated activity levels, the starting point should always be the preparation of a scattergraph. The **scattergraph** is merely a graph with the vertical axis indicating the cost being analyzed (the **dependent variable**) and the horizontal axis indicating the volume or level of activity (the **independent variable**). The actual cost observations from the past will be dots at the coordinates of the respective levels of activity and related cost. A scattergraph for the Rupert Company example of repairs and maintenance costs for 19X6 is shown in Exhibit 3–7 (page 56).

Note on Exhibit 3–7 that the cost (the dependent variable) is plotted on the vertical or y-axis and that the activity measure (the independent variable) is plotted on the horizontal or x-axis. This should be true for any scattergraph. The cost "depends" on the activity level or is a function of the activity level and is therefore referred to as the dependent variable. Rupert has chosen direct labor hours as the independent variable because they think that it has the most influence on the amount of repair and maintenance costs incurred. Part of the problem of good cost analysis and the development of

EXHIBIT 3—7

Scattergraph of Repairs and Maintenance Cost Monthly for 19X6

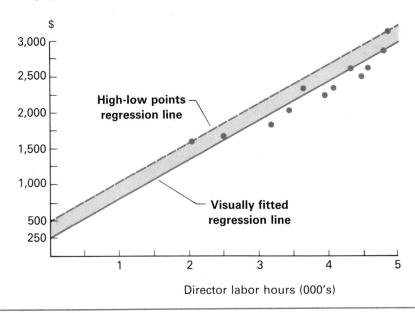

cost functions is to choose the best independent variable, the activity measure that seems to have the closest relationship with the change in the cost being analyzed. More will be said about this in the discussion of the regression method.

The preparation of Exhibit 3—7 discloses some pertinent facts. First, it appears that a linear representation of the repairs and maintenance cost is entirely legitimate. Second, it discloses that the high-low points method was not a good estimator for the cost. The dotted line connecting the high and low volume points represents the cost function derived using the high-low points method. All the actual repairs and maintenance costs (other than the two points) fall below the line.

If the scattergraph were to be used as the sole technique to analyze the cost and develop a cost function, the next step after plotting the data for 19X6 would be to draw a representative line through the points. The line, referred to as a **regression line,** is actually a line of averages with the average variable cost per direct labor hour represented by the slope of the line and the average total fixed cost represented by the point where the regression line intersects the y-axis. The line would be drawn by visually trying to get an equal number of points on each side of the line (therefore, the technique is often referred to as visual fit). A transparent ruler or a string can be used to help determine the location of the line. The solid line on Exhibit 3—7 represents an attempt to draw the regression line.

Once the regression line is drawn, a cost function can be developed. The easier approach might be to use the y-intercept as the amount of fixed cost ($250) and to then analyze the total cost at some point on the regression line to determine the amount of variable cost. If the total cost associated with 5,000 direct labor hours was used, the variable cost would be computed as follows:

Total cost at 5,000 DLH (from regression line)	$2,850
Less fixed costs	250
Total variable cost element at 5,000 DLH	$2,600

$$\$2,600/5,000 = \$.52/DLH$$

The cost function for monthly repairs and maintenance derived from the data on the scattergraph is, therefore:

Total monthly repairs and maintenance cost $= \$250 + \$.52(DLH)$

Using the scattergraph overcomes some of the weaknesses of the high-low points method. We are able to obtain more confidence in regard to our cost estimates: all of the information has an effect on the final calculation. We would regard the cost function as acceptable for ball-park estimates. We must realize, of course, that our cost function is only as accurate as our construction of the graph and visual fitting of the regression line. We can not be sure that we have drawn a "line of best fit" when we draw the regression line, and no statements can be made about the percentage of change in the total repair and maintenance costs (the dependent variable) that has been explained by the changes in the direct labor hours (the independent variable). The use of statistical regression techniques overcomes both of these weaknesses.

Statistical Regression Analysis

We can think of **statistical regression analysis** as being similar to using the scattergraph with the exception being that the regression line is mathematically described as opposed to being visually fitted. The line is truly a "line of best fit." A graphical illustration and discussion will help to clarify this statement. Exhibit 3–8 (page 58) is a typical scattergraph of a cost plotted against levels of activity. In Exhibit 3–8 and in the discussion that follows, the following notation is used:

Y_i = actual cost at X_i level of activity
a = y-intercept, the amount of fixed cost
b = slope of the line, the variable cost per unit of activity
X_i = a particular level of activity (independent variable)
$\hat{Y}_i$ = estimated cost at X_i activity (per regression line)
N = number of observations (pairs of cost and activity level)

We indicated that in statistical regression analysis we *mathematically* describe the regression line on the scattergraph. The formula for a straight

EXHIBIT 3–8

Underlying Concept of Statistical Regression Analysis

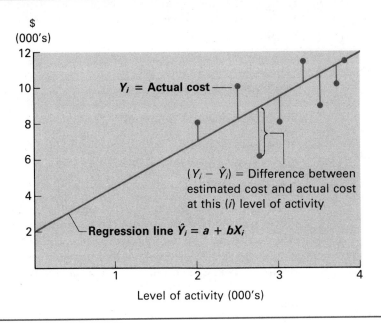

line is $Y = a + bX$. On the scattergraph in Exhibit 3–8, the Y values are actual dollars of cost at some particular level of activity X_i, so we refer to the points as Y_i. The regression line we wish to describe is to give us *estimated* values for particular levels of activity X_i. We will therefore describe the regression line with the formula $\hat{Y}_i = a + bX_i$, ($\hat{Y}_i$ indicating an estimated value). The difference between the actual cost plotted on the graph for a particular level of activity and the associated estimated value from the regression line for that same level of activity can be expressed as $(Y_i - \hat{Y}_i)$. These differences can be regarded as the estimation or prediction error (if all the actual values fell exactly on the regression line there would be no prediction error). Remember that we would try to get an equal number of points on each side of the regression line when trying to visually fit it on the scattergraph. If the line is properly drawn, this would mean that the sum of the prediction errors $(Y_i - \hat{Y}_i)$ on each side of the line would be equal and would algebraically sum to zero. Because these deviations from the regression line are both positive and negative, the individual prediction errors are squared, $(Y_i - \hat{Y}_i)^2$, leaving only positive numbers. The object, then, is to describe a regression line such that the sum of the squared differences

$$\sum_{i=1}^{n} (Y_i - \hat{Y}_i)^2$$

is the lowest value of any line that could be drawn through the points on the scattergraph. As a result, this technique is often referred to as the **Method of Least Squares.**

What we are trying to do is minimize the value of the equation

$$\sum_{i=1}^{n} (Y_i - \hat{Y}_i)^2$$

Remember that $\hat{Y}_i = a + bX_i$; therefore, we are looking for those values for a and b where the prediction error equation

$$\sum_{i=1}^{n} [Y_i - (a + bX_i)]^2$$

is at a minimum.

From the calculus, the following two normal equations are derived:

$$\Sigma Y = Na + b\Sigma X$$

$$\Sigma XY = a\Sigma X + b\Sigma X^2$$

These equations contain two unknowns: a = the y-intercept or the amount of the fixed costs, and b = the slope of the regression line or the variable cost per unit of activity X. Because the two equations are not linear transformations of one another, we can solve them as we would any other set of simultaneous equations.

In the discussion to this point we have assumed one X value — one independent variable. In the Rupert Company illustration, the independent variable is direct labor hours. When only one activity measure or independent variable is used to explain the change in cost, the technique is referred to as **simple linear regression.**

Simple Linear Regression

Statistical regression analysis utilizing simple linear regression will be illustrated by applying the method to the Rupert Company data previously used. The data is repeated here as Exhibit 3–9 along with the extensions required for the normal equations. The normal equations are

$$\sum Y = Na + b \sum X \qquad\qquad\qquad 3\text{--}1$$

$$\sum XY = a \sum X + b \sum X^2 \qquad\qquad\qquad 3\text{--}2$$

Substituting the values from Exhibit 3–9:

$$26{,}550 = 12a + 45{,}600b \qquad\qquad\qquad 3\text{--}1a$$

$$105{,}110{,}000 = 45{,}600a + 181{,}980{,}000b \qquad\qquad\qquad 3\text{--}2a$$

EXHIBIT 3–9

Data for Solving Simple Regression Analysis
X = Direct Labor Hours; Y = Repairs and Maintenance Cost

Month	DLH X	$Cost Y	X · Y	X²
January	2,000	$ 1,500	$ 3,000,000	4,000,000
February	2,500	1,600	4,000,000	6,250,000
March	3,500	2,000	7,000,000	12,250,000
April	3,200	1,800	5,760,000	10,240,000
May	3,700	2,250	8,325,000	13,690,000
June	4,000	2,150	8,600,000	16,000,000
July	4,500	2,500	11,250,000	20,250,000
August	5,000	3,000	15,000,000	25,000,000
September	4,200	2,500	10,500,000	17,640,000
October	4,700	2,750	12,925,000	22,090,000
November	4,400	2,400	10,560,000	19,360,000
December	3,900	2,100	8,190,000	15,210,000
Totals	45,600	$26,550	$105,110,000	181,980,000

In order to solve the equations, it will be necessary to eliminate one of the unknown terms (a or b). Because $45,600a$ divided by $12a$ is 3,800, the (a) term can be eliminated by multiplying equation 3–1a by 3,800 and then subtracting equation 3–2a from equation 3–1a as shown below:

Multiply 3–1a by 3,800: $100,890,000 = 45,600a + 173,280,000b$

Equation 3–2a as is: $105,110,000 = 45,600a \pm 181,980,000b$

Subtract 3–2a from 3–1a: $-4,220,000 =$ $-8,700,000b$

Divide both sides by $-8,700,000$ for solution: $\$.4850574 = b$

According to our solution, the slope of the regression line and the variable cost per direct labor hour is just over $.48. The unknown value of (a), the y-intercept (the fixed cost), can be determined by substituting the solution value for (b) in either equation 3–1 or 3–2 and solving for (a). Equation 3–1 has smaller numbers, so we will use it:

$26,550 = 12a + 45,600b$

$26,550 = 12a + 45,600(.4850574)$

$26,550 = 12a + 22,118.62$

$4,431.38 = 12a$

$369.28 = a$

This indicates that the y-intercept (and the amount of the fixed cost element) is $369.28. The regression line equation is, therefore, $Y = \$369.28 +$

$.4851X. If we restate the mathematical formula for the regression line in terms of a cost function for the monthly repairs and maintenance cost for the Rupert Company, it would be:

Total monthly repairs and maintenance cost = $369.28 + $.4851(DLH)

where the direct labor hours could vary over the relevant range of 2,000 to 5,000.

Excluding the industrial engineering approach, we have now illustrated three techniques that can be used to analyze cost behavior and develop cost functions. Note the difference in the identified cost elements for the three different analysis techniques:

	Fixed Cost	Variable Cost per DLH
High-low points method	$500.00	$.50
Scattergraph	250.00	.52
Simple linear regression	369.28	.4851

The analysis has been applied to a simple set of data. It is not difficult to see that the disparity among the answers could be greater given a larger, more complex, and more widely dispersed set of data.

Coefficient of Correlation and Determination

The use of statistical regression analysis results in an objectively determined (mathematically correct) cost function. All the cost observations are considered in the analysis. A further benefit from using this technique is the ability to measure how well the activity base used does, in fact, explain the change in the related cost. In the Rupert Company repairs and maintenance example, we can get some idea of the degree of relationship between changes in direct labor hours and the change in the repairs and maintenance cost by computing the correlation coefficient. The **correlation coefficient** is a standard measure of the degree to which two variables move together and can take on values between -1 and $+1$. In management accounting we are primarily interested in positive correlation, which implies that the two variables move in the same direction. In the Rupert Company repairs and maintenance case, this would mean that as the direct labor hours increase, the repairs and maintenance cost also increases. A zero correlation coefficient would mean that the movement of the two variables is unrelated; a correlation coefficient of $+1$ would mean perfect correlation (all actual repairs and maintenance costs fall exactly on the regression line).

The correlation coefficient merely gives some indication of the relationship between the two variables. For example, a correlation coefficient of $+.92$ means that there is a better relationship between the independent and dependent variable than a correlation coefficient of $+.80$. It does not indicate that the relationship is causal, nor does it disclose the percentage of the change in the dependent variable that is explained by the change in the independent variable. If the correlation coefficient is computed, it is easy to take the analysis one step further and compute the coefficient of determination. The **coefficient of determination** is found by merely squaring the coefficient of correlation. It discloses the percentage of the change in the dependent variable that is explained by the change in the independent variable. If, for example, the correlation coefficient for the regression line computed for the repairs and maintenance cost of the Rupert Company had been +.9, the coefficient of determination would be .81. This tells us that 81% of the variability of the repairs and maintenance cost is explained by the change in direct labor hours. Appendix 3—A illustrates the calculation of the coefficient of correlation and the coefficient of determination for the Rupert Company repairs and maintenance data.

The coefficients of correlation and determination can be very useful information in helping select the activity base used in the cost analysis process. If we find that only 50% of the variation in the dependent variable is explained by the activity base we have chosen, management may be very reluctant to place much stock in our estimates, especially if it involves a particularly high cost or if they are bidding on a contract on a very tight profit margin. If the coefficient of determination seems too low, we might search for an activity base that gives us a better relationship. For example, we could try using machine hours or direct materials cost as possible activity bases. The use of statistical regression analysis also may allow us to apply further statistical techniques employing the standard error of the estimate, leading to the determination of confidence intervals for our estimates. This topic is addressed in any elementary statistics textbook or in more advanced managerial or cost accounting textbooks.

We could run into the situation where we cannot find a suitable single independent variable, that is, the costs may vary because of more than one factor. In these cases, if the situation warrants the added time and cost, we might move from simple regression to multiple regression analysis.

Multiple Regression Analysis

Multiple regression analysis is merely a further application and expansion of simple regression analysis, which allows the consideration of more than one independent variable. In multiple regression analysis, the formula for the regression line used in simple regression, $Y = a + bX$, is expanded to include more than one independent variable. In the Rupert Company case, for example, we might expand the equation to $Y = a + bX + cZ$, where the Z could refer to the number of machine hours and c would refer to the amount of repairs and maintenance cost added per machine hour.

The "least squares" concept is essentially the same for a number of independent variables as it is for only one. If the second independent variable is added in the repairs and maintenance cost analysis as suggested above, the arithmetical computations become significantly more complex because we now have three unknowns and will have a set of three equations to deal with in finding our solution. In addition, we could no longer show the relationship on a two dimensional graph. Most management accountants now have access to a computer, however, and there is a good deal of software available for statistical regression analysis including multiple regression.

Just as with simple regression, coefficients of correlation and determination can be computed for multiple regression analysis. If there is not significant improvement in the degree of correlation by the use of multiple regression, the analyst can always revert to the simpler technique.

Considerations in the Application of Analysis Techniques

The management accountant should not get so absorbed in the mechanics of analyzing cost behavior that he or she forgets to exercise careful judgment in the process. The analysis techniques we have illustrated assume *linearity*. Economists often criticize this assumption by stating that total costs are more likely to be incurred as represented in Exhibit 3–10. Although their claim is no doubt correct, the management accountant has compensated for this nuance of cost behavior by the use of the relevant range concept. As indicated in Exhibit 3–10, this limits us to a smaller section of the total cost curve where the costs tend to approach linearity (as suggested by the dotted line in the relevant range). We have indicated that if the data and circumstances dictate, we should be ready to drop the linearity assumption and move to curvilinear analysis.

The cost analyst must also keep in mind that these techniques have all been applied to *past costs*. A meticulous definition of past costs is of little use for future periods if those costs will *change* in the future. Businesses are constantly faced with changing prices and technology. The analysis of past costs is merely the starting point in the prediction of future costs.

EXHIBIT 3–10
Economist's Cost Pattern and the Relevant Range

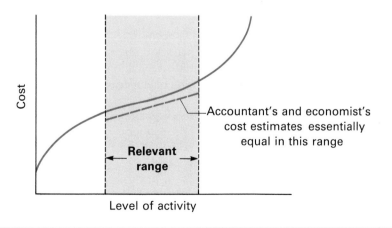

As in many other applications, the use of more sophisticated mathematical techniques along with the use of the computer in applying those techniques sometimes introduces an aura of infallibility regarding the output or solution. A very high coefficient of correlation between two variables or a high coefficient of determination does not prove that one causes the other — changes in the two variables may very well be caused by a third variable. The correlation might also be the result of a chance event that may never occur again, or the relationship may change considerably in the future because of changes in the economic or technical environment. The management accountant must be alert to possible improper application of the analysis techniques or to improper conclusions that may be drawn from the application of those techniques.

Summary

Business activity requires the incurrence of costs. If management is to effectively plan and control costs, it must know how costs respond to changes in activity.

Four types of costs were identified in this chapter that behave differently as activity levels change. In general, fixed costs do not change in response to changes in activity level during a given time period. Step costs are constant *within* a given range of activity but are different *between* ranges of activity. Variable costs are costs that, in total, change in direct proportion to changes in activity levels. Mixed costs contain both fixed and variable elements; they are positive when there is zero activity, and they increase in a linear fashion as activity increases. Variable costs per unit remain constant as the activity level changes, but unit fixed costs decrease as activity levels increase, but not in direct proportion to the activity changes.

Four techniques were discussed that can be used to classify cost behavior and develop cost functions — the industrial engineering approach, high-low points method, scattergraph, and statistical regression analysis. Application of these techniques should disclose which cost pattern best describes the cost behavior. The industrial engineering approach is costly and therefore has limited application. It would work well in those situations where there are strong engineering relationships between inputs and outputs.

Because most planning and control techniques employed by modern management require a cost breakdown into either fixed or variable costs, the fixed and variable cost elements of mixed costs need to be separately identified. The high-low points method is a simple approach to accomplish this task but suffers from the fact that it considers only two pairs of observations from the data set. Because it does not investigate the possibility of a curvilinear cost function, the method assumes that the cost structure is linear — the variable cost is constant per unit of activity.

The scattergraph and statistical analysis techniques take into consideration all the observed data pairs. The scattergraph gives visual evidence of the appropriateness of the linearity assumption but is limited in accuracy, in the ability to statistically express the relationship between the variability of the cost (the dependent variable), and in the change in activity base used (the independent variable). The use of simple or multiple regression analysis assures a mathematically defined "line of best fit." The ability to express the relationship between the variability of the cost being analyzed and the activity base that is believed to be related to it is measured by computing the coefficient of correlation or the coefficient of determination.

Those responsible for analyzing cost behavior and developing cost functions that are to be used for purposes of planning and control must exercise careful judgment in the application of the analysis techniques. They need to be aware that the behavior descriptions based on past costs are only the starting point for predictions of cost behavior and amounts for the future.

Appendix 3–A
Coefficient of Correlation and Coefficient of Determination for Repairs and Maintenance Cost, Rupert Company

As was mentioned in the chapter, the coefficient of correlation is a standard measure of the degree to which two variables move together and can take on the values between -1 and $+1$. The nearer the coefficient is to either of these extremes, the better the relationship. If we are concerned about the choice of an activity base (independent variable) to use for explaining the change in a particular cost (dependent variable), we would want to choose a base that seems to have a high degree of correlation with that particular cost (a coefficient of correlation close to $+1$). We will illustrate this concept further by computing the coefficient of correlation to determine the relationship between repairs and maintenance cost and direct labor hours for the Rupert Company using the data observations given in the chapter.

Mathematicians have developed the following equation to calculate the coefficient of correlation:

$$r = \frac{\sum_{i=1}^{n} (X_i - \overline{X}) \cdot \sum_{i=1}^{n} (Y_i - \overline{Y})}{\sqrt{\sum_{i=1}^{n} (X_i - \overline{X})^2 \cdot \sum_{i=1}^{n} (Y_i - \overline{Y})^2}}$$

where:

X_i = the independent variable (direct labor hours = DLH)

Y_i = the dependent variable (repairs and maintenance cost = R&M)

$\overline{X}$ = the average of the DLH, computed by dividing the sum of the monthly DLH by 12

$\overline{Y}$ = the average of the R&M cost, computed by dividing the sum of the monthly R&M cost by 12

$\sum_{i=1}^{n} (X_i - \overline{X}) \cdot \sum_{i=1}^{n} (Y_i - \overline{Y})$ = the sum of each difference between the individual values of the DLH and the average of the DLH multiplied by the corresponding difference between the individual R&M cost and the average of the R&M cost

$\sum_{i=1}^{n} (X_i - \overline{X})^2$ = the sum of the squared differences between the DLH and the average of the DLH

$\sum_{i=1}^{n} (Y_i - \overline{Y})^2$ = the sum of the squared differences between the R&M costs and the average of the R&M costs

Exhibit 3–11 shows the monthly direct labor hours and the related repairs and maintenance costs for 19X6, along with the extensions providing the information necessary to solve the coefficient of correlation formula.

Substituting the numbers from Exhibit 3–11 into the formula results in the following:

$$r = \frac{4,220,000}{\sqrt{8,700,000 \times 2,225,625}} = .959$$

This indicates a very good relationship between the repairs and maintenance costs and direct labor hours. It does not indicate that the change in direct labor hours *causes* the change in repairs and maintenance; it merely indicates that direct labor hours seem to do a good job of *explaining* the change in repairs and maintenance costs.

If we would like to know the percentage of change in repairs and maintenance cost that is explained by the change in direct labor hours, we could compute the coefficient of determination or r^2:

$$r^2 = .959^2 = .9197$$

This coefficient of determination indicates that nearly 92% of the variability in the repairs and maintenance cost of Rupert Company is explained by the changes in direct labor hours. It would appear that direct labor hours is a very good activity base to use for the analysis of repairs and maintenance cost and, given the caveats mentioned in the chapter, a good base to use for estimation purposes.

EXHIBIT 3–11
Data for Computation of Correlation Coefficient

Month	DLH X	$(X - \bar{X})$	$(X - \bar{X})^2$	Cost Y	$(Y - \bar{Y})$	$(Y - \bar{Y})^2$	$(X - \bar{X}) \cdot (Y - \bar{Y})$
January	2,000	−1,800	3,240,000	$ 1,500	−$712.5	$ 507,656.25	$1,282,500
February	2,500	−1,300	1,690,000	1,600	−612.5	375,156.25	796,250
March	3,500	−300	90,000	2,000	−212.5	45,156.25	63,750
April	3,200	−600	360,000	1,800	−412.5	170,156.25	247,500
May	3,700	−100	10,000	2,250	37.5	1,406.25	−3,750
June	4,000	200	40,000	2,150	−62.5	3,906.25	−12,500
July	4,500	700	490,000	2,500	287.5	82,656.25	201,250
August	5,000	1,200	1,440,000	3,000	787.5	620,156.25	945,000
September	4,200	400	160,000	2,500	287.5	82,656.25	115,000
October	4,700	900	810,000	2,750	537.5	288,906.25	483,750
November	4,400	600	360,000	2,400	187.5	35,156.25	112,500
December	3,900	100	10,000	2,100	−112.5	12,656.25	−11,250
Totals	45,600		8,700,000	$26,550		$2,225,625	$4,220,000
Average	3,800			$2,212.5			

Key Terms

Coefficient of correlation (correlation coefficient)   is a standard statistical measure of the degree to which two variables move together.

Coefficient of determination   discloses the percentage of the change in the dependent variable that is explained by the change in the independent variable. It is found by squaring the coefficient of correlation.

Committed fixed costs   are fixed costs that arise from long-term commitments. They represent investments in productive capacity including key management and operating personnel.

Dependent variable   is the cost whose behavior is being analyzed.

Discretionary (managed) fixed costs   are those fixed costs that are set at some fixed amount each year at the discretion of management.

High-low points method   establishes a regression line for mixed costs by examining the change in costs between representative high and low volume points.

Independent variable   is the output or volume level of activity against which changes in the dependent variable, the cost being analyzed, are gauged.

Industrial engineering (or work measurement) approach   is an engineering approach that studies the relationships between inputs and outputs in order to determine how costs behave.

Method of Least Squares   is another name for statistical regression analysis.

Mixed (semivariable) costs   are those costs that contain specific fixed and variable cost segments.

Multiple regression analysis   is an expansion of simple regression analysis that allows the consideration of more than one independent variable.

Regression line   is a line whose slope specifies the variable cost rate per unit. It is derived by methods such as visual fitting on a scattergraph or by the more precise statistical regression methods.

Scattergraph   has a vertical axis that indicates the costs being analyzed (dependent variable) and a horizontal axis that indicates the volume or level of activity factor (independent variable). Each past cost observation is shown as a dot at the coordinates of the respective levels of activity and related cost.

Simple linear regression   is a statistical method for splitting mixed costs into fixed and variable components. Also known as the method of least squares.

Statistical regression analysis   refers to statistical methods (simple and multiple regression analysis) for mathematically deriving a regression line.

Step costs   are constant within a range of activity but change between ranges of activity. Are fixed costs with relatively narrow relevant ranges of activity.

Questions

Q3–1   Briefly describe four widely used total cost behavior patterns.

Q3–2   Chart the four costs mentioned in Q3–1 above on a graph with activity plotted on the horizontal axis and cost on the vertical axis.

Q3–3   What effect does a *decrease* in volume have on the following?

    a. Total variable costs
    b. Unit variable costs
    c. Total fixed costs
    d. Unit fixed costs

Q3–4   Define what is meant by *relevant range*. What does this concept have to do with cost analysis and estimation?

Q3–5   Under what circumstances are step costs approximated as variable costs? As mixed or semivariable costs?

Q3–6   If step costs are not approximated by variable or mixed costs, how are they included in cost functions if the relevant range spans more than one step?

Q3–7   Economists tend to represent total cost curves as curvilinear. How can accountants justify their representation of total costs as linear?

Q3–8   Fixed costs are classified as discretionary or committed. Distinguish between the two classifications.

Q3–9   What methods are available for identifying the fixed and variable elements of a mixed cost?

Q3–10   What are the major disadvantages of using the high-low points method in describing cost behavior? Is the method *ever* acceptable, and if so, when?

Q3–11   Why should a scattergraph always be prepared when analyzing cost behavior? How are cost functions developed from a scattergraph?

Q3–12   What is the *minimum* number of observations of past cost data combinations that would be necessary in order to estimate the fixed and variable elements of a semivariable cost?

Q3–13   What is meant by the term *activity base* in regard to cost behavior analysis?

Q3–14   Why does the industrial engineering approach have limited usefulness in analyzing cost behavior?

Q3–15   What advantages does the scattergraph approach have over the high-low points method of cost analysis?

Q3–16   What is the least squares criterion?

Q3–17   Why is a regression line defined using the method of least squares regarded as more accurate than one visually fitted on a scattergraph?

Q3–18   Distinguish between coefficient of correlation and coefficient of determination citing the usefulness of each in relation to cost behavior analysis.

Q3–19   What is multiple linear regression, and when would you consider its use in cost behavior analysis?

Q3–20   What must be considered when cost functions developed by cost behavior analysis are used for cost prediction?

Exercises

E3–1   **Committed and discretionary fixed costs.** Indicate whether the following fixed costs are usually committed (C) or discretionary (D).

_____   1. Salary of the chairman of the board of directors
_____   2. Insurance on the plant property
_____   3. Fundamental research (not applicable to a specific product)
_____   4. Contract with an advertising agency for this year's advertising
_____   5. Repairs and maintenance of buildings and equipment
_____   6. Depreciation of plant and equipment
_____   7. Plant superintendent's salary
_____   8. Company calendars given as customer Christmas gifts
_____   9. Annual corporate United Way contribution
_____ 10. Cost of management development seminars

E3–2   **Identifying cost behavior patterns.** For each situation listed below, select the most appropriate cost behavior pattern. Lines on the graphs represent cost behavior patterns. The vertical axis represents total costs. The horizontal axis represents total volume. Where shown, dots represent actual costs. A pattern may be used more than once.

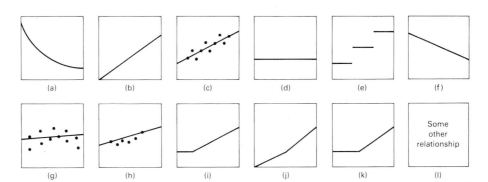

(a)   (b)   (c)   (d)   (e)   (f)

(g)   (h)   (i)   (j)   (k)   (l)

_____ 1. Total fixed costs
_____ 2. Total variable costs
_____ 3. Total mixed costs
_____ 4. Unit fixed costs
_____ 5. Unit variable costs
_____ 6. A service contract with a flat fee of $500 a month for the first 10 hours and $25 per hour thereafter
_____ 7. Incorrect use of method of least squares to describe a regression line
_____ 8. Rent of warehouse space for the winter
_____ 9. Salaries of foremen where each foreman can supervise 15 employees
_____ 10. Correct use of method of least squares to describe a regression line
_____ 11. Salesperson is guaranteed a base salary plus a commission on all sales made
_____ 12. Employees are paid $8 per hour for the first 40 hours worked each week and $12 per hour thereafter
_____ 13. An independent computer serviceperson is paid $100 per hour with a guaranteed fee of $1,000 per month
_____ 14. High-low points regression line influenced by unusual observations

E3–3   **High-low points estimation.** Three-Day-Max Freight Company operates a small fleet of trucks and has the following information available about operating costs:

Year	Miles	Operating Costs
19X6	800,000	$700,000
19X5	1,000,000	850,000

Required: Use the high-low points method to develop a cost function for the operating costs for Three-Day-Max Freight Company.

E3–4   **High-low points method estimation.** Amwell Company has supplied the following information about its maintenance and repair cost for the year 19X6:

Month	Direct Labor Hours	Maintenance and Repair Cost
May (High)	20,100	$29,290
November (Low)	13,800	23,620

Required: Use the high-low points method to develop a cost function for the monthly maintenance and repair cost for Amwell Company.

E3–5   **High-low points method — cost behavior and estimation.** The following information is available regarding one of the costs incurred by the Jackson Printing Company:

	Direct Labor Hours	Cost
High Activity	2,145	$2,681.25
Low Activity	1,358	1,697.50

Required: Using the high-low points method to analyze the cost:

     1. Identify the cost according to its cost behavior.
     2. Develop a cost function for this cost.

E3–6   **High-low points method estimation.** Jackson, Inc. is preparing a flexible budget for 19X1 and requires a breakdown of the cost of steam used in its factory into the fixed and variable elements. The following data on the cost of steam used and direct labor hours worked are available for the last six months of 19X6:

Month	Cost of Steam	Direct Labor Hours
July	$ 15,850	3,000
August	13,400	2,050
September	16,370	2,900
October	19,800	3,650
November	17,600	2,670
December	18,500	2,650
Total	$101,520	16,920

Required: Use the high-low points method to develop a cost function for the monthly cost of steam.

(CPA Adapted)

E3–7 **High-low points method estimation.** The Lowe Company operates a number of machines in their machine shop and the following monthly power costs were incurred for the year 19X6:

Month	Machine Hours	Power Costs
January	3,300	$ 9,150
February	2,800	9,200
March	2,600	8,900
April	3,700	10,550
May	3,400	10,100
June	2,900	9,350
July	2,500	8,750
August	3,200	9,800
September	2,200	8,800
October	3,800	10,700
November	3,900	10,850
December	4,200	12,000

Required:
1. Using the high-low points method, develop the cost function for the monthly power costs.
2. What would be the expected power costs for a month in which the machine hours totaled 3,650?

E3–8 **Scattergraph and high-low points method.** Refer to the data for Lowe Company in Exercise 3–7.

Required:
1. Prepare a scattergraph using the data for Lowe Company power costs for the year 19X6. (The independent variable is machine hours plotted on the x-axis, and the power cost is the dependent variable plotted on the y-axis.) Visually fit a regression line to your plotted points.
2. What is the approximate monthly fixed cost of power? The approximate variable cost of power per machine hour? Express in a cost function formula.
3. Why does your cost function differ from the one developed in Exercise 3–7? Which method (high-low points or scattergraph) seems most appropriate for developing a cost function for power costs for Lowe Company?

E3–9   **Unit fixed and variable costs.** Tandor Company produces and sells one product and operates within a relevant range of 2,000 to 6,000 units.

Required: Complete the following schedule reflecting the company's total and unit costs:

	Units Produced and Sold		
	2,000	4,000	6,000
Total fixed costs	$45,000	$_____	$_____
Total variable costs	40,000	_____	_____
Total costs	$85,000	$_____	$_____
Cost per unit:			
Fixed costs	$_____	$_____	$_____
Variable costs	_____	_____	_____
Total cost per unit	$_____	$_____	$_____

E3–10   **Estimating automobile operating costs using high-low points method.** Carlson Company is a wholesaling firm with a number of salespeople on the road calling on customers. The company furnishes a standard automobile for all salespeople and absorbs the associated expenses. Carlson has found that if an automobile is driven 60,000 miles per year the operating costs average 16⅓ cents per mile. If an automobile is driven 30,000 miles, the operating costs average 21⅓ cents per mile.

Required: 1. Using the high-low points method, determine the fixed and variable elements of operating an automobile and express them in a cost estimation function.

2. Using the cost function developed above, what would be the expected total operating costs if a salesperson drove an automobile 48,000 miles during a year?

E3–11   **Estimating step costs.** Brandees Department Store employs a number of people to do gift wrapping at Christmas time each year. The gift wrapping is available for three hours each evening from 7 to 10 P.M. Gift wrappers are paid $10 per hour for the three hours and can wrap a maximum of 15 packages per hour. Brandees would like to develop a cost estimation function for the labor cost associated with gift wrapping based on packages wrapped.

Required: 1. The labor costs are obviously a step cost with each step encompassing 45 packages (three hours times 15 packages per hour). Develop a cost estimation function where the labor costs are treated as a mixed cost.

2. Using the cost function developed above, estimate the total cost of wrapping 405 packages and 406 packages. What is the amount of error associated with your two approximations?

E3–12   **Developing a cost function using method of least squares.** Komputer Kare is trying to determine the cost of normal microcomputer repair jobs. The following information is available regarding the past six months:

Month	Computers Repaired	Labor Hours
January	15	45
February	5	20
March	10	35
April	20	60
May	15	40
June	25	70
	90	270

Required: 1. Using the method of least squares simple regression model, develop a function to estimate the total time required to repair microcomputers between the relevant range of 5 and 25 computers.

2. If repairpersons are paid $25 per hour, what is the expected labor cost if 22 computers are repaired in the following month?

E3–13 **Coefficient of correlation and coefficient of determination.** Sundby Company has developed a cost function to estimate the company's electricity expense using the method of least squares. Direct labor hours have been used as the independent variable. The company's total electricity expense for the past 18 months has been $38,000. Direct labor hours during the period totaled 150,000 hours. The direct labor hour differences from average multiplied by the electricity expense differences from its average and summed

$$\left[\sum_{i=1}^{n} (x_i - \bar{x}) \cdot \sum_{i=1}^{n} (y_i - \bar{y}) \right]$$

is 5,027. The direct labor hour differences from average squared and summed

$$\left[\sum_{i=1}^{n} (x_i - \bar{x})^2 \right]$$

is 26,000. The electricity expense differences from average squared and summed

$$\left[\sum_{i=1}^{n} (y_i - \bar{y})^2 \right]$$

is 1,200.

Required: 1. Compute the coefficient of correlation, r, and the coefficient of determination, r^2, for direct labor hours as it relates to electricity expense.

2. What can be said about direct labor hours as an activity base to use for estimating electricity expense?

Problems

P3–14 **Cost behavior analysis using high-low points method and unit activity base.** Tasty Corn Dogs is a relatively new company that is marketing a new corn dog made with a special Polish sausage and a batter from a secret recipe. They are considering franchising their operation and need to have a better understanding of cost behavior for discussion with potential franchisees. Tasty has accumulated the following data:

Monthly sales of corn dogs in units	50,000	80,000	100,000
Food cost in corn dogs	$40,000	$ 64,000	$ 80,000
Wages and fringe benefits of employees	30,000	37,200	42,000
Delivery expense	8,000	12,800	16,000
Depreciation of equipment	1,000	1,000	1,000
Utility expense	1,500	2,100	2,500
Rent of building	1,500	1,500	1,500
Supplies (cleaning, napkins, etc.)	1,200	1,400	1,700
Administration	1,800	1,800	1,800
	$85,000	$121,800	$146,500

Required:
1. Identify each of the costs as being fixed, variable, or mixed.
2. Develop a schedule listing each cost and the fixed element of each and the variable element per corn dog. Total the amounts of each element and express them as a cost estimation function for the total monthly costs (activity base is the number of corn dogs).
3. Based on your analysis to this point, what would be the expected total costs if 95,000 corn dogs were sold?

P3–15 **Cost behavior analysis using high-low points method and dollar activity base.** Harry's Hardware has the following income statements available for two months of 19X6:

	February	December
Sales	$70,000	$120,000
Cost of goods sold	38,500	66,000
Gross margin	$31,500	$ 54,000
Operating expenses:		
Utilities	$ 5,600	$ 6,600
Advertising	1,000	1,000
Supplies	700	950
Depreciation	3,700	3,700
Salaries and commissions	5,000	7,500
Delivery expense	1,800	2,800
Administration	2,200	2,200
Total expenses	$20,000	$ 24,750
Net income	$11,500	$ 29,250

Required:
1. Identify each of the costs as being fixed, variable, or mixed.
2. Develop a schedule listing each cost and the fixed element of each and the variable element *per sales dollar.* Total the amounts of each cost element and express them as a cost estimation function for the total monthly cost associated with the hardware store (remember that the activity basis is *sales dollars*).
3. Based on the cost function developed in (2) above, what would be the total estimated costs when sales revenue totaled $115,000?

P3–16 **High-low points method of analyzing cost behavior.** Crannon Manufacturing has incurred the following overhead costs for the past six months:

Month	Machine Hours	Total Overhead Cost
January	60,000	$215,000
February	50,000	195,000
March	70,000	235,000
April	80,000	255,000
May	65,000	225,000
June	45,000	185,000

The total overhead costs consist of depreciation, supervisors' salaries, power and water, and repairs and maintenance. Crannon analyzed these costs at the 50,000 machine hour level and determined the following:

Depreciation	$ 20,000
Supervisors' salaries	55,000
Power and water	60,000
Repairs and maintenance	60,000
Total overhead costs	$195,000

The company is sure that depreciation and supervisors' salaries are fixed costs and that power and water costs are variable. The repairs and maintenance costs, however, do not seem to be fixed *or* variable. Crannon has heard about mixed costs and has appealed to you as their managerial accounting consultant to analyze this cost further.

Required:

1. Determine the amount of total overhead costs at the high level of activity (80,000 machine hours) and the low level of activity (45,000 machine hours) that was due to repairs and maintenance costs.

2. With the information obtained in (1) above, and using the high-low points method, determine the fixed cost element of repairs and maintenance and the variable cost element per machine hour. Express your findings as a cost function for repairs and maintenance.

3. How much repairs and maintenance cost and total overhead costs would be expected to be incurred at 78,000 machine hours?

P3–17 High-low points method analysis with changing prices. Dr. Manly Meddling is a well-known psychiatrist who travels extensively giving stress management seminars. He was concerned that the stress management seminars would gradually lose their popularity, so in 19X1 he started a counseling service. He employed licensed psychologists giving them a guaranteed base salary plus an hourly payment for each hour of counseling (each patient receives one hour of counseling at each appointment). Dr. Meddling gave salary and hourly increments at the beginning of 19X3 and 19X5. He is now being asked to increase the guaranteed base salaries by 15% and to increase the hourly wages by 20% for 19X7. The number of hours of counseling and the salaries and wages paid for the last six years are given below:

Year	Counseling Hours	Counseling Salaries and Wages
19X1	3,000	$ 65,000
19X2	3,800	67,000
19X3	3,500	92,000
19X4	5,000	122,000
19X5	4,800	144,200
19X6	4,000	124,200

Required:

1. Develop a cost function for counselors' salaries and wages costs for 19X7 if the increase is granted.

2. Dr. Meddling would like to know the counselors' salaries and wages costs for 19X7 if there are 4,500 hours of counseling. Use your cost function developed in (1) above to arrive at the estimated amount.

P3–18 Identifying cost behavior patterns. The graphs below represent a number of cost behavior patterns that might be experienced by a company. The vertical axes of the graphs represent total dollars of cost, and the horizontal axes represent levels of activity or volume. In all cases the zero point is at the intersection of the two axes.

Required: For each situation described below, select the graph that illustrates the cost pattern described. The graphs may be used more than once.

_____ 1. Lease of a piece of production equipment where the lease stipulates a minimum charge of $2,000 for up to 1,000 hours of machine time. After 1,000 hours there is an additional charge of $1.50 per hour up to 2,000 hours. There is no further charge for additional hours of use.

_____ 2. Electricity bill — a flat fixed charge, plus a variable cost after a certain number of kilowatt hours are used

_____ 3. City water bill, which is computed as follows:

First 1,000,000 gallons or less	$1,000 flat fee
Next 10,000 gallons	.003 per gallon used
Next 10,000 gallons	.006 per gallon used
Next 10,000 gallons	.009 per gallon used
etc.	etc.

_____ 4. Cost of raw materials used

_____ 5. Cost of special gear lubricant, where the cost per pound decreases by $.03 per pound until 300 pounds are used. At this point there are no further cost reductions.

_____ 6. Depreciation of equipment, where the amount is computed by the straight-line method. When the depreciation rate was established, it was anticipated that the obsolescence factor would be greater than the wear-and-tear factor.

_____ 7. Rent on a factory building donated by the city, where the agreement calls for a fixed-fee payment unless 200,000 man-hours are worked, in which case no rent need be paid

_____ 8. Salaries of repairpersons, where one repairperson is needed for every 1,000 machine-hours or less (that is, 0 to 1,000 hours requires one repairperson, 1,001 to 2,000 hours requires two, and so forth)

_____ 9. Cost of raw materials used where the first 200 units cost $10 each, the next 200 units cost $9 each, and the next 200 units cost $8 each. There is no further quantity discount for amounts used over 600 units.

_____ 10. Rent on a factory building donated by county, where agreement calls for rent of $100,000 less $1 for each direct-labor hour worked in excess of 200,000 hours, but minimum rental payment of $20,000 must be paid

(CPA Adapted)

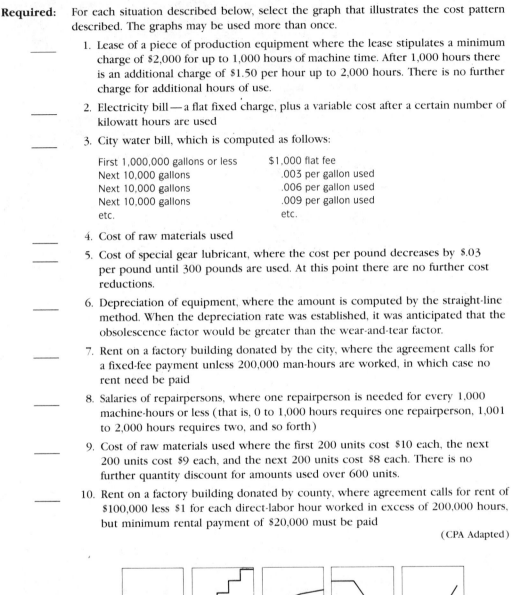

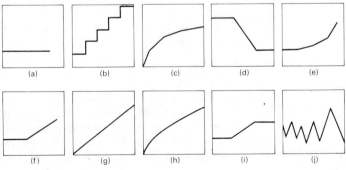

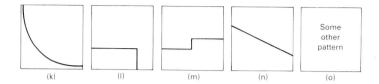

(k)   (l)   (m)   (n)   (o) Some other pattern

P3–19 **Scattergraph and simple regression analysis.** Perry Johnson operates a small feed-lot for finishing beef for a specialty food chain. He has the facilities to handle 1,500 feeder cattle at one time but varies the number he puts in his feedlot at one time depending on his assessment of future demand and prices. He has kept on a schedule of holding each lot of cattle for six months.

Perry has had some difficulty predicting the medical related costs associated with the number of cattle finished. The medical related costs are the result of a retainer with the local veterinary, lot preparation each time a new group of cattle are added to the lot, costs of medicine and extra veterinary charges, and normal medical supplements added to the feeding ration. Perry believes that the cost should be variable, but that has not proven to be the case. He has supplied the following data for the last ten lots of cattle he has finished:

Lot No.	Number of Feeders	Medical Related Costs
1	600	$22,500
2	500	22,000
3	1,100	37,000
4	1,200	43,000
5	900	32,500
6	800	31,000
7	1,000	37,000
8	1,300	43,500
9	700	30,000
10	950	34,500

Required:
1. Prepare a scattergraph using the data supplied by Perry. Visually fit a regression line to the plotted points.

2. The graph indicates that the medical related cost is what kind of cost? Using your scattergraph, develop a cost estimation function for these costs for Perry.

3. Using the above data and the method of least squares, develop a cost estimation function for the medical related costs. Is there a significant difference between the cost function developed using the scattergraph and the one developed using the method of least squares? Why is this?

4. The data used in your cost analysis covers a five-year span. Should you advise Perry Johnson of potential inaccuracies in your cost estimation function? If so, why?

P3–20 **Mixed cost analysis using three methods.** Decatur Seeds is a large producer of corn, wheat, and soybean hybrid seeds with headquarters located in midwestern United States. Randy Anderson is the plant manager of a seed conditioning plant and is in the process of budgeting costs for the 19X8 fiscal year. He has had problems with estimating the monthly costs of the utilities expense in the past and has had arguments with his plant controller regarding the cost behavior of utilities expense. Randy thinks that the expense should be variable, but the controller says that it is more fixed than variable, so he proposes putting it in the monthly budget as a fixed expense.

You are an enterprising management trainee working in the corporate offices of Decatur Seeds, and on a visit to Randy's plant site you are asked if you have a solution to the problem. You ask Randy and the controller if they have past data available regarding the amount of utilities expense and the bushels of seed conditioned in the plant. They provide you with the following data for the last fiscal year:

Month	Bushels of Seed Conditioned (000's)	Utilities Expense
August	120	$7,200
September	160	9,000
October	150	7,500
November	130	7,000
December	140	7,400
January	90	6,000
February	110	6,700
March	100	6,500
April	80	5,600
May	70	5,500
June	60	5,400
July	50	5,500

You explain to Randy and the controller that you can show them three techniques that could be used to develop a cost estimation function for utilities expense. They are anxious to see and hear your explanation.

Required:

1. Develop a cost estimation function for utilities expense using the high-low points method.

2. Prepare a scattergraph by plotting the above data on a graph. Visually fit a regression line to the plotted points. Express your regression line in terms of a cost estimation function for the utilities expense.

3. Develop a cost estimation function for utilities expense using the method of least squares.

4. In your discussion with Perry and the controller, advise them on the following questions:
   a. What kind of cost is utilities expense?
   b. Which of the three methods you have used in your analysis is most appropriate for *this* data? Why?

P3–21   **High-low points method, scattergraph, and regression analysis.** The JBC Company manufactures a wide range of products at several plant locations. The Singapore plant, which manufactures electrical components, has been experiencing difficulties with fluctuating monthly overhead costs. The fluctuations have made it difficult to estimate the level of overhead that will be incurred for any one month.

Management needs to be able to estimate overhead costs accurately if they wish to improve their planning of operations and financial requirements. JBC subscribes to a trade association magazine that indicates that for companies manufacturing electrical components, overhead tends to vary with direct labor hours. Accordingly, one member of the accounting staff has proposed that the cost behavior pattern of the overhead costs be determined and that budgeted direct labor hours be used as the activity base for prediction purposes.

Another member of the accounting staff has suggested that a good starting place for determining the cost behavior pattern of overhead costs would be an analysis of historical data. The historical cost behavior pattern would provide a basis for estimating future overhead costs. The methods that have been proposed for determining the cost behavior pattern include the high-low points method, the scattergraph method, simple linear regression, multiple regression, and exponential smoothing. Of these methods, JBC has decided to employ the high-low points method, the scattergraph method, and simple linear regression. Data on direct labor hours and the respective overhead costs incurred have been collected for the past two years. The raw data are as follows:

	19X1		19X2	
Month	Direct Labor Hours	Overhead Costs	Direct Labor Hours	Overhead Costs
January	20,000	$84,000	21,000	$86,000
February	25,000	99,000	24,000	93,000
March	22,000	89,500	23,000	93,000
April	23,000	90,000	22,000	87,000
May	20,000	81,500	20,000	80,000
June	19,000	75,500	18,000	76,500
July	14,000	70,500	12,000	67,500
August	10,000	64,500	13,000	71,000
September	12,000	69,000	15,000	73,500
October	17,000	75,000	17,000	72,500
November	16,000	71,500	15,000	71,000
December	19,000	78,000	18,000	75,000

All equipment in the Singapore plant is leased under an arrangement calling for a flat fee up to19,500 direct labor hours of activity in the plant, after which rental charges are assessed on an hourly basis. Rental expense is a major item of overhead cost.

Required:

1. Using the high-low points method, determine the cost formula for overhead in the Singapore plant.

2. Repeat (1) above, this time using the least squares method. Your assistant has computed the following amounts, which may be helpful in your analysis:

$$\Sigma X = 435,000$$

$$\Sigma Y = \$1,894,000$$

$$\Sigma XY = \$35,170,500,000$$

$$\Sigma X^2 = 8,275,000,000$$

3. Prepare a scattergraph, including on it all data for the two-year period. Fit a regression line to the plotted points by visual inspection.

4. Assume that the Singapore plant works 20,500 direct labor hours during a month. Compute the expected overhead cost for the month, using the cost formulas developed above with

    a. High-low points method,

    b. The least squares method,

    c. The scattergraph method.

5. Of the three proposed methods, which one should the JBC Company use to estimate monthly overhead costs in the Singapore plant? Explain fully, indicating the reasons why the other methods are less desirable.

6. Would the relevant range concept probably be more or less important in the Singapore plant than in most companies?

(CMA Adapted)

P3–22   **Cost behavior analysis using method of least squares.** Joyce Company's plant management wishes to develop a cost estimation function to use to predict the factory overhead that can be expected to be incurred at various activity levels. The function is to be developed using the method of least squares. Sufficient evidence is available to conclude that factory overhead varies with direct labor hours, and monthly data for the last three years were provided from plant records.

    The three-year period contained various occurrences not uncommon to many businesses. During the first year, production was severely curtailed for two months because of wildcat strikes. In the second year, production was reduced in one month because of material shortages and materially increased (overtime scheduled) during two months to meet the units required for a one-time sales order. At the end of the second year, employee benefits were raised significantly as the result of a labor agreement. Production during the third year was not affected by any special circumstances.

    Various members of Joyce's staff raised some issues regarding the historical data collected for the cost behavior analysis.

    a. Some believed that the use of data from all 36 months would provide a more accurate portrayal of cost behavior. Although they recognized that any of the monthly data could include efficiencies and inefficiencies, they believed that these efficiencies and inefficiencies would tend to balance out over a longer period of time.

    b. Others suggested that only those months that were considered normal should be used, so that the analysis would not be distorted.

    c. Still others felt that only the most recent 12 months should be used because they were the most relevant.

    d. Some questioned whether historical data should be used at all to form the basis for a cost estimation function.

    The Accounting Department ran two methods of least squares analyses of the data — one using the data from all 36 months and the other using only the data from the last 12 months. The following information was derived:

	Data from All 36 Months	Data from Most Recent 12 Months
Fixed cost	$123,810	$109,020
Variable rate	$ 1.6003	$ 4.1977
Coefficient of correlation	.4710	.6891

Required: 1. From the analysis that used data from all 36 months, determine

    a. The cost function to use in estimating monthly factory overhead,

    b. The factory overhead estimate when 23,500 direct labor hours are worked.

2. Select the analysis results (36 months versus 12 months) to be preferred as a basis for cost behavior estimation.

3. Comment on the four specific issues raised by members of Joyce's staff.

(CMA Adapted)

P3–23   **Choosing the appropriate activity base; cost behavior analysis.** The Budget and Analysis Department of Potter Corporation is trying to arrive at the best activity base to use for developing a cost estimation function for the company's supplies expense. The following information about past expenses and two potential activity bases has been supplied:

Month	Supplies Expense	Direct Labor Hours	Machine Hours
March	$ 2,500	3,900	2,100
April	2,400	4,200	2,000
May	2,600	4,200	2,100
June	2,550	3,950	2,000
July	2,450	3,800	1,950
August	2,450	3,900	2,000
September	2,500	4,200	2,050
October	2,550	4,300	2,100
November	2,650	4,250	2,400
December	2,550	4,300	2,300
Totals	$25,200	41,000	21,000

Required:

1. Compute the coefficient of correlation, r, and the coefficient of determination, r^2, between supplies expense and each of the two potential activity bases.

2. Which of the two activity bases above should be used as the activity measure for a cost estimation function?

3. Using the activity base selected in (2) above, develop a cost estimation function using the method of least squares.

CHAPTER 4

Cost-Volume-Profit Analysis for Short-Run Planning

Learning Objectives

After reading this chapter you should be able to:

1. Understand the meaning of break-even and its extension to cost-volume-profit analysis in single product situations.

2. Be able to apply cost-volume-profit analysis in multiproduct situations.

3. Understand the importance and application of cost-volume-profit analysis as a short-run planning tool.

4. Have knowledge of the diagrammatic methods for presenting cost-volume-profit analysis.

5. Comprehend the use and limitation of individual product line cost-volume-profit analysis in multiproduct situations.

6. Appreciate the underlying assumptions of cost-volume-profit analysis.

T he ability to break costs down into fixed and variable components discussed in the preceding chapter leads to many useful applications involving both short-run and long-run planning and also control (comparing actual results against plan). The first of these uses that we shall examine is cost-volume-profit analysis, a short-run planning tool.

Cost-volume-proft (C-V-P) analysis helps to answer questions concerning the amount of sales necessary to generate particular amounts of profit. Moreover, it is a tool that enables management to assess the effect on profits of possible changes that can be undertaken quite rapidly. These include changes in selling price of products or services, changes in advertising expenditures on the various product lines, changes in variable costs such as substituting a less expensive direct material for a more costly one, changes in sales mix of the firm's product lines, and changes in the structure of fixed and variable costs resulting from changes in production methods. C-V-P analysis is extremely useful when employed in conjunction with the budgetary process because it is a dynamic tool for assessing "what if" types of questions raised by operating management. Furthermore, the availability of spreadsheet computer programs has greatly improved the flexibility of this type of analysis. However, it should be stressed that underlying assumptions such as the effect on sales volume of a change in price must be reasonable if this form of analysis is to be helpful in aiding managerial decision making.

We begin by examining the most limiting type of C-V-P application: determination of the break-even point in a single-product firm. C-V-P is next extended to determining levels of sales needed to attain particular profit levels on both before- and after-tax bases. The analysis is then extended to multiproduct situations. We next illustrate several situations where key variables are changed. Graphic methods of presenting C-V-P analysis are then discussed. The special problem of whether individual product line C-V-P analysis in multiproduct situations can or should be determined is also examined. Finally, the limiting assumptions of C-V-P analysis are enumerated and discussed.

Cost-Volume-Profit (C-V-P) Analysis in a One-Product Enterprise

Break-Even Analysis

If all costs (expenses) of a firm can be classified into either the fixed or variable category, operations at a zero level of profit — called the break-even point — can be depicted by the following formula:

$$R = VC + FC \qquad\qquad 4\text{--}1$$

where

R   = Total revenues

VC = Total variable costs

FC = Total fixed costs

At the **break-even (B-E) point,** revenues equal total expenses (fixed costs and variable costs). A simple illustration should clarify the concept. Assume that the XYZ Company manufactures a single product, called the A-1, which sells for $50 per unit. Variable costs are $20 per unit, and fixed costs are expected to be $1,800,000 for the year. To determine the number of units that must be sold in order to break even, we would solve for x (the number of units) in the following break-even equation:

$$\$50x = \$20x + \$1,800,000 \qquad\qquad\qquad 4\text{--}1a$$

and

$$\$50x - \$20x = \$1,800,000$$

$$\$30x = \$1,800,000$$

$$x = \frac{\$1,800,000}{\$30}$$

$$x = 60,000 \text{ units}$$

The break-even point is 60,000 units. The $30 amount divided into the total fixed costs is determined by subtracting the variable costs per unit from the revenue per unit. This is known as the contribution margin per unit. **Contribution margin per unit** represents the increase in working capital resulting from the excess of revenues per unit over the variable cost per unit generated by the sale of a unit of product. Hence the break-even point reduces to FC/(R − VC). This might also be expressed as FC/CM with CM being the designation for the contribution margin. The latter is a more general expression than the former because it refers to both the per unit and percentage approaches (discussed next), whereas the former expresses only the per unit contribution margin approach. It is also important to note that the **contribution margin** concept is frequently used on an aggregated basis: (total) revenues minus (total) variable costs equal (total) contribution margin.

Contribution Margin as a Percentage of Revenues

The contribution margin in break-even analysis can be expressed as a percentage per dollar of revenue as well as an amount per unit of sale. The contribution margin per unit of $30 is divided by the revenue per unit of $50 to arrive at the **contribution margin ratio** of 60%. The 60% represents the portion of each dollar of sales that is the contribution margin. The budgeted fixed costs of $1,800,000 are then divided by the 60% to arrive at the break-even point of $3,000,000 of sales. Note that $3,000,000 of sales multiplied by the contribution margin percentage (60%) gives $1,800,000, the amount left over after covering variable costs, which is equal to the fixed costs. Both approaches are used in C-V-P analysis: contribution margin per unit to arrive at the number of units that must be sold in order to attain a particular goal as well as contribution margin percentage in order to determine the necessary dollars of sales for achieving a goal. The results, of course, are closely related and easily transformable into the other number: 60,000 units times $50 per unit equals $3,000,000 of total revenues at the B-E point. The two approaches illustrated in this section and the previous one, utilizing the XYZ Company example, are summarized in Exhibit 4–1.

Variable costs are often expressed as a percentage or ratio of sales VC/R. Because revenues minus variable costs equal the contribution margin, the contribution margin ratio CM/R is complementary to the **variable cost ratio.** Thus VC/R + CM/R = 1.

Profit Analysis

Although break-even point determination is useful, the analysis is easily extended to the C-V-P realm: deriving the number of units or dollars of sales necessary to reach any desired level of profit by extending equation 4–1 to:

$$R = VC + FC + DP \qquad 4-2$$

where

DP = Desired point level

Continuing with the same example but assuming that management would like to know how many units must be sold in order to attain a profit of $2,700,000, we would have

$$\$50x = \$20x + \$1,800,000 + \$2,700,000 \qquad 4-2a$$

EXHIBIT 4–1
The Two Approaches to C-V-P Analysis

Expressing Contribution Margin in **Units** *of Sales*		*Expressing Contribution Margin in* **Dollars** *of Sales*	
Revenue per unit	$50	Contribution margin per unit	$30
− Variable cost per unit	20	÷ Revenue per unit	$50
= Contribution margin per unit	$30	= Contribution margin as a percentage	60%
Break-even in units	$\dfrac{\$1,800,000}{\$30}$	Break-even in dollars of revenues	$\dfrac{\$1,800,000}{.60}$

and

$$\$30x = \$4,500,000$$

$$x = \frac{\$4,500,000}{\$30}$$

$$x = 150,000 \text{ units}$$

The $2,700,000 may have been selected because it represents a certain percentage of the total investment in the firm's assets. If this were the case management would be striving to attain a particular *return on assets.* Of course, to say that it takes the sale of 150,000 units to attain a profit of $2,700,000 is not quite the same as saying that this is a realistic goal given existing marketing conditions.

Expressing the desired profit level in terms of necessary sales, we would divide the total of fixed costs and desired profit (totalling $4,500,000) by the contribution margin of 60% to arrive at a sales level of $7,500,000. Of course, 150,000 units multiplied by a selling price of $50 also gives the same total sales requirement of $7,500,000.

A Simple Example of C-V-P Analysis

The power of C-V-P analysis can be demonstrated with a simple illustration. Assume that the firm in our example is deliberating whether to raise advertising expenditures — a fixed cost — for the forthcoming period by an amount of $60,000. In order for the expenditure to be worthwhile, it must boost sales by at least 2,000 units. This is the case because $60,000 divided by a contribution margin of $30 per unit equals 2,000 units. If the additional sales are above 2,000 units, profit would be higher than it would have been without the increased expenditure. Similarly, if incremental sales are less than 2,000 units, profit would be lower than it would have been without the increased advertising expenditure. The 2,000 unit amount, then, is a differential break-even point that can be used as a benchmark for assessing whether or not the additional advertising expenditure should be made. Several other illustrations using C-V-P analysis for analyzing potential changes will be presented later in this chapter.

Profit Analysis on an After-Tax Basis

The desired profit level expressed in equation 4–2 ignores income taxes. Consequently, it is a before-tax approach. If it is desired to determine the level of sales needed to attain a certain level of income on an after-tax basis, the desired profit term in equation 4–2 is modified by dividing it by the complement of the tax rate (1 minus the tax rate) and becomes

$$R = VC + FC + \frac{DP}{1 - T}$$

where

T = The differential tax rate

Assume in the example above that management wants to know how many units must be sold in order to attain a profit of $2,700,000 after allowing for taxes at a 40% rate. The formula becomes

$$\$50x = \$20x + \$1,800,000 + \frac{\$2,700,000}{1 - .40}$$

and

$$\$30x = \$1,800,000 + \$4,500,000$$

$$x = \frac{\$6,300,000}{\$30}$$

$$x = 210,000 \text{ units}$$

In total required sales dollars, the $6,300,000 would be divided by 60% showing necessary sales of $10,500,000. Two points deserve to be mentioned relative to determining desired after-tax levels of profit.

Note first that the complement of the tax rate $(1 - .40)$ is another example of the contribution margin concept. It defines the percentage of a dollar of pretax income that is kept after satisfying tax requirements. Thus, $2,700,000 of desired after-tax profit when divided by .6 gives $4,500,000. This amount is the required before-tax profit necessary to generate the desired after-tax profit ($4,500,000 × .6 = $2,700,000).

Second, many firms do C-V-P analysis on a before-tax rather than an after-tax basis. There are several reasons underlying the before-tax choice. Although income taxes are an extremely important aspect of business, they are generally not a primary operating consideration except in the very special area of long-term capital investment projects. By *operating considerations* we mean attempts to increase income by increasing revenues or reducing incurred expenses. Tax decisions are generally separate from operating decisions and may be intertwined with what may be termed *accounting policy* questions, such as the choice between LIFO and FIFO inventory costing methods.

Another reason that the before-tax approach is frequently employed is that different amounts of income have been subject to different income tax rates. For example, the first $50,000 of income of corporations is taxed at 15%, with amounts between $50,001 and $75,000 taxed at 25%. Amounts above $75,000 are taxed at 34%. Furthermore, in situations where firms have suffered income tax losses in previous years, income taxes can be completely avoided in succeeding profitable years. Suffice it to say that tax questions are complex and often are separate from or do not affect primary operating questions concerning increasing revenues or decreasing incurred expenses.

Cost-Volume-Profit Analysis in Multiproduct Enterprises

In today's modern industrial economy, single product firms are indeed rare. Nevertheless, it serves as a good introduction to the multiproduct situation. We shall introduce one more product, B-2, to the XYZ Company illustration used in the previous section. Product B-2 sells for $120 with a variable cost of $30 per unit. We will also assume that periodic fixed costs are expected to be $3,000,000.

Although the principles in a multiproduct C-V-P situation are exactly the same as in the single product case, one crucial element must be added: the **sales mix** or proportion in which the various products are expected to be sold. In our example, assume that XYZ's marketing management expects 60% of the number of units sold to be A-1's. Contribution margin analysis can be set up in the format shown in Exhibit 4–2. Individual contribution margins are multiplied by the appropriate weighting factor (the 60% to 40% ratio of A-1's to B-2's reduces to 3 to 2).

The grand total column is the key. If the break-even point is desired in sales dollars, the fixed costs of $3,000,000 are divided by the weighted average contribution margin percentage of .6923077, or $4,333,333 dollars of sales. If desired in units, the $3,000,000 is divided by the weighted average contribution margin of $54 resulting in 55,556 units. In turn, this total is divided into 60% A-1's (33,334) and 40% B-2's (22,222). This basic example will be used in several contexts throughout the chapter.

The importance of the sales mix in Exhibit 4–2 should now be apparent. The stronger the weighting in favor of the high-margin product—B-2 in our example—the higher the weighted average contribution margin percentage (or margin per unit), the lower the break-even point.

Calculations of desired profit levels on either a before-tax or after-tax basis could likewise be done using a weighted average contribution margin in

EXHIBIT 4–2

Weighted Average Contribution Margin Analysis (WACM)[a]

	A-1	× Weight	= Total	B-2	× Weight	= Total	Grand Total
Revenue	$50 ×	3	= $150	$120 ×	2	= $240	$390
Variable cost	20 ×	3	= 60	30 ×	2	= 60	120
Contribution margin	$30 ×	3	= $ 90	$ 90 ×	2	= $180	$270

WACM%

WACM per unit[b]

$$\frac{CM}{R} = \frac{\$270}{\$390} = .6923077 \qquad \$270 \div 5 \text{ units} = \$54$$

[a]The 60% to 40% ratio of A-1's to B-2's reduces to 3 to 2.
[b]The 5 units are the sum of the 3 A-1's and 2 B-2's.

either percentage or dollars per unit terms. For very large firms with literally thousands of products, C-V-P analysis will often be done for divisions of the firm. C-V-P analysis for individual product lines will be discussed later in the chapter.

Applications of Cost-Volume-Profit Analysis

This section examines one frequently used sensitivity measure used in conjunction with C-V-P analysis—the margin of safety ratio. Then several hypothetical or "as if" types of changes are demonstrated to illustrate the flexibility of C-V-P analysis.

Margin of Safety Ratio

The **margin of safety ratio** provides management with a simple measure in percentage terms of how far sales can drop until the break-even point is reached. The measure is calculated in the following fashion:

$$\text{Margin of safety ratio} = \frac{\text{Expected sales} - \text{Sales at the break-even point}}{\text{Expected sales}}$$

In the multiproduct situation previously discussed, assume that projected sales for the forthcoming period are $5,000,000. The margin of safety ratio would then be:

$$\frac{\$5,000,000 - \$4,333,333}{\$5,000,000} = 13.33\%$$

Hence, budgeted sales, at the assumed mix, could decline by 13.33% before hitting the break-even point. **Margin of safety** can also be expressed in dollar terms as the difference between budgeted sales and break-even sales. This amount would be $666,667 in our example ($5,000,000 − $4,333,333).

The margin of safety ratio gives management a simple and effective measure for evaluating the amount of "comfort" that they have in terms of expected operating profitability. Thus, if the margin were too tight, consideration might be given to evaluating alternative courses of action.

Changes in Selling Price

Perhaps the easiest factor to change in the short run is the selling price of one or more products. Management should, of course, very carefully attempt to assess the effect on volume resulting from potential price changes. Furthermore, changes in the price of one product may bring about changes in the demand for other products. For example, if a stove manufacturer includes economy and deluxe stoves in its product line, cutting the price of the inexpensive item may have a negative effect upon sales of the deluxe stove. This is due to the substitution effect because the products are competitive with each other. Hence, care and caution must be exercised when price changes are being contemplated. Wherever possible, market research should be used in order to provide insights relative to the demand for the affected products.

Referring once again to the XYZ Company and its two products, the A-1 and the B-2, let us assume that management is contemplating an increase in the price of the A-1 from $50 to $60. On a budgetary basis, the perceived effect of the present pricing structure and the proposed change are shown in Exhibit 4–3. It is assumed the increase in price of the A-1 will change the sales mix to the 5:4 ratio shown in Exhibit 4–3. The new weighted average contribution margin data are shown in Exhibit 4–4.

Expected profit for the two situations can be determined by multiplying budgeted sales by the contribution margin percentage and deducting the fixed costs. Budgeted profit, break-even point, and margin of safety ratio for the two alternatives are shown in Exhibit 4–5. Raising the selling price of A-1 would result in a modest gain in income and slight improvements in terms of lowering the break-even point and raising the margin of safety ratio. Hence, if the two predictions were equally reliable, raising the selling price of A-1 to $60 would appear to be marginally beneficial without presenting any drawbacks.

EXHIBIT 4–3
Estimated Effects of a Price Change

		Original Prices	New Prices
Selling price		A-1 $ 50	A-1 $ 60
		B-2 $120	B-2 $120
Total revenues		$5,000,000	$4,850,000
Sales mix in units (A-1; B-2)		3:2	5:4

EXHIBIT 4–4
Revised Weighted Average Contribution Margin Analysis
(Change in Selling Price and Sales Mix)

	A-1	× Weight	=	Total	B-2	× Weight	=	Total	Grand Total
Revenue	$60 ×	5	=	$300	$120 ×	4	=	$480	$780
Variable cost	20 ×	5	=	100	30 ×	4	=	120	220
Contribution margin	$40 ×	5	=	$200	$ 90 ×	4	=	$360	$560

WACM%

$$\frac{CM}{R} = \frac{\$560}{\$780} = .71794$$

WACM per unit

$$\$560 \div 9 \text{ units} = \$62.222$$

EXHIBIT 4–5
Analysis of Potential Change of Price

	Original Assumptions	Revised Assumptions
Budgeted profit		
(Budgeted sales × WACM%)	($5,000,000 × .6923)	($4,850,000 × .71794)
– fixed costs	– $3,000,000 = $461,500	– $3,000,000 = $482,000
Break-even point	$3,000,000 ÷ .6923	$3,000,000 ÷ .71794
	= $4,333,333	= $4,178,855

Margin of safety ratio	$\dfrac{\$5,000,000 - \$4,333,333}{\$5,000,000} = 13.33\%$		$\dfrac{\$4,850,000 - \$4,178,855}{\$4,850,000} = 13.83\%$	

Changing Advertising Costs

Returning to the original budgetary figures with the weighted average contribution margin of .6923077 from Exhibit 4–2, assume that management is attempting to assess whether it would be beneficial to spend an additional $200,000 in advertising costs. If the additional advertising is not expected to affect the sales mix, one way to get a handle on the problem would be by means of dividing the $200,000 by the weighted average contribution margin of .6923077 to arrive at required incremental sales of $288,889. This is the break-even point on the differential advertising appropriation in the short run. If additional advertising expenditures of $200,000 were expected to generate incremental sales of $350,000 during the period without affecting the sales mix, the resulting profit would be approximately $42,000:

Contribution margin on sales	
($350,000 × .6923077)	$242,213
Less: Incremental advertising expenditures	200,000
Incremental profit	$ 42,213

Of course, if the advertising increment is intended to have a long-run impact on sales, short-run analysis should not be employed in evaluating the expenditure.

If the incremental advertising costs are being considered for specific product lines, the break-even notion can be applied to individual product lines in a fashion similar to the single-product situation illustrated previously. The amounts can be divided by the respective contribution margins of the individual product lines to determine required sales for each product line in order to determine product-line differential break-even points: $30/$50 = 60% for A-1 and $180/$240 = 75% for B-1 as shown in Exhibit 4–2. Thus, $100,000 of advertising committed to A-1 should generate at least $166,667 dollars of sales to break-even ($100,000 ÷ .6), and $100,000 directed to B-2 would have to raise $133,333 in order to break even ($100,000 ÷ .75). If additional advertising expenditures of $100,000 in A-1 were expected to generate sales of $250,000, the incremental contribution margin would be $150,000 ($250,000 × .6). On the other hand, if the $100,000 were assigned to B-2 with an expectation of increasing sales by $175,000, contribution margin would be increased only by $131,250 ($175,000 × .75). The break-even approach does provide a useful benchmark for assessing the success of each possible course of action.

Changes in Production Methods

As firms become more automated, fixed costs for depreciation of machinery and equipment replace direct labor costs. The result is higher fixed costs per period along with a higher contribution margin percentage. Assume in the XYZ case that as a result of automating a process, the fixed costs for the period would increase to $3,250,000. Variable costs per unit of output decrease by $2 for the A-1 and $3 for the B-2. The new weighted average contribution margin percentage is shown in Exhibit 4–6.

The break-even point with the new equipment would be $4,494,724 ($3,250,000 ÷ .72307). However, a second type of break-even point can be determined in situations involving automation of processes: the point where total sales using either the original technology or the new automated equipment will result in the same total profit. This level of sales is determined by setting up an equation where the profit is the same for both alternatives:

$$CM_1 - FC_1 = CM_2 - FC_2$$

where

CM_1 = Contribution margin with original technology

FC_1 = Fixed costs with original technology

CM_2 = Contribution margin with new technology

FC_2 = Fixed costs with new technology.

EXHIBIT 4–6
Revised Weighted Average Contribution Margin
(Lower Variable Costs Resulting from Automation)

	A-1 × Weight		=	Total	B-2 × Weight		=	Total	Grand Total
Revenue	$50 ×	3	=	$150	$120 ×	2	=	$240	$390
Variable cost	18 ×	3	=	54	27 ×	2	=	54	108
Contribution margin	$32			$ 96	$ 93			$186	$282

WACM%	WACM per unit
$\dfrac{CM}{R} = \dfrac{\$282}{\$390} = .72307$	$282 ÷ 5 = $56.40

Substituting (and letting R = total revenues) we would have:

$$.6923077R - \$3,000,000 = .72307R - \$3,250,000$$

Solving for R, the level of sales where profits would be the same for either technology would be $8,126,831, resulting in profits of $2,626,268.

When sales are above $8,126,831, the automated equipment will generate higher profits. Similarly, at sales levels below this amount, the older approach is more profitable. Consequently, the decision will be affected by managerial expectations of future sales relative to the break-even level of sales for the two production methods.

The Diagrammatic Approach to Cost-Volume-Profit Analysis

A handy way to literally give management the "big picture" relative to C-V-P analysis is by means of the diagram or **C-V-P graph** shown in Exhibit 4–7. The dollars of sales on the horizontal axis represents the various output levels of activity. Units can be used on the horizontal axis for a single product firm but sales dollars are generally used in multiproduct situations. Potential revenues generated and costs incurred are measured on the vertical axis. The revenue line begins at the intersection of the axes. The slope is defined by the change in sales dollars for the particular mix of 3 A-1's and 2 B-2's. The total cost line does not begin at the intersection of the two axes. Instead, it starts at a point on the vertical axis equal to the fixed costs of the period. This is somewhat of a simplification because if the firm were operating at a zero output level, many fixed costs would be cut back or eliminated. As long as the firm is operating within the relevant range of its fixed costs, the simplification presents no problems. The slope of the total cost line is equal to the rate of increase in the variable costs for the given sales mix. The crossing of the revenue and total cost lines marks the break-even point. Thereafter, the vertical distance between the two lines marks the total profit for the particular level of sales, such as the $4,952,610 profit at the level of $9,752,610 of sales shown on the exhibit. Total profit can be easily determined for any given level of output.

An alternative way of showing the C-V-P graph appears in Exhibit 4–8 (page 95). In this approach, variable costs and fixed costs are switched. Both the variable costs and revenues begin at the intersection of the vertical and horizontal axes. The fixed costs are represented by the difference between the variable cost and total cost lines. Notice that these lines are parallel, giving an equal vertical distance between them that means that the fixed costs remain the same in total throughout the diagram. As in Exhibit 4–7, the amount of profit or loss is the difference between the lines on the vertical axis for the indicated level of output on the horizontal axis, again a profit of $4,952,610 for sales of $9,752,610. One additional benefit of Exhibit 4–8 over Exhibit 4–7 is that the contribution margin, the difference between the

EXHIBIT 4–7
C-V-P Graph

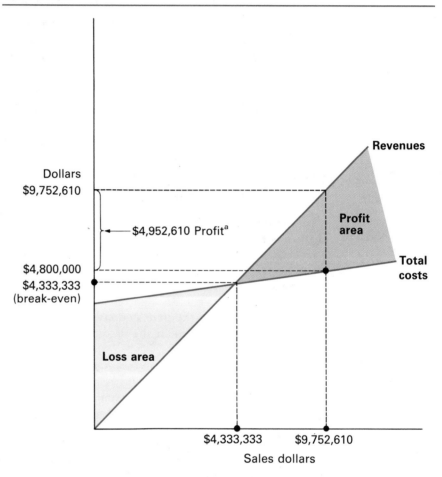

ᵃProfit is the differential between revenues and total costs as measured on the vertical axis.

revenue and variable cost lines, can also be read on the vertical axis for any level of output such as the $6,752,610 for a sales level of $9,752,610 shown in the profitgraph.

The profit picture can be shown in a more compact and easily readable form in the **profitgraph** shown in Exhibit 4–9 (page 96). The profit line shown in Exhibit 4–9 would be equal at all sales dollar points to the revenue line minus the total costs line shown in Exhibit 4–7. The line starts at the −$1,800,000 point at zero sales dollars because that is the amount of the fixed costs per period. The slope of the profit line is equal to the contribution margin rate because the fixed costs are constant throughout the range of the chart.

The advantage of the profitgraph is that income for any level of sales can

EXHIBIT 4–8
Revised C-V-P Graph

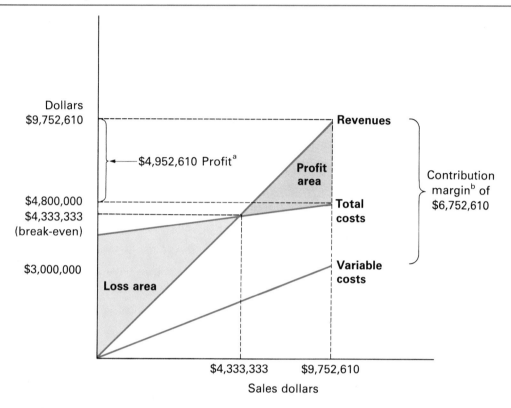

[a]Profit is the differential between revenues and total costs measured on the vertical axis.
[b]Contribution margin is the differential between revenues and variable costs measured on the vertical axis.

easily be read as a single figure on the vertical axis. The disadvantage of the profitgraph, as opposed to the previous C-V-P graphs, is that detail on revenues and variable costs is lost. Contribution margin can be determined on the profitgraph by adding back the fixed costs of $1,800,000 to the profit for any level of output.

Individual Product Line Cost-Volume-Profit Analysis in Multiproduct Situations

In C-V-P analysis involving more than one product, dividing the fixed costs by the weighted average contribution margin treats the fixed costs as joint or common to the individual products. Thus, the fixed costs are applicable to all the products together with no assignment to individual products. The ques-

EXHIBIT 4–9
Profitgraph

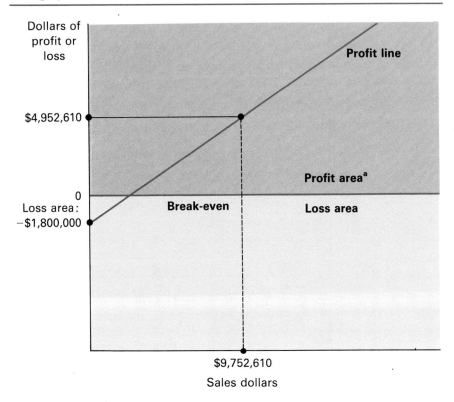

ᵃProfit (or loss) is now a single point on the vertical axis. At a sales level of $9,752,610, profit would be $4,952,610.

tion thus arises as to whether individual product C-V-P analysis can or should be done.

It should first be noted that if separate product C-V-P analysis is done and the fixed costs are allocated among the product lines, the individual product results will generally not add up to the total for the firm. This will be illustrated by means of our break-even example.

In the case of the XYZ Company, the total firm break-even point was $4,333,333. The only way that the individual product line break-even points will add up to this total is if the fixed costs are allocated between the products on a basis that is proportionate to their individual product contribution margins for the given sales mix.

Referring to Exhibit 4–2, it can be seen that B-2 is expected to contribute two-thirds of the total contribution margin ($180 of the total of $270). Therefore, if—and only if—two-thirds of the fixed costs of $3,000,000 are assigned to B-2 with the remainder to A-1 will the separate product line break-even points equal the combined enterprise total of $4,333,333:

A-1	$1,000,000 ÷ .6	= $1,666,666
B-2	$2,000,000 ÷ .75	= 2,666,667
Total		$4,333,333

However, dividing fixed costs strictly in proportion to the contribution margins for the given sales mix is unrealistic. The key point relative to fixed costs is whether they are direct or indirect to particular products. Assume in the XYZ case that products A-1 and B-2 are manufactured in separate factories. As a result, a relatively high proportion of the fixed costs of the enterprise are direct relative to the two product lines. A cost analysis showed the following break-down of budgeted fixed costs:

Direct fixed costs of A-1	$1,000,000
Direct fixed costs of B-2	1,400,000
Indirect (common) administrative and marketing costs	600,000
Total	$3,000,000

For C-V-P analysis purposes, only the direct fixed costs of a product should be assigned to it. Break-even points, in units, for the two products would be:

A-1: $1,000,000 ÷ $30 = 33,333 units

B-2: $1,400,000 ÷ $90 = 15,556 units

Again, it should be stressed that indirect fixed costs should not be allocated to the individual products because any assignment of common costs is purely arbitrary. Also, the fact that the individual break-even points do not add up to the enterprise total should not be a concern. Important information relative to the profitability of each product line can be determined from this analysis by working with just the direct fixed costs of the various product lines.

On the other hand, if the A-1 and the B-2 were manufactured in the same plant and went through many of the same production departments, a high proportion of the fixed costs would be indirect relative to the individual products. If this were the case, individual product C-V-P analysis should not be attempted.

Hence, the desire for individual product C-V-P analysis will be based on the degree of fixed costs that are direct relative to the individual product lines. The higher the percentage of direct fixed costs, the more meaningful will be the analysis. Judgment must be exercised by management for each enterprise relative to undertaking individual product or product line C-V-P analysis.

The most useful application of C-V-P analysis at less than firm-wide levels would be for major conglomerate firms made up of numerous large divisions or segments. Again, however, indirect corporate fixed costs should not be assigned to the operating divisions. Any division among the segments will be arbitrary and can easily lead to dissension and bickering among the affected units.

Limiting Assumptions of Cost-Volume-Profit Analysis

There are several assumptions underlying C-V-P analysis. They will be listed first and then briefly discussed:

1. Costs can be segregated into their fixed and variable components.
2. There is no change in selling price per unit of output and variable cost per unit of input throughout the time period and for all levels of production.
3. There is no change in efficiency of the variable factors of production.
4. Fixed costs remain within the relevant range.
5. The sales mix remains constant during the period and for all levels of sales.
6. Inventory levels do not significantly change during the period.

If costs could not be segregated into their fixed and variable components, neither C-V-P analysis nor budgeting, among other managerial tools, could be utilized. Fortunately, tools such as regression analysis are able to provide us with relatively accurate divisions of fixed and variable costs.

Assumptions 2 through 5 are necessary to maintain linear cost and revenue functions. Linearity simplifies C-V-P without reducing the accuracy and utility of the tool to any significant degree. In those cases where linear functions will not suffice, greater accuracy can be attained by applying mathematical formulas for curvilinear functions.

The second assumption refers to the per unit selling price of product and cost per unit of variable factors such as direct materials and direct labor. If changes in either selling price or variable cost factors are expected, they should be averaged out to maintain the linearity of the cost or revenue line.

The maintenance of efficiency in assumption 3 is likewise necessary to maintain the linearity of the variable cost function. If direct labor were able, at some point, to increase its hourly output, the variable cost per unit of output would decrease even though the cost of direct labor per hour were to remain constant.

The relevant range assumption pertaining to fixed costs in assumption 4 was discussed in Chapters 2 and 3. Fixed costs, by definition, should be within their relevant range unless productivity is expected to be unusually high or low during the period.

The sales mix is also assumed to remain constant throughout the range of total sales in assumption 5 in order to keep the revenue line linear. Changing the sales mix would change the average revenue per unit sold, affecting the linear pattern of the revenue line.

The most subtle of the assumptions is number 6, in which the inventory level does not change significantly during the period. Under the traditional form of income reporting for manufacturing firms, inventory increases result in fixed manufacturing overhead costs remaining in inventory accounts. In these situations, the incurred fixed manufacturing overhead exceeds the amount that becomes expensed. The opposite effect occurs if inventory levels decrease. Assumption 6 avoids the problem of the effect on income of changing levels of inventory. However, this assumption makes C-V-P analysis totally consistent with variable costing, an income reporting method that does not include fixed manufacturing overhead among product costs (variable costing is covered in Chapter 11). Variable costing is not acceptable for either income tax or external reporting purposes. However, this method has become extremely popular for managerial accounting (internal profit reporting) purposes. Traditional income reporting methods in terms of handling fixed manufacturing overhead and the variable costing approach are discussed later in this book.

The assumptions underlying C-V-P analysis are intended to maintain the simplicity of the method. However, simplicity does not prevent it from being a powerful tool for exploring the effects on profits of changing various alternatives in the short run. Although economists stress curvilinear cost and revenue relationships in C-V-P analysis, the linear assumptions have proved to be eminently practical and highly useful in the great majority of actual business applications.

Summary

C-V-P analysis provides an excellent tool for examining operations in the short run. It enables the firm to determine the sales necessary to attain any desired level of profit. Therefore, it is extremely helpful in terms of assessing the effect of operating changes on profits. These operating changes include such things as changing selling prices, advertising budgets, and the introduction of new equipment that increases fixed costs per period and lowers variable costs per unit of output.

C-V-P work can be done on a before-tax or after-tax basis. The before-tax basis is frequently used because operating decisions and tax questions fall into somewhat different areas of responsibility. Therefore, the before-tax approach focuses on considerations that are of primary importance to operating management.

In situations where firms manufacture more than one product, the sales mix is an important consideration affecting the attainment of desired profits.

C-V-P is used for both entire enterprises and for large divisions of major conglomerate firms. Extreme care should be exercised when considering the use of C-V-P for individual products. It should be done only if a large proportion of fixed costs of the firm (or major division) are direct relative to the product lines. Arbitrary allocation of indirect fixed costs to products can be misleading when viewed from the managerial standpoint.

C-V-P analysis is subject to several simplifying assumptions. These assumptions keep the analysis clear and understandable without sacrificing usefulness in most real-world situations.

Finally, C-V-P employs the contribution margin approach where variable costs are subtracted from the revenues of the various product lines. This same approach is also used in certain types of income statements prepared for management called *variable costing*. An important link thus exists between planning (C-V-P) and control (variable costing) tools where the same costing method is used.

Key Terms

Break-even (B-E) point   is the point of zero profit where revenues equal total expenses.

Contribution margin   is revenues minus variable costs.

Contribution margin per unit   is revenue per unit minus variable cost per unit.

Contribution margin ratio   is contribution margin divided by revenues. It is used in a planning context as part of C-V-P analysis on either an individual product line or a weighted average basis where several product lines exist. It can also be done on an after-the-fact basis by dividing actual total contribution margin by total revenues.

Cost-volume-profit (C-V-P) analysis   is the technique for deriving the number of units or dollars of sales necessary to reach any desired level of profit.

Cost-volume-profit (C-V-P) graph   is a type of graph used to illustrate C-V-P analysis that shows total revenues, total costs and dollars of profit for extensive ranges of output.

Margin of safety   is the difference between budgeted sales and break-even sales, both measured in dollars.

Margin of safety ratio   is a simple measurement in percentage terms of how far revenues can drop, from a planned sales standpoint, until the break-even point is reached.

Profitgraph   is a very simple type of graph showing the level of profits for extensive ranges of outputs.

Sales mix   is the proportion of different product lines constituting the expected (or actual) sales output of an enterprise.

Variable cost ratio   is variable costs divided by revenues on either a unit or total basis. It is the complement of the contribution margin ratio.

Questions

Q4–1   Why is C-V-P analysis useful to management for short-run planning purposes?

Q4–2   How can the contribution margin be expressed for C-V-P purposes?

Q4–3   How does the contribution margin differ from gross profit?

Q4–4   Why are the contribution margin ratio and the variable cost ratio complementary?

Q4–5   How is break-even analysis extended into cost-volume-profit (C-V-P) analysis?

Q4–6   Why is one minus the tax rate $(1 - T)$ similar to the contribution margin concept?

Q4–7   Why is C-V-P frequently done on a before-tax basis rather than an after-tax basis?

Q4–8   Why must the sales mix be taken into account in multiproduct C-V-P analysis?

Q4–9   What does the margin of safety measure?

Q4–10   If changing the price of a product is contemplated, what factors must be very carefully considered?

Q4–11   How can the break-even concept be applied for assessing additional advertising expenditures?

Q4–12   Describe the different ways that C-V-P analysis can be shown in diagrammatic form.

Q4–13   How must fixed costs be allocated among product lines in order to make individual product line break-even points agree with the product line break-even points computed in regular (firm-wide) C-V-P analysis?

Q4–14   When might separate product line break-even or C-V-P be employed?

Q4–15   Why might separate product line break-even or C-V-P be useful to management?

Q4–16   Should indirect corporate fixed costs be assigned to operating divisions of major conglomerate firms for C-V-P analysis?

Q4–17   Which underlying assumptions of C-V-P analysis are necessary to maintain the linearity of variable costs?

Q4–18   Why do we assume that inventory levels do not change during the period for C-V-P analysis purposes?

Exercises

E4–1   **Single product B-E and C-V-P.** Vosmik Company produces a single type of automobile battery used by certain compact motor car manufacturers. The battery sells for $30. Vosmik's variable costs per battery are

Direct materials	$12
Direct labor	5
Variable manufacturing overhead	3

During 19X8 the budgeted fixed manufacturing overhead is estimated to be $800,000, and budgeted fixed selling, general and administrative costs are expected to be $400,000. Variable selling costs are $4 per battery.

Required:
1. Determine the break-even point in units.
2. What dollar level of sales must be attained in order to make a profit of $600,000?

E4–2   **Single product C-V-P after taxes.** Refer to the data in E4–1. Answer the following questions:
1. What dollar level of sales must be attained in order to generate a profit of $600,000 after allowing for income taxes that are at the rate of 40% of net income?
2. What dollar level of sales must be attained in order to make a profit equal to 10% of sales after allowing for income taxes at the rate of 40% of net income?

E4–3   **Justifying additional advertising expenditures.** Refer again to the data in E4–1. The sales manager of Vosmik believes that sales can be increased by placing additional advertising in automotive trade magazines. He would like to place an additional $30,000 of advertising in these magazines. He felt the additional advertising would increase sales by 4,000 batteries.

Required:
1. As the executive vice-president, would you be inclined to go along with the sales manager's request? Show figures.
2. What is the minimum allowable number of additional batteries that must be sold in order to justify the sales manager's request? Show figures.

E4–4   **Changing selling prices and margin of safety.** Refer again to the data in E4–1. Sales in units during 19X8 were expected to be 225,000 units at the price of $30 per battery. The sales manager felt that this price was too low. He therefore advocated raising the selling price to $36 per battery. Market research showed that sales would decline to 180,000 units at this price.

Required:
1. Compute the margin of safety ratio for the two different pricing policies.
2. Assuming that you had equal confidence in the accuracy of the budgeted level of sales, which pricing policy would you prefer?
3. Are there any other factors that might affect your decision? Discuss.

E4–5   **Changing fixed costs.** Refer again to the data in E4–1. The production manager of Vosmik wants to acquire a new piece of machinery that is more efficient than presently owned equipment. The new equipment costs $1,000,000 and has a five-year life with no salvage value. It would be depreciated on a straight-line basis. The new equipment would replace equipment having an annual depreciation of $40,000. Direct labor cost would be $4.50 per unit with the new equipment and variable manufacturing overhead would be $2.50 per unit.

Required:
1. Compute the break-even point (in units) if the new equipment is acquired.
2. At what level of sales (in units) are profits the same between the two alternatives (keeping the old equipment or acquiring the new equipment)?
3. Would you be inclined to acquire the new equipment if annual sales were expected to be around 150,000 units each year?

E4–6   **Single product break-even (working backwards).** Carey Company manufactures a stylus for record players. During 19X6 the company had $1,200,000 of fixed manufacturing, marketing, and administrative costs. Total variable costs per unit were $8. The break-even point was 60,000 styluses.

Required: 1. What was the selling price per stylus?

E4–7   **Multiple choice, two products.** Taylor, Inc., produces only two products, Acdom and Belnom. These account for 60% and 40% of the total sales dollars of Taylor, respectively. Variable costs (as a percentage of sales dollars) are 60% for Acdom and 85% for Belnom. Total fixed costs are $150,000. There are no other costs.

Required: 1. What is Taylor's break-even point in sales dollars?

   a. $150,000
   b. $214,286
   c. $300,000
   d. $500,000

   2. Assuming that the total fixed costs of Taylor increase by 30%, what amount of sales dollars would be necessary to generate a net income of $9,000?

   a. $204,000
   b. $464,000
   c. $659,000
   d. $680,000

(CPA Adapted)

E4–8   **Two products, break-even and pricing.** The Iguana Motel has fifty available rooms. Half rent for $10 per day and the remainder for $8 per day. Variable costs per room are

	Maid Service per Day of Use	Laundry per Day of Use
$10 rooms	$1.50	.50
$ 8 rooms	1.00	.50

Fixed costs per month are

Depreciation	$3,000
Taxes and insurance	2,500
Utilities	875
Maintenance	1,600

Required: 1. What is the number of rooms per month that must be rented if the motel is to break even? Assume that the rentals, in number of rooms, are divided evenly between the $10 and $8 rooms at the break-even point.

   2. During the motel's slack season, one price is charged for all rooms. Williams, the owner, on the basis of past experience, states that 5,050 rooms will be rented during this six-month period. What must this price be if the motel is to break even during this period? Assume that total variable costs per room used per day are $2. Monthly fixed costs remain as stated above.

   3. Assume the same cost facts as stated in requirement 2 above. Gardner, the motel manager, submits the following demand estimates for the slack season:

Daily Rate	Total Six-Month Rentals
$10	6,000 rooms
8	8,300 rooms
6	11,500 rooms

Based on Gardner's estimates, what should the daily room rate be?

E4–9   **Single product C-V-P, solving for unknown.** White Company manufactures a single product that sells for $5 per unit. During 19X2, the firm expected to sell 1,000,000 units. Total fixed costs, both manufacturing and nonmanufacturing, are expected to be $1,600,000. White projected its income at $2,000,000 after income taxes at $33\frac{1}{3}\%$.

Required: Determine the variable costs per unit of product.

E4–10   **Single product C-V-P, solving for unknown.** Overbach Company manufactures one product. The product sells for $3 per unit. The firm has its budget for 12,000,000 units sales during 19X0. There is no expected change in inventory levels. Shown below are product costs per unit and other information.

Cost per unit of product	
Direct materials	$ .40
Direct labor	.50
Variable manufacturing overhead	.25
Fixed manufacturing overhead	.60
Variable selling costs per unit	.05
Total fixed selling, general, and administrative costs	?
Tax rate	40%
Projected after-tax income	$600,000

Required: Determine the total fixed selling, general, and administrative costs.

Problems

P4–11   **Straightforward C-V-P with two products.** The Coolidge Vacuum Cleaner Company makes two types of vacuum cleaners, which it sells to wholesalers and to large retailers. Data for the two product lines for 19X9 are

	Regular	Deluxe
Selling price per unit	$30	$60
Variable costs per unit	18	25
Contribution margin per unit	$12	$35

The company expects fixed costs of $3,000,000 during 19X7. The firm expects 60% of its sales (in units) to be Regular vacuum cleaners.

Required: 1. Determine the break-even point in units.
2. Determine the level of sales (in dollars) necessary to generate a profit of $1,500,000.
3. Determine the level of sales (in dollars) necessary to generate a profit of $1,500,000 after allowing for income taxes at a rate of 40%.

P4–12   **Separate product-line break-even points.** Refer to the data in P4–11, and answer the following questions.

1. Assume that the two products are manufactured in separate factories. As a result, $1,800,000 of the firm's expected fixed costs are direct to the Deluxe line,

$900,000 are direct to the Regular line, and $300,000 are common to both. Compute the break-even point for each product line.

2. Now assume that the vacuum cleaners are manufactured in the same plant. As a result, $700,000 of fixed costs are direct to the Deluxe line and $300,000 are direct to the Regular line. The other $2,000,000 of fixed costs are direct to both lines. Would you now compute separate product-line break-even points? Discuss.

3. What is the benefit of separate product-line break-even analysis points? Discuss.

P4–13   **Change in advertising costs.** Refer again to P4–11. The sales manager would like to have his advertising budget increased by $100,000.

Required: 1. Assuming that the advertising will benefit both products and would generate additional sales in the same mix as previously anticipated (60% of the units would be Regular), what is the minimum acceptable amount of total sales (in units) that would have to be generated by the additional advertising in order to justify the expenditure?

2. Assume that the additional advertising expenditure of $100,000 would go to either the Regular or Deluxe line. If it goes to the Regular line, it is expected that sales of 10,000 additional units would arise. If it goes to the Deluxe line, 5,000 additional unit sales are expected. How should the $100,000 be spent based on the sales estimates?

P4–14   **Two products, sales mix in dollars rather than units.** Dunne Company is a manufacturer of two small household appliances: blenders and mixers. The sales manager expects 60% of its sales (in dollars) to be blenders and 40% in mixers. Blenders sell for $12 each and mixers sell for $20 each.

Total variable costs are $6 per blender and $8 per mixer. Total fixed costs are $1,000,000 for the year.

Required: 1. Determine the break-even point in units.
2. What dollar level of sales is necessary to generate a profit of $1,500,000?
3. What level of sales is necessary to generate a profit equal to 15% of sales after taxes? The tax rate is 40%.
4. If $10,000 of additional advertising costs were going to be spent for mixers, what is the minimum allowable level of sales that it should generate to justify the expenditure?

P4–15   **Evaluation of short-run changes upon income.** Moss Company anticipates the following income during the year 19X8 (the projected income statement has been set up by separating fixed and variable costs in order to facilitate managerial decision making).

MOSS COMPANY
Projected Income Statement
19X8

Revenues	$500,000
Variable costs	
Variable manufacturing costs	$200,000
Variable selling costs	50,000
Total variable costs	$250,000

Contribution margin	$250,000
Fixed costs	
Fixed manufacturing costs	$150,000
Fixed selling, general, and administrative costs	98,000
Total fixed costs	$248,000
Net income	$ 2,000

The projected income statement was based on sales of 100,000 units. Moss Company has the capacity to make and sell 150,000 units during the year. Each of the following questions is independent of the others.

Required:

1. Management is unhappy with the results presently anticipated. It is choosing two possible courses of action.

   a. If the selling price is cut by $.85 per unit, sales would increase to capacity.
   b. If selling price is raised by 5% per unit, annual advertising costs are raised by $25,000, and commissions are raised to 15% of selling price from the present level of 10%, it is believed that sales, in units, can be increased by 20% above the present budget.

   Which alternative would you choose? Show figures.

2. Moss Company has a chance to make a large sale in a foreign market that would not affect domestic sales. The foreign company wants a price quote for 20,000 units of product. Selling commissions would be avoided, but Moss would pay shipping costs of $.20 per unit. Foreign licenses and fees would total $10,000. What is the minimum acceptable price that would allow Moss to make a profit of $15,000 on *all* its operations?

3. Moss does not want to change its selling price. It does believe that increasing advertising costs will increase sales. If sales could be increased by 20%, by how much could advertising be increased if the firm desired a profit equal to 5% of sales?

4. Is the process in requirement 3 realistic or unrealistic? Discuss.

P4–16 **Analyzing changing sales mix.** The Golf Department of the Donham Sporting Goods Company sells three types of golf club sets. Individual sales by type for March and April showed the following results:

	Joltin Jack	Slammin Sam	Bantam Ben	Total
March	20	50	60	130
April	100	30	40	170

Cost and selling price per bag of three sets were

	Joltin Jack	Slammin Sam	Bantam Ben
Selling price	$90	$150	$200
Cost	$70	$ 75	$ 80

The store manager has looked over the results for March and April. He is pleased to see that sales in units and in dollars has gone up from March to April (sales were $21,300 in March and $21,500 in April). However, profits were down, going from

$6,350 in March to $4,050 in April. The fixed costs for the department, mainly salaries, remained constant at $5,000. The store manager was quite perplexed.

Required:
1. Explain as carefully as you can, why profits are down for the Golf Department in April as compared to March. Show figures.
2. Compute the break-even point for the department for each month.
3. Compute the margin of safety ratio for each month.

P4–17   Break-even and C-V-P analysis with two technologies. Candice Company has decided to introduce a new product. The new product can be manufactured by either a capital-intensive method or labor-intensive method. The manufacturing method will not affect the quality of the product. The estimated manufacturing costs by the two methods are as follows:

	Capital Intensive		*Labor Intensive*	
Raw materials		$5.00		$5.60
Direct labor	.5DLH @ $12	6.00	.8DLH @ $9	7.20
Variable overhead	.5DLH @ $ 6	3.00	.8DLH @ $6	4.80
Directly traceable incremental fixed manufacturing costs	$2,440,000		$1,320,000	

Candice's market research department has recommended an introductory unit sales price of $30. The incremental selling expenses are estimated to be $500,000 annually plus $2 for each unit sold regardless of manufacturing method.

Required:
1. Calculate the estimated break-even point in annual unit sales of the new product if Candice Company uses the

   a. Capital-intensive manufacturing method,
   b. Labor-intensive manufacturing method.

2. Determine the annual unit sales volume at which Candice Company would be indifferent between the two manufacturing methods.
3. Determine the level of sales under each of the two methods that would generate income of $100,000 after allowing for income taxes at the rate of 40%.
4. What other factors would enter into your decision of choosing between the two?
(CMA Adapted)

P4–18   Evaluation of short-run changes. The following is the income statement for the Davanna Company during 19X3. The company had sales of 1,800 tons of product. They can produce up to 3,000 tons of product per year. The income statement shown below was prepared in a contribution margin format to facilitate C-V-P analysis.

DAVANNA COMPANY
Statement of Income
For the Year Ended December 31, 19X4

Sales	$900,000
Variable costs:	
Manufacturing	$315,000
Selling costs	180,000
Total variable costs	$495,000

Contribution margin	$405,000
Fixed costs:	
Manufacturing	$ 90,000
Selling	112,500
Administration	45,000
Total fixed costs	$247,500
Net income before income taxes	$157,500
Income taxes (40%)	63,000
Net income after income taxes	$ 94,500

Required: (Each question is independent.)

1. Determine the break-even point in tons of product.
2. Determine the after-tax net income for 19X5 if 2,100 units are sold and fixed costs remain the same in total and variable cost per unit is the same.
3. Davanna is considering whether to market its product in a new territory. It would have to spend $61,500 per year on advertising and pay a sales commission of $25 per ton. How many tons would it have to sell in the new territory to maintain total firm net income at $94,500.
4. Davanna is considering replacing a highly labor-intensive process with a machine. This would result in an increase of $58,500 annually in fixed manufacturing costs. The variable manufacturing costs would decrease $25 per ton. Determine the new break-even volume in tons.
5. Ignore the facts presented in requirement 4 and now assume that Davanna estimates that the per-ton selling price would decline 10% next year. Variable costs would increase $40 per ton, and the fixed costs would not change. What dollar sales volume would be required to earn an after-tax net income of $94,500 next year?

(CMA Adapted)

P4–19   **Hospital break-even with step costs.** The Melrose Hospital operates a general hospital but rents space and beds to separate entities for specialized areas such as pediatrics, maternity, and psychiatric. Melrose charges each separate entity for common services to its patients such as meals and laundry and for administrative services such as billings and collections. All uncollectible accounts are charged directly to the entity. Space and bed rentals are fixed for the year.

For the entire year ended June 30, 19X3, the Pediatrics Department at Melrose Hospital charged each patient an average of $65 per day, had a capacity of 60 beds, operated 24 hours per day for 365 days, and had revenue of $1,138,800.

Expenses charged by the hospital to the Pediatrics Department for the year ended June 30, 19X3, were as follows:

Basis of Allocation

	Patient-days	Bed capacity
Dietary	$ 42,952	
Janitorial		$ 12,800
Laundry	28,000	
Laboratory, other than direct charges to patients	47,800	
Pharmacy	33,800	

	Patient-days	Bed capacity
Repairs and maintenance	5,200	7,140
General administrative services		131,760
Rent		275,320
Billings and collections	40,000	
Bad-debt expense	47,000	
Other	18,048	25,980
	$262,800	$453,000

The only personnel directly employed by the Pediatrics Department are supervising nurses, nurses, and aides. The hospital has minimum personnel requirements based on total annual patient-days. Hospital requirements beginning at the minimum expected level of operation follow.

Annual Patient-Days	Aides	Nurses	Supervising Nurses
10,000–14,000	21	11	4
14,001–17,000	22	12	4
17,001–23,725	22	13	4
23,726–25,550	25	14	5
25,551–27,375	26	14	5
27,376–29,200	29	16	6

The staffing levels above represent full-time equivalents, and it should be assumed that the Pediatrics Department always employs only the minimum number of required full-time equivalent personnel.

Annual salaries for each class of employees follows: supervising nurses—$18,000; nurses—$13,000; and aides—$5,000. Salary expense for the year ended June 30, 19X3, for supervising nurses, nurses, and aides was $72,000, $169,000, and $110,000, respectively.

The Pediatrics Department operated at this full 60-bed capacity for 100 days during 19X3. During 90 of these days the demand averaged 18 patients more than capacity and was as high as 20 patients more on some days. The hospital has 20 beds available for rent for the next year.

Required:

1. Calculate the minimum number of patient days required for the Pediatrics Department to break even for the year ending June 30, 19X4, if the additional 20 beds are not rented. Patient demand is unknown, but assume that revenue per patient-day, cost per patient-day, cost per bed, and employee salary rates will remain the same as for the year ended June 30, 19X3. Make sure that the step costs are consistent with your answer.

2. Assuming for purposes of this problem that patient demand, revenue per patient-day, cost per patient-day, cost per bed, and employee salary rates for the year ending June 30, 19X4, remain the same as for the year ended June 30, 19X3, should the Pediatrics Department rent the additional 20 beds? Show the incremental gain or loss from the additional beds.

(CPA Adapted)

P4–20   Changes in sales mix, income taxes. Elmo Electronics manufactures two products— tape recorders and electronic calculators—and sells them nationally to wholesalers and retailers. The Elmo management is very pleased with the company's performance for the current fiscal year. Projected sales through December 31, 19X7, indicate that 70,000 tape recorders and 140,000 electronic calculators will be sold this year. The projected earnings statement, which appears below, shows that Elmo will exceed its earnings goal of 9% on sales after taxes.

ELMO ELECTRONICS
Projected Earnings Statement
For the Year Ended December 31, 19X7

	Tape Recorders		Electronic Calculators		
	Total Amount ($000)	Per Unit	Total Amount ($000)	Per Unit	Total ($000)
Sales	$1,050	$15.00	$3,150	$22.50	$4,200.0
Production costs:					
Materials	$ 280	$ 4.00	$ 630	$ 4.50	$ 910.0
Direct labor	140	2.00	420	3.00	560.0
Variable overhead	140	2.00	280	2.00	420.0
Fixed overhead	70	1.00	210	1.50	280.0
Total production costs	$ 630	$ 9.00	$1,540	$11.00	$2,170.0
Gross margin	$ 420	$ 6.00	$1,610	$11.50	$2,030.0
Fixed selling and administrative expenses					1,040.0
Net income before income taxes					$ 990.0
Income taxes (55%)					544.5
Net income					$ 445.5

The tape recorder business has been fairly stable the last few years, and the company does not intend to change the tape recorder price. However, the competition among manufacturers of electronic calculators has been increasing. Elmo calculators have been very popular with consumers. In order to sustain this interest in its calculators and to meet the price reductions expected from competitors, management has decided to reduce the wholesale price of its calculator from $22.50 to $20 per unit effective January 1, 19X8. At the same time, the company plans to spend an additional $57,000 on advertising during fiscal year 19X8. As a consequence of these actions, management estimates that 80% of its total revenue will be derived from calculator sales, as compared to 75% in 19X7. As in prior years, the sales mix is assumed to be the same at all volume levels.

The total fixed overhead costs will not change in 19X8, nor will the variable overhead cost rates (applied on a direct labor-hour base). However, the cost of materials and direct labor is expected to change. The cost of solid-state electronic components will be cheaper in 19X8. Elmo estimates that material costs will drop 10% for the tape recorders and 20% for the calculators in 19X8. However, direct labor costs for both products will increase 10% in the coming year.

Required: 1. How many tape recorder and electronic calculator units did Elmo Electronics have to sell in 19X7 to break even?

2. What volume of sales is required if Elmo Electronics is to earn a profit in 19X8 equal to 9% on sales after taxes?

3. How many tape recorder and electronic calculator units will Elmo have to sell in 19X8 to break even?

(CMA Adapted)

P4–21 **Multiple products, effect of new product on break-even point and margin of safety ratio.** Orsini Brothers are manufacturers of two types of very fine California wines called Chateau Loire and Mellow Bordeaux. Contribution margin information per bottle for each of the two products in 19X3 is as follows:

	Chateau Loire	Mellow Bordeaux
Revenue	$20	$30
Variable costs	8	10
Contribution margin	$12	$20

Orsini's budgeted fixed costs are $10,000,000 for the year. Orsini expects to sell 600,000 bottles of Chateau Loire and 300,000 bottles of Mellow Bordeaux.

Fred Conte, the sales manager of the firm, is aware that the firm has excess productive capacity that can be utilized for other products. Consequently, he developed a product utilizing additional wine production coupled with various fruit juices to be called Sonoma Spritzer. Sonoma would sell for $18 a bottle with a variable cost of $12 per bottle. The new product would have no effect on either Orsini's fixed costs or the expected sales of the two wines. Conte believes that he can sell 300,000 bottles of Sonoma Spritzer during the year.

Required:

1. How much incremental income should the new product bring in?
2. Compute the break-even point in sales dollars if just the two wine products are manufactured.
3. Compute the break-even point in sales dollars with the Sonoma Spritzer included.
4. Compute the margin of safety ratio without the new product.
5. Compute the margin of safety ratio with the new product.
6. Comment on the above results, particularly why the break-even point increased as a result of adding the new product line without any additional fixed costs.
7. Even if productive capacity were sufficient to handle the production of the new product, what type of fixed costs would you expect as a result of introducing the new product line?

CHAPTER 5

Budgeting for Short-Run Goals

Learning Objectives

After reading this chapter you should be able to:

1. Appreciate the major role budgeting plays in the planning process.

2. Distinguish between short-run budgeting and capital budgeting.

3. Understand the concepts of responsibility accounting and participatory budgeting.

4. Understand the idea of a master budgeting system and how the various budgets in the system relate to each other.

5. Identify, and be able to prepare, the individual budgets in a master budget system.

One of the central themes of this book is the efficient planning of operations. We consider in this chapter one of the most important tools used by management to aid in the planning process: budgeting. Budgets play an important role not only in the planning of operations, but also in the control of operations. In other words, feedback concerning the difference between planned results, as reflected in a budget, and actual results is crucial to the process.

We will begin the study of budgeting by examining the nature of budgets and their role in the modern business enterprise. Next, we will examine the concept of an integrated master budget system. Finally, the various individual budgets that make up a master budget system will be illustrated.

The Nature of Budgeting

A **budget** is a financial plan that specifies and quantifies how the resources of an organization will be managed over a future period of time. Some budgets are concerned with the inflows of resources, whereas others deal with the outflows of resources. The resources in a budget will vary depending on the type of budget. For example, one of the most crucial resources that an organization must manage is cash. Thus, the cash budget is an important component in the total budgeting system. Other budgets are concerned with the control of physical resources, such as raw materials, or the control of manpower, such as direct labor. Each of these resources is the subject of a budget. The time horizon of budgets also varies and will be considered at a later point.

Who Budgets?

All organizations budget. The bud
stant attention from the media. 7
Congress over the federal budg
pect. With federal budgeted an
not difficult to understand the
will the money be raised to su
be raised? Or will we be bet
tures? Should cuts be made i
in the area of public welfare
cial to the planning of the f
to plan for the future.

Budgeting is just as i
tor. Management of a l
resources of stockholders
resources to earn a prof

adept at the use of sophisticated techniques to aid them in their jobs, and one of the most important tools they use is the budget.

Finally, budgeting is not confined to organizations. Most of us, as individuals and as families, budget whether we recognize it or not. Planning for a college education is one of the most significant tasks that many families will ever face. Some families prepare elaborate budgets to aid them in the planning process, whereas others are not quite as formal in their plans. Still, the decision to commit large dollars to a college education requires foresight.

Why Budget?

The three examples above were intended to give you some appreciation of the need for budgeting, although we will concentrate our attention on budgeting in private sector organizations rather than in government or in families. As mentioned at the beginning of this chapter, budgeting is important both as a planning device as well as a control tool. These two components in the efficient operation of a business, and in particular their relationship to budgeting, need to be understood before we look at the actual preparation of budgets.

One important reason for planning operations is to coordinate the activities of the various parts of the organization. It is absolutely essential that the overall goals of a company be communicated to the parts of the company. For example, many companies have goals for growth in both sales and income. These goals are an important part of the planning process and must be communicated to the various operating divisions. It then becomes the responsibility of the divisions to incorporate these goals into their individual budgets. If, for example, management has set a goal for the year of 10% growth in sales, it is imperative that this be communicated to the managers of the divisions and that they in turn find ways to increase their sales. Thus, coordination and communication are two important reasons for budgeting.

It is worth noting that the techniques discussed in the last chapter are a form of budgeting. Cost-volume-profit (C-V-P) analysis is an important planning tool for management and is often the first step in the overall budgeting process. For example, a manager may want to calculate the amount of profit at a number of different levels of sales before constructing a sales budget for the division. Although C-V-P analysis can be an important first step, the procedures and assumptions used in the overall budgeting process are more involved. Budgeting involves not just planning for sales and costs but also planning for the cash effects of these items. Budgeting for sales and the various operations of the business (such as buying materials and scheduling ...) is sometimes called **operational budgeting.** Planning the timing of ... ows and outflows, as well as planning for any cash excess or cash ... is referred to as **financial budgeting.**

... to coordination, another important reason for budgeting is to ... s. Used properly, budgets can be an invaluable motiva- ... ny. However, used improperly, budgets can be a negative force in an organization and serve to destroy employee morale. For example, superiors have been known to use the budget as an instrument for "flogging" subordinates if they do not attain the goals set out in the budget. Used in this fashion, the budget can actually be an instrument that promotes dissension and discord rather than harmony and achievement. It is obvious that budgeting requires much more than simply an understanding of accounting concepts. The behavior of individuals in an organizational setting is an important element to be considered in setting budgets.

Finally, we must not lose sight of the importance of the control aspect of budgeting. Control implies follow through. In other words, it is not enough to draw up elaborate budgets in the planning phase without any verification after the period is ended. Once the actual results for a period of time are recorded, they must be compared with the original budgeted amounts if the budgeting process is to be of any value in future periods. Communication, in the form of feedback as to the difference between budget and actual, is as important to the control aspect of budgeting as it is to planning.

Responsibility Accounting and Budgeting

The budgeting process is often thought of as a laborious mechanical task carried out by the company accountants. However, the role of the accountant in the budgetary process should be advisory rather than primary. Although the accountant can aid in the generation of the numbers that go into budgetary reports, it must be the managers of the divisions of the company that take primary responsibility for preparing the reports.

Central to the notion that managers should take part in the budgeting process is the concept of **responsibility accounting.** Responsibility accounting is a system of accounting that recognizes the importance of the individual in the control of operations and attempts to assign costs and revenues to the individuals who have the most control or influence over them. One of the terms defined in Chapter 2 was *controllable cost.* A controllable cost was defined as one that can be influenced by a particular manager. Note that it is not necessary for a manager to have total control over a cost to be held accountable for its level—only that the manager be able to influence its level of expenditure.

Participatory Budgeting

Participatory budgeting is the alternative to handing managers a budget for the year and judging their performance on whether they operated within it. Several advantages accrue to a company that successfully incorporates the idea of participation by those who will be held accountable for actual results compared to budgeted results:

1. Those individuals closest to the operations of a particular segment are most familiar with that part of the business and are often most qualified when it comes to setting realistic goals for their operations.

2. Studies have shown that employees are more motivated to "make the budget" if they have a hand in the setting of the budget. It is human nature to assume more responsibility for something that one has helped organize. Thus, the idea behind the self-imposed budget is to involve employees in the setting of the budget so that they will feel more responsibility for attaining the goals in the budget.

3. One of the important ideas in budgeting is the assignment of responsibility for variances of actual results from the budgeted amounts. By involving the managers in the setting of the budgets the company has identified in advance who is responsible for certain areas rather than trying to do this after the fact.

Although many benefits accrue from the participation of employees in the setting of budgets, certain problems can also arise. It is important that the managers involved in the process understand their role and be as realistic as possible in setting their budgets. Managers, for example, may try to build slack into a cost budget so that they will not look bad if costs are higher than they anticipate. Similarly, managers may be unrealistically conservative in budgeting sales if they are overly concerned about not attaining their goal. In short, it is important to involve managers in the setting of budgets in order to make them aware of the need to be as realistic as possible in budgeting their results.

The Flow of Budgetary Information

The concepts of responsibility accounting and participatory budgeting imply a certain direction in the flow of information in a company. The flow is naturally from bottom to top, that is, employees at lower levels in the organization prepare budgetary information that is aggregated with the reports prepared by others at the same level and passed on up to the next highest level.

Consider an example of a production facility turning out a single product. A direct labor budget might originate with the shift supervisors. Next, the budgets of the three shifts (assuming the company works three eight-hour shifts) would be aggregated by the line supervisor for all three shifts. The product manager responsible for all the lines that work on a particular product would then aggregate the budgets of all line supervisors and pass them up to the next level of management. The titles of the personnel at the various levels will of course vary from one company to the next, but the concept should be clear — the flow of information in a responsibility system of accounting is from bottom to top.

The Time Horizon in Budgetary Reports

The horizon of a budget can vary from as short as one month into the future to as long as ten or twenty years into the future. **Capital budgeting** deals with the planning of major expenditures for buildings, property, and even other businesses and naturally involves a time horizon of many years. The techniques involved in capital budgeting are quite different from those involved in short-run budgeting and are covered in detail in Chapters 13 and 14. Our concern in this chapter is with budgets that generally reach no further than one year into the future.

The yearly budget period is often broken down into shorter subunits, such as months or quarters of the year. We will look at a budgetary system in which all amounts are budgeted for a three-month period and then aggregated in a yearly budget. The illustration will assume a static budget in which the budgetary process is completed before the start of the period. However, **continuous budgets** are becoming increasingly popular. The idea is to continually add another month or quarter as each period ends. For example, if a company used a monthly budgeting system, a budget for January of the following year would be prepared during January of the current year. At the end of January, a new twelve-month budget would be released, with February of the current year as the first month and January of the following year as the twelfth month in the budget. One important advantage of continuous budgeting is that it keeps managers constantly involved in the planning and control of operations rather than something that they think about only once a year.

The Master Budget System

A **master budget system** consists of a series of individual budgets that are aggregated to form a complete set of budgeted financial statements for the current period. The order in which the individual budgets are prepared is crucial to the process. For example, the first budget to be prepared is the sales budget. Many of the cost budgets, such as the direct materials and direct labor budgets, depend directly on the level of sales. Exhibit 5–1 illustrates the relationships among the individual budgets in a master budget system.

You should study the exhibit at this point to get a general understanding of how the various budgets relate to each other. After the budgets have been illustrated you should return to the exhibit and review these relationships. Note that the capital budget is included in the system, although discussion of it will be deferred until later in the book. Also note that the system includes some components that are called *budgets* whereas others are referred to as *schedules* and still others as *financial statements.*

The Sales Forecast

Preparation of a sales forecast is the first step in the budget process. The objective in forecasting sales is to estimate the volume of sales for the period based on all the factors, both internal and external to the business, that could potentially affect the level of sales. The projected level of sales is then combined with estimates of selling prices to form the sales budget.

EXHIBIT 5–1
A Master Budget System

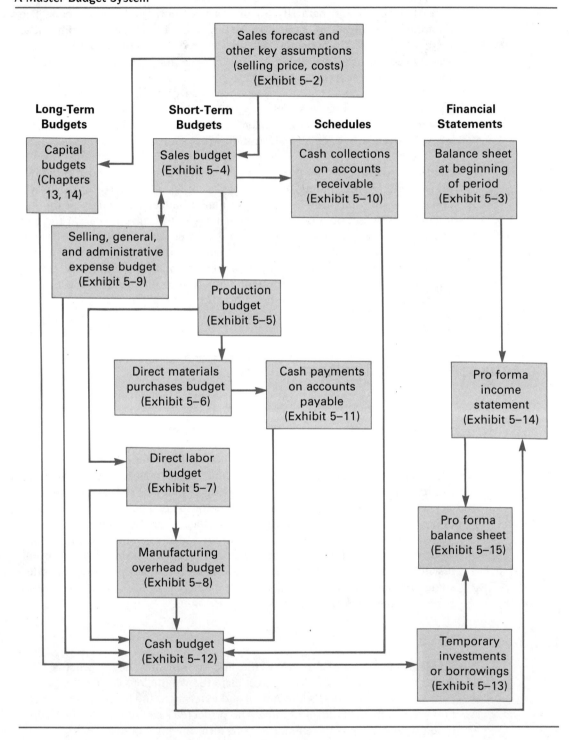

Large companies often employ full-time specialists, normally trained in economics, to forecast demand for the company's products and services. The forecaster must consider a wide range of factors that can affect demand. Some of the factors are:

External factors

1. General outlook for the economy,
2. General outlook for the industry,
3. Pending changes in legislation (such as the tax law),
4. Relations between the United States and foreign countries with which the company deals.

Internal factors

1. Existing backlog of unfilled orders,
2. Planned level of advertising and promotion,
3. Potential for strikes by unionized employees,
4. Past pricing policies and plans for future policies,
5. Existing productive capacity and any plans for expansion,
6. Findings of recent market research studies.

Forecasters employ a wide range of techniques to aid them in integrating all of the various factors into a forecast of sales. Although judgment is an important part of the process, forecasters also use various mathematical tools as well. **Time series analysis,** for example, is based on the extrapolation of historical data into the future. The forecaster uses statistical techniques to attempt to predict future sales based on past trends. Another popular statistical tool is regression analysis, which was discussed in Chapter 3. The forecaster tries to identify certain key variables that are highly correlated with sales, such as changes in selling price and the rate of growth in the industry. Some of the mathematical techniques used in forecasting will be considered further in Chapter 17.

Not all companies can afford to employ full-time specialists in forecasting. Many firms use more rudimentary techniques to forecast sales, such as periodic feedback from their salespeople. Although such an approach may be more subjective than the statistical techniques, the people in the field are often in a position to best evaluate future sales prospects.

Estimates of Selling Price and Costs

We now turn to the illustration of a complete set of budgets for a hypothetical company. For simplicity, we will illustrate the process for a manufacturer selling one product: men's suits. The accounting department has started the process by gathering information on the expected selling price for the suits

EXHIBIT 5–2

BAILEY COMPANY
Selling Price and Cost Data
For the Year Ended December 31, 19X9

(1) Selling price per suit $200

(2) Variable production costs:

Direct material:	3 yards at $10 per yard	= $ 30
Direct labor:	4 hours at $15 per hour	= $ 60
Variable overhead:	4 hours at $2.50 per hour	= $ 10
	Total variable production costs	$100

(3) Other variable costs:
    Selling, general, and administrative expense per suit = $5
    Bad debts expense = 5% of budgeted sales

(4) Fixed costs:
    Overhead (salaries, insurance, and depreciation) $18,675 per quarter
    Selling, general, and administrative expense $20,000 per quarter

---

and the various cost components. These data are shown in Exhibit 5–2. A balance sheet at the beginning of the budget year is shown in Exhibit 5–3.

Note the temporary investments of $11,000 on the balance sheet. The company's policy is to maintain a minimum cash balance of $10,000 at all times. Any excess of cash receipts over cash disbursements for a quarter, after considering this desire to maintain a $10,000 cash balance, is invested in bonds that are assumed to earn a 10% return. Also note on the balance sheet the income taxes payable of $5,000. The company makes quarterly installment payments, and this is assumed to be the amount due from the fourth quarter of the prior year.

Illustration of a Master Budget System

We now turn our attention to the preparation of a series of four quarterly budgets for the Bailey Company. The starting point is the sales budget. Refer back to Exhibit 5–1 as each budget is discussed to see how each budget fits into the integrated system.

Sales Budget

A **sales budget** for each of the four quarters of the year, and the total for the year, is shown in Exhibit 5–4. The budget is based on a sales forecast, after taking into consideration general economic conditions, the condition of the garment industry, and other key factors. Note the seasonal nature of sales. The company expects sales to peak in the second quarter as their customers,

EXHIBIT 5–3

BAILEY COMPANY
Balance Sheet
January 1, 19X9

Cash	$ 10,000	
Temporary investments	11,000	
Accounts receivable, less allowance of $6,000	24,000	
Inventories: raw materials (1,000 yards)	10,000	
finished goods (250 suits)	32,500	
Total current assets		$ 87,500
Land	$150,000	
Plant and equipment	$400,000	
Less: accumulated depreciation	(150,000)	250,000
Total long-term assets		400,000
Total assets		$487,500
Accounts payable	$ 14,000	
Income taxes payable	5,000	
Total current liabilities		$ 19,000
Common stock, no par	$300,000	
Retained earnings	168,500	
Total stockholders' equity		468,500
Total liabilities and stockholders' equity		$487,500

EXHIBIT 5–4

BAILEY COMPANY
Sales Budget
For the Year Ended December 31, 19X9

	Quarters				
	First	*Second*	*Third*	*Fourth*	*Total*
Budgeted sales in units	700	900	400	500	2,500
Times selling price per unit	$ 200	$ 200	$ 200	$ 200	$ 200
Budgeted sales	$140,000	$180,000	$80,000	$100,000	$500,000

wholesalers of suits, attempt to build up their inventory. In turn, the wholesalers have peak sales to retailers in the summer months (the second quarter) as the retailers stock their shelves for the fall season when their sales are at their highest. Budgeted sales in dollars are computed by multiplying sales in units by the expected selling price of $200 per suit.

Production Budget

Budgeted sales are the basis for the **production budget,** as shown in Exhibit 5–5. To budget the necessary production of finished goods, the company takes into account desired levels of ending inventory. The inventory level is based on Bailey's policy of maintaining a stock of suits at the end of a quarter equal to 30% of the following quarter's expected sales. Notice that the ending inventory of one quarter becomes the beginning inventory of the following quarter.

Bailey's desire to stock 30% of the next quarter's sales is an attempt to relate production directly to sales. Inventory levels and production increase in anticipation of increases in sales. Inventories and production go down in advance of planned decreases in sales. This is not the only approach to planning inventory levels. Another approach is to schedule production at a fairly constant level throughout the year. The general approach a company uses depends on the relative costs associated with each alternative.

Consider what would happen if Bailey scheduled production for each quarter exactly equal to one-fourth of the budgeted yearly sales of 2,500 units, or 625 suits per quarter. Assuming the same beginning inventory of 250 suits to start the year, note what would happen to inventory at the end of the second quarter:

	First Quarter	Second Quarter
Beginning inventory	250	175
Add: production of suits	625	625
Equals: suits available to sell	875	800
Less: sales of suits	(700)	(900)
Ending inventory	175	(100)

EXHIBIT 5–5

BAILEY COMPANY
Production Budget – Units of Finished Goods
For the Year Ended December 31, 19X9

	Quarters				
	First	Second	Third	Fourth	Total
Budgeted sales, in units (Exhibit 5–4)	700	900	400	500	2,500
Add: desired ending inventory = 30% of next quarter's needs	270	120	150	240[b]	240
Total units needed	970	1,020	550	740	2,740
Less: beg. inventory	250[a]	270	120	150	250
Units to be produced	720	750	430	590	2,490

[a]First quarter from the beginning balance sheet, Exhibit 5–3.
[b]Fourth quarter based on sales of 800 units, first quarter next year.

Although this is an extreme example, it does illustrate a major problem with scheduling level production (in this case, 625 suits per quarter). Inventory may not be sufficient to meet the demands of the period, resulting at the best in a need to schedule overtime work (costing the company a premium in wages) and at the worst, lost sales. For example, if Bailey schedules production of only 625 suits per quarter and it does not have the ability to schedule overtime, the firm stands to lose sales of 100 suits because only 800 are available to sell.

Conversely, certain problems can arise if production is not stabilized. Erratic production results in physical facilities, as well as labor resources, being stretched to their limits in peak periods of production and the facilities and labor available remaining idle in periods of low production. Certainly there is no perfect answer to the choice between scheduling production relative to sales of the next period, as opposed to scheduling level production. A compromise somewhere between the two extremes is probably best in most cases.

Note the logic employed in preparing the production budget, assuming the original case that production is related to sales of the next quarter. Production needs are found by adding the budgeted sales of the period to the desired level of ending inventory. The beginning inventory is then subtracted from the production needs to find how many units must be produced. Similar logic could be used to find the purchase needs of a retailer. The only significant difference is in the end result—the units to be *purchased* rather than the units to be *produced*:

Retailer

Budgeted sales
Add: Desired level of ending inventory of merchandise
= Total needs for the period
Less: Beginning inventory of merchandise
= Units to be purchased

Direct Materials Purchases Budget

A purchases budget for direct materials follows directly from the production budget. A **direct materials purchases budget** for Bailey is shown in Exhibit 5–6 (page 124).

The first step is to convert the number of units to be produced, from Exhibit 5–5, to an equivalent number of yards of material. Each unit to be produced requires 3 yards of material (fabric, because we are making suits), as shown in Exhibit 5–2. Bailey desires to carry an inventory of material at the end of any one quarter equal to 50% of the needs for the next quarter's production. The desired level of ending inventory is added and the level of beginning inventory is subtracted—just as was done on the production budget earlier. Finally, the yards of material to be purchased are multiplied by the cost per yard of $10 to find the cost of material to be purchased each quarter.

EXHIBIT 5—6

BAILEY COMPANY
Purchases Budget for Direct Materials
For the Year Ended December 31, 19X9

	Quarters				
	First	*Second*	*Third*	*Fourth*	*Total*
Units to be produced (Exhibit 5–5)	720	750	430	590	2,490
Times: yards of material per unit	3	3	3	3	3
Yards of material needed for production	2,160	2,250	1,290	1,770	7,470
Add: desired ending inventory = 50% of next quarter's needs	1,125	645	885	1,425[a]	1,425
Total yards needed	3,285	2,895	2,175	3,195	8,895
Less: beginning inventory of raw material in yards	1,000	1,125	645	885	1,000
Yards to be purchased	2,285	1,770	1,530	2,310	7,895
Times: cost per yard	$ 10	$ 10	$ 10	$ 10	$ 10
Cost of raw material purchases	$22,850	$17,700	$15,300	$23,100	$78,950

[a]Estimated for the fourth quarter.

Why does Bailey attempt to maintain an inventory of material equal to 50% of the following quarter's production needs? Why do they aim for an inventory of finished goods equal to 30% of the next period's sales? Maintenance of the "ideal" level of both materials and finished goods is an important concern of management and one to which considerable time and effort is devoted. Answers to these questions require a company to think clearly about the costs associated with the management of inventory.

If the inventory of finished goods is not sufficient to meet demand, the company will lose sales. However, to retain the customers, the company might schedule the labor force to work overtime at a premium pay rate. On the other hand, there are certain costs in carrying too much inventory, such as high storage costs and property taxes. In addition, there is always the risk that inventory may become obsolete and have to be sold at a reduced price.

Similar costs must be considered in deciding on the level of materials inventory. For example, if inventory of materials is not sufficient to meet production needs, the company may have to pay more for the material by not buying enough to get their normal quantity discount. Each additional order placed will result in additional clerical costs and transportation charges. But again, as was the case with finished goods, excessive storage and other costs will be associated with carrying too much materials.

Many companies use various operations research techniques to aid in the overall management of inventory. One of these techniques, economic order quantity (EOQ) analysis, is discussed in the appendix to Chapter 9.

Direct Labor Budget

The production budget is not only the basis for the direct materials budget but also for the **direct labor budget,** as illustrated in Exhibit 5–7. Recall from Exhibit 5–2 that each unit requires four hours of direct labor time at a rate of $15 per hour, or a total of $60 per unit.

We discussed earlier the effect that scheduling production around the next period's sales will have on labor requirements. Note the varying number of labor hours needed each quarter. Requirements range from a high of 3,000 hours in the second quarter to a low of 1,720 hours in the third quarter. Assuming that the company feels that scheduling production according to sales is better than scheduling level production, it must make the appropriate plans to meet the varying labor needs. For instance, it might consider adding a second shift during the first six months of the year and then cutting back during the second half when production is down.

Manufacturing Overhead Budget

The **manufacturing overhead budget** is the third and final budget to flow from the production budget. Once it has been prepared, the three elements of the cost of production will be budgeted — direct materials, direct labor, and overhead. The manufacturing overhead budget is shown in Exhibit 5–8.

Note the distinction on the budget between fixed and variable overhead costs. Variable overhead is applied to production on the basis of a rate of $2.50 per direct labor hour (see Exhibit 5–2). Some of the more common variable overhead costs are: indirect materials and supplies, indirect labor, overtime premiums, and some service department costs. These costs are assumed to vary directly in proportion to the number of hours worked and are therefore budgeted on the basis of labor hours — at a rate of $2.50 per labor hour.

EXHIBIT 5–7

BAILEY COMPANY
Direct Labor Budget
For the Year Ended December 31, 19X9

	First	*Second*	*Third*	*Fourth*	*Total*
			Quarters		
Units to be produced (Exhibit 5–5)	720	750	430	590	2,490
Times direct labor hours per unit	4	4	4	4	4
Direct labor hours needed	2,880	3,000	1,720	2,360	9,960
Times labor cost per hour	$ 15	$ 15	$ 15	$ 15	$ 15
Total direct labor cost	$43,200	$45,000	$25,800	$35,400	$149,400

EXHIBIT 5–8

BAILEY COMPANY
Manufacturing Overhead Budget
For the Year Ended December 31, 19X9

	Quarters				
	First	Second	Third	Fourth	Total
Budgeted direct labor hours (Exhibit 5–7)	2,880	3,000	1,720	2,360	9,960
Times variable overhead rate	$ 2.50	$ 2.50	$ 2.50	$ 2.50	$ 2.50
Budgeted variable overhead	$ 7,200	$ 7,500	$ 4,300	$ 5,900	$24,900
Budgeted fixed overhead:					
Supervisor's salary	$ 9,675	$ 9,675	$ 9,675	$ 9,675	$38,700
Insurance	3,000	3,000	3,000	3,000	12,000
Depreciation	6,000	6,000	6,000	6,000	24,000
Total fixed overhead	$18,675	$18,675	$18,675	$18,675	$74,700
Total budgeted overhead	$25,875	$26,175	$22,975	$24,575	$99,600

Bailey's budgeted fixed overhead consists of three costs: the salary of the supervisor on the production line, insurance on the factory equipment, and depreciation of the equipment. These costs are budgeted to be $74,700 for the year, and because they do not vary with the level of production they are simply allocated equally to each quarter of the year.

Selling, General, and Administrative Expense Budget

In addition to product costs, Bailey also has a budget for various operating expenses, called selling, general, and administrative expenses (S,G&A). As was the case with overhead costs, these costs also have a variable and a fixed portion. Variable costs include such items as freight, packaging, and clerical costs on each unit sold, as well as the commission paid to the salesperson who sells the product. Therefore, the variable portion of the S,G&A expense is based on the budgeted sales, in units. A **selling, general, and administrative expense budget** is presented in Exhibit 5–9.

The company has one other variable expense not included in the amount budgeted of $5 per unit. Because it sells on credit, the company estimates that 5% of all sales will be uncollectible. Because bad debts expense is based on sales *dollars,* rather than sales in *units,* it is shown separately on the budget.

Four expense items make up the total budgeted fixed portion of S,G&A: office salaries, advertising, utilities, and office rent. Keep in mind the key point relative to the definition of fixed costs: they will remain the same within a given time period, provided that sales are within a relevant range.

EXHIBIT 5–9

BAILEY COMPANY
Selling, General, and Administrative Expense Budget (S,G&A)
For the Year Ended December 31, 19X9

	Quarters				
	First	Second	Third	Fourth	Total
Budgeted sales in units (Exhibit 5–4)	700	900	400	500	2,500
Times variable S,G&A per unit[a]	$ 5	$ 5	$ 5	$ 5	$ 5
Budgeted variable expense	$ 3,500	$ 4,500	$ 2,000	$ 2,500	$ 12,500
Bad debts expense[b]	$ 7,000	$ 9,000	$ 4,000	$ 5,000	$ 25,000
Fixed S,G&A expenses:					
Office salaries	$10,000	$10,000	$10,000	$10,000	$ 40,000
Advertising	5,000	5,000	5,000	5,000	20,000
Utilities	2,000	2,000	2,000	2,000	8,000
Office rent	3,000	3,000	3,000	3,000	12,000
Budgeted fixed S,G&A	$20,000	$20,000	$20,000	$20,000	$ 80,000
Total budgeted S,G&A	$30,500	$33,500	$26,000	$27,500	$117,500

[a]Consists of commissions, packaging, freight, and secretarial costs.
[b]Sales, in dollars (Exhibit 5–4) times 5% estimated uncollectible.

For example, Bailey assumes that the current office staff will be sufficient to support sales between the low of 400 units in the third quarter to a high of 900 units in the second quarter and therefore has budgeted office salaries at $40,000 for the year, or $10,000 per quarter.

At this point, refer back to the diagram of the master budget system in Exhibit 5–1. Note the arrows going both from the sales budget to the S,G&A budget, as well as from the S,G&A budget to the sales budget. The amount budgeted for S,G&A is not only affected *by* the level of sales but also has an effect *on* the sales. For example, if the company's efforts are successful, the amount spent on advertising will have an effect on the level of future sales.

Cash Budget

The central focus of a master budgeting system is the **cash budget.** After the sales budget and all of the cost budgets have been prepared, attention turns to the aggregation of these budgets into the cash budget. For example, how much are the estimated cash receipts from the budgeted sales? What are the estimated cash disbursements for the purchases of inventory? And how much cash will be expended for the manufacturing overhead costs and the S,G&A costs?

Cash Collections on Accounts Receivable

A schedule of the cash collections on accounts receivable is presented in Exhibit 5–10. This schedule serves two purposes: (1) the cash collections from the sales of each quarter are computed for inclusion on the cash budget and (2) the ending balance in accounts receivable at the end of each quarter is also computed.

Based on past experience, Bailey estimates that 75% of the cash from the sales of any one quarter will be collected in that same three-month period. One of the key factors in this estimate is the credit terms extended by the company to its customers. For example, assume that Bailey requires its customers to pay their bills within sixty days. Cash from sales made in January would normally be collected by the end of the first quarter on March 31. Cash from some of February sales would be collected and relatively less from sales in March. Bailey estimates that 20% of the sales made in the previous quarter will be collected in the following quarter. Sales for the fourth quarter of the previous year were assumed to be $120,000, and collections in the first quarter of this year on those sales therefore are estimated to be 20% or

EXHIBIT 5–10

BAILEY COMPANY
Cash Collections on Accounts Receivable
For the Year Ended December 31, 19X9

	Quarters				
	First	*Second*	*Third*	*Fourth*	*Total*
Accounts receivable, beginning of quarter	$ 30,000[a]	$ 35,000	$ 45,000	$ 20,000	$ 30,000
Add: sales (from Exhibit 5–4)	140,000	180,000	80,000	100,000	500,000
Total amounts due from customers	$170,000	$215,000	$125,000	$120,000	$530,000
Deduct: cash collections: 75% of sales for current quarter	$105,000	$135,000	$ 60,000	$ 75,000	$375,000
20% of sales for previous quarter	24,000	28,000	36,000	16,000	104,000
Total cash collections	($129,000)	($163,000)	($ 96,000)	($ 91,000)	($479,000)
Deduct: write-offs: 5% of previous quarter's sales	($ 6,000)	($ 7,000)	($ 9,000)	($ 4,000)	($ 26,000)
Accounts receivable, end of quarter	$ 35,000	$ 45,000	$ 20,000	$ 25,000	$ 25,000

[a]Sales in fourth quarter of previous year assumed to be $120,000, of which 25% or $30,000 remains uncollected to start this year.

$24,000. Finally, recall from the budget for S,G&A expenses that Bailey estimates that 5% of all accounts will be uncollectible. This explains why Exhibit 5–10 shows a total of only 95% of any one quarter's sales being eventually collected (that is, 75% in the quarter of the sale and 20% in the following quarter).

To find the ending balance in accounts receivable each quarter, budgeted sales are added to the beginning accounts receivable balance and budgeted cash collections are deducted. Write-offs of bad debts must also be subtracted to arrive at the ending balance. Bailey assumes that their estimate of 5% of sales for bad debts expense is accurate. Therefore, they will write off 5% of the prior quarter's sales during each quarter. For example, the bad debts expense of $7,000 in the first quarter (Exhibit 5–9) is the amount estimated to be written off in the second quarter (Exhibit 5–10). Write-offs of $6,000 in the first quarter are based on 5% of the $120,000 in sales in the fourth quarter of last year.

Cash Payments on Accounts Payable

The logic used to prepare this schedule is the same as that used for the schedule of cash collections on accounts receivable. Purchases of direct materials, as budgeted in Exhibit 5–6, are added to the beginning balance of accounts payable each quarter. Estimated cash payments for the purchases are then deducted to arrive at the ending balance in accounts payable. Bailey estimates that they will pay for 40% of all purchases in the same quarter the purchases are made. The other 60% of purchases are paid for in the following quarter. The schedule of cash payments on accounts payable is shown in Exhibit 5–11 (page 130).

Summary Cash Budget

Cash collections on accounts receivable and cash payments on accounts payable are now aggregated with other cash inflows and outflows in a summary cash budget, as shown in Exhibit 5–12.

The amounts for cash collections on accounts receivable and cash payments on accounts payable come directly from the two schedules. Because wages must be paid as the work is done (unlike purchases of materials, there is no credit period extended), the cash paid for direct labor is taken directly from the direct labor budget. Similarly, variable overhead costs are assumed to be paid in the period incurred and therefore are the same amounts as shown on the overhead budget.

Note, however, that the amounts on the cash budget for fixed overhead and variable selling, general, and administrative expense are not the same amounts as appear on their respective budgets. Each of these costs include an item that will not require a cash outlay. Depreciation of $6,000 per quarter was included in the overhead budget but does not require cash—cash is paid when the fixed asset is purchased (unless financed by long-term debt) and would appear in a capital budget. The fixed overhead in the cash budget

EXHIBIT 5—11

BAILEY COMPANY
Cash Payments on Accounts Payable
For the Year Ended December 31, 19X9

	Quarters				
	First	*Second*	*Third*	*Fourth*	*Total*
Accounts payable, beginning of quarter	$14,000[a]	$13,710	$10,620	$ 9,180	$14,000
Add: purchases (Exhibit 5–6)	22,850	17,700	15,300	23,100	78,950
Total amount owed	$36,850	$31,410	$25,920	$32,280	$92,950
Deduct: cash payments:					
40% of purchases for the quarter	$ 9,140	$ 7,080	$ 6,120	$ 9,240	$31,580
60% of purchases for previous quarter	14,000	13,710	10,620	9,180	47,510
Total cash payments	($23,140)	($20,790)	($16,740)	($18,420)	($79,090)
Accounts payable, end of quarter	$13,710	$10,620	$ 9,180	$13,860	$13,860

[a]Purchases in the fourth quarter of previous year are assumed to be $23,333, of which 60% or $14,000 remains unpaid to start this year.

of $12,675 per quarter consists of the supervisor's salary of $9,675 and insurance of $3,000. Similarly, bad debts expense is an expense to be included on the S,G&A budget in Exhibit 5–9. However, it does not require any cash outlay and is not included in the cash budget. All of the fixed S,G&A expenses are assumed to require the payment of cash in the period incurred and are included in Exhibit 5–12.

Three items are included in the cash payments section of the cash budget that have not been included on previous budgets: income taxes, dividends, and acquisition of land. The amounts paid for income taxes require an estimate of income, and we will therefore defer discussion of these amounts until we have prepared a budgeted income statement. The amount of dividends stems from the dividend policy of the board of directors, whereas the plans to acquire land would be based on a capital budget.

If cash collections added to the beginning cash balance in any one period exceed the total cash payments, the company may have excess cash to invest. This depends on the minimum level of cash that the company feels it must maintain as a cushion. A certain minimum of cash must be maintained in case sales lag or costs are higher than budgeted. Also, many banks require that their customers maintain a minimum balance and charge a monthly fee if the balance falls below this amount.

EXHIBIT 5–12

BAILEY COMPANY
Cash Budget
For the Year Ended December 31, 19X9

	From Exh.	First	Second	Third	Fourth	Total
				Quarters		
Cash balance, beg. of quarter		$ 10,000[a]	$ 10,035	$ 10,320	$ 10,555	$ 10,000
Add: cash collected on accounts receivable (Exhibit 5–10)		129,000	163,000	96,000	91,000	479,000
Cash available		$139,000	$173,035	$106,320	$101,555	$489,000
Deduct: cash payments:						
Material purchases	5–11	$ 23,140	$ 20,790	$ 16,740	$ 18,420	$ 79,090
Direct labor	5–7	43,200	45,000	25,800	35,400	149,400
Variable overhead	5–8	7,200	7,500	4,300	5,900	24,900
Fixed overhead[b]	5–8	12,675	12,675	12,675	12,675	50,700
Variable S,G&A[c]	5–9	3,500	4,500	2,000	2,500	12,500
Fixed S,G&A	5–9	20,000	20,000	20,000	20,000	80,000
Income taxes		10,750	5,750	5,750	5,750	28,000
Dividends		2,500	2,500	2,500	2,500	10,000
Acquisition of land		0	25,000	0	0	25,000
Total cash payments		$122,965	$143,715	$ 89,765	$103,145	$459,590
Excess cash (deficiency)		$ 16,035	$ 29,320	$ 16,555	$ (1,590)	$ 29,410
Investing activities:						
Investment in bonds		(6,000)	(19,000)	(6,000)	0	(31,000)
Redemption of bonds		0	0	0	12,000	12,000
Ending cash balance		$ 10,035	$ 10,320	$ 10,555	$ 10,410	$ 10,410

[a]First quarter balance from beginning balance sheet (Exhibit 5–3). Company policy is to maintain a $10,000 balance at end of each quarter.

[b]Excludes $6,000 of depreciation each quarter (noncash expense).

[c]Excludes bad debts expense each quarter (noncash expense).

We have assumed that Bailey wants to keep a balance of $10,000 on hand at all times. Any excess is assumed to be invested in government bonds that will earn 10% annually. All interest is assumed to be automatically reinvested and therefore does not come back to the company in the form of cash. We have further assumed that these investments can be made only in denominations of $1,000 each. Therefore, the excess cash of $16,035 at the end of the first quarter can be used to buy $6,000 of bonds and still leave the company with a balance of $10,035 in cash. Note the need to sell $12,000 of the bonds in the fourth quarter in order to maintain the minimum cash balance of $10,000.

Some companies do not find themselves in Bailey's position with excess cash to invest. They must borrow on a short-term basis in order to maintain a minimum cash balance. Any necessary borrowings would be shown in the same section of the cash budget as the investing activities, but as an addition to cash rather than a deduction.

Schedule of Temporary Investments

The investing section of the cash budget is the basis for preparing a schedule of the company's temporary investments. Because earnings on the bonds are reinvested, they are added to the beginning balance each quarter along with any additional investments made, as indicated on the cash budget. Any redemptions are a reduction in the temporary investments. A schedule of temporary investments is shown in Exhibit 5–13.

Pro Forma Income Statement – Contribution Margin Format

Once the cash budget is completed, budgeted financial statements can be prepared. Projected or budgeted income statements and balance sheets are often called **pro forma statements.** A pro forma income statement for the year is shown in Exhibit 5–14.

The pro forma income statement was prepared using the contribution margin format approach. Recall from Chapter 4 the meaning of contribution margin: revenues less variable expenses. Note the division on the income statement between variable expenses and fixed expenses. The objective is to

EXHIBIT 5–13

BAILEY COMPANY
Temporary Investments
For the Year Ended December 31, 19X9

	Quarters				
	First	*Second*	*Third*	*Fourth*	*Total*
Beginning balance	$11,000	$17,275	$36,707	$43,625	$11,000
Add: 10% interest on beginning balance[a]	275	432	918	1,091	2,716
Add: investments (Exhibit 5–12)	6,000	19,000	6,000	0	31,000
Deduct: redemptions (Exhibit 5–12)	0	0	0	(12,000)	(12,000)
Ending balance	$17,275	$36,707	$43,625	$32,716	$32,716

[a]Interest of 10% compounded quarterly (or 2.5% per quarter) is reinvested.

EXHIBIT 5–14

BAILEY COMPANY
Pro Forma Income Statement – Contribution Margin Format
For the Year Ended December 31, 19X9

Sales revenue		$500,000
Variable expenses:		
Production expenses[a]	$250,000	
S,G&A expenses	12,500	
Bad debts expense	25,000	(287,500)
Contribution margin		$212,500
Fixed expenses:		
Manufacturing overhead	$ 75,000	
S,G&A expenses	80,000	(155,000)
Operating income		$ 57,500
Interest income		2,716
Net income before tax		$ 60,216
Income tax expense		(24,086)
Net income		$ 36,130

[a]Consists of $30 direct materials, $60 direct labor and $10 variable overhead (see Exhibit 5–2).

---

classify costs on the income statement according to their *behavior* (that is, variable or fixed), rather than according to their *function* (that is, production, selling, and so forth). The reader of this statement can quickly tell that sales activity of the period provided the company with $212,500 in contribution margin to apply toward fixed costs and profits.

One of the two fixed costs, manufacturing overhead, needs further explanation. Fixed manufacturing overhead costs, per Exhibit 5–8, are $74,700. Why does the income statement show $75,000? The answer lies in the concept of the application of manufacturing overhead—a concept we will explore in detail in Chapter 6. For now, however, recall from Exhibit 5–8 that total variable overhead was found by multiplying the rate of $2.50 times 9,960 budgeted direct labor hours. Applying the same concept, we find that the budgeted fixed overhead rate is the actual fixed overhead of $74,700 divided by 9,960 hours or $7.50 per hour. Because four direct labor hours are required to produce a unit of product, the rate per unit is $7.50 times 4 or $30. Finally, $30 per unit times 2,500 units of product sold yields the amount charged to the income statement of $75,000. Summarizing:

Total fixed overhead costs incurred	$74,700
Divided by: direct labor hours	9,960 hours
= Fixed overhead rate per hour	$7.50 per hour
× Hours required per unit	4 hours
= Fixed overhead rate per unit	$30 per unit
× Number of units sold	2,500 units
= Fixed overhead charged to the income statement	$75,000

Income is assumed to be taxed at a rate of 40%, resulting in income tax expense of $24,086 for the year. Keep in mind, however, that this is not necessarily the amount of tax Bailey will pay during the year. Companies must make quarterly installment payments to the government, based on an estimate of their annual earnings.

Referring back to the cash budget in Exhibit 5–12, we see the amount of taxes paid each quarter. For simplicity, we have assumed that Bailey makes quarterly payments based on an estimate of their income before considering any interest income. (If the bonds are municipal bonds, any interest earned will be tax exempt—otherwise Bailey will have to pay tax on the interest earned on the bonds.) Therefore, the total payments are 40% of the operating income of $57,500, or $23,000. Each quarterly payment is one-fourth of $23,000, or $5,750. Note, however, that the first installment is $10,750. It includes $5,000 to pay off the amount due at the end of last year—the current liability shown on the balance sheet in Exhibit 5–3.

Pro Forma Balance Sheet

The final budgeted statement in the process is the balance sheet. A pro forma balance sheet is presented in Exhibit 5–15. Most of the amounts in the statement can be traced directly to one of the other exhibits. For example, the cash balance comes directly from the cash budget and the balance in temporary investments comes from the schedule of temporary investments. Other accounts, such as plant and equipment and common stock, are unchanged from the beginning of the year balance sheet in Exhibit 5–3.

Finally, an observation about this textbook illustration should be made. The entire set of budgets was prepared without any revisions. In practice, budgeting is a give-and-take process in which many iterations may be necessary before the numbers are finalized. If the budget system is to be an effective planning tool, "fine tuning" is often necessary to make it an accurate reflection of the company's goals.

The Use of the Computer in Budgeting

Probably no other area of accounting lends itself as well to the use of the computer as does budgeting. Two important advances in the computer industry have had profound effects on accounting and budgeting in particular. One of these advances is the equipment itself, or hardware, where smaller and smaller units continue to flood the marketplace. For many applications, the larger mainframe computers are being replaced by minicomputers, microcomputers, desktop computers, and even some that fit in a briefcase. Regardless of their names, these scaled-down versions are often just as powerful as their predecessors and sold at a cost that makes them much more accessible to small companies to aid in the budgeting process.

EXHIBIT 5–15

BAILEY COMPANY
Pro Forma Balance Sheet
December 31, 19X9

Cash (Exhibit 5–12)		$ 10,410
Temporary investments (Exhibit 5–13)		32,716
Accounts receivable, less allowance of $5,000 (Exhibit 5–10)		20,000
Inventories: raw materials (1,425 yards)		14,250
finished goods (240 suits)		31,200
Total current assets		$108,576
Land	$175,000	
Plant and equipment	$400,000	
Less: accumulated depreciation	174,000	226,000
Total long-term assets		401,000
Total assets		$509,576
Accounts payable (Exhibit 5–11)		$ 13,860
Taxes payable[a]		1,086
Total current liabilities		$ 14,946
Common stock, no par	$300,000	
Retained earnings[b]	194,630	
Total stockholders' equity		494,630
Total liabilities and stockholders' equity		$509,576

[a]Beginning balance of $5,000 plus expense of $24,086 less payments of $28,000.
[b]Beginning balance of $168,500 plus net income of $36,130 less dividends of $10,000.

The second important advance is the software that has been written for the smaller computers. Software is a set of logically written instructions that tell the computer how to perform a particular function. A computer standing alone is dumb. It must be told how to add, subtract, order data, and perform other important tasks. One type of software application, spreadsheet analysis, is ideally suited to aid in the budgeting process. The software package allows the user to develop templates for various managerial accounting applications.

Even more important, these programs allow the user to ask any number of "what if" questions and have the answers in a matter of seconds. For example, one of the assumptions used in our problem was that 75% of the cash from the sales of a quarter is collected in the same quarter. What if Bailey was considering granting more liberal credit terms to their customers? What effect would this have on the level of sales and thus on the sales budget? On the negative side, what if this change resulted in only 50% of the sales being collected in the same quarter? What effect would this have on the cash budget for each of the quarters? A spreadsheet can be used to provide answers to these questions much faster than ever would have been possible by making all of the necessary changes in the numbers manually.

Finally, the computer is a very efficient device for updating continuous budgets. Because actual results seldom agree exactly with budgeted amounts, the beginning cash balance must be corrected each month. This necessitates changing many of the other numbers in the master budget as well. The computer facilitates this process and saves considerable time otherwise spent in erasing and replacing numbers manually.

Zero-Base Budgeting

Zero-base budgeting is an alternative approach to budgeting that became particularly prominent during the administration of President Carter. The concept has been applied by some corporations, as well as by governmental units, but has never achieved the widespread popularity that its advocates had envisioned for it.

Traditional budgeting relies on the use of an incremental approach to cost justification. For example, in our problem fixed selling, general, and administrative expenses were budgeted to be $20,000 per quarter. In a traditional budgeting system, $80,000 would be the starting point for budgeting these costs for the following year, and the manager would have to justify any increases above this amount. In contrast, in a zero-based budgeting environment, the manager must start at ground level and justify all expenses, not just those over and above last year's amount. In other words, no programs are sacred—all activities must be reviewed periodically and justified on a cost/benefit basis if they are to be continued. Whether or not zero-based budgeting is used as the sole method for the budgeting process, the underlying concept of periodically reviewing programs from the ground up is a useful one.

Summary

Budgeting is one of the most important tools that management has at its disposal in planning for the attainment of the company's goals. We concentrated our attention in this chapter on short-run budgeting as opposed to capital budgeting, which is concerned with company goals over a time horizon longer than the next year. Crucial to the success of any budgeting system, short or long run, is the active involvement in the process by those individuals who will be responsible for meeting the goals set out in the budget. The concepts of responsibility accounting and participatory budgeting were introduced in the chapter to emphasize the importance of the personnel in the process.

The master budget system was introduced in the chapter to show how the various individual budgets fit together and ultimately lead to the preparation of budgeted or pro forma financial statements for the period. For brevity, the process was illustrated for a quarterly budgeting system, but in practice monthly budgets are more common. We saw how the starting point in the process is the sales budget and how all other budgets depend to some extent on an accurate forecast of sales. Once the individual cost budgets were prepared, the cash budget followed, with the aid of schedules of cash collections on accounts receivable and cash payments on accounts payable. A contribution margin income statement was illustrated to emphasize the important distinction in managerial accounting between variable and fixed costs.

Budgeting is crucial to both the efficient planning of operations as well as to the control of those operations. Neither the size of an organization nor the lack of sophistication in its accounting system is a good excuse for ignoring this important tool. A company that argues that it does not have the time to budget fails to understand the importance of planning to the overall success of the business.

Key Terms

Budget is a financial plan as to how the resources of an organization will be managed over a future period of time.

Capital budgeting is a type of budgeting concerned with the planning of major expenditures, such as new plant and equipment — the time horizon may be as long as twenty or thirty years.

Cash budget is a summary budget of the planned cash receipts and cash payments.

Continuous budget is a type of budget in which an additional time period, such as a month or quarter, is added on to the budget as the previous month or quarter ends.

Direct labor budget is a budget of the planned expenditures for direct labor, usually indicating the number of hours to be worked and the hourly rate.

Direct materials purchases budget is a budget of the expected costs for direct materials, usually indicating the number of units, such as pounds or yards, of material and the cost per unit.

Financial budgeting plans the timing of cash inflows and outflows, as well as planning for any cash excess or cash deficiencies.

Manufacturing overhead budget is a budget of the planned expenditures for variable and fixed overhead.

Master budget system is a series of individual budgets aggregated to form a complete set of budgeted financial statements for the current period.

Operational budgeting is a type of budgeting concerned with sales and the various operations of the business, such as buying materials and scheduling labor.

Participatory budgeting is a system of budgeting in which those individuals who will be held accountable for the differences between budgeted and actual results are allowed to take part in the setting of the budgets.

Production budget is a budget indicating the number of units of finished product to be manufactured, taking into account expected sales and desired levels of inventory.

Pro forma statement is a projected or budgeted financial statement, such as an income statement or a balance sheet.

Responsibility accounting is a system of accounting that recognizes the importance of the individual in the control of operations and that attempts to assign costs and revenues to the individuals who have the most control or influence over them.

Sales budget is a budget of the planned sales of product, usually indicating the number of units to be sold and the selling price.

Selling, general, and administrative expense budget is a budget of the planned expenditures for operating costs such as commissions (variable) and office salaries (fixed).

Time series analysis is a statistical technique useful in forecasting sales in which the forecaster tries to predict future sales based on past trends.

Zero-base budgeting is an alternative form of budgeting, in which all expenses must be justified, not just those over and above the amount spent in the prior period.

Questions

Q5–1   How is C-V-P analysis, discussed in Chapter 4, related to budgeting?

Q5–2   What is the difference between operational budgeting and financial budgeting?

Q5–3   The budget manager for a large corporation makes the following statement: "Setting a budget requires as much understanding of organizational behavior as it does knowledge of accounting." Evaluate this statement.

Q5–4   Explain the relationship of responsibility accounting to budgeting. What is the significance of controllable costs to this relationship?

Q5–5   List the various advantages to a company in using a participatory budgeting system.

Q5–6   What is the underlying concept behind a continuous budget? Why do companies use a continuous budgeting system?

Q5–7   Explain why, in a master budgeting environment, the sales forecast is the starting point. What is the difference between a sales forecast and a sales budget?

Q5–8   Two budget managers are talking about their jobs. One argues that today's sophisticated environment calls for sophisticated forecasting techniques, such as regression analysis and time series analysis. The other manager says that the only way to forecast sales is to ask the people in the field, the salespeople, what they are going to sell next month. Evaluate the two positions. Who is right?

Q5–9   Explain the importance of seasonality to budgeting sales.

Q5–10   One critical link in a master budget is the relationship between the sales budget and the production budget. Explain this relationship.

Q5–11   A company is considering two approaches to scheduling monthly production for a year. One approach would involve relatively even or level production throughout the year. The other alternative would involve determining production needs for each month on the basis of the next month's budgeted sales. Which approach do you favor? Why?

Q5–12 What budget would replace the production budget for a retailer?

Q5–13 When budgeting purchases, a company must weigh the relative costs of carrying too much inventory against the costs of not carrying enough. What are some of the costs associated with each of these possibilities?

Q5–14 What problems does scheduling production relative to the next period's sales create in planning labor requirements?

Q5–15 Why is it important in a selling, general, and administrative expense budget to separate variable and fixed costs? Give some examples of each.

Q5–16 Explain the meaning of the following statement: "The selling, general, and administrative expense budget is unique because it is the only cost budget that both is affected by the level of sales and also has an effect on sales."

Q5–17 Why are the credit terms that a company extends to its customers a key factor in budgeting cash collections?

Q5–18 What are the costs associated with carrying a relatively large cash balance? A relatively small cash balance? Why is cash management such a crucial concern of all businesses?

Q5–19 A budget manager makes the following statement: "The most valuable aspect of using a computer software program to aid in budgeting is the ability to ask numerous 'what if' questions." What does the manager mean by this? Give some examples of such questions.

Q5–20 Evaluate the following statement: "The development of the smaller computers has revolutionized the budgeting process. The human element in the process has been replaced by the electronic capabilities of the computer and the process is now primarily a mechanical one."

Q5–21 What is meant by zero-base budgeting? How does it differ from the traditional form of budgeting?

Exercises

E5–1 **Purchases budget for a retailer.** Hal's Bike Shop budgets bicycle sales for six months at a time. Peak sales occur in April in anticipation of the summer riding season and again in December for the holiday season. Budgeted sales for the first six months of 19X9 are as follows:

Month	Budgeted Sales (in units)
January	50
February	80
March	125
April	175
May	150
June	130

Hal starts 19X9 with an inventory of 20 bicycles and attempts to maintain a safety stock at the end of any given month equal to 20% of the next month's budgeted sales. Budgeted sales for July of 19X9 are 110 units.

Required: Prepare a purchases budget (in units), by month and in total, for the first six months of 19X9.

E5–2 **Production and purchases budgets for a manufacturer.** FineOaks manufactures dining room tables, selling them to wholesalers nationwide. The company employs a continuous budgeting system with a four-month time horizon. Their top-of-the-line table requires 20 square feet of oak, at a cost to the company of $25 per square foot. FineOaks has budgeted sales of the tables for the first five months of 19X0 as follows (the extra month is needed to estimate the ending inventory for April):

Month	Budgeted Sales (units)
January	300
February	450
March	500
April	700
May	850

Required: 1. Prepare a production budget, in units, by month and in total, for the first four months of 19X0. Assume that the company wants to maintain an inventory of tables at the end of each month equal to 10% of the following month's sales and that 60 tables are on hand at the beginning of the year.

2. Prepare a purchases budget, in dollars, for direct materials, by month and in total, for the first four months of 19X0. Assume that FineOaks feels that they need to maintain an inventory of lumber at the end of each month equal to 30% of the next month's needs and that 1,500 square feet of oak are on hand to start the year. FineOaks estimates an inventory of oak on hand at the end of April of 4,950 square feet.

E5–3 **Direct labor and overhead budgets.** The Webster Manufacturing Company has completed its production budget for the first four months of the year. The budget, in units of finished product, is:

January: 1,200
February: 1,500
March: 1,650
April: 2,000

Each unit of finished product requires 3 hours of direct labor at a cost of $9 per hour. Variable manufacturing overhead is budgeted on the basis of direct labor hours, at a rate of $4 per direct labor hour. Monthly fixed overhead consists of three supervisors' salaries at $3,000 each, depreciation on the production facility of $15,000, and insurance of $5,000.

Required: 1. Prepare a direct labor budget, by month and in total, for the first four months of the year.

2. Prepare a manufacturing overhead budget, by month and in total, for the first four months of the year.

E5–4 **Cash collections on accounts receivable.** Budgeted sales, in dollars, for the first quarter of the year for the Wilson Auto Parts Company are as follows:

> January: $60,000
> February: $75,000
> March: $85,000

Wilson normally collects 70% of each month's sales in that month with 25% collected the following month. Five percent of all sales turn out to be uncollectible and are written off in the following month. The company started the year with a balance in accounts receivable of $12,000, which represents 30% of the sales of December of last year.

Required: Prepare a schedule of the cash collections on accounts receivable, by month, and in total, for the first quarter of the year.

E5–5 **Cash payments on accounts payable (with cash discounts).** Griswold Distributing's budget for purchases, before any cash discounts, for the last four months of 19X3 is:

> September: $80,000
> October: $95,000
> November: $110,000
> December: $90,000

Griswold buys from two primary suppliers, each of which extends credit terms of 2/10, net 30. Griswold's policy is to take advantage of all cash discounts. Due to the timing of purchases in any given month, this policy results in 80% of the *net* purchases being paid for in the month of the purchase with the other 20% paid for in the following month. The balance in accounts payable at the end of August is $14,000, which represents 20% of that month's *net* purchases.

Required: Prepare a schedule of the cash payments on accounts payable, by month and in total, for the last four months of 19X3.

E5–6 **Production budget for two products.** The Kelley Company manufactures two products, A and B. Kelley has budgeted sales for 19X4, by quarter, as:

Quarter	Product A	Product B
First	150	80
Second	250	100
Third	180	140
Fourth	120	200

The company expects a 20% increase in sales of each product in each quarter of 19X5 over the corresponding quarter of 19X4.

Required: Prepare a production budget, in units of each product by quarter and in total, for the year 19X4. Kelley wants to maintain an inventory of each product at the end of each quarter equal to 30% of the next quarter's sales. The inventory to start the year consists of 40 units of Product A and 50 units of Product B.

E5–7 **Pro forma income statement.** The Norris Corporation is in the process of compiling a set of budgets for the coming year. Norris's single product sold last year for

$10 per unit. Total sales were 500,000 units. The vice-president of sales has requested that the company consider a 10% price reduction in order to stay competitive with new entrants into the market. She is confident that such a reduction will increase sales volume by 20%.

Variable production costs this past year were

Direct material	$4
Direct labor	$2
Variable overhead	$1

The only other variable cost incurred is the 10% commission paid to the salespeople on each unit sold. Although no increase in either the commission or direct labor are expected in the upcoming year (a new contract was signed last year with the union), a 15% increase in the cost of direct materials is expected. Variable overhead is a function of direct labor hours worked. Fixed costs the past year were $250,000 and are expected to increase by 10% in the next year.

Required:

1. In parallel columns, prepare an income statement for the past year and a pro forma income statement for the upcoming year, using the contribution margin format. Assume a 30% tax rate.
2. Should the company follow through with the proposed price reduction? Explain your answer.

E5–8   **Cash budget for a rental business.** Henry Hill is considering opening a video rental store. He has noted the tremendous popularity of home videos in the past year and that his city with a population of 10,000 does not currently have an outlet. He has $5,000 to invest and has approached the local bank for additional money. They have told him that he must submit a detailed cash budget for the first six months.

Hill estimates monthly rentals of videos to be

	Unit Rentals
April	5,000
May	4,000
June	2,500
July	2,000
August	2,500
September	3,500

Each video will rent for $3. Hill will invest in April in 1,000 titles at a cost to him of $20 each. In addition to his own time in the store he plans on hiring 5 employees. Each employee will initially work 30 hours per week at a rate of $8 per hour. During the summer months of June, July, and August each employee will only work 20 hours per week (assume four weeks in each month). The rent on the store will be $1,000 per month. Other expenses, including insurance and utilities, are estimated to be $500 per month.

Required:

1. Prepare a detailed cash budget for the first six months of the new business, assuming no borrowing from the bank.
2. How much should Hill ask to borrow from the bank? Justify your recommendation.

E5–9 **Cash collections with discounts.** The Brody Company sells merchandise for cash as well as with credit terms of 2/10, net 20. In the past, cash sales have accounted for approximately 20% of total sales. The credit terms have resulted in the following normal collection pattern:

Credit Sales Collected in:	Percentage
Same month as sold	60%
Month following the sale	30
Two months following the sale	8
Written off as uncollectible	2

Budgeted total sales for the first quarter of 19X6 are

Month	Budgeted Sales
January	$600,000
February	750,000
March	800,000

Total sales in November of 19X5 were $400,000 and in December amounted to $500,000.

Required: Prepare a schedule of cash collections, by month and in total, for the first quarter of 19X6. Assume 75% of credit sales collected in the same month as sold will receive the discount.

E5–10 **Investment of excess cash.** The Gotitmade Company is putting together budgets for 19X9. The budget manager has produced the following estimates for the first six months of 19X9:

Month	Cash Collections	Cash Disbursements
January	$200,000	$160,000
February	280,000	230,000
March	375,000	310,000
April	300,000	285,000
May	245,000	250,000
June	220,000	250,000

Any cash excess at the end of each month is invested in a money market account, which currently pays 6% compounded monthly. The company's policy is to maintain a cash balance at the end of each month of $20,000 to cover contingencies and any inaccuracies in the budgeting system. Any deficiencies at the end of a month that need to be made up to maintain the $20,000 cushion result in a withdrawal from the money market account.

Required:
1. Prepare a cash budget, by month and in total, for the first six months of 19X9. Assume that exactly $20,000 is budgeted as the cash balance at the end of each month (any amount can be invested in the money market account—even denominations are not necessary). Interest is reinvested. The cash balance on December 31, 19X8, is $20,000.
2. Prepare a schedule to show the beginning and ending balance in the money market account, by month and in total, for the first six months of 19X9. The balance in the account on December 31, 19X8, is $150,000.

Problems

P5–11   **Set of budgets for two products.** The Scarborough Corporation manufactures and sells two products, Thingone and Thingtwo. In July 19X7 Scarborough's budget department gathered the following data in order to project sales and budget requirements for 19X8:

19X8 Projected Sales:

Product	Units	Price
Thingone	60,000	$ 70
Thingtwo	40,000	$100

19X8 Inventories – in units:

Product	Expected January 1, 19X8	Desired December 31, 19X8
Thingone	20,000	25,000
Thingtwo	8,000	9,000

In order to produce one unit of Thingone and Thingtwo, the following raw materials are used:

Raw Material	Unit	Amount Used Per Unit Thingone	Thingtwo
A	lbs.	4	5
B	lbs.	2	3
C	each		1

Projected data for 19X8 with respect to raw materials is as follows:

Raw Material	Anticipated Purchase Price	Expected Inventories January 1, 19X8	Desired Inventories December 31, 19X8
A	$8	32,000 lbs.	36,000 lbs.
B	$5	29,000 lbs.	32,000 lbs.
C	$3	6,000 each	7,000 each

Projected direct labor requirements for 19X8 and rates are as follows:

Product	Hours per Unit	Rate per Hour
Thingone	2	$3
Thingtwo	3	$4

Overhead is applied at the rate of $2 per direct labor hour.

Required: Based on the above projections and budget requirements for 19X8 for Thingone and Thingtwo, prepare the following budgets for 19X8:

1. Sales budget (in dollars)
2. Production budget (in units)
3. Raw materials purchase budget (in quantities)

4. Raw materials purchase budget (in dollars)
5. Direct labor budget (in dollars)
6. Budgeted finished goods inventory at December 31, 19X8 (in dollars)

(CPA Adapted)

P5–12   **Quarterly cash budgets for a service business.** Prime Time Court Club (PTCC) has been in business for five years. The club has experienced cash flow problems each year, especially in the summer when court use is quite low and new membership sales are insignificant. Temporary loans have been obtained from the local bank to cover the summer shortages. Additional permanent capital has also been invested by the owners.

The owners and the bank have decided some action needs to be taken at this time to improve PTCC's net cash flow position. They would like to review a quarterly cash budget based on a revised fee structure that hopefully would increase club revenues. The purpose of the cash budget would be to better anticipate both the timing and amounts of the probable cash flow of the club and to determine if the club can survive.

John Harper, club manager, recommended that the membership dues be increased and that the hourly court time fees be replaced with a monthly charge for unlimited court use. He believes that this plan will increase membership and that the cash flow and timing problem should be reduced. The proposed fee schedule, which is consistent with rates at other clubs, is presented below. In his opinion, the proportions of the different membership categories should not change, but the total number of members will increase by 10%. Court use will also increase an estimated 20% as a result of this new program. The pattern of use throughout the year is not expected to change.

The present fee structure, the distribution among membership categories, and the projected 19X3 operating data including membership status, court usage, and estimated operating costs are presented below. The projected operating data presented in the table were based on the present fee structure before Harper's proposed fee schedule was recommended.

Proposed Fee Schedule

Membership Category	Annual Membership Fees	Monthly Court Charges
Individual	$ 75	$10
Youth	45	8
Family	150	18

Present Fee Structure

Annual Membership Dues

Individual	$ 45
Youth	30
Family	100

Court Time Fees

Prime	$10 per hour
Regular	6 per hour

Membership Distribution

Individual	50%
Youth	20
Family	30
	100%

Projected Operating Data

Quarter	Membership Renewal or New Memberships	Court Time in Hours		Costs	
		Prime	Regular	Fixed Costs[a]	Variable Costs
1	600	5,500	6,000	$ 56,500	$ 57,500
2	200	2,000	4,000	56,500	30,000
3	200	1,000	2,000	56,500	15,000
4	600	5,500	6,000	56,500	57,500
	1,600			$226,000	$160,000

[a]Includes a quarterly depreciation charge of $12,500.

Required:

1. Construct a cash budget, by quarter and for the year in total, for PTCC assuming the new fee structure is adopted and John Harper's estimates of increases in membership and court use occur. Assume the transition from the old to the new fee structure is immediate and complete when preparing the budget.
2. Will John Harper's proposal solve the summer cash shortfall problem? Explain your answer.
3. Will John Harper's proposal support a conclusion that the club can become profitable and survive in the long run. Explain your answer.

(CMA Adapted)

P5–13 **Production scheduling alternatives.** The Cutter Company is a manufacturer of high-quality lawn mowers for residential use. Sales are seasonal with peak sales in April with the beginning of spring. Cutter's sales manager anticipates the following pattern for sales in the first seven months of 19X7:

Month	Budgeted Sales (in units)
January	2,500
February	3,200
March	6,500
April	8,500
May	7,000
June	5,300
July	4,500

At its monthly meeting in December of 19X6, the company's management team discussed the scheduling of production for 19X7. The production manager argues that production should be stabilized as much as possible to prevent the need to hire additional workers during busy periods and lay off employees during slack times. "The quality of our product suffers if we do not stabilize production," he says. "During busy times workers cannot keep up and turn out an inferior product if they feel rushed.

And if we have to hire part-timers to help out who don't know enough about our product, quality will likewise suffer."

On the other side, the sales manager believes that scheduling production evenly throughout the year could create serious problems for the company. He argues, "Inventory levels must be sufficient at all times to satisfy our distributors. If we turn out the same number of mowers every month we are bound to run short in peak months. Not only will we lose a sale this year to a key distributor, but we run the risk of losing their business next year as well."

To resolve the dilemma, the president of the company has asked for your help in comparing the effects of scheduling production around sales versus level production. The inventory of mowers on January 1, 19X7, is expected to be 200.

Required:

1. Prepare a production budget, by month and in total, for the first six months of 19X7, assuming that the company decides to maintain an inventory of mowers equal to 10% of the following month's sales.

2. Prepare a schedule to compute the ending inventory of mowers, by month and in total, for the first six months of 19X7, assuming that the company decides to schedule production each month equal to the average budgeted monthly sales for the first six months of the year.

3. Based on your work in (1) and (2), what recommendation would you make to the president? Support your recommendation.

P5–14   **Cash budget for a professional sports team.** The Kane County Colonels is a minor league baseball franchise operating in a market with a total population of 100,000. The ball park seats a maximum of 10,000. The club has enjoyed considerable success, both on the field as well as at the box office, in recent years. This success is attributable to the players that have been with the franchise as well as the management team. However, because of escalating player salaries and the competing sources of entertainment, the club has fallen on harder times the last two years.

Management is in the process of putting together a loan proposal to present to the local bank. The concern has been expressed that the team may not be able to meet its payroll for the coming season, and it decided to approach its bank. The bank in turn has asked for a detailed cash budget for the six-month period beginning April 1 and ending September 30. The baseball season begins the first week of May and concludes in the middle of September.

Single-game tickets for the upcoming season will be $5 for reserved seats and $3 for bleacher seats. In addition to single-game sales, the club offers two types of season ticket plans: (1) a full-season ticket plan for all 50 home games at a reduced price of $200 and (2) a weekend plan for the 20 weekend games at a reduced price of $80. The campaign to sell season tickets begins in April and continues into the first two weeks of May. The ticket manager has projected season ticket sales, by month of sale, to be

Month	Plan Type	Estimated Sales
April	Full season	500
	Weekends	1,200
May	Full season	200
	Weekends	700

Single-game sales, by month sold, are projected to be

Month	Estimated Sales
May	15,000
June	25,000
July	32,000
August	36,000
September	10,000

In the past, approximately 60% of the single-game sales have been for the reserved seats and 40% for the bleachers.

An independent concessionaire sells all food, drinks, and souvenirs in the ball park and remits 10% of all sales to the club for the privilege of operating the concession. The club's 10% share of concessions for the upcoming season is estimated to be

Month	Share of Concessions
May	$ 6,000
June	9,000
July	11,000
August	14,000
September	4,000

The largest cost to the club is player salaries. The total payroll, including front office personnel and coaches, is expected to be $780,000. All employees are paid monthly, with the first check on April 30 and the last on September 30.

The ball park is rented from the city at a cost of $20,000 per month. Overhead costs include field maintenance, utilities, and insurance and are estimated at $32,000 per month. Both rent and overhead are incurred evenly each month, except April and September when only one-half of the normal monthly cost is incurred for each.

Required:

1. Prepare a detailed cash budget, by month and in total, for the months of April through September for the Kane County Colonels. Show all supporting calculations. The cash balance on hand to start the season is $50,000.
2. How much should the club ask to borrow from the bank? Assuming that the bank approves a loan, when should the club borrow the money? Support your recommendations.
3. Based on the budget prepared in (1) above, are the club's cash flow problems of a seasonal nature or more long term in scope? What recommendations can you make to help the club remedy their cash flow problems?

P5–15   **Master budget for a wholesaler.** The Sunshine Company distributes a wide range of electronic components to various manufacturers. The company has a budgeting horizon of three months and is now putting together a set of budgets for the first quarter of 19X9. Sunshine's financial position at December 31, 19X8, is

Cash	$ 15,000
Accounts receivable	60,200
Inventories	80,000
Total current assets	$155,200

Land		$200,000
Plant and equipment	$450,000	
Less: accumulated depreciation	(130,000)	320,000
Total long-term assets		$520,000
Total assets		$675,200
Accounts payable		$ 30,000
Commissions payable		21,500
Taxes payable		10,000
Total current liabilities		$ 61,500
Common stock, no par		$200,000
Retained earnings		413,700
Total stockholders' equity		$613,700
Total liabilities and stockholders' equity		$675,200

As the first step in the budget process, the sales manager has budgeted sales for the first four months of the year as

Month	Budgeted Sales
January	$265,000
February	320,000
March	415,000
April	520,000

Normally 70% of sales are on credit and the remainder are cash sales. Credit terms of net 30 result in 60% of credit sales being collected in the month of the sale with the remainder collected in the following month. The accounts receivable balance at December 31, 19X8, represents the uncollected credit sales from December. Total sales in December were $215,000.

The gross profit rate has averaged 40% in recent years. Normally, 80% of a month's purchases are paid for in the month of purchase with the remainder in the following month. The accounts payable balance at December 31, 19X8, represents December purchases not paid for that month. The company's policy is to maintain an inventory at the end of each month equal to 50% of the next month's budgeted sales (at cost).

Variable selling costs equal to 10% of sales are paid in the month following a sale. Fixed selling, general, and administrative costs are $35,000 per month and, with the exception of $10,000 of this amount which is depreciation, are paid in the month incurred. Estimated tax payments equal to 40% of the estimated income for the quarter are made at the end of each quarter. The tax liability on the balance sheet at the end of 19X8 will be paid in March 19X9.

Required: 1. Prepare the following schedules, by month and in total, for the first quarter of the year:

    a. Cash collections on accounts receivable

    b. Cash payments on accounts payable. Note: In order to prepare this schedule it will be necessary to compute each month's purchases. Use the following format to find each month's purchases:

Budgeted cost of goods sold (60% of month's sales)
Add: desired ending inventory (50% of next month's cost of goods sold)
Total needs
Less: beginning inventory
Total purchases for the month

2. Prepare a cash budget, by month and in total, for the first quarter of the year. The amount of taxes paid in March cannot be determined until the income statement for the quarter is prepared (see 3 below).

3. Prepare the following pro forma financial statements:

   a. Income statements, by month and in total, for the first quarter of the year, using the contribution margin format.

   b. Balance sheet at March 31, 19X9.

P5–16   Master budget for a manufacturer. The Webster Company manufactures a single product. The product is sold for $50 per unit, and sales are budgeted for the first four months of the year as

Month	Budgeted Sales (units)
January	75,000
February	63,000
March	58,000
April	50,000

Each unit of finished product requires 5 pounds of raw material, at a cost of $4 per pound. Each unit requires one-half hour of direct labor at a cost of $10 per hour to the company. Variable overhead is applied on the basis of direct labor hours at a rate of $2 per hour. Fixed manufacturing overhead is $300,000 per month and is paid in the month incurred with the exception of $100,000 of this amount, which is depreciation. Variable selling, general, and administrative costs amount to $4 per unit. Fixed selling, general, and administrative costs are $150,000 per month. All selling, general, and administrative costs are paid in the month incurred.

To satisfy its distributors' needs, the company attempts to maintain a stock of finished product at the end of each month equal to 20% of budgeted sales units for the next month. At the beginning of the year 15,000 units of finished product are on hand. Because of the uncertainty relative to Webster's supply of raw material, the company tries to maintain an inventory at the end of each month equal to the next month's budgeted production needs. The supply of raw material to start the year consists of 350,000 pounds. The company desires to end the first quarter with an inventory of 290,000 pounds of raw material.

The accounts receivable balance at the beginning of the year is $1,200,000. Approximately 60% of the sales of any given month are collected in that month with the remainder collected in the following month. Accounts payable at the beginning of the year is $1,100,000. Webster normally pays for only 20% of all purchases in the month of purchase and the balance in the following month. Webster attempts to maintain a cash balance of $200,000 at all times, with any excess at the end of each month being invested in debt securities. The investments can only be made in denominations of $10,000 each. The actual cash balance to start the year is $204,000.

Required: Prepare the following budgets and schedules, by month and in total, for the first quarter of the year:

1. Sales budget (in dollars)
2. Production budget (in units)
3. Purchases budget for raw materials (in dollars)
4. Direct labor budget
5. Schedule of cash collections on accounts receivable
6. Schedule of cash payments on accounts payable
7. Cash budget

P5–17 **Master budget for a new business.** Two business associates have decided to form a partnership to operate a distributorship. To acquire the necessary plant and equipment, each partner invested $250,000. Next they approached a bank for a working capital loan. The bank has agreed to advance the new company $150,000 to finance the purchase of inventory. The loan principal and 3% simple interest (12% annual rate) are to be repaid on the first day of the fourth month of business. As a condition of the loan the partners must submit a comprehensive budget to the bank, complete with an income statement and a cash budget, as evidence of the company's ability to repay the loan from successful operations.

The partners have approached you and asked for your help in putting together the budget. You are able to determine the following:

1. Sales for the first four months are estimated to be:

Month	Budgeted Sales
One	$200,000
Two	280,000
Three	320,000
Four	380,000

2. The partners will offer credit terms of net 20. They expect these terms to result in 80% of all sales being collected in the month of the sale, 18% in the month following the month of sale, and 2% of all sales to be uncollectible.
3. The gross profit rate is expected to average 30%. The partners expect to get credit terms from their manufacturers of net 20. This policy should result in 80% of the purchases being paid for in the month of purchase with the other 20% paid for in the following month.
4. The partners are concerned about building a loyal customer base in their first year in business and want to avoid any risk of being out of stock. Therefore, they decide that it is necessary to be conservative and carry inventory at the end of each month equal to 100% of the next month's expected sales (at cost).
5. Salespeople will be paid a commission of 5%, payable at the beginning of the month following a sale.
6. Fixed selling, general, and administrative costs are expected to be $25,000 per month and, with the exception of $15,000 of this amount that is depreciation, are to be paid in the month incurred.
7. Because the business is organized as a partnership, the company will not incur any income tax. Instead, any profits will flow through to the individual partners.
8. The partners intend to use the $150,000 from the bank to buy inventory. Note: In working the problem, assume that this is to be the beginning inventory — that this is *in addition* to the first month's purchases. Also, assume that all of the cash of $150,000 is used to pay for all of the inventory, that is, none is put on account.

Required: 1. Prepare the following schedules, by month and in total, for the first quarter of the year:

a. Cash collections on accounts receivable (estimated uncollectible accounts are set up as an allowance at the end of each month, and actual uncollectible amounts are written off in the month following the sale)

b. Cash payments on accounts payable. Note: In order to prepare this schedule it will be necessary to compute each month's purchases. Use the following format to find each month's purchases:

Budgeted cost of goods sold (70% of month's sales)
Add: desired ending inventory (100% of next month's cost of goods sold)
Total needs
Less: beginning inventory
Total purchases for the month

2. Prepare a cash budget, by month and in total, for the first quarter of the year. Assume that the loan will not be repaid until the first day of the fourth month.

3. Prepare the following pro forma financial statements:

a. Income statements, by month and in total, for the first quarter of the year, using the contribution margin format. (Remember to account for interest each month)

b. Balance sheet at the end of the first three months.

4. Does it appear as if the partners will be able to pay off the loan at the end of the first ninety days of business? If not, what recommendation(s) would you make to the partners?

P5–18   **Cash budget for nonprofit organization.** United Business Education, Inc. (UBE) is a nonprofit organization that sponsors a wide variety of management seminars throughout the United States. In addition, it is heavily involved in research into improved methods of educating and motivating business executives. The seminar activity is largely supported by fees and the research program from member dues.

UBE operates on a calendar year basis and is in the process of finalizing the budget for 19X9. The following information has been taken from approved plans that are still tentative at this time.

SEMINAR PROGRAM

Revenue. The scheduled number of programs should produce $12,000,000 of revenue for the year. Each program is budgeted to produce the same amount of revenue. The revenue is collected during the month the program is offered. The programs are scheduled so that 12% of the revenue is collected in each of the first five months of the year. The remaining programs, accounting for the remaining 40% of the revenue, are distributed evenly through the months of September, October, and November. No programs are offered in the other four months of the year.

Direct expenses. The seminar expenses are made up of three segments:

Instructors' fees are paid at the rate of 70% of the seminar revenue in the month following the seminar. The instructors are considered independent contractors and are not eligible for UBE employee benefits.

Facilities fees total $5,600,000 for the year. They are the same for each program and are paid in the month the program is given.

Annual promotional costs of $1,000,000 are spent equally in all months except June and July, when there is no promotional effort.

RESEARCH PROGRAM

Research grants. The research program has a large number of projects nearing completion. The other main research activity this year includes the feasibility studies for new projects to be started in 19X0. As a result, the grant expense of $3,000,000 for 19X9 is expected to be paid out at the rate of $500,000 per month during the first six months of the year.

SALARIES AND OTHER UBE EXPENSES

Office lease. Annual amount of $240,000 paid monthly at the beginning of each month.

General administrative expenses (telephone, supplies, postage, etc.). $1,500,000 annually or $125,000 a month.

Depreciation expense. $240,000 a year.

General UBE promotion. Annual cost of $600,000 paid monthly.

Salaries and benefits.

Number of Employees	Annual Salary Paid Monthly	Total Annual Salaries
1	$50,000	$ 50,000
3	40,000	120,000
4	30,000	120,000
15	25,000	375,000
5	15,000	75,000
22	10,000	220,000
50		$960,000

Employee benefits amount to $240,000 or 25% of annual salaries. Except for the pension contribution, the benefits are paid as salaries are paid. The annual pension payment of $24,000, based on 2.5% of salaries (included in the total benefits and the 25% rate), is due April 15, 19X9.

OTHER INFORMATION

Membership income. UBE has 100,000 members, each of whom pays an annual fee of $100. The fee for the calendar year is invoiced in late June. The collection schedule is as follows:

July	60%
August	30%
September	5%
October	5%
	100%

Capital expenditures. The capital expenditures program calls for a total of $510,000 in cash payments to be spread evenly over the first five months of 19X9.

Cash and temporary investments. At January 1, 19X9, they are estimated at $750,000.

Required:
1. Prepare a budget of the annual cash receipts and disbursements for UBE, Inc. for 19X9.
2. Prepare a cash budget for UBE, Inc. for January 19X9.

3. Using the information you developed in requirement 1 and 2, identify two important operating problems of UBE, Inc.

(CMA Adapted)

P5–19   **Pro forma income statement and balance sheet.** Einhard Enterprises has a comprehensive budgeting program. Pro forma statements of earnings and financial position are prepared as the final step in the budget program. Einhard's projected financial position as of June 30, 19X2, is presented below. Various 19X2–19X3 master budget schedules based on the plans for the fiscal year ending June 30, 19X3, are also included.

All sales are made on account. Raw material, direct labor, factory overhead, and selling and administrative expenses are credited to vouchers payable. Federal income tax expense is charged to income taxes payable. The federal income tax rate is 40%.

EINHARD ENTERPRISES
Pro Forma Statement of Financial Position as of June 30, 19X2
($000 omitted)

Assets

Cash	$ 800
Accounts receivable	750
Direct material inventory	506
Finished goods inventory	648
Total current assets	$ 2,704
Land	$ 1,500
Property, plant & equipment	11,400
Less accumulated depreciation	(2,250)
Total long-term assets	$10,650
Total assets	$13,354

Liabilities and Equity

Vouchers payable	$ 1,230
Income taxes payable	135
Notes payable (due 12/30/X2)	1,000
Total liabilities	$ 2,365
Common stock	$10,200
Retained earnings	789
Total equity	$10,989
Total liabilities and equity	$13,354

Sales Schedule in Units and Dollars

Unit Sales	Selling Price Per Unit	Total Sales Revenue
2,100,000	$16	$33,600,000

Production Schedule in Units and Dollars

Production in Units	Cost Per Unit	Total Manufacturing Cost
2,110,000	$12.00	$25,320,000

Raw Material Purchases Schedule in Units and Dollars

Purchases in Pounds	Cost Per Pound	Total Purchase Cost
4,320,000	$2.75	$11,880,000

Two pounds of raw material are needed to make one unit of finished product.

Direct Labor Schedule in Units and Dollars

Production in Units	Direct Labor Cost Per Hour	Total Direct Labor Cost
2,110,000	$8	$8,440,000

Each unit requires one-half hour of direct labor time.

Manufacturing Overhead Schedule in Dollars
(expected activity level — 1,055,000 direct labor hours)

Variable expenses	$2,954,000[a]
Depreciation	600,000
Other fixed expenses	1,721,000[a]
Total manufacturing overhead	$5,275,000

[a]All require cash expenditures. The manufacturing
overhead rate is $5 per direct labor hour
($5,275,000 divided by 1,055,000).

Selling and Administrative Expense Schedule in Dollars

Selling expenses	$2,525,000
Administrative expenses	2,615,000
Total	$5,140,000

All selling and administrative expenses require the expenditure of cash.

Beginning Inventory Schedule in Units and Dollars

	Quantity	Cost per Unit	Total Cost
Direct material	184,000 pounds	$2.75 per lb.	$506,000
Finished goods	54,000 units	$12.00 per unit	$648,000

Cash Receipts and Disbursements Schedule
($000 omitted)

Cash balance 7/1/X2 (estimated)		$ 800
Cash receipts		
Collection of accounts receivable	33,450	
Total cash available		$34,250
Cash disbursements:		
Payment of vouchers payable:		
Direct material	$11,900	
Direct labor	8,400	
Manufacturing overhead	4,650	
Selling and administrative expenses	5,200	
Total vouchers payable	$30,150	

Income taxes	1,100	
Purchase of equipment	400	
Cash dividends	820	
Total cash disbursements		$32,470
Excess cash		$ 1,780
Financing:		
Repayment of notes payable 12/30/X2	$ 1,000	
Interest expense	50	
Total financing cost		$ 1,050
Projected cash balance 6/30/X3		$ 730

1. Prepare a pro forma income statement for Einhard Enterprises for the fiscal year ended June 30, 19X3. Show all supporting computations.
2. Prepare a pro forma statement of financial position for Einhard Enterprises as of June 30, 19X3. Show all supporting computations.

(CMA Adapted)

P5–20   **Cash budgeting and setting goals.** The Triple-F Health Club (Family, Fitness, and Fun) is a nonprofit family-oriented health club. The club's board of directors is developing plans to acquire more equipment and expand the club facilities. The board plans to purchase about $25,000 of new equipment each year and wants to begin a fund to purchase the adjoining property in four or five years. The adjoining property has a market value of about $300,000.

The club manager, Jane Crowe, is concerned that the board has unrealistic goals in light of its recent financial performance. She has sought the help of a club member with an accounting background to assist her in preparing a report to the board supporting her concerns.

The club member reviewed the club's records, including the cash basis income statements presented below. The review and discussions with Jane Crowe disclosed the additional information which follows the statement.

TRIPLE-F HEALTH CLUB
Statement of Income (Cash Basis)
For Years Ended October 31
($000 omitted)

	19X0	19X9
Cash revenues:		
Annual membership fees	$355.0	$300.0
Lesson and class fees	234.0	180.0
Miscellaneous	2.0	1.5
Total cash received	$591.0	$481.5
Cash expenses:		
Manager's salary and benefits	$ 36.0	$ 36.0
Regular employees' wages and benefits	190.0	190.0
Lesson and class employee wages and benefits	195.0	150.0
Towels and supplies	16.0	15.5
Utilities (heat and light)	22.0	15.0
Mortgage interest	35.1	37.8
Miscellaneous	2.0	1.5
Total cash expenses	$496.1	$445.8
Cash income	$ 94.9	$ 35.7

ADDITIONAL INFORMATION

Other financial information as of October 31, 19X0:

> Cash in checking account, $7,000
> Petty cash, $300
> Outstanding mortgage balance, $360,000
> Accounts payable arising from invoices for supplies and utilities which are
> unpaid as of October 31, 19X0, $2,500

No unpaid bills existed on October 31, 19X9.

The club purchased $25,000 worth of exercise equipment during the current fiscal year. Cash of $10,000 was paid on delivery and the balance was due on October 1 but has not been paid as of October 31, 19X0.

The club began operations in 19X4 in rental quarters. In October 19X6 it purchased its current property (land and building) for $600,000, paying $120,000 down and agreeing to pay $30,000 plus 9% interest annually on November 1 until the balance was paid off.

Membership rose 3% during 19X0. This is approximately the same annual rate the club has experienced since it opened.

Membership fees were increased by 15% in 19X0. The Board has tentative plans to increase the fees by 10% in 19X1.

Lessons and class fees have not been increased for three years. The board policy is to encourage classes and lessons by keeping the fees low. The members have taken advantage of this policy, and the numbers of classes and lessons have grown significantly each year. The club expects the percentage of growth experienced in 19X0 to be repeated in 19X1.

Miscellaneous revenues are expected to grow at the same percentage as experienced in 19X0.

Operating expenses are expected to increase. Hourly wage rates and the manager's salary will need to be increased 15% because no increases were granted in 19X0. Towels and supplies, utilities, and miscellaneous expenses are expected to increase 25%.

Required:
1. Construct a cash budget for 19X1 for the Triple-F Health Club.
2. Identify any operating problem(s) that this budget discloses for the Triple-F Health Club. Explain your answer.
3. Is Jane Crowe's concern that the board's goals are unrealistic justified? Explain your answer.

(CMA Adapted)

P5–21 Master budget with preprinted schedules. Valley Company has a budgeting horizon of three months and is now putting together a set of budgets for the third quarter of 19X9. Valley's financial position at June 30, 19X9, is

Cash		$ 30,000
Accounts receivable		126,000
Inventories		160,000
Total current assets		$ 316,000
Land		$ 400,000
Plant and equipment	$900,000	
Less: accumulated depreciation	(260,000)	640,000
Total long-term assets		$1,040,000
Total assets		$1,356,000

Accounts payable	$ 60,000
Commissions payable	70,000
Total current liabilities	$ 130,000
Common stock, no par	$ 400,000
Retained earnings	826,000
Total stockholders' equity	$1,226,000
Total liabilities and stockholders equity	$1,356,000

As the first step in the budget process, the sales manager has budgeted sales for the next four months of the year as

Month	Budgeted Sales
July	$400,000
August	480,000
September	625,000
October	780,000

Normally 60% of sales are on credit and the remainder are cash sales. Credit terms of net 30 result in 70% of credit sales being collected in the month of the sale with the remainder collected in the following month. The accounts receivable balance at June 30, 19X9, represents the uncollected credit sales from June. Total sales in June were $700,000.

The gross profit rate has averaged 25% in recent years. Normally, 80% of a month's purchases are paid for in the month of purchase with the remainder in the following month. The accounts payable balance at June 30, 19X9, represents June purchases not paid for that month. The company's policy is to maintain an inventory at the end of each month equal to 50% of the next month's budgeted sales (at cost).

Variable selling costs equal to 10% of sales are paid in the month following a sale. Fixed selling, general, and administrative costs are $55,000 per month and—with the exception of $5,000 of this amount, which is depreciation—are paid in the month incurred. Estimated tax payments equal to 40% of the estimated income for the quarter are made at the end of each quarter.

Required: 1. Complete the following schedules, budgets, and statements, by month and in total, for the third quarter of the year:

a. Cash Collections on Accounts Receivable

	July	August	September	Total
Accounts receivable, beginning of month	$126,000			
Add: sales	400,000			
Due from customers	$526,000			
Deduct: cash collections				
Cash sales	$160,000			
Credit sales:				
Month of sale	168,000			
Prior month	126,000			
Total cash collections	$454,000			
Accounts receivable, end of month	$ 72,000			

b. Purchases Budget

	July	August	September	Total
Budgeted cost of sales	$300,000			
Add: desired ending inventory	180,000			
Total needs	$480,000			
Less: beginning inventory	160,000			
Total purchases	$320,000			

c. Cash Payments on Accounts Payable

	July	August	September	Total
Accounts payable, beginning of month	$ 60,000			
Add: purchases	320,000			
Total amount owed	$380,000			
Deduct: cash payments				
Current month's purchases	$256,000			
Prior month's purchases	60,000			
Total cash payments	$316,000			
Accounts payable, end of month	$ 64,000			

d. Cash Budget

	July	August	September	Total
Cash balance, beginning of month	$ 30,000			
Add: cash collected	454,000			
Cash available	$484,000			
Deduct: cash payments				
Accounts payable	$316,000			
Commissions	70,000			
Fixed selling, general, and administrative	50,000			
Income taxes[a]	–0–			
Total cash payments	$436,000			
Cash balance, end of month	$ 48,000			

[a]Note: The amount of taxes to be paid in September cannot be determined until the income statement for the quarter is prepared (see e below).

e. Pro Forma Income Statements

	July	August	September	Total
Sales revenue	$400,000			
Cost of sales	$300,000			
Commissions	40,000			
Total variable expenses	$340,000			
Contribution margin	$ 60,000			
Fixed expenses	55,000			
Net income before tax	$ 5,000			
Income tax expense	$ 2,000			
Net income	$ 3,000			

2. Prepare a pro forma balance sheet as of September 30, 19X9.

3. What recommendations would you make to the Valley Company with regard to their cash balance at the end of the third quarter?

CHAPTER 6

Cost Accumulation and Allocation

Learning Objectives

After reading this chapter you should be able to:

1. Differentiate between cost accumulation, allocation, and control.

2. Understand a general model for determining the cost of a product.

3. Differentiate between the cost elements necessary for production, that is, direct materials, direct labor, and manufacturing overhead.

4. Explain why predetermined overhead rates are used and how they are developed.

5. Develop predetermined overhead rates based on various concepts of capacity and activity bases.

6. Compute under- or overapplied overhead and determine its disposition at the end of the accounting period.

7. Explain the difference between service and producing departments and understand why it is necessary to allocate service department costs to producing departments.

8. Allocate service department costs using the direct method, step method, and the reciprocal method (Appendix 6–A).

In this chapter we develop a general model for determining the cost of producing a product. Chapters 7 through 11 develop specific cost systems used for this purpose. We must be able to accumulate costs by some cost objective (that is, department, division, or product) so that comparisons may be made between planned and actual activity. With this information we have the ability to hold someone responsible for explanations of variations between planned and actual performance. This is the control aspect of management accounting. It is carried out by means of the budgetary process (Chapter 5) in which actual results are compared against budget for each organizational unit. We return to this topic in Chapter 10 when flexible budgeting is discussed.

In addition, the cost accounting aspect is involved with allocating or applying the accumulated costs to units of product so that we can determine the cost of producing a unit of product. This unit cost number is of interest for managerial purposes such as pricing. It is also extremely important to the financial accountant in determining income and in reporting inventory values on the balance sheet. Hopefully, our management accounting system will meet this dual role of providing information useful for planning and control as well as for financial reporting purposes.

In this chapter, the costs of production (direct materials, direct labor, and manufacturing overhead) are examined in terms of how they are assigned to product. The most difficult area is manufacturing overhead because these costs are, by definition, indirect to product. Manufacturing overhead is therefore assigned to product by means of overhead rates. Both actual and predetermined overhead rates are examined. Further ramifications of predetermined overhead are then scrutinized. These include problems of capacity concept and disposition of overapplied and underapplied overhead. The scope of overhead rates—plantwide versus departmental—is also examined as well as different possible overhead bases such as direct labor hours, machine hours, and direct labor costs. Finally, the problem of assigning service department costs to producing departments is mentioned with more detail being supplied in Appendix 6–A.

Costs of Production

The production of a product requires the use of three basic cost elements: direct materials, direct labor, and manufacturing overhead. A custom cabinet builder, for example, needs the wood products used to make the cabinets, and he needs specially trained helpers to cut, fit, assemble, and perhaps finish and install the cabinets. He also needs a shop of some kind in which to operate. This means that he incurs costs for heat, light and power, depreciation, insurance, maintenance and repairs, property taxes, and so forth. When he completes the cabinets for a particular house, he needs to know the total costs associated with that particular custom job, and he also would like to know if he was able to produce the cabinets in an efficient manner, that is, whether he was able to control his costs. In this chapter, the definitions given for these three basic cost elements will be reviewed and reinforced. Consideration is given to the practical complexities of tracking the costs of these basic elements from incurrence to final product, allowing for control through the manufacturing process. Specific control documents will be illustrated more fully as specific cost systems are developed in subsequent chapters.

Direct Materials

As previously defined, direct materials are those material inputs that become part of and are relatively easy to trace to the finished product. For the custom cabinet builder, for example, this would consist of plywood sheets, oak and other solid wood pieces, formica for cabinet tops, door and drawer hardware, and glass and decorative inserts for cabinet doors. The builder will need to carry an inventory of these items to ensure that materials are available as needed by the shop crew. As materials are purchased, the costs will be accumulated in the accounting system in one of two possible accounts—materials or purchases. If you remember your first course in financial accounting, you learned that there were two inventory methods—periodic and perpetual. You most likely dealt almost exclusively with the periodic inventory method. With this method, as merchandise was acquired, the cost was entered in an account called *purchases*. To determine the cost of goods sold (or used in the manufacturing setting), you added purchases for the period to the beginning inventory to determine goods available for sale (use). A physical count of the merchandise on hand then had to be made, and a dollar value determined (which many of you have no doubt learned is no small task!). The ending inventory value was then subtracted from goods available for sale to determine cost of goods sold. The same procedure could be followed in the manufacturing setting, but remember that we are interested in not only determining the total costs for product costing purposes but are also concerned with controlling costs and operations. Management may wish to know how much of a particular material is on hand at any time. It may be costly to have to make a physical count every time that piece of information is desired. Perhaps a greater inconvenience from a management control standpoint is the inability to determine the cost of materials used until a physical count is made. The custom cabinet builder has a twofold problem. Providing information at the end of an accounting period about the cost of materials used (in total) is of little information value. He needs to know at the time he completes a job what materials were used on that particular job. With this information he is able to compare his actual costs with his planned (estimate or bid) to see how well he is doing as each job is completed. Therefore, the periodic inventory method is usually abandoned in a manufacturing setting for the perpetual inventory method.

As indicated by its name, the perpetual inventory method means that the management accountant has "perpetual" knowledge of the balance of materials on hand. A materials account is used, and as materials are purchased they are added to the materials account, thus accumulating the cost of materials purchased but not yet associated with a product or cost center. Documents such as purchase requisitions, purchase invoices, and receiving reports will support (authorize) such entries. As materials are issued and used in the manufacturing process, a document called a *materials requisition* will support the entries to reduce the materials account and will indicate where or on what job the materials were used, thus allocating the materials costs to different products, jobs, or cost centers. These underlying documents are illustrated in Chapter 7.

Direct Labor

Direct labor consists of major work effort going into product that helps to transform direct materials into final output. Again, for our custom cabinet builder, this would consist of time spent by employees in sawing, fitting and assembling, finishing, and installing cabinets.

If the builder needed to know simply total direct labor cost, he could have a time clock at the entrance to his shop, and as workers came and left work they could clock on and off a time or clock card. A payroll accountant could then calculate the time in the shop for the pay period and multiply it by the hourly rate of the individual employee directly working on cabinets. If all these individual direct labor earnings were added up, the total could be called *total direct labor* and entered in an account called, for example, *payroll.* But again, as in the case of direct materials, this accumulated total does not have much management information value for our cabinet builder. You should now begin to appreciate the problem. The cabinet maker needs to know how much labor cost to associate with a particular job in order to determine the total cost of the job just completed. Again, with this information, he is able to compare his actual labor cost with his planned (estimate or bid) cost to see how well he is doing on each job completed.

How is he able to do this? Remember that there may be five or ten different custom jobs being worked on in the shop at any one time. Some record must be provided then for how much time each employee spends on each job each day—a cost allocation problem. What is needed then is another document to accumulate time spent on each job during the day. This document is usually called a *job ticket.* Employees would enter on the job ticket, either manually or electronically, when they start and when they complete or quit on each particular job they work on during the day. Job tickets can then be sorted by particular jobs or department so that total time on individual jobs may be determined.

Note the added control feature built into this system. If only clock cards are used, the employee could clock in to the shop or factory in the morning and spend considerable nonproductive time. If job tickets are used, hours can be accumulated by the employee each day from his job ticket, and this figure should agree with the time shown on his clock card total for that day. This not only provides a record of what each employee has worked on during the day but also makes it more difficult for "friends" to clock in for an employee. It is rather difficult to both clock in and out on the clock card and to also fill in job tickets for the day. The clock card and job tickets are illustrated in the next chapter.

Manufacturing Overhead

All costs other than direct materials and direct labor that are associated with the manufacturing process are referred to as *manufacturing overhead* (also *factory overhead* or *factory burden*). Chapter 2 gives a representative list of manufacturing overhead items. Although direct materials are easily identified with the finished product either by sight or through materials requisition documents, and direct labor is traceable directly to the finished product through job tickets, manufacturing overhead is not easily traceable to specific units of output. Paying the insurance premium or property taxes, recording depreciation for the period, or maintaining a maintenance and repair department does not guarantee that any production will take place. Indeed, facilities, management, and a skeleton work force must be provided in order for any production to take place. Even when production is taking place, however, there is little relationship between manufacturing overhead costs and the amount of production. In fact, even though production activity fluctuates, manufacturing overhead tends to remain relatively constant (depending somewhat on the type of manufacturing, of course). This implies that a fairly large portion of manufacturing overhead is fixed as opposed to variable.

Remember that as materials were purchased the cost of those materials was accumulated in the materials account. Also remember that as direct labor costs were incurred, these costs were accumulated in an account we called *payroll.* If the same logic is followed for manufacturing overhead, as actual overhead costs are incurred we will accumulate them in an account called *manufacturing* or *factory overhead.* This, then, is the accumulation phase for manufacturing overhead. When heat, light, and power bills are recorded, the cost is added to the manufacturing overhead account. The same is true when property taxes on the factory are recorded, or when factory depreciation, repairs, or insurance are recorded. But once again there is an allocation problem—we must determine the amount of overhead to associate with a particular unit of output for product costing purposes. Accountants call this procedure *applying overhead to product.* It is a special type of allocation of overhead—the final step in tracing costs to products as distinguished from allocating costs to cost centers, departments, divisions, or territories. The application of overhead may be done one of two ways: using an actual rate or a predetermined rate.

The word *rate* implies a relationship between two numbers. In this context, it is the relationship between the manufacturing overhead and the volume of activity. Activity may be expressed in terms of units of output, direct labor hours, direct labor cost, machine hours, or units of input. The point is to use an activity measure that seems to have the highest relationship (correlation) with the amount of overhead cost incurred. The cabinet builder, for example, might expect to determine his application rate by using an activity measure of direct labor hours worked or square feet of plywood used. Units of output would not be feasible because of the different sizes of cabinets produced.

Actual Overhead Rates

The rate for applying overhead to product could be accurately determined at the end of the accounting period after all manufacturing overhead costs had been determined along with the actual level of activity attained. Rates of this type are known as **actual overhead rates.** For instance, if the cabinet builder had decided to use direct labor hours as the activity base, the formula would appear as follows:

$$\frac{\text{Actual total manufacturing overhead}}{\text{Actual total direct labor hours}} = \frac{\$100,000}{20,000} = \$5/\text{DLH}$$

This would mean that each time that one direct labor hour was associated with a job or product, $5 of manufacturing overhead would have to be added or applied to that job or product.

Although this may be an accurate method of applying overhead to product, it may again be useless from a management information standpoint. If the cabinet builder had to wait until the end of each accounting period to know what it cost to produce the cabinets for a particular home, he would not know if his cost estimates were correct or incorrect, that is, was his price too low allowing no profit or too little profit, or was he tending to bid so high he was likely to lose bids to his competitors? In other words, he would have cost information that would reflect the actual costs incurred but would receive it too late to affect any marketing or operating decision he perhaps should make during the year. As a result, most manufacturers use what is referred to as a *predetermined overhead application rate.*

Predetermined Overhead Rate

A **predetermined overhead rate** is one in which the overhead application rate is determined in advance—before production begins. This means that the numbers to use in the application rate formula must be estimated rather than actual. The formula, as illustrated previously for the cabinet builder, becomes

$$\frac{\text{Estimated total manufacturing overhead}}{\text{Estimated total direct labor hours}} = \frac{\text{Predetermined}}{\text{overhead rate}}$$

The use of a predetermined overhead rate does correct the problems associated with using actual overhead rates — that is, costs of products can be determined on completion rather than having to wait until the end of the year. It does, however, introduce some other interesting complexities that must be understood and resolved before using a predetermined application rate. These complexities are (1) budget capability, (2) time horizon, (3) capacity concept, and (4) under- and overapplied overhead.

Budget capability   Obviously, if total manufacturing costs are to be determined in advance, the firm must be able to estimate total overhead associated with some level of activity chosen for the denominator of the overhead rate formula. In other words, the firm must be able to budget. As outlined in Chapter 3, this requires a knowledge of cost behavior — which costs are variable and which are fixed. If the cost is a combination (has both fixed and variable portions), the component parts must be identifiable.

Time horizon   Management also must decide what period of time will be covered by the overhead rate formula — should it be one week, one month, one quarter, one year, or some other time period? It is not too difficult to see that the shorter the time period covered, the more volatile the overhead rate. From the standpoint of the numerator of the formula, costs are likely to be incurred in uneven chunks at various times of the year. For example, insurance may be paid once a year, property taxes may be paid twice a year, vacation and holiday pay may concentrate in certain times of the year depending on the location of the company, heating costs may be high in winter months and air conditioning costs high in summer months, repairs and maintenance costs may be erratic, supplies requisitioned in one month may be used over two or three following months, and so forth. If a weekly or monthly rate were to be used, the rate could fluctuate considerably from week to week or month to month just because of costs expected to be incurred in each of those weeks or months. It does not seem wise to have overhead rates vary (and therefore unit cost of products vary each week or month they are produced) just because of the way certain costs are incurred during the year. This tends to suggest that the time period should perhaps be long enough to smooth out the "chunks and lumps" effect of cost incurrence and that this would require a period of a year in most cases.

There is also a problem associated with the denominator of the overhead rate formula. Keep in mind that a good portion of the manufacturing overhead costs may be fixed. Many businesses naturally have seasonal variations in levels of activity. Does it seem reasonable, for instance, that a unit produced in August when production might be at its peak should cost less to produce than a unit produced in February when production activity is at its lowest level? If overhead rates were determined on a monthly basis, this phenomenon would occur because of spreading the fixed portion of manufacturing overhead over varying levels of activity. Also, if a monthly period were used in the rate calculation, there could be a variation in the overhead rate just because of the calendar variance between months (more work days during some months as opposed to others). Because of the above reasons, it seems justifiable to use the year as the time period in calculating the predetermined overhead rate. This averages out the effects of month-to-month fluctuations in production volume and the possible erratic incurrence of a number of the overhead costs.

Capacity concepts   Even though the decision is made to use a year as the time period to be covered in the overhead rate calculation, a problem still remains regarding the level of activity estimate for the year. This estimate may be based on three possible activity assumptions:

1. The physical capacity of the plant to produce,
2. An average level of production that will meet projected sales demand over some time period beyond a year,
3. The projected (budgeted) level of activity for the next year.

The first activity assumption, **physical capacity,** is often designated as either theoretical or practical. **Theoretical (or ideal) capacity** implies that production continues "full steam ahead" twenty-four hours a day, seven days a week, fifty-two weeks a year. This may perhaps be an ideal utilization of physical facilities but certainly not very feasible and will not be considered further as a possible choice. A more realistic concept might be practical capacity. This allows for the usual nuances of the particular manufacturing process. Some processes such as a foundry in a steel mill may actually operate on a basis similar to theoretical capacity. Other manufacturers may normally operate only eight hours a day, five days a week, with allowances for some expected down time of machines and break time for employees. **Practical capacity,** then, refers to the physical ability of the plant to produce with the current equipment during normal operating hours of that particular manufacturing process.

Note that this is not affected by what management actually intends to produce during the next year—it merely indicates what the plant is physically capable of producing given various assumptions.

The second activity assumption, the activity level based on projected sales for several years, is often referred to as **normal volume** or **normal capacity.** It is the level of capacity utilization that will satisfy average sales demands over some intermediate time period (three to five years) allowing for seasonal, cyclical, and trend factors. Note that the only relationship between normal volume and practical capacity is that practical capacity becomes the upper constraint on normal volume—the only way to push activity levels above practical capacity is to start extending hours through overtime or add additional shifts. At any rate, the important point regarding normal volume is that it is a sales-based figure as opposed to a physical capacity-based figure.

The third activity assumption is often referred to as **expected capacity** — the level of activity used to drive the production budget for the following year. In other words, what do we need to produce next year to meet projected sales demand after allowing for desired ending inventory levels?

Exhibit 6–1 illustrates the effect on the predetermined overhead rate assuming different capacity concepts are utilized in the denominator of the overhead rate formula. Note how the overhead cost per unit of product produced varies. Note also that it is because of the fixed overhead that the rate varies — the variable component is always $1 per unit.

What capacity concept should be used for the predetermined overhead rate calculation? It seems that the answer is, "It depends on where management wishes to place information value." If management is convinced that it is important to operate at full (usually practical) capacity, and this level of operation gives the only correct cost of product as far as they are concerned, then perhaps practical capacity should be used to calculate the overhead rate.

If, however, management feels that there should be emphasis on the longer-run (average) costs of production and that this has an important bearing on their pricing decisions, then they will perhaps want to use normal capacity as an activity measure. On the other hand, management may wish to compare actual results with budget as a means of analyzing and controlling costs. Remember that the budget is the principal short-run planning and control tool that should have been set initially after careful analysis of sales opportunities for the current year. Managers are aware of, and feel obligated to attain, the budgeted figures because they know they will be evaluated on the basis of budget achievement. Therefore, it seems that if management is interested in the control aspects associated with manufacturing overhead, they will want to use expected capacity as the level of activity in the predetermined overhead rate calculation. Prediction of expected activity will usually be more accurate than intermediate-term sales predictions needed for normal capacity. The authors feel that the emphasis on control is a compelling reason to use the expected capacity concept. This capacity concept will be used in further discussions and illustrations.

EXHIBIT 6–1
Predetermined Overhead Rates Assuming Various Capacity Concepts

	Practical	Normal	Expected
Estimated overhead:			
Variable ($1 per unit)	$100,000	$ 80,000	$ 70,000
Fixed	500,000	500,000	500,000
Total	$600,000	$580,000	$570,000
Divide by estimated units of activity	100,000	80,000	70,000
Predetermined rate per unit produced	$ 6.00	$ 7.25	$ 8.143

Under- and overapplied overhead   When actual overhead rates are used, it is a rather simple procedure at the end of the period to allocate the accumulated actual overhead to job or product by the overhead application procedure outlined—all actual overhead accumulated in the manufacturing overhead account is applied in the process. This is most likely not true when a predetermined overhead rate is used. Remember that the predetermined rate is arrived at by using estimates of both manufacturing overhead dollar amounts as well as level of activity. If either the estimated overhead costs (numerator) or the estimated level of activity used (denominator) in the calculation of the predetermined overhead rate differs from the actual cost or the actual level of activity attained for the period, the predetermined overhead rate will be inaccurate. Being inaccurate means that either more or less overhead will be applied to product than is actually incurred. This is referred to as **under- or overapplied overhead.** The following illustration will help to explain the problem:

	Company X	Company Y
Activity base to be used	Sq. ft. wood	Dir. lab. hrs.
Estimated manufacturing overhead cost for 19X6	$150,000 (a)	$200,000 (a)
Estimated square feet of wood to be used in 19X6	50,000 (b)	—
Estimated direct labor hours for 19X6	—	80,000 (b)
Predetermined overhead rate (a/b)	$ 3/sq. ft.	$ 2.50/DLH

Let us assume that the actual overhead costs and actual levels of activity for the two companies for the year 19X6 were as follows:

	Company X	Company Y
Actual manufacturing overhead costs	$148,000	$200,000
Actual sq. ft. of wood used	50,000	—
Actual direct labor hours worked	—	70,000

Notice that for Company X the actual overhead costs were less than estimated but the level of activity was exactly as estimated. For Company Y the actual overhead costs were exactly as estimated, but the level of activity actually attained differed from the estimate. Computation of the under- or overapplied overhead follows:

	Company X	Company Y
Actual manufacturing overhead costs	$148,000	$200,000
Manufacturing overhead applied to product during 19X6:		
50,000 actual sq. ft. of wood × $3	150,000	—
70,000 actual DLH × $2.50	—	175,000
Underapplied (overapplied) overhead	(2,000)	25,000

Herein lies the under- or overapplied problem associated with using a predetermined overhead application rate. For Company X more overhead than was actually incurred has been allocated to product thus overstating the actual costs of the product. In the case of Company Y less overhead than was actually incurred was allocated to product. In this situation, the total of the unit costs of production for the period is less than the total actual costs incurred. How can management solve this dilemma? The under- or over-applied overhead may be handled one of two ways:

1. Added to (deducted from) the cost of product sold during the period, or
2. Allocated among inventories of work still proceeding through the factory and work already completed and sitting in finished goods inventory and to the cost of product already sold.

Adding or deducting from cost of product sold is the typical disposition of the under- or overapplied amount, mainly because it is much simpler than the allocation process. This is an appropriate procedure to follow if most of the product manufactured has been sold or if the amount involved is relatively insignificant.

If most of the product worked on during the period is still either being worked on in the factory or is still sitting unsold in finished goods inventory, there could be a material misstatement of the profits for the year if the under- or overapplied balance were all closed to cost of goods sold. Under these circumstances it is more appropriate to allocate the under- or overapplied overhead among the work in process, finished goods, and cost of goods sold.

For example, assume that Company Y at the end of the period has $150,000 of work in process, finished goods of $225,000, and cost of goods sold of $375,000. The $25,000 of underapplied overhead would be *added* to each of the three inventories in proportion of each to the total of the three inventories:

$$\text{Work in process } \frac{\$150,000}{\$750,000} \times \$25,000 = \$5,000$$

$$\text{Finished goods } \frac{\$225,000}{\$750,000} \times \$25,000 = \$7,500$$

$$\text{Cost of goods sold } \frac{\$375,000}{\$750,000} \times \$25,000 = \$12,500$$

If manufacturing overhead is overapplied, the same procedure is used to reduce the balance of the three inventories.

Plantwide versus Departmental Overhead Rates

The discussion in this chapter has assumed that a **plantwide (or single) overhead rate** was being used throughout the entire plant. This may not be an equitable method of allocating overhead to product. Consider the case of our cabinet builder. It was previously suggested that there would be producing departments such as cutting, fitting and assembling, finishing, and installation. The builder might bid his jobs as finished and installed, assembled and installed but not finished, or simply assembled and unfinished at the buyer's choice. This would mean that not all jobs would pass through all operations and therefore should not have overhead added for the missed production operations or departments.

There is also the possibility that the cutting department or operation is much more machine intensive than finishing, for instance, which would tend to be more labor intensive. It would seem more equitable in these cases to develop different application rates—**departmental overhead rates**—for the different producing departments or operations, applying overhead to the product according to the producing departments through which it passes. Because of this situation many manufacturing companies will utilize predetermined overhead rates calculated on a departmental basis using different overhead bases rather than a plantwide basis. Labor-intensive departments often employ direct labor hours or direct labor dollars bases whereas capital-intensive departments may well use machine hours.

Type of Overhead Base

In our discussion thus far we have assumed that the overhead base used was direct labor hours. Certainly many of the variable manufacturing overhead elements such as indirect labor, the employer's share of payroll taxes, and supplies could be correlated with labor time spent on product. However, other types of bases may be more applicable to particular overhead application situations if they are either better predictors of total manufacturing overhead incurred (thus minimizing over- or underapplied overhead) or are fairer methods for assigning overhead to product. Two of the more frequently used overhead bases, in addition to direct labor hours, are machine hours and direct labor costs.

Machine hours   Under capital-intensive conditions, direct labor hours may not be a relevant basis for assigning overhead to product. In these circumstances fixed manufacturing overhead elements such as depreciation and property taxes may predominate in dollar terms among the individual components of manufacturing overhead. If this is the case, machine time spent on product may be a fairer basis of assigning manufacturing overhead to product. There generally is, however, added clerical costs involved in tracking machine time spent on individual jobs and production runs.

Direct labor cost   If direct labor rates are uniform for most manufacturing operations, direct labor dollars should result in approximately the same results as usage of direct labor hours as the overhead application base. If direct labor costs differ significantly among the manufacturing operations and fringe labor costs such as payroll taxes are an important element of manufacturing overhead, direct labor costs may be a better indicator of overhead assignment to product than direct labor hours.

It should be noted that labor-oriented bases such as direct labor hours and direct labor cost are decreasing in importance as overhead bases. This is a result of increasing automation—overhead bases such as machine hours are thus growing in frequency of usage.

Service Department Costs

Manufacturing overhead was defined as all costs other than direct materials and direct labor that are associated with the manufacturing process. In the cost accumulation and allocation model developed so far, it has been assumed that all departments within the factory have been directly engaged in production and were referred to as producing departments. Departments may exist within the factory that are not directly engaged in production but render services or assistance that facilitate the activities of producing departments. Examples of such departments or services would be cost accounting, personnel, materials handling, repairs and maintenance, internal auditing, and cafeteria. Because these services are regarded as an integral and necessary part of the manufacturing process, costs related to these services should become part of the completed unit cost of production. This is another cost accumulation/allocation problem. It is covered in Appendix 6–A of this chapter.

Summary

The management accounting system needs to be designed so that management is able to ascertain the cost of producing a unit of product. This is an important piece of information for management information purposes as well as for the financial accountant who uses this information in preparing financial statements shared with those outside the organization. A general information model was developed in this chapter to provide this information. The first phase involved a procedure for accumulating the costs of the three basic elements of manufacturing—direct materials, direct labor, and manufacturing overhead. The second phase in the development of the model was to find a method to allocate these accumulated costs to the production activity of the period in such a way that costs could be identified with individual jobs or products. Exhibit 6–2 (page 174) is a pictorial illustration of the model.

In the cost accumulation phase, the actual costs for materials, labor, and manufacturing expenses are marshaled or assembled by category as incurred. In the allocation/reallocation phase the costs are identified with product: direct materials used on a particular product are identified through the use of materials requisitions; direct labor used to perform operations on the material to transform it into finished product is identified with the product through the use of job tickets; and a portion of the manufacturing overhead expenses are associated with the finished product by using a predetermined application rate based on some measure of activity (time spent on the product by workers or machines, cost of material used, cost of direct labor used, and so forth). When the product is finished and ready to go to the

EXHIBIT 6–2
General Model
Cost of Producing a Unit of Product

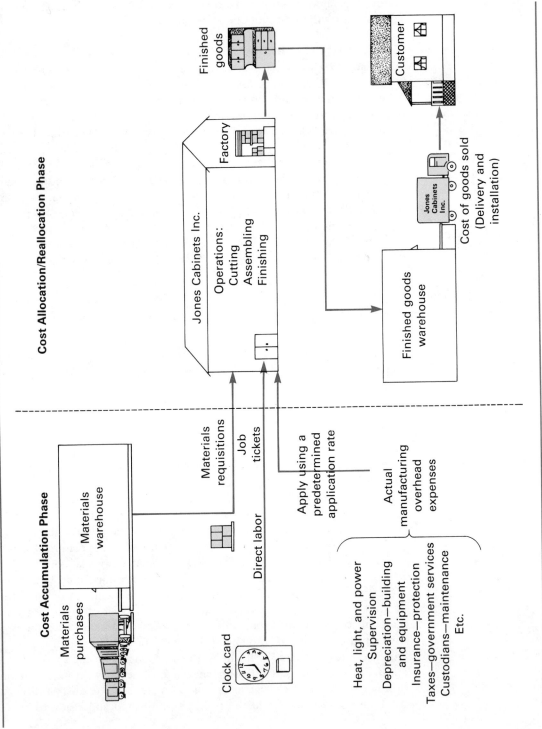

finished goods warehouse (or directly to the customer in the case of special orders), management has immediate feedback available to use in comparing actual results with planned activity.

The use of a predetermined rate for overhead application introduced complexities of budget capability, time horizon, capacity concept, and under- or overapplied overhead. Most production companies will need to use multiple (departmental) overhead rates for the application of overhead rather than a single plantwide rate.

Appendix 6—A
Allocating Service Department Costs
to Producing Departments

It was noted in the chapter that service departments may exist in a factory and that these departments were necessary in order to keep the factory operating smoothly. Costs of operating these service departments should then be viewed as manufacturing costs and should become part of the unit costs of production. In the model developed in the chapter, manufacturing costs were allocated to products as the product passed through producing departments only. How, then, can costs of service departments be allocated to product? It seems logical to conclude that we must somehow first allocate the service department costs to producing departments where these costs can then be identified with product as the output passes through the producing departments.

Do not forget that predetermined overhead application rates were developed for the producing departments. This means that prior to calculating the predetermined rate we must estimate the costs of the service departments and allocate them to the producing departments in order to allow for application of all costs of production (service department costs as well as producing departments). An example will help illustrate the problem.

Let us assume that we have a factory with two producing departments (cutting and finishing, and assembling) and two service departments (personnel, and repairs and maintenance). The following diagram illustrates the provision of service by the service departments to the producing departments and other service departments. Personnel and repairs and maintenance are designated as Service Departments 1 and 2, and cutting and finishing and assembling are designated as Producing Departments A and B.

The arrows on the diagram indicate that Service Department 1 performs service for Producing Departments A and B as well as performing service for Service Department 2. Service Department 2, on the other hand, performs service for Producing Departments A and B as well as Service Department 1. We have indicated that these services are not free—they are necessary for production to take place and therefore should be added to the cost of the

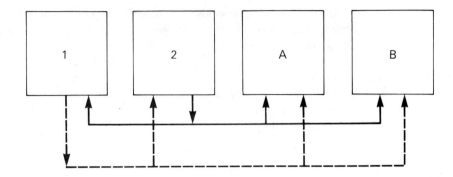

product. The problem is how to allocate the service department costs to the producing departments on some equitable and rational basis.

Three methods have been developed for this allocation process:

1. Direct method,

2. Step (step-down, sequential) method, and

3. Reciprocal (double distribution, cross-allocation, or matrix) method.

In an effort to keep our discussion and illustrations simple, we will ignore the fact that fixed costs of a service department should be allocated on a lump-sum basis (using predetermined or agreed percentages) and that the variable costs should be allocated on a basis that coincides with the amount of service rendered or received. For example, the variable costs of the personnel department could be allocated on the basis of the number of employees in each department served, or the variable costs in a repairs and maintenance department could be allocated on the basis of repair hours of service rendered. The fixed-cost portion of the service department costs would then be allocated based on some estimate of the needs of the departments that made the creation of the service department necessary. In other words, the fixed costs of service departments would tend to be allocated on a rather constant dollar amount basis, whereas the variable costs of service departments would be allocated based on percentages of total service rendered to the other departments. Notice in both cases that we are allocating a percentage of total fixed or variable cost to each department served, so that if you acquire a general understanding of the allocation techniques on a percentage basis you will be able to apply the specific techniques to either of the two kinds of costs.

Let us assume that in budgeting for the upcoming year the information in Exhibit 6–3 was assembled. Note from the data that Service Department 1 (personnel) costs are to be allocated on the basis of number of employees and that Service Department 2 (repairs and maintenance) are to be allocated on the basis of repair hours worked. Note also that overhead is to be applied in the producing departments on the basis of direct labor hours worked.

EXHIBIT 6–3
Information for Service Department Cost Allocation

	Departments			
	Service		Producing	
	1	2	A	B
Budgeted overhead cost directly identified with department	$50,000	$20,000	$60,000	$40,000
Number of employees to be served by Service Dept. 1		18	30	12
Percentages		30%	50%	20%
Estimated hours of repair and maintenance service to be provided by Service Dept. 2	500		4,000	500
Percentages	10%		80%	10%
Estimated direct labor hours			30,000	12,000

Direct Method

The **direct method** of allocation of service department costs ignores all reciprocal relationships; that is, it ignores the fact that Service Department 1 performs service for Service Department 2 and vice versa. This makes the allocation very simple. It would appear as shown in Exhibit 6–4.

EXHIBIT 6–4
Direct Method of Service Department Cost Allocation

	Departments			
	Service		Producing	
	1	2	A	B
Overhead cost directly identified with department	$50,000	$20,000	$ 60,000	$40,000
Allocate Service Dept. 1 (5/7, 2/7)[a]	($50,000)		35,714	14,286
Allocate Service Dept. 2 (8/9, 1/9)[b]		(20,000)	17,778	2,222
Total overhead costs to apply in producing departments (a + b)			$113,492	$56,508
Divide by estimated DLH			30,000	12,000
Predetermined overhead rate			$ 3.7831	$4.7090

[a] The base is 30 + 12 = 42 employees; 30/42 = 5/7, 12/42 = 2/7.
[b] The base is 4,000 + 500 = 4,500 repair hours; 4,000/4,500 = 8/9, 500/4,500 = 1/9.

Note in the direct method that the fraction used to allocate the service department costs is determined by considering producing departments only. To allocate Service Department 1 costs, employees in producing departments only are considered. Therefore, if Producing Department A has 30 employees and Producing Department B has 12 employees (making a total of 42 employees), the fraction (percentage) of Service Department 1 costs allocated to Producing Department A becomes 30/42 or 5/7 and to B, 12/42 or 2/7. The same procedure is followed for Service Department 2.

Step Method

The **step method** gives at least partial recognition to the reciprocal relationships among service departments. This method is illustrated in Exhibit 6–5. Note that with the step method, the first allocation of service department cost (Service Department 1) gives recognition to the services rendered to Service Department 2. Once the costs of a service department are allocated, however, we never return to that department with further allocations. That is why we said that the step method gives partial recognition to reciprocal relationships between service departments. This method does create some question regarding the sequencing of allocations of the various service department costs. Theoretically, the service department rendering service to the greatest number of other service departments would be the first candidate for allocation, and so on. As a practical matter, the service department

EXHIBIT 6–5
Step Method of Service Department Cost Allocation

| | Departments | | | |
| | Service | | Producing | |
	1	2	A	B
Overhead cost directly identified with department	$50,000	$20,000	$ 60,000	$40,000
Allocate Service Dept. 1 (3/10, 5/10, 2/10)[a]	(50,000)	15,000	25,000	10,000
Total cost now in Dept. 2		35,000		
Allocate Service Dept. 2 (8/9, 1/9)[b]		(35,000)	31,111	3,889
Total overhead to apply in producing departments (a + b)			$116,111	$53,889
Divide by DLH			30,000	12,000
Predetermined overhead rate			$ 3.870	$ 4.491

[a] The base is 18 + 30 + 12 = 60 employees; 18/60 = 3/10, 30/60 = 5/10, 12/60 = 2/10.
[b] Because Service Department 1 is now closed, the base becomes 4,000 + 500 = 4,500; 4,000/4,500 = 8/9, 500/4,500 = 1/9.

with the greatest total costs would be allocated first and the assumption made that the department with the greatest cost is rendering the greatest amount of service to other service departments.

Reciprocal Method

As you would expect, the **reciprocal method** gives full recognition to the reciprocal relationships of services rendered among service departments. It requires the use of simultaneous equations (or matrix algebra) to complete the allocation. The simultaneous equations for giving full recognition to the reciprocal service relationships between the service departments are shown in Exhibit 6–6. The reciprocal service department allocations are shown in Exhibit 6–7 (page 180).

Note that after solving the mathematical equations the total costs identified with the two service departments is $89,690 ($53,608 + $36,082), whereas there is only $70,000 of costs to be allocated ($50,000 + $20,000). Do not be alarmed at this phenomenon. This inflated total comes from the mathematical recognition of the reciprocal service relationships. Note further that only 70% of S1 costs are allocated ($37,526) and 90% of S2 costs are allocated ($32,474). These total to $70,000, the total of service department costs that we set out to allocate.

EXHIBIT 6–6
Determining Reciprocal Costs of Service Departments

Let S1 = costs associated with Service Department 1
Let S2 = costs associated with Service Department 2
Then

(1) S1 = 50,000 + .1S2
(2) S2 = 20,000 + .3S1

Restating equations to get the unknowns on the same side of the equal sign:

(1) S1 − .1S2   = 50,000
(2) −.3S1 + S2 = 20,000

Eliminate one unknown and solve:

Multiply (1) by   .3 = .3S1 − .03S2 = 15,000
Repeat (2) unmodified = −.3S1 +   S2 = 20,000
Add   .97S2 = 35,000
Solve   S2 = 36,082

Substitute in (1) to solve for S1:

S1 = 50,000 + .1S2
S1 = 50,000 + .1(36,082)
S1 = 50,000 + 3,608
S1 = 53,608

EXHIBIT 6–7
Reciprocal Method of Service Department Cost Allocation

	Producing Department	
	A	B
Overhead directly identified with department	$ 60,000	$40,000
Allocate Service Dept. 1 (50%, 20%)[a]	26,804	10,722
Allocate Service Dept. 2 (80%, 10%)[b]	28,866	3,608
Total overhead to apply in producing departments (a + b)	$115,670	$54,330
Divide by DLH	30,000	12,000
Predetermined overhead rate	$ 3.8557	$4.5275

[a] From the solution as determined above, S1 = $53,608. Therefore, 50% × $53,608 = $26,804; 20% × $53,608 = $10,722.

[b] From the solution as determined above, S2 = $36,082. Therefore, 80% × $36,082 = $28,866; 10% × $36,082 = $3,608.

Choosing among the Methods

Which of the three allocation methods should be used? One way to answer this question is to observe the sensitivity of the predetermined overhead application rates to the various service department cost allocation methods. The calculated rates for our example are summarized below by allocation method.

Allocation Method	Predetermined Overhead Rate by Producing Departments	
	A	B
Direct	$3.7831	$4.7090
Step	3.8700	4.4910
Reciprocal	3.8557	4.5275

From the summary above it appears that the variation in overhead rates is rather insignificant. However, given a different set of service department relationships and overhead costs, we could very well find the rates affected significantly by the method of allocation used. Obviously, the reciprocal method should be most accurate. It would seem then that the method to be used depends on the sensitivity of the decisions to be made to the results obtained through the use of the allocation method. If management is pricing a product that has minimal margins or making a decision regarding purchasing services internally or externally, the numbers could have a significant effect on major decisions and should therefore be as accurate as possible. This would suggest the use of the reciprocal method or at least a check of the results obtained using the reciprocal method versus the other methods. Under less sensitive circumstances, and from a purely practical standpoint, the step or direct method may suffice.

We have illustrated the three methods that may be used to allocate service department costs to producing departments. It was stressed that this allocation must be done in order to calculate a predetermined overhead application rate and therefore would need to be done during the budget period. The process involved four steps:

1. Prepare departmental budgets (producing and service departments).
2. Choose an allocation base for the allocation of the service department cost.
3. Allocate the budgeted service department costs to the producing departments using one of the three methods discussed above.
4. Calculate a predetermined overhead application rate to be used in each producing department to apply the total overhead costs to product produced.

At the end of the accounting period, this process of allocating service department costs will need to be repeated using actual costs and actual activity levels achieved. This allocation process at the end of the accounting period is made primarily for the purpose of comparing actual with planned performance.

Key Terms

Actual overhead rate is one where manufacturing overhead is assigned to product at the end of the accounting period when total actual manufacturing overhead for the period is known.

Departmental overhead rate is a separate rate often used where plantwide rates are inequitable in terms of charging manufacturing overhead to product.

Direct method of service department cost allocations to producing departments ignores reciprocal relations between departments.

Expected capacity is a capacity base geared to an anticipated productive factor for the forthcoming year.

Normal capacity (or volume) is the average expected productive output for an intermediate time period such as three to five years.

Overapplied overhead occurs when applied overhead exceeds actual overhead for the period.

Physical capacity is maximum productive capacity for a year on either a practical or theoretical capacity basis.

Plantwide (or single) overhead rate is a single overhead rate used for all departments and operations in a plant.

Practical capacity refers to an overhead base geared to the physical ability of the plant to produce with current equipment during normal operating hours of that particular manufacturing process.

Predetermined overhead rate (applied overhead rate) refers to an overhead rate determined in advance for the year using budgetary information.

Reciprocal method   of service department cost allocations gives full recognition to the reciprocal relationships of services rendered among service departments.

Step method   of service department cost allocations gives partial recognition to reciprocal relationships among service departments. Departments closed out first have some of their costs allocated to service departments whose costs have not yet been allocated.

Theoretical (or ideal) capacity   is an overhead base calculated from the standpoint of production continuing on a twenty-four-hour basis for 365 days per year.

Underapplied overhead   occurs when actual overhead exceeds applied overhead for the period.

Questions

Q6–1   Identify the three basic cost elements necessary for the production of a product and briefly describe each.

Q6–2   What is included in the cost accumulation phase of product costing?

Q6–3   How is direct material identified with a finished product? Direct labor?

Q6–4   "Applying overhead is an indirect allocation process." Explain what is meant by this statement.

Q6–5   What is meant by a *predetermined overhead rate* and how is it computed?

Q6–6   What are the benefits or advantages associated with using a predetermined overhead rate?

Q6–7   What is the alternative to allocating overhead to product using a predetermined rate? What are the disadvantages of using this alternative?

Q6–8   Savy Company's overhead application rate is $8 per direct labor hour; Slippery Company's rate is $6 per machine hour. For each company identify the production activity base and describe probable characteristics of each company's manufacturing process.

Q6–9   What factors should be considered in selecting the activity measure or base to use in computing the predetermined overhead rate?

Q6–10   What time horizon should be selected in estimating the amount of manufacturing overhead and the level of the activity measure or base to use in the computation of the predetermined overhead rate? Why?

Q6–11   Distinguish between ideal, practical, normal, and expected capacity. Which capacity concept is more useful for long-run product costing? Which is more useful for performance evaluation and control in the short run? Why?

Q6–12   Why is a knowledge of cost behavior important in the computation of a predetermined overhead rate?

Q6–13   What is meant by *overapplied overhead?* By *underapplied overhead?* Describe several reasons why manufacturing overhead might be overapplied.

Q6–14   Uang Company uses a predetermined overhead rate to apply manufacturing overhead and ends the year with overapplied manufacturing overhead. Nearly all of the production activity of the period resulted in completed products that have been sold. How would Uang dispose of the overapplied overhead at the end of the year?

Q6–15 Distinguish between departmental predetermined overhead rates and a plantwide rate. Why would a company use several departmental overhead rates rather than a single plantwide rate?

Q6–16 Satu Company used a predetermined overhead rate to apply manufacturing overhead and ends the year with underapplied manufacturing overhead. Much of the product worked on during the period is still not complete, some has been completed, and very little has been sold. How would Satu dispose of its underapplied overhead at the end of the year? If your answer is different from the answer given for Q6–14 above, why is it different?

Q6–17 What is the difference between a producing department and a service department? Give illustrations of each.

Q6–18 Why is it considered necessary to allocate service department costs to producing departments?

Q6–19 What questions must be resolved in selecting the bases to use for the allocation of service department costs?

Q6–20 What methods can be used for allocating service department costs to producing departments? Which would you recommend and why?

Exercises

E6–1 **Actual overhead rates.** Slow Company allocates manufacturing overhead to product based on an actual overhead rate. The company incurred $210,000 of manufacturing overhead during the year, and the plant used 30,000 hours of direct labor costing $300,000. Slow applies overhead using direct labor hours as the activity base.

Required: 1. What is Slow's manufacturing overhead application rate?
2. When would the rate be computed?
3. What are the problems associated with using an actual overhead application rate as opposed to a predetermined overhead application rate?

E6–2 **Capacity concepts and overhead rates.** Hasty Company expects to utilize 40,000 direct labor hours next year. They have analyzed their manufacturing overhead costs well and have developed the following cost estimate function:

Total manufacturing overhead $= \$400,000 + \$5X$

where X equals the number of direct labor hours. Therefore, Hasty expects to incur $600,000 of manufacturing overhead next year. The theoretical capacity of Hasty's plant is 60,000 direct labor hours, the practical capacity is 50,000 direct labor hours, and the average projected sales for the next five years would require the output from 45,000 direct labor hours (normal capacity).

Required: 1. What would be Hasty's predetermined overhead application rate if it is based on
                     a. Theoretical capacity?
                     b. Practical capacity?
                     c. Normal capacity?
                     d. Expected capacity?
                  2. Which capacity level would you recommend that Hasty Company use to
                     determine their overhead application rate and why?

E6–3   **Overhead rates based on normal capacity versus expected capacity.** Krandall
         Manufacturing has estimated the cost function for total manufacturing overhead to be
         $100,000 + $8X$, where X equals machine hours. They are trying to decide whether
         to use a predetermined overhead application rate based on a normal projected capac-
         ity of 125,000 machine hours or on the expected capacity next year of 100,000 ma-
         chine hours.

Required: 1. Compute the total predetermined overhead rate based on normal capacity and
                     on expected capacity.
                  2. Compute separate fixed overhead and variable overhead predetermined appli-
                     cation rates for each of the two capacity levels.
                  3. What conclusions can be drawn from a comparison of the overhead application
                     rates you have calculated?

E6–4   **Time horizon and overhead application rates.** Beta Company wants to initiate the
         use of a predetermined overhead rate in applying manufacturing overhead to pro-
         duction. The manufacturing process requires substantial amounts of hand labor, so
         the company feels that direct labor hours is an appropriate activity base to use for the
         application of overhead. The following estimates have been made for next year:

	1st Qtr.	2d Qtr.	3d Qtr.	4th Qtr.	Total
Est. mfg. overhead	$155,000	$115,000	$220,000	$200,000	$690,000
Est. direct lab. hours	25,000	25,000	40,000	60,000	150,000

Required: (Show computations)
                  1. If Beta Company uses a time horizon of one year in determining the predeter-
                     mined overhead rate, how much overhead will be applied to production for
                     each direct labor hour worked?
                  2. If Beta Company uses a time horizon of three months, how much overhead will
                     be applied to production for each direct labor hour worked in each of the
                     quarters?
                  3. Why do the predetermined overhead application rates that you computed vary?
                     Which time horizon should Beta Company use and why?

E6–5   **Determining cost function and fixed and variable overhead application rates.**
         Refer to the information given in E6–4.

Required: 1. Why are the estimated manufacturing overhead expenses in the first quarter
                     greater than the estimated manufacturing overhead expenses in the second
                     quarter when direct labor hours are the same? Further, how can the estimated
                     manufacturing overhead expenses be more for the third quarter than they are
                     for the fourth quarter when direct labor hours are 20,000 greater in the fourth
                     quarter?

2. Is it possible to determine the cost function that Beta Company used in computing the manufacturing overhead numbers for each quarter and for the year? If not, why not?

E6–6 **Underapplied or overapplied overhead.** Dandy Company estimated total manufacturing overhead for their next year of operations (19X7) at $321,000 using the following cost estimation function:

Total manufacturing overhead = $107,000 + $2X

where X equals direct labor hours. Dandy applies manufacturing overhead to production using direct labor hours as an activity base and used a predetermined overhead application rate of $3 during 19X7.

During 19X7 Dandy actually incurred $297,000 of manufacturing overhead and worked 95,000 direct labor hours.

Required:
1. Dandy based its predetermined overhead application rate on how many estimated direct labor hours?
2. How much manufacturing overhead was applied to production during 19X7?
3. Did Dandy Company end the year with underapplied or overapplied manufacturing overhead? How much?
4. If you compare the overhead costs actually incurred for 95,000 direct labor hours with Dandy's cost estimation function, it appears that Dandy incurred the exact amount of manufacturing overhead that would have been estimated for 95,000 direct labor hours. How can Dandy have underapplied or overapplied manufacturing overhead under these circumstances?

E6–7 **Disposition of underapplied or overapplied overhead.** Rachael Industries incurred total manufacturing overhead costs during the year of $450,000. At the end of the year Rachael had the following selected account balances:

Manufacturing overhead (credit)	$ 60,000
Work in process inventory	200,000
Finished goods inventory	400,000
Cost of goods sold	600,000

Required:
1. Was manufacturing overhead underapplied or overapplied for the year? Explain.
2. It was mentioned in the chapter that underapplied or overapplied overhead could be closed at the end of the year to cost of goods sold or allocated between the various inventories and cost of goods sold. If Rachael does the latter,
   a. Determine how much is allocated to each of the inventories and to cost of goods sold.
   b. Are the amounts allocated added or subtracted from the respective accounts? Why?

E6–8 **Plantwide versus departmental overhead rates.** Ralee Company operates a plant where specialty bicycles are assembled and painted for different brand name distributors. Some of the distributors wish to have the bicycle painted by Ralee, whereas others prefer to paint them themselves.

Ralee has two major departments in its plant—assembly and painting. Assembly requires a good deal of hand work, but the painting is well mechanized. Ralee applies manufacturing overhead to production using a plantwide predetermined rate based on direct labor hours. The predetermined rate for the current year was based on the following estimates:

	Assembly	Painting	Plantwide Total
Estimated mfg. overhead	$200,000	$150,000	$350,000
Estimated direct labor hours	35,000	5,000	40,000

At the end of the year Ralee had incurred $375,000 of actual manufacturing overhead and had applied only $340,000.

Required:
1. What was Ralee Company's overhead application rate?
2. What are some possible reasons that Ralee has a significant amount of under-applied overhead for the year?
3. What suggestions could you make to Ralee to improve its overhead application procedure?

E6–9 **Selecting overhead application base.** Grandberg Apples has several orchards lo-cated in the midwest. At harvest time the apples are picked and transported to a cen-tral plant where they are first sorted by size in a highly mechanized sizing department. The apples then go to a packing department where a good deal of human intervention is required in the packing process. Grandberg wished to apply overhead to produc-tion by the use of a predetermined rate. The following estimates are available for Grandberg for the next year:

	Sizing	Packing
Estimated manufacturing overhead	$60,000	$ 40,000
Estimated machine hours	15,000	4,000
Estimated labor hours	3,000	20,000
Estimated direct labor costs	$24,000	$180,000

Required:
1. Calculate a predetermined manufacturing overhead application rate for each department for each of the following basis:
   a. Machine hours
   b. Direct labor hours
   c. Direct labor costs
2. What base would you recommend using to calculate the predetermined application rate? Explain why you *do not* recommend those that you exclude.

E6–10 **Schedule of cost of goods manufactured.** The Ellis Company has provided you with the following data regarding its manufacturing activities for the year 19X7:

Inventories:	
Raw materials, January 1	$ 8,000
Raw materials, December 31	10,000
Work in process, January 1	14,000
Work in process, December 31	12,000

Manufacturing overhead costs incurred during 19X7:	
Supplies	$ 5,000
Utilities	10,000
Insurance	7,000
Depreciation	30,000
Indirect labor	12,000
Total	$ 64,000

Other factory related costs incurred
during the year:

Purchase of raw materials	$ 50,000
Direct labor costs (15,000 hours)	105,000

Ellis Company uses a predetermined overhead application rate to apply overhead costs to production. The rate used in 19X7 was $3 per direct labor hour.

Required:
1. Does Ellis Company have underapplied or overapplied overhead at the end of 19X7? If so, how much?
2. Prepare a schedule of cost of goods manufactured for 19X7. (Remember that manufacturing overhead is added to work in process in the ledger using the predetermined rate, so be careful of your treatment of total manufacturing costs in the schedule.)

E6–11 **Allocation of service department costs—direct method.** Hartford Company distributes the service department overhead costs directly to producing departments without allocation to the other service department. Information for the month of January 19X7 is as follows:

	Service Departments	
	Maintenance	Utilities
Overhead costs incurred	$18,700	$9,000
Service provided to:		
Maintenance department	–0–	10%
Utilities department	20%	–0–
Producing department A	40%	30%
Producing department B	40%	60%
Total	100%	100%

Required: Determine the amount of utilities department costs that are distributed to each of the producing departments for 19X7.

(CPA Adapted)

 E6–12 **Allocation of service department costs—step method.** Complex Manufacturing has three service departments: Personnel, Power, and Repairs and Maintenance. They also have two producing departments: Fabrication and Assembly. Selected data for the five departments is presented below:

	Producing Departments		Service Departments		
	Fabrication	Assembly	Personnel	Power	Maintenance
Manufacturing overhead	$60,000	$100,000	$70,000	$60,000	$50,000
Number of employees	200	400	40	45	20
Units of power consumed	6,000	13,000	500	200	1,000
Machine hours	8,000	12,000	–0–	–0–	–0–

Complex allocates service department costs by the step method in the following order:

1. Personnel, based on number of employees
2. Power, based on units of power consumed
3. Repairs and maintenance, based on machine hours

Required: Using the step method, set up a schedule showing the allocation of the service department costs to the producing departments. Make your schedule so that it shows the total overhead costs that must be applied to production in the fabrication and assembly departments.

Problems

P6–13   **Disposition of underapplied or overapplied overhead.** Rex Company uses predetermined overhead rates to apply manufacturing overhead to production. The rates are based on direct labor hours. Estimates for the year 19X7 are given below:

Estimated manufacturing overhead	$300,000
Estimated direct labor costs	450,000
Estimated direct labor hours	50,000

During 19X7 Rex Company used 55,000 direct labor hours. At the end of 19X7 Rex Company records revealed the following actual costs and other operating data:

Manufacturing overhead	$308,000
Direct labor cost	500,500
Cost of goods sold	575,000
Finished goods inventory	315,000
Work in process	110,000
Raw materials inventory	50,000

Required: 1. What was Rex's predetermined overhead rate for 19X7?
2. Determine the amount of underapplied or overapplied manufacturing overhead for 19X7.
3. If Rex decides that it is necessary to allocate the underapplied or overapplied overhead to the appropriate accounts, identify the accounts that will be affected and compute the amount to be allocated to each. Is the amount allocated added to or subtracted from each account?
4. What will be the difference in Rex Company's net income if it closes all the underapplied or overapplied manufacturing overhead to cost of goods sold rather than allocating it as suggested in 3 above? Which method of disposing of the underapplied or overapplied manufacturing overhead would you recommend under the circumstances?

P6–14   **Plantwide versus departmental overhead rates.** Hi-Cam is a manufacturer of parts used to convert standard automobile engines to high-performance engines, specializing particularly in crankshafts and camshafts. The company has three departments: Molding, Lathe and Grinding, and Sanding and Polishing. Some of the camshafts and crankshafts must stay within very close tolerances, which requires more time in the sanding and polishing departments where many sanding and polishing materials are required.

     The high-performance parts business is very competitive, and Hi-Cam is concerned about internal costing policies—particularly the application of manufacturing overhead. The company bids on orders by taking 125% of the total cost of manufacturing (which includes direct materials, direct labor, and applied manufacturing overhead). If each order is not charged with its equitable share of manufacturing overhead, the bid may be so high that Hi-Cam loses the bid to a competitor, or it may be so low that Hi-Cam may make no profit or even actually incur a loss on the order. The company has been applying manufacturing overhead on the basis of direct labor cost and made the following estimates for the current year:

	Molding	Lathe & Grinding	Sanding & Polishing	Total
Manufacturing overhead	$200,000	$300,000	$370,000	$870,000
Direct labor cost	250,000	250,000	100,000	600,000

Hi-Cam has just received a request for a bid proposal on an order of camshafts. It is an order that has relatively liberal tolerances, so not as much time needs to be spent in sanding and polishing. The engineers have indicated that the order will require the following direct materials and direct labor in each department:

	Molding	Lathe & Grinding	Sanding & Polishing	Total
Direct materials	$60,000	$ 5,000	$10,000	$ 75,000
Direct labor	80,000	65,000	10,000	155,000

Required:

1. If Hi-Cam uses a plantwide application rate,
   a. Calculate the predetermined application rate for the current year.
   b. Determine the amount of manufacturing overhead that would be applied to the above camshaft order based on the plantwide rate.
   c. Determine the total cost on which the bid would be based using the applied manufacturing overhead determined in b above.
2. If Hi-Cam were to use separate departmental rates (still based on direct labor cost in each department),
   a. Calculate the predetermined overhead application rate for each of the three departments.
   b. Determine the amount of manufacturing overhead that would be applied to the above camshaft order using the departmental rates.
   c. Determine the total cost on which the bid would be based using the applied manufacturing overhead determined in 2b above.
3. Assuming that Hi-Cam bids using its standard bid policy and that a competitor has bid $520,000 for the job,
   a. Will Hi-Cam get the order if it bases its bid on overhead applied using a plantwide rate?
   b. Will Hi-Cam get the order if it bases its bid on overhead applied using departmental rates? Show your computations for each.

P6–15 **Schedule of cost of goods manufactured.** Zepada Company installed a management accounting system at the beginning of 19X7 and is anxious to see the first statements produced from the system. The company manufactures and sells a single product. You have been assigned the task of preparing a schedule of cost of goods manufactured for the month of January 19X7. You are aware that Zepada uses a predetermined overhead application rate that applies $9 of manufacturing overhead for each direct labor hour worked. The following information is available pertaining to the month of January 19X7:

   a. 6,000 units of product were produced. Each unit of product requires two units of raw materials.

b. The raw materials inventory on January 1 was 3,000 units valued at $8 each.

c. Three purchases of raw materials were made during January:

January 4	5,000 units @ $9
January 15	5,000 units @ $8.50
January 20	3,000 units @ $8.25

d. The beginning and ending work in process inventories were

January 1	3,000 units @ $20
January 31	4,000 units @ $30

e. The finished goods inventory at January 1 consisted of 2,000 units valued at $44 each.

f. The company uses the perpetual inventory system for all inventories.

g. Depreciation is calculated on a straight-line basis and an estimated life of ten years. Zepada owns the following depreciable property (at its original cost):

Office equipment	$ 12,000
Factory equipment	300,000

h. Other information:

Sales (7,000 units)	$560,000
Direct labor (12,100 hours)	122,000
Interest expense	3,000
Delivery expense	1,500
Indirect labor	54,000
Power, heat, and light	4,000
Rent (factory)	10,000
Freight-in	1,000
Sales commissions	23,000
Sales returns and allowances	6,000
Bad debts expense	2,000
Supplies (factory)	4,000
Insurance (factory)	2,500
Property taxes (factory)	1,500
Miscellaneous factory overhead	7,000

Required:

1. Prepare in good form a schedule of cost of goods manufactured for the month of January. Where necessary, show supporting computations. (Assume that Zepada closes its underapplied or overapplied manufacturing overhead to cost of goods sold.)

2. Determine the unit cost of goods manufactured during January.

P6–16   Types of manufacturing overhead application rates. Schweiger, Inc. has engaged the services of an accounting firm for the design and installation of a management accounting system. A preliminary investigation of Schweiger's manufacturing operations has disclosed these facts:

a. The company makes a line of light fixtures and lamps. The materials cost of any particular item ranges from 15% to 60% of total factory cost, depending on the kind of metal and fabric used.

b. The business is subject to wide cyclical fluctuations because the sales volume follows new housing construction.

c. About 60% of the manufacturing is normally finished during the first quarter of the year.

d. For the whole plant, the direct labor wage rates range from $7.50 to $13 an hour. However, within each of the eight individual departments, the spread between the high and low wage rate is less than 5%.

e. Each product requires the use of all eight of the manufacturing departments, but not proportionately.

f. Within the individual manufacturing departments, manufacturing overhead ranges from 30% to 80% of prime cost (direct materials plus direct labor).

Required: Prepare a letter for the president of Schweiger, Inc., explaining whether its management accounting system should use the following procedures, including the reasons supporting each of the recommendations made:

1. A predetermined manufacturing overhead rate or an actual manufacturing overhead rate — departmental or plantwide.

2. A method of applying manufacturing overhead based on direct labor hours, direct labor cost, or prime cost.

(CPA Adapted)

P6–17   **Should we allocate or not — selecting bases.** Cook Associates recently reorganized its computer and data processing activities. In the past, small computer systems were located in the accounting departments at the firm's plant and subsidiary locations. These systems have been replaced with a centralized data processing department at corporate headquarters. The new department has been in operation for two years and has been regularly producing reliable and timely data for the past twelve months.

Because the department has focused its activities on converting applications to the new system and producing reports for the plant and subsidiary managements, little attention has been devoted to the costs of the department. Now that the data processing activities are operating relatively smoothly, company management has requested that the departmental manager recommend a cost accumulation system to facilitate cost control and the development of suitable charging rates for users.

For the past two years, the data processing costs have been recorded in one account. The costs have then been allocated to user departments on the basis of computer time used. The costs and charging rate for the current year are given below:

a. Salaries and benefits	$ 622,600
b. Supplies	40,000
c. Equipment maintenance contract	15,000
d. Insurance	25,000
e. Heat and air conditioning	36,000
f. Electricity	50,000
g. Equipment and furniture depreciation	285,400
h. Building improvements depreciation	10,000
i. Building occupancy and security	39,300
j. Corporate administrative charge	52,700
Total cost	$1,176,000

Computer hours for user processing*		2,750
Hourly rate ($1,176,000/2,750)		$ 428
*Use of available computer hours:		
Testing and debugging programs	250	
Setup of jobs	500	
Processing jobs	2,750	
Downtime for maintenance	750	
Idle time	742	
Total	4,992	

The department manager recommends that the department's costs be accumulated by five activity centers within the department: Systems Analysis, Programming, Data Preparation, Computer Operations (processing), and Administration. He also suggests that the costs of Administration activity should be allocated to the other four activity centers before a separate rate for charging users is developed for each of the first four activities. The manager explained that the subsidiary accounts within the department contained the following charges:

a. Salaries and benefits — the salary and benefit costs of all employees in the department.
b. Supplies — punch card costs, paper costs for printers, and a small amount for miscellaneous other costs.
c. Equipment maintenance contracts — charges for maintenance contracts covering all equipment.
d. Insurance — cost of insurance covering the equipment and furniture.
e. Heat and air conditioning — a charge from the corporate heating and air conditioning department estimated to be the differential costs that meet the special needs of the computer department.
f. Electricity — the charge for electricity, based on a separate meter within each department.
g. Equipment and furniture depreciation — the depreciation for all owned equipment and furniture within the department.
h. Building improvements depreciation — the depreciation charges for all building changes that were required to provide proper environmental control and electrical service for the computer department.
i. Building occupancy and security — the department's share of the depreciation, maintenance, heat, and security costs of the building; these costs are allocated to the department on the basis of square feet occupied.
j. Corporate administrative charges — the Computer Department's share of the corporate administrative costs that are allocated to the department on the basis of the number of employees.

Required:

1. For each of the ten cost items (lettered *a* through *j*), state whether or not it should be allocated to the five activity centers. For each cost item that should be allocated, recommend the basis on which it should be allocated. Justify your answer in each case.

2. Assume that the costs of the Computer Operations (processing) activity will be charged to the user departments on the basis of computer hours. Using the analysis of computer utilization shown as a footnote to the department cost schedule above, determine the total number of hours that should be employed

to compute the charging rate for Computer Operations (processing). Justify your answer.

(CMA Adapted)

P6–18   **Service department allocations and predetermined overhead rates.** Sy-Lac Associates produces a new drug used in the medical profession. The drug must be processed under extremely controlled conditions. Workers must wear special uniforms and have daily medical checks because of slight possibilities of reactions to any exposure to the drug as it is processed. The whole manufacturing area is kept extremely clean. As a result, Sy-Lac has three service departments supporting the two producing departments: Medical Services, Uniforms, and Maintenance. The company wants to compute predetermined manufacturing overhead application rates for the producing departments for the next year. The monthly estimated costs and other pertinent operating data are given below:

	Service Departments			Producing Departments	
	Medical Services	Uniforms	Maintenance	Extraction	Mixing & Blending
Direct materials				$100,000	$150,000
Direct labor				40,000	30,000
Medical supplies	$ 5,000				
Uniform cleaning & refurbishing		$ 8,000			
Maintenance supplies			$ 4,000		
Maintenance labor			12,000		
Miscellaneous overhead costs	9,000	12,000	10,000	80,000	100,000
Totals	$14,000	$20,000	$26,000	$220,000	$280,000
Direct labor hours				2,000	1,200
Floor space occupied	600	1,200	1,000	4,600	5,200
No. of uniforms processed:					
Currently	7	18	20	45	30
Peak period expectations	15	30	24	60	45
No. of employees:					
Currently employed	3	8	10	15	10
Long-run needs	5	10	12	20	15

Medical supplies, uniform cleaning and refurbishing, maintenance supplies, and maintenance labor costs are considered variable costs. All other costs in the service departments are considered to be fixed. Sy-Lac allocates service department costs to producing departments using the step method. Inasmuch as all service departments furnish services to all other departments, Sy-Lac allocates service department costs by starting with the department with the most total cost and proceeds in order by those service departments with lesser cost. The bases used for allocation of the different service department costs are given on the next page.

Department	Type of Cost	Basis for Allocation
Maintenance	Variable	Direct labor hours
	Fixed	Square feet of floor space occupied
Uniforms	Variable	Number of items processed
	Fixed	Items expected to be processed in peak periods
Medical Services	Variable	Number of employees currently employed
	Fixed	Expected long-run employee needs

Required:

1. Prepare a schedule showing the allocation of the service department costs for the purpose of determining the predetermined manufacturing overhead application rates.
2. At the end of the next year, would it be necessary to prepare the same schedule only using actual costs? Explain.
3. Compute the predetermined application rate to be used by each of Sy-Lac's producing departments.

P6–19 **Service department cost allocation by direct and step methods.** B-Compat Company has two production departments and three service departments. A summary of costs and other data for each department prior to allocation of service department costs for the year ended December 31, 19X7, is shown below:

	Producing Departments		Service Departments		
	Fabrication	Assembly	General Factory Administration	Factory Maintenance	Factory Cafeteria
Direct labor costs	$2,100,000	$3,075,000	$90,000	$123,150	$130,500
Direct materials costs	3,130,000	950,000	–0–	65,000	91,000
Manufacturing overhead costs	1,650,000	1,850,000	70,000	56,100	62,000
Direct labor hours	562,500	437,500	31,000	27,000	42,000
Number of employees	280	200	12	8	20
Square footage occupied	88,000	72,000	1,750	2,000	4,800

The costs of General Factory Administration, Factory Maintenance, and Factory Cafeteria are allocated on the basis of direct labor hours, square footage occupied, and number of employees, respectively.

Required:

1. Assuming that B-Compat decides to distribute service department costs directly to production departments without recognizing reciprocal departmental relationships, how much Factory Maintenance cost would be allocated to the Fabricating Department?
2. Assuming the same method of allocation as above, how much General Factory Administration cost would be allocated to the Assembly Department?
3. Assuming that B-Compat elects to distribute service department costs to other service departments (starting with the service department with the greatest total costs) as well as to the production departments, how much Factory Cafeteria cost would be allocated to the Factory Maintenance Department? How much Factory Maintenance cost would be allocated to the Factory Cafeteria Department?

(CPA Adapted)

P6–20 **Allocating service department costs — reciprocal method.** Barry Corporation is developing departmental overhead rates based on direct labor hours for its two production departments — Molding and Assembly. The Molding Department employs twenty people, and the Assembly Department employs eighty people. Each person in these two departments works 2,000 hours per year. The production-related overhead costs for the Molding Department are budgeted at $200,000, and the Assembly Department costs are budgeted at $320,000. Two service departments — Repair and Power — directly support the two production departments and have budgeted costs of $48,000 and $250,000, respectively. The production departments' overhead rates cannot be determined until the service department's costs are properly allocated. The following schedule reflects the use of the Repair Department's and Power Department's output by the various departments:

	Department			
	Repair	*Power*	*Molding*	*Assembly*
Repair hours	–0–	1,000	1,000	8,000
KWH	240,000	–0–	840,000	120,000

Required:

1. Calculate the overhead rates per direct labor hour for the Molding Department and the Assembly Department using the direct allocation method to charge the production departments for service department cost.
2. Calculate the overhead rates per direct labor hour for the Molding Department and the Assembly Department using the reciprocal distribution method to charge service department costs to each other and to the production departments.
3. Explain the difference between the methods and indicate the arguments that are generally presented to support the reciprocal method over the direct allocation method.

(CMA Adapted)

P6–21 **Plantwide versus departmental overhead rates with service departments.** Executiff Corporation manufactures a complete line of fiberglass attache cases and suitcases. Executiff has three manufacturing departments — Molding, Component, and Assembly — and two service departments — Power and Maintenance.

The sides of the cases are manufactured in the Molding Department. The frames, hinges, locks, and so forth are manufactured in the Component Department. Varying amounts of materials, time, and effort are required for each of the various cases. The Power Department and Maintenance Department provide service to the three manufacturing departments.

Executiff has always used a plantwide overhead rate. Direct labor hours are used to assign the overhead to its product. The predetermined rate is calculated by dividing the company's total estimated overhead by the total estimated direct labor hours to be worked in the three manufacturing departments.

Whitney Smart, manager of cost accounting, has recommended that Executiff use departmental overhead rates. The planned operating costs and expected levels of activity for the coming year have been developed by Smart and are presented by department in the schedules below (000s omitted):

| | Manufacturing Departments | | |
	Molding	Component	Assembly
Departmental activity measures:			
Direct labor hours	500	2,000	1,500
Machine hours	875	125	–0–
Departmental costs:			
Raw materials	$12,400	$30,000	$ 1,250
Direct labor	3,500	20,000	12,000
Variable overhead	3,500	10,000	16,500
Fixed overhead	17,500	6,200	6,100
Total departmental costs	$36,900	$66,200	$35,850

| | Manufacturing Departments | | |
	Molding	Component	Assembly
Use of service departments:			
Maintenance:			
Estimated usage in labor hours for coming year	90	25	10
Power (in kilowatt hours):			
Estimated usage for coming year	360	320	120
Maximum allotted capacity:	500	350	150

| | Service Departments | |
	Power	Maintenance
Departmental activity measures:		
Maximum capacity	1,000 KWH	Adjustable
Estimated usage in coming year	800 KWH	125 hours
Departmental costs:		
Materials and supplies	$ 5,000	$1,500
Variable labor	1,400	2,250
Fixed overhead	12,000	250
Total service department costs	$18,400	$4,000

Required: 1. Calculate the plantwide overhead application rate for Executiff Corporation for the coming year using the same method as in the past.

2. Whitney Smart has been asked to develop departmental overhead application rates for comparison with the plantwide rate. The following steps are to be followed in developing the departmental rates:

   a. The Maintenance Department costs should be allocated to the three manufacturing departments using the direct method.

   b. The Power Department costs should be allocated to the three manufacturing departments using the dual method, that is, the fixed costs allocated according to long-term capacity and the variable costs according to planned usage.

   c. Calculate departmental overhead rates for the three manufacturing departments using a machine hour base for the Molding Department and a direct labor hour base for the Component and Assembly Departments.

3. Should Executiff Corporation use a plantwide rate or departmental rates to allocate manufacturing overhead to its products? Explain your answer.

(CMA Adapted)

CHAPTER 7

Job Order Costing

Learning Objectives

After reading this chapter you should be able to:

1. Comprehend the difference between the major types of costing systems: job order and process costing.

2. Understand cost flows in a job order costing system.

3. Understand the accounting entries for materials, labor, and overhead in job order costing systems.

4. Have knowledge of the source documents underlying the accounting entries for materials, labor, and overhead.

5. Understand how the subsidiary ledgers tie together with their appropriate control accounts in a job order cost system.

In the previous chapter we developed a general model for determining the cost of producing a unit of product and emphasized the importance of this information to decision makers. The model illustrated how costs need to be accumulated as incurred and how the costs are finally allocated and traced to individual units of product. The model also assumed that all costs related to manufacturing became part of the cost of the finished product: direct material, direct labor, and manufacturing overhead. This approach to product costing is referred to as **absorption or full costing.** We will later develop an approach (called *direct or variable costing*) where this is not the case—variable manufacturing overhead will become part of the cost of the product, but fixed manufacturing overhead will be charged off as an expense of the period in which it is incurred.

In this chapter we develop a job order costing system using the full or absorption costing approach referred to above. The documents and accounts necessary for this subset of the formal information system are illustrated as the system is developed. The complete job order costing cycle is illustrated as costs are traced from incurrence to the finished product and finally to the customer through sales. The difference between job order costing and process costing is also explained.

The Major Costing Systems

Not all manufacturing processes are alike. In the previous chapter we illustrated the manufacture of custom built cabinets—each set of cabinets was *uniquely* designed for a particular house. In this case, each set of cabinets had to be identified separately as a particular job. In other words, the cost object was the particular job—total costs incurred were allocated to each unique job going through the factory.

Contrast the cabinet-making situation above with the processing of crude oil. In the latter, a steady stream of crude oil flows into the refinery, and a continuous stream of products—various grades of gasoline, fuel oil, kerosene, diesel fuel, and so forth—is produced. The mix of the products produced can be varied somewhat by changing the refining process, but basically a barrel of kerosene produced today is the same as a barrel produced last month or last year. It is obvious in this case that there is no single unique product aimed at a particular buyer. The cost object therefore cannot be the job. In these situations the cost object becomes the *process* instead of the job.

It is not coincidental then that two major cost systems have developed. A **job order cost system** (where the cost object is the job) is used in those manufacturing settings where separate jobs are identifiable—a set of custom cabinets for a house, a special order print job, shipbuilding, aircraft manufacture, furniture manufacture, or the manufacture of special order agricultural equipment. A **process cost system** (where the cost object is the process) is used where a basically homogeneous product flows evenly through the production process on a fairly continuous basis. Examples of the latter would be the manufacture of paint, textiles, steel, mining, cement, canneries, bricks, oil, or chemicals. Process costing is also for mass production of like units such as toasters and radios.

The important point to remember is that product costing under both cost systems is an averaging process. To determine a unit cost, the accumulated costs must be divided by some measure of production. Where the job is the cost object, the divisor may be a very small number — such as 1, in the case of a specially built piece of agricultural equipment. It could be 100 if the job consisted of 100 one-half horsepower capacitor electric motors. If the cost object is a process such as refining crude oil, the costs are allocated to a process (the cost object), and these total costs are divided by the throughput of the process for a period of time. The throughput might be thousands of gallons or hundreds of barrels. This cost system is discussed in the following chapter.

An Overview of Cost Flows — Job Order

The preceding chapter illustrated a general model for determining the cost of producing a product. We will now take that general model and make it more specific, that is, we will set up the accounts necessary to accumulate the information in the ledger, and we will design the appropriate documents to help in the recording and controlling of costs. The point was made as the general model was developed that there are three cost elements necessary in order to produce a product — materials, labor, and manufacturing overhead. It therefore would seem that we need those three accounts in our job order cost system as a basic starting point. We will call them, not surprisingly, Materials, Payroll, and Manufacturing Overhead. As materials and labor are used in the factory, and as overhead is applied, we will transfer the three basic elements of cost to an account called Work in Process. As the jobs are completed, the costs associated with each job are transferred to an account called Finished Goods. And finally, as the product is sold, the costs are transferred from Finished Goods to an account you are already familiar with, Cost of Goods Sold. Exhibit 7–1 pictorially illustrates the accounts used and their relationships in a basic job order cost system.

In the development of our job order costing system we will assume that perpetual inventory methods are used throughout. It should also be pointed out that each of the six accounts illustrated in Exhibit 7–1 is a control account. You will perhaps remember that when we refer to an account as a "control" account, we expect to see a subsidiary ledger that provides us with the details of the control account. The example you might remember at this point is the accounts receivable control account with its related accounts

EXHIBIT 7–1
General Model
Job Order System Cost Flows

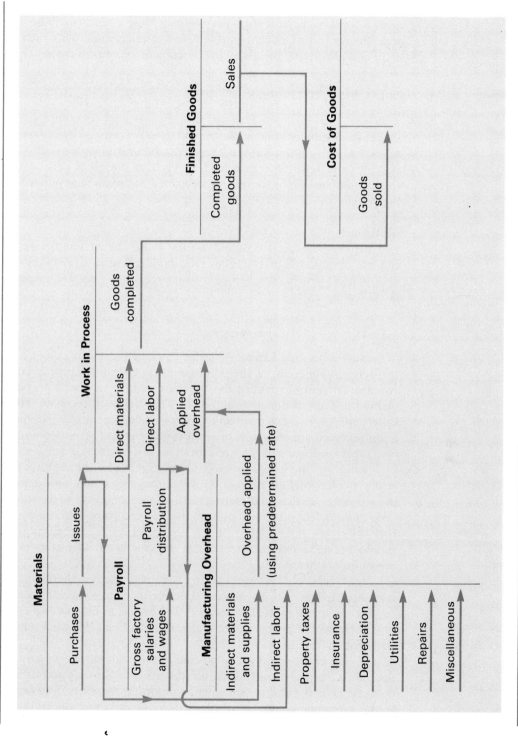

receivable subsidiary ledger or the accounts payable control account and its related accounts payable subsidiary ledger. These concepts will be developed and illustrated in the sections that follow by beginning with each cost element and illustrating the associated document and cost flows.

Specific Document and Cost Flows — The Cost Elements

The custom cabinet builder illustrated in the preceding chapter will be used as the basis for illustrating the document and cost flows for a job order cost system. Only selected transactions in each of the areas will be illustrated so that sufficient competence can be gained in the use and understanding of the system.

Materials

The materials (or stores) control account is used to account for the purchase and use of materials and supplies. The purchase of twelve sheets of $3/4'' \times 4' \times 8'$ oak plywood for $45 per sheet on January 5, 19X6 would result in the following entry:

(1)	1/5	Materials	540	
		Accounts Payable		540

As illustrated in Exhibit 7–2, this entry will result in a debit to the control account Materials for the purchase invoice total. For proper control, the company should not record the purchase until it has been properly documented that the materials ordered are what has been received. This is typically done by using a receiving report—a document that verifies that all items received are what was ordered—quantity and quality. There also may be a separate document that indicates that prices charged agree with quoted prices and that the extensions and additions made by the supplier in arriving at the invoice total are correct. This documentation may vary depending on the size, organization, and management of the company. There should, however, be sufficient documentation so that the company does not accept materials that were not ordered or pay for materials not received. There also should be signatures on the control documents so that responsibility for errors may be fixed.

If the materials account is truly a "control" account, there must be some subsidiary ledger that documents the receipt of this specific material. This might consist of a **materials ledger card** similar to Exhibit 7–3 (page 204).

There would be a separate materials ledger card for each item of material kept in inventory—Exhibit 7–3 is the subsidiary record for $3/4'' \times 4' \times 8'$ oak plywood only. The posting to the materials ledger card would be done on a daily basis and would use the purchase invoice and its supporting documents as the source document supporting the entry. Entering PO4567 in the reference column on January 5 pinpoints the supporting document

EXHIBIT 7–2

Materials Documents and Cost Flows
Job Order Costing

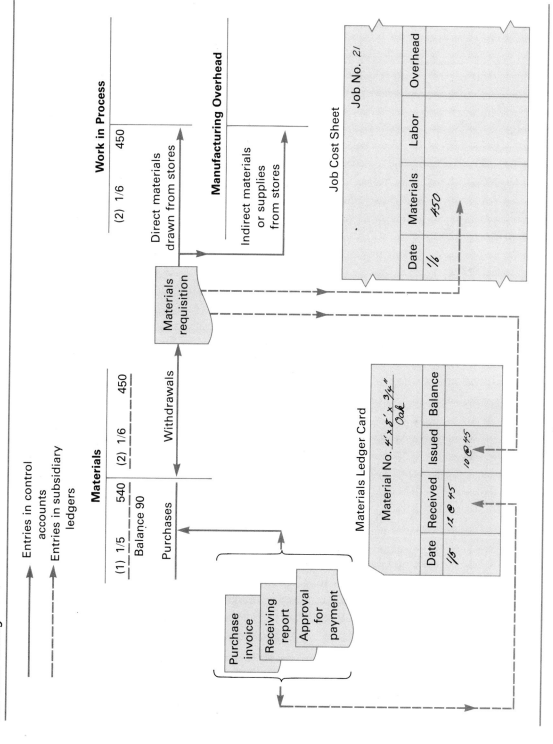

EXHIBIT 7–3

Materials Ledger Card

Date	Reference	Received			Issued			Balance		
		Qty	Unit cost	Total cost	Qty	Unit cost	Total cost	Qty	Unit cost	Total cost
1/5	PO 4567	12	45	540				12	45	540
1/6	R 1078				10	45	450	2	45	90

Item ¾″ × 4′ × 8′ Oak Plywood   Location Bay 5

used to make the entry. There might well have been a beginning balance on the materials ledger card because of inventory on hand, but it has been assumed that there was none for the sake of simplicity.

Many of the indirect materials such as glue, nails, screws, and supplies such as sandpaper, lubricants, and cleaning supplies will not be kept on a perpetual inventory basis. These items may be expensed immediately to the department where they are used, or their cost may be determined by using the periodic inventory method (beginning inventory plus purchases minus ending inventory equals amount used). There should be document support so that the cost of these items may be properly determined and controlled.

Just as there is documentation to support receipts of materials, there must also be documentation to track the issuance of materials from the storeroom. Let us say that on January 6, 19X6, Job No. 21 is to be started in our cabinet factory. The foreman determines from the blueprints and specifications that ten sheets of 3/4″ × 4′ × 8′ oak plywood are needed for this job. To draw this material from the storeroom he will fill out a materials requisition as shown in Exhibit 7–4.

Note that the **materials requisition form** indicates the job on which the material is to be used, the type of material issued, the account to be charged (Work in Process for direct materials and Manufacturing Overhead for indirect materials or supplies), and the signature of someone authorized to draw materials from the storeroom. This source document will result in the following entry:

```
(2)   1/6   Work in Process      450
                 Materials                    450
```

Again, as in entry (1) on January 5, control accounts are affected by entry (2). First, the Work in Process account is debited or increased and Ma-

EXHIBIT 7–4

Materials Requisition Form

Requisition No. _1078_			Job No. _21_
Date _1/6/86_			
Account charged _Work in Process_			
Authorized by _Harry Wolfe_			

Description	Quantity	Unit cost	Total cost
3/4" x 4' x 8' Oak	10 sheets	45	450.⁰⁰

terials is credited or decreased. As we learned in entry (1), if control accounts are increased or decreased, their supporting subsidiary ledgers must also be updated. We are already familiar with the subsidiary ledger supporting the materials account (the materials ledger cards), so that record will be updated first. Using a copy of the materials requisition, we enter the information on the materials ledger card for $3/4'' \times 4' \times 8'$ oak plywood sheets as indicated in Exhibit 7–3 on January 6.

Just as materials ledger cards are subsidiary records for the materials account, **job order cost sheets** are subsidiary records for the Work in Process control account. Exhibit 7–5 is an example of a job order cost sheet.

The job order cost sheet will be used to accumulate costs applicable to each job started in the factory. The entry in the materials section of Exhibit 7–5 (the job order cost sheet for Job No. 21) on page 206 used a copy of Exhibit 7–4 (Materials Requisition No. 1078) as the source document for making the entry on the job cost sheet. If our record keeping is up to date, we now have a document that shows all of the costs that have been charged to Job No. 21 or to any other job that is in process in the factory.

We have now illustrated the source documents and accounts that apply to the use of direct materials in the manufacturing process. You may wish to review Exhibits 7–1 and 7–2 to be sure you understand the accounting for materials in the job order cost system before moving on to accounting for labor.

Labor

Exhibit 7–6 presents the detail of the documents, control accounts, and subsidiary ledgers associated with accounting for labor incurred in a factory or production setting. It is suggested that you review this exhibit (page 207) before proceeding with the discussion that follows.

EXHIBIT 7–5

Job Order Cost Sheet

			Job Cost Sheet			

Job No. _____21_____   Date started _____1/6/86_____

Contractor ___J. Weitz Co___   Date completed _____1/10_____

Customer ___Spec Homes___

Address ___5208 Boulder___

Materials			Direct labor			Manufacturing overhead		
Date	Req. No.	Amount	Date	Number	Amount	Hours	Rate	Amount
1/6	1078	450.00	1/6	1254	32	4	2.50	10.00
			1/7	1256	32	4		10.00
			1/7	1260	32	4		10.00
			1/7	1262	16	2		5.00
			1/8	1266	32	4		10.00

Summary of Costs

Direct materials $ 450.00

Direct labor   144.00

Applied overhead   45.00

TOTAL $ 639.00

Many of you have no doubt worked for a factory or a business where you had to clock in in the morning or beginning of a shift and clock out at the end of the day or shift. You might also have worked for a smaller contractor where you manually filled in a clock card. The **clock card** gives a record of time spent on the job and is necessary for the preparation of payroll checks for employees working by the hour. A manually prepared clock card for an employee of our cabinet builder is shown in Exhibit 7–7 on page 208.

Each day of the week Mr. Beech fills in his clock card with the hours worked. At the end of the week, the payroll department (or the accountant in a smaller company) will complete the card by determining the total hours and the total gross pay (including the overtime premium of $8.00) as Ex-

EXHIBIT 7–6
Labor Document and Cost Flows
Job Order Costing

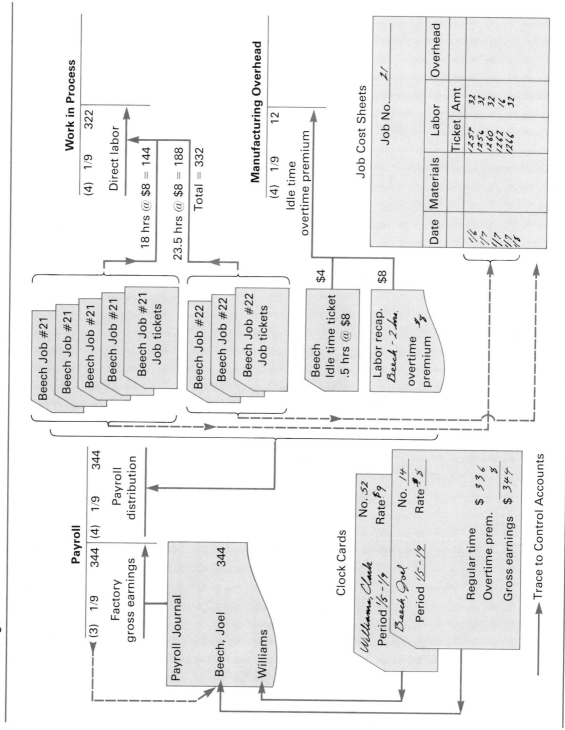

EXHIBIT 7—7
Clock Card

Name _Beech, Joel_				Employee No. _14_			
Pay period _1/5 - 1/9_				Pay rate/hr. _$8.00_			

	A.M.		P.M.		Overtime		Total
Date	In	Out	In	Out	In	Out	hours
1/5	8:00	12:00	1:01	5:02			8
1/6	7:59	12:00	12:59	5:01			8
1/7	7:58	12:01	1:00	5:03	7:00	9:00	10
1/8	8:01	12:02	1:01	5:02			8
1/9	8:00	12:00	1:00	5:00			8

Regular time _42_ hrs @ _$8.00_ $ _336.00_
Overtime premium _2_ hrs @ _$4_   _8.00_
Gross earnings $ _344.00_

hibit 7—7 has been extended and summarized. This document becomes the basis for making an entry in the payroll journal at the end of the pay period. We are not illustrating the payroll journal. The payroll journal merely lists all employees, their gross pay, deductions, and net pay. For our job order cost system, we are concerned with gross pay—the cost associated with having the employee in the factory or on the production job for the pay period. The amount of the deductions from the employee's pay and who is to receive those deductions is a matter for the payroll department or the financial accountants to handle.

The payroll journal for the factory will become the basic document used to record the gross earnings or payroll for the period 1/5 to 1/9 for our cabinet builder. This total covers all the factory or production employees, but we are going to illustrate one employee only. You can imagine that in practice the entries would be the same except that the dollar amounts would be much larger. The entry to record the earnings for the week would be

(3)	1/9	Payroll	344	
		Withholdings (assumed)		154
		Cash		190

As illustrated in Exhibit 7–6, this entry is posted as a debit to the Payroll account. The detail underlying the Payroll account comes from the payroll journal. In turn, the clock cards are the source of payroll data going into the payroll journal. The payroll journal contains gross earnings for all employees as well as other payroll related information.

We have now accumulated the costs associated with production labor. The next step is to allocate or distribute the labor costs to the appropriate jobs or to manufacturing overhead. At this point we do not know whether Joel Beech worked on Job No. 21 in the cabinet factory, worked on some other job, or was not productively engaged. When we developed the general model for determining the cost of producing a product (in Chapter 6), we indicated that production workers would be required to fill out job tickets each day. These **job tickets** would indicate what job(s) was being worked on each day. A ticket for Joel Beech is illustrated below as Exhibit 7–8.

The job ticket serves two purposes. First, it indicates how the labor costs should be allocated — that is, what job should be charged with particular direct labor costs. If the employee is idle, he will fill out an idle time ticket (a job ticket that might be a different color) to indicate that during the time shown on the idle time ticket the employee was not working on any particular job. Idle time is typically charged to Manufacturing Overhead. The job tickets would be sorted each day by job so that entries could be made on the job cost sheets for the direct labor cost, and the tickets can then be accumulated so that once a week a summary entry could be made to distribute the labor costs to the proper accounts.

A second purpose served by the job tickets is one of control. All job and idle time tickets would be added for each day for each employee, and the total time checked against the total time that each employee shows on the clock card for that day. If the two do not reconcile, the employee and his supervisor would need to be able to explain the discrepancy.

EXHIBIT 7–8

Job Ticket

Job Ticket No. _1254_	Date _1/6_
Employee No. _14_	Name _J. Beech_
Job No. _21_	Account _Work in Process_
Operation _Cutting/Gluing_	Rate/hour _$8.00_
Start time _8:00 A.M._	Stop time _12:00_
Hours on job _4_	Amount $ _32.00_

We have illustrated a manually prepared job ticket. There could, of course, be many variations of recording time on the job ticket. It might be done by designing the ticket so that time could be entered from a typical time clock, that is, the clock would mechanically punch the time on the job ticket when inserted into the clock. In modern computerized factories, the employee might go to a terminal, insert his badge in a slot in the terminal, and key in the job number and *start*. The computer would read his badge, identify him, and record the time that he started on the job. The same process would be followed for clocking off the job.

Let's say for the week ending January 9, Joel Beech had job tickets indicating 18 hours worked on Job No. 21, 23.5 hours worked on Job No. 22, and .5 hours of idle time. Remember also (from Exhibit 7–7) that Joel's rate was $8 per hour and that he had overtime premium pay of $8. The overtime premium consisted of 2 hours at $4 per hour. The entry to allocate or distribute the payroll cost for the week is shown below.

(4)	1/9	Work in Process (41.5 × $8)	332	
		Manufacturing Overhead		
		[(.5 × $8) + $8]	12	
		Payroll		344

Before we post the entry, remember again that we are dealing with control accounts. When the $332 is added to Work in Process as indicated in Exhibit 7–6, the subsidiary ledger for Work in Process must also be updated. As indicated previously, the subsidiary ledger for Work in Process is a file of job order cost sheets. The job order cost sheet for Job No. 21 would have been updated on a daily basis as shown in the direct labor section of the job cost sheet for Job No. 21 (Exhibit 7–5). Notice again that we have illustrated only one job ticket, but five job tickets have been entered on the job cost sheet for Job No. 21. The additional job tickets were entered to make the illustration more realistic. The other job tickets for the week that were applicable to Job No. 22 have also not been illustrated but would have been recorded on the job cost sheet for Job No. 22 in the same manner.

When Mr. Beech worked the two hours of overtime on January 7 (see his clock card in Exhibit 7–7), Job No. 21 was charged the straight time rate of $8 per hour. The overtime premium pay of $8 [(.5 × $8) × 2 hrs.] is part of the charge to Manufacturing Overhead as indicated in entry (4) above. The rationale for this approach is that the factory was generally behind in work and the overtime was necessary in order to try to catch up and meet scheduled deliveries. If this were so, there is no reason why Job No. 21 should be charged for all the overtime premium just because it happened to be the job going through the factory at the time there was an effort to speed up production in general. If, however, the sales staff had guaranteed a shorter than usual delivery time for this particular job and it was necessary to work overtime to meet that schedule, it would be correct to charge all of the overtime premium to that particular job.

We have indicated that entry (4) distributes the gross pay for the period to Work in Process as direct labor and therefore to particular jobs or to Manufacturing Overhead as indirect labor, overtime premium, or idle time. When the distribution entry is recorded, the Payroll account is, in fact, reduced to a zero balance. The Payroll account is used then as a type of clearing account — it is debited with the gross factory payroll to accumulate the total labor cost and then credited with that total factory pay when the distribution entry is made.

A further point needs to be made regarding the portion of the gross pay distributed to Manufacturing Overhead. We have illustrated the overtime premium and idle time cases but have not as yet indicated how we arrive at the other "indirect" labor amounts. You may have been wondering by now how we handle the supervisors, foremen, materials handlers, security guards, and janitors — these people will not be filling in job tickets or idle time tickets. This requires an analysis of payroll and a recapitulation of the total labor costs to determine the amount of pay applicable to these individuals, and this becomes the basis for the remainder of the distribution to the Manufacturing Overhead control account.

Exhibit 7–6 illustrates the posting of the overtime premium and idle time charges to the Manufacturing Overhead account but does not illustrate the subsidiary ledger for this control account. This will be illustrated in the section that follows.

Manufacturing Overhead

The accumulation phase of manufacturing overhead costs is fairly straightforward. As actual overhead costs are incurred, the manufacturing overhead control account is debited. Exhibit 7–9 (page 212) presents the detail of the documents, control accounts, and subsidiary records for the accounting for manufacturing overhead in a job order cost system.

We have already covered two sources of actual manufacturing overhead costs — the use of indirect materials and/or supplies covered in the section on materials, and the use of indirect labor, overtime premium, and idle time covered in the preceding section on labor. Some other sources of manufacturing overhead for our cabinet factory would be from invoices received from outside vendors illustrated in the following list with some assumed dollar amounts:

Utilities (water, light, heat, power)	$ 4,000
Property taxes	3,500
Repairs	1,400
Equipment rental	1,200
Miscellaneous expenses	400
Total	$10,500

The following summary entry would be made to record these costs at the end of January:

(5)	1/31	Manufacturing Overhead Control	10,500	
		Accounts Payable		10,500

EXHIBIT 7–9
Manufacturing Overhead   Document and Cost Flows
Job Order Costing

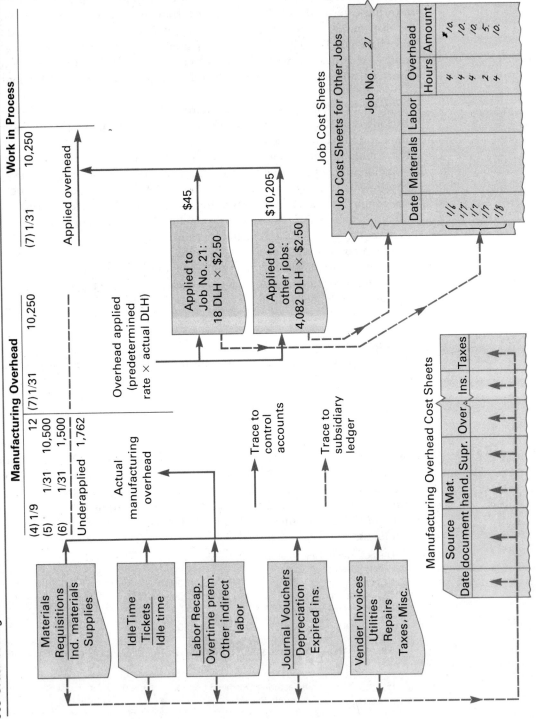

Exhibit 7–9 illustrates this amount posted to the Manufacturing Overhead Control account as entry (5). Other sources of manufacturing overhead would be from internal transfers. Examples would be journal vouchers or special memos from the chief accountant to record items such as depreciation and expiration of prepaid insurance. The entry to record such items at the end of the month of January is given below.

(6)	1/31	Manufacturing Overhead Control	1,500	
		Accumulated Depreciation – Bldg.		500
		Accumulated Depreciation – Equip.		600
		Prepaid Insurance		400

The entry has been posted to the Manufacturing Overhead control account as entry (6) in Exhibit 7–9. Once again, if the manufacturing overhead account is a control account, there must be some type of subsidiary ledger that will give us the detail of the costs. Notice that entries (5) and (6) are summary type entries and, therefore, if we merely look at the manufacturing overhead account we do not know the breakdown of the total costs listed there. The subsidiary ledger for the manufacturing overhead control account may be nothing more than a spreadsheet that gives a breakout of the summary entries in the control account along with the source documents supporting the various amounts. Separate subsidiary ledger accounts or spreadsheets should be kept for each department or organizational unit incurring manufacturing overhead costs. Exhibit 7–10 illustrates a possible manufacturing overhead expense analysis sheet.

The grand total of the columns of the **manufacturing overhead expense analysis sheet** should agree with the total actual charges to the Manufacturing Overhead control account. If the factory is departmentalized, there would be a manufacturing overhead expense analysis sheet for each department.

We now have a system for accumulating the actual manufacturing overhead costs incurred by the cabinet builder. The next step, as in the case of direct materials and direct labor, is to allocate these overhead costs to

EXHIBIT 7–10

Manufacturing Overhead Expense Analysis Sheet

Date	Source Document	Material Handling	Supervision	Overtime	Idle Time	Other Labor	Repairs	Depr.	Util.	Ins.	Taxes
1/9	Idle time ticket				4						
1/9	Labor recap	xx	xx	8		xx					
1/31	Invoice						1400		4000		3500
1/31	Journal voucher							1100		400	
Totals											

specific jobs. In the preceding chapter we developed a system for applying manufacturing overhead. You might want to review that section at this time. Remember that we said that we could not wait until the end of the accounting period to determine the total actual amount of overhead incurred and then allocate it to the different jobs passing through the factory during the year. That might mean that management would not know the cost of producing a job until long after it had been sold. We solved that problem by the use of a predetermined overhead application rate. This rate is established at the beginning of the period by estimating the amount of overhead cost expected to be incurred during the year and dividing this estimate by some estimated base common to all jobs, such as square feet of wood used or direct labor hours worked. As work progresses during the year, overhead is allocated to each job by multiplying the square feet of wood used or the direct labor hours worked on each job by the predetermined rate set at the beginning of the period. This process of overhead application made it possible for us to know the approximate cost of a job at its completion date.

If we follow the illustration used in the preceding chapter where we developed a predetermined rate of $2.50 per direct labor hour, and if we assumed that 4,100 direct labor hours were worked during the month of January, the summary entry to apply overhead would be

(7)	1/31	Work in Process ($2.50 × 4,100)	10,250	
		Manufacturing Overhead Control		10,250

The total overhead applied has been entered in the Work in Process account on Exhibit 7–9 as entry (7). This, of course, represents the total overhead applied for the month of January and applies to all the jobs that were being worked on during the month. Remember again that Work in Process is a control account, so that we need to be aware that the subsidiary ledger (the job cost sheets) is affected by this activity. The entry we have made in (7) is a monthly summary entry — the job cost sheets are updated on a daily basis. As we post each job ticket for direct labor, we would also apply overhead on the cost sheet on the basis of direct labor hours indicated on the job ticket. It also would be acceptable, and more convenient, to wait until the job is complete and make one entry on the job cost sheet to apply all overhead; that is, for Job No. 21 we could add the direct labor hours and take this sum of 18 hours times the predetermined rate of $2.50 and apply $45 of overhead at the completion of the job instead of applying overhead each time a job ticket was recorded on the cost sheet. The remaining $12,205 of applied overhead not allocated to Job No. 21 will be similarly applied to each job cost sheet for each of the jobs worked on during January.

Notice in Exhibit 7–9 that the Manufacturing Overhead control account has a debit balance of $1,762 at the end of January. Overhead is thus underapplied by $1,762 at this point. The period covered has been one month only, and the period used in calculating the predetermined rate was one year. It could be that the utility bill is unusually high in January and that the property taxes were paid and recorded in one lump sum during January instead of being accrued over some period of time. On the other hand, it may be that January is a month of typically low activity and it is expected that actual overhead would exceed the overhead applied during that month. At any rate, we hope by the end of the year that manufacturing overhead applied is close to the amount of actual overhead incurred. If it is not, we must close out the under- or overapplied overhead to Cost of Goods Sold or allocate it among inventories of Work in Process and Finished Goods along with Cost of Goods Sold. These procedures were well developed in the preceding chapter. If necessary, we suggest that you turn to the preceding chapter and review that section at this time.

Specific Document and Cost Flows — Completion of Product to Sales

We have now traced the documents and cost flows to the point that we have product in the factory that has been completed and is ready for transfer to the finished goods storeroom. Job No. 21 was completed on January 10, 19X6. Technically, Job No. 21 is a special order job and would be shipped directly to the customer site, but we are going to treat it as a normal stock item so that you can see all the documents and cost flows for a normal stock item. Exhibit 7–11 (page 216) illustrates the detail of documents, control accounts, and subsidiary records affected as the product moves from the factory to the customer.

When Job No. 21 is completed, it is sent to the finished goods storeroom. We know that if the product is no longer in the factory, the costs associated with the product should be transferred from Work in Process to Finished Goods. The question then becomes, "How many *dollars* should be transferred out of the factory to finished goods?" You may have already figured out the answer. We used a job cost sheet for Job No. 21 and recorded on it all of the costs that we allocated to that job. Now that the job is complete, we merely need to summarize all of the Direct Materials, Direct Labor, and Manufacturing Overhead associated with the job to know how much it cost to complete Job No. 21. The costs have been summarized on the job cost sheet for Job No. 21 in Exhibit 7–5, and the total amounts to $639. We now have the document and the numbers to make the following entry:

    (8)   1/10   Finished Goods   639
                       Work in Process   639

The posting of entry (8) has been completed on Exhibit 7–11. Notice that the job cost sheet for Job No. 21 is the source document used as support for the entry. Now that costs have been transferred from the control account, Work in Process, the subsidiary ledger must also reflect that fact. Remember that our subsidiary ledger for Work in Process was a file of job order cost sheets. What we need to do now is remove the job cost sheet for Job No. 21 from the active "in process" file and put it in an inactive "completed" file. In other words, our subsidiary ledger for Work in Process is now going to con-

EXHIBIT 7–11

Document and Cost Flows
Completion of Product to Sales
Job Order Costing

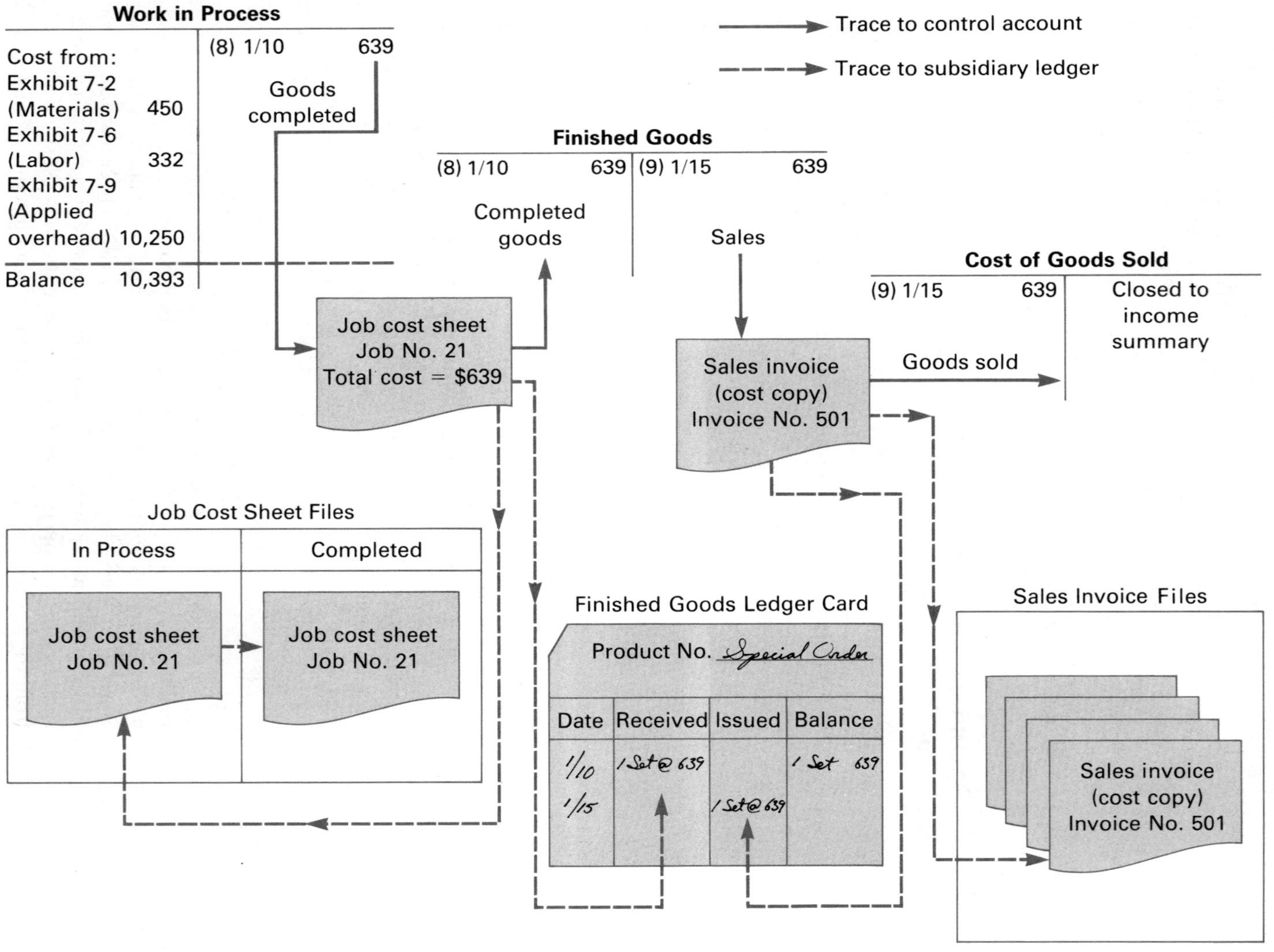

→ Trace to control account

⇢ Trace to subsidiary ledger

Work in Process

(8) 1/10	639

Cost from:
Exhibit 7-2
(Materials) 450
Exhibit 7-6
(Labor) 332
Exhibit 7-9
(Applied
overhead) 10,250

Balance 10,393

Goods completed

Job cost sheet
Job No. 21
Total cost = $639

Job Cost Sheet Files

In Process	Completed
Job cost sheet Job No. 21	Job cost sheet Job No. 21

Finished Goods

(8) 1/10	639	(9) 1/15	639
			639

Completed goods

Sales

Sales invoice
(cost copy)
Invoice No. 501

Finished Goods Ledger Card

Product No. *Special Order*

Date	Received	Issued	Balance
1/10	1 Set @ 639		1 Set @ 639
1/5		1 Set @ 639	1 Set 639

Cost of Goods Sold

(9) 1/15	639		Closed to income summary

Goods sold

Sales Invoice Files

Sales invoice
(cost copy)
Invoice No. 501

sist of a file of jobs that are not yet complete. The file for completed jobs will be for future reference only. On Exhibit 7–11 we have indicated that the cost sheet for Job No. 21 has been moved to the completed file. It should be mentioned that the total cost of all jobs completed for the period represents the cost of goods manufactured for the period.

The Work in Process control account will have a balance at the end of the period if any work is still on the floor of the factory. The total value of that work in process inventory should be the total of the job cost sheets in the "in process" file, which should also, of course, agree with the balance in the Work in Process account. The work in process balance at the end of the period will be included in the current asset section of the company's balance sheet as well as being shown on the schedule of cost of goods manufactured.

The $639 added to the Finished Goods control account must also be reflected in a subsidiary ledger. We used materials ledger cards as the subsidiary ledger for the Materials account. It would seem appropriate to use **finished goods ledger cards** as the subsidiary ledger for the Finished Goods control account. Exhibit 7–12 illustrates how the job order cost sheet for Job No. 21 is used to update the finished goods ledger card for the cabinets finished on Job No. 21.

Let's say that the cabinets were sold on January 15 (even though we know they were technically already sold at the time that they were ordered) and that the selling price was $1,200. Let us also say that this information was captured on Sales Order No. 501. Multiple copies could be made of the sales order, and one of the copies retained by the cabinet builder could be a copy reflecting the cost of the cabinets from Job No. 21. You have no doubt seen copies of sales invoices where a cross-hatched column obviously has some printing in it that is illegible. What has probably happened is just what we are

EXHIBIT 7–12
Finished Goods Ledger Card

		Received			Issued			Balance		
			Unit	Total		Unit	Total		Unit	Total
Date	Reference	Qty	cost	cost	Qty	cost	cost	Qty	cost	cost
1/10	Job Order 21	1-Set	639	639				1-Set	639	639.00
1/15	S 501				1-Set	639	639			

Item *Cabinets for 5208 Boulder* Location *Bay 15*

talking about. The cost of the items has been entered on the form but will be legible only on one or two copies where the column was clear prior to printing. These copies would be retained by the seller, and one of these could then be used as the source document supporting entry (9).

(9)	1/15	Cost of Goods Sold	639	
		Finished Goods		639

The entry has been posted on Exhibit 7–11. Now that $639 has been removed from the finished goods storeroom, we will use a copy of the sales invoice to update the finished goods ledger card for the item. This has been indicated on both Exhibit 7–11 and 7–12. Because we have followed through on one job only, our Finished Goods control account and subsidiary ledger indicate a zero balance at the end of January. If some production is for stock, we normally would expect a balance in finished goods inventory at the end of a period. If there were a balance, it would be reflected as a current asset on the balance sheet of the company at the end of the period and also would be shown in the cost of goods sold section of the income statement.

Entry (9) has indicated a debit to Cost of Goods Sold. Remember that when we use a perpetual inventory system and record a sale, two entries are necessary. One entry records the sale at its selling price debiting Accounts Receivable and crediting Sales. We will again let the financial accountants record that entry. Our concern is with the *cost* side of the transaction, and that is what has been recorded. The sales invoice has not been illustrated because all of you have seen a sales invoice of one kind or another. Note again that the Cost of Goods Sold is a control type account, meaning that there must be a subsidiary ledger of some kind for detail. We are suggesting, and have illustrated in Exhibit 7–11, that the subsidiary ledger could be merely a file of the costed sales invoices. Of the six control accounts illustrated in Exhibit 7–1, Cost of Goods Sold is the only expense account. Its balance is closed to income summary at the end of the accounting period and has a zero balance at the beginning of the next period. This suggests that its subsidiary ledger will also begin anew each year. The file of costed sales invoices will be labeled as the prior year sales invoices and a new file begun for the current year. Because Cost of Goods Sold is an *expense* account, it will appear on the company's income statement only.

Summary

Determination of the unit cost of manufacturing a product requires the assembling of information regarding costs incurred and output achieved. The information system designed to produce this information must "fit" the manufacturing process. A job order cost system is designed for those manufacturing situations where units of product differ from each other such as the building of custom cabinets for houses or special order agricultural equipment. A process costing system is designed for those manufacturing situations where a basically homogeneous product flows evenly through production on a fairly continuous basis, such as the manufacture of paint, textiles, or chemicals.

The design of the information system also includes the design of documents so that information is properly captured and proper authorization is obtained and retained for audit, analysis, and management control purposes.

The job order costing system required the use of six control accounts. The materials account shows purchases of materials and supplies supported by purchase invoices and receiving reports with approval documentation. Entries reflecting issues of materials from this account are authorized and documented by the use of materials requisitions. These withdrawals can result in direct materials being charged to Work in Process or indirect materials and/or supplies charged to Manufacturing Overhead. The subsidiary ledger supporting the Materials control account is the materials ledger cards.

Debits to the Payroll account represent the total or gross factory wages for the period and are supported by the payroll journal. Credits to the payroll account represent distributions of the total payroll. Job tickets are used to obtain the detail necessary to charge Work in Process for direct labor. Idle time tickets and labor recapitulations are used to support the charges to Manufacturing Overhead for idle time charges, overtime premium, and all other indirect labor. The Payroll account should be "cleared out" after the distribution entry.

Manufacturing Overhead is debited for actual overhead costs incurred. These charges are supported by idle time tickets, labor recaps, vendor invoices, or internally generated journal vouchers. The detail of the actual overhead costs summarized in the control account is shown in the manufacturing overhead expense analysis sheets. Manufacturing Overhead is applied to Work in Process (production) using a predetermined rate developed by dividing the estimated overhead expenses for the period by the estimated activity base such as direct labor hours, materials used, or direct labor cost.

Because estimates are used in the determination of the predetermined rate, actual overhead costs may be more or less than the amount of overhead applied, resulting in under- or overapplied overhead. This balance in the control account is closed to Cost of Goods Sold or allocated among Cost of Goods Sold, Finished Goods, and Work in Process.

The above activity results in charges to Work in Process for direct materials, direct labor, and manufacturing overhead. The subsidiary ledger for the control account is the file of job order cost sheets. As goods are completed and sent to the warehouse, costs are transferred from Work in Process to Finished Goods. The subsidiary ledger for the Finished Goods control account is the finished goods ledger cards.

Finally, as goods are sold, the sales invoice is the documentation for the sale and is the basis for the entry transferring costs from Finished Goods to Cost of Goods Sold. A file of costed sales invoices provides the detail of the charges to the Cost of Goods Sold control account. Of the six control accounts needed for the job order costing system, Cost of Goods Sold is the only expense account.

The chapter has illustrated a complete job order costing cycle with the appropriate documents and ledger accounts. Exhibit 7–13 is a summary of the entries in a job order cost cycle with the related source documents.

EXHIBIT 7–13
Job Order Cost Cycle Sample Entries

Transaction	Source Document	General Ledger Entry	Subsidiary Ledger
1. Purchase of materials	Approved purchase invoice and receiving report	Materials Accounts payable	Materials ledger cards
2. Issue direct materials	Materials requisition	Work in Process Materials	Job order cost sheets Materials ledger cards
3. Issue indirect materials or supplies	Materials requisition or purchase invoice	Mfg. Overhead Materials	Mfg. overhead exp. analysis sheets Materials ledger cards

4. Recording payroll	Payroll journal
	Clock cards
		Payroll
		  Withholdings
		  Cash
			Payroll journal
			Employee earnings records

5. Distribution of labor	Job tickets Idle time cards Labor recap.	Work in Process Mfg. Overhead Payroll	Job cost sheets Mfg. overhead exp. analysis sheets
6. Record employer payroll taxes	Journal voucher	Mfg. Overhead Payroll Tax Pay	Mfg. overhead exp. analysis sheets

7. Depreciation — factory equip. and building	Journal voucher (depr. schedule)	Mfg. Overhead
		  Acc. Depr. — Bldg.
		  Acc. Depr. — Equip.
			Mfg. overhead exp. analysis sheets

8. Utilities	Approved vendor invoice	Mfg. Overhead Accounts Payable	Mfg. overhead exp. analysis sheets
9. Expired insurance	Journal voucher (lapsing sched.)	Mfg. Overhead Prepaid Ins.	Mfg. overhead exp. analysis sheets
10. Overhead applied to product	Predetermined rate calc. Job tickets	Work in Process Mfg. Overhead	Job cost sheets
11. Completion of product	Job cost sheet	Finished Goods Work in Process	Finished goods ledger cards Job cost sheets
12. Sale of product	Sales invoice (costed copy)	Cost of Goods Sold Finished Goods	File of sales invoices Finished goods ledger cards

Key Terms

Absorption (full) costing   is any of the several systems in which fixed manufacturing overhead — as well as direct materials, direct labor, and variable manufacturing overhead — is charged to product.

Clock cards   give a record of time at work for each employee.

Finished goods ledger cards   comprise the subsidiary ledger for Finished Goods. Basis for this information is completed job order cost cards.

Job order cost sheets   comprise the subsidiary ledger for Work in Process. Direct materials, direct labor, and (applied) manufacturing overhead for each job are charged to a job order cost sheet.

Job order cost system   comprises those systems where costs are tracked by specific job. Each customer order is generally discrete and different from other customer orders.

Job tickets   are filled in for direct labor time performed on each job by the employee.

Manufacturing overhead expense analysis sheet   is used to keep track of actual manufacturing overhead items classified by type of cost incurred for each organizational unit.

Materials ledger card   is the subsidiary ledger record tracking purchases and dispositions of materials into production.

Materials requisition form   is the form used to draw direct materials from the storeroom for each particular job.

Process cost system   is one where basically homogeneous units flow through production on a fairly continuous basis.

Questions

Q7–1   In a costing system environment, what is meant by a *cost object?* What is the cost object in a job order costing system?

Q7–2   Describe the difference between job order costing and process costing.

Q7–3   What is the rationale supporting the use of process costing instead of job order costing for product costing purposes?

Q7–4   What is the primary objective in job order costing?

Q7–5   Progressive Company uses the perpetual inventory system throughout its job order costing system. What "inventory" accounts is Progressive likely to have for its costing system?

Q7–6   Trace the flow of manufacturing costs through the control accounts into cost of goods sold. Which control accounts are primarily for cost accumulation as opposed to cost allocation?

Q7–7   How does a company "control" the issuance of materials from the storeroom to the factory?

Q7–8   Distinguish between a clock card and job tickets pointing out the purpose served by each.

Q7–9   Costs such as direct materials and direct labor can easily be traced to and identified with a job. How are *indirect* costs identified with jobs?

Q7–10   What purpose is served by job cost sheets, and what is their relationship to work in process inventory?

Q7–11   What is meant by *distributing payroll?* What entry is made when payroll is distributed? (Assume that there is both direct and indirect labor.)

Q7–12   What journal entry is made to record the transfer of jobs completed in the factory to the finished goods warehouse? How is the dollar amount determined for the entry?

Q7–13   If a portion of materials previously issued for use on a job is returned to the storeroom, what supporting document would be used as the authority for making a journal entry? Make the journal entry, and identify which subsidiary records would be affected by your entry.

Q7–14   At the end of each period, what should be the balance in the payroll account? Why?

Q7–15   Which document would be used as support for recording a sale of product? What entry(ies) is made at the time of sale? What subsidiary ledgers are affected?

Q7–16   The Schedule of Cost of Goods Manufactured shows total manufacturing costs to be $290,000 and the cost of goods manufactured to be $250,000. If the company completed twenty jobs during the period, how can we determine the unit costs associated with *one* of the jobs?

Q7–17   How is manufacturing overhead associated with a particular job in a job order costing system? What accounts and subsidiary ledgers are affected when manufacturing overhead is associated with a particular job?

Q7–18   Penway Company uses a job order costing system and has three producing departments, each of which uses its own predetermined overhead application rate. Is Penway likely to have underapplied or overapplied overhead at the end of the accounting period under these circumstances? Why? Where will it be found in the ledger?

Q7–19   A job was still in process at the end of a period, and the job cost sheet shows that $5,000 of direct materials has been added to the job along with $8,000 of direct labor. The company applies manufacturing overhead on the basis of 150% of direct labor. If this were the only job in process in the factory, what would be the balance in the Work in Process account?

Q7–20   At the beginning of a period the job cost sheet for Job No. 15 indicated that $3,000 of direct materials had been issued to the job last period and $4,000 of manufacturing overhead had been applied. The job was completed during the period requiring $5,000 more in materials and the application of $8,000 of manufacturing overhead. Overhead is applied on the basis of 80% of direct labor cost. The job consisted of 1,000 units. What was the *unit* cost of product from Job No. 15?

Exercises

E7–1 **Job order costing or process costing.** For each of the following manufacturing businesses, indicate whether job order costing or process costing is more appropriate:

  a. An oil refinery
  b. A processor of instant mashed potatoes
  c. A ready-mix cement plant
  d. A "one-size fits all" hosiery mill
  e. A custom home builder
  f. A textbook publisher
  g. An aircraft repair and maintenance center
  h. A manufacturer of recreational sail boats
  i. A manufacturer of life-vests for various retail chains
  j. A fertilizer processing company

E7–2 **Total job costs — missing direct labor cost.** Woodbury uses a job order cost system and applies manufacturing overhead to production orders on the basis of direct labor cost. The overhead rates for 19X7 are 20% for department A and 50% for department B. Job No. 321, started and completed during 19X7, was charged with the following costs:

	Department	
	A	*B*
Direct materials	$25,000	$ 5,000
Direct labor	?	30,000
Manufacturing overhead	40,000	?

Required: What are the total manufacturing costs associated with Job No. 321?

(CPA Adapted)

E7–3 **Direct materials cost missing in ending Work in Process.** Amfelt Corporation has a job order cost system. The following debits (credits) appeared in the general ledger account, Work in Process, for the month of January 19X7:

January 1, balance	$ 12,000
January 31, direct materials	40,000
January 31, direct labor	30,000
January 31, manufacturing overhead	27,000
January 31, to finished goods	(100,000)

Amfelt applies overhead to production at a predetermined rate of 90% based on the direct labor cost. Job No. 543, the only job still in process at the end of January 19X7, has been charged with manufacturing overhead of $2,250.

Required: What was the amount of direct materials charged to Job No. 543?

(CPA Adapted)

E7–4 **Reconciling time cards and job/idle-time tickets.** Randy Akers works as a machinist for Albany Manufacturing Company. One of Randy's clock cards in March 19X7 contained the selected information shown on the next page.

	In	Out	In	Out
March 14	7:59A	12:02P	12:58P	6:02P
March 15	8:00A	12:00P	12:59P	7:00P

Randy had job tickets or idle-time tickets for the above two days as follows:

	On	Off
March 14:		
Job No. 10	8:00A	9:30A
Job No. 12	9:32A	12:00P
Job No. 12	1:00P	4:00P
Job No. 14	4:30P	6:00P
March 15:		
Job No. 14	8:02A	8:30A
Job No. 19	8:33A	12:30P
Job No. 19	1:02P	2:30P
Job No. 23	2:35P	5:58P

Required:

1. Assume that your task is to reconcile clock cards with job tickets and idle-time tickets. Is there a problem with Randy's time data? If so, what?
2. If there are discrepancies, what are some possible explanations?

E7–5   **Application of manufacturing overhead.** Plasticon utilizes a job order costing system and applies overhead on the basis of direct labor hours. When establishing the predetermined overhead application rate, management estimated that 100,000 direct labor hours would be worked and $350,000 of manufacturing overhead costs would be incurred.

During the year, the company actually worked 110,000 direct labor hours. At the end of the period the company's Manufacturing Overhead and Work in Process accounts contained the following amounts:

Manufacturing Overhead

Indirect labor	90,000	?
Indirect materials	60,000	
Insurance	20,000	
Utilities	48,000	
Repairs & maintenance	36,000	
Depreciation	100,000	

Work in Process

Direct materials	400,000	Finished goods	1,200,000
Direct labor	950,000		
	?		

Required:

1. Determine the amount for the question marks in each of the above accounts. What are these amounts called?
2. Determine the amount of underapplied or overapplied overhead for the year.
3. Make the journal entry that would most likely be made to close out the manufacturing overhead account at the end of the year.

E7–6   **Journal entries for job order costing cycle.** Kolinski Company manufactures toys and uses a job order costing system. The following transactions occurred during August 19X7:

a. Raw materials purchased (on account), $85,000
b. Direct materials issued to the factory, $90,000
c. Indirect materials issued during the month, $10,000
d. Factory payroll costs for the month, $120,000 ($100,000 direct, $20,000 indirect)
e. Other manufacturing overhead costs incurred during the month, $55,000 (for simplicity assume that Accounts Payable is credited)
f. Kolinski applies manufacturing overhead to production on the basis of $10 per direct labor hour and worked 8,000 direct labor hours during the month.
g. Jobs completed and transferred to the finished goods warehouse during the month, $250,000
h. Toys that had cost $260,000 to manufacture were shipped to customers during the month. Kolinski prices its toys on the basis of 200% of the cost. All of Kolinski's sales are made on account.

Required:
1. Prepare journal entries to record the transactions for the month.
2. Prepare T-accounts for Manufacturing Overhead, Work in Process, and Finished Goods. Post the appropriate entries to these accounts. (Work in Process and Finished Goods had beginning balances of $5,000 and $15,000, respectively.) Indicate the ending balance in each of these accounts.

E7–7 **Total job cost with departmental overhead rates.** Tammy Corporation uses a job order costing system and has two producing departments, M and A. Budgeted manufacturing costs for 19X7 are as follows:

	Department	
	M	A
Direct materials	$700,000	$100,000
Direct labor	200,000	800,000
Manufacturing overhead	600,000	400,000

The actual material and labor costs charged to Job No. 234 during 19X7 were as follows:

Direct material		$25,000
Direct labor:		
Department M	$ 8,000	
Department A	12,000	20,000

Tammy applies manufacturing overhead to production orders on the basis of direct labor cost using departmental rates predetermined at the beginning of the year based on the annual budget.

Required: What are the total manufacturing costs associated with Job No. 234 for 19X7?

(CPA Adapted)

E7–8 **Journal entries based on information in job cost sheet.** Renuz Company started Job No. 29 on November 20, 19X7, and completed it on December 15 the following month. Renuz applies manufacturing overhead on the basis of direct labor cost and does so at the end of each month and as jobs are completed. The additional information listed on the next page is available in the job cost sheet for Job No. 29.

Direct materials:
11/20	$2,000	
12/10	500	
Total		$ 2,500

Direct labor:
11/21	$ 200	
11/28	1,000	
12/05	1,100	
12/12	900	
12/15	300	
Total		3,500

Manufacturing overhead:
11/30	1,440	
12/15	2,760	
Total		4,200
Total for Job No. 29		$10,200

Required:

1. Prepare the journal entries to record all transactions associated with Job No. 29 during December 19X7.
2. What was the predetermined manufacturing overhead rate used by Renuz Company?

E7–9 Control accounts and subsidiary ledgers. Selected transactions from a job order costing system are listed in the left-hand column of the table below. At the right are spaces to indicate the control accounts and the subsidiary ledgers or records that are affected by the transaction. The first transaction is filled in as an example.

	Control Account		Subsidiary Ledger	
Transaction	*Increase*	*Decrease*	*Increase*	*Decrease*
1. Purchased material	Materials Acct. Pay.		Mat. ledger card Acct. Pay. Ledger	
2. Issued direct material on Requisition No. 10				
3. Distributed payroll (both direct and indirect labor)				
4. Applied manufacturing overhead				
5. Return direct material to storeroom (previously issued on Requisition No. 10)				
6. Completed Job No. 30				

Required: Number your answer sheet from 1 to 6 and put headings on four columns similar to the preceding table. Fill in the appropriate control accounts and subsidiary ledgers or records to complete the table as illustrated by the first transaction.

E7–10 **Departmental overhead rates and job order costing.** Scott Manufacturing Company uses a job order costing system. There are two production departments, Cutting and Stamping, and a predetermined overhead application rate is used in each department. The Cutting Department bases its rate on direct labor hours, and the Stamping Department bases its rate on machine hours. The company made the following estimates at the beginning of the current year:

	Cutting	Stamping
Machine hours	8,000	53,000
Direct labor hours	32,000	4,000
Manufacturing overhead cost	$320,000	$424,000

Job No. 217 was started and completed during August, and the following information for each department is extracted from the job cost sheet:

	Cutting	Stamping
Machine hours	40	300
Direct labor hours	180	20
Direct materials	$1,800	–0–
Direct labor cost	$2,000	$260

Required:
1. What was the predetermined manufacturing overhead rate used by each producing department?
2. Compute the total cost of completing Job No. 217.
3. If Scott Manufacturing Company had used a plantwide predetermined overhead rate based on direct labor hours, would total cost of Job No. 217 have been significantly different? Would you expect this to be the case with all jobs completed by Scott Manufacturing? Why?

E7–11 **Journal entries and individual unit costs of a job.** Electric Motors, Incorporated, produces electric motors for various brand name suppliers. The customer furnishes specifications, and Electric Motors manufactures according to those specifications and places the customer's brand name on the motor. The company received an order from a customer in September for 1,000 one-half horse-power capacitor motors. The order was started through the plant on September 25 as Job No. 318.

During September, $20,000 of costs were charged to the job. Electric Motors worked on Job No. 318 exclusively during October, finishing the job on October 30. The company applies manufacturing overhead on the basis of direct labor hours. Estimates for the year were 100,000 direct labor hours and $650,000 of manufacturing overhead. The following activity took place during October:

a. Materials purchased on account, $60,000
b. Materials requisitioned by the factory, $50,000 (90% direct materials and 10% indirect)
c. Factory payroll costs, $30,000 (80% direct labor and 20% indirect)
d. Depreciation for the month, $4,000
e. Other manufacturing costs, $5,000 (assume a credit to Accounts Payable)
f. Direct labor hours worked, 2,400

Required: 1. Prepare journal entries to record all the activity for October.

2. What is the total cost of the job cost sheet for Job No. 318 at the completion of the job? What is the production cost for *one* of the motors in Job No. 318?

E7–12   **Cost of goods manufactured — overapplied or underapplied overhead.** Jackson Company uses a job order costing system. Manufacturing overhead is applied to production at a predetermined rate of 150% of direct labor cost. Any overapplied or underapplied overhead is closed to the Cost of Goods Sold account at the end of each month. Additional information is available as follows:

a. Job No. 101 was the only job in process at January 31, 19X7, with accumulated costs as follows:

Direct materials	$4,000
Direct labor	2,000
Applied manufacturing overhead	3,000
Total	$9,000

b. Job Nos. 102, 103, and 104 were started during February.
c. Direct materials requisitions for February totaled $26,000.
d. Direct labor cost of $20,000 was incurred for February.
e. Actual factory overhead was $32,000 for February.
f. The only job still in process at February 28, 19X7, was Job No. 104, with costs of $2,800 for direct materials and $1,800 for direct labor.

Required: 1. Prepare a schedule of cost of goods manufactured for the month of February 19X7.

2. How much overapplied or underapplied overhead should be closed to the cost of goods sold account at February 28, 19X7?

(CPA Adapted)

Problems

P7–13   **Job order costing — journal entries and job costs.** Wallace Industries uses a job order costing system and charges work in process for the actual cost of direct materials and direct labor used, but uses a predetermined rate to charge manufacturing overhead to work in process. Wallace uses machine hours as the basis for applying overhead. When the predetermined rate was computed at the beginning of the year, Wallace had estimated manufacturing overhead for the year would be $56,000 and that 7,000 machine hours would be utilized.

The following information is available for August of the current year:

	Job No. 801	*Job No. 802*	*Job No. 803*
Work in process, August 1	$9,500	$7,500	$3,500
August production activity:			
Materials requisitioned	2,100	3,400	6,000
Direct labor costs	1,980	3,870	990
Direct labor rate per hour	$9	$9	$9
Machine hours	200	650	150

The actual manufacturing overhead cost incurred in August was $13,000.

Required:

1. Compute the predetermined overhead application rate.
2. Prepare journal entries to record the activity for the month of August.
3. Job Nos. 801 and 802 were completed during August. What was the cost of each job?
4. What is the balance of Work in Process at August 31?
5. If there was no balance in the Manufacturing Overhead account on August 1, what is its balance at August 31? Does the balance represent underapplied or overapplied overhead?

P7–14 **Journal entries, job cost sheets, and ending inventories.** Pfester Company uses a job order costing system and had the following inventories on May 1, 19X7:.

Raw Materials	$12,000
Work in Process	21,035
Finished Goods	20,000

The job cost sheets for the beginning work in process inventory indicated the following detail:

	Job Number		
	486	**487**	**488**
Direct material	$3,600	$2,700	$2,100
Direct labor	2,300	3,100	1,250
Applied manufacturing overhead	2,070	2,790	1,125
Totals	$7,970	$8,590	$4,475

The following information pertains to operational activity during May:

a. Materials purchased, $35,000
b. Job No. 489 was started during the month.
c. Materials requisitioned, $32,000. Of this amount, $2,800 was for indirect material. The remainder was distributed as follows:

Job No.	Amount
486	$5,400
487	7,500
488	9,200
489	7,100

d. Materials returned to the storeroom from factory, $800. These materials had been requisitioned for Job No. 489.
e. Factory payroll for the month, $34,900. Indirect labor made up $10,000 of the total payroll. The balance was distributed as follows:

Job No.	Amount
486	$5,700
487	6,000
488	8,200
489	5,000

f. The employer taxes and contributions related to the payroll, $5,235. The amount is treated as manufacturing overhead.
g. Adjusting entries made at the end of May recorded the expenses listed on the next page.

Depreciation	$2,500
Expired insurance	800

h. Bills (as yet unpaid) for other manufacturing overhead, $3,470
i. Pfester applies manufacturing overhead based on a predetermined rate of 90% of direct labor cost.
j. Job Nos. 486, 487, and 488 were completed during the month and transferred to the finished goods storeroom.
k. Job Nos. 486 and 487 were sold during May at a selling price based on 150% of the manufacturing cost.

Required:

1. Prepare skeleton job cost sheets and enter the beginning inventory data.
2. Journalize the May transactions and post to the job cost sheets where appropriate.
3. Prepare a schedule of the ending inventory balances. Pfester uses a FIFO perpetual inventory system. Be sure that you can support the Work in Process inventory with the detail by job.

P7–15 **Job order costing and applying overhead—multiple choice.** Maxwell Company uses a job order costing system for its production costs. A predetermined overhead application rate is used to apply overhead to individual jobs. A flexible budget was prepared for 19X7 (the current year) as follows:

Direct labor hours	100,000	120,000	140,000
Variable overhead costs	$325,000	$390,000	$455,000
Fixed overhead costs	216,000	216,000	216,000
Total overhead	$541,000	$606,000	$671,000

Management determined 120,000 direct labor hours as the expected level of activity for the year. The following information is for April 19X7. Job Nos. X7–50 and X7–51 were completed during the month.

Inventories April 1, 19X7:		
Raw materials and supplies	$ 10,500	
Work in process (Job No. X7–50)	54,000	
Finished goods	112,500	
Purchases of raw materials and supplies:		
Raw materials	$135,000	
Supplies	15,000	
Materials and supplies requisitioned for production:		
Job No. X7–50	$ 45,000	
Job No. X7–51	37,500	
Job No. X7–52	25,500	
Supplies	12,000	
Factory direct labor hours:		
Job No. X7–50		3,500 DLH
Job No. X7–51		3,000 DLH
Job No. X7–52		2,000 DLH
Labor costs:		
Direct labor wages	$ 51,000	
Indirect labor wages (4,000 hours)	15,000	
Supervisor salaries	6,000	

Building occupancy costs (heat, light, depreciation, etc.):

Factory facilities	$ 6,500
Sales offices	1,500
Administrative offices	1,000
Factory equipment costs:	
Power	$ 4,000
Repairs and maintenance	1,500
Depreciation	1,500
Other	1,000

Required: Answer the following multiple choice questions.

1. The predetermined overhead rate to be used to apply overhead to individual jobs during the year is
   (a) $5.41 per DLH.   (b) $5.05 per DLH.   (c) $3.25 per DLH.
   (d) $4.69 per DLH.   (e) none of these.

   Note: Without prejudice to your answer to 1, assume that the predetermined overhead rate is $4.50 per direct labor hour. Use this amount in answering 2 through 6.

2. The total cost of Job No. X7–50 is
   (a) $81,750.   (b) $142,750.   (c) $146,750.   (d) $135,750.
   (e) none of these.

3. The manufacturing overhead costs applied to Job No. X7–52 during April were:
   (a) $8,000.   (b) $47,500.   (c) $46,500.   (d) $9,000.
   (e) none of these.

4. The total amount of overhead applied to jobs during April was
   (a) $56,250.   (b) $38,250.   (c) $47,250.   (d) $29,250.
   (e) none of these.

5. Actual manufacturing overhead incurred during April was
   (a) $50,500.   (b) $47,500.   (c) $38,000.   (d)$41,500.
   (e) none of these.

6. At the end of the year, Maxwell Company had the following account balances:

Overapplied overhead	$ 1,000
Cost of goods sold	980,000
Work in process inventory	38,000
Finished goods inventory	82,000

The most common treatment of overapplied overhead would be to

a. Prorate it between Work in Process Inventory and Finished Goods Inventory.
b. Prorate it between Work in Process Inventory, Finished Goods Inventory, and Cost of Goods Sold.
c. Carry it as miscellaneous operating revenue on the income statement.
d. Credit it to Cost of Goods Sold.
e. None of these.

(CMA Adapted)

P7–16 **Job order costing and disposition of underapplied or overapplied overhead.** Rubin Industries uses a job order costing system and a predetermined manufacturing overhead rate based on machine hours. The estimated manufacturing overhead for 19X7 was $490,000, and the estimated machine hours were 70,000. On January 1, 19X7, Rubin had the inventories listed on the next page.

Raw materials and supplies	$25,000
Work in process (Job No. 42)	8,000
Finished goods	42,000

The following information pertains to the company's activities for the month of January 19X7:

a. Purchased raw materials on account, $80,000
b. Purchased supplies on account, $8,200
c. Issued raw materials to work in process, $72,000. These were distributed to jobs as follows:

Job No. 42	$20,000
Job No. 43	42,000
Job No. 44	10,000

d. Issued supplies to the factory, $4,000
e. Factory payroll totaled $120,000 for the month. The direct labor was distributed as follows:

Job No. 42	$35,000
Job No. 43	45,000
Job No. 44	20,000

f. Other manufacturing costs were

Utilities	$ 4,000
Repairs & maintenance	3,000
Miscellaneous	5,000
Depreciation	18,000

(Other than depreciation, the items required cash.)

g. The company used 5,800 machine hours. The hours used on each job in process were

Job No. 42	1,200 MH
Job No. 43	3,600 MH
Job No. 44	1,000 MH

h. Job Nos. 42 and 43 were completed.
i. Goods costing $123,600 were sold during the month.

Required:

1. Prepare journal entries to record the manufacturing activities of Rubin Industries for the month of January 19X7.
2. Prepare T-accounts for the Manufacturing Overhead, the inventory accounts, and Cost of Goods Sold. Enter beginning balances (where appropriate) and post the transactions for January.
3. Does the ending balance in the manufacturing overhead account represent underapplied or overapplied overhead? Prepare journal entries to dispose of the underapplied or overapplied overhead under the following two assumptions:
   a. It is written off to Cost of Goods Sold.
   b. It is allocated to Work in Process, Finished Goods, and Cost of Goods Sold. (Round calculations to two decimal places.)

P7–17   **Journal entries from job cost sheets.** Wallboom Company uses a job order costing system and applies manufacturing overhead using a predetermined rate based on a percentage of direct materials cost. During April 19X7 the company worked on three jobs—Job No. 183 was started in March, and Job Nos. 184 and 185 were started in April. Job Nos. 183 and 184 were completed during April; Job No. 185 was still in process at April 30. The actual manufacturing overhead cost incurred in April was $15,000. The balances in the inventory accounts on April 1 were

Materials	$ 7,000
Work in process	?
Finished goods	32,000

The following information is available from the job cost sheets for the three jobs:

	Job No. 183		Job No. 184		Job No. 185	
	March	April	March	April	March	April
Direct materials	$2,200	$3,700	–0–	$8,050	–0–	$2,850
Direct labor	3,600	2,500	–0–	8,150	–0–	3,300
Manufacturing overhead applied	2,420	?	–0–	?	–0–	?

Required:

1. Prepare T-accounts for the three inventory accounts above and for Manufacturing Overhead. Enter the balances as of April 1, 19X7, in the inventory accounts.
2. Prepare a summary journal entry to record the actual manufacturing overhead and post to the appropriate T-account. (Assume a credit to accounts payable.)
3. Prepare summary journal entries to record the issuance of direct material to the factory and the distribution of payroll (no indirect labor). Post to the appropriate T-accounts.
4. What is the amount of the predetermined overhead application rate? Use this rate and prepare a summary journal entry to apply manufacturing overhead for the month of April. Post to the appropriate T-account(s).
5. Prepare a summary journal entry to record the completion of Job Nos. 183 and 184. Post to the proper T-accounts.
6. What is the balance of Manufacturing Overhead, Work in Process, and Finished Goods? Does Work in Process reconcile with the subsidiary ledger? Explain.

P7–18 **Entries directly in T-accounts; schedule of cost of goods manufactured.** Famway Associates started the year 19X7 with the following trial balance:

	Debits	Credits
Cash	$ 12,000	
Accounts receivable	22,000	
Raw materials and supplies	15,000	
Work in process	21,000	
Finished goods	28,000	
Prepaid insurance	10,000	
Plant and equipment	350,000	
Accumulated depreciation		$145,000
Accounts payable		42,000
Capital stock		200,000
Retained earnings		71,000
Totals	$458,000	$458,000

Famway worked on Job No. 27 all year, completing it on December 31, 19X7. No other jobs were started during the year. The following transactions took place during 19X7:

a. Raw materials purchased on account, $75,000
b. Supplies purchased on account, $5,000
c. Raw materials and supplies requisitioned, $87,500 ($82,500 was direct materials, the remainder was supplies)
d. Cost for salaries and wages were as follows:

Direct labor	$102,000
Indirect labor	23,000
Sales salaries & commissions	55,000
Administrative salaries	42,000

e. Straight-line depreciation is based on the original cost of the plant and equipment using a ten-year life; 10% of the plant and equipment is used by sales and administration.
f. Unexpired insurance at December 31, 19X7, $2,000. Of the expired insurance, $2,000 was applicable to sales and administration.
g. Utility costs for the factory for the year, $15,000
h. Famway uses a predetermined rate of $2.50 per direct labor hour to apply manufacturing overhead to production. The company worked 33,000 direct labor hours during the year.
i. Goods with a manufacturing cost of $300,000 were sold for $450,000.
j. Miscellaneous selling expenses incurred, $14,000

Required:

1. Prepare T-accounts for those accounts required to provide information for preparing a schedule of cost of goods manufactured.
2. Enter beginning balances in the T-accounts you set up in (1) if they have any. Record the transactions for the year directly in the accounts. Key the entries in your accounts to the letter of the transaction (such as (a), (c), etc.). Record only those transactions necessary to provide information needed in the preparation of the schedule of costs of goods manufactured.
3. Is the manufacturing overhead underapplied or overapplied for the year? Make an entry to close out the underapplied or overapplied manufacturing overhead. (You needn't make an entry to Cost of Goods Sold if it is not necessary for the preparation of the schedule of cost of goods manufactured.)
4. What were the costs associated with Job No. 27 at its completion? Prepare a schedule of cost of goods manufactured for 19X7. Why does the total of cost of goods manufactured for the year equal the costs associated with Job No. 27 only?

P7–19   **Reconstructing journal entries from T-accounts — cost flows.** Selected accounts from the ledger of Sandstone Company for the year 19X7 are presented below:

Raw Materials and Supplies

Balance 1/1	15,000	19X7 credits	?
19X7 debits	150,000		
Balance 12/31	12,000		

Factory Payroll

19X7 debits	225,000	19X7 credits	?

Manufacturing Overhead

19X7 debits:		19X7 credits	?
Depreciation	55,000		
Insurance	24,000		
Utilities	36,000		
Maintenance	28,000		
Other	?		

Work in Process

Balance 1/1	20,000	19X7 credits	?
Direct materials	144,000		
Direct labor	205,000		
Other	?		
Balance 12/31	33,000		

Finished Goods

Balance 1/1	?	19X7 credits	?
19X7 debits	500,000		
Balance 12/31	30,000		

Cost of Goods Sold

19X7 debits	510,000		

Sandstone Company applies manufacturing overhead using a predetermined rate based on direct labor cost.

Required:

1. From the above information, prepare the journal entries that were made by Sandstone Company to
   a. Record the purchase and issuance of raw materials and supplies.
   b. Record the incurrence and distribution of factory labor.
   c. Record all the actual manufacturing overhead incurred during the year (credit accounts payable when necessary).
   d. Apply manufacturing overhead to production.
   e. Record the completion of jobs during the year.
   f. Record the sale of goods (cost of the sale only).

2. Is manufacturing overhead overapplied or underapplied? What rate does Sandstone use to apply overhead?

3. What was the beginning balance of Finished Goods inventory? If the ending balance of Work in Process consists of only one job that was started during 19X7 and direct labor costs of $12,000 have been used so far on the job, what are the amounts of direct material and manufacturing overhead associated with this job?

P7–20   **Incomplete data—knowledge of cost flows.** You have applied for a position in the management accounting department of the Relaxed Manufacturing Company and have an interview scheduled with the director of the department, George Wellington III. When you arrive for the interview, Mr. Wellington promptly informs you that he is "of the old school" and that he has a little test he gives all prospective employees in his department. It requires an understanding of job order costing and manufacturing cost flows in general. He advises you that you have no more than thirty minutes to answer the questions proposed in the test. At this point he leaves you in the conference room with the following information and directions and says he will be back in thirty minutes to pick up your answers.

Relaxed Company uses a job order costing system and uses a predetermined manufacturing overhead rate based on 120% of direct labor cost. The following selected accounts and entries in those accounts are provided for the month of August 19X7:

Raw Materials

Balance 8/1	10,000	
	120,000	

Manufacturing Overhead

Indirect materials	6,000	
Indirect labor	20,000	

Work in Process

Balance 8/1	4,960	
Direct materials	115,000	
Direct labor	62,000	

Finished Goods

Balance 8/1	30,000	

Relaxed Company worked on three jobs during August—Job Nos. 8, 9, and 10. Job No. 8 was in process at the beginning of August and the other two jobs were started in August. Job Nos. 8 and 9 were completed in August. Partial job cost sheets for Job Nos. 8 and 10 are given below:

	Job No. 8	Job No. 10
Beginning balance 8/1	$ 4,960	–0–
Direct materials	45,000	$12,000
Direct labor	24,600	6,000

The total actual manufacturing overhead incurred by Relaxed Company for August was $72,000. The company sold goods during August with a manufacturing cost of $176,160. Relaxed uses the FIFO perpetual inventory system throughout its costing system.

Required: 1. The job cost sheet for Job No. 9 seems to be lost. Prepare a skeleton job cost sheet for Job No. 9 showing the direct material and direct labor used on the job and the amount of manufacturing overhead applied to the job.

2. Reconcile the ending work in process balance with the job cost sheet for Job No. 10.
3. What is the balance in the Finished Goods account at August 31?
4. After closing the underapplied or overapplied manufacturing overhead to Cost of Goods Sold, what is the amount of cost of goods sold for August?
5. What is the balance of Raw Materials at August 31?

P7–21 **Comprehensive problem: journal entries; T-accounts; job cost sheets; schedule of cost of goods manufactured; cost of goods sold section of the income statement.** Hanover Gear Company uses a job order costing system and applies manufacturing overhead to production on the basis of machine hours. At the beginning of 19X7, the following estimates were made as a basis for determining the predetermined overhead rate for the year: manufacturing overhead costs, $360,000; machine hours, 90,000. The balances in the inventory accounts at January 1, 19X7 were

Raw materials	$ 98,000
Work in process	45,000
Finished goods	115,000

Job No. 15 was started in 19X6 and at the end of the year had been charged with direct materials of $18,000, direct labor of $14,000, and $13,000 of applied manufacturing overhead. Job Nos. 16, 17, and 18 were started in 19X7. Job Nos. 17 and 18 are still in process at the end of 19X7. The following transactions occurred during the year (all purchases and sales are on account):

a. Purchases of raw materials and supplies, $400,000
b. Raw materials and supplies issued to the factory during the year totaled $395,000
c. Factory payroll for the year:

Direct labor	$315,000
Indirect labor	52,000

d. Information regarding direct materials, direct labor, and machine hours associated with each job is given below:

	Job No. 15	Job No. 16	Job No. 17	Job No. 18
Direct material	$67,000	$150,000	$84,000	$62,000
Direct labor	$65,000	$130,000	$70,000	$50,000
Machine hours	17,500	45,000	22,000	10,500

e. Utility bills, $48,000
f. Insurance, $36,000
g. Repairs and maintenance, $42,000
h. Property taxes, $62,000
i. Depreciation, $96,000
j. Miscellaneous manufacturing overhead, $3,000
k. Direct material issued for Job No. 16 returned to the storeroom, $2,000
l. All of the beginning inventory of finished goods was sold as well as Job No. 15 and one-half of Job No. 16.
m. Supplies issued to the factory and returned to the storeroom, $1,000

Required: 1. Prepare journal entries to record the above transactions.

2. Post your entries to T-accounts (use only the manufacturing related control accounts and be sure to post opening balances where appropriate).
3. Prepare skeleton job cost sheets for the four jobs, posting the transactions where appropriate.
4. Determine the ending balances in the inventory accounts and in the Manufacturing Overhead account.
5. Determine the cost of completing Job Nos. 15 and 16. Reconcile the amount shown on the job cost sheet for Job Nos. 17 and 18 with the ending balance in Work in Process.
6. Prepare a schedule of cost of goods manufactured for 19X7.
7. Prepare a journal entry to close the overapplied or underapplied manufacturing overhead to Cost of Goods Sold. Prepare the cost of goods sold section as it would appear in the income statement for the year.

P7–22   **Underapplied or overapplied overhead and ending inventory balances in job order costing system.** Green-Gro manufactures lawn equipment. A job order system is used because the products are manufactured on a batch rather than a continuous basis. The balances in selected general ledger accounts for the eleven-month period ended November 30, 19X7, are presented below:

Raw materials inventory	$ 32,000
Work in process inventory	1,200,000
Finished goods inventory	2,785,000
Manufacturing overhead control	2,260,000
Cost of goods sold	14,200,000

The work in process inventory consists of two jobs:

Job No.	Units	Items	Accumulated Cost
3005–5	50,000	Estate sprinklers	$ 700,000
3006–4	40,000	Economy sprinklers	500,000
			$1,200,000

The finished goods inventory consists of five items:

Items	Quantity and Unit Cost	Accumulated Cost
Estate sprinklers	5,000 units @ $22 each	$ 110,000
Deluxe sprinklers	115,000 units @ $17 each	1,955,000
Brass nozzles	10,000 gross @ $14 per gross	140,000
Rainmaker nozzles	5,000 gross @ $16 per gross	80,000
Connectors	100,000 gross @ $5 per gross	500,000
		$2,785,000

The factory cost budget prepared for the year 19X7 is presented below. The company applies manufacturing overhead on the basis of direct labor hours. The activities during the first eleven months of the year were quite close to the budget. A total of 367,000 direct labor hours have been worked through November 30, 19X7.

Factory Cost Budget
For the Year Ending December 31, 19X7

Direct materials	$ 3,800,000
Purchased parts	6,000,000
Direct labor (400,000 hours)	4,000,000
Manufacturing overhead:	
Supplies	190,000
Indirect labor	700,000
Supervision	250,000
Depreciation	950,000
Utilities	200,000
Insurance	10,000
Property taxes	40,000
Miscellaneous	60,000
Total factory costs	$16,200,000

The December 19X7 transactions are summarized below:

a. All direct materials, purchased parts, and supplies are charged to raw materials inventory. The December purchases were as follows.

Materials	$410,000
Purchased parts	285,000
Supplies	13,000

b. The direct materials, purchased parts, and supplies were requisitioned from raw materials inventory as shown in the table below.

	Purchased Parts	Materials	Supplies	Total Requisitions
3005–5	$110,000	$100,000	–0–	$210,000
3006–4	–0–	6,000	–0–	6,000
4001–3 (30,000 gross rainmaker nozzles)	–0–	181,000	–0–	181,000
4002–1 (10,000 deluxe sprinklers)	–0–	92,000	–0–	92,000
4003–5 (50,000 ring sprinklers)	163,000	–0–	–0–	163,000
Supplies	–0–	–0–	20,000	20,000
	$273,000	$379,000	$20,000	$672,000

c. The payroll summary for December is as follows:

	Hours	Cost
3005–5	6,000	$ 62,000
3006–4	2,500	26,000
4001–3	18,000	182,000
4002–1	500	5,000
4003–5	5,000	52,000
Indirect	8,000	60,000
Supervision	—	24,000
Sales and administration	—	120,000
		$531,000

d. Other factory costs incurred during December were

Depreciation	$62,500
Utilities	15,000
Insurance	1,000
Property taxes	3,500
Miscellaneous	5,000
	$87,000

e. Jobs completed during December and the actual output were:

Job No.	Quantity	Items
3005–5	48,000 units	Estate sprinklers
3006–4	39,000 units	Economy sprinklers
4001–3	29,500 gross	Rainmaker nozzles
4003–5	49,000 units	Ring sprinklers

f. The following finished products were shipped to customers during December:

Items	Quantity
Estate sprinklers	16,000 units
Deluxe sprinklers	32,000 units
Economy sprinklers	20,000 units
Ring sprinklers	22,000 units
Brass nozzles	5,000 gross
Rainmaker nozzles	10,000 gross
Connectors	26,000 gross

Required:

1a. Calculate the overapplied or underapplied overhead for the year ended December 31, 19X7. Be sure to indicate whether the overhead is overapplied or underapplied.

b. What is the appropriate accounting treatment for this overapplied or underapplied overhead balance? Explain.

2. Calculate the dollar balance in the work in process inventory account as of December 31, 19X7.

3. Calculate the dollar balance in the finished goods inventory as of December 31, 19X7, for the estate sprinklers using a FIFO basis.

(CMA Adapted)

CHAPTER 8

Process Costing

Learning Objectives

After reading this chapter you should be able to:

1. Comprehend how job order costing and process costing differ.

2. Appreciate the different product flows in process costing situations.

3. Comprehend the procedures and documentation in process costing situations.

4. Understand the meaning of and how to calculate equivalent production in both weighted average and FIFO process costing situations.

5. Understand the cost of production report in both weighted average and FIFO process costing situations.

6. Understand what joint products are and how joint costs are allocated among them for product costing purposes (Appendix 8–A).

7. Understand what by-products are (Appendix 8–A).

The organization of a manufacturing firm and the type of product manu-factured dictate the type of costing system that will be used. If the firm is engaged in the manufacture of products such as custom cabinets for homes, printing, custom built homes, shipbuilding, or specially built agricul-tural equipment, a job order costing system is used. In this system, the cost object is the *job,* and the information system is designed to identify costs with individual jobs. If, however, the firm is involved in manufacturing a fairly homogeneous product on a continuous basis such as paint, steel, bricks, or the processing of meat, the cost object can no longer be an individual job because the "job" is continuous and theoretically never complete. The costing system is then designed to identify costs with the *process* rather than the job. A process is a series of actions or operations on a product requiring the use of materials and/or labor and manufacturing overhead to achieve some degree of completion of the product. A processing department is any location in the factory where some process takes place. The activity or opera-tion performed in a processing department must be performed uniformly on all of the product passing through the department and the output must be homogeneous.

In this chapter we develop the information system necessary to deter-mine unit costs of output when the cost object is the *process* rather than the job. It will be assumed that the reader is familiar with a job order costing sys-tem and all of the accounts and documentation required in that system. If this is not the case, it is suggested that you review the previous chapter on job order costing before proceeding.

Process Costing versus Job Order Costing

It may be comforting to know that if you are familiar with a job order costing system you are well on the way to understanding a process costing system. The manufacture of nearly any product will require the three elements of cost—direct materials, direct labor, and manufacturing overhead. This fact cannot be changed just because a firm is manufacturing unique products ver-sus homogeneous look-alikes. As a result, you would expect that the process cost system would need accounts for Materials, Payroll, and Manufacturing Overhead just as were needed for a job order costing system. The underlying support documents would also be the same. The major differences between the two systems are the result of the difference in cost objects—in job order the cost object is the *job.* The system was designed, therefore, to trace costs to a job, and if a job consisted of more than one unit, the unit cost was found by dividing the total costs associated with a job by the number of units in the job. All documentation as well as accounts used were to emphasize and make it possible to identify costs with jobs. The general model for a job order cost system is shown in Exhibit 7–1. It is suggested that you refer to that model and review it before proceeding.

The general model for a process costing system is illustrated in Exhibit 8–1 (page 244). Refer to it now and identify how this model differs from the job order costing model.

It is not difficult to see that the process costing model has a work in process account for each process as opposed to only one in the job order costing model. This again illustrates the notion of designing the information system to "fit" the process about which information is being gathered. As mentioned above, when we have a manufacturing process continuously turning out a homogeneous product, there is no "job" as such for which costs can be identified. We then must concentrate on the process, so the cost elements (direct materials, direct labor, and manufacturing overhead) are added to the first process. When this process is completed, the product is transferred to the next process where additional processing occurs. This results in labor and overhead cost and perhaps some more material added in the second process, and so forth. Therefore, the "finished product" of one process becomes the "raw material" of the following process. When all processing is complete, the product moves to finished goods as it does in a job order costing system resulting in an addition to the work in process in the receiving department and a reduction in work in process in the sending (or completing) department.

You can now appreciate why the additional work in process accounts are necessary. The Work in Process–Department 1 account is used to accumulate processing costs in department number one. Upon completion of processing there, the unfinished product moves on to Processing Department 2. This means that the costs accumulated in the first process are transferred on to the second process. As additional processing costs are incurred in the second department, these costs are also charged to Work in Process–Department 2. As processing is completed in the second processing department, the product moves on to the third processing department with the costs from both Processing Departments 1 *and* 2, and the procedure is repeated until the product is fully complete and moves to finished goods. The general model illustrates three processing departments. Obviously, this could be less than three or more than three depending on the product being manufactured.

When processing proceeds on a continuous basis, there must be a way to determine the unit cost of production. In job order costing we accumulated costs by jobs, and if the job consisted of one unit, the unit cost was equal to the total costs accumulated on the job cost sheet. If the job consisted of a number of units, we divided the total costs on the job cost sheet by the number of units in the job to obtain the average unit cost. In the process costing environment, we will determine unit costs for each process by dividing the costs incurred in a process *during a certain time period* by the units completed in that process during that time period. This means that we obtain an average unit cost in each process for each time period—a number that is useful for planning and control purposes. The total unit cost for a product is accumulated in each process through which the product passes during manufacturing.

EXHIBIT 8–1
General Model
Process System Cost Flows

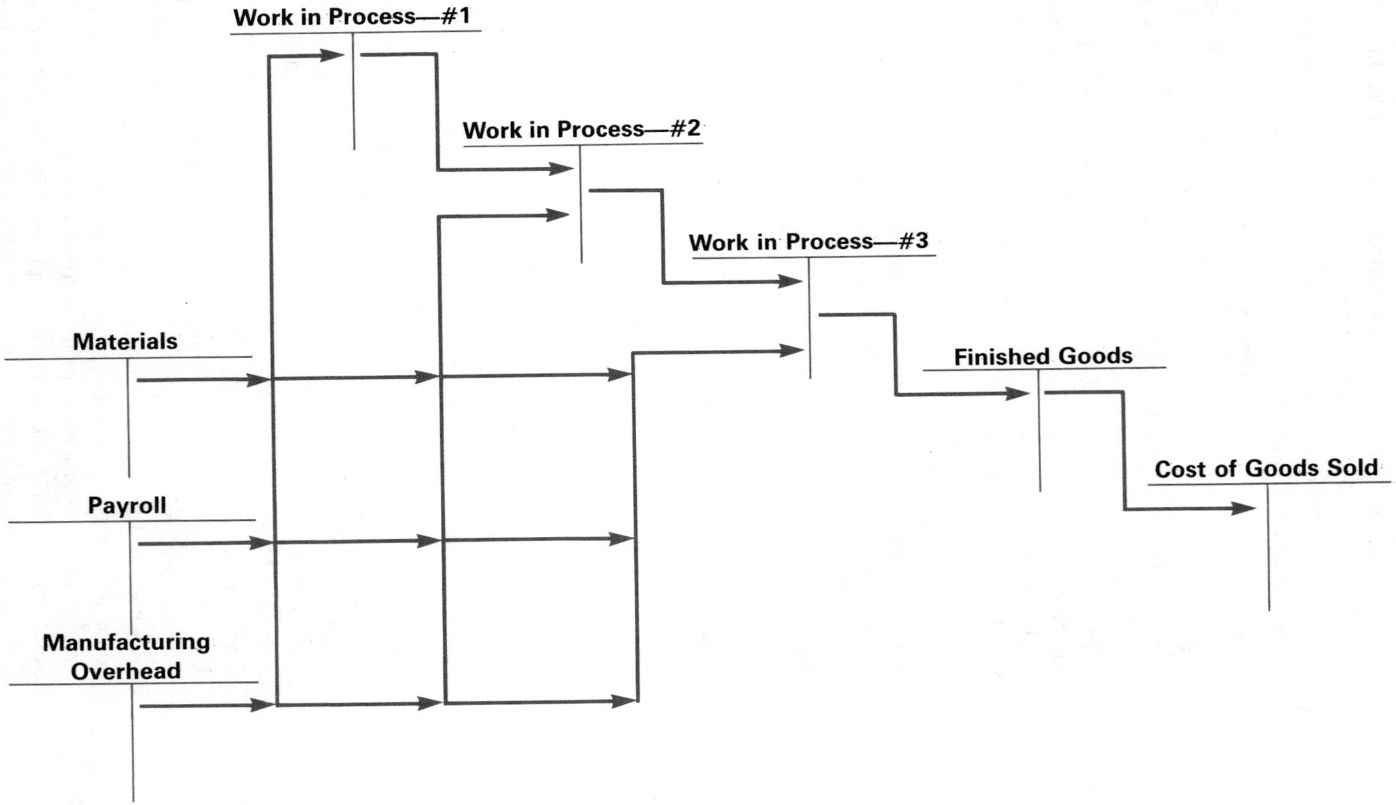

Another difference between job order costing and process costing that is not visible by looking at the general model is the detail documentation for the Work in Process accounts. In the job order system the support for the activity in the Work in Process account was found on the job order cost sheet—one sheet for each job. The support for the detail in each Work in Process account in a process cost system is found on a cost of production report, a supporting document that will be explained and illustrated shortly.

The major differences between process costing and job order costing can be summarized as follows:

Process Costing	***Job Order Costing***
1. One or a few identical products are produced on a continuous basis for extended periods of time.	1. One or a number of unique jobs are worked on during a time period.
2. Costs are accumulated by processing department.	2. Costs are accumulated by individual job.
3. Unit costs are determined by individual processing departments and added together to obtain total unit cost.	3. Unit costs are determined by dividing the total costs on the job cost sheet by the number of units in the job.
4. The cost of production report provides the detail for the Work in Process account for each processing department.	4. The job cost sheet provides the detail for the Work in Process account.

Flow of Product in a Process Costing Environment

It is often inferred in a process costing environment that the product moves through the factory in some kind of assembly line where all products begin in Processing Department 1 and move through all processing departments and finally to finished goods on completion. This is not always the case—the product may flow through processing departments on a sequential, parallel, or selective basis. The point to remember is that the same basic costing procedures are applied to all types of product flow methods.

Sequential Flow

If the product moves through the factory in the same series of steps (that is, from process 1 to 2 to 3, etc.), it is referred to as a **sequential product flow** and can be diagrammed as shown on the next page.

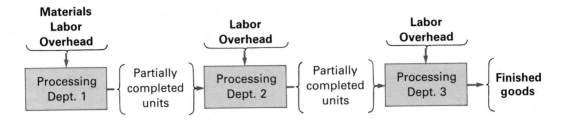

The diagram suggests that materials, labor, and manufacturing overhead are added in the first process, but only labor and manufacturing overhead are added in the other processing departments. This, of course, depends on the manufacturing process. Processing Department 3, for instance, might be a painting department where additional material would be added.

Parallel Product Flow

In a **parallel product flow,** raw material may be processed in Processing Department 1, whereupon two different products emerge and then flow through their own series of processing departments for completion. The meat packing industry or the refining of crude oil might be an example of this type of flow. This particular product flow is diagrammed below:

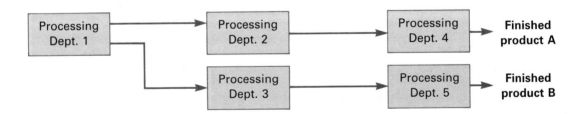

Note in this particular product flow that raw material(s) is added in Processing Department 1 and more than one product emerges from the process. This creates a joint cost/joint product situation, which is discussed in Appendix 8–A.

Another example of parallel product flow could be the situation where various portions of the work could be done simultaneously and then brought together in a final process or processes before moving on to finished goods. An example could be certain chemical industries where various chemicals are produced and finally mixed together to make a finished product. The product flow is diagrammed on the next page.

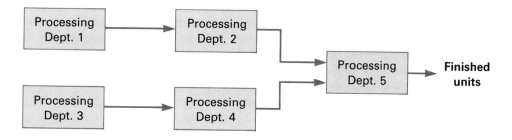

Selective Product Flow

In the **selective product flow** the product moves to different processing departments within the plant, depending on what is desired for final product. An example might again be a meat processor who slaughters, dresses, and processes a fairly complete line of meat products. A possible product flow is diagrammed below:

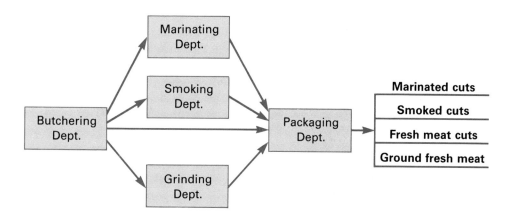

The diagram illustrates a number of possibilities for this industry. You can see other possible combinations for curing bacon, hams, and so forth. Again, the point to remember is that no matter what the product flow method, the same basic process costing procedures are applied—a unit cost is determined for each process and the cost of the finished product is the total of the unit costs accumulated as the product passes through each processing department.

Process Costing Cost Flows and Procedures

It has already been mentioned that the basic procedures used in process costing are, with a few exceptions, generally similar to job order costing. An example will be used to demonstrate the procedures and documentation in a process costing system as well as to emphasize the differences from job order.

An Illustration

Randolph Manufacturing, Inc. produces a homogeneous product on a continuous basis that requires two processes—cutting, and sanding and polishing. All material is added at the beginning of processing in the Cutting Department with only conversion costs (direct labor and manufacturing overhead) added in the Sanding and Polishing Department. The following information pertains to the month of January 19X7:

	Cutting	Sanding and Polishing
Work in process — beginning:		
Units in process	1,000	2,000
Stage of completion	50%	30%
Costs in beginning inventory:		
Cost from preceding dept.	–	$ 8,500
Materials	$ 1,000	–
Direct labor	800	1,170
Manufacturing overhead	1,000	1,755
Total costs in process	$ 2,800	$11,425
Units started in production during this period	15,000	
Units received from Cutting Department this period		14,000
Units transferred to Sanding and Polishing Department	14,000	
Costs added to production this period:		
Materials	$15,800	–
Direct labor	22,140	$29,630
Manufacturing overhead applied:		
125% of direct labor	27,675	
150% of direct labor		44,445
Work in process — ending:		
Units in process	2,000	1,500
Stage of completion	40%	60%

It is assumed that you are familiar with the entries to record the accumulation of the actual costs for purchases of materials and labor and the incurrence of manufacturing overhead. These entries will not be repeated here. If further review is necessary you may want to refer to the previous chapter on job order costing. We shall first consider the entries necessary to record the activity in the Cutting Department. It should be noted from the example information that there is a beginning inventory of work in process in the Cutting Department. This amount has been carried over from the previous period. In other words, at the beginning of January 19X7, the Work in Process—Cutting Department had a debit balance of $2,800.

Materials

The withdrawal of materials from stores will require a materials requisition, but the requisition need only show that the material is for use in the Cutting Department—it need not show any particular job number as in job order costing. From the information given for Randolph Manufacturing, the following entry is made to record the requisition of material for the month of January in the Cutting Department:

| (1) | Work in Process – Cutting | 15,800 | |
| | Materials | | 15,800 |

Labor

Again, because there is no individual job as such, direct labor need only be identified with the processing department and not the job. Therefore, job tickets are unnecessary. The direct labor costs to charge to a department can be obtained by doing a labor recapitulation to determine the amount to be charged to each processing department (as well as how much indirect labor is to be charged to the Manufacturing Overhead account). In our example for Randolph Manufacturing, direct labor costs for the Cutting Department for January 19X7 are $22,140 and would be recorded by the following entry:

| (2) | Work in Process – Cutting | 22,140 | |
| | Payroll | | 22,140 |

Manufacturing Overhead Applied

Randolph Manufacturing is using a predetermined rate for applying overhead. The rate is 125% of direct labor cost in the Cutting Department and 150% of direct labor cost in the Sanding and Polishing Department. The direct labor cost for the Cutting Department in January was $22,140. Therefore, the overhead applied to Cutting would be $27,675 ($22,140 × 125%) and would be recorded by the following entry:

| (3) | Work in Process – Cutting | 27,675 | |
| | Manufacturing Overhead | | 27,675 |

It is possible that some firms might charge Work in Process for the actual manufacturing overhead cost incurred for the period instead of using a predetermined rate to apply overhead. For this procedure to work well, it would require that production would remain fairly stable from period to period and that manufacturing overhead be incurred uniformly throughout the year. If these conditions are not met, we run into the same problem as in the job order case—units processed in January may appear to cost far more or less than units processed in June, for instance, if large amounts of fixed manufacturing overhead were incurred or paid in January or if January production was much larger or smaller than the June production. It would seldom happen that these two prerequisites would be met, so we will assume throughout our discussion in this chapter that each processing department will use a predetermined rate for applying manufacturing overhead.

We have indicated that unit costs of materials, labor, and manufacturing overhead would be determined for each processing department and that to find these unit costs we would divide the costs incurred in a process during a certain time period by the units completed in the process during that time period. This requires an understanding of an important concept used in process costing—equivalent production.

Equivalent Production

Equivalent production is the expression of all activity of a processing department during a period in terms of fully completed units. Simply stated, it means that two units one-half complete are equal to one unit fully complete. If we are to determine unit costs for the period, it would not make sense to divide total cost incurred for the period by fully completed units only—some of the costs incurred would have been spent on bringing some units to a partially complete stage. The concept of equivalent production allows us, then, to express all activity for which costs were incurred in terms of fully completed units. Once this very important number is determined, the calculation of unit costs is relatively simple. Note that it is because of the existence of partially completed beginning and ending inventories of work in process that makes the equivalent production calculation crucial to process costing. If all work started during the period were always completed at the end of the period, there would be no work in process inventories and the equivalent production number would equal the units completed during the period. Very few manufacturing firms will ever be in this situation, however, so it is important that you acquire a good understanding of this important concept.

There are two ways of determining equivalent production. These two methods are referred to as the *weighted average method* and the *first-in first-out (FIFO) method.*

Weighted Average Method

The **weighted average method** implies that there is some kind of averaging taking place. This occurs because the units in beginning work in process inventory are treated as though they were started *and* completed during the current period. An example will make this more clear. Consider the following facts regarding the Casting Department in a manufacturing company for the month of January 19X7:

	Units	Percentage Complete	
		Materials	Conversion
Work in process, beginning	1,000	100	40
Started into production during period	10,000		
Completed and transferred to next department	9,000		
Work in process, ending	2,000	100	60

Note, as is often the case, that beginning and ending inventories of work in process are at different stages of completion in terms of conversion costs (direct labor and manufacturing overhead) but are both 100% complete as to materials. This would suggest that all material is added at the beginning of production and conversion costs are incurred uniformly as a particular process is being completed. The equivalent production figures for this process would be determined as indicated in Exhibit 8–2.

Note in Exhibit 8–2 that of the 9,000 units completed and transferred, all material had been added to 1,000 of the units last period, and enough labor and overhead had been added to complete 400 units (1,000 × 40%). These costs are merely "averaged in" with costs incurred this period to complete the 9,000 units and, therefore, the name *weighted average* for this method. This calculation of equivalent production for the weighted average is rather simple as a result—merely add the units completed and transferred to the equivalent units in ending work in process inventory for each cost element.

First-In First-Out Method

This method is an extension of the weighted average method. Remember that we said that in the weighted average method that some costs and activity of last period are "averaged in" with the current period's costs and activity. This does not give a clear look at this period's performance exclusively. When the

EXHIBIT 8–2
Equivalent Production – Casting Department
For the Month of January 19X7 (Weighted Average Method)

	Materials	Conversion
Units completed and transferred to next department	9,000	9,000
Equivalent units in ending work in process:		
Materials – 2,000 × 100%	2,000	
Conversion – 2,000 × 60%		1,200
Equivalent production	11,000	10,200

FIFO method is used, equivalent production indicates the activity of this period only—no activity from last period is included. This requires that the work done last period on this period's beginning work in process inventory must be removed in determining equivalent production for this method. The calculation is illustrated in Exhibit 8–3 using the information given in the weighted average example.

As indicated in Exhibit 8–3, equivalent production under the FIFO method merely requires that the calculation of equivalent production using weighted average be carried one step further—the equivalent units in beginning work in process are subtracted from equivalent production on the weighted average basis. As we shall see in the calculation of unit costs, the FIFO method, as compared to the weighted average method, adds some complexity to our calculations. It can be argued, however, that this method results in more accurate unit costs for the period, which provides "better numbers" for cost comparisons between periods and better information for performance evaluation.

The Cost of Production Report

We now return to the earlier example involving Randolph Manufacturing. Before digressing to illustrate the calculation of equivalent production, we had charged the Work in Process—Cutting Department account for Randolph Manufacturing for all of the materials, direct labor, and manufacturing overhead applied for the month of January. The Work in Process—Cutting Department is a control account, which means that there should be some underlying document that provides the detail for the entries in this account. In the job order costing system the detail for the work in process account was found on job order cost sheets. In a process costing system, the detail and support for each work in process account is found on a cost of produc-

EXHIBIT 8–3
Equivalent Production – Cutting Department
For the Month of January (FIFO Method)

	Materials	Conversion
Units completed and transferred to next department	9,000	9,000
Equivalent units in ending work in process:		
Materials – 2,000 × 100%	2,000	
Conversion – 2,000 × 60%		1,200
Total	11,000	10,200
Less: Equivalent units in beginning work in process:		
Materials – 1,000 × 100%	(1,000)	
Conversion – 1,000 × 40%		(400)
Equivalent Production	10,000	9,800

tion report. This report is considered to be one of the more complex parts of a process costing system, and it is suggested that you study its structure and content carefully. It is not possible to fully understand a process costing system without an understanding of this important document.

As you might expect, the cost of production report will vary somewhat depending on whether the report is for the first or succeeding departments and whether the weighted average method or the FIFO method is used.

Cost of Production Report – Weighted Average Method

The **cost of production report** summarizes all the costs charged to a department during a period, determines unit costs, determines the dollar amount to be transferred on to the next department or finished goods, and computes the ending work in process inventory value. The report consists of four major sections: the quantity schedule, equivalent production, costs charged to the department, and a section called *costs accounted for as follows* (a reconciliation with the costs charged to the department). Exhibit 8–4 (page 254) illustrates a cost of production report for the Cutting Department (the first processing department) for the month of January 19X7 using the weighted average method.

The quantity schedule, section 1 of the cost of production report, merely traces whole physical units through each processing department and is not concerned with the stage of completion of those units (although notice that the stage of completion is shown parenthetically within the schedule). This schedule makes it possible for management to easily see how many units passed through the department during the period. It also is useful to the preparer of the cost of production report to keep track of the physical flow of units so that cost flows will be appropriate. This schedule may seem rather simplistic at this point, but as the physical flow becomes more complex it becomes almost essential that a quantity schedule is prepared. We suggest that you get into the habit of always preparing a quantity schedule before proceeding with the rest of the cost of production report.

The calculation of equivalent production, section 2 of the cost of production report, follows the example given previously for the weighted average method and is self-explanatory.

Section 3, the costs charged to the department, details the costs in beginning inventory and the costs added during the period in this department. Note the calculation of the unit cost for each element of cost. For materials, for instance, the materials cost associated with beginning inventory is added to (averaged with) materials costs added this period and is divided by the equivalent production for materials to get the average materials unit cost of $1.05 for January. The individual unit costs are added together to get the unit cost in the Cutting Department for January of $4.5375. After completion of section 3 of the report we also know that we have to account for total costs of $68,415.

EXHIBIT 8—4

Cost of Production Report — Cutting Department
For the Month of January 19X7 (Weighted Average Method)

(1) Quantity schedule:
    Units to be accounted for:

Units in process, beginning (100% materials, 50% conversion)	1,000
Units started in process during January	15,000
Total units to be accounted for	16,000

    Units accounted for as follows:

Units transferred to Sanding & Polishing	14,000
Units in process, ending (100% materials, 40% conversion)	2,000
Total units accounted for	16,000

	Materials	Conversion
(2) Equivalent production:		
Units completed and transferred	14,000	14,000
Units in ending work in process:		
Materials — 2,000 × 100%	2,000	
Conversion — 2,000 × 40%		800
Equivalent Production	16,000	14,800

	Total Cost	÷	Equivalent Units	=	Unit Cost
(3) Cost charged to the department:					
Cost added by department:					
Materials:					
Work in process, beginning	$ 1,000				
During current period	15,800				
Total materials added	$16,800	÷	16,000	=	$ 1.05
Direct labor:					
Work in process, beginning	$ 800				
During current period	22,140				
Total direct labor added	$22,940	÷	14,800	=	$ 1.55
Manufacturing overhead:					
Work in process, beginning	$ 1,000				
During current period	27,675				
Total manufacturing overhead added	$28,675	÷	14,800	=	$1.9375
Total cost to be accounted for	$68,415				$4.5375

(4) Cost accounted for as follows:

Completed and transferred to Sanding & Polishing (14,000 × $4.5375)		$63,525
Work in Process — Ending Inventory:		
Materials — 2,000 × 100% × $1.05	$ 2,100	
Direct labor — 2,000 × 40% × $1.55	1,240	
Manufacturing overhead — 2,000 × 40% × $1.9375	1,550	4,890
Total cost accounted for		$68,415

Section 4 of the cost of production report explains what happens to the costs charged to the Cutting Department. We know by looking at the quantity schedule that 14,000 units were completed and transferred to the Sanding and Polishing Department. It is not difficult to see that the costs to be transferred to the next department should be 14,000 units times the unit cost of $4.5375 or $63,525. This gives us the basis for the journal entry to transfer the costs to the Sanding and Polishing Department:

| (4) | Work in Process – Sanding and Polishing | 63,525 | |
| | Work in Process – Cutting | | 63,525 |

Remember, we had $68,415 of costs to account for in section 3 of the report—which means that we have not yet accounted for costs totaling $4,890. The only explanation for these costs not yet accounted for must be that they are in ending work in process. We proceed, therefore, to explain the make-up of the ending work in process inventory. Our quantity schedule tells us that there are 2,000 physical units in ending work in process and that these units are 100% complete as to materials and 40% complete as to direct labor and manufacturing overhead. The report shows that when we consider these facts and apply unit costs for the period, the ending work in process inventory does in fact total $4,890. We now have accounted for all costs charged to the Cutting Department. Note that the total of section 4, costs accounted for as follows, should always agree with the total of section 3, costs charged to the department. If these two amounts do not reconcile, you need to check your work for errors. Obviously, unit costs for materials, direct labor, and manufacturing overhead will seldom come out to even cents, so it often will be necessary to carry your computations to six or seven decimal places to make sections 3 and 4 of the cost of production report reconcile. We have done this throughout the chapter.

We can now illustrate the relationship between the Work in Process—Cutting Department control account and the detail shown in the cost of production report. The Work in Process—Cutting Department account is shown below with the January 19X7 entries posted:

Work in Process – Cutting Department

Beginning balance	2,800	(4) Cost transferred	63,525
(1) Materials	15,800	Ending balance (fwd)	4,890
(2) Direct labor	22,140		
(3) Overhead applied	27,675		
	68,415		68,415
Balance brought forward	4,890		
Total cost to be accounted for – section 3 of the cost of production report		Total cost accounted for – section 4 of the cost of production report	

Note that the total debits to the Work in Process—Cutting account agree with the total costs shown in section 3 of the cost of production report—costs charged to the department. The cost of production report shows the detail of the beginning inventory of $2,800. It should be apparent at this point that the costs in section 3 of the cost of production report explain the *debits* to the work in process account to which it is related.

Also note that the credits to the Work in Process account agree with the total costs shown in section 4 of the cost of production report — the section called *costs accounted for as follows.* The cost of production report shows how the costs to be transferred out are determined and how the value of the ending work in process inventory is assembled. Section 4 of the cost of production report, then, should agree with the *credits* to the Work in Process account (including the ending balance of the account to be carried forward to the next period).

The cost of production report for the Sanding and Polishing Department for the month of January is illustrated in Exhibit 8–5. It is a bit more complex because this department not only adds its own costs to the product but must account for costs transferred in from the prior department. Again, the information given in the Randolph Manufacturing example on page 248 is used to develop the illustration. No material is added in this department, so there need be no calculation of equivalent production for materials.

This cost of production report has some information in section 3 that is not required in the report for the Cutting Department. Sanding and Polishing is the second processing department, so there are **transferred-in costs** from the Cutting Department to account for along with costs added in the Sanding and Polishing Department. The weighted average unit cost from the Cutting Department was $4.5015625. Do not be misled by the unit cost figures for beginning work in process ($4.25) and those transferred in this period ($4.5375). These are for management information purposes only. The *weighted average* unit cost for units from the Cutting Department is $4.5015625.

Because there are costs from a preceding department, the total unit cost associated with units as they are completed and leave the Sanding and Polishing Department includes the average unit costs from the Cutting Department ($4.5015625) *and* the average unit costs for the Sanding and Polishing Department ($5.00), or a total unit cost at this point of $9.5015625.

Section 4 of the cost of production report is also affected by the costs from the Cutting Department. When calculating the ending work in process inventory for Sanding and Polishing, we now need to include the costs from Cutting along with the costs added by the Sanding and Polishing Department as indicated in Exhibit 8–5.

The journal entries to summarize the detail of the activity shown in the cost of production report for the Sanding and Polishing Department for the month of January are illustrated below. You should trace the numbers to the cost of production report as was done for the Cutting Department.

(1)	Work in Process — Sanding & Polishing	63,525	
	Work in Process — Cutting		63,525
	This entry is the same as entry (4) for the Cutting Department and is shown here for information only.		

EXHIBIT 8–5

Cost of Production Report – Sanding and Polishing Department
For the Month of January 19X7 (Weighted Average Method)

(1) Quantity schedule:
    Units to be accounted for:

Units in process, beginning (30% converted)	2,000
Units transferred in from Cutting Dept.	14,000
Total units to be accounted for	16,000

    Units accounted for as follows:

Units transferred to finished goods	14,500
Units in process, ending (60% converted)	1,500
Total units accounted for	16,000

(2) Equivalent production:

	Transferred in	Conversion
Units completed and transferred to finished goods	16,000	14,500
Units in ending work in process:		
Conversion costs – 1,500 × 60%	–	900
Equivalent production	16,000	15,400

(3) Costs charged to the department:

	Total Cost	÷	Equivalent Units	=	Unit Cost
Costs from preceding department:					
Work in process – beginning	$ 8,500				$4.25
Transferred in during period	63,525				4.5375
Total preceding department costs	$ 72,025	÷	16,000	=	$4.5015625
Cost added by department:					
Direct labor:					
Work in process, beginning	$ 1,170				
During current period	29,630				
Total direct labor added	$ 30,800	÷	15,400	=	$2.00
Manufacturing overhead:					
Work in process, beginning	$ 1,755				
During current period	44,445				
Total manufacturing overhead added	$ 46,200	÷	15,400	=	3.00
Total cost added	$ 77,000				$5.00
Total cost to be accounted for	$149,025				$9.5015625

(4) Cost accounted for as follows:

Completed and transferred to Finished Goods (14,500 × $9.5015625)		$137,772.65
Work in process – ending:		
Cost from Cutting Department (1,500 × $4.5015625)	$6,752.35	
Direct labor (1,500 × 60% × $2.00)	1,800.00	
Manufacturing overhead (1,500 × 60% × $3.00)	2,700.00	11,252.35
Total cost accounted for		$149,025.00

(2)	Work in Process — Sanding & Polishing	74,075	
	Payroll		29,630
	Manufacturing Overhead		44,445
	To record the direct labor and manufacturing overhead costs added in the Sanding and Polishing Department this period.		
(3)	Finished Goods	137,772.65	
	Work in Process — Sanding & Polishing		137,772.65
	To record units completed in Sanding and Polishing and transferred to the finished goods storeroom.		

This completes the illustration of the weighted average method. We shall now consider the FIFO method of determining equivalent production and unit cost determination.

Cost of Production Report — FIFO Method

In the discussion of equivalent production, it was pointed out that when the FIFO method is used, the emphasis is on the activity and unit costs *for the current period only.* It was emphasized that unit costs would reflect costs of the current period only — no cost from the prior period is to be averaged in with costs of the current period. The cost of production report will be very similar to the cost of production report prepared under the weighted average method, but there is some complexity added — especially in section 4 of the report. To illustrate, a cost of production report will be prepared using the information from the Randolph Manufacturing example on page 248. When we have completed the cost of production report on a FIFO basis you should be able to see where the differences are between the weighted average and the FIFO approaches. Exhibit 8–6 is a cost of production report for the Cutting Department for the month of January 19X7, using the FIFO method.

The quantity schedule, section 1 of the cost of production report, is exactly the same as it is under the weighted average method. As was men-

EXHIBIT 8–6
Cost of Production Report — Cutting Department
For the Month of January 19X7 (FIFO Method)

(1) Quantity schedule:	
Units to be accounted for:	
Units in process, beginning (100% materials, 50% conversion)	1,000
Units started in process during January	15,000
Total units to be accounted for	16,000
Units accounted for as follows:	
Units transferred to Sanding & Polishing	14,000
Units in process, ending (100% materials, 40% conversion)	2,000
Total units accounted for	16,000

EXHIBIT 8–6, continued

	Materials	Conversion
(2) Equivalent production:		
Units completed and transferred	14,000	14,000
Units in ending work in process:		
Materials – 2,000 × 100%	2,000	
Conversion – 2,000 × 40%		800
Total	16,000	14,800
Units in beginning work in process:		
Materials – 1,000 × 100%	(1,000)	
Conversion – 1,000 × 50%		(500)
Equivalent production (FIFO)	15,000	14,300

	Total Cost	÷	Equivalent Units	=	Unit Cost
(3) Cost charged to the department:					
Work in process – beginning	$ 2,800				
Cost added by department:					
Materials	$15,800	÷	15,000	=	$1.05333
Direct labor	22,140	÷	14,300	=	1.54825
Manufacturing overhead	27,675	÷	14,300	=	1.93532
Total cost added	$65,615				$4.53690
Total cost to be accounted for	$68,415				$4.53690

(4) Cost accounted for as follows:		
Completed and transferred to Sanding & Polishing Department:		
From beginning inventory –		
Inventory value	$2,800.00	
Direct labor (1,000 × 50% × $1.54825)	774.13	
Manufacturing overhead (1,000 × 50% × $1.932532)	967.67	$ 4,541.80
From current production (13,000 × $4.5369)		58,979.70
Total costs transferred		$63,521.50[a]
Work in process – ending:		
Materials (2,000 × 100% × $1.05333)	$2,106.65	
Direct labor (2,000 × 40% × $1.54825)	1,238.60	
Manufacturing overhead (2,000 × 40% × $1.93532)	1,548.25	4,893.50
Total cost accounted for		$68,415.00

[a]Note that the unit cost transferred to the Sanding and Polishing Department really turns out to be an average of the FIFO cost – the costs associated with the beginning inventory ($4,541.80) plus the costs from current production ($58,979.70) divided by the total units completed and transferred (14,000) give a unit cost of $4.53725 on the 14,000 units transferred to Sanding and Polishing during January. This has led some authors to refer to this method as the modified FIFO method.

tioned previously, the quantity schedule deals only with physical units and therefore is not affected by the stage of completion of units. The stage of completion is shown for information purposes in completing equivalent production calculations.

Equivalent production under FIFO costing concentrates on activity of the current period, so as illustrated earlier, the work completed in previous periods on the beginning work in process is subtracted from equivalent production on a weighted average basis to arrive at equivalent production on a FIFO basis. This has been done in section 2 of the report.

Section 3 of the cost of production report (cost charged to the department) is actually simpler on a FIFO basis than on a weighted average basis. The total costs associated with beginning work in process ($2,800) are merely listed so that they can be included as part of the costs to be accounted for — no unit cost calculations are necessary because these costs are from the prior period, not the current period. The unit cost for each element of cost is determined by dividing the cost added during the period by the equivalent production of the period. On Exhibit 8–6 we see that the total cost to complete a unit in the Cutting Department during January 19X7 was $4.5369.

The complexity added by using the FIFO method is illustrated in section 4 of the cost of production report. The quantity schedule tells us that at the beginning of January there were 1,000 units in process and that these units were 100% complete as to materials and 50% complete as to direct labor and manufacturing overhead. From the information given in the example we also know that it took $2,800 to get the 1,000 units that far along in the manufacturing process during the previous period. On a FIFO basis, we need to determine how much more costs must be added *this period* to finish off these 1,000 units. The units already have all material added, so none had to be added in January. Therefore, to complete the 1,000 units, the Cutting Department had to add labor and overhead necessary to do the equivalent of starting from scratch and completing 500 units (1,000 × 50%) during January. The report shows that this required $774.13 of direct labor and $967.67 of manufacturing overhead. Total costs associated with the first 1,000 units transferred out then amounted to a total of $4,541.80.

The quantity schedule indicates that 14,000 units were completed and transferred to the Sanding and Polishing Department during January. So far we have dealt with only 1,000 of those units — those that were in process at the beginning of the month. The remaining 13,000 units transferred out were from production that was started and completed entirely during January. The cost associated with these 13,000 units is the total unit cost determined for January ($4.5369) times 13,000 or $58,979.70. The total cost associated with the 14,000 units transferred is the total of the 1,000 units from beginning inventory plus the 13,000 units started and completed this period or $63,521.50.

This illustrates the complexity referred to earlier that is added by the use of the FIFO method. If there is a beginning work in process inventory, the costs transferred out of the department will consist of two layers—one associated with the beginning inventory and another associated with the units started and completed during the current period. As indicated in the note to the cost of production report, the two layers of cost are combined and the Sanding and Polishing Department will be receiving 14,000 units with a total cost of $63,521.50 (or an overall cost per unit of $4.53725). The procedure to calculate the ending work in process inventory is the same as for the weighted average method.

The journal entries to record the activity in the Cutting Department will be exactly the same as they were for the weighted average method as far as costs added during the period, that is, materials, direct labor, and manufacturing overhead. The only difference will be the amount of cost transferred to the Sanding and Polishing Department. Therefore, the entries will not be repeated. The Work in Process—Cutting Department account is illustrated below so that you may see all of the entries and compare them to the cost of production report.

Work in Process – Cutting Department

Beginning balance	2,800.00	Costs transferred	63,521.50
Materials	15,800.00	Ending balance (fwd.)	4,893.50
Direct labor	22,140.00		
Overhead applied	27,675.00		
	68,415.00		68,415.00
Balance brought forward	4,893.50		

Sanding and polishing   The cost of production report for the Sanding and Polishing Department for the month of January on a FIFO basis is illustrated in Exhibit 8–7 (page 262). Note how this department incorporates the costs transferred in from the Cutting Department and how these transferred-in costs are handled in determining the ending work in process inventory value.

So that you may again compare the control account with the detail in the cost of production report, the Work in Process—Sanding and Polishing account is illustrated below with all of the entries for the month of January 19X7.

Work in Process – Sanding and Polishing

Beginning balance	11,425.00	Costs transferred	
Transferred in	63,521.50	out	137,711.06
Direct labor	29,630.00	Ending balance	
Manufacturing overhead applied	44,445.00	carried forward	11,310.44
	149,021.50		149,021.50
Balance brought forward	11,310.44		

Evaluation of the Weighted Average and FIFO Methods

The calculation of equivalent production and the total cost of goods transferred out of a processing department in particular seemed to be quite different under the two methods. When we look at the unit cost for direct

EXHIBIT 8–7

Cost of Production Report – Sanding & Polishing Department
For the Month of January 19X7 (FIFO Method)

	Transferred in	Conversion
(1) Quantity schedule:		
Units to be accounted for:		
Units in process, beginning (30% converted)		2,000
Units transferred in from Cutting Dept.		14,000
Total units to be accounted for		16,000
Units accounted for as follows:		
Units transferred to finished goods		14,500
Units in process, ending (60% converted)		1,500
Total units accounted for		16,000

	Transferred in	Conversion
(2) Equivalent production:		
Units completed and transferred to finished goods	14,500	14,500
Units in ending work in process:		
Conversion costs – 1,500 × 60%	1,500	900
Total	16,000	15,400
Units in beginning work in process:		
Conversion costs – 2,000 × 30%	(2,000)	(600)
Equivalent production (FIFO)	14,000	14,800

	Total Cost	÷	Equivalent Units	=	Unit Cost
(3) Cost charged to the department:					
Work in process, beginning	$ 11,425				
Cost from preceding department:					
Transferred in during month	$ 63,521.50	÷	14,000	=	$4.53725
Cost added by department:					
Direct labor	$ 29,630.00	÷	14,800	=	$2.002027
Manufacturing overhead	44,445.00	÷	14,800	=	3.0030405
Total cost added	$ 74,075.00				$5.0050675
Total cost to be accounted for	$149,021.50				$9.5423175

EXHIBIT 8–7, continued

(4)	Cost accounted for as follows:		
	Completed and transferred to finished goods:		
	From beginning inventory:		
	Inventory value	$11,425.00	
	Direct labor (2,000 × 70% × $2.002027)	2,802.84	
	Manufacturing overhead (2,000 × 70% × $3.0030405)	4,204.26	$ 18,432.10
	From current production (12,500 × $9.5423175)		119,278.96
	Total costs transferred		$137,711.06[a]
	Work in process — ending:		
	Cost from cutting department (1,500 × $4.53725)	$ 6,805.88	
	Direct labor (1,500 × 60% × $2.002027)	1,801.82	
	Manufacturing overhead (1,500 × 60% × $3.0030405)	2,702.74	11,310.44
	Total cost accounted for		$149,021.50

[a]Unit cost transferred to finished goods equals the costs associated with beginning inventory ($18,432.10) plus costs from current production ($119,278.96) divided by total units completed and transferred (14,500) giving a unit cost of $9.4973144.

materials, direct labor and manufacturing overhead added in each department or the total unit costs, the total costs transferred out, or the value of the ending work in process, however, we see very little difference between the two methods. Exhibit 8–8 (page 264) summarizes these various costs by department for the two methods for the month of January 19X7.

As long as the costs seem to be so similar, and if the weighted average is regarded as an easier method, why should the FIFO method be used? Many manufacturing firms have asked this question, and, by far, the majority have concluded that they are happy to opt for the weighted average method. As long as the price of the various cost elements does not fluctuate erratically, the two methods will give very similar results. If, however, some of the cost element prices vary greatly from month to month, and if ending work in process inventories vary significantly from period to period, the two methods could produce significantly different results. When the prices of the basic cost elements do vary significantly, the use of the weighted average method does tend to mask the true costs of the current period because of the "averaging in" of some last-period costs with this period. This tends to destroy some of the value of the information for control purposes. For control and performance evaluation purposes, we would like to be able to concentrate on an evaluation of the current period's activity *only*. In this sense, the FIFO method is preferable. Each firm must decide which method they feel better serves their information needs.

EXHIBIT 8–8
Comparison of Costs by Department for January 19X7
Weighted Average versus FIFO Method

	Costing Method	
	Weighted Average	FIFO
Cutting Department:		
Basic cost element unit costs:		
Material	$1.05	$1.05333
Direct labor	1.55	1.54825
Manufacturing overhead	1.9375	1.93532
Total unit costs (transferred)	4.5375	4.53725
Total cost transferred	$63,525.00	$63,521.50
Ending inventory (WIP)	4,890.00	4,893.50
Sanding and Polishing Department:		
Basic cost element unit costs:		
Direct labor	$2.00	$2.002027
Manufacturing overhead	3.00	3.0030405
Total unit costs (transferred)	9.5015625	9.4973144
Total cost transferred	$137,772.65	$137,711.06
Ending inventory (WIP)	11,252.35	11,310.44

Summary

A process costing system will be used by those manufacturing firms engaged in the production of homogeneous products on a continuous basis. The same accounts and supporting documents are used in the design of a process costing system as in the job order system with the exception of the number of work in process accounts and the detail ledger for these accounts. Because the cost object in a process system is the process rather than the job, a work in process account is required for each process and unit costs are determined by process rather than job. In a job order costing system the job cost sheets contain the detail for the Work in Process account. In a process costing system the cost of production report contains the detail for each work in process account. An important point to remember is that both systems are striving to accomplish the same basic purposes: determine the unit cost of the completed product and provide management with information useful for decision making.

Unit costs are determined by departments in a process costing system by dividing the total cost incurred in a process during a period by the equivalent production in that department for that period. Equivalent production was defined as the expression of all activity of a processing department during a period in terms of fully completed units. Equivalent production can be determined on the weighted average method or the FIFO method. The weighted average method includes the partially completed units in beginning work in process inventories with the activity for the current period to determine equivalent production whereas the FIFO method concentrates on this period's activity exclusively.

The activity represented by each work in process account is detailed on a cost of production report. The cost of production report consists of four major sections. The first section is the quantity schedule, which merely tracks the physical units through each processing department for the period. The second section consists of a documentation of the determination of equivalent production for each of the cost elements. Section 3 summarizes all the costs charged to the department for the period and explains the debits to the respective work in process account. The fourth section gives the detail of costs transferred out of the department as well as determining the ending work in process inventory value. This section gives the detail of the credits to the work in process account and reconciles the credits with the debits for the period.

If the cost of the basic cost elements remain fairly stable over time, the two methods give very similar results. It would seem then that the "easiest" method would be used. If costs and ending work in process do fluctuate, however, the FIFO method may be more useful for cost control and performance evaluation because of the concentration on the current period's activity only.

It should be pointed out that there are a number of additional topics associated with process costing. The coverage here, however, should give you sufficient background to work with and understand this particular accounting system.

Appendix 8–A
Joint and By-products

Joint Products and Joint Costs

In the discussion of product flow in a process costing environment we illustrated the situation where raw materials were added in a process and two or more separate products emerged. This was described as a joint product/joint cost situation.

Joint products are two or more products of significant value produced simultaneously by a common manufacturing process and coming from a common input. An example of joint products could be different cuts of meat resulting from a butchering process or crude oil products such as fuel oil, gasoline, diesel, and kerosene that result from a common refining process.

The costs incurred in the production of joint products are called **joint costs.** These costs can create problems for cost or managerial accountants. By their very nature, these costs cannot be identified with any particular joint product—they are incurred prior to the separation of the joint products from the common input. This suggests, therefore, that costs incurred are inseparable up to the point where separate joint products are identifiable (the split-off point). For managerial decision making, these costs are irrelevant and may remain identified as joint costs, that is, they are not allocated to the individual products. We also know, however, that for product costing purposes and for external financial reporting all costs of production need to be identified with finished product. As a result, it is necessary to allocate the joint costs to the respective joint products. Because of the inseparable nature of joint costs, any allocation procedure will be arbitrary. The most we can hope for is that the allocation method we use has some reasonable and logical basis and is not spurious.

Joint costs are allocated to joint products at the point of **split-off.** To illustrate the allocation process assume that Heal-All, Inc. is a drug manufacturer that produces Drug A and Drug B from a common manufacturing process illustrated below:

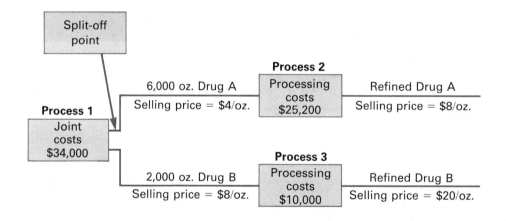

As illustrated above, the joint products (Drug A and Drug B) emerge as separate products from Process 1 where joint costs of $34,000 are incurred. The products can be sold at the split-off point at the price indicated or they can be processed further and sold as Refined Drugs A and B.

Various methods have been proposed for allocating joint costs to joint products. Two of the most popular methods will be discussed here. They are referred to as the **physical quantity method** and the **relative sales value method.**

Physical Quantity Method

Under the physical quantity method, joint costs are allocated on the basis of some physical quantity characteristic such as units of product, a volume measure or a weight measure. The physical quantity measure for Drugs A and

B for Heal-All is ounces of product. Using the physical quantity method, Heal-All would allocate $25,500 of joint costs to Drug A and $8,500 to Drug B as follows:

Product	Quantity (Ounces)	Relative Quantity		Joint Cost		Allocated Joint Costs
Drug A	6,000	.75	×	$34,000	=	$25,500
Drug B	2,000	.25	×	34,000	=	8,500
	8,000	1.00				$34,000

Note that each ounce of product has joint costs of $4.25 associated with it at this point (split-off point), that is, $25,500/6,000 and $8,500/2,000. It is perhaps obvious at this point that we could determine the costs to be allocated to each unit of product merely by first dividing the total joint costs ($34,000) by the total physical measure quantity produced (8,000 ounces) to obtain the cost allocated to each ounce of product ($4.25). The amount allocated to each joint product would then be determined as follows:

Product	Quantity		Cost/Unit		Joint Cost
Drug A	6,000	×	$4.25	=	$25,500
Drug B	2,000	×	4.25	=	8,500
					$34,000

Allocating joint costs by the physical quantity method may produce distortions in gross profit computations. Note the consequences of the method for Heal-All Inc.:

	Drug A	Drug B	Total
Sales	$24,000	$16,000	$40,000
Cost of Goods Sold	25,500	8,500	34,000
Gross Profit	($ 1,500)	$ 7,500	$ 6,000

It appears that Drug A has a negative gross profit and Drug B a positive gross profit. Any time there is a significant difference in the selling price of the joint products (in our case Drug B is selling for twice as much as Drug A at the split-off point), this situation will occur. Where the two products together produce a gross profit of $6,000 and one cannot be produced without the other, it seems unreasonable to assume that one is produced at a loss while the other is produced at a profit. It appears, therefore, that the physical quantity method is a reasonable and logical allocation method only when the selling price per unit of physical quantity measure is equal or not significantly different.

Relative Sales Value Method

As the name implies, using the relative sales value method results in an equal amount of joint cost assigned to each sales dollar resulting in equal gross profit percentages per dollar of sales value. The allocation of joint costs to

Drug A and Drug B for Heal-All is illustrated below. Note that the sales value for each product is determined at the split-off point. For Drug A it is $24,000 (6,000 oz. × $4 per oz.) and $16,000 for Drug B (2,000 oz. × $8 per oz.). Drug A, therefore, has 60% of the total sales value ($24,000/$40,000) and Drug B has the other 40% ($16,000/$40,000).

Product	Sales Value	Relative Sales Value		Joint Costs		Allocated Joint Costs	Unit Cost
Drug A	$24,000	.60	×	$34,000	=	$20,400	$3.40
Drug B	16,000	.40	×	34,000	=	13,600	6.80
	$40,000	1.00				$34,000	

Under this method of joint cost allocation, the partial income statement for Heal-All would appear as follows:

	Drug A	Drug B	Total
Sales	$24,000	$16,000	$40,000
Cost of goods sold	20,400	13,600	34,000
Gross profit	$ 3,600	$ 2,400	$ 6,000
Gross profit %	15%	15%	15%

The use of the relative sales value method results in the joint products being equally profitable up to point of split-off. The "reasonable and logical" basis for this method seems to be that joint products should be allocated joint costs on the basis of their economic value at the split-off point. This seems a fair basis when the nature of joint costs are considered.

It will often happen that joint product(s) cannot be sold at the point of split-off, that is, there is no market for them in their uncompleted state. This presents a problem in using the relative sales value (at split-off) method. When this situation occurs, an approximate sales value at the split-off point is determined by taking the sales value of the completed product and subtracting the costs of processing beyond the split-off point. If we assumed in the Heal-All case that Drug A could not be sold at the split-off point we would approximate a sales value at the point of split-off as shown in Exhibit 8–9.

EXHIBIT 8–9

Relative Sales Value Method Where There Is No Market Value at Split-Off

Product	(1) Sales Value	(2) Costs After Split-Off	(3) = (1) − (2) Relative Sales Value	(4) Relative Sales Value Percents		(5) Joint Costs	(6) Allocated Joint Costs
Drug A	$48,000	$25,200	$22,800	.432	×	$34,000	$14,688
Drug B	40,000	10,000	30,000	.568	×	34,000	19,312
			$52,800				$34,000

The sales value (column 1) for each product is what the final product sells for. For Drug A it is $48,000 (6,000 oz. × $8 per oz.) and $40,000 for Drug B (2,000 oz. × $20 per oz.). The relative sales value percentages were determined by taking each product's relative sales value divided by the total. Thus Drug A's 43.2% is $22,800/$52,800 and Drug B's 56.8% is $30,000/$52,800.

Managerial Decisions of Whether to Process Further

It was mentioned at the beginning of this discussion that joint costs needed to be allocated to joint products for product costing and financial reporting purposes, but these costs were usually irrelevant for internal decision making purposes. The illustration for Heal-All, Inc. indicated that Drugs A and B could be sold at the split-off point or processed further and sold as Refined Drugs A and B. The joint costs are irrelevant in making the decision of whether to process further—the decision turns on whether the additional revenue exceeds the additional costs of processing further. For Drug A, the cost to process the 6,000 ounces further is given as $25,500. The additional revenue generated by processing further is $24,000 [($8 − $4) × 6,000]. It is therefore unprofitable to process Drug A further. Note that the joint costs were not considered in making this decision. This concept is further illustrated in Chapter 12.

By-products

A product of minor economic value that is produced as a result of the production of the main or joint products is referred to as a **by-product.** An example would be the production of bark slabs, sawdust, and wood shavings in the lumber industry. Some by-products may be sold for minor amounts, some may be given away, and in a number of cases it may be necessary to incur costs to dispose of the by-product.

If the by-product can be sold, the treatment that is considered to be conceptually best from a *cost accounting* standpoint is to reduce the cost of the process resulting in the by-product by the net realizable value of the by-product production for the period. **Net realizable value** is the total revenue expected to be generated from the sale of the by-product units produced during the period reduced by any costs to complete or dispose of the units.

A simple illustration using the Heal-All, Inc. example for joint products should demonstrate the procedure. Assume, in the first case, that 1,000 ounces of a by-product are produced in Process 1. The by-product sells for $1 per ounce with selling and disposal costs of $.30 per ounce. In this situation, the joint costs of Process 1 would be reduced by $700 (1,000 oz. × $.70) to $33,300 ($34,000 − $700). The handling of the joint products would proceed exactly as before with the $33,300 being divided between Drug A and Drug B in the same percentages as in Exhibit 8–9 (43.2% for Drug A and 56.8% for Drug B).

Assume, in the second case, that the 1,000 ounces of the by-product are produced in Process 2. In this situation the costs of Process 2 would be reduced to $24,500 ($25,200 − $700). The allocation of the joint costs from Process 1 would proceed as before. The relative sales value percentages would, of course, differ.

In either of these cases, any unsold by-products would be carried in inventory at their net realizable value of $.70 per unit. Other treatments of by-products are simpler than the preferred treatment. They are often treated as elements of Other Revenues and Expenses on the income statement with no effect on the allocation of joint costs among joint products.

Occasionally, by-products may become main products as a result of new technology or demand. If this occurs, the product is then treated as a joint product, and joint costs will be allocated to it as any other joint product.

If the by-product cannot be sold and it is necessary to incur costs to dispose of it, these costs will need to be added to the costs of producing the main products.

Key Terms

By-product is a joint product with relatively minor economic value.

Cost of production report summarizes all the costs charged to a department during a period, shows the dollar amount to be transferred to the next department or finished goods, and shows the computations for ending work in process inventory.

First-in first-out (FIFO) method in product costing separates beginning inventory work in determining equivalent units and calculating equivalent unit rates.

Equivalent production is the expression of activity of a processing department during a period in terms of fully completed units. Beginning inventory work is added in under weighted average but omitted under FIFO.

Joint costs are costs assignable to two or more product lines produced together.

Joint products are two or more products of significant value produced simultaneously by a common manufacturing process and coming from a common input.

Net realizable value is the total revenue expected to be generated from the sale of the by-product units produced during the period reduced by any costs to complete or dispose of the units.

Parallel product flow occurs when products come from a common department and then flow through their own separate series of departments or go through their own separate series of departments and eventually flow through a common department.

Physical quantity method can be used in assigning joint costs to joint products where joint costs are allocated on a physical quantity characteristic such as units or pounds. Where used, the economic value should be proportional to the physical quantity characteristic selected.

Relative sales value method can be used in assigning joint costs to joint products on the basis of economic value at split-off or a simulation of economic value at split-off.

Selective product flow is when product moves to different processing departments based on the final product desired.

Sequential product flow   occurs when product moves in one specified series of steps from process to process.

Split-off   is the point at which joint products separate.

Transferred-in costs   are the direct materials, direct labor, and manufacturing overhead coming from all previous processes that are assigned to units coming into a process.

Weighted average method   combines beginning work in process inventory costs and units with the costs and units of currently started work.

Questions

Q8–1   In a job order costing system, the cost object is the job. What is the cost object in a process costing system?

Q8–2   What product and manufacturing characteristics would support the use of a process costing system?

Q8–3   In what ways is process costing similar to job order costing?

Q8–4   Distinguish among sequential, parallel, and selective product flow in the production process.

Q8–5   When materials are requisitioned in a job order costing environment, a materials requisition is needed to indicate which job should be charged for the materials cost. Are materials requisitions necessary in a process costing environment? Why or why not?

Q8–6   A job time ticket is not important in a process costing system. Do you agree? Why or why not?

Q8–7   If a company is using a process costing system, how many work in process accounts would it have in its general ledger?

Q8–8   It has been suggested that the cost allocation phase is easier using process costing as opposed to job order costing. Do you agree? Why or why not?

Q8–9   What is meant by *equivalent units of production?*

Q8–10   Explain the difference between equivalent units in process and equivalent units manufactured.

Q8–11   What is the *basic* difference between the weighted average method of process costing and the FIFO method?

Q8–12   Explain the difference between weighted average and FIFO process costing in terms of the treatment of beginning work in process inventory.

Q8–13   What is a quantity schedule and what purpose does it serve?

Q8–14   How does the calculation of equivalent units of production under the weighted average method differ from the FIFO method?

Q8–15   What is a cost of production report? What is its counterpart in job order costing?

Q8–16   Which record in a process costing system provides the information for the dollar amount to be transferred from Work in Process to Finished Goods on the completion of product?

Q8–17   From a performance and evaluation standpoint, it was suggested that the FIFO method may be superior to the weighted average method. Why might this be so?

Q8–18   Why is the FIFO method sometimes referred to as *modified FIFO?*

Q8–19   Under what circumstances would a department (or process) show transferred-in costs in its cost of production report?

Q8–20   Distinguish between joint products and by-products.

Q8–21   What are joint costs? What problem is there in using a "physical units" basis for allocating joint costs?

Q8–22   Joint costs are often allocated using the relative sales value method at the point of split-off. What is meant by the *split-off point?* What if the product cannot be sold at the split-off point; that is, it has no sales value at that point?

Exercises

E8–1   **Quantity schedule for one department.** Dwight Company manufactures a product that goes through two processing departments, Lathe and Polishing. The following information pertains to the Lathe Department for the month of June 19X7:

	Units
Work in process, June 1 (100% complete for materials, 40% labor and overhead)	4,000
Started during June	80,000
Work in process, June 30 (100% complete for materials, 55% labor and overhead)	6,000

Required: Prepare a quantity schedule for the Lathe Department for the month of June.

E8–2   **Quantity schedule for two departments.** Lendler Industries manufactures a product that goes through three processes: cutting, grinding, and treating. Material is all added at the beginning of processing in the Cutting Department. The following information is available for the Cutting and Grinding Departments for the month of August 19X7:

		Percentage Complete	
	Units	Materials	Conversion
Cutting Department:			
Work in process, August 1	8,000	100	30
Started during August	50,000		
Work in process, August 31	10,000	100	40
Grinding Department:			
Work in process, August 1	4,000	—	50
Work in process, August 31	2,000	—	60

Required: Prepare a quantity schedule for the Cutting and Grinding Departments for the month of August. (Prepare one schedule with columns for each department.)

E8–3   **Equivalent units — weighted average.** Sussex Corporation's production cycle starts in the Mixing Department. The company uses a process costing system, and the following information is available for the month of April 19X7:

	Units
Work in process, April 1 (50% complete)	40,000
Started in April	240,000
Work in process, April 30 (60% complete)	25,000

Materials are added at the beginning of processing in the Mixing Department.

Required: Using the weighted average method, what are the equivalent units of production for direct materials, direct labor, and manufacturing overhead in the Mixing Department for the month of April 19X7?

(CPA Adapted)

E8–4   **Equivalent units — FIFO method.** The Fabrication Department is the first stage in the production cycle for the Dale Company. Material is added at the beginning of processing. The following information is available for the Fabrication Department for the month of October 19X7:

	Units
Work in process, October 1 (60% complete)	20,000
Started in October	250,000
Work in process, October 31 (40% complete)	30,000

Required: Using the FIFO method, determine the equivalent units of production for direct materials, direct labor, and manufacturing overhead for the Fabrication Department for the month of October 19X7.

E8–5   **Budgeted equivalent units.** Lempir Company produces canned tomato soup and is budgeting sales of 250,000 units for the month of January 19X7. Actual inventory units at January 1 and budgeted inventory units at January 31 are as follows:

	Units
Actual inventory at January 1:	
Work in process (40% complete)	10,000
Finished goods	75,000
Budgeted inventory at January 31:	
Work in process (75% complete)	16,000
Finished goods	6,000

Materials are added evenly throughout the production process.

Required: How many equivalent units of production (for all elements of manufacturing) is Lempir budgeting for January 19X7?

(CPA Adapted)

E8–6   **Equivalent units; cost of material, labor, and overhead — weighted average.** Tandry Company manufactures a product that requires processing in two departments, Cooking and Mixing. Materials are added at the beginning of processing in the Cooking Department. The information on the next page is available regarding the Cooking Department for the month of March 19X7.

	Units	Cost
Work in process, March 1 (60% processed)	10,000	
Direct materials		$ 41,000
Direct labor		31,700
Manufacturing overhead		14,150
Total work in process, March 1		$ 86,850
Started in production during March	70,000	
Costs added:		
Direct materials		$355,000
Direct labor		284,000
Manufacturing overhead		213,000
Total costs added during March		$852,000
Work in process, March 31 (80% processed)	15,000	

Required: Determine the cost per equivalent unit of production for direct materials, direct labor, and manufacturing overhead in the Cooking Department for the month of March if Tandry uses the weighted average method of process costing.

E8–7 **Equivalent units; cost of material, labor, and overhead—FIFO.** Refer to the data in E8–6 for Tandry Company.

Required: Determine the cost per equivalent unit of production for direct materials, direct labor, and manufacturing overhead in the Cooking Department for the month of March if Tandry uses the FIFO method of process costing.

E8–8 **Journal entries to record flow of product through processes.** Stick-All Industries manufactures a special glue used in the wood products industry. The glue is processed in two departments: Cooking and Blending. Materials are added at the beginning of processing in both the Cooking Department and the Blending Department. The T-accounts below show the flow of costs through the two processes for the month of September 19X7:

Work in Process – Cooking

Balance 9/1	23,000	Transferred to	
Direct materials	72,000	Blending	245,000
Direct labor	85,000		
Manufacturing overhead	68,000		

Work in Process – Blending

Balance 9/1	32,000	Completed and	
From Cooking	245,000	transferred to	
Direct materials	33,000	Finished Goods	375,000
Direct labor	25,000		
Manufacturing overhead	48,000		

Required: Prepare journal entries to reflect all of the activity in the two processing departments for the month of September 19X7.

E8–9 **Unit costs transferred out—weighted average.** Ray Company manufactures Product X in a two-step production cycle in Departments A and B. Ray uses the weighted average method of process costing. Conversion costs for Department B were 50% complete as to the 6,000 units in the beginning work in process and 75% as to the 8,000 units in the ending work in process; 12,000 units were completed and transferred out of Department B during February 19X7. An analysis of the costs relating to work in process and production activity in Department B for February 19X7 follows:

		Costs	
	Transferred In	Materials	Conversion
Work in Process, February 1	$12,000	$2,500	$1,000
February costs added	29,000	5,500	5,000

Required: Determine the cost per equivalent unit of Product X transferred to finished goods during February 19X7. (Round answers to the nearest penny.)

(CPA Adapted)

E8–10 **Allocation of joint costs — physical units method.** Dumont Chemical Company produces two chemicals, Jo-Po and Jo-Go, from a joint process, boiling. The joint products can be sold at this point or processed further. Dumont elects to process further, and Jo-Po goes on to an extraction process and Jo-Go is processed further in a blending process. A by-product, By-Gone, also emerges from the boiling process but as yet has no commercial value and is hauled away free of charge by local farmers who use it to help keep cattle feedlots dry.

Because the joint products have similar sales values at the split-off point, and also because the joint products are both measured in gallons, Dumont allocates the joint costs on the basis of physical units. The following information pertains to the Boiling Department for the month of July 19X7:

No beginning and ending inventories of work in process
Costs added during the month:

Raw material	$ 55,000
Direct labor	38,000
Manufacturing overhead	27,000
Total costs added	$120,000

Production units:

Jo-Po	59,800 gallons
Jo-Go	55,200 gallons
By-Gone	5,000 tons

Required: 1. Determine the amount of joint costs to be allocated to the joint products.
2. Make the journal entries to record the activity in the Boiling Department for the month of July 19X7.

E8–11 **Equivalent units and unit costs — weighted average.** Grandy Products manufactures a single product that requires shaping and assembling and uses a process costing system to account for the manufacturing activity. All material is added at the beginning of processing in the Shaping Department. A quantity schedule for the month of October for the Shaping Department is given on the next page.

QUANTITY SCHEDULE
Shaping Department
For the month of October 19X7

Units to be accounted for:

Units in process, October 1 (all materials, 80% converted)	12,000
Units started in process during October	120,000
Total units to be accounted for	132,000

Units accounted for as follows:

Units transferred to Assembling Department	112,000
Units in process, October 31 (all material, 40% labor and overhead)	20,000
Total units accounted for	132,000

The following dollar amounts pertain to the Shaping Department for October 19X7:

Work in process, October 1:

Direct material	$ 57,000
Direct labor	70,800
Manufacturing overhead	51,600
Total	$ 179,400

Costs added during October:

Direct material	$ 900,000
Direct labor	883,200
Manufacturing overhead	662,400
Total costs added	$2,445,600

Required:

1. Assume that Grandy uses the weighted average method of process costing. Prepare a schedule showing the equivalent units of production for direct materials, direct labor, and manufacturing overhead in the Shaping Department for the month of October.

2. Complete the "costs charged to the Shaping Department" section of the cost of production report given below:

	Total Cost	Unit Cost
Cost Added by Shaping Department:		
Materials:		
Work in process, beginning	$ 57,000	
During current period	900,000	
Total materials added	$957,000	?
Direct labor:		
Work in process, beginning	?	
During current period	?	
Total direct labor added	?	?
Manufacturing overhead:		
Work in process, beginning	?	
During current period	?	
Total overhead added	?	?
Total cost to be accounted for	?	?

E8–12 **Costs transferred out and ending work in process—weighted average.** This is a continuation of Exercise 8–11. Refer to the data in E8–11 and the solution to that exercise.

Required:

1. Complete the "cost accounted for as follows" section of the cost of production report given below:

Cost Accounted for as Follows:

Completed and transferred to Assembling Department		?
Work in Process — Ending Inventory:		
Direct materials	?	
Direct labor	?	
Manufacturing overhead	?	?
Total cost accounted for		?

2. Compare the "total cost accounted for" determined above with the "total cost to be accounted for" in E8–11. Do they agree? If not, see if you can determine the cause of the difference and correct your error(s).

E8–13 **Equivalent units and unit costs—FIFO.** Refer to the data for Grandy Products in Exercise 8–11.

Required:

1. Assume that Grandy uses the FIFO method of process costing. Prepare a schedule showing the equivalent units of production for direct materials, direct labor, and manufacturing overhead in the Shaping Department for the month of October 19X7.
2. Complete the "costs charged to the Shaping Department" section of the cost of production report given below:

	Total Cost	Unit Cost
Costs Charged to the Shaping Department:		
Work in process, beginning	$179,400	
Cost added by Shaping Department:		
Direct materials	$900,000	?
Direct labor	?	?
Manufacturing overhead	?	?
Total cost added	?	?
Total cost to be accounted for	?	?

E8–14 **Costs transferred out and ending work in process—FIFO.** This is a continuation of Exercise 8–13. Refer to the data for Grandy Products in Exercise 8–11 and to the solution to Exercise 8–13.

Required:

1. Complete the "cost accounted for as follows" section of the cost of production report on page 278 (assuming that the FIFO method of process costing is used).

Cost Accounted for as Follows:

Completed and transferred to Assembling Department:
From beginning inventory:

Inventory value	$179,400	
Direct labor	?	
Manufacturing overhead	?	
Total		?
From current production		?
Total cost transferred out		?
Work in process, ending:		
Direct materials	?	
Direct labor	?	
Manufacturing overhead	?	
Total ending work in process		?
Total cost accounted for		?

2. Compare the "total cost accounted for" determined above with the "total cost to be accounted for" in Exercise 8–13. Do they agree? If not, see if you can determine the cause of the difference and correct your error(s).

Problems

P8–15   **Cost of production report—weighted average (no beginning work in process).** Agra Industry manufactures a liquid fertilizer used especially by truck gardeners for the growing of vegetables. The fertilizer is produced in a continuous process entirely in one mixing and blending department. All material is added at the beginning of processing. Production and cost information for Agra for the month of January 19X7 are given below:

	Gallons
Production information:	
Started during January	80,000
Completed and transferred to storage tanks	65,000
In process, end of January (100% complete for materials, 66⅔% for direct labor and manufacturing overhead	15,000
Costs added during January:	
Direct materials	$400,000
Direct labor	112,500
Manufacturing overhead applied on the basis of 150% of direct labor cost	

Required: Prepare a complete cost of production report for the Mixing and Blending Department for the month of January 19X7. The cost of production report should include:

a. Quantity schedule
b. Schedule showing the calculation of equivalent units
c. Cost to account for with a determination of unit costs
d. Cost accounted for showing costs transferred out and the detail of the ending work in process, if any

P8-16 **Cost of production report—FIFO (no beginning work in process).** Refer to the data in P8-15. Change the degree of completion of the units in ending work in process from 66⅔% complete to 80% complete. All other information remains the same.

Required:

1. Prepare a complete cost of production report for the Mixing and Blending Department for the month of January 19X7. The cost of production report should include:
   a. Quantity schedule
   b. Schedule showing the calculation of equivalent units
   c. Cost to account for with a determination of unit costs
   d. Cost accounted for showing costs transferred out and the detail of the ending work in process inventory
2. With no beginning inventories and one processing department, what is the difference between the weighted average method and the FIFO method of process costing?

P8-17 **Detailed manufacturing and unit costs from incomplete data.** Conrad Company manufactures a single product on a continuous basis in a single department. The company knows that its cost per equivalent unit processed in December 19X7 for materials was $9. All material is added at the beginning of processing. There was no work in process at the beginning of December. During the month, 18,000 units of product were finished and ending work in process contained 5,000 units that were 40% complete as to direct labor and manufacturing overhead. The total cost for the units transferred to finished goods during the month and the work in process at the end of the month was $447,000. Conrad applies manufacturing overhead on the basis of 60% of direct labor cost.

Required:

1. Determine the equivalent units of production for direct materials, direct labor, and manufacturing overhead for Conrad Company for the month of December.
2. Determine the total cost added to production for December for direct materials, direct labor, and manufacturing overhead.
3. Determine the cost per equivalent unit of production for the month for direct materials, direct labor, and manufacturing overhead.
4. Show the computation for the costs transferred to Finished Goods during the month.
5. Show the detail of costs for the ending Work in Process.

P8-18 **Cost of production report with beginning work in process—weighted average.** Square-B manufactures bricks used in the building of houses and commercial buildings. The bricks are formed in a mixing and shaping process and then are fired in a kiln. Square-B measures the volume of bricks by the pallet. At the beginning of April 19X7 the company had 200 pallets of bricks in process. All the material is added at the beginning of processing in the Mixing and Shaping Department. The work in process at April 1 was 60% complete as to direct labor and manufacturing overhead, and the following costs had been applied to the production process:

Direct materials	$11,150
Direct labor	3,739
Manufacturing overhead	5,223

During the month of April 1,500 pallets were started into production. The costs on page 280 were charged to production during the month.

Direct materials	$90,000
Direct labor	48,425
Manufacturing overhead	58,855

At April 30, 300 pallets were in process and were 70% complete as to direct labor and manufacturing overhead.

Required: Prepare a complete cost of production report for the Mixing and Shaping Department of Square-B for the month of April 19X7, assuming that the company uses the weighted average method of process costing. The cost of production report should include
a. Quantity schedule
b. Schedule showing the computation of equivalent units
c. Costs to account for with a determination of units costs
d. Cost accounted for showing costs transferred out of the department during the month and the detail of the ending Work in Process

P8–19 **Cost of production report with beginning work in process — FIFO.** Refer to the information given for P8–18.

Required: Prepare a complete cost of production report for the Mixing and Shaping Department of Square-B for the month of April 19X7, assuming that the company uses the FIFO method of process costing. The cost of production report should include
a. Quantity schedule (if you have done P8–18 you already have completed a quantity schedule and need not repeat it here)
b. Schedule showing the computation of equivalent units
c. Cost to account for with a determination of unit costs
d. Cost accounted for showing costs transferred out of the department during the month and the detail of the ending Work in Process

P8–20 **Analysis of Work in Process account — weighted average.** Reyab Drug Company manufactures a popular tablet for relief of headaches. The ingredients are all added in the Mixing Department. The compound then goes to the Forming and Drying Department where the compound is made into tablets and then on to a third department where the tablets are packaged. Information for the Mixing Department for the month of January is given below:

Work in Process – Mixing

January 1 balance		Completed and transferred	
(100,000 units 40%		to forming and drying	
converted)	143,500	(b) units	(c)
Direct materials			
(1,000,000 units)	1,250,000		
Direct labor	(a)		
Manufacturing			
overhead	437,500		
February 1 balance			
(200,000 units 70%			
converted)	(d)		

The beginning balance in Work in Process — Mixing consisted of the following:

Direct materials	$103,000
Direct labor	20,400
Manufacturing overhead	20,100
Total	$143,500

Reyab made some changes in the materials ingredients as well as processing techniques starting January 1, so they are expecting some changes in costs per unit compared to last year. The company started applying overhead on the basis of 175% of direct labor cost at the beginning of January.

Required:

1. Assume Reyab Drug Company uses the weighted average method of process costing. Determine the missing values for the letters (a) through (d) in the Work in Process—Mixing account above, and the unit costs of production during January. Show your work (prepare a cost of production report if you find it necessary).

2. When a company changes the manufacturing process as Reyab did, what problems are there from a performance evaluation and control standpoint in using the weighted average method?

P8–21 **Analysis of work in process account—FIFO.** Refer to the data for the Reyab Drug Company given in P8–20.

Required:

1. Assume that Reyab Drug Company uses the FIFO method of process costing. Determine the missing values for the letters (a) through (d) in the Work in Process—Mixing account and the unit costs of production during January. Show your work (prepare a cost of production report if it is necessary).

2. If you completed P8–20, compare the unit costs that you just determined under FIFO with those you obtained using the weighted average method. You should now be able to better understand the question posed in P8–20—"When a company changes the manufacturing process as Reyab did, what problems are there from a performance evaluation and control standpoint in using the weighted average method?"

P8–22 **Cost of production report and journal entries; second department—weighted average.** Comp-Con Electronics manufactures a small hand-held computer that the company feels will soon capture a sizable portion of the educational computer market. The computers are processed in two departments: Fabrication and Assembly.

Comp-Con started the month of August 19X7 with 5,000 units in process in the Assembly Department, 52% complete as to conversion. Because the Assembly Department only assembles the fabricated parts, no material is added in this department. The following schedule gives the detail of the costs associated with the beginning work in process and of the costs added to the Assembly Department during August:

Beginning work in process (5,000 units):		
Transferred in from Fabrication		$ 290,000
Costs added in Assembly:		
Direct labor	$100,400	
Manufacturing overhead	51,600	
Total cost added		152,000
Total beginning work in process		$ 442,000

August activity:
Transferred in from Fabrication
(15,000 units) $ 900,000
Costs added in Assembly:
Direct labor $604,800
Manufacturing overhead   489,600
Total cost added   1,094,400
Total transferred in and costs
added in Assembly during
August $1,994,400

At August 31, 19X7, there were 6,000 units in process in Assembly 60% complete as to direct labor and manufacturing overhead.

Required: 1. Prepare a complete cost of production report for the month of August for the Assembly Department of Comp-Con Electronics assuming that the company is using the weighted average method of process costing. The cost of production report should include
a. Quantity schedule
b. Schedule showing the computation of equivalent units
c. Cost to account for with a determination of unit costs
d. Cost accounted for showing costs transferred out of the department during the month and the detail of the ending Work in Process
2. Prepare journal entries to record all of the activity in the Assembly Department for the month of August.

P8–23   Cost of production report and journal entries; second department—FIFO. Refer to the data for Comp-Con Electronics in P8–22.

Required: 1. Prepare a complete cost of production report for the month of August for the Assembly Department of Comp-Con Electronics assuming that the company is using the FIFO method of process costing. The cost of production report should include
a. Quantity schedule (if you did P8–22, you already have a quantity schedule and need not do it again)
b. Schedule showing the computation of equivalent units
c. Costs to account for with a determination of unit costs
d. Cost accounted for showing costs transferred out of the department during the month and the detail of the ending work in process
2. Prepare journal entries to record all of the activity in the Assembly Department for the month of August.

P8–24   Cost of production report, journal entries, work in process T-accounts; two departments—weighted average. Shakway Pharmaceutical manufactures a multiple vitamin in tablet form. The company mixes the contents in the Mixing Department and then shapes the compounds in tablet form in the Shaping/Drying Department. The tablets are then packaged in various containers and packages in the Packaging Department. The quantity schedule for the Mixing and Shaping/Drying Departments for the month of March is given on the next page.

Quantity Schedule

	Mixing	Shaping/Drying
Units to be accounted for:		
Units in process, March 1:		
Mixing (80% converted)	50,000	
Shaping/Drying (40% converted)		60,000
Units started in process in March	900,000	
Units transferred in from Mixing		870,000
Total units to be accounted for	950,000	930,000
Units accounted for as follows:		
Units completed and transferred		
to Shaping/Drying	870,000	
Units completed and transferred		
to Packaging		890,000
Units in process, March 31:		
Mixing (60% converted)	80,000	
Shaping/Drying (70% converted)		40,000
Total units accounted for	950,000	930,000

All material is added at the beginning of processing in the Mixing Department. As a result, only direct labor and manufacturing overhead are added in the Shaping/Drying Department. The costs in Work in Process at March 1 in each department based on the use of either the weighted average or FIFO method of process costing are given below:

	Mixing Department	
	Weighted Average	FIFO
Work in Process, March 1:		
Materials	$ 81,000	$ 81,000
Direct labor	39,180	39,180
Manufacturing overhead	28,820	28,820
Total	$149,000	$149,000

	Shaping/Drying Department	
	Weighted Average	FIFO
Work in Process, March 1:		
Costs transferred in from		
Mixing Department	$230,100	$225,600
Direct labor	23,580	21,300
Manufacturing overhead	39,180	37,600
Total	$292,860	$284,500

The costs added by each department during the month of March were as follows:

	Mixing	Shaping/Drying
Materials	$1,800,000	$ –0–
Direct labor	658,500	536,400
Manufacturing overhead	834,100	1,117,500
Total costs added	$3,292,600	$1,653,900

Required:

1. Assuming that Shakway uses the weighted average method of process costing, prepare a cost of production report for both Mixing and Shaping/Drying for the month of March. The quantity schedule was already done for you, so your cost of production report should include
   a. Schedule showing computation of equivalent units
   b. Costs to account for with a determination of unit costs
   c. Costs accounted for showing costs transferred out of the department during the month and the detail of the ending Work in Process
2. Prepare the journal entries to summarize the activities in the two departments for the month of March.
3. Prepare T-accounts for work in process for the Mixing and Shaping/Drying Departments. Enter the beginning balances and post the entries for the month from your journal entries. Make sure that the balance of each Work in Process account at March 31 agrees with the March 31 work in process inventory shown in the respective cost of production report.

P8–25   **Cost of production report, journal entries, work in process T-accounts; two departments — FIFO.** Refer to the data for Shakway Pharmaceutical in P8–24.

Required:

1. Assuming that Shakway uses the FIFO method of process costing, prepare a cost of production report for both the Mixing and Shaping/Drying Departments for the month of March. The quantity schedule was already done for you, so your cost of production report should include
   a. Schedule showing computation of equivalent units
   b. Cost to account for with a determination of unit costs
   c. Cost accounted for showing costs transferred out of the departments during the month and the detail of the ending Work in Process
2. Prepare the journal entries to summarize the activities in the two departments for the month of March.
3. Prepare T-accounts for the Work in Process for the Mixing and Shaping/Drying Departments. Enter the beginning balances and post the entries for the month from your journal entries. Make sure that the balance of each work in process account at March 31 agrees with the March 31 work in process inventory shown in the respective cost of production report.

P8–26   **Joint cost allocation — relative sales value method.** Wainwright Corporation manufactures products C, D, and E from a joint process. Joint costs are allocated on the basis of relative sales value at split-off. Additional information is as follows:

		Product		
	C	D	E	Total
Units produced	6,000	4,000	2,000	12,000
Joint costs	$ 72,000	?	?	$120,000
Sales value at split-off	?	?	$30,000	$200,000
Additional costs if processed further	$ 14,000	$10,000	$ 6,000	$ 30,000
Sales value if processed further	$140,000	$60,000	$40,000	$240,000

Required: How much of the joint costs should Wainwright allocate to joint products D and E?

(CPA Adapted)

P8–27 **Verification of stated inventory values using weighted average process costing.** Spanner Corporation manufactures a digital watch. You are a member of the internal audit team for Spanner and are attempting to verify the costing of the ending inventory of work in process and finished goods that were recorded on Spanner's books as follows:

	Units	Cost
Work in process (50% complete as to labor and overhead)	300,000	$ 660,960
Finished goods	200,000	$1,009,800

Materials are added to production at the beginning of the manufacturing process and manufacturing overhead is applied to each product at the rate of 60% of direct labor costs. There was no finished goods inventory on January 1, 19X7. A review of Spanner's inventory cost records disclosed the following information:

		Costs	
	Units	Materials	Labor
Work in process January 1, 1987 (80% complete as to labor and overhead)	200,000	$ 200,000	$ 315,000
Units started in production	1,000,000		
Materials costs		$1,300,000	
Labor costs			$1,995,000
Units completed	900,000		

Required: 1. Prepare schedules as of December 31, 19X7, to compute the following:
   a. Equivalent units of production using the weighted average method
   b. Unit costs of production of materials, labor, and manufacturing overhead
   c. Costing of the finished goods inventory and work in process inventory
2. Prepare the journal entry that you would propose to correctly state the inventory of finished goods and work in process, assuming that the books have not been closed.

(CPA Adapted)

CHAPTER 9

Standard Costing – Materials and Labor

Learning Objectives

After reading this chapter you should be able to:

1. Explain how a standard costing system relates to a job order or process costing system.

2. Differentiate between ideal standards and currently attainable standards.

3. Explain how direct material and direct labor standards are determined.

4. Distinguish between standard costs and standard cost cards.

5. Compute direct materials price and quantity variances and explain their significance.

6. Compute direct labor rate and efficiency variances and explain their significance.

7. Prepare journal entries to record direct material and direct labor transactions using a standard costing system.

8. Explain how management decides whether or not it should investigate a variance.

9. Enumerate the advantages and appreciate the possible negative aspects of using a standard costing system.

10. Have knowledge of economic order quantity and just-in-time approaches to inventory management (Appendix 9–A).

11. Comprehend the learning curve phenomenon (Appendix 9–B).

There are two basic cost systems used to determine unit costs of production: job order costing and process costing. We established previously that a job order costing system is used in those manufacturing situations where units of product differ from each other such as the building of custom cabinets for houses or special ordered agricultural equipment; and a process costing system is used in those manufacturing situations where a basically homogeneous product flows evenly through production on a fairly continuous basis such as the manufacture of paint, textiles, or chemicals. In both of these costing systems, the unit cost of production was, more or less, the actual cost incurred in the production process. We say "more or less" because the product cost included the actual cost of direct materials used and the actual cost of direct labor incurred, but overhead was charged to the product using a predetermined rate. If the actual overhead incurred and the actual activity achieved turned out exactly as estimated when the overhead rate was calculated, then the unit cost for overhead would, in fact, be the actual costs incurred. However, if either the actual overhead costs or the actual activity achieved varied from estimate there would be an element of under- or overapplied overhead. Manufacturing overhead unit costs determined by either of the costing systems can be converted to actual unit costs by allocating the under- or overapplied overhead to the various inventories and to cost of goods sold.

Although the actual cost to produce a unit of product is useful information, it perhaps does not provide management with the degree of information content it would like. It does not tell management, for instance, that the price paid for materials and labor was as expected. Nor does it tell management whether the time required to manufacture units was as expected or whether more or less material than estimated was used in the manufacturing process. The basic costing systems are not designed to capture this information—it would be available only with a good deal of analysis outside the costing system itself.

In this chapter we begin to explore a costing system designed to capture some of this additional information. It is referred to as *standard costing.* An important point that needs to be emphasized immediately is that a standard costing system is not a "third" costing system. Just as air conditioning, power steering, power brakes, and so forth are accessories added to a basic automobile to make it easier to operate and control, standard costing is an "accessory" that can be added to either job order costing or process costing to enhance these basic costing systems. In this chapter we develop the concept of standard costing and variance analysis with respect to materials and labor. In the following chapter we extend the application to manufacturing overhead.

Two appendixes conclude the chapter. Materials standards are concerned with minimizing material costs per unit consistent with the quality of inputs and quantities in which materials are acquired. Appendix 9–A is concerned with determining appropriate order sizes for materials and when purchase orders should be instituted. Appendix 9–B discusses the learning curve, an important phenomenon involving complex labor operations (and therefore labor standards) where employee performance improves as more output is produced. Hence these appendixes deal with issues of cost estimation and minimization that are closely related to standard cost issues.

Standard Costs

Before we can explain and illustrate a standard costing system, we need to understand what is meant by the term *standard cost.* It is perhaps useful to emphasize the two words—*standard* and *cost. Standard* refers to a predetermined quantity of materials or time required to manufacture one unit of product or to perform one unit of service. We have all encountered standards in one way or another. If we take our automobile to the garage to have a new clutch installed, for example, and we ask for an estimate to do the job, the shop foreman will most likely refer to a manual that lists the "standard time" to complete the task. If you have worked in a restaurant, you may have heard the managers refer to *portion control.* They might have been referring to the standard amount of french fries that are to be served with various sandwiches or dinner combinations or the ounces of sliced beef that should be placed on each French Dip sandwich. We speak in terms of standards for ourselves: the normal time it takes to get ready for work in the morning, the normal time to get to work by public or private transport, or the normal time it takes us to complete our three-mile run in the morning. As you might expect, many manufacturing firms have developed standards for the quantity of materials and the amount of time required to produce a unit of product.

The word *cost* in the term *standard cost* refers to the predetermined dollar amount associated with each unit expressed in the standard quantity. For example, a manufacturer may have determined that material A should cost $3.00 per pound (the standard price), and that it takes five pounds of material A to manufacture a unit of product X. The standard quantity of material required is five pounds of material A and the standard price is $3.00 per pound—the standard cost of materials for product X, then, is $15.00 (standard quantity × standard price). The term **standard cost** can now be defined as the expected or budgeted cost of materials, labor, or manufacturing overhead to produce one unit of product. Notice the emphasis on *one* unit of product. When we prepare a formal list of the standard cost for materials, labor, and manufacturing overhead to produce one unit of product and add them together, we arrive at the total standard cost for one unit of product and refer to it as a **standard cost card.**

The Standard Setting Process

We have referred to standard costs as expected or predetermined quantity and dollar amounts necessary to produce one unit of product. These standards must, of course, be determined by someone. Although the accountant may be able to contribute a good deal of useful information to help determine the standard, he or she is ill equipped to be the final standard setter. For instance, the accountant may be able to assemble historical information regarding quantities and dollar amounts of materials, labor, and manufacturing overhead used in the past to produce a unit of output and might even have some insight into what costs might be in the immediate future. This, however, is only one piece of information that might be used in the setting of a standard. It could be that production has been very inefficient in the past or that future production processes will be entirely different because of changed factory technology. The firm would not wish to perpetuate past inefficiencies. What else, then, is required in the standard setting process?

Before we can answer this question fully we need to know what kind of standard management wishes to set. There are basically two choices that management can make—ideal standards or currently attainable standards.

Ideal Standards

Just as the name suggests, **ideal standards** are similar to the perfect 10 in gymnastics—virtually unattainable. In industry, the ideal standard would be based on the kind of efficiency that managers dream of—no work stoppages due to material shortages, highly skilled and efficient employees who work at peak performance all of the time, and efficient machinery that can operate at peak capacity with no breakdowns. Most managers would agree, however, that although this is nice to dream about, reality would suggest that it is not practical. In fact, such a standard may even be counterproductive. If employees know (and they will learn very quickly) that a standard is not attainable, serious morale problems can be created. Employees may feel that if they are going to perform below standard anyway, they might just as well "miss the mark" a good deal and let management know that their expectations are unfair. Under these conditions, the standard may give rise to low morale and even sabotage instead of being a motivational force to give employees a goal to achieve. In addition, deviations from such standards are difficult to analyze. Management would have to decide what part of the deviation from standard is expected because they know the standard is really unattainable, and what part is due to inefficiencies (or efficiencies). The alternative is to choose a currently attainable standard.

Currently Attainable Standards

Currently attainable standards discount some of the dreams built into ideal standards. For instance, time is allowed for normal machine down-time and for employee rest periods. This does not mean, however, that all employees can achieve standard—it would require diligent effort by a normal worker who is efficient and well trained. In other words, the standard is tight but attainable. Notice that this standard is called *currently* attainable. This means that the standard is current—it is up-to-date. It would not be useful to compare current performance with a two-year-old standard if prices or the production process has changed over the years. Not only would it be unfair for those whose performance is being measured, but it introduces confusion into the information furnished to management. The deviations from standard would not measure current efficiencies or inefficiencies only — they would include legitimate deviations because of uncontrollable changes that have occurred over time.

We will assume throughout our discussion of standard costing the use of currently attainable standards. Now that we are familiar with what we mean by *standards* and *standard costs,* we will next illustrate the setting of standards for direct materials and direct labor.

Setting Direct Materials Standards

In the definition of standard costs it was stressed that there would need to be a standard for the quantity of materials that should be used as well as a standard price for the material. In a medium to large manufacturing firm the standard quantity might be determined by engineers who can establish very specific relationships between inputs and outputs. They might be able to say, for example, that three pounds of material A *will* produce a unit of product X *if* a certain quality of material A is used and if the manufacturing process is followed as prescribed by the engineering staff. In a smaller firm, the standard might be arrived at much less scientifically. Management might agree on a standard by obtaining information about the past from the accountant, by consulting with line supervisors in the plant, and by considering possible changes they expect will occur in the future. However the standard is set, it should make allowances for normal waste or spoilage and for normal rejects. If a manufacturing firm is stamping out jar covers from metal sheets, there is bound to be some scrap, and once in a while the product may not meet specifications at inspection points because of machine failure. This is especially true if the product being manufactured requires a high degree of precision. With these considerations in mind, the determination of a standard quantity could appear as follows:

Standard Quantity of Material per Unit of Product X

	Pounds
Material A in final product X	3.0
Allowance for waste	.2
Allowance for rejects (normal)	.1
Standard quantity per unit product X	3.3

The standard price per unit of material should reflect the total cost of acquiring the material: the basic price less discounts plus freight, receiving and handling. Remember that in setting the quantity standard we have designated a specific *quality* material, so the price must coincide with the specified material. We would also set the standard price based on the quantities that we normally order and using the mode of shipment best suited to our needs (costs and time considered). The standard price, therefore, might be determined as follows:

Standard Price per Pound of Material A

	Price per Pound
Purchase price, grade AA, 100 pound lots	$5.50
Less purchase discounts	(.50)
Freight — United Trucking Company	.26
Receiving and handling	.04
Standard price per pound	$5.30

The $5.30 standard price per pound is theoretically correct. Not all firms, however, will add the freight costs and receiving and handling costs to the cost of raw material inventory because of the additional accounting costs involved. The freight-in and receiving and handling costs may merely be included in manufacturing overhead and become part of the cost of finished product through the normal application of manufacturing overhead. If this is the case, the standard price for material would consist of the purchase price less any discounts.

Now that we have established the standard quantity of material A as 3.3 pounds and the standard price to be $5.30 per pound, we can determine the standard cost of material for a unit of product X by multiplying the standard quantity by the standard price:

$$3.3 \text{ lbs.} \times \$5.30 = \$17.49 \text{ per unit}$$

The above would appear on the standard cost card for product X as the standard materials component.

Setting Direct Labor Standards

Various approaches may be taken to set the standard time for the production of a product just as in the case of setting the standard quantity for direct materials. Larger manufacturing firms that have engineers on their staff may do comprehensive studies of the manufacturing process. The engineers may actually go to the factory floor with stop watches, observing and timing the various operations to arrive at a standard time. The exact handling procedure, placement of tools, body position, and so forth, may have been designed for the worker to follow. Another procedure could be to break down the required direct labor into the most basic of body movements, and by referring to published standard tables for the movements, the total time to do a job can be determined by adding up the time required by the various movements. Medium to small firms may find either of these approaches too costly and may, as in the case of direct materials, turn to accountants, line supervisors, and personnel to compile information suitable for the determination of the standard time. Whatever approach is used to set the standard, time required must give consideration to the usual coffee breaks, personal needs of employees, adjustment or cleanup time, expected down-time for the machinery, and normal time required for reworking. The standard time might be calculated as follows:

Standard Quantity of Direct Labor per Unit of Product X

	Hours
Actual direct labor time required	3.5
Allowance for breaks and personal needs	.2
Allowance for reworking	.1
Allowance for clean-up and down-time	.2
Standard hours per unit of product X	4.0

The standard cost for direct labor is usually referred to as the *standard rate*. This rate should theoretically include the wages earned as well as the other related labor costs such as employer payroll taxes and employee fringe benefits. Remember that various direct labor operations may require different degrees of skill and training. This must be considered when determining the standard rate. We will assume that we are using the same type labor for the production of a unit of product X. The rate, therefore, is the same for all labor required. It could happen that considerably different operations are involved, and the standard for each could vary accordingly. In addition, rates on the same operation could vary in practice because of seniority or perhaps some other union or management agreements. The determination of the standard rate for direct labor might include the following:

Standard Rate per Hour for Direct Labor

	Rate per Hour
Basic rate	$10.00
Employer payroll taxes @ 8% of basic rate	.80
Employee fringe benefit package (35% of basic rate)	3.50
Standard rate per direct labor hour	$14.30

Management may find the inclusion of employer payroll taxes and employee fringe benefit costs in the standard rate administratively objectionable. As with direct materials, the direct labor standard rate may include only the basic wage rate and the employer taxes, and employee fringe benefit costs may be included in manufacturing overhead. This, of course, makes the deviations from standard much easier to calculate and the information more easily assembled for the calculation.

We have now established for product X a standard direct labor time of 4.0 hours and a standard rate of $14.30 per hour. The standard direct labor cost for a unit of product X would be determined by multiplying the standard time by the standard rate as follows:

$$4.0 \text{ hours} \times \$14.30 = \$57.20 \text{ per unit}$$

The above would appear on the standard cost card for product X as the direct labor component.

Setting Manufacturing Overhead Standards

Even though it is often referred to in the literature, there can be no standards for manufacturing overhead in the true sense of the word. With direct materials and direct labor, we can establish an input/output relationship. That is, we can expect that by adding certain amounts of direct materials and direct labor a certain output should be forthcoming. Stated another way, given a certain output we can surmise that a certain amount of direct material and direct labor would have been required to produce that amount of output. In other words, there is a direct relationship between inputs of direct material and direct labor and the output or finished product. This is not the case, however, with manufacturing overhead. We certainly cannot relate the amount of fixed manufacturing overhead expenses incurred—such as supervisors' salaries, property taxes, or straight-line depreciation expense—to the amount of output. Even those items that we generally consider variable manufacturing overhead (such as power, normal waste or scrap, and factory supplies) are considered more a function of the direct materials and direct labor incurred rather than an input that should result in certain output. As a result, manufacturing overhead is related to direct material or direct labor inputs in a standard costing system by using an application rate tied to one of the direct material or direct labor standards. For instance, if it has been determined that the variable manufacturing overhead incurred is a function of the number of direct labor hours worked and that the amount of variable overhead is $8 per direct labor hour, the "standard cost" for variable manufacturing overhead would be $8 times the number of standard hours allowed for the production of one unit of product X. The authors do not consider this a true standard cost—it is a cost *related* to a standard for another cost item such as direct materials or direct labor. Because there is at least an indirect relationship between the amount of variable manufacturing overhead and completed production and the fact that the amount of variable manufacturing overhead incurred is a function of the standard amount of direct materials or direct labor required for production, we will include it in the standard cost card. Because there is little or no relationship between fixed manufacturing overhead and the volume of completed production, it will be excluded from the standard cost card for this chapter. Chapter 10 considers in detail how manufacturing overhead is handled in a standard costing system.

At this point we can now summarize and illustrate the standard cost card for one unit of product X. It is given on page 294 as Exhibit 9–1.

EXHIBIT 9–1
Standard Cost Card
Variable Production Cost for One Unit of Product X

	Standard Cost
Direct material:	
3.3 lbs. material A @ $5.30/lb.	$ 17.49
Direct labor:	
4.0 hours @ $14.30/hour	57.20
Variable manufacturing overhead:	
4.0 hours × $8 per direct labor hour	32.00
Total standard variable cost per unit product X	$106.69

Determining and Recording Variances in a Standard Costing System

The Basic Variance Model

We stated previously that standard cost refers to the expected or budgeted cost of direct materials, direct labor, or manufacturing overhead to produce one unit of product. The *standard* gives us a benchmark for quantity used or price paid against which performance may be measured. When we compare actual performance against the benchmark (standard) and there is a difference, this difference is referred to as a *variance.* There are basically two possible variances: quantity or price. If there is a difference when we compare the actual inputs to the amount of inputs that should have been used for the production actually achieved, we have a quantity variance. If there is a difference when we compare the actual price paid for the inputs with what should have been paid according to the established standard, we have a price variance. The general model for the basic variable cost variance calculations is illustrated in Exhibit 9–2.

It is very important that you grasp the ideas expressed in Exhibit 9–2 before proceeding further. Note that the exhibit depicts only two basic variances for the variable production costs, price, and quantity and that the model can be applied to direct materials, direct labor and variable manufacturing overhead with only slight differences in specific names of the variances.

Exhibit 9–2 shows that the **price variances** are determined using the following formula:

$$\text{Price variance} = (AQ \times AP) - (AQ \times SP)$$

For this variance we are interested in whether or not we paid the standard price for the inputs acquired. Therefore, we want to compare the actual costs

EXHIBIT 9–2

General Model for Basic Variable Cost Variances

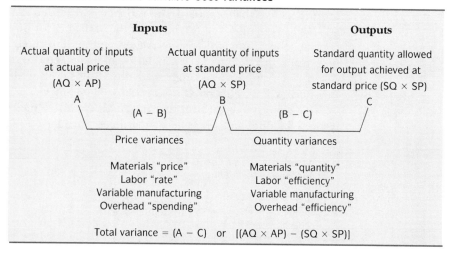

of the inputs (AQ × AP) with what the inputs should have cost according to the standard price (AQ × SP). The variable that we are concerned with here is price, so we can simplify the formula by factoring out the common term (actual quantity or AQ) so that the basic formula reduces to

$$\text{Price variance} = AQ(AP - SP)$$

This is referred to as the *short-cut method* of determining the price variance and emphasizes the fact that the price variance results from paying more or less than the standard price for the actual quantity of inputs purchased.

Exhibit 9–2 indicates that the **quantity variance** is expressed as

$$\text{Quantity variance} = (AQ \times SP) - (SQ \times SP)$$

In this variance we are interested in seeing whether we used the quantity of inputs allowed according to standard. In other words, we compare what we did use (AQ × SP) with what we should have used for the production achieved (SQ × SP). We do not want to have the variance influenced by price variations (this is determined in the price variance calculation), so to put a dollar value on the variances we multiply the quantities by the standard price. This variance can be shortened to the following formula:

$$\text{Quantity variance} = SP(AQ - SQ)$$

Again, this emphasizes the fact that the quantity variance results from a difference between the quantities we actually used and what we should have used according to the standard.

As you might expect, if the actual price or quantity exceeds standard, the variance is regarded as unfavorable. Conversely, if the actual price or quantity is less than standard, the variance is regarded as favorable.

The calculation and recording of the variances for direct material and direct labor in a standard costing system will be illustrated using the information from the following example. The manufacturing overhead variance calculations and analysis along with the disposition of all the standard cost variances will be illustrated in the following chapter.

P.T. Alun is a small firm that produces exclusive men's shirts made from genuine Indonesian batik. The standard cost card for one shirt is given below:

Standard Variable Cost Card
Indonesian Batik Shirt

Direct material: 2½ yards batik @ $8 per yard	$20.00
Direct labor: 3 hours @ $10 per hour	30.00
Variable manufacturing overhead: $5 per DLH	15.00
Standard variable cost per shirt	$65.00

The following information pertains to P. T. Alun for the month of January 19X7:

Shirts produced: 600

Batik purchased: 2,000 yards costing $15,900

Batik used: 1,600 yards

Direct labor purchased: 1,750 hours costing $18,375

Variable manufacturing overhead incurred: $8,925

Direct Materials Transactions and Variances

Direct Materials Purchased

Variances should be calculated at the earliest point possible so that management may take action to correct any situation that is out of control. For materials, this means that the price variance should be calculated at the time of the purchase. Management has the option of waiting until the time the materials are used to calculate the price variance, but this may destroy some of the value of using the standard costing system—several additional purchases may be made before any of the material in the current purchase is used. In such a case, management would not have the opportunity to correct the problem before it occurs again (perhaps several times). For P. T. Alun, the **materials price variance** would be calculated as follows:

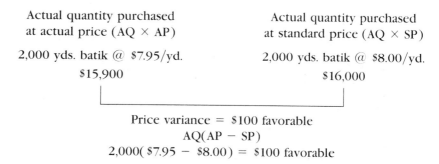

Actual quantity purchased at actual price (AQ × AP)	Actual quantity purchased at standard price (AQ × SP)
2,000 yds. batik @ $7.95/yd.	2,000 yds. batik @ $8.00/yd.
$15,900	$16,000

Price variance = $100 favorable

AQ(AP − SP)

2,000($7.95 − $8.00) = $100 favorable

The actual price paid per yard of batik was $7.95 ($15,900/2,000 yards). Therefore, P. T. Alun paid $.05 less per yard than standard on the 2,000 yards purchased. The shorter variance calculation is also indicated above. The entry to record the purchase of batik in the standard costing system would be

Materials	16,000	
Materials Price Variance		100
Accounts Payable		15,900

Note that the Materials control account is debited at the standard price. This makes it possible to keep the subsidiary materials inventory detail records on a quantity basis only because all items will come into and go out of stores at the standard price. We need only make a note on the subsidiary record of that standard price. Notice also that the materials price variance is favorable, and it is a credit in the journal entry. This suggests that favorable variances will be credits and unfavorable variances will be debits.

Direct Materials Used

The **materials quantity variance** is calculated at the time that materials are issued or used in the manufacturing process. Materials may be issued to production on the basis of a bill of materials. A **bill of materials** merely lists all of the material that should be issued for a given job or units of production in a production run. It would be compiled, of course, based on standard quantities allowed. The amount of materials specified on the bill of materials could be issued at the start of the production run (or job). If additional material was needed to complete the job, additional materials requisitions could be issued in a different color—for example, to indicate that a quantity of material above standard is being used. Likewise, if material is returned to stores as extra material not necessary to complete the production run or job, a materials return form would be initiated indicating that less than the standard quantity of material was used. Our example company, P. T. Alun, could use this procedure for production runs consisting of so many shirts from each type material.

The materials quantity variance for January would be determined as shown on page 298.

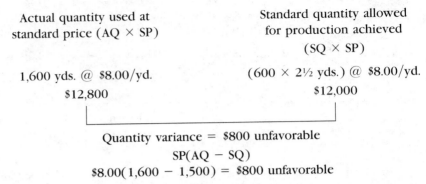

Actual quantity used at
standard price (AQ × SP)

Standard quantity allowed
for production achieved
(SQ × SP)

1,600 yds. @ $8.00/yd.
$12,800

(600 × 2½ yds.) @ $8.00/yd.
$12,000

Quantity variance = $800 unfavorable
SP(AQ − SQ)
$8.00(1,600 − 1,500) = $800 unfavorable

The variance is unfavorable because it took 1,600 yards of batik to make 600 shirts instead of the standard quantity of 1,500 yards (600 × 2½ yards per shirt). The entry to summarize the use of material for the month of January would be:

Work in Process	12,000	
Materials Quantity Variance	800	
Materials		12,800

Notice again that Work in Process is debited at the *standard cost* of material allowed for the production actually achieved. In this case, the variance is unfavorable so it is debited in the recording process.

Direct Labor Transactions and Variances

Direct Labor Purchased

After calculating the variances and recording direct materials purchased and used, the determination of the variances and the recording of direct labor purchased and used will seem relatively simple. The same basic general model is followed to determine the direct labor variances except that the "price" variance for labor will be more appropriately referred to as a *rate* variance and the "quantity" variance is referred to as an *efficiency variance.* The rate variance is calculated as follows:

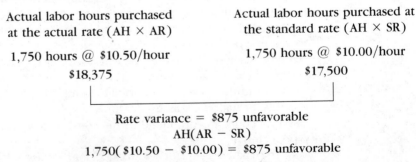

Actual labor hours purchased
at the actual rate (AH × AR)

Actual labor hours purchased at
the standard rate (AH × SR)

1,750 hours @ $10.50/hour
$18,375

1,750 hours @ $10.00/hour
$17,500

Rate variance = $875 unfavorable
AH(AR − SR)
1,750($10.50 − $10.00) = $875 unfavorable

The **direct labor rate variance** indicates that P. T. Alun paid $875 over the standard amount for the actual hours of labor purchased, so the variance is unfavorable. The journal entry to record the direct labor purchased (with the variance) would be as follows (no payroll deductions are recorded):

Payroll	17,500	
Labor Rate Variance	875	
Accrued Payroll		18,375

As with materials, the payroll control account is debited at the standard price. The rate variance is unfavorable, so it is debited.

Direct Labor Used

The "quantity" variance for direct labor is referred to as the *efficiency* variance because it furnishes information about the efficiency of the direct labor. If the production is completed within the standard time, we would surmise that the labor is efficient — that is, that the work is being done within the standard time allowed. If it takes longer than standard time to complete the product, of course, we would tend to think that we were "inefficient." The **direct labor efficiency variance** for P. T. Alun for January 19X7 is calculated below:

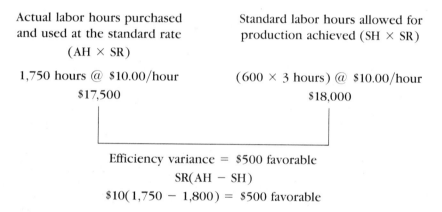

Actual labor hours purchased and used at the standard rate (AH × SR)

Standard labor hours allowed for production achieved (SH × SR)

1,750 hours @ $10.00/hour
$17,500

(600 × 3 hours) @ $10.00/hour
$18,000

Efficiency variance = $500 favorable

SR(AH − SH)

$10(1,750 − 1,800) = $500 favorable

The variance indicates that the 600 shirts were produced in 50 hours less direct labor time than standard, which translates into a favorable efficiency variance of $500. The entry to distribute the direct labor for January would be

Work in Process	18,000	
Labor Efficiency Variance		500
Payroll		17,500

It is useful to calculate the total direct labor variance for reconciliation and proof. We indicated in the general model diagram (Exhibit 9–2) that the total variance would compare the actual inputs purchased at the actual price (AQ × AP) with the standard inputs allowed for the production actually achieved at the standard price (SQ × SP). In the case of direct labor for P. T. Alun for January, the total labor variance would be

Actual hours purchased at the actual price	$18,375
Standard hours allowed for the production	
achieved: (600 × 3) × $10	18,000
Total direct labor variance	$ 375 U

We have broken this total variance down into the following:

Labor rate variance	$875 U
Labor efficiency variance	500 F
Net labor variance	$375 U

The total of the rate and efficiency variances reconcile with the total overall labor variance. This illustrates the importance of doing the individual rate and efficiency variances rather than merely calculating a total overall variance. The overall variance might be insignificant because the individual variances may offset one another giving management the indication that they are in control as far as labor is concerned when, in fact, there could be serious problems.

The total variance was not illustrated for material because very seldom will the material used equal the amount of material purchased. If this does happen to be the case, then the total variance can be calculated for materials as was done above for labor.

The Problem of Mutual Price-Quantity Variances

There are those who suggest that the way that price and quantity variances are calculated can lead to arguments regarding responsibility for the variances. This can be illustrated by graphically presenting the direct labor variances calculated for P. T. Alun for the month of January 19X7, above. The variances are graphically presented in Exhibit 9–3.

Refer to the shaded area in the upper right-hand corner of the graph in Exhibit 9–3. In P.T. Alun's case for the month of January, the labor efficiency variance is favorable and the labor rate variance is unfavorable. The production supervisor might claim that she not only saved the company $500 by being efficient (saved 50 hours @ $10.00 per hour = $500), but she also saved the company another $25 [50 hours × ($10.50 − $10.00) = $25] that would have shown up as a rate variance if the additional 50 standard hours had been necessary. The situation is usually illustrated with both the variances being unfavorable. In that case, there is an overlapping of price (rate) and quantity (efficiency) variances in the shaded area. If that had been the case for P.T. Alun, the personnel department might argue that they should not be held responsible for the rate variance for time taken beyond the standard hours allowed for the production achieved and that it should be the responsibility of the production supervisor for being inefficient. The authors feel that this is usually an empty argument. Unless the inefficiency of the production supervisor causes the personnel department to have to hire additional hours of direct labor at a price above what they would normally have to pay (or

EXHIBIT 9–3

Graphical Presentation of Direct Labor Rate and Efficiency Variances
For the Month of January 19X7

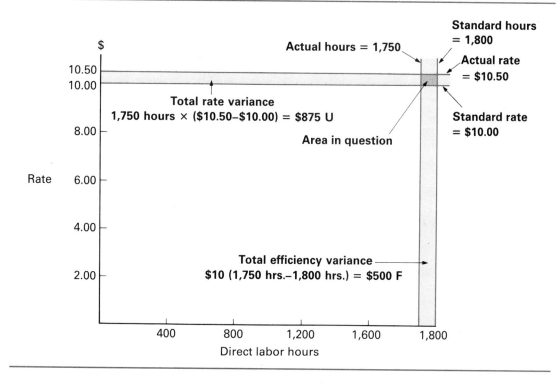

in the case of materials, the purchasing agent to have to make an unplanned purchase of materials at a premium price), there is little to be gained by the additional refinement in the analysis of the variances. It is usually considered the responsibility of purchasing to obtain whatever materials are needed and personnel to hire whatever direct labor is necessary to keep production moving and to do so at the standard price or rates.

Variance Analysis

Variances are the result of deviations of actual prices or quantities incurred or used from the standard prices or quantities that should have been incurred or used (inputs) for the activity level achieved (outputs). What does the variance tell management? Just exactly that—that there is a discrepancy between actual and plan (the budget or standard). Stated another way, there is an exception to management's plan. The variance does not reveal the cause of the exception; it only alerts management to the fact that things are not going according to plan. We can consider it the same as when the so-called idiot light for the battery or temperature appears on the dashboard of our automobile, or a red flag is waved by a flagman as we approach a section of highway construction or repair—we are being warned that things are not as we would expect. There is an exception or deviation from normal. Our response is to take some kind of action. We stop and investigate to see if we can determine why our alternator is not charging, why the car is apparently heating, or we slow down for the construction area. We may ignore the warnings and take no action, but it may prove costly for us in the not so distant future.

Periodic performance reports to managers make possible **management by exception.** This management technique merely means that if there are no exceptions or deviations from planned performance, management need not spend precious time where it is not needed. They can devote their time, instead, to creative thinking and plans for improvements in the future. When variances do appear on performance reports, however, how does management decide on a course of action (investigate the variance or do not investigate the variance)?

We have indicated that the variance does not indicate its *cause.* Just because there is a favorable direct materials price variance does not necessarily mean that the purchasing manager is doing a great job. Nor does it mean that if there is an unfavorable materials quantity variance that the production supervisor is at fault. It may be discovered, on investigation, that the purchasing manager bought inferior quality materials resulting in a good deal of waste in the production process. The point is that we discover *causes* of variances by investigation.

For example, an unfavorable labor efficiency variance may indicate that workers have been poorly trained or supervised, equipment is faulty or defective, materials have been substandard, or excessive work interruptions have occurred. If any of these or similar factors create an unfavorable labor efficiency variance, the situation can be corrected resulting in future cost savings. This is the potential benefit of investigating unfavorable variances. What criteria should management follow in deciding whether they should incur the cost of investigating the variance or take the risk of "letting it ride" for the time being? We suggest five criteria that management might utilize in making this decision: materiality, pattern over time, profit sensitivity, ability to influence, and probability of occurrence associated with cost alternatives. The criteria are not mutually exclusive, and management may use a combination of them to make the decision on whether or not to investigate variances. The point should be made that favorable as well as unfavorable variances are subject to this decision. Underspending a standard or budgeted amount may be as critical to a company as overspending.

Materiality

One obvious way to decide whether or not to investigate a variance is to consider its size — if it is large, then investigate and if small, ignore the variance. Management must decide what it considers to be the threshold point — that is, how large does the variance need to be before it is material and should be investigated? This will vary depending on the size of the firm and the management within each firm. An example of this approach would be to say that any variance over $1,000 will be investigated. This, however, ignores the fact that the total cost of some items may be $1,000,000 and for others, $10,000. To overcome this problem, management might say that any variance that is more than 5% of the budgeted item to which it is related will be investigated. In practice, management may use a combination of these two approaches to materiality. For example, it may request that any variance that is more than 5% of the standard or budgeted amount to which it is related, or that is more than $1,000, is to be investigated.

Pattern Over Time

Management may observe the pattern of the variance over time and could, in fact, decide to investigate before it reaches the materiality threshold referred to above. If an unfavorable variance occurs in one period and keeps on repeating and growing, it would suggest that the cost is already out of control and should be investigated. Prolonging the investigation will only add to production costs because the variance will soon cross the materiality threshold anyway. The plot of the pattern of the variance over time, however, might disclose that the variance fluctuates a good deal, even perhaps from favorable to unfavorable. This may suggest that the variance is due to random causes, and investigation may disclose that no corrective action is possible. When a variance is subject to this type fluctuation, statistical control chart techniques may be used to help management make the investigation decision based on a range of acceptable variations. The techniques are beyond the scope of this text and will not be explained further here.

Profit Sensitivity

Some costs that deviate from standard or budget may have a significant immediate or long-run effect on the overall profitability of the company. For example, the firm may be supplying a component on a government contract at a very competitive price, and one item of direct material may be a large percentage of the total cost of the component. If the price increases above standard, profit may be eliminated quickly. In this case, management may set the threshold for investigation of the variance lower than some other cost items.

The same may be true for maintenance and repairs. Favorable variances here might save money in the short run, but management may realize that in the long run this could be very costly. As a result, they might wish to monitor these variances carefully.

This criteria could also apply to costs outside the production area, such as advertising. Again, favorable variances might increase profitability in the short run, but on a long-run basis revenue could be materially affected. As a result, management may want to know the cause of any cost variances in this area very quickly.

Ability to Influence

There is little that management can do if a new union contract is signed giving labor a 10% pay increase or if a prolonged strike in the steel industry causes unforeseen increases in the cost of steel. In the last few years, and sometimes rather suddenly, there have been significant changes in the cost of electricity and gas as well as telephone. These are outside of management's ability to control. If the firm has stayed within quantity expectations, virtually nothing can be accomplished by investigating the price variances for these items. The variances will appear on performance reports for general information purposes.

Probability of Occurrence Associated with Cost Alternatives

Management may have to shut down the production process to investigate a variance to determine whether or not the process is out of control or out of adjustment. This, of course, costs money. Also, some production costs may vary from standard due to random causes. What management would like to know in these cases is the probability of variances of certain sizes occurring due to random causes (which suggest that the process is not out of control and the variance should not be investigated). The possible courses of action that management may take are (1) to investigate and adjust if necessary and (2) do not investigate. Associated with these management alternatives are two possible states of the production environment: (1) the production process is in adjustment, or (2) the process is out of adjustment. If management can determine the probability of the process's being in adjustment or out of adjustment and the costs associated with investigating or not investigating the variance, payoff tables can be constructed to summarize these alternative courses of action and production environment states. Payoff tables are illustrated in Chapter 17, along with an example of their use in investigating variances.

Evaluation of the Standard Costing System

With a basic understanding of the nuances of a standard costing system, we should now be able to evaluate its advantages and possible disadvantages. Throughout the chapter a number of advantages or purposes of using standard costing were cited or inferred. The advantages or uses that might be listed for the use of a standard costing system could include the following:

1. Standard costing and the associated reports linked with variance analysis can assist in the performance evaluation process by providing an important part of the information needed in the overall performance evaluation system. It fits well with the concept of responsibility accounting — the performance reports indicating variances can be designed by areas of responsibility.

2. The variances that are an important part of the information output of a standard costing system make possible the concept of *management by exception.* Once planning has been completed (the budget adopted) and policies set, management need only be involved in day to day operations to monitor and take action on the exceptions from the plan. This leaves them free to use their time more productively.

3. Once standards are set, the costing system may be more economical and simpler to operate than job order or process costing systems not utilizing standards. It was pointed out previously that the control accounts can be kept at prices shown on the standard cost cards with all movement through the system at these standard costs. This means that the subsidiary records for these control accounts need only show quantities — if the dollar value is desired, all that needs to be done is multiply the quantity shown on the subsidiary record by the standard prices. This holds true from the raw materials inventory control account on through finished goods inventory control and the cost of goods sold account.

4. Standard costing can be a tremendous aid in the budgeting or bidding and pricing process. Standard costs are really a budget for *one unit* of product. If we want to budget for a number of units, we need only multiply. The bidding process is greatly simplified as well because the firm has already done a careful analysis of its cost structure in setting the standard cost, so it is better informed for making competitive bids or for pricing.

5. Currently attainable standards can be a motivating force for employees by providing goals or targets to work toward. This can help control costs and perhaps also help promote cost reductions.

The list of advantages or uses cited above would seem to compel us toward using a standard costing system. However, a few disadvantages or caveats should be enumerated.

1. Although it is less costly to *use* a standard costing system once it is in place, it is costly to install. The determination of reliable standards is not an easy task, and many firms never get beyond the standard setting process or perhaps they establish standards in a very casual manner. The variances calculated and the information disseminated in standard costing reports is useful only to the extent that the standards are reliable and realistic representations of the firm's potential.

2. Emphasis on performance evaluation based on standards can produce morale and productivity problems. If standards are too ideal or emphasis is only placed on *unfavorable* variances, the standard costing system and the standard may become the whipping boy for all that is wrong in the company. For this reason, a number of companies involve all affected in the setting of standards so that employees internalize the standard as their own personal goals.

3. Closely related to (2) above, if too much emphasis is placed on unfavorable variances or exceptions, employees and supervisors may try to hide or cover up (and therefore not report) activity that leads to unfavorable variances. This, of course, defeats the purpose of using the standard costing system. Workers and supervisors may even collude in protecting their good records or try to avoid being called on the carpet. A good deal of selling, involvement, and informing should precede the installation of a standard costing system so that employees up through middle managers see it as an aid to help them increase efficiency and control costs rather than as the C.I.A for top management.

Summary

Standard costing systems are basic job order or process costing systems with the additional use of the concept of standard costs. This marriage results in an information system capable of furnishing management with data not ordinarily captured in the basic costing systems. The additional information obtained is useful for implementation of the concept of management by exception, performance evaluation, budgeting and forecasting, and for product costing and pricing.

A standard cost can be interpreted as the budget for one unit of product or service. The standard cost consists of a predetermined quantity at a predetermined price (the inputs), which should result in the production of one unit of product (the outputs). The standard may be an ideal standard (one that would be nice to work toward but realistically is not practical) or a currently attainable standard (one that is tight yet attainable if the inputs are managed as stated in the standard). A formal summary of the standard costs allowed for the production of one unit of product is a standard cost card.

As production takes place, actual inputs in terms of prices and quantities are compared with the standard inputs that would be allowed based on the output actually achieved. Differences between actual inputs and the standard inputs based on the output actually achieved are variances. The basic variances for variable production costs are price and quantity. The variances alert management to the fact that actual performance is deviating from plan. The cause of the variance, and therefore who is responsible, can usually be determined only through an investigation. Management determines whether variances should be investigated using criteria such as materiality, pattern of the variance over time, profit sensitivity, and ability to influence.

A standard costing system has the potential of motivating the work force and promoting efficiency and cost control. However, care must be taken in the implementation and utilization of the system by providing an understanding of what is trying to be accomplished. Misunderstanding of the system and emphasis on only the negative variances can cause serious behavioral problems among the work force, which may negate many of the potential benefits associated with the use of a standard costing system.

Appendix 9–A
Economic Order Quantity, Reorder Point, and Safety Stock

In the discussion on setting the standard price for direct materials, it was mentioned that the standard price would be determined based on the specific quality of goods desired and purchased from reliable suppliers for the best price obtainable *in the quantities that the company normally buys.* Management must try to determine the order size and its corollary, how often orders should be placed, not only to obtain the most favorable price per unit for materials but to minimize the total costs associated generally with inventory.

It is possible to think of these total costs associated with inventory as being composed of two *conflicting* kinds of cost: the costs associated with carrying inventory and the costs associated with carrying inadequate amounts of inventory. Examples of these conflicting costs are shown in the following comparison:

Costs of Carrying Inventory	*Costs of Carrying Insufficient Amounts of Inventory*
Return on investment in inventory	Lost sales
Insurance	Loss of customer goodwill
Property taxes	Extra purchasing and handling costs to expedite shipments
Costs of storage space	Higher unit cost because of smaller quantities purchased
Handling	
Breakage	Frequent stock-outs, which may disrupt production schedules causing overtime and additional set-up time
Evaporation or spoilage	
Obsolescence	Additional costs of customer call-backs and back-order procedures

Management faces a difficult task in trying to arrive at tradeoffs between these conflicting costs, particularly when the costs associated with carrying insufficient inventory tend to be very difficult to quantify. What often happens is that those who are concerned with controlling costs associated with inventory will use their personal judgment in assessing the effect of the costs of not carrying sufficient inventory but will tend to concentrate on those costs that can be more objectively determined. These are the total costs associated with placing orders and the costs of carrying inventory. One of the first applications of operations research techniques in the management accounting area was a model referred to as the **economic order quantity.** The objective of the model is to help answer questions as to "how much" and "when to order" in regard to inventory purchases so that the total inventory ordering and carrying costs can be minimized.

How Much?

It is possible to take a trial-and-error tabular approach to answering these questions. This approach will be illustrated first, followed by the mathematical model. The following notation is used throughout the illustration:

E = order size

A = annual requirements in units

S = annual cost of carrying one unit in stock for one year

P = cost of placing and receiving a purchase order

TC = the total annual ordering and carrying costs

Both solution approaches are based on the following assumptions:

1. There are no quantity discounts.
2. The demand rate is known and it is uniform.
3. Ordering costs are a function of the number of orders placed and are variable.
4. Carrying costs are a function of the *average* inventory.
5. Management does not intentionally plan occasional stock-outs.

Let us assume that Boti Company, a bicycle manufacturer, is producing 6,000 bicycles per year. A special light costing $12 is installed on each bicycle. The following costs have been determined:

Costs to place an order

Clerical, postage, stationery, telephone, receiving, etc. (per order)	$10.00

Cost of carrying a unit in inventory for one year

Insurance, taxes, breakage, etc. (per year)	$ .30
Desired annual return on investment (10% × $12)	1.20
Total carrying cost per unit per year	$ 1.50

EXHIBIT 9–4

Total Ordering and Carrying Cost for Various Order Sizes

Explanations							
E = Order size	100	200	250	300	500	1,000	6,000
$E/2$ = Average inventory units	50	100	125	150	250	500	3,000
A/E = Number of purchase orders	60	30	24	20	12	6	1
$S(E/2)$ = Annual carrying cost at $1.50 per unit	$ 75	$150	$188	$225	$375	$ 750	$4,500
$P(A/E)$ = Annual cost of placing purchase order @ $10	600	300	240	200	120	60	10
TC = Total annual costs of carrying & purchasing	$675	$450	$428	$425	$495	$ 810	$4,510

Exhibit 9–4 illustrates the trial-and-error tabular approach for determining the most economic order size. Exhibit 9–4 suggests that the most economic order size should be somewhere between 250 and 500. Other order sizes within this range would need to be explored to find the actual order size where total costs are at a minimum. The exhibit illustrates other points that should be explained. It is apparent that the two costs, ordering and carrying inventory, are also conflicting in terms of cost management. Order size can be increased to decrease ordering costs, but in the process the carrying costs increase. The object is to balance these two costs so that total cost is minimized. Exhibit 9–5 illustrates this point more clearly, disclosing the fact that the total cost seems to be at a minimum where ordering costs and carrying costs are equal.

The mathematical approach leads directly to an economic order size. Remember that the object is to minimize total costs. Exhibit 9–4 indicates that the total ordering costs per year can be expressed as $P(A/E)$, and the total carrying costs per year as $SE/2$. Therefore, the total costs could be expressed as:

$$TC = \frac{PA}{E} + \frac{SE}{2}$$

9.1

We are interested in the value of E (the economic order quantity) where the total costs are at a minimum. To find this value of E, we take the first derivative of the total cost equation with respect to E, set it equal to zero, and solve for E:

First derivative of 9.1:
$$\frac{dTC}{dE} = \frac{-PA}{E} + \frac{S}{2}$$

9.2

Set 9.2 = zero:
$$\frac{S}{2} - \frac{PA}{E} = 0$$

9.3

Solve for E:

(a) Common denominator:
$$\frac{SE^2 - 2PA}{2E^2} = 0$$

EXHIBIT 9–5
Relationship of Inventory Ordering, Carrying, and Total Costs

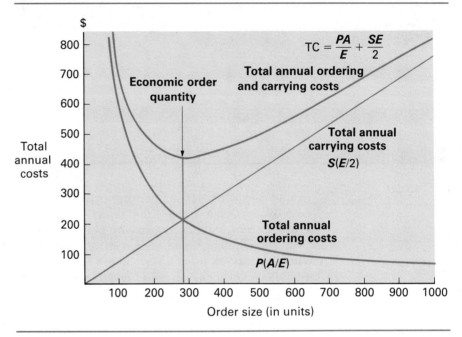

(b) Multiply both sides of
equation by $2E$ and
solve for E:

$$SE^2 - 2PA = 0$$

$$SE^2 = 2PA$$

$$E^2 = \frac{2PA}{S}$$

$$E = \sqrt{\frac{2PA}{S}}$$

Substituting the data for Boti Company in the economic order model results in the following:

$$E = \sqrt{\frac{2 \times 10 \times 6{,}000}{1.50}} = \sqrt{80{,}000} = 282$$

This confirms the order size depicted on the graph in Exhibit 9–5, and pinpoints the ball-park number suggested in the trial and error tabular approach shown in Exhibit 9–4.

Many companies will round off the economic order size to some even number. This will not usually cause significant changes in the total annual cost and can be verified by looking at Exhibit 9–5. Notice there is a fairly broad range around the economic order quantity where the total cost line is quite flat, illustrating that the model is quite insensitive to minor changes in the economic order quantity.

The economic order quantity model can also be used to determine the most economic size of a production run. It usually requires set-up time to switch from the production of one product to another. Management would like to produce the optimum number of units each time that it starts a new production run such that the total costs associated with set up and carrying completed inventory are minimized. The economic order quantity model does this nicely — the only change needed in the formula is to substitute the set-up costs for starting a production run for the order costs associated with purchasing (PA/E) as already discussed. The switch in application is straightforward and will not be illustrated.

Keep in mind the assumptions on which this solution is based. If the company can obtain significantly different quantity discounts depending on order size, the model can be extended to accommodate that fact. Both approaches become somewhat more complex, and the student is referred to more advanced managerial accounting texts if that analysis is desired.

When to Order

For purposes of convenience, Boti Company has decided that as long as the economic order model is quite forgiving, they will order the bicycle lights in quantities of 300. If Boti is producing 6,000 bicycles per year and puts in 240 working days per year, it means that on average the company will need 25 bicycle lights per day. On that basis, an order will need to be placed every 20 days (6,000/300). However, this does not tell the management of Boti Company *when* orders should be placed. They cannot wait until they have installed the last light on a bicycle before placing an order for more (unless the supplier is next door and would deliver in minutes). Determining when to order (or to start a production run) involves a consideration of the *reorder point* and possibly *safety stock.* The **reorder point** merely refers to the quantity level at which a new order should be placed and is dependent on three factors: the economic order quantity, the lead time, and the rate of usage during the lead time. **Lead time** is the interval between placing an order and its delivery and availability for use.

The Boti Company produces 25 bicycles per working day on average (6,000/240). Sometimes, however, production can exceed that amount. For instance, it occasionally produces 30 bicycles per day for a few days at a time. In this case, the rate of usage during the lead time is not constant. Boti is also not in control of the lead time. Orders usually arrive in five working days, but sometimes it has taken seven days for delivery. If management is trying to minimize the costs of carrying insufficient inventory, these fluctuations in rate of usage and lead time require establishing a minimum or buffer inventory to serve as a cushion for preventing possible stock-outs. This buffer or cushion is referred to as a **safety stock.**

The information from Boti Company and the following notation will be used to illustrate these concepts:

ROP = reorder point

SS = safety stock

d_m = maximum expected usage of lights per day = 30

d_n = normal expected usage of lights per day = 25

L_m = maximum expected lead time in working days = 7

L_n = normal expected lead time in working days = 5

If demand or usage did not vary from 25 lights per day, and if the lead time was always five days, the reorder point would merely be

$$ROP = d_n L_n$$

$$= 25 \times 5 = 125$$

Section (a) of Exhibit 9–6 illustrates this stable assumption. Note that the order arrives just at the point where the inventory of lights is exhausted. The

EXHIBIT 9–6
Reorder Point and Safety Stock with Variable Rate of Usage

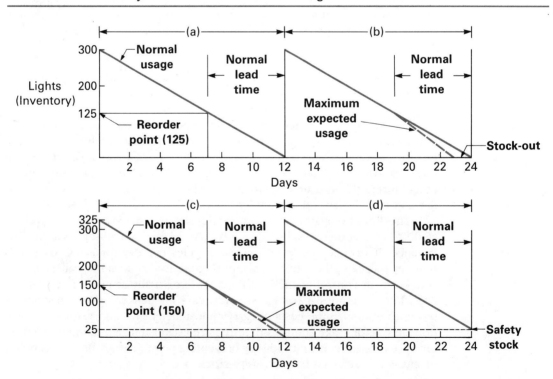

information about Boti indicates, however, that the rate of usage may increase to 30 per working day. Section (b) of Exhibit 9–6 illustrates what the
consequences of this can be. If at the date an order was placed, production
did increase to 30 bicycles per day, the company would run out of lights the
day before the order arrived. To allow for this contingency, a safety stock
would be determined as follows:

$$SS = L_n(d_m - d_n)$$
$$= 5(30 - 25)$$
$$= 25, \text{ and the reorder point becomes:}$$
$$ROP = d_n L_n + SS$$
$$= d_n L_n + L_n(d_m - d_n)$$
$$= (25 \times 5) + 5(30 - 25)$$
$$= 150$$

Section (c) of Exhibit 9–6 illustrates how the safety stock provides the cushion for the change in rate of usage so that a stock-out does not occur. Section (d) illustrates how the process stabilizes again with the arrival of the
new order and the rate of usage reverting to the usual rate of 25 per day.

If the lead time seems to be the main problem, management could minimize the chance of stock-outs by calculating the safety stock so that it would
provide for normal usage during the possible extended lead time. With this
emphasis, the safety stock for Boti Company would be

$$SS = d_n(L_m - L_n)$$
$$= 25(7 - 5)$$
$$= 50, \text{ and the reorder point would then become:}$$
$$ROP = d_n L_n + d_n(L_m - L_n)$$
$$= (25 \times 5) + 25(7 - 5)$$
$$= 175$$

Exhibit 9–7 illustrates this situation. Section (a) shows the extended lead
time of seven days and the safety stock providing a cushion to prevent a
stock-out. Section (b) illustrates again the stabilization of the lead time.

The reorder point model has been illustrated where safety stock allows
for variability in either rate of usage or lead time, but not both. The model
can accommodate this situation, although the mathematics does get slightly
more complicated. The point in this discussion is to give you a sound basic
introduction to the techniques available to management to help plan and
control costs in this area.

EXHIBIT 9–7
Safety Stock with Variable Lead Time

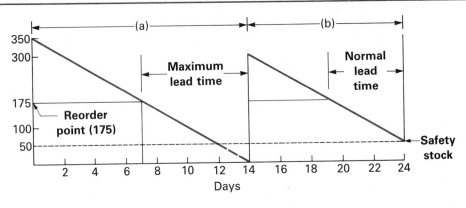

Just-in-Time Approach to Inventory Management

In the wake of foreign industrial challenges to the United States, new approaches to production and purchasing are beginning to be used in this country. One method that is receiving considerable attention is **just-in-time** (JIT) production. The essence of JIT is to manufacture products or components thereof only as needed. Hence the need for a product or part in either finished goods or a production department triggers action "upstream" in prior departments to fill the need. Several important factors stem from this production policy.

First, inventories of finished goods, parts, and raw materials are minimized. Ideally JIT would lead to zero inventory levels. Lower inventories mean considerable cost savings. These include lower investment in inventories, less insurance and property taxes, less need for storage facilities, and lower obsolescence costs.

Second, vendors of raw materials or parts for firms employing JIT must be relied on for frequent deliveries and high quality. These inputs will go virtually immediately into production, by-passing the storeroom. Hence JIT production leads to JIT purchasing, which requires extremely close and cooperative arrangements between vendor and manufacturer.

Third, the "stripped down" nature of inventories puts very strong pressures throughout the production process to insure extremely high quality. JIT would be totally untenable without this feature.

Fourth, the emphasis on high quality of production means that a high degree of cooperation and involvement must be forthcoming from direct labor and other employees in terms of maintaining quality control. Materials quantity variances arising from faulty work on direct materials and labor efficiency variances should be slashed to a minimum under a set of currently attainable standards.

JIT production and purchasing policies are still at a very early stage on the U.S. industrial scene. It remains to be seen how widely they can be adapted to our particular cultural circumstances. If they can be applied here successfully—including the ability of the manufacturing firm to still satisfy its customers needs—the benefits in terms of both cost savings and higher quality could be enormous.

Appendix 9–B
Learning Curves –
Setting Direct Labor Standards and
Evaluating Labor Efficiency Variances

Often the fact is overlooked that positive direct labor efficiency variances may materialize even though the work force has made no special effort to increase efficiency. In fact, they might even be producing at less than normal efficiency. This situation can occur in certain types of manufacturing (or service) industries where learning takes place—that is, the direct laborer becomes more efficient because he or she *learns* as a job is repeated a second and third time.

The **learning curve** phenomenon was first identified and quantified by the aircraft industry where it was discovered that, as production quantities doubled, cumulative average time per unit was reduced to 80% of the previous cumulative average. The aircraft industry is one where there are relatively few products produced (the 747 jetliner, for example), and the product is complex. The learning curve is applicable, then, in those situations where workers become more efficient each time they move on to another unit of output. If you enjoy working with wood, for instance, and designed and built an ornate grandfather's clock out of rough sawn walnut, you would find that if you decided to produce a number of the same clocks, the second and third ones would take less time to produce. On the other hand, if you are only sawing boards into one-foot lengths, the time required to saw each piece would change very little because of learning taking place (assuming that you know how to use a saw when you start). Therefore, the learning curve is not applicable to small, repetitive type tasks performed in assembly-line manufacturing environments. Learning curve theory has many interesting applications in business, particularly in production planning and control. Our objective here is to give a basic introduction to the theory and to develop an appreciation of how it can be applied to management accounting.

Exhibit 9–8 illustrates an 80% learning curve where the first lot of 10 units is produced in 100 hours (assuming that 80% learning applies as quantities double). The learning percentage may vary between industries and may be applicable when production is tripled, quadrupled, and so forth.

The cumulative average hours to produce a unit of product is particularly pertinent to the development of standard labor times and evaluating

EXHIBIT 9–8

**Illustration of Effect of 80% Learning Curve
on Cumulative Average Production Time per Unit**

Lot No.	No. In Lot	Cumulative Units	Cumulative Average Hours per Unit	Cumulative Total Production Hours
1	10	10	10.	100
2	10	20	8.	160
3	20	40	6.4	256
4	40	80	5.12	409.6
5	80	160	4.096	655.36
6	160	320	3.277	1,048.58

labor efficiency variances. Exhibit 9–9 illustrates graphically the relationship of cumulative average hours as production doubles.

The graph in Exhibit 9–9 illustrates that once cumulative production reaches approximately 160 units, very little reduction in average time to produce a unit of output occurs after that point. It is important, therefore, for management to know where they are on their learning curve when they are setting standards or evaluating variances from standards. A firm at the start of the learning curve will tend to estimate the standard time too high and should, if workers are efficient, find that they have favorable labor efficiency variances (and as we see in the following chapter, favorable variable manufac-

EXHIBIT 9–9

An 80% Learning Curve

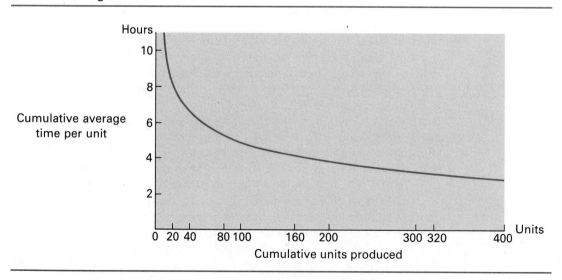

Cumulative average time per unit

Cumulative units produced

turing overhead efficiency variances as well). Management may be euphoric about performance when, in fact, it would have been expected if they had applied learning curve theory to their situation.

It may also be crucial for management to be aware of this phenomenon if they are bidding on a production contract. If a new firm is at the point where it has produced 20 units (average cumulative time to produce one unit is now eight hours), and it is bidding against a firm that has produced over 300 units, it is at a distinct disadvantage. If it is not aware of the learning curve phenomenon, it will surely lose on a competitive bid situation. If it is aware of learning, however, it may bid on a very low margin (or even at a loss), knowing it is the only way that they are going to be competitive.

In addition to being applicable to only certain manufacturing or service industries, it goes without saying that learning curve theory assumes a fairly stable work force. If there is a very high turnover rate, or if the company is expanding rapidly and adding new workers, it is not possible for "learning" to take place or, at least, to take place at a constant rate.

Key Terms

Bill of materials   lists the materials that should be issued for a given job or units of production in a production run. It would be in standard where a standard costing system were in use.

Currently attainable standards   are tight but attainable by an efficiently operating work force.

Direct labor efficiency variance   is a quantity type variance that measures direct labor hours and costs above or below the standard hours allowed for production achieved.

Direct labor rate variance   is a price type variance showing the effect on direct labor costs of being above or below the standard hourly rate.

Economic order quantity   attempts to minimize the cost of ordering and carrying inventories by determining the inventory order size that minimizes the total costs associated with inventories.

Ideal standards   are geared to theoretical peaks of efficiency. They are virtually unattainable.

Just-in-time   refers to a production and purchasing approach that minimizes carrying inventories. Emphasis is on high quality of output and rapid delivery of any raw materials or parts needs.

Lead time   is the interval between placing an order and its delivery and availability for use.

Learning curve   refers to efficiencies in labor as more units are produced resulting from the benefits of experience in complex production situations.

Management by exception   refers to restricting management attention to situations that are potentially "out of control." One way of implementing this is by examining the relative and absolute sizes of variances on performance reports and concentrating attention on the most important situations.

Materials price variance   is a price type variance showing the effect on materials costs of being above or below standard materials costs per unit of input acquired or used.

Materials quantity variance   is a quantity type variance that measures direct materials costs above or below the standard costs of direct materials allowed for production achieved.

Price variances   refers to variances measuring whether the cost per unit of input is above or below standard. These include materials price, labor rate, and variable manufacturing overhead spending variances.

Quantity variances   refers to variances measuring whether the quantities of input used for production achieved are above or below standard. These include material quantity, labor efficiency, and variable manufacturing overhead efficiency variances.

Reorder point   refers to the quantity level of inventory on hand when a new order should be placed. To minimize inventory costs this can be done in accordance with EOQ models.

Safety stock   refers to a level of inventory over and above the amount expected to be used up during the lead time period. It is a "buffer" inventory intended to serve as a cushion against possible stockouts.

Standard cost   refers to the expected or budgeted cost of materials, labor, or manufacturing overhead to produce one unit of product. Standard costing systems can be instituted in both job order and process costing situations.

Standard cost card   is a formal list of the standard cost for direct materials, direct labor, and manufacturing overhead to produce a unit of product.

Questions

Q9–1   What are standard costs?

Q9–2   Explain how standard costing relates to job order and process costing.

Q9–3   The president of a company was quoted as making the following statement: "In our company we feel that the accountants should have the responsibility for setting material and labor standards because they deal with costs associated with these items on a continuous basis." Comment on the president's viewpoint.

Q9–4   What is a variance?

Q9–5   Distinguish between ideal standards and currently attainable standards.

Q9–6   There are two basic variances—price and quantity. Describe each, giving examples.

Q9–7   Why is the total labor variance generally segregated into a rate variance and an efficiency variance?

Q9–8   What is a standard cost card?

Q9–9   What does a standard bill of materials have to do with a standard costing system?

Q9–10   Why should a materials price variance be determined at the time of materials purchases rather than at the time of the use of the material?

Q9–11   "Our firm is too small to use a standard costing system. We save clerical costs by using our 'actual' costing system." Comment on this statement.

Q9–12   How do variances relate to the concept of "management by exception"?

Q9–13   What might be suggested by the fact that a firm has a favorable labor rate variance and an unfavorable labor efficiency variance?

Q9–14   What benefits are associated with the use of a standard costing system?

Q9–15   How does management decide who is responsible for a particular variance?

Q9–16   A firm will motivate its employees toward increased productivity by using ideal standards rather than currently attainable standards. Do you agree? Why or why not?

Q9–17   How does management determine whether or not a variance should be investigated?

Q9–18   What are some costs associated with a company's inventory policy that are not reflected in the financial statements?

Q9–19   What is meant by the term *economic order quantity?* What costs are equal (or nearly equal) at the economic order quantity?

Q9–20   What is meant by the statement that the economic order quantity is a relatively insensitive model? Of what value is this fact to a company?

Q9–21   Describe what is meant by *safety stock?* Would most firms establish a safety stock with the idea that stock-outs would never occur? Why?

Q9–22   What benefit is there in calculating a reorder point? What factors enter into its determination?

Q9–23   What is the just-in-time approach to inventory management?

Q9–24   What are the benefits of the just-in-time approach to inventory management?

Q9–25   The learning curve phenomenon applies to what kind of manufacturing processes?

Q9–26   How does learning curve theory apply to standard costing?

Exercises

E9–1   **Setting the materials standard.** One of the products manufactured by Atwood Furniture Company is a large executive office desk. The desk requires 21 board feet of walnut, 30 board feet of mahogany, and 50 square feet of cedar. The cedar is ordered in 4′ × 7′ sheets that are one-half inch thick. Two of the cedar sheets are required for each desk in order to get all of the various pieces required.

Atwood buys the wood from different suppliers. The walnut costs $3 per board foot, and freight costs $10 per 100 board feet. The supplier gives a 2% cash discount, and Atwood takes all discounts. The mahogany costs $1.75 per board foot, and the supplier pays the freight. This supplier gives no cash discounts. The cedar sheets cost $28 per sheet, and the freight costs are $8.40 per dozen sheets. The supplier allows a 10% cash discount.

Required: 1. Compute the standard price for
   a. A board foot of walnut.
   b. A board foot of mahogany.
   c. A square foot of cedar. ·
2. Prepare the direct materials portion of a standard cost card for the executive desk.

E9–2   **Setting the labor standard.** Cajun Company is developing standards for the assembly of product X in the Assembly Department. A good deal of handwork is involved, so Cajun is interested in controlling the direct labor costs. The company's industrial engineer has done an analysis of the motions required to complete the assembly process. The motion categories and the standard time suggested for each is listed below:

No. Required	Motion	Standard Time/Each
2	A	3 minutes
5	B	2 minutes
3	C	4 minutes
11	D	30 seconds
7	E	1 minute
3	F	$1\frac{1}{2}$ minutes

For every 15 minutes of work, there is an average of one minute of break time. Every 90 minutes that an employee is in the department, four minutes will be taken up with either personal time, machine down time, clean-up, or adjustment. The workers average $12 per hour in the Assembly Department, and a management study indicates that fringe benefits amount to 30% of the base wage.

Required: 1. Compute the standard labor cost per hour for the Assembly Department. (Cajun includes all direct labor related costs in the standard for direct labor.)
2. Prepare the direct labor portion of a standard cost card for product X for Cajun Company.

E9–3   **Materials variances.** Belfry Manufacturing uses a standard costing system. The materials section of the standard cost card follows:

Product Y
Partial Standard Cost Card

8 lbs. material A @ $20 per lb $160

The following information pertains to activity for the month of August 19X7:

Material A purchased:	4,000 lbs. costing $82,480	
Material A used:	3,750 lbs.	
Product Y produced:	487	

Required: Compute the direct materials price and quantity variances for the month.

E9–4   **Labor variances.** The direct labor portion of the standard cost card for Bates Manufacturing is given below:

Product Z
Partial Standard Cost Card

3 – 4′ × 6′ quarter-inch sheet steel @ $55 $165
4 – hours direct labor @ $11.50 per hour   46

During the month of July Bates manufactured 265 units of product Z. The company paid $12,097.75 for 1,085 hours of direct labor.

Required:
1. Compute the direct labor rate and efficiency variances for the month of July.
2. Calculate the overall labor variance and check to see that it reconciles with the total of your rate and efficiency variances.

E9–5 **Materials variances — incomplete data.** The following information is available regarding direct materials for Able Industries for the month of September:

Standard unit price	$ 5.40
Materials price variance (unfavorable)	360.00
Materials quantity variance (favorable)	302.40
Actual quantity purchased	2,400
Actual quantity used	2,500

Required:
1. What was the actual purchase price per unit of materials purchased?
2. How many units of material *should* have been used during the month?

E9–6 **Labor variances — incomplete data.** The following information is available regarding direct labor for Yardley Manufacturing for the month of March 19X7:

Standard direct labor rate per hour	$ 8.50
Direct labor rate variance (favorable)	32.50
Direct labor efficiency variance (unfavorable)	212.50
Standard direct labor hours allowed	625

Required:
1. How many actual direct labor hours were worked during March?
2. What was the actual rate of pay per hour during March?

E9–7 **Standard costing journal entries.** Selected accounts from the ledger of Candy Manufacturing are given below. The entries represent beginning balances, specific entries, or summary entries for the month of January.

Direct Materials

1/1 Bal	12,000	Issued	89,500
1/15	85,000		

Materials Price Variance

1/15	1,700		

Payroll

1/31	98,500	1/31	98,500

Accounts Payable

		1/15	86,700

Work in Process

1/31	88,000		
1/31	98,200		

Materials Quantity Variance

1/31	1,500		

Accrued Payroll

		1/31	98,500

Labor Rate Variance

		1/31	1,500

Labor Efficiency Variance

		1/31	1,200

Required: 1. Prepare journal entries to reflect all the activity for direct materials and direct labor for the month.
2. What do the four variances tell management?

E9–8   **Materials and labor variances, journal entries.** Paul Bunyan Industries makes, among other things, a "Paul Bunyan" men's plaid flannel shirt. The company uses a standard costing system and a partial standard cost card is given below:

"Paul Bunyan" Men's Plaid Flannel Shirt Partial Standard Cost Card

2 1/2 yards plaid flannel @ $3.50	$ 8.75
2 hours direct labor @ $7.50	15.00
	$23.75

During the month of September 19X7 the company had the following activity for the "Paul Bunyan" shirts:

a. Purchased 2,000 yards of plaid flannel costing $7,240.
b. Manufactured 950 shirts.
c. Used 2,280 yards of plaid flannel.
d. Worked 1,950 direct labor hours costing $14,430.

Required: 1. Determine the materials price and quantity variances.
2. Determine the labor rate and efficiency variances.
3. Prepare journal entries for all of the activity related to direct materials and direct labor for the month of September.

E9–9   **Causes of standard costing variances.** Adler Company uses a standard costing system and for the month of April 19X7 recorded the following standard cost variances:

	Debit	Credit
Materials price variance		$500
Materials quantity variance	$600	
Labor rate variance	800	
Labor efficiency variance		700

Required: 1. Explain what each variance means.
2. List two possible causes for each variance.
3. How will management know for sure what caused each variance and who is responsible for it?

E9–10   **Classification of costs associated with inventory.** P. T. Garuda is a car dealer. The sales manager and chief accountant have been having a discussion regarding the number of cars to have in inventory at any one time and have been discussing the costs related thereto. For each of the instances listed below, classify them as (a) costs associated with new car inventory or (b) costs associated with carrying an insufficient inventory of new cars:

_____   1. Losses incurred at the end of the model year by discounting the "old" models.
_____   2. Fire, theft, and natural disaster insurance on the inventory.
_____   3. Loss of factory incentive discounts because of buying a small number of cars at a time.
_____   4. Loss of customers because salespeople often have to say "I can order one for you."
_____   5. Interest on the "floor-plan contract" (financing of the inventory through the local bank).

_____ 6. Frequent telephone calls and "driving trips" trying to pick up cars from other dealers.

_____ 7. Customer dissatisfaction and loss of customers because "your colors and options selection is never as good as Joe's on the East Side."

_____ 8. Loss of interest that could be earned if money was invested in tax exempt bonds rather than automobiles.

_____ 9. "Nickel and dime" damages to vehicles resulting from soiling of fabric by customers, nicks and scratches on paint, general deterioration because of exposure to the elements, and so forth.

_____ 10. State and/or local personal property taxes on the inventory.

_____ 11. Washing and polishing of vehicles in inventory.

_____ 12. A model becomes an especially hot item and the automobile manufacturer puts dealers on a quota based on past levels of inventory carried.

E9–11   **Economic order quantity.** Bingston Industries manufactures a variety of plastic products and buys plastic granules in bulk that are processed into liquid for forming into the various plastic products. Bingston buys the plastic granules in 100-pound bags and has need for 100,000 of these per year. The granules are used fairly evenly throughout the year.

The company has determined the average cost to carry a 100-pound bag of plastic granules in inventory per year is $2 and that it costs $10 to place an order.

Required: 1. What is the economic order quantity in 100-pound bags?

2. If Bingston works 250 days per year, how many bags of plastic granules are used per working day?

3. From your answers to (1) and (2) above, how often will Bingston be placing orders for plastic granules?

E9–12   **Reorder point and safety stock.** Elroy Manufacturing has grown from a small welding shop to a builder of specialized farm tillage equipment. The company uses approximately 210,000 pounds of two-inch angle iron per year and has had difficulty with stock-outs of this item which interfered with delivery dates on some of the orders. The company works 250 days per year, and the usage of the two-inch angle iron has been fairly uniform. Delivery of the angle iron, however, has varied from six working days to as much as twelve.

Required: 1. If Elroy Manufacturing wishes to avoid the majority of the stock-outs of the two-inch angle iron, it should carry a safety stock of how many pounds?

2. If Elroy opts to establish the safety stock determined in (1) above, what will be the reorder point for the two-inch angle iron?

E9–13   **Learning curve application.** National Parts plans to begin production of a new product during 19X8. They have produced a prototype that required 1,000 hours of direct labor. The company feels that it could sell seven units of this product if it were available in 19X8 (the prototype is not for sale). Management wishes to budget or set labor standards for the production of the seven units.

Required: 1. If 80% learning takes place on doubled quantities, how many standard hours of direct labor should be required to produce the seven more units? (Assume a stable work force.)

2. If National Parts did not recognize the learning factor, it may have set a standard for how many hours of direct labor?

Problems

P9–14   **Setting labor standards.** The Mansfield Company is going to expand its punch press department. The company is about to purchase several new punch presses from Turner Manufacturing. The engineers from Turner Company report that their mechanical studies indicate that for Mansfield's intended use, the output rate for one press should be 1,000 pieces per hour. The Mansfield Company has similar presses now in operation. At present, production from these presses averages 600 pieces per hour.

A detailed study of the Mansfield Company's experience shows that the average is derived from the following individual outputs:

Worker	Output per Hour (pieces)
J. Smith	750
L. Brown	750
C. Jones	600
T. Hardy	550
P. Clark	500
B. Randall	450
Total	3,600
Average	600

Mansfield's management also plans to institute a standard cost accounting system in the near future. The company's engineers are supporting a standard based on 1,000 pieces per hour; the accounting department is arguing for a standard of 750 pieces per hour; and the department supervisor is arguing for a standard of 600 pieces per hour.

Required: 1. What argument would each proponent be likely to use to support his or her case?
2. Which alternative best reconciles the needs of cost control and motivation for improved performance? Explain the reasons for your choice.

(CMA Adapted)

P9–15   **Standard cost card and materials and labor variances.** Bancroft Company manufactures product Y based on standard costs and specifications. The following information is available for the month of July:

	Quantity	Standard Prices
Inventories, July 1:		
Finished Goods (at standard variable costs)	8,000	$208,000
Materials	12,000	48,000

The actual and standard quantities and costs for the month of July were as follows:

	Quantity		Costs	
	Actual	Standard	Actual	Standard
Materials purchases	50,000		$205,000	$200,000
Materials requisitioned	52,000	51,000		
Direct labor (hours)	50,500	51,000	310,575	306,000
Variable manufacturing overhead			155,550	

Bancroft manufactured 25,500 units of product during July. There was no beginning or ending work in process in July. The same standards are utilized throughout the calendar year.

Required:

1. Prepare a standard variable cost card for product Y.
2. Show the calculation of the variances for direct materials and direct labor for the month of July.

P9–16 **Revision of standard costs.** One of Castner Company's products has a standard labor cost of $58 per 100 units. Beginning in January, the cost is to increase to $62.50, and because of the use of a greater percentage of less skilled workers, only 90 units are expected to be produced in the same time period previously required for producing 100 units.

In addition, Castner Company was notified by its materials supplier that a lower quality material would be supplied after January 1, with an estimated 5% of the units manufactured being rejected on final inspection because of defective material. The rejected units must be junked and have no commercial value. In the past, no units were lost for this reason.

In January Castner plans to produce 42,750 units of this product.

Required:

1. Compute the standard labor cost *per unit* of product after January 1. Assume that the standard is determined based on the expected good product produced (that is, the good units must absorb the costs associated with the 5% rejected). If necessary, round off your answers to three decimal places.
2. Compute the amount of expected labor costs under the previous and the revised standards, indicating the amount of the change associated with the material change and with the labor changes.

(CMA Adapted)

P9–17 **Straightforward standard variable costing—variances and journal entries.** Don Chemical manufactures a chemical product called Zip. The standard variable cost card for Zip is given below:

Standard Variable Cost Card
One gallon of Zip

Materials:[a]		
1 gallon chemical A @ $12/gallon	$12.00	
2 quarts chemical H @ $5/quart	10.00	$22.00
Direct labor: .5 hours @ $14/hour		7.00
Variable manufacturing overhead ($12/DLH)		6.00
Total standard variable cost/gallon Zip		$35.00

[a]During the manufacturing process the one gallon and two quarts of liquid added evaporate to one gallon of finished product Zip.

The company records materials price variances at the time of purchase. The following activity took place during the month of October:

Materials purchases: Chemical A — 26,000 gallons costing $317,200
Chemical H — 40,000 quarts costing $196,800

Materials used: Chemical A — 25,750 gallons
Chemical H — 41,100 quarts

Zip produced: 25,500 gallons

Direct labor: 12,600 hours costing $170,100

Actual variable manufacturing overhead: $154,000

Required:
1. Calculate the direct materials price and quantity variances for *each* chemical and in total.
2. Calculate the direct labor rate and efficiency variances and reconcile them to the total direct labor variance.
3. Determine the amount of underapplied or overapplied overhead.
4. Prepare journal entries to record all the activity related to Zip for the month of October.

P9–18   Revision of standard costs. The standard cost of QNG-4, manufactured by New Mexico Company, is as follows:

	Prime Cost	Manufacturing Overhead (50%)	Total
Material A	$10.00		$10.00
Material B	5.00		5.00
Material C	2.00		2.00
Direct labor — cutting	8.00	$ 4.00	12.00
Direct labor — shaping	4.00	2.00	6.00
Direct labor — assembling	2.00	1.00	3.00
Direct labor — boxing	1.00	.50	1.50
Total	$32.00	$ 7.50	$39.50

The company manufactured 10,000 units of product QNG-4 during the period under review. Materials A, B, and C are issued in the Cutting Department.

The following variances relating to this product appear on the books for the period:

	Unfavorable	Favorable
Materials price variance:		
Due to a favorable purchase of total requirements of material A		$19,500
Materials quantity variance:		
Excessive waste during period	$ 6,000	
Labor rate variance:		
5% wage increase to direct workers	7,500	
Labor efficiency variance:		
Due to shutdown caused by strike	17,000	
Manufacturing overhead variance — fixed:		
Due to shutdown caused by strike	8,000	
Manufacturing overhead variance — variable:		
Due to permanent savings in cost of certain services		18,000

Required: Taking the above variances and causes into consideration, prepare a schedule of revised standard costs for product QNG-4 for New Mexico Company for the next period. The schedule should clearly indicate the cumulative standard for each successive operation.

(CPA Adapted)

P9–19   **Variance calculation and analysis; variance control responsibility.** Maypole
Corporation manufactures and sells a single product, using a standard costing system.
The standard variable cost per unit of product is:

Materials: 1 pound of plastic @ $2	$ 2.00
Direct labor: 1.6 hours @ $4	6.40
Variable manufacturing overhead cost per unit	3.00
Total	$11.40

The variable manufacturing overhead cost per unit was calculated from the following annual overhead cost budget for a 60,000 volume:

Variable manufacturing overhead cost:	
Indirect labor (30,000 hours @ $4)	$120,000
Supplies (oil – 60,000 gallons @ $.50)	30,000
Allocated variable service department cost	30,000
Total variable manufacturing overhead cost	$180,000

The variable charges to the Manufacturing Department for November, when
5,000 units were produced, were:

Materials (5,300 pounds @ $2)	$10,600
Direct labor (8,200 hours @ $4.10)	33,620
Indirect labor (2,400 hours @ $4.10)	9,840
Supplies (oil – 6,000 gallons @ $.55)	3,300
Allocated variable service department cost	3,200
Total	$60,560

The Purchasing Department normally buys about the same quantity of plastic as
is used in production during a month. In November 5,200 pounds were purchased at
a price of $2.10 per pound.

The company has divided its responsibilities so that the Purchasing Department
is responsible for the price at which materials and supplies are purchased, whereas
the Manufacturing Department is responsible for the quantities of materials used.

The Manufacturing Department manager performs the timekeeping function, and,
at various times, an analysis of manufacturing overhead and direct labor variances has
shown that the manager has deliberately misclassified labor hours (such as direct
labor hours might be classified as indirect labor hours and vice versa), so that only
one of the two labor variances is unfavorable. It is not economically feasible to hire a
separate timekeeper.

Required: 1. Calculate these variances from standard costs for the data given: (a) materials
price variance; (b) materials quantity variance; (c) direct labor rate variance;
and (d) direct labor efficiency variance.
2. Explain whether the division of responsibilities should solve the conflict
between price and quantity variances.
3. Suggest a solution to the company's problem involving the classification of labor
hours.

(CMA Adapted)

P9–20   **Standards and variances from incomplete data.** Handicraft Company produces,
among other hand crafts, a yarn kit for latch hooked rugs of a standard size. Yarn is cut

into the proper length strips and packaged by color for the kit. All colors cost the same amount. An incomplete standard variable cost card for a kit is given below:

(Incomplete) Standard Variable Cost Card
Latch-hooked Rug Kit

30 yarn packets @ $.?? per packet	?
? hours of direct labor @ $8.00 per hour	?
Variable manufacturing overhead: $3 per DLH	?
Total standard variable cost per rug kit	$28.00

During the month of November Handicraft Company manufactured and sold 1,000 of the kits. There was no beginning or ending inventory of yarn or work in process. The company used 31,000 packets of yarn to produce the 1,000 kits. The actual variable costs per kit for the November production was $.62 less than the standard variable cost per kit. Other information regarding the rug kit activity for November is given below:

	Materials	Labor	Variable Manufacturing Overhead
Total standard cost	$22,500	?	$1,500
Actual cost incurred		$4,080	1,600
Materials quantity variance	750 U		
Labor efficiency variance		160 F	

Required:

1. What was the total standard cost of direct labor for November?
2. How many hours of direct labor are required per kit?
3. What was the labor rate variance for November?
4. What is the standard price per yarn packet?
5. What was the materials price variance for November?
6. Was variable manufacturing overhead underapplied or overapplied and by how much?
7. Complete the standard variable cost card for a latch-hooked rug kit.

P9–21 Variance analysis; multiple lots. Valley Fashions manufactures ladies' blouses of one quality, produced in lots to fill each special order from its customers, comprised of department stores located in various cities. Valley sews the particular stores' labels on the blouses. The standard variable costs for a dozen blouses are:

Direct materials	24 yards @ $1.10	$26.40
Direct labor	3 hours @ $4.90	14.70
Variable manufacturing overhead	3 hours @ $2.40	7.20
Standard variable cost per dozen		$48.30

During June 19X7 Valley worked on three orders, for which the month's job cost records disclose the following:

Lot No.	Units in Lot (dozens)	Materials Used (yards)	Hours Worked
12	1,000	24,100	2,980
13	1,700	40,440	5,130
14	1,200	28,825	2,890

The following information is also available:

1. Valley purchased 95,000 yards of material during June at a cost of $106,400. The materials price variance is recorded when goods are purchased. All inventories are carried at standard cost.
2. Direct labor during June amounted to $55,000. According to payroll records, production employees were paid $5.00 per hour.
3. Variable manufacturing overhead during June amounted to $29,100.
4. A total of $345,600 was budgeted for variable manufacturing overhead for the year based on estimated production of 48,000 dozen blouses. Manufacturing overhead is applied on the basis of direct labor hours.
5. There was no work in process at June 1. During June lots 12 and 13 were completed. All material was issued for lot 14, which was 80% completed as to direct labor.

Required:
1. Prepare a schedule showing the computation of standard variable costs of lots 12, 13, and 14 for June 19X7.
2. Determine the materials price variance for June. Indicate whether the variance is favorable or unfavorable.
3. Prepare a schedule showing, for each lot produced during June, computations of the
   a. Material quantity variance in yards.
   b. Labor efficiency variance in hours.
   c. Labor rate variance in dollars.
   Indicate whether each variance is favorable or unfavorable.
4. Determine whether variable manufacturing overhead was overapplied or underapplied and by how much.

(CPA Adapted)

P9–22 **Economic order quantity and reorder point.** SaPane Company is a regional distributor of automobile window glass. With the introduction of the new subcompact car models and the expected high level of consumer demand, management recognizes a need to determine the total inventory cost associated with maintaining an optimal supply of replacement windshields for the new subcompact cars introduced by each of the three major manufacturers. SaPane is expecting a daily demand for 36 windshields. The purchase price of each windshield is $50.

Other costs associated with ordering and maintaining an inventory of these windshields are as follows:

a. The historical ordering costs incurred in the Purchase Order Department for placing and processing orders are as follows:

Year	Orders Placed and Processed	Total Ordering Costs
19X5	20	$12,300
19X6	55	12,475
19X7	100	12,700

Management expects the ordering costs to increase 16% over the amounts and rates experienced the last three years.

b. The windshield manufacturer charges SaPane a $75 shipping fee per order.
c. A clerk in the Receiving Department receives, inspects, and secures the windshields as they arrive from the manufacturer. This activity requires 8 hours per

order received. This clerk has no other responsibilities and is paid at the rate of $9 per hour. Related variable overhead costs in this department are applied at the rate of $2.50 per hour.

d. Additional warehouse space will have to be rented to store the new windshields. Space can be rented as needed in a public warehouse at an estimated cost of $2,500 per year plus $5.35 per windshield.

e. Breakage cost is estimated at 6% of the average inventory value.

f. Taxes and fire insurance on the inventory are $1.15 per windshield.

g. The desired rate of return on the investment in inventory is 21% of the purchase price.

Six working days are required from the time the order is placed with the manufacturer until it is received. SaPane uses a 300-day work year when making economic order quantity computations.

Required:

1. Calculate the following values for SaPane Company:
   a. The value for ordering cost that should be used in the economic order quantity formula.
   b. The value for storage cost that should be used in the economic order quantity formula.
   c. The economic order quantity.
   d. The minimum annual relevant cost at the economic order quantity point.
2. Determine the reorder point in units for windshields.

(CMA Adapted)

P9–23   Economic order quantity; reorder point including safety stock. Bender Corporation is concerned about its inventory controls procedures. In connection with engaging you to install a complete accounting system, the management has asked you to help them determine indicators of how much inventory to order and when to order it. The following information is furnished for one item, called a satusonic, that is carried in inventory:

a. Satusonics are sold by the gross (12 dozen) at a list price of $960 per gross, FOB shipper. Bender receives a 50% trade discount off list price on purchases in gross lots.

b. Freight cost is $20 per gross from the shipping point to Bender's plant.

c. Bender uses about 5,000 satusonics during a 259-day production year but must purchase a total of 36 gross per year to allow for normal breakage. Minimum and maximum usages are 12 and 28 satusonics per day, respectively.

d. Normal delivery time to receive an order is 20 working days from the date that a purchase request is initiated. A stockout (complete exhaustion of the inventory) of satusonics would stop production, and Bender would purchase satusonics locally at list price rather than shut down.

e. The cost of placing an order is $30.

f. Space storage cost is $24 per year per average gross in storage.

g. Insurance and taxes are approximately 12% of the net delivered cost of average inventory, and Bender expects a return of at least 8% on its average investment.

Required:

1. Use the economic order quantity formula to determine the most economic lot size to order.
2. Determine the reorder point for satusonics (include a safety stock in your calculation so that Bender can guard against a stock-out).

(CPA Adapted)

P9–24 **Learning curve.** The Kempton Company plans to manufacture a product called Spectrocal, which requires a substantial amount of direct labor on each unit. Based on the company's experience with other products that required similar amounts of direct labor, management believes that there is a learning factor in the production process used to manufacture Spectrocal.

Each unit of Spectrocal requires 50 square feet of raw material at a cost of $30 per square foot for a total material cost of $1,500. The standard direct labor rate is $25 per direct labor hour. Variable manufacturing overhead is assigned to products at a rate of $40 per direct labor hour. The company adds a markup of 30% on variable manufacturing cost in determining an initial bid price for all products.

Data on the production of the first two lots (16 units) of Spectrocal is as follows:

a. The first lot of eight units required a total of 3,200 direct labor hours.

b. The second lot of eight units required a total of 2,240 direct labor hours.

Based on prior production experience, Kempton anticipates that there will be no significant improvement in production time after the first 32 units. Therefore, a standard for direct labor hours will be established based on the average hours per unit for units 17 to 32.

Required:

1. What is the basic premise of the learning curve?

2. Based upon the data presented for the first 16 units, what learning rate appears to be applicable to the direct labor required to produce Spectrocal? Support your answer with appropriate calculations.

3. Calculate the standard for direct labor hours that Kempton should establish for each unit of Spectrocal.

4. After the first 32 units have been manufactured, Kempton Company was asked to submit a bid on an additional 96 units. What price should Kempton bid on this order of 96 units? Explain your answer.

5. Knowledge of the learning curve phenomenon can be a valuable management tool. Explain how management can apply the learning curve in planning and controlling of business operations.

(CMA Adapted)

CHAPTER 10

Standard Costing – Manufacturing Overhead and Flexible Budgeting

Learning Objectives

After reading this chapter you should be able to:

1. Prepare a flexible budget and explain why it is preferred over a static budget.

2. Understand the relationship of flexible budgeting to a standard costing system.

3. Use flexible budgeting techniques to prepare performance reports.

4. Understand the various analysis levels at which variances can be computed and analyzed.

5. Compute spending and efficiency variances and explain their significance.

6. Determine budget and volume variances and interpret their meaning.

7. Differentiate between a product costing procedure and a performance and evaluation technique.

8. Understand how variances recorded in the standard costing system are treated at the end of the accounting period.

It was mentioned in the previous chapter that engineering relationships could be established between inputs and outputs for direct materials and direct labor, that is, that engineers could establish that if a certain amount of direct materials and direct labor were utilized according to specifications, a certain amount of product would be forthcoming. For purposes of performance evaluation and control, it is useful to rearrange the statement and say that for a certain amount of production, certain amounts of direct material and direct labor should have been used. In a standard costing system, standards are established for these input/output relationships and are utilized to, among other things, evaluate actual performance.

There is not, however, tight engineering input/output relationships between the amount of manufacturing overhead incurred and the amount of production expected. As a result, we look to another technique to analyze performance for the manufacturing overhead component in the standard costing system — the flexible budget. Therefore, a standard costing system achieves its main advantages of performance evaluation and control, simplification of budgeting and forecasting, and aiding in product costing and pricing by utilizing standard costs for direct materials and direct labor and flexible budgeting for manufacturing overhead.

Much of the discussion in this chapter regarding flexible budgeting and manufacturing overhead relies on basic techniques and concepts explored in Chapter 3 on cost behavior and Chapter 6 on cost accumulation and allocation. A brief review of those chapters may prove useful before you continue.

This chapter explains the flexible budget and the flexible budgeting process and how it is utilized in a standard costing system. It also explains the variance calculations and analysis for manufacturing overhead. The chapter concludes by summarizing how and to whom the variances are communicated and explains how to dispose of the "booked" variances at the end of the accounting period.

Flexible Budgeting

The example of P. T. Alun, the manufacturer of Indonesian batik shirts, used in the previous chapter will be continued and expanded to illustrate the flexible budgeting concept and how it is applied to manufacturing overhead in a standard costing system. Assume that during December 19X6 the management of P. T. Alun prepared the budget for manufacturing overhead for the month of January 19X7, shown as Exhibit 10–1 (page 334).

The budget in Exhibit 10–1 is called a **static budget**. It is rather obvious why it is called a static budget: it is a budget based on one level of activity only (the production of 800 shirts). If we were to prepare a performance report on manufacturing overhead for the month of January 19X7 based on the static budget, it would appear as shown in Exhibit 10–2.

EXHIBIT 10–1

Manufacturing Overhead Budget
For the Month Ending January 31, 19X7

Budgeted production of shirts	800
Budgeted Manufacturing Overhead	
Indirect materials	$ 6,000
Factory supplies	3,600
Power	2,400
Repairs and maintenance	1,400
Rent	3,500
Insurance	1,000
Depreciation	3,400
Supervisory Salaries	7,500
Total	$28,800

EXHIBIT 10–2

Manufacturing Overhead Performance Report
For the Month Ending January 31,19X7

	Budget	Actual	Variance
Production of shirts	800	600	200 U
Manufacturing overhead:			
Indirect materials	$ 6,000	4,200	$1,800 F
Factory supplies	3,600	2,800	800 F
Power	2,400	1,925	475 F
Repairs and maintenance	1,400	1,600	200 U
Rent	3,500	3,500	–0–
Insurance	1,000	1,000	–0–
Depreciation	3,400	3,400	–0–
Supervisory salaries	7,500	7,800	300 U
Totals	$28,800	$26,225	$2,575 F

You can no doubt point out a number of problems with the performance report shown in Exhibit 10–2. First, we see that P. T. Alun did not produce the expected 800 shirts during January — it produced only 600. By using the static budget against which to compare the actual manufacturing overhead costs incurred, we are comparing budgeted costs for one level of activity (800 shirts produced) with actual costs incurred for a different level of activity (600 shirts produced). Supervisory personnel may be proud of the fact that they have some significant favorable individual variances and a favorable overall variance for manufacturing overhead, but the variances are obviously meaningless. Therefore, the report has little information value beyond telling management that the budgeted production level was not achieved. If, as a student, you had a budget from your parents to purchase books and supplies for eighteen semester hours of course work, but you only registered for twelve semester hours, you would *expect* that you should spend less than budget. The same is true for P. T. Alun: we would *expect* that there should be favorable variances. From a performance evaluation and cost control standpoint, we would like to see a comparison of actual manufacturing overhead costs incurred with what *would have been budgeted* for the production of 600 shirts. If the report were prepared on that basis, we would be comparing costs on a comparable basis, and the report would then have significant information value.

The static budget illustrated in Exhibit 10–2 has other deficiencies as well. There is no information given regarding cost behavior. We cannot tell by looking at the report which costs are variable and which costs are fixed. It is true that we may have some notion as to behavior, but we should not expect that the reader of the report is to determine this. In fact, the determination of the classification of the individual costs as fixed or variable should have been done before the budget was prepared. Because the costs are not identified as variable or fixed, we lose information regarding possible cost controllability. We must look, then, for an approach to budgeting that overcomes these deficiencies. That approach is called *flexible budgeting*.

Preparation of the Flexible Budget

As the name suggests, a **flexible budget** is a budget prepared to cover a *range* of activity. This means that if we have the information correctly identified and assembled to prepare a flexible budget, we can quickly convert a proposed budget for one level of activity to some other level of activity. If the budgeted level of activity is 800 shirts, for example, and the actual number produced is 600, we can quickly convert the proposed budget for 800 shirts to what would have been proposed for the production of 600 shirts.

Some basic analysis is necessary to identify and assemble the information needed to prepare the flexible budget. Costs must be analyzed, as was illustrated in Chapter 3, to determine whether they are variable or fixed. If the cost is mixed, it must be broken into its variable and fixed components. In the process of analyzing the costs, the relevant range should be determined. We do not want to take the risk of extending our cost predictions beyond the range where we have some confidence in the reliability of our estimates.

Assume that P. T. Alun has done an analysis of the manufacturing overhead costs included in the static budget illustrated previously. The results of its analysis resulted in the information shown in Exhibit 10–3 (page 336).

The analysis in Exhibit 10–3 indicates that there are fixed manufacturing overhead costs of $16,800 and that the variable costs are budgeted at the rate of $5.00 per direct labor hour. This reconciles with the standard variable cost card shown in the previous chapter where variable manufacturing overhead

EXHIBIT 10–3
Analysis of Manufacturing Overhead Costs
Expected Production of 800 Shirts (2,400 Direct Labor Hours)[a]

	Fixed	Variable (per DLH)
Indirect material		$2.50
Factory supplies		1.50
Power		1.00
Repairs and maintenance	$ 1,400	
Rent	3,500	
Insurance	1,000	
Depreciation	3,400	
Supervisory salaries	7,500	
Totals	$16,800	$5.00

[a]Relevant range = 500 to 1,000 shirts or 1,500 to 3,000 direct labor hours.

was included in the standard cost of the product at the rate of $5.00 per direct labor hour.

At this point we can express the flexible budget for manufacturing overhead as a formula based on the simple equation:

$$\text{Total costs} = \text{Fixed cost} + \text{Variable costs}$$

For the manufacturing overhead flexible budget, the formula becomes (using FMO for fixed manufacturing overhead and VMO as variable manufacturing overhead per direct labor hour)

$$\text{Total manufacturing overhead} = \text{FMO} + \text{DLH(VMO)}$$

Therefore, for P. T. Alun the flexible budget equation is

$$\text{Total manufacturing overhead} = \$16,800 + \text{DLH}(\$5.00)$$

P. T. Alun can now determine the total budgeted manufacturing overhead for any level of activity within the relevant range by merely entering the desired activity level (direct labor hours) and solving the simple equation. For example, if we wish to know the budgeted manufacturing overhead for the production of 600 shirts, we first determine that the production of 600 shirts will require 1,800 standard direct labor hours (600 $\times$ 3 DLH per shirt). Substituting in the formula we obtain

$$\text{Total budgeted manufacturing overhead} = \$16,800 + 1,800(\$5.00)$$

$$= \$25,800$$

This calculation of total manufacturing overhead may suffice for our variance calculations later, but more detail is generally needed for performance evaluation purposes. Manufacturing overhead is composed of a number of smaller separate costs, which are often controllable by different managers. For performance reports, the flexible budget can be prepared in detail for whatever level of activity is needed for comparison purposes. This is illustrated in Exhibit 10–4 where manufacturing overhead is budgeted for three different levels of activity. Note that the variable manufacturing overhead costs have been determined using the information assembled in Exhibit 10–3. If P. T. Alun had produced 1,000 shirts during January, it would have compared their actual manufacturing overhead costs incurred against the flexible budget based on that level of activity, and variances could be determined for the individual costs. Note, as expected, the fixed costs do not change at the various levels of activity because they are expected to remain within the relevant range.

Relating the Flexible Budget to Standard Costing

We have stated that it is virtually impossible to establish any engineering relationship between inputs and outputs for manufacturing overhead. This also means that true quantity standards for manufacturing overhead cannot be established. We solve this problem by resorting to the use of a predetermined

EXHIBIT 10–4

Flexible Budget for Manufacturing Overhead
(Various Levels of Activity)

		Direct Labor Hours[a]		
	Cost per DLH	1,800	2,400	3,000
Variable mfg. overhead:				
Indirect material	$2.50	$ 4,500	$ 6,000	$ 7,500
Factory supplies	1.50	2,700	3,600	4,500
Power	1.00	1,800	2,400	3,000
Total var. mfg. overhead	$5.00	$ 9,000	$12,000	$15,000
Fixed mfg. overhead:				
Repairs and maintenance		$ 1,400	$ 1,400	$ 1,400
Rent		3,500	3,500	3,500
Insurance		1,000	1,000	1,000
Depreciation		3,400	3,400	3,400
Supervisory salaries		7,500	7,500	7,500
Total fixed mfg. overhead		$16,800	$16,800	$16,800
Total manufacturing overhead		$25,800	$28,800	$31,800

[a]It takes 3 hours of direct labor to produce a shirt, so the manufacturing overhead budget for 600 shirts is based on 1,800 direct labor hours, for 800 shirts it is based on 2,400 hours, and so forth.

overhead application rate as it was developed in Chapter 6. We tie the application of manufacturing overhead into our standard costing system by basing the application of manufacturing overhead on some quantity standard related to either direct materials or direct labor. For instance, we could apply manufacturing overhead based on the standard quantity of direct materials used, the standard price of direct materials allowed, the standard hours allowed or a percentage of the standard direct labor costs. The base used will vary with the manufacturing process and the desires of the management team. It should, however, take into consideration whether or not there is a causal relationship between the base selected and the amount of variable manufacturing overhead, whether the relationship is stable, and the ease of using the base.

In the case of P. T. Alun, direct labor hours were chosen for applying overhead. The making of shirts is more labor than capital intensive, so we expect that there should be a positive causal relationship between direct labor hours and the amount of variable manufacturing overhead incurred. It would be possible to use a percentage of direct labor cost, but this can tend to violate the idea of a "stable relationship." Labor rates may change during the period because of inflation or new union contracts with no proportionate change in the manufacturing overhead costs. This will cause overhead to be over- or underapplied just because of the change in the labor rate; that is, the base being used does not have a stable relationship with the amount of manufacturing overhead incurred. The base chosen should be as simple to apply as possible and, of course, should be the base that is used for the preparation of the flexible budget.

In a standard costing system, we calculate a separate application rate for the variable and fixed manufacturing overhead. You will appreciate why as we illustrate the manufacturing overhead variances. Suffice it to say at this point that these two costs react entirely differently, so they should be analyzed differently.

The variable manufacturing overhead rate is determined as we analyze cost behavior. In the P. T. Alun case, we have determined that $5.00 of variable manufacturing overhead is incurred for each direct labor hour worked. The fixed manufacturing overhead rate is a different matter, however. To determine this rate we will need to again utilize the formula developed in Chapter 6 (using FMOR for fixed manufacturing overhead rate):

$$\text{Predetermined FMOR} = \frac{\text{Estimated fixed manufacturing overhead}}{\text{Estimated direct labor hours}}$$

We already have our estimate of fixed manufacturing overhead for P. T. Alun for the month of January (the numerator of the above fraction). The denominator or estimated direct labor hours could be based on the various capacity concepts — theoretical or ideal, practical, normal or expected. These concepts were discussed fully in Chapter 6 and will not be reviewed here. Because we are particularly interested in performance evaluation and control if we are using a standard costing system, it would seem that we would want to use a rate based on *expected* capacity—the level of activity that we expect (and are budgeting) to reach next period. P. T. Alun is expecting to manufacture 800 shirts during January. Therefore, its fixed manufacturing overhead predetermined rate would be

$$\text{FMOR} = \frac{\$16,800}{2,400} = \$7.00 \text{ per direct labor hour}$$

It should be noted that for simplicity we are determining the manufacturing overhead rates for the month of January. As was mentioned in the discussion of predetermined overhead rates in Chapter 6, the fixed rate particularly needs to be determined on a yearly basis to compensate for the "chunks and lumps" manner in which fixed costs are likely to be incurred along with the possible variations in actual production at different times of the year (seasonal variation). We will assume that neither of these factors are significant in our example.

In the previous chapter we prepared a standard *variable* cost card for the batik shirts produced by P. T. Alun. Exhibit 10–5 is a complete standard cost card including all manufacturing overhead.

Manufacturing Overhead Transactions and Variances

The information regarding P. T. Alun for the month of January 19X7 will be used again to illustrate the journal entries and variance analysis for manufacturing overhead. The information given in the example in the prior chapter is repeated with additional information regarding fixed manufacturing costs for the month in Exhibit 10–6 (page 340).

The variances associated with manufacturing overhead are not usually "booked" through journal entries. This probably stems from the fact, as we mentioned above, that the application rates are not standards in the true sense of the word and that the rates cover a number of separate costs needing individual analysis. This makes the recording of manufacturing overhead applied a simple matter. It is the same procedure as was used in the job order

EXHIBIT 10–5
Standard Cost Card
Indonesian Batik Shirt

Direct material: 2 1/2 yards batik @ $8.00 per yard	$20.00
Direct labor: 3 hours @ $10.00 per hour	30.00
Variable manufacturing overhead ($5.00 per DLH)	15.00
Fixed manufacturing overhead ($7.00 per DLH)	21.00
Total standard cost for one batik shirt	$86.00

EXHIBIT 10–6

Production Information for January

Shirts produced: 600
Batik purchased: 2,000 yards costing $15,900
Batik used: 1,600 yards
Direct labor purchased: 1,750 hours costing $18,375
Variable manufacturing overhead incurred $8,925
Fixed manufacturing overhead incurred $17,300
    (The detail for the actual costs of individual items of variable and fixed manufacturing
    overhead were reflected in the static budget performance report shown in
    Exhibit 10–2.)

and process costing systems, with one exception. Manufacturing overhead is applied based on the standard hours allowed for the production achieved rather than on the actual hours worked. In the case of P. T. Alun, they produced 600 shirts during January. The application rate is based on direct labor hours. The standard direct labor hours allowed for the production achieved during January would be $600 \times 3 = 1,800$. The overall manufacturing overhead rate of $12.00 (FMOR + VMOR) would be used and the amount applied for January for P. T. Alun would be $12.00 \times 1,800$ hours or $21,600. The entry to apply manufacturing overhead using the standard costing system would be:

Work in Process	21,600	
Manufacturing Overhead Control		21,600

The charges to Work in Process for the month of January include direct materials at standard, direct labor at standard, and manufacturing overhead determined on a flexible budgeting basis and applied using a rate based on standard hours allowed for the production achieved. The summarized manufacturing overhead control account is illustrated in Exhibit 10–7.

Before we do any other variance analysis, we see that P. T. Alun has underapplied overhead of $4,625. The performance report based on a flexible budget would appear as shown in Exhibit 10–8. Notice the budgeted figures are the ones shown in the column for 1,800 hours in Exhibit 10–4.

EXHIBIT 10–7

Manufacturing Overhead Control

Manufacturing Overhead Control			
Actual total costs	26,225	Applied overhead costs	21,600
		(Underapplied overhead	4,625)

EXHIBIT 10–8

Manufacturing Overhead Performance Report
For the Month Ending January 31, 19X7

	Based on 1,800 Direct Labor Hours		
	Budget	Actual	Variance
Variable manufacturing costs:			
Indirect materials	$ 4,500	$ 4,200	$300 F
Factory supplies	2,700	2,800	100 U
Power	1,800	1,925	125 U
Total variable costs	$ 9,000	$ 8,925	$ 75 F
Fixed manufacturing costs:			
Repairs and maintenance	$ 1,400	$ 1,600	$200 U
Rent	3,500	3,500	–0–
Insurance	1,000	1,000	–0–
Depreciation	3,400	3,400	–0–
Supervisory salaries	7,500	7,800	300 U
Total fixed costs	$16,800	$17,300	$500 U
Overall total	$25,800	$26,225	$425 U

The individual variances for variable manufacturing overhead look significantly different than they do in Exhibit 10–2, where the actual costs were compared against a static budget based on 800 shirts budgeted for production rather than the 600 shirts actually produced. We shall now illustrate another kind of performance evaluation and control technique that ties in with the standard costing approach — the calculation of manufacturing overhead variances. It should be pointed out before beginning the next section that so far in our discussion of manufacturing overhead we have prepared detailed performance reports utilizing the flexible budget to determine the budgeted amounts for each item of manufacturing overhead. When we compared actual costs against budgeted costs for each of the separate cost items, we referred to this difference as a variance. This is the total variance for each of those cost items that includes, in the case of variable manufacturing overhead, both a price or spending variance and a quantity or efficiency variance. To avoid confusion because of the use of the word *variance* in what seems like different situations, think of the variances calculated for manufacturing overhead to this point as being on a very detailed level. We might refer to it as a Level 3 Analysis. We are now going to look at the total variances for variable manufacturing overhead and fixed manufacturing overhead separately. This starts to aggregate the individual costs, so we could refer to this amount of detail as a Level 2 Analysis — the variance analysis approach when we look at total variable manufacturing overhead and total fixed manufacturing overhead separately. If we moved up one more level of aggregation, we could refer to a comparison of the total manufacturing overhead incurred with the total manufacturing overhead applied as a Level 1 Analysis — a highly summarized comparison which furnishes little information in the way of performance evaluation and cost control. Exhibit 10–9 summarizes pictorially these analysis levels. To help put this classification scheme in perspective, Exhibit 10–8 is a Level 3 Analysis. Exhibit 10–7, indicating underapplied manufacturing overhead of $4,625, is a Level 1 Analysis. We are now about to illustrate the Level 2 Analysis — the variances associated with total variable and total fixed manufacturing overhead. On completion of the illustration of the variances for the Level 2 Analysis, we should be able to see how all the manufacturing overhead "variances" articulate.

Determining Variable Manufacturing Overhead Variances

We indicated in the general model for variable cost variances in Chapter 9 that there were two basic variances associated with variable costs — price

EXHIBIT 10–9
Manufacturing Overhead Variance Levels of Analysis

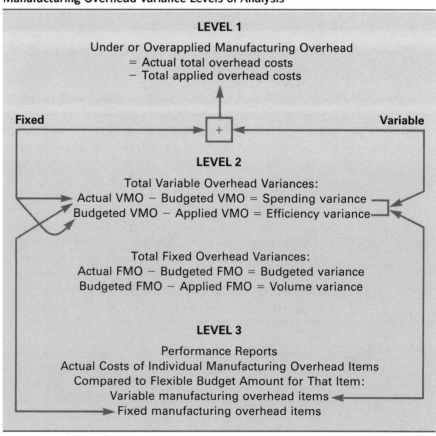

LEVEL 1

Under or Overapplied Manufacturing Overhead
= Actual total overhead costs
− Total applied overhead costs

Fixed   Variable

LEVEL 2

Total Variable Overhead Variances:
Actual VMO − Budgeted VMO = Spending variance
Budgeted VMO − Applied VMO = Efficiency variance

Total Fixed Overhead Variances:
Actual FMO − Budgeted FMO = Budgeted variance
Budgeted FMO − Applied FMO = Volume variance

LEVEL 3

Performance Reports
Actual Costs of Individual Manufacturing Overhead Items
Compared to Flexible Budget Amount for That Item:
Variable manufacturing overhead items
Fixed manufacturing overhead items

and quantity. For variable manufacturing overhead we will refer to these two variances as the spending variance and the efficiency variance. When these basic variances are calculated for direct materials and direct labor, we look to the standard cost card to help us determine the standard price as well as the standard quantity that should have been used for the production level achieved. With manufacturing overhead we will also need to refer to the flexible budget.

Variable Manufacturing Overhead Spending Variance

The **variable manufacturing overhead spending variance** should tell management whether the amount spent for variable manufacturing overhead was within the budgeted price guidelines. For instance, P. T. Alun has determined that it will incur $5.00 for total variable manufacturing overhead for each hour of direct labor _actually_ worked. Notice the emphasis on the direct labor hours actually worked—this variance is to analyze whether we are paying the _budgeted price_ for the variable manufacturing overhead used. The spending variance for P. T. Alun for the month of January would be determined as follows:

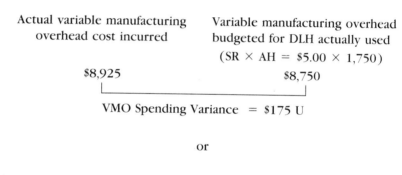

Actual variable manufacturing overhead cost incurred

Variable manufacturing overhead budgeted for DLH actually used

$(SR \times AH = \$5.00 \times 1,750)$

$8,925 $8,750

VMO Spending Variance = $175 U

or

$AH(AR - SR)$

$1,750(\$5.10 - \$5.00) = \$175 \text{ U}$

Short Calculation Method

Note in the calculation of the budgeted amount allowed for the actual hours of direct labor worked that we are dealing with the _total_ variable manufacturing overhead. As a result, we can use the total manufacturing overhead budget equation developed earlier in the chapter:

Total manufacturing overhead = FMO + DLH(VMO)

Because the current analysis deals with variable manufacturing overhead, we need only use the variable portion of the equation [DLH(VMO)] to determine the variable manufacturing overhead budgeted for the actual hours worked. As indicated in the variance calculation, we multiply the actual direct labor hours worked (1,750) times the budgeted variable overhead rate ($5.00) to obtain the variable manufacturing overhead that would be budgeted for the actual direct labor hours worked.

The spending variance indicated that P. T. Alun spent more than what would have been budgeted for the 1,750 actual direct labor hours worked. Again, this does not indicate cause or who is responsible. It merely identifies that an exception or deviation from budget has occurred. The variance could result from an unforeseen increase in the price of some of the supplies, poor purchasing decisions, or any number of other causes. The variance would need to be investigated to determine cause and fix responsibility.

Variable Manufacturing Overhead Efficiency Variance

The **variable manufacturing overhead efficiency variance** does not tell management how efficient they are in the use of variable overhead. What it really tells management is the savings or extra variable manufacturing overhead expenses incurred because there was efficient or inefficient use of the *base* on which variable manufacturing overhead is applied. In the P. T. Alun example, manufacturing overhead is applied using direct labor hours as a base. We already determined in the previous chapter that P. T. Alun had a favorable direct labor efficiency variance of $500 for January. This resulted from taking 1,750 actual direct labor hours to produce output that should have required 1,800 standard direct labor hours. The saving of 50 direct labor hours at a standard direct labor rate of $10.00 per direct labor hour results in the labor efficiency variance of $500. Once the labor efficiency variance is calculated, management knows that there will also be a favorable variable manufacturing overhead efficiency variance. It is only a matter of establishing the dollar value. The variance calculation follows:

Variable manufacturing overhead budgeted for DLH actually used (AH × SR = 1,750 × $5.00)	Variable manufacturing overhead budgeted for standard DLH allowed for production achieved (SH × SR = 1,800 × $5.00)
$8,750	$9,000

VMO efficiency variance = $250 F

$$SR(AH - SH)$$
$$\$5.00(1,750 - 1,800) = \$250 \text{ F}$$

It must be emphasized that the *cause* of the variable manufacturing overhead efficiency variance results from the efficient use of the *base* on which variable manufacturing overhead is budgeted—in this case direct labor hours. Therefore, the responsibility for the variance should be credited to whoever is responsible for the direct labor efficiency variance.

The total variable manufacturing overhead variance for P. T. Alun for January 19X7 can be determined just as the overall direct labor variance was determined:

Actual variable manufacturing overhead cost incurred	$8,925
Variable manufacturing overhead budgeted based on standard hours allowed for production achieved: (600 × 3) × $5.00	9,000
Total variable manufacturing overhead variance	$ 75 F

We have broken this variance down into the following:

Variable manufacturing overhead spending variance	$ 175 U
Variable manufacturing overhead efficiency variance	250 F
Total variable manufacturing overhead variance	$ 75 F

The total of the variable manufacturing overhead spending and efficiency variances reconciles with the total overall variable manufacturing overhead variance. The total variable manufacturing overhead variance calculated above also agrees with the aggregate variance calculated from each of the individual variable manufacturing overhead items shown in Exhibit 10–8.

Determining Fixed Manufacturing Overhead Variances

The analysis of manufacturing overhead to this point has dealt with variable manufacturing costs only, that is, direct materials, direct labor, and variable manufacturing overhead. We indicated that management has the ability in the short run to make decisions to influence both the price paid for these items and the quantity used. The price and quantity variances determined using the standard costing system furnished information helpful to management in its endeavors to influence or control these costs. The analysis of fixed manufacturing overhead, however, differs from the analysis of variable manufacturing overhead. The analysis is different because the cost is entirely different, both from the standpoint of its behavior and by its short-run controllability. If we were to force the analysis of fixed manufacturing overhead into the same model that we used for the variable manufacturing costs, the variances would have little information value and could be misleading. Two variances are generally calculated for fixed manufacturing overhead — a budget variance and a volume variance.

Fixed Manufacturing Overhead Budget Variance

The **fixed manufacturing overhead budget variance** merely compares the actual fixed manufacturing overhead to the fixed manufacturing overhead that would have been budgeted for the level of production actually achieved. The latter number is available, of course, in the flexible budget. Utilizing the information given for P. T. Alun in Exhibit 10–6, and the analysis of manufacturing overhead done in Exhibit 10–3, we would calculate the budget variance as shown on the next page.

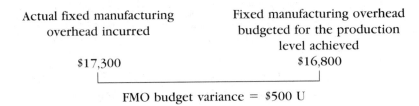

Actual fixed manufacturing overhead incurred

$17,300

Fixed manufacturing overhead budgeted for the production level achieved

$16,800

FMO budget variance = $500 U

Remember that the flexible budget equation for P. T. Alun was

$$\text{Total manufacturing overhead} = \$16,800 + \text{DLH}(\$5.00)$$

This tells us that throughout the relevant range, at least, the fixed manufacturing overhead does not change. Therefore, for any level of utilization of direct labor hours between 1,500 and 3,000 (the relevant range cited in Exhibit 10–3), the fixed portion of the flexible budget remains constant at $16,800.

What information does this variance provide management? We would have to conclude, "Not a great deal." Management usually has little ability to influence these costs in the short run, so the variance does little more than indicate to management the total effect of changes in price factors. It is possible that there could be significant information value for variances from some of the discretionary fixed overhead such as repairs and maintenance but that information is found on the performance reports where individual costs are listed — not in an aggregated fixed manufacturing overhead variance.

Fixed Manufacturing Overhead Volume Variance

The other variance often calculated for fixed manufacturing overhead, and of questionable value, is the **fixed manufacturing overhead volume variance.** Supposedly, it is a measure of the utilization of the plant facilities. For P. T. Alun, it would be calculated as follows:

Fixed manufacturing overhead budgeted for the production level achieved

$16,800

Fixed manufacturing overhead applied based on standard hours allowed for production level achieved
(SH × FMOR = 1,800 × $7.00)

$12,600

FMO volume variance = $4,200 U

Another way that this variance can be determined, which may help understand it, is as follows:

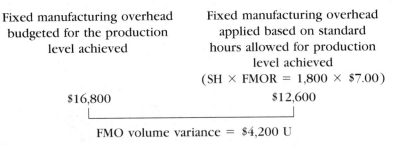

$$\text{FMO volume variance} = \text{FOR}\left(\begin{array}{c}\text{Expected capacity}\\ \text{(denominator DLH used} \\ \text{in FOR determination)}\end{array} - \begin{array}{c}\text{Standard hours allowed}\\ \text{for production level}\\ \text{achieved}\end{array}\right)$$

For P. T. Alun this would be

$$\text{FMO volume variance} = \$7.00(2,400 - 1,800) = \$4,200 \text{ U}$$

The volume variance can be very misleading if the same thinking is applied to the analysis of the variance as has been utilized to this point. The inference may be that it "cost" P. T. Alun $4,200 because it did not operate at its expected level of activity. Nothing could be further from the truth. The budgeted fixed manufacturing overhead of $16,800 is incurred whether P. T. Alun utilizes 1,500 direct labor hours or 3,000 — there is no "cost" or "savings" associated with the variance. This is an example of confusing a product costing technique with a performance evaluation and control technique.

Recall in our earlier discussion that we calculated a predetermined rate for applying fixed manufacturing overhead. This was necessary in order to have product costs on an interim basis. To calculate the predetermined rate for fixed manufacturing overhead we used the budgeted fixed manufacturing overhead costs in the numerator of the fraction and the expected level of activity in the denominator. In the P. T. Alun case, the expected denominator level was 2,400 direct labor hours. With budgeted fixed manufacturing costs of $16,800 and a denominator level of 2,400, it meant that we needed to apply $7.00 of fixed manufacturing overhead every direct labor hour worked in order to allocate to products or absorb all the fixed manufacturing overhead budgeted during the period. The fixed manufacturing overhead rate then becomes a function of the denominator level chosen for applying overhead — a product costing purpose. As it turned out, P. T. Alun did not operate at the denominator level — they fell short of that goal by 600 standard direct labor hours. So the variance does not tell management that it cost P. T. Alun $4,200 because it operated at a level 600 standard direct labor hours below expectations. It merely tells management that it did not operate at the expected level of activity — a fact they are most likely well aware of without the calculation of this variance!

A graphical presentation of these concepts may be helpful. The first graph in Exhibit 10–10 illustrates the budget variance that may be regarded as a legitimate (though limited) piece of information useful in performance evaluation and control. The actual fixed manufacturing overhead costs of $17,300 are compared against the budgeted fixed manufacturing overhead of $16,800. The unfavorable budget variance of $500 applies to any level of activity in the relevant range. The second graph depicts the gradual applying of fixed manufacturing overhead to the product as production progresses. As it happens, P. T. Alun doesn't get all the fixed manufacturing overhead applied because it did not attain the denominator activity level of 2,400 direct labor hours. So the shortfall in applying the budgeted fixed manufacturing overhead can be determined by multiplying the difference between expected direct labor hours of 2,400 and the standard direct labor hours achieved of 1,800 by the $7 fixed overhead rate. Note that if P. T. Alun had used a denominator level of 1,800 direct labor hours, they would have applied all the bud-

EXHIBIT 10–10

Graphical Analysis of Fixed Manufacturing Overhead Variances

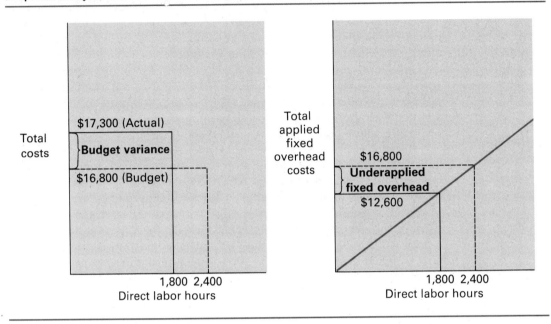

geted fixed manufacturing overhead [($16,800/1,800) × 1,800 = $16,800], and there would have been no volume variance. It seems, then, that this variance has little information value for management. If we wished to put a meaningful dollar value on the fact that P. T. Alun did not operate at the expected or denominator level, we might more appropriately express the shortfall in production in terms of lost contribution margin.

Summarizing the Manufacturing Overhead Variances

Exhibit 10–9 was a conceptual illustration of the manufacturing overhead variances determined at the various levels of analysis. Exhibit 10–11 repeats this analytical framework using the manufacturing overhead variances actually determined for P. T. Alun for the month of January 19X7. The exhibit shows how the various variances at the different levels of analysis relate and "tie together." Notice that the standard cost variances at analysis Level 2 all "tie" to the total variances on the performance reports at analysis Level 3 except for the fixed manufacturing overhead volume variance. This reinforces the point made earlier that the volume variance in particular is *not* useful for performance evaluation and control — it is a child of an overhead application technique necessary for product costing.

EXHIBIT 10–11

P. T. ALUN
Manufacturing Overhead Variance Summary
For the Month of January 19X7

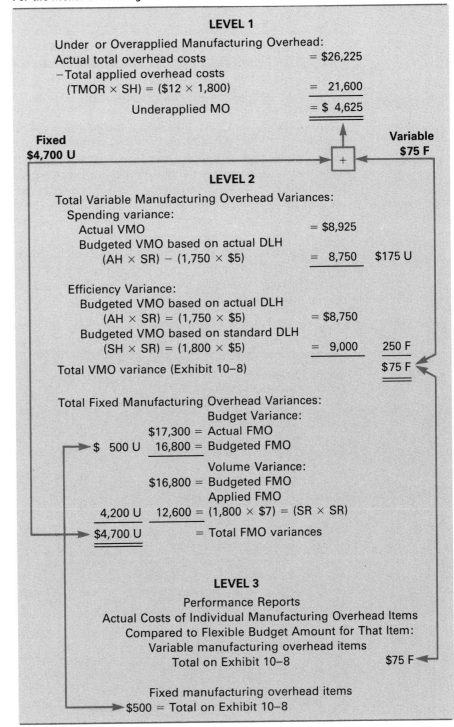

LEVEL 1

Under or Overapplied Manufacturing Overhead:
Actual total overhead costs = $26,225
−Total applied overhead costs
  (TMOR × SH) = ($12 × 1,800) = 21,600
                Underapplied MO = $ 4,625

Fixed
$4,700 U

Variable
$75 F

+

LEVEL 2

Total Variable Manufacturing Overhead Variances:
  Spending variance:
    Actual VMO = $8,925
    Budgeted VMO based on actual DLH
      (AH × SR) − (1,750 × $5) = 8,750 $175 U

  Efficiency Variance:
    Budgeted VMO based on actual DLH
      (AH × SR) = (1,750 × $5) = $8,750
    Budgeted VMO based on standard DLH
      (SH × SR) = (1,800 × $5) = 9,000   250 F

Total VMO variance (Exhibit 10–8) $75 F

Total Fixed Manufacturing Overhead Variances:
                Budget Variance:
    $17,300 = Actual FMO
$ 500 U 16,800 = Budgeted FMO

                Volume Variance:
    $16,800 = Budgeted FMO
             Applied FMO
4,200 U 12,600 = (1,800 × $7) = (SR × SR)
$4,700 U   = Total FMO variances

LEVEL 3

Performance Reports
Actual Costs of Individual Manufacturing Overhead Items
Compared to Flexible Budget Amount for That Item:
Variable manufacturing overhead items
Total on Exhibit 10–8 $75 F

Fixed manufacturing overhead items
$500 = Total on Exhibit 10–8

Manufacturing Overhead Variance Communication and Disposition

As production progresses, performance reports similar to Exhibit 10–8 will be furnished to management on a periodic basis and, if deemed appropriate, analyzed for causes and corrective action taken where possible. The reports will be designed to fit the particular areas of responsibility. This would suggest that the content of the report could vary according to the information considered necessary for the particular area of responsibility covered by the report. Exhibit 10–8 illustrates both variable and fixed manufacturing overhead cost elements on the report—this may not be considered necessary. Some firms like to include the fixed costs on the performance report for information purposes even though the person receiving the report does not have control of these costs (and will not be held accountable). In general, only those costs over which the recipient of the report has control are included on his or her report. As you might then expect, usually only variable costs will appear on performance reports.

The standard cost variances are often also included on the income statement generated for internal use by top management. Exhibit 10–12 illustrates such an income statement for P. T. Alun for the month of January, assuming that all 600 shirts produced are sold.

EXHIBIT 10–12

P. T. ALUN
Income Statement
For the Month Ending January 31, 19X7

Sales (600 × $150)			$90,000
Cost of goods sold (at standard = 600 × $86)		$51,600	
Plus net unfavorable standard cost variances:			
Materials price variance	$ 100 F		
Materials quantity variance	800 F		
Labor rate variance	875 U		
Labor efficiency variance	500 F		
Variable overhead spending variance	175 U		
Variable overhead efficiency variance	250 F		
Fixed overhead budget variance	500 U		
Fixed overhead volume variance	<u>4,200</u> U		
Total variances		<u>4,100</u> U	
Cost of goods sold at actual cost			55,700
Gross margin			$34,300
Less operating expenses:			
Selling[a]		9,000	
General and administrative[a]		<u>14,000</u>	<u>23,000</u>
Net income			$11,300

[a]Assumed.

Exhibit 10–12 summarizes for top management the effect of the variances on profit. Note that this report is for internal use by management. Standard costing techniques are not acceptable in most cases for external reporting, so the income statement prepared for external users would be prepared based on actual costs rather than standard costs.

A final consideration is the disposition of the "booked" variances in the standard costing system. We have illustrated journal entries that recorded direct materials and direct labor variances. The manufacturing overhead variances were determined for management information purposes by a separate analysis. What is done with these booked variances (along with the underapplied overhead) at the end of the accounting period?

As indicated in Chapter 6, the under- or overapplied overhead is normally closed to cost of goods sold. This is acceptable if the under- or overapplied overhead is insignificant or if all of the production of the period is sold. If, however, the under- or overapplied overhead is a material amount and significant amounts of product are still in work in process or finished goods, the under- or overapplied overhead should be prorated on the basis of the percentage of production activity of the period still included in each of these inventories and cost of goods sold.

The same is true for the other standard cost variances. P. T. Alun sold all their production for the period, so closing the variances to cost of goods sold is acceptable. If much of the production for the period was still in work in process and finished goods, then any significant variances should be prorated to work in process, finished goods, and cost of goods sold with one possible exception. A portion of the materials price variance would have to be prorated to the raw materials inventory as well as the other inventories and cost of goods sold if a significant part of the materials purchased during the period had not been used.

There are those who argue that the standard costing variances should be closed to income summary (and, therefore, be shown on the income statement as items of expense or revenue) rather than charged to cost of goods sold or prorated to the inventories and cost of goods sold. The argument is based on the assumption that if the standards are carefully set, the standard cost should be the *recorded* product cost and inefficiencies or efficiencies in the production process should not be allowed to affect that recorded product cost. This argument may have merit for internal reporting purpose, but as long as standard costing is not acceptable for external reporting, where cost of goods sold and the inventories must be at actual cost, the argument loses credibility.

Summary

Engineering relationships cannot be established for manufacturing overhead. Therefore, these costs are best controlled by means of a flexible budget. A flexible budget is defined as a budget that can be adjusted to any desired level, measured either in input or output terms. It is necessary to set the budget at a level geared to actual output in order to facilitate control. Thus the actual costs for the level attained are compared against what costs should be for this output.

Although the flexible budget is the primary control tool for manufacturing overhead, the standard costing idea is extended to manufacturing overhead by basing the predetermined overhead rate on a quantity standard having at least a general causal relation to the manufacturing overhead such as direct labor hours. This base should be the same base that is used in preparing the flexible budget.

In a standard costing system, separate overhead rates should be computed for fixed and variable manufacturing overhead. This is because the variances differ due to behavioral differences between fixed and variable overhead. The manufacturing overhead variances are at a more aggregated level than variances stemming from the flexible budget. However, the separation of variable overhead differences between the flexible budget and actual costs into spending and efficiency variances does provide a useful supplementary control tool for management.

The fixed overhead variances have little control significance. The fixed overhead budget variance is merely an aggregation of differences between the flexible budget and actual costs. The fixed overhead volume variance provides little if any information that is relevant for control purposes and may be misleading because it does not measure costs saved or squandered due to efficient or inefficient operations.

In an effort to review standard costing and all of the variances calculated in both Chapter 9 and Chapter 10, the P. T. Alun example will be extended to the month of February 19X7. The standard cost card is repeated below for convenience:

P. T. Alun
Standard Cost Card
Indonesian Batik Shirt

Direct material: 2 1/2 yards batik @ $8.00 per yard	$20.00
Direct labor: 3 hours @ $10.00 per hour	30.00
Variable manufacturing overhead ($5.00 per DLH)	15.00
Fixed manufacturing overhead ($7.00 per DLH)	21.00
Total standard cost for one batik shirt	$86.00

The flexible budget equation is the same as for January:

$$\text{Total manufacturing overhead} = \$16{,}800 + \text{DLH}(\$5.00)$$

The fixed manufacturing overhead is to be applied on the expected capacity of 800 shirts produced (2,400 direct labor hours) resulting in the same fixed manufacturing overhead application rate of $7.00 per direct labor hour. The activity for P. T. Alun for the month of February is given on the next page.

Shirts produced: 900

Batik purchased: 2,100 yards costing $17,010

Batik used: 2,200 yards

Direct labor hours purchased: 2,800 hours costing $27,720

Variable manufacturing overhead incurred: $13,500

Fixed manufacturing overhead incurred: $16,700

The variances will be calculated using the shorter method where possible.

Direct Materials Variances

Materials price variance:
$$AQ(AP - SP) = 2,100(\$8.10 - \$8.00) = \$210 \text{ U}$$
Materials quantity variance:
$$SP(AQ - SQ) = \$8(2,200 - 2,250) \quad = \$400 \text{ F}$$

Total materials variance $\underline{\underline{\$190 \text{ F}}}$

Direct Labor Variances

Labor rate variance:
$$AH(AR - SR) = 2,800(\$9.90 - \$10.00) = \$ \ 280 \text{ F}$$
Labor efficiency variance:
$$SR(AH - SH) = \$10(2,800 - 2,700) \quad = \ \underline{1,000 \text{ U}}$$

Total labor variance $= \$ \ \underline{\underline{720 \text{ U}}}$

Manufacturing Overhead Variance Analysis

Over- or underapplied overhead:

Total actual manufacturing overhead incurred	$30,200
Total overhead applied: (SH × SR) = (2,700 × $12)	32,400
Total overapplied manufacturing overhead	$ 2,200 F

Variable manufacturing overhead variances:
Spending variance:

Actual variable manufacturing overhead	$13,500	
VO budgeted based on actual DLH:		
(2,800 × $5)	14,000	$ 500 F

Efficiency variance:

VO budgeted based on actual DLH	$14,000	
VO budgeted based on standard DLH:		
(900 × 3) × $5	13,500	500 U

Fixed manufacturing overhead variances:
Budget variance:

Actual fixed manufacturing overhead	$16,700	
Budgeted fixed manufacturing overhead	16,800	100 F

Volume variance:

FMOR(denominator DLH − standard DLH):		2,200 F
$7(2,400 − 2,700)		

Total manufacturing overhead variances
(reconciles with overapplied overhead above) $ 2,200 F

Key Terms

Fixed manufacturing overhead budget variance   is the difference between actual and budgeted fixed manufacturing overhead.

Fixed manufacturing overhead volume variance   is the difference between budgeted fixed manufacturing overhead and standard applied fixed manufacturing overhead for output achieved. It is a measure of utilization of plant and equipment and is not useful for control purposes.

Flexible budget   is a budget that can easily be adapted to a range of activity. It is extremely important for control purposes in order to compare actual costs with a budget geared to this same level of activity rather than the original budget determined at the start of the year.

Static budget   is a budget based on only one level of activity.

Variable manufacturing overhead efficiency variance   is an efficiency type variance based on the difference between the *actual* base of operations (direct labor hours, for example) achieved multiplied by the variable manufacturing overhead rate and the standard base of operations for production achieved multiplied by the variable manufacturing overhead rate.

Variable manufacturing overhead spending variance   is a rate type variance based on the difference between actual variable overhead and the actual base of operations achieved multiplied by the variable overhead rate.

Questions

Q10–1   What is a static budget? What are its weaknesses?

Q10–2   What is a flexible budget? How does it differ from a static budget?

Q10–3   "Give me the cost formulas used in developing the flexible budget, and I'll give you a budget for any level of activity." What is the problem with this statement?

Q10–4   Where is the "flex" in the flexible budget?

Q10–5   "Why do we need to use flexible budgeting techniques in the analysis of manufacturing overhead in our standard costing system? We don't need it for direct materials and direct labor!" Comment on the quote.

Q10–6   What factors should be considered in choosing an activity base for the application of manufacturing overhead?

Q10–7   Why should the activity base used to apply manufacturing overhead in a standard costing system be the same activity base as that used for the preparation of the flexible budget?

Q10–8   What is meant by *standard hours allowed*?

Q10–9   Distinguish between standard hours allowed based on expected capacity and standard hours allowed for the production achieved.

Q10–10   Why are manufacturing overhead variances usually not "booked" (entered in the journal and posted to the general ledger)?

Q10–11   If manufacturing overhead variances are not booked, what is the difference in accounting for overhead in a standard costing system as opposed to a costing system not using standard costs?

Q10–12   What is a manufacturing overhead performance report? What is its use?

Q10–13   Explain the difference between the three levels of analysis of manufacturing overhead giving examples of each level of analysis.

Q10–14   Underapplied or overapplied manufacturing overhead can be broken down into what four variances? Is it possible to have no under- or overapplied overhead and still have overhead variances? Explain.

Q10–15   Why are actual variable manufacturing overhead costs compared against variable overhead budgeted for actual hours worked rather than standard hours allowed for the production achieved in determining the spending variance?

Q10–16   "I don't need to calculate a variable overhead efficiency variance. I get that information from the labor efficiency variance." Is the statement correct? Explain.

Q10–17   What does the fixed overhead budget variance measure? Is any part of this variance controllable by management? Explain.

Q10–18   "All the volume variance tells me is whether or not I operated at the denominator level of activity!" Do you agree with this statement? Justify your stand.

Q10–19   A production supervisor made the following statement: "There should be an efficiency variance for fixed manufacturing overhead—a line supervisor can efficiently use his or her resources." Comment on the production supervisor's statement.

Q10–20   If a volume variance is to be calculated, what might be a better measure of its dollar value than the traditional method of calculation?

Q10–21   What is the essential difficulty in applying fixed overhead to product and the typical error made in analyzing fixed overhead variances?

Q10–22   Why would a company allocate variances to inventories and cost of goods sold rather than closing them all to cost of goods sold?

Exercises

E10–1   **Critique of a performance report.** Kelli Company's management is concerned about the performance reports it is receiving. The company uses a fixed or static budget to measure its performance against the budget objectives and to help in cost control. At the end of a recent month, management received the following report comparing actual performance with budgeted figures:

Item	Budget	Actual
Units produced	24,000	21,500
Direct materials	$48,000	$47,300
Direct labor	26,400	25,800
Indirect labor	1,500	1,450
Repairs and maintenance	2,400	2,500
Factory supplies	1,800	1,850
Property taxes	500	510
Insurance	800	800
Rent	2,500	2,500
Depreciation	3,000	3,000
Total	$86,900	$85,710

Required: 1. What useful information does this report provide?
                  2. What are the weaknesses of this type budget and performance report?

E10–2   **Flexible budgets given cost formulas.** Berger Company has done an analysis of its manufacturing overhead costs and determined the cost formulas shown below. Berger has also determined that the cost formulas are valid over a relevant range of 12,000 to 16,000 direct labor hours.

Indirect labor	$12,000 plus $.20 per direct labor hour
Utilities	$ 800 plus $.18 per direct labor hour
Supplies	$.25 per direct labor hour
Repairs and maintenance	$ 8,000 plus $.15 per direct labor hour
Insurance	$ 4,000
Rent	$ 5,000
Depreciation	$10,000

Required: 1. What is the cost formula for total manufacturing overhead?
                  2. Prepare a flexible budget for all the manufacturing overhead costs for 12,000, 14,000, and 16,000 direct labor hours.

E10–3   **Flexible budget for one activity level given the budget for other activity levels.** Olen Industries uses flexible budgeting with its standard costing system to help in the determination and control of costs. The following flexible budget for manufacturing overhead is provided for 80% and 100% of expected capacity:

	Expected Capacity	
	80%	100%
Units of production	4,000	5,000
Indirect labor	$ 5,000	$ 6,000
Utilities	2,800	3,300
Repairs and maintenance	2,700	3,200
Supplies	1,600	2,000
Insurance	800	800
Rent	2,000	2,000
Depreciation – plant and equipment	3,500	3,500
Miscellaneous factory costs	1,400	1,500
Total budgeted manufacturing overhead	$19,800	$22,300

Required: 1. Prepare a flexible budget for the manufacturing overhead assuming that 4,600 units are produced in the current period.
                  2. If the manufacturing overhead application rate were based on the expected capacity (100%) and the actual manufacturing overhead costs were equal to the budget allowed for 4,600 units, would there be any overapplied or underapplied overhead? If so, how much?

E10–4   **Performance report—variable manufacturing overhead.** Ikan Company budgets variable manufacturing overhead costs on the basis of direct labor hours. One unit of product requires three hours of direct labor. The cost formulas for the variable overhead items are given on page 357.

Variable Overhead Costs	Per Direct Labor Hour
Indirect materials	$.30
Utilities	.20
Indirect labor	.10
Repairs and maintenance	.25
Total variable overhead costs	$.85

During November 19X7 Ikan budgeted for a production of 6,000 but produced 6,500 units of product. The actual variable manufacturing overhead costs were:

Indirect materials	$ 5,900
Utilities	3,800
Indirect labor	2,025
Repairs and maintenance	5,275
Total	$17,000

Required:

1. Prepare a performance report for the variable manufacturing overhead for the period (Level 3 Analysis). Indicate whether the individual variances are favorable or unfavorable.

2. With the information given, can you tell whether the individual variances are the result of spending or efficiency or both? Could some of the variances be related to other variances? Explain.

E10–5 **Determining amount of manufacturing overhead applied.** Ulfex Company uses a standard costing system. The following manufacturing overhead costs and production data are available for August 19X7:

Standard fixed manufacturing overhead rate per DLH	$1.00
Standard variable manufacturing overhead rate per DLH	$4.00
Budgeted monthly direct labor hours (expected capacity)	40,000
Actual direct labor hours worked	39,500
Standard DLH allowed for actual production	39,000
Overall manufacturing overhead variance (overapplied)	$ 2,000

Required: Determine the amount of manufacturing overhead applied during August.

E10–6 **Determining actual manufacturing overhead costs incurred.** At the end of the current period, Donaldson Company has total underapplied manufacturing overhead of $15,000. Additional information is as follows:

Variable manufacturing overhead:	
Applied based on standard direct labor hours allowed for production achieved	$42,000
Budgeted variable overhead based on actual direct labor hours worked	38,000
Fixed manufacturing overhead:	
Applied based on standard direct labor hours allowed for production achieved	30,000
Budgeted fixed overhead based on expected capacity	27,000

Required: What were the total actual manufacturing overhead costs incurred during the period?

(CPA Adapted)

E10–7   **Variable manufacturing overhead variances.** Everdale Company uses a standard costing system and bases its standard variable manufacturing overhead costs on direct labor hours. The standard cost card indicates that variable manufacturing overhead costs are $18 per unit of finished product ($6 per direct labor hour for the three hours of direct labor allowed to produce one unit).

During the last month, Everdale produced 2,000 units of product requiring 6,100 hours of direct labor. The actual variable manufacturing overhead costs incurred were as follows:

Indirect materials	$ 4,200
Indirect labor	17,800
Supplies	3,950
Utilities	7,200
Repairs and maintenance	3,200
Miscellaneous	1,250
Total	$37,600

Required: 1. Determine the variable manufacturing overhead spending variance.
2. Determine the variable manufacturing overhead efficiency variance.
3. If Everdale discovered a way to use only half as many supplies as the standard called for, which variance (spending or efficiency) would reflect these cost savings? Explain.

E10–8   **Relationship of direct labor and variable overhead efficiency variances.** Rex Company manufactures men's blended silk ties and uses a standard costing system. The standard cost card for one tie is given below:

Standard Cost Card
Men's Blended Silk Tie

1/2 yard blended silk material @ $10 per yard	$ 5.00
1/2 hour of direct labor @ $12 per hour	6.00
Manufacturing overhead @ $6 per direct labor hour	
($4 variable, $2 fixed)	3.00
Total standard cost	$14.00

During September 19X7 Rex Company used 1,300 direct labor hours to produce 2,400 ties.

Required: 1. Determine the direct labor efficiency variance. Is it favorable or unfavorable?
2. Determine the variable manufacturing overhead efficiency variance. Is it favorable or unfavorable?
3. What can be said about the relationship of the variable overhead efficiency variance and the direct labor efficiency variances?

E10–9   **Fixed manufacturing overhead variances.** Parker Manufacturing uses standard costs for cost control and internal reporting. The flexible budget equation for manufacturing overhead for an expected capacity of 9,000 units is $40,500 + $5(DLH)$, where DLH represents direct labor hours. It requires two hours of direct labor for each unit of product produced.

During December 19X7 actual fixed costs were $42,500, and the actual production was 10,000 units of product.

Required:
1. Determine the fixed manufacturing overhead budget variance. Was it affected because Parker operated above the expected capacity of 9,000 units?
2. Determine the fixed manufacturing overhead volume variance. Is it favorable or unfavorable? Why?

E10–10 **Variable manufacturing overhead analysis.** Anders Manufacturing uses flexible budgeting techniques along with its standard costing system to help with cost estimating and in performance evaluation and control. The flexible budget is based on direct labor hours. It takes two standard direct labor hours to produce one unit of finished product. During the current period Anders produced 4,750 units of product. It took the company 500 hours above standard to achieve this output. The variable manufacturing overhead spending variance was $1,500 unfavorable. The actual variable manufacturing overhead was $31,025.

Required:
1. What is the variable manufacturing overhead rate per direct labor hour?
2. Compute the variable overhead spending variance. Is it favorable or unfavorable?
3. With this information regarding variable manufacturing overhead, what can be said about the direct labor variance?

E10–11 **Fixed manufacturing overhead analysis: working back from variances.** Beatreese Company's flexible budget equation for total manufacturing overhead expenses per month is $60,000 + $5(DLH)$, where (DLH) is direct labor hours. The budget is based on an expected capacity of 15,000 direct labor hours per month. For March, Beatreese had determined that the fixed manufacturing overhead budget variance was $2,000 unfavorable and the volume variance was $4,000 unfavorable.

Required:
1. What is the fixed manufacturing overhead application rate?
2. How much were the actual fixed manufacturing overhead costs for March?
3. How many standard direct labor hours were worked in March?

E10–12 **Fixed manufacturing overhead analysis.** Information regarding Farner Company's manufacturing overhead costs for the June 19X7 production activity is as follows:

Budgeted fixed manufacturing overhead	$84,000
Standard fixed manufacturing overhead rate per direct labor hour	$ 7
Standard variable manufacturing overhead rate per direct labor hour	$ 6
Actual fixed manufacturing overhead in June	$84,500
Standard direct labor hours allowed for the production achieved in June	12,500

Farner bases its manufacturing overhead application rate on expected capacity.

Required:
1. What is Farner's expected capacity per month expressed in direct labor hours?
2. What is the budget variance for June? (Favorable or unfavorable?)
3. What is the volume variance for June? Indicate whether the volume variance is favorable or unfavorable and explain what it means.

E10–13 **Variable and fixed manufacturing overhead variances.** Normandie Company bases its manufacturing overhead cost function on direct labor hours. The flexible budget equation for total manufacturing overhead for one month is expressed as $33,000 + $2.40(DLH)$, where (DLH) refers to direct labor hours. An abbreviated flexible budget listing only total variable and fixed manufacturing costs for three levels of activity within the relevant range follows on page 360.

	Direct Labor Hours		
	10,000	11,000	12,000
Manufacturing overhead costs:			
Variable	$24,000	$26,400	$28,800
Fixed	33,000	33,000	33,000
Total manufacturing overhead	$57,000	$59,400	$61,800

Normandie expected to utilize 11,000 direct labor hours per month during the current year and determined its manufacturing overhead rates accordingly. The standard time to produce one unit of product at Normandie is two direct labor hours.

During the current year the company's operating results were

Actual direct labor hours	10,400
Units produced	5,100
Actual variable manufacturing overhead costs	$24,480
Actual fixed manufacturing overhead costs	$30,600

Required:
1. Compute the variable manufacturing overhead spending and efficiency variances.
2. Compute the fixed manufacturing overhead budget and volume variances.
3. Is manufacturing overhead underapplied or overapplied for the period? How is this possible when you have balances for all four manufacturing overhead variances?

E10–14 **Disposition of variances.** Dallas Corporation uses a standard costing system in accounting for its product — Waco. Dallas follows the common practice of "booking" its direct materials and direct labor variances but prefers to analyze underapplied or overapplied manufacturing overhead on separate schedules outside the general ledger. Dallas applies overhead on the basis of direct labor hours. Variances (including underapplied or overapplied overhead) are allocated to cost of goods sold and ending inventories at the end of the accounting period.

The following information was available from the books of Dallas Company at the end of the current period:

Variance	Debit	Credit
Materials price variance		$3,000
Materials quantity variance	$ 4,000	
Labor rate variance	1,000	
Labor efficiency variance		2,000
Underapplied overhead	10,000	

The following inventories were on hand at the end of the period:

Finished goods	2,000 units
Work in process	2,000 units
Raw materials	None

The work in process inventory was 100% complete as to materials but only 50% complete as to direct labor and manufacturing overhead. The company sold 2,000 units of the production during the period.

Required:
1. Determine the dollar amount of the variances that will be allocated to each of the inventories and to cost of goods sold.
2. Prepare the journal entry to allocate the variances.

Problems

P10–15 **Flexible budget for performance evaluation.** The University of Edwardsville offers an extensive continuing education program in many cities throughout the state. For the convenience of its faculty and administrative staff and to save costs, the university employs a supervisor to operate a motor pool. The motor pool operated with 20 vehicles until October, when an additional automobile was acquired. The motor pool furnishes gasoline, oil, and other supplies for its automobiles. A mechanic does routine maintenance and minor repairs. Major repairs are done at a nearby commercial garage.

Each year the supervisor prepares an operating budget that informs the university administration of the funds needed for operating the motor pool. Depreciation (straight-line) on the automobiles is recorded in the budget in order to determine the cost per mile.

The following schedule presents the annual budget approved by the university, with November's actual costs compared to one-twelfth of the annual budget:

University Motor Pool
Budget Report for November

	Annual Budget	One-Month Budget	November Actual	(Over) Under
Gasoline	$ 52,500	$ 4,375	$ 5,323	$(948)
Oil, minor repairs, parts, and supplies	3,600	300	380	(80)
Outside repairs	2,700	225	50	175
Insurance	6,000	500	525	(25)
Salaries and benefits	30,000	2,500	2,500	—
Depreciation	26,400	2,200	2,310	(110)
	$121,200	$10,100	$11,088	$(988)
Total miles	600,000	50,000	63,000	
Cost per mile	$ .2020	$ .2020	$ .1760	
Number of automobiles	20	20	21	

The annual budget was constructed upon these assumptions:

a. 20 automobiles in the pool.
b. 30,000 miles per year per automobile.
c. 16 miles per gallon per automobile.
d. $1.40 per gallon of gasoline.
e. $.006 per mile for oil, minor repairs, parts, and supplies.
f. $135 per automobile for outside repairs.

The supervisor is unhappy with the monthly report comparing budget and actual costs for March, claiming that it presents an unfair picture of performance. A previous employer used flexible budgeting to compare actual costs to budgeted amounts.

Required: 1. Prepare a performance report showing budgeted amounts, actual costs, and monthly variations for November, using flexible budgeting to compare actual costs to budgeted amounts.
2. What seems to be the basis for the budget for outside repairs?

(CMA Adapted)

P10–16 **Flexible budgeting: evaluating selling expenses.** Ritson Company employs flexible budgeting techniques to evaluate the performance of several of its activities. The selling expense flexible budgets for three representative monthly activity levels are shown below.

Representative Monthly Flexible Budgets for Selling Expenses

Activity measures:			
Unit sales volume	400,000	425,000	450,000
Dollar sales volume	$10,000,000	$10,625,000	$11,250,000
Number of salespersons	75	75	75
Number of orders	4,000	4,250	4,500
Monthly expenses:			
Advertising and promotion	$ 1,200,000	$ 1,200,000	$ 1,200,000
Administrative salaries	57,000	57,000	57,000
Sales salaries	75,000	75,000	75,000
Sales commissions	200,000	212,000	225,000
Salespersons' travel	170,000	175,000	180,000
Sales office expense	490,000	498,750	507,500
Shipping expense	675,000	712,500	750,000
Total Selling Expenses	$ 2,867,000	$ 2,930,250	$ 2,994,500

The following assumptions were used to develop the selling expense flexible budgets:

a. The average size of Ritson's salesforce during the year was planned to be 75.

b. Salespersons are paid a monthly salary plus commission on gross dollar sales.

c. The travel costs are best characterized as a step variable cost. The fixed portion is related to the number of salespersons while the variable portion tends to fluctuate with gross dollar sales.

d. Sales office expense is a mixed cost with the variable portion related to the number of orders processed.

e. Shipping expense is a mixed cost with the variable portion related to the number of units sold.

A sales force of 80 persons generated a total of 4,300 orders resulting in a sales volume of 420,000 units during November. The gross dollar sales amounted to $10.9 million. The selling expenses incurred for November were as follows:

Advertising and promotion	$1,350,000
Administrative salaries	57,000
Sales salaries	80,000
Sales commissions	218,000
Salespersons' travel	185,000
Sales office expense	497,200
Shipping expense	730,000
Total	$3,117,200

Required:

1. Explain why flexible budgeting is a useful management tool.

2. Explain why the selling expense flexible budget presented above would not be appropriate for evaluating Ritson Company's November selling expenses, and indicate how the flexible budget would have to be revised.

3. Prepare a selling expense report for November that Ritson Company can use to evaluate its control over selling expenses. The report should have a line for

each selling expense item showing the appropriate budgeted amount, the actual selling expense, and the dollar variation for the month.

(CMA Adapted)

P10–17 **Flexible versus fixed budget.** Stuarts Inc. is a regional chain of restaurants, each with a carryout delicatessen department. Company management has prepared the following budget for a typical unit:

Typical Stuarts Restaurant – Deli
Budgeted Income Statement for the Year

	Restaurant	Delicatessen	Total
Sales	$2,500,000	$1,000,000	$3,500,000
Purchases	$1,000,000	$ 600,000	$1,600,000
Hourly wages (variable)	875,000	50,000	925,000
Franchise fee	75,000	30,000	105,000
Advertising (fixed)	200,000	100,000	300,000
Utilities (variable)	125,000	70,000	195,000
Depreciation	75,000	50,000	125,000
Lease expense	50,000	30,000	80,000
Salaries (fixed)	50,000	30,000	80,000
Total	$2,450,000	$ 960,000	$3,410,000
Income before income tax	$ 50,000	$ 40,000	$ 90,000

All units are approximately the same size, with a uniform style of building and facilities. The corporation charges a franchise fee, which is a percentage of sales, for use of the company name, the building and facilities design, and advertising advice.

The Minneapolis, Minnesota, unit was selected to test the budget program. Its performance for the year just ended, compared to the typical budget, is as follows:

STUARTS RESTAURANT – DELI, MINNEAPOLIS, MINNESOTA
Income Statement for the Year Ended December 31, 19X7
(in 000's)

	Actual				Over (Under)
	Restaurant	Delicatessen	Total	Budget	Budget
Sales	$2,000	$1,200	$3,200	$3,500	$(300)
Purchases	$ 800	$ 780	$1,580	$1,600	$ (20)
Hourly wages	700	60	760	925	(165)
Franchise fee	60	36	96	105	(9)
Advertising	200	100	300	300	—
Utilities	100	76	176	195	(19)
Depreciation	75	50	125	125	—
Lease expense	50	30	80	80	—
Salaries	50	30	80	80	—
Total	$2,035	$1,162	$3,197	$3,410	$ (213)
Income before tax	$ (35)	$ 38	$ 3	$ 90	$ (87)

A review of the report and a discussion of its meaning by Stuarts' management led to the conclusion that a more meaningful comparison would result if a flexible budget analysis for each of the two lines were performed.

Required:

1. Prepare an income statement for the Minneapolis unit's deli line, comparing actual performance to a flexible budget.
2. Discuss whether or not a complete report, comparing the performance of each of the two lines to its flexible budget, would make Minneapolis's operating problems easier to identify.
3. What are the advantages of comparing actual performance to a flexible budget as a part of the regular annual as well as monthly reporting system?

(CMA Adapted)

P10–18   Using the flexible budget. Department A, one of fifteen departments in the manufacturing plant, is involved in the production of all of the six products manufactured by Agus Products Inc. Because Department A is highly mechanized, its output is measured in direct machine hours. Flexible budgets are utilized throughout the plant in planning and controlling costs, but this problem's focus is on the application of flexible budgets in Department A only.

On March 15, 19X7, the following flexible budget was approved for Department A to be used throughout the fiscal year 19X7–X8, beginning on July 1, 19X7. This flexible budget was developed through the cooperative efforts of Department A's manager, the supervisor, and members of the Budget Department.

Flexible Budget for Department A
For Fiscal Year 19X7–X8

Controllable Costs	Fixed Amount per Month	Variable Rate per Direct Machine Hour
Employees' wages (direct labor)	$20,000	$.08
Indirect salaries	10,000	—
Indirect materials	—	.10
Other costs	5,000	.05
Total	$35,000	$.23

On May 5, 19X7, the annual sales plan and the production budget were completed. To continue preparation of the annual profit plan, which was detailed by month, the production budget was translated to planned activity for each of the fifteen departments. The planned activity for Department A was:

	July	August	September	October–June	For Twelve Months Ending June 30, 19X8
Planned output in direct machine hours	22,000	25,000	29,000	260,000	336,000

On August 31, 19X7, Department A's manager was informed that the planned September output had been revised to 34,000 direct machine hours. On September 30, 19X7, Department A's accounting records showed the following actual data for September:

Actual output in direct machine hours	32,000
Actual controllable costs incurred:	
Employees' wages	$22,750
Indirect salaries	10,300
Indirect materials	3,200
Other costs	7,100
Total	$43,350

Required: (The following requirements relate primarily to the potential uses of the flexible budget for the period March through September 19X7.)

1. Explain how the range of the activity base to which the variable rates per direct machine hour are relevant should be determined.
2. Explain and illustrate the use of the flexible budget in:

   a. Budgeting costs when the annual sales plan and production budget are completed (about May 5, 19X7 or shortly thereafter).
   b. Budgeting a cost revision based upon a revised production budget (about August 31, 19X7 or shortly thereafter).
   c. Preparing a cost performance report for September 19X7. (Prepare a cost performance report for September 19X7, to illustrate.)

(CPA Adapted)

P10–19 **Preparing and analyzing a detailed performance report.** Tipton Products, Inc., operates a number of production plants throughout the country. The company's Plainview Plant has been in operation for fifteen months. Performance in the plant during the first six months was affected by the usual problems associated with a new operation. Although operations are now running smoothly, the Plainview Plant has not been able to produce profits on a consistent basis. As the production requirements to meet sales demand have increased, the profit performance has deteriorated.

At a staff meeting attended by the plant general manager, the corporate controller, and the corporate budget director, the plant production manager commented that production in the plant changes somewhat from month to month according to sales demand. He noted that this makes it more difficult to control manufacturing expenses. He further noted that the overhead budget for the plant, included in the company's annual profit plan, was static in nature and thus was not useful for judging the plant's performance because of the month-to-month changes in operating levels. The meeting resulted in a decision to redo the budget on a flexible basis and to prepare a report each month that would compare actual manufacturing expenses with budgeted expenses based on actual direct labor hours in the plant.

The plant production manager and the plant accountant studied the cost patterns for recent months, as well as volume and cost data from other Tipton plants. Then they prepared the following flexible budget schedule:

		Direct Labor Hours		
Overhead Costs	Per Direct Labor Hour	150,000	200,000	250,000
Variable costs:				
Indirect labor	$0.80	$120,000	$160,000	$200,000
Supplies	0.13	19,500	26,000	32,500
Power	0.07	10,500	14,000	17,500
Total variable costs	$1.00	150,000	200,000	250,000

Overhead Costs (continued)	Direct Labor Hours (continued)		
	150,000	200,000	250,000
Fixed costs:			
Supervisory labor	69,000	69,000	69,000
Heat and light	15,000	15,000	15,000
Property taxes	6,000	6,000	6,000
Total fixed costs	90,000	90,000	90,000
Total overhead costs	$240,000	$290,000	$340,000

The plant expected to work 200,000 planned production hours in a typical month, which at standard would result in 50,000 units of output.

The manufacturing expense reports prepared for the first three months after the flexible budget program was approved were pleasing to the plant production manager. They showed that except for small variations, the manufacturing expenses were in line with the flexible budget allowances. This is also reflected in the report prepared for November, which is presented below, when 50,500 units were manufactured. However, the plant is still not producing an adequate profit (due in part to excessive overhead costs), and management is beginning to wonder whether the flexible budget was a good idea after all.

PLAINVIEW PLANT
Manufacturing Expense Report
November 19X7
(220,000 Actual Direct Labor Production Hours)

Overhead Costs	Actual Costs	Budgeted Costs	(Over) Under Budget
Variable costs:			
Indirect labor	$177,000	$176,000	$(1,000)
Supplies	27,400	28,600	1,200
Power	16,000	15,400	(600)
Total variable costs	220,400	220,000	(400)
Fixed costs:			
Supervisory labor	70,000	69,000	(1,000)
Heat and light	15,500	15,000	(500)
Property taxes	6,000	6,000	–
Total fixed costs	91,500	90,000	(1,500)
Total overhead costs	$311,900	$310,000	$(1,900)

Required:

1. From the standpoint of performance evaluation and control, explain the advantages of the flexible budget approach over the static or fixed budget approach.
2. Criticize the overhead expense report above. How could the report be improved to provide management with more information about overhead costs?
3. Prepare a new overhead expense report for November. On your report, show the total excess over standard incurred for manufacturing expense items during the

month. Add two more columns to the expense report, one for spending variance and one for efficiency variance. Break down the "over or under budget" into spending and efficiency variances where appropriate.

4. Suggest what the management of the Plainview Plant should do to reduce

   a. The spending (or budget) variance.
   b. The efficiency variance.

(CMA Adapted)

P10-20 **Manufacturing overhead variances.** Nolden Products developed its overhead application rate from the current annual budget. The budget is based on an expected actual output of 720,000 units requiring 3,600,000 direct labor hours (DLH). The company is able to schedule production uniformly throughout the new year.

A total of 66,000 units requiring 315,000 DLH was produced during May. Actual overhead costs for May amounted to $375,000. The actual costs as compared to the annual budget and one-twelfth of the annual budget are shown below:

	Annual Budget				**Actual Costs for May 19X7**
	Total Amount	*Per Unit*	*Per DLH*	*Monthly Budget*	
Variable:					
Indirect labor	$ 900,000	$1.25	$ .25	$ 75,000	$ 75,000
Supplies	1,224,000	1.70	.34	102,000	111,000
Fixed:					
Supervision	648,000	.90	.18	54,000	51,000
Utilities	540,000	.75	.15	45,000	54,000
Depreciation	1,008,000	1.40	.28	84,000	84,000
Total	$4,320,000	$6.00	$1.20	$360,000	$375,000

Required:

1. Calculate the absorbed (applied) overhead costs for May 19X7.
2. Compute the following variances and label each as favorable (F) or unfavorable (U):

   a. Variable overhead spending variance.
   b. Fixed overhead budget variance.
   c. Variable overhead efficiency variance.
   d. Volume variance.

(CMA Adapted)

P10-21 **Manufacturing overhead application rates and variances.** Armada Corporation manufactures a product with the following standard costs:

Direct materials: 20 yards @ $1.35 per yard	$27
Direct labor: 4 hours @ $9.00 per hour	36
Manufacturing overhead: applied at five-sixths of direct labor.	
Ratio of variable costs to fixed costs: 2 to 1	30
Total standard cost per unit of output	$93

Standards are based on expected monthly production requiring 2,400 direct labor hours (600 units of output).

The information on the next page pertains to the month of July 19X7.

Direct materials purchased: 18,000 yards @ $1.38 per yard $24,840
Direct materials used: 9,500 yards
Direct labor: 2,100 hours @ $9.15 per hour $19,215
Actual manufacturing overhead:
    Fixed $ 6,200
    Variable   10,450 $16,650

500 units of the product were actually produced in July 19X7.

Required:

1. Prepare schedules to compute

   a. Variable manufacturing overhead rate per direct labor hour.
   b. Total fixed manufacturing overhead based on expected activity.

2. Prepare schedules to compute the following variances for the month of July 19X7 [be sure to label your variances as favorable (F) or unfavorable (U)]:

   a. Variable manufacturing overhead spending and efficiency variances.
   b. Fixed manufacturing overhead budget and volume variances.

(CPA Adapted)

P10–22 **Standard manufacturing overhead variance calculations.** Edney Company employs a standard absorption costing system for product costing. The standard cost of its product is as follows:

Raw materials $14.50
Direct labor: 2 DLH @ $8   16.00
Manufacturing overhead: 2 DLH @ $11   22.00
    Total standard cost $52.50

The manufacturing overhead rate is based on an expected activity level of 600,000 direct labor hours for the year. Edney planned to produce 25,000 units each month during 19X7. The budgeted manufacturing overhead for 19X7 is as follows:

Variable $3,600,000
Fixed   3,000,000
   Total $6,600,000

During November 19X7, Edney Company produced 26,000 units. Edney used 53,500 direct labor hours in November at a cost of $433,350. Actual manufacturing overhead for the month was $260,000 fixed and $315,000 variable.

Required:

1. Compute the variable overhead spending and efficiency variances.
2. Determine the *total* variance due to *efficiency* for the month of November. Comment on possible causes and those responsible for the overall efficiency (or inefficiency as the case may be).
3. Calculate the fixed manufacturing overhead budget and volume variances.
4. Check to see that the total of your overhead variances agree with the amount of underapplied or overapplied overhead.

(CMA Adapted)

P10–23 **Fixed manufacturing overhead analysis with graphing.** Kristi Manufacturing has done an analysis of its manufacturing overhead costs and has determined that most of the variable manufacturing overhead costs are a function of direct labor hours (DLH). Therefore, the flexible budget equation for total monthly manufacturing overhead was finally determined to be $60,000 + $2.50(DLH). The company feels that the relevant range for this budget equation is 10,000 to 15,000 direct labor hours.

Kristi manufactures a model airplane called the Air-Buss. It requires 5 pounds of material at a standard cost of $3 per pound and 2 hours of direct labor at a standard rate of $7.50 per hour. In accordance with the overhead cost analysis referred to above, the company applies manufacturing overhead on the basis of direct labor hours. The following actual information is available for December 19X7:

Units produced:	5,000
Direct labor hours:	10,500
Fixed manufacturing overhead costs:	$58,000

Required:

1. Assuming that Kristi develops its predetermined overhead application rate on the basis of an expected capacity (denominator level) of 12,000 direct labor hours:

   a. Calculate the predetermined manufacturing overhead application rate and break it down into the fixed and variable elements.
   b. Prepare a standard cost card for one Air-Buss.
   c. Calculate the fixed overhead budget and volume variances.
   d. Prepare a graph similar to the one shown in Exhibit 10–10 showing the budgeted fixed overhead costs through the relevant range and the applied fixed overhead costs from zero to the expected denominator level of activity. Indicate on your graph the volume variance computed in (c) above. Why does Kristi have a volume variance in December?

2. Assuming that Kristi had used an expected capacity (denominator level of activity) of 10,000 direct labor hours rather than 12,000,

   a. Calculate the predetermined manufacturing overhead application rate and break it down into the fixed and variable elements.
   b. Calculate the fixed overhead budget and volume variances.
   c. Prepare another graph similar to the one prepared in (1d) above using the expected capacity of 10,000 direct labor hours as the denominator activity. Does your graph agree with your volume variance calculated in (2b) above?
   d. What can you now say about the cause of volume variances and their usefulness from a performance evaluation and control standpoint?
   e. Add one line to each of your graphs that will illustrate the budget variance. What information does this variance provide to management?

P10–24 **Comprehensive manufacturing overhead analysis by levels.** Seacom Industries is a highly mechanized company making high precision tools. Management of Seacom has been concerned about trying to control manufacturing overhead costs and has hired you as a consultant to help in the process. The company already uses standard costing for direct materials and direct labor.

After a good deal of research and analysis you have determined that there is a close relationship between the amount of variable manufacturing overhead and machine hours worked. From your analysis of the individual manufacturing overhead items you developed the following monthly cost functions:

Overhead Item	Cost Function
Indirect labor	$15,000 + $.20(MH)
Utilities	$ 800 + $.40(MH)
Indirect materials	$ 1,000 + $.30(MH)
Lubricants and supplies	$.18(MH)
Repairs and maintenance	$10,000 + $.25(MH)
Insurance	$ 3,000
Rent	$ 6,000
Depreciation	$12,000

You consider the cost functions to be reliable within a relevant range of 15,000 to 25,000 machine hours. Seacom has indicated that it expects to operate at a level of 20,000 machine hours per month and wishes to determine the predetermined manufacturing overhead application rate on that basis.

The following information pertains to Seacom Company during the month following your analysis:

	Total	Fixed	Variable
Actual overhead costs incurred:			
Indirect labor	$19,000	$15,200	$ 3,800
Utilities	8,200	800	7,400
Indirect materials	6,400	900	5,500
Lubricants and supplies	3,400	–	3,400
Repairs and maintenance	14,890	10,100	4,790
Insurance	3,100	3,100	–
Rent	6,000	6,000	–
Depreciation	12,000	12,000	–
Total	$72,990	$48,100	$24,890

Actual machine hours	19,000
Standard machine hours allowed for production achieved	18,000

Required:

1. Compute the predetermined manufacturing overhead application rate and show the breakdown between the fixed overhead rate and the variable overhead rate.
2. Prepare a Level 1 Analysis of manufacturing overhead for the month. (Determine whether manufacturing overhead is over- or underapplied and by how much.) Explain what this level tells management.
3. Prepare a Level 2 Analysis of manufacturing overhead for the month. (Calculate variable overhead spending and efficiency variances and fixed overhead budget and volume variances.) Be sure that your four variances algebraically total to the Level 1 Analysis in (2). Explain what this level of analysis tells management.
4. Prepare a Level 3 Analysis of manufacturing overhead for the month (a manufacturing overhead performance report). Be sure that it reconciles with the Level 2 Analysis as indicated in Exhibit 10–11. Who would be most interested in this report and what information does it provide that is not provided in the Level 2 Analysis?
5. The Level 3 Analysis could be expanded to show the spending and efficiency variances for each variable overhead item. Calculate the spending and efficiency variances for the indirect labor and lubricants and supplies items in the performance report prepared for (4) above. What information does this possible further analysis provide management that is not provided in the performance report as you prepared it for (4) above?

P10–25   Allocating variances. Cordan Corporation commenced business on December 1. The corporation uses a standard costing system for the manufacturing costs of its only product, Cordex. The standard costs for a unit of Cordex are

Materials: 10 kilograms @ $.70	$ 7
Direct labor: 1 hour @ $8	8
Manufacturing overhead (applied on the basis of $2 per direct labor hour)	2
Total	$17

Cordan had budgeted a production level of 3,000 units for the month. The company sold 1,500 units of Cordex during the month. The following additional data was extracted from the corporation's books for December:

	Debit	Credit
Sales		$45,000
Materials price variance	$1,620	
Materials quantity variance	660	
Direct labor rate variance	250	
Manufacturing overhead overapplied		300

Inventory data at December 31 indicate that the following inventories were on hand:

Finished goods	900 units
Work in process	1,200 units
Materials	None

The work in process inventory was 100% complete as to materials and 50% as to direct labor and manufacturing overhead. The corporation's policy is to allocate variances to the cost of goods sold and ending inventories—that is, work in process and finished goods.

Required: Prepare the following schedules:

1. Allocating the variances to the ending inventories and to cost of goods sold.
2. Computing the cost of goods manufactured at standard cost and at actual cost for December. Amounts for materials, labor, and manufacturing overhead should be shown separately.
3. Computing the actual cost of materials, labor, and manufacturing overhead included in the work in process inventory and in the finished goods inventory at December 31.

(CPA Adapted)

P10–26 **Comprehensive standard costing problem: materials, labor, and manufacturing overhead variances, journal entries, disposition of variances.** Executive Accessories specializes in the making of pen and pencil desk sets. The set consists of a base of select walnut with a marble inset. The company buys the walnut by the board foot and the marble in 3-foot strips that are one-half inch thick and four inches wide. The final cutting and finishing is done by Executive Accessories in the manufacturing process. The pens and pencils are a customer supplied item. The standard cost card for a desk set follows:

Standard Cost Card
Pen and Pencil Desk Set

1 board foot of walnut @ $3.50	$3.50	
12" of 1/2" × 4" marble @ $6/ft	6.00	$ 9.50
2 hours of direct labor @ $7.50		15.00
Manufacturing overhead @ $5 per DLH ($3 variable, $2 fixed)		10.00
Total standard cost		$34.50

At the start of the current period, the company had 500 board feet of walnut and 200 strips of marble on hand. There was no beginning work in process, and there were 100 desk sets in finished goods. The following information is available regarding the company's operations for the period:

Desk sets produced: 4,600
Material purchased:
  Walnut: 5,000 board feet costing $18,000
  Marble: 1,600 strips costing $28,000
Material used:
  Walnut: 4,800 board feet
  Marble: 1,550 strips
Direct labor: 9,350 hours costing $61,190
Manufacturing overhead:
  Variable: $27,900
  Fixed: 19,500

Executive Accessories had budgeted fixed manufacturing overhead for the period at $20,000 and computes the predetermined overhead application rates on the basis of expected capacity. At the end of the period there was no work in process, and 4,200 desk sets were sold. The FIFO perpetual inventory method is applied throughout the company.

Required:

1. What was the expected capacity for the period? (Express in either units or direct labor hours.)
2. Prepare schedules showing the determination of
   a. Materials price and quantity variances.
   b. Labor rate and efficiency variances.
   c. Variable manufacturing overhead spending and efficiency variances.
   d. Fixed manufacturing overhead budget and volume variances.
3. Prepare journal entries to record all the activity for the period.
4. Is manufacturing overhead underapplied or overapplied and by how much?
5. Prepare a journal entry to allocate the variances (including under- or overapplied manufacturing overhead) to inventories and cost of goods sold.

CHAPTER 11

Variable Costing and the Contribution Approach to Income Reporting

Learning Objectives

After reading this chapter you should be able to:

1. Understand the basic difference between absorption and variable costing, which is the treatment of fixed manufacturing overhead as a period cost or a product cost.

2. Understand the cost behavior (contribution margin) format of the income statement under variable costing versus the cost function under absorption costing.

3. Appreciate how income will vary under variable costing as opposed to absorption costing.

4. Understand why the variable costing format is more useful than absorption costing for managerial accounting purposes.

5. Have knowledge of the contribution margin format for segment reporting purposes.

One of the purposes of a management accounting system is to determine the cost of producing a unit of product and therefore the value of inventory. As inventory is sold, the costs associated with the inventory that is sold are matched with the revenue generated by sales. It is obvious then that the valuation of inventory has an effect on income measurement of the company.

The costing systems discussed and illustrated to this point have considered all production costs as product costs; that is, the direct material used, the direct labor incurred, and the variable *and* fixed manufacturing overhead incurred were associated with the finished product in some rational manner. A costing system designed to produce an inventory value that consists of *all* manufacturing costs is referred to as an absorption (or full) costing system. Even though this is the inventory value necessary for external financial reporting purposes, it has been questioned whether this method of determining product costs (inventory values) is the most useful for internal decision making purposes. It has been suggested that a costing system referred to as variable (or direct) costing is more appropriate for collecting and furnishing information that is helpful to management in their planning and control functions as well as providing information for determining the income of the company.

This chapter defines, analyzes, and compares absorption and variable costing. The effects of each method on inventory valuation and income measurement are illustrated, and the advantages and limitations of each are explored. Finally, it is illustrated how reports prepared in the variable costing format provide management with better information for evaluating the profitability of segments of a company such as territories, divisions, or individual products.

Absorption versus Variable Costing

As indicated above, all manufacturing costs become product costs under absorption or full costing. Fixed and variable selling expenses and fixed and variable administrative expenses are treated as period costs (costs that are charged off to expense in the period in which they are incurred).

Under **variable or direct costing**, only those manufacturing costs that vary with the level of production activity become product costs, that is, direct materials, direct labor, and variable manufacturing overhead. The fixed manufacturing overhead is treated as a period cost along with the fixed and variable selling expense and fixed and variable administrative expense. Exhibit 11–1 summarizes the treatment of the various costs under the two methods.

The dotted lines in Exhibit 11–1 emphasize the fact that the major difference between the two systems for product cost determination is the treatment given the fixed manufacturing overhead. Under absorption costing the fixed manufacturing overhead is treated as a product cost, becoming part of

EXHIBIT 11-1

Cost Treatment Under Absorption and Variable Costing

	Costing Method	
	Absorption	*Variable*
Included in product costs?		
Direct material	Yes	Yes
Direct labor	Yes	Yes
Variable manufacturing overhead	Yes	Yes
Fixed manufacturing overhead	Yes- - - - - - - - - - - - - -No	
Included in period costs?		
Fixed manufacturing overhead	No- - - - - - - - - - - - - -Yes	
Fixed selling expenses	Yes	Yes
Variable selling expenses	Yes	Yes
Fixed administrative expenses	Yes	Yes
Variable administrative expenses	Yes	Yes

the inventory value, and is charged to expense as the inventory is sold. Under variable costing, the fixed manufacturing costs never become product costs—they are charged off to expense in the period incurred.

To better understand how these two costing methods result in different unit costs (inventory value) and cost of goods sold, an illustration is developed based on the following information for Beacon Company for the year 19X7:

Variable costs per unit:		
Direct materials	$	5
Direct labor		10
Variable manufacturing overhead		8
Variable selling expense		4
Variable administrative expense		1
Fixed costs per year:		
Manufacturing overhead		$60,000
Selling expense		12,000
Administrative expense		15,000
Units in beginning inventory		–0–
Units produced in 19X7		10,000
Units sold in 19X7		8,000
Selling price per unit	$	43

Beacon would determine its cost per unit under each of the costing methods as follows:

	Absorption	Variable
Direct materials	$ 5	$ 5
Direct labor	10	10
Variable manufacturing overhead	8	8
Fixed manufacturing overhead − ($60,000/10,000)	6	—
Total cost per unit	$29	$23

Note that if Beacon does not sell all of its production in 19X7, the ending inventory values are going to be different under the two methods. If Beacon uses absorption costing, each unit will be included in ending inventory at $29, but if they use variable costing each unit will be included at $23.

Now that we have illustrated how product costs per unit determined under absorption and variable costing may vary, Exhibit 11–2 illustrates the income statements for the year under the two costing methods.

EXHIBIT 11–2

BEACON COMPANY
Income Statements
For the Year Ended December 31, 19X7

Absorption Costing

Sales ($43 × 8,000)			$344,000
Cost of goods sold:			
Beginning inventory		–0–	
Cost of production ($29 × 10,000)		$290,000	
Goods available for sale		$290,000	
Ending inventory ($29 × 2,000)		58,000	232,000
Gross profit			$112,000
Expenses:			
Selling:			
Fixed	$ 12,000		
Variable ($4 × 8,000)	32,000	44,000	
Administrative:			
Fixed	$ 15,000		
Variable ($1 × 8,000)	8,000	23,000	
Total expenses			67,000
Operating income			$ 45,000

Variable Costing

Sales ($43 × 8,000)			$344,000
Less variable expenses:			
Cost of goods sold:			
Beginning inventory	–0–		
Cost of production ($23 × 10,000)	$230,000		
Available for sale	$230,000		
Ending inventory ($23 × 2,000)	46,000	$184,000	
Variable selling expense ($4 × 8,000)		32,000	
Variable administrative expense ($1 × 8,000)		8,000	
Total variable expenses			224,000
Contribution margin			$120,000
Fixed expenses:			
Manufacturing overhead		$ 60,000	
Selling		12,000	
Administrative		15,000	
Total fixed expenses			87,000
Operating income			$ 33,000

Differences in Determination of Cost of Goods Sold

The differences in the calculation of cost of goods sold for Beacon Company under the two methods are summarized in Exhibit 11–3.

It has been emphasized that the difference between absorption and variable costing is the treatment of fixed costs. Note in Exhibit 11–3 that the total costs of production vary by the amount of fixed manufacturing costs ($60,000). The ending inventory values differ by $12,000, the amount of fixed manufacturing costs in ending inventory ($6 per unit × 2,000 units). This $12,000 of fixed manufacturing cost is carried forward as an asset in ending inventory of finished goods resulting in a deferral of charging the costs to expense until the inventory is sold in the following year. The cost of goods sold under absorption costing is $48,000 ($6 per unit × 8,000 units sold) greater than under variable costing.

Differences in Income Statement Format

You have no doubt observed that the cost of goods sold is not the only difference between the income statements for the Beacon Company. Under absorption costing, costs are classified according to their business function, that is, manufacturing, selling, and administrative. There is no breakdown by cost behavior. In other words, both fixed and variable costs are included in each of the functional classifications. In the typical functional income statement, cost of goods sold is subtracted from sales to determine gross profit, and selling and administrative expenses are subtracted from gross profit to obtain net income.

When variable costing is used, the income statement is normally prepared using a contribution margin format. In the contribution approach, costs are classified by behavior. Note in Exhibit 11–2 under the variable costing

EXHIBIT 11–3

Differences in Manufacturing Costs Expensed
Absorption versus Variable Costing

	Absorption Costing	Variable Costing	Difference
Beginning inventory	$ –0–	$ –0–	$ –0–
Cost of production	290,000	230,000	60,000
Available for sale	290,000	230,000	60,000
Ending inventory	58,000	46,000	12,000
Cost of goods sold	232,000	184,000	48,000
Fixed manufacturing overhead treated as period cost		60,000	(60,000)
Total manufacturing costs expensed (also the income difference)	$232,000	$244,000	$12,000

income statement that all variable expenses (manufacturing, selling, and administrative) are subtracted from sales to arrive at the contribution margin. You may remember from Chapter 4 that the contribution margin was defined as the difference between revenue and the variable costs and it was very useful for management analysis purposes. Another way of defining contribution margin is to say that it is the amount of sales revenue left after covering variable costs that is available to contribute toward covering fixed costs and profit. Accordingly, in the Beacon Company income statement, all fixed costs are subtracted from the contribution margin to arrive at the profit of $33,000.

One further comparison can be made between the two statements—the amount of net income. The difference is $12,000 ($45,000 − $33,000). One way to explain this difference is to consider the amount of fixed costs charged to expense during the period as shown in Exhibit 11–4.

The difference of $12,000 in the amount of fixed costs charged to expense explains the difference in net income under the two methods. A shorter method of explaining the difference will be illustrated later.

Absorption versus Variable Costing — Extended Illustrations

Now that you have a basic understanding of the difference between absorption and variable costing and the related income statement format, a three-year comparison will be developed to better illustrate the two methods and provide a better background for evaluation purposes. The basic information pertaining to the Beacon Company will again be used. For convenience, the information is repeated below:

Sales price per unit	$ 43
Variable costs per unit:	
Manufacturing (including direct materials,	
direct labor, and variable overhead)	23
Selling	4
Administrative	1
Fixed costs per year:	
Manufacturing	60,000
Selling	12,000
Administrative	15,000

Production Constant and Sales Vary

Remember that the product cost using variable costing is $23 and for absorption costing it is $29 ($23 plus $60,000 divided by 10,000 normal production units). For simplicity we will assume that the selling price and costs do not change during the three-year period. We will also assume that Beacon is beginning the year 19X8 with no inventory of finished goods on hand. Income statements for the three years under absorption and variable costing are shown in Exhibit 11–5 (page 380).

In 19X8 sales and production were equal. As a result, there is no deferral

EXHIBIT 11-4
Fixed Costs Charged to Expense During 19X7
Absorption Versus Variable Costing

	Costing Method	
	Absorption	*Variable*
Fixed costs:		
Manufacturing	$48,000[a]	$60,000[b]
Selling	12,000	12,000
Administrative	15,000	15,000
Total	$75,000	$87,000

[a]$6 per unit times 8,000 units sold.
[b]Always charged off in total under variable costing.

of fixed manufacturing costs in inventory. In addition to the variable costs, all fixed costs were charged to expense under both methods. Therefore, net income is the same under both methods.

In 19X9 production exceeds sales by 6,000 units. Under absorption costing, unit product costs include $6 of fixed manufacturing overhead. Every unit of product carried over to the next year includes this $6 of fixed cost resulting in $36,000 of fixed costs being deferred in inventory (and carried forward to the next year as an asset). Under variable costing, all fixed manufacturing overhead is charged to expense as a period cost, resulting in total expenses being $36,000 greater under variable costing as opposed to absorption costing. This explains the difference in income under the two methods ($9,000 profit under absorption costing and $27,000 loss under variable costing). A simpler way to explain the difference is to consider the change in the units of inventory from the beginning of the period to the end. In 19X9 the units in inventory increased by 6,000 units (from 0 to 6,000). Each unit increase in inventory results in the deferral of $6 of fixed manufacturing costs to be released next period when the unit is sold. In 19X9 this meant a total of $6 × 6,000 or $36,000 (the difference in income under the two methods).

In 19X0, sales exceed production. In fact, all inventory carried over is sold as well as all production of the period. This means that under absorption costing, not only will all fixed manufacturing costs of the period be charged to expense through cost of goods sold, but the $36,000 deferred in 19X9 will also be expensed. As a result, income under absorption costing will be $36,000 less than the income under variable costing. Note that the difference in incomes in 19X0 according to Exhibit 11-5 is in fact $36,000 ($153,000 − $117,000). This can also be explained by the fact that the units in inventory decreased during 19X0—there were 6,000 units in beginning inventory and none left in ending inventory. The decrease of 6,000 units times $6 per unit of fixed cost explains the difference in income under the two methods.

EXHIBIT 11–5
Production Constant — Sales Vary

Basic Unit Information

	19X8	19X9	19X0	Three Years Together
Beginning inventory in units	–0–	–0–	6,000	–0–
Units produced during the year	10,000	10,000	10,000	30,000
Units sold during the year	10,000	4,000	16,000	30,000
Ending inventory in units	–0–	6,000	–0–	–0–

Income Statements
Absorption Costing

	19X8	19X9	19X0	Three Years Together
Sales	$430,000	$172,000	$688,000	$1,290,000
Beginning inventory	–0–	–0–	174,000	–0–
Cost of production	290,000	290,000	290,000	870,000
Goods available for sale	290,000	290,000	464,000	870,000
Ending inventory	–0–	174,000	–0–	–0–
Cost of goods sold	290,000	116,000	464,000	870,000
Gross profit	140,000	56,000	224,000	420,000
Selling expenses	52,000	28,000	76,000	156,000
Administrative expenses	25,000	19,000	31,000	75,000
Total expenses	77,000	47,000	107,000	231,000
Operating income	$ 63,000	$ 9,000	$117,000	$ 189,000

Variable Costing

	19X8	19X9	19X0	Three Years Together
Sales	$430,000	$172,000	$688,000	$1,290,000
Less variable expenses:				
Beginning inventory	–0–	–0–	138,000	–0–
Cost of production	230,000	230,000	230,000	690,000
Goods available for sale	230,000	230,000	368,000	690,000
Ending inventory	–0–	138,000	–0–	–0–
Cost of goods sold	230,000	92,000	368,000	690,000
Selling expenses	40,000	16,000	64,000	120,000
Administrative expenses	10,000	4,000	16,000	30,000
Total variable expenses	280,000	112,000	448,000	840,000
Contribution margin	150,000	60,000	240,000	450,000
Fixed expenses:				
Manufacturing	60,000	60,000	60,000	180,000
Selling	12,000	12,000	12,000	36,000
Administrative	15,000	15,000	15,000	45,000
Total fixed expenses	87,000	87,000	87,000	261,000
Operating income (loss)	$ 63,000	$ (27,000)	$153,000	$ 189,000

Break-Even Analysis with Absorption and Variable Costing

Exhibit 11–5 illustrates an interesting problem in the use of absorption costing as opposed to variable costing. In 19X9 income calculated using absorption costing is $9,000 whereas there is a loss of $27,000 using variable costing. We learned in Chapter 4 that we could calculate break-even in units by dividing total fixed costs by the contribution margin per unit. Using the data pertaining to Beacon Company, break-even is determined as follows:

$$\frac{\text{Total fixed costs}}{\text{Contribution margin per unit}} = \frac{\$87,000}{\$43 - \$28} = 5,800 \text{ units}$$

We see that in 19X9 Beacon only sold 4,000 units, yet according to the absorption costing method, there was positive income of $9,000! How can this happen? This phenomenon has already been explained. The explanation lies in the fact that under absorption costing, $36,000 of fixed manufacturing overhead costs were deferred in inventory and did not appear as charges against income in 19X9. By deferring these costs, Beacon was able to show a profit even though it sold less than the break-even quantity. This suggests that the only way that absorption costing data can be used in break-even analysis is to assume that there is no change in inventory during the period. This, in fact, was a key assumption of C-V-P analysis discussed in Chapter 4. In practice, this is not very likely to be the case.

It is worth noting that this problem does not occur when variable costing is used. The variable costing numbers tell us that when 4,000 units are sold, Beacon needs $27,000 more contribution margin in order to break even. We can verify that this is the case by calculating the number of additional units necessary to accumulate that amount of contribution by again using the break-even formula:

$$\frac{\text{Contribution required}}{\text{Contribution margin per unit}} = \frac{\$27,000}{\$15} = 1,800 \text{ units}$$

Adding 1,800 units to the 19X9 sales of 4,000 units coincides with the 5,800 units required to break even according to the original break-even calculation. Therefore, the variable costing income figures are symmetrical with the break-even analysis.

Sales Constant and Production Varies

Exhibit 11–5 compared absorption and variable costing in the situation where production remained constant and sales varied. We shall now consider the case where sales remain constant and production varies (Exhibit 11–6, page 382). Again, we use the information from Beacon Company and assume that they begin the year 19X8 with no inventory of finished goods on hand.

In 19X8 sales and production are equal. This is identical to the year 19X8 in Exhibit 11–5 and will not be discussed again here. In 19X9 production exceeds sales. Even though sales are the same as in 19X8 (and prices have not changed), we see that net income goes up $10,000 as we look at the

EXHIBIT 11–6
Sales Constant – Production Varies

Basic Unit Information

	19X8	19X9	19X0	Three Years Together
Beginning inventory in units	–0–	–0–	2,000	–0–
Units produced during the year	10,000	12,000	8,000	30,000
Units sold during the year	10,000	10,000	10,000	30,000
Ending inventory in units	–0–	2,000	–0–	–0–
Cost of producing one unit:				
Using absorption costing:				
Variable manufacturing costs	$23.00	$23.00	$23.00	
Fixed manufacturing costs – $60,000 spread over units produced each year	6.00	5.00	7.50	
Total cost per unit	$29.00	$28.00	$30.50	
Using variable costing:				
Variable manufacturing costs only	$23.00	$23.00	$23.00	

Income Statements
Absorption Costing

	19X8	19X9	19X0	Three Years Together
Sales	$430,000	$430,000	$430,000	$1,290,000
Beginning inventory	–0–	–0–	56,000	–0–
Cost of production	290,000	336,000	244,000	870,000
Goods available for sale	290,000	336,000	300,000	870,000
Ending inventory	–0–	56,000	–0–	–0–
Cost of goods sold	290,000	280,000	300,000	870,000
Gross profit	140,000	150,000	130,000	420,000
Selling expenses	52,000	52,000	52,000	156,000
Administrative expenses	25,000	25,000	25,000	75,000
Total expenses	77,000	77,000	77,000	231,000
Operating income	$ 63,000	$ 73,000	$ 53,000	$ 189,000

absorption costing statement. Can you now explain why this happens? We see that when Beacon increased its production to 12,000 units, the fixed manufacturing overhead was spread over 12,000 instead of 10,000 units making the fixed manufacturing cost $5 per unit. There is an increase in inventory of 2,000 units. Therefore, under absorption costing, Beacon is able to defer $10,000 of fixed cost in inventory ($5 × 2,000) to be released to expense at a later date. As a result, net income in 19X9 is $10,000 greater using absorption costing as opposed to variable costing.

EXHIBIT 11—6 (continued)

Variable Costing

	19X8	19X9	19X0	Three Years Together
Sales	$430,000	$430,000	$430,000	$1,290,000
Less variable expenses:				
Beginning inventory	–0–	–0–	46,000	–0–
Cost of production	230,000	276,000	184,000	690,000
Goods available for sale	230,000	276,000	230,000	690,000
Ending inventory	–0–	46,000	–0–	–0–
Cost of goods sold	230,000	230,000	230,000	690,000
Selling expense	40,000	40,000	40,000	120,000
Administrative expense	10,000	10,000	10,000	30,000
Total variable expenses	280,000	280,000	280,000	840,000
Contribution margin	150,000	150,000	150,000	450,000
Fixed expenses:				
Manufacturing	60,000	60,000	60,000	180,000
Selling	12,000	12,000	12,000	36,000
Administrative	15,000	15,000	15,000	45,000
Total fixed expenses	87,000	87,000	87,000	261,000
Operating income	$ 63,000	$ 63,000	$ 63,000	$ 189,000

In 19X0 sales exceed production. The $10,000 of fixed manufacturing cost deferred in inventory at the end of 19X9 is now released to expense. Because all inventory is sold in 19X0, there is $10,000 more fixed manufacturing cost charged to expense under absorption costing than under variable costing, and net income is reduced accordingly.

Absorption versus Variable Costing — Some Observations

After analysis of the comparative illustrations above, we can make some observations regarding these two costing methods:

1. When sales equal production, there is no difference in net income under the two methods. (This assumes that any beginning inventory units have the same cost per unit as currently manufactured units under each of the two methods).

2. When production exceeds sales, net income reported under absorption costing will generally be higher than net income reported under variable costing (see the results for the year 19X9 in both Exhibits 11–5 and 11–6). As we mentioned above, the reason this happens is because part of the fixed manufacturing costs are deferred in inventory leaving only a portion of the fixed manufacturing costs to be expensed through

cost of goods sold. Under variable costing, all the fixed manufacturing costs are expensed each year.

3. When sales exceed production, net income reported under variable costing will generally exceed net income reported under absorption costing (see the results for the year 19X0 in both Exhibits 11–5 and 11–6). The reason for this is that when absorption ending inventory unit balances decrease, fixed manufacturing costs that were deferred in prior years are now released to expense. As a result, the total fixed manufacturing costs charged to expense during the year that sales exceed production will be more under absorption costing than under variable costing and the net income will be less, accordingly.

4. Under absorption costing, net income is affected by variations in *production* as well as sales. If prices remain unchanged, we see that net income is affected only by the amount of *sales* when variable costing is used.

5. Over an extended period of time, net income reported under both methods tends to be the same. Exhibits 11–5 and 11–6 both indicate that for the three-year period where Beacon started and ended the period with no finished goods inventory, the total net income for the three years was the same under both methods. The difference results from the *timing* of the release of fixed manufacturing costs to expense. We know, of course, that over a longer period of time, sales and production must approach equality. We can observe, however, that net income in any given year can vary a great deal under the two costing methods.

An Evaluation of Variable Costing

Over the years there has been a great deal of controversy regarding the use of variable costing. Twenty years ago, for instance, numerous articles were appearing in leading accounting journals arguing the merits of variable costing. The central issue is, of course, the omission of fixed manufacturing costs from inventory by the variable costers. The variable coster would argue that fixed manufacturing costs do not add value to inventory because the incurrence of the fixed cost in the current period does not avoid the necessity of incurring the cost in a future period. In other words, if current production exceeds sales, deferring fixed manufacturing costs in inventory has no effect at all on the amount of fixed manufacturing cost that must be incurred next period if we are going to maintain production readiness in the manufacturing plant. This argument seems to have a good deal of merit.

The absorption costers, however, feel that a product is not fully costed until it has been allocated a share of the fixed costs necessary in order to manufacture the product. The standard setting agencies in the financial accounting area agree with this conclusion along with the Internal Revenue Service, so for all practical purposes, the use of absorption costing is mandatory for external reporting. The argument about the use of either of the methods has subsided, and it is probably safe to say at this point that absorption costing will be used for external reporting but variable costing will be used internally for management information purposes. Why is this so? The following points may help to answer this question.

1. Data needed for cost-volume-profit analysis as discussed in Chapter 4 is most likely not available if an absorption costing system is used. It is necessary to have costs classified by behavior (fixed or variable) in order to do cost-volume-profit analyses. As we have mentioned, this classification is not necessary under absorption costing.

2. A variable costing system supports the concept of flexible budgeting — it is impossible to utilize the techniques of flexible budgeting if costs are not classified according to behavior. The budgeting process is greatly facilitated by having an information base designed according to the requirements of variable costing.

3. Management can do a better job of pricing and bidding competitively if they are aware of the "out-of-pocket" (usually variable) costs associated with a product or service.

4. Management is more aware of the effect of fixed manufacturing costs on profit because this fixed cost appears on the income statement as a total rather than being buried as an unidentifiable part of inventories or cost of goods sold.

5. Management is better able to appraise performance of divisions, products, or personnel by using contribution margin — a number that is not confused or obscured by the allocation of fixed costs that do not change as a result of changes in production in the short run.

6. If prices do not fluctuate, profit for the period is a function of the sales achieved and is not affected by variation in the amount of production. It is difficult to explain to a manager that his net income may fall when he has increased sales and managed to keep his expenses within budget. This can easily happen when absorption costing is used and sales exceed production.

You may now appreciate more fully the general conclusion that absorption costing is used for external reporting and variable costing for internal uses. This does not mean that a company will keep "two sets of books." It merely means that the accounting information system will need to be designed so that data may be marshaled in whatever manner needed — either for internal reports or for external reports. This provides more opportunities in the accounting profession for persons who appreciate the importance of the design of the accounting information system and the ability of the computer to expand the limits of information processing to meet requirements.

The Contribution Approach to Reporting

If a company produces only one product and sells that product to a rather homogeneous clientele located in a limited geographical area, the following discussion may be of limited application or relevance. Modern businesses, however, usually handle multiple products, have complex organization structures, can be located over wide geographical areas, and are likely to do business with different types of customers located across the United States or even the world. With the expansion of business has come the need for information that will help management determine which product lines are profitable and which are not, which divisions are operating inefficiently, which sales territories require attention, or where expansion is attractive. Management usually turns to reports that focus on the *segments* of their company to discover problem areas or to obtain information to help answer these questions. The preparation of such reports is known as segmental reporting.

A **segment** can be defined as any part of an organization about which management seeks data. Examples of a segment could be a particular division, a sales territory, a manufacturing plant, a producing department within that plant, or merely a cost center consisting of similar machines within a producing department. Fortunately, in this chapter we have become familiar with a method of reporting that management finds very useful and one that adapts well to segmental reporting—the income statement prepared on a contribution approach (an approach possible when a variable costing accounting information system is in place).

Segment Report Configuration

Segmented reports can be prepared at any of the levels of the organization or any center of activity suggested above—division, product, plants within a division, and so forth. As we move from reports prepared for smaller segments of the organization to larger, we might expect to see some possible variations in format or terminology. To illustrate this concept, consider the case of Pionaire Hybrid company. It produces, conditions, and sells seed corn and soybean seed. It has two divisions, Central and Plains, and each division has two plants at which seed corn is conditioned and one plant at which soybean seed is conditioned. Exhibit 11–7 illustrates possible segmental income statements for the company.

Several terms appear in the segmental income statements illustrated in Exhibit 11–7 that need explanation before proceeding further. The first part of each statement is similar to those of Beacon Company prepared in a contribution format earlier in the chapter, that is, sales minus variable expenses equal contribution margin. However, new terms are introduced following contribution margin: direct fixed expenses, common fixed expenses, and various segment margins.

Direct fixed expenses (or costs) are defined as costs that can be specifically identified with a particular segment and arise because of the exis-

EXHIBIT 11–7
Segmental Income Statements

a. Segments defined as divisions of Pionaire Hybrid (first level)

	Divisions		
	Central	Plains	Total Company
Sales	$800,000	$650,000	$1,450,000
Less variable expenses:			
Variable cost of goods sold	$340,000	$290,000	$ 630,000
Other variable expenses	160,000	130,000	290,000
Total variable expenses	$500,000	$420,000	$ 920,000
Contribution margin	$300,000	$230,000	$ 530,000
Less direct fixed expenses	120,000	140,000	260,000
Division segment margin	$180,000	$ 90,000	$ 270,000
Less common fixed expenses			80,000
Operating income			$ 190,000

b. Segments defined as products of the Central Division of Pionaire Hybrid (second level)

	Corn	Soybeans	Central Division
Sales	$500,000	$300,000	$800,000
Less variable expenses:			
Variable cost of goods sold	$180,000	$160,000	$340,000
Other variable expenses	70,000	90,000	160,000
Total variable expenses	$250,000	$250,000	$500,000
Contribution margin	$250,000	$ 50,000	$300,000
Less direct fixed expenses	50,000	30,000	80,000
Product segment margin	$200,000	$ 20,000	$220,000
Less common fixed expenses			40,000
Division segment margin			$180,000

c. Segments defined as corn plants within the Central Division of Pionaire Hybrid (third level)

	Plant 1	Plant 2	Corn
Sales	$290,000	$210,000	$500,000
Less variable expenses:			
Variable cost of goods sold	$110,000	$ 70,000	$180,000
Other variable expenses	40,000	30,000	70,000
Total variable expenses	$150,000	$100,000	$250,000
Contribution margin	$140,000	$110,000	$250,000
Less direct fixed expenses	10,000	15,000	25,000
Plant segment margin	$130,000	$ 95,000	$225,000
Less common fixed expenses			25,000
Product segment margin			$200,000

tence of that segment. Another way of expressing this would be to say that the direct fixed costs would not be incurred if the particular segment were discontinued. In the first level segmental income statements for Pionaire Hybrid, for example, the $120,000 of direct fixed cost would be eliminated if Central Division were discontinued. Included in the direct fixed cost classification would be such costs as the division president's salary, depreciation, insurance, property taxes, and repairs and maintenance.

Common (or indirect) fixed costs (also referred to as indirect fixed costs) are those fixed costs that benefit more than one segment and cannot be specifically identified with any one segment. Often, they are costs incurred at one level for the benefit of two or more segments at a lower level. The corporate controller's salary, for instance, cannot be specifically traced to either the Central Division or Plains Division. The only way that her salary could be assigned to each division would be to allocate it on some arbitrary basis. Other examples of common fixed costs at the first level would be the corporate president's salary, depreciation on corporate offices and equipment, and brand advertising emphasizing the corporate image.

Segment margin (or income) is the amount of segment contribution margin remaining after covering the direct fixed costs of the segment (division, product, plant, etc.); that is, it is the amount that the segment contributes toward the common fixed costs and profit. Although the segment contribution margin is more useful in making short-run operating decisions such as accepting or rejecting orders at special prices, the segment margin is generally viewed as being the best measure of the long-run profitability of the segment. It would seem obvious that if, in the long run, the segment cannot cover its direct fixed expenses, it is a candidate for being discontinued. The exception, of course, would be the case where the segment somehow supports profitable activity of some other segment or segments.

Now that we understand all the terminology used in the segmental income statements, let us again focus our attention on the statements for Pionaire Hybrid in Exhibit 11–7. You will note in the first-level statements that the Central Division shows direct fixed expenses of $120,000. When we move to the second level segmental income statements where the focus is on the products of the Central Division, notice that the $120,000 has been divided between direct fixed expenses for the two products of $80,000 ($50,000 to corn and $30,000 to soybeans) and the remaining $40,000 is now classified as a common fixed expense for Central. This should seem logical. Consider the depreciation expense on the corn and soybean conditioning plants. It is a fixed expense that we can specifically identify with either seed corn or soybean seed and therefore is a direct fixed expense when the segment statements are for products within the Central Division. However, let us consider the salary of the president of the Central Division. The first-level segmental income statements would properly classify his salary as a direct fixed expense for the Central Division because his salary can be specifically identified with the Central Division. When we prepare the second level statements, however, the president's salary benefits both the seed corn segment and the soybean seed segment of the Central Division and now must be classified as a common fixed expense.

The same thing happens when we go from the second-level statements to the third level. In the second-level statements (each product is a segment), we see direct fixed expenses for corn in the Central Division of $50,000. When we move to the third-level statements (the segments are corn plants in the Central Division), the direct fixed expenses have again been partially reclassified—$25,000 has moved to the common fixed expense classification. Let us say that included in the direct fixed expenses for corn on the second-level statements was the salary for a production superintendent who was in charge of production and conditioning at both the corn plants in the Central Division and that there was media advertising specifically for corn in the Central Division. These are direct fixed costs specifically identifiable with corn when the segment definition was products (corn and soybeans). When the segment definition is changed to corn plants, however, these costs cannot be traced to a specific plant—the costs are incurred to benefit both corn plants, so they must now be classified as part of the common fixed expenses for this segment definition.

Basic Steps in the Preparation of Segmental Reports

You may have discovered at this point that there are some basic steps to be followed when segmental reports are to be prepared:

1. Identify the segment(s) being reported on. In the case of Pionaire Hybrid, for instance, it is crucial for us to know whether our reporting objective is a corn plant in the Central Division, the product seed corn in the Central Division, all products in the Plains Division, and so forth. The precise definition of our reporting objective is necessary so that we seek and obtain only that information from our accounting information system that is relevant to the reporting segment(s).

2. Determine the direct fixed costs that can be assigned to the reporting segment(s). This task can appear to be an illusion and only comes into clear focus as we precisely define the reporting segments. Remember in the Pionaire Hybrid example how costs classified as direct fixed when the reporting segment was defined one way became common fixed costs when segments were defined differently.

3. Do *not* allocate common or indirect fixed costs—if a fixed cost cannot be traced directly to some segment, then it is treated as a common cost and kept separate from the segments themselves. In the Pionaire Hybrid first-level segmental income statements, we mentioned specifically that we would not allocate the salary of Pionaire's president to each division—his salary benefits both divisions and would most likely continue even though one of the divisions was abolished. From a management viewpoint, any arbitrary allocation of common costs

would simply destroy the value of the segment margin as a guide to long-run segment profitability.

In this chapter we have attempted to develop a sound basic understanding of the variable costing method and how it can lead to the use of the contribution approach for reporting. Specific applications of these concepts are illustrated further in Chapter 12, which deals with relevant costs for short-run decisions, and in Chapter 15, which is concerned with controlling decentralized operations.

Segmental Reporting – Establishing Limits

We have seen that segmental income statements prepared on a contribution format basis have great potential in aiding management in making day-to-day routine decisions regarding planning and control, as well as the nonroutine type decisions such as accepting or rejecting special orders, continuing or discontinuing a segment, and so forth. The point to remember is that segmental reporting requires a versatile and flexible accounting information base — an information base from which we have the ability to draw information and classify and arrange it in many different ways. A well-designed computerized information base gives us the potential capability to provide many, many combinations of segmented data. In fact, the format and frequency of segmental reports may be limited only by management's willingness to pay for the reports. We would expect, however, that management would subject this cost to the usual analysis — the benefits to management of the requested information must equal or exceed the cost of obtaining it. Some further discussion and examples of segmental variable costing income statements appears in Chapter 15.

Summary

Absorption costing and variable costing are two alternative methods of arriving at the cost of producing a unit of product. The main difference between these two methods is in the timing of the release of fixed manufacturing costs to expense. Under absorption costing, the fixed manufacturing costs are assigned to product and are only released to expense when the product is sold. Under variable costing, the fixed manufacturing costs are immediately released to expense as period costs — they never become part of the finished goods inventory.

In spite of the fact that absorption costing is required for external and income tax reporting, variable costing continues to be used a great deal for internal reporting. Its popularity undoubtedly stems from the fact that it provides information required for cost-volume-profit analysis and the preparation of income statements in the contribution format.

As businesses have become more complex and diversified both in product lines and geographically, management has increasingly needed tools to help with their functions of planning and control. One of the tools that has proven helpful is segmental reporting. A segment was defined as any part of an organization about which management seeks data. Through segmental income statements prepared on a contribution format basis, management is able to see the contribution margin of a segment and the segment contribution. The segment contribution margin provides information useful in assessing performance and in making short-run operating decisions such as accepting or rejecting orders at special prices. The segment margin provides information that is useful to management in assessing the long-run profitability of a segment.

Direct fixed costs are those that can be specifically identified with a segment of the business. Common fixed costs are costs that cannot be traced to a particular segment and are to remain identified with a segment level where allocation is unnecessary. Preparation of segmental reports requires (1) a careful definition of the segment, (2) a determination of the direct fixed costs that can be assigned to the defined segment, and (3) the resistance of the tendency to allocate common fixed costs to segments where the costs cannot be specifically traced.

The continued development of computer technology has provided management with the ability to assemble larger and more sophisticated data bases at continually decreasing costs. This makes it more feasible to design an accounting information base that can capture, classify, and provide information that will support reports prepared in nearly any way that management desires. Management must be prepared to justify the cost of providing the information requested.

Key Terms

Common (indirect) fixed costs are fixed costs that benefit more than one segment or organizational unit and cannot be traced or specifically identified with any one segment or organizational unit.

Direct fixed expenses (costs) are costs that can be specifically identified with a particular segment or organizational unit and arise because of the existence of that segment or organizational unit.

Segment is any part of an organization about which management seeks data. Segments include divisions, product lines, sales territories, and plants.

Segment margin or income is the segment contribution margin remaining after covering the direct fixed costs of the segment.

Variable (direct) costing is an income measurement method that treats fixed manufacturing overhead as a period cost rather than a product cost. Variable costing is closely related to the contribution margin format of income statement preparation, which deducts variable expenses from revenues to arrive at contribution margin. Fixed expenses (including fixed manufacturing overhead) are then deducted from contribution margin to arrive at operating income.

Questions

Q11–1   Distinguish between product costs and period costs.

Q11–2   Does a company that uses an absorption costing system have any period costs? Explain, giving examples, if any.

Q11–3   What is the basic difference between absorption and variable costing?

Q11–4   "We are not interested in a costing system where the unit costs vary. Our full costing system gives us fairly stable unit costs." Comment on this statement.

Q11–5   What is the relationship between variable costing and the contribution approach to reporting?

Q11–6   How can the difference in net income between variable costing and absorption costing methods of inventory valuation be reconciled?

Q11–7   What is meant by a *segment* in the context of internal reporting?

Q11–8   Distinguish between contribution margin, product margin, and segment margin.

Q11–9   What is the difference between direct fixed costs and common fixed costs?

Q11–10   Might a company have more than one type of first-level statement in segment reporting? Explain.

Q11–11   What can be said about the detail of information as you move from lower to higher levels of segmented statements (that is, level 3 to level 2 to level 1)?

Q11–12   Why is it important to identify the reporting objective in segment reporting?

Q11–13   The ending inventory of finished goods has less fixed costs than the beginning inventory of finished goods. Is the company using absorption costing or variable costing? Were sales less than, equal to, or greater than production of the period?

Q11–14   If production exceeds sales of the period, which method (absorption costing or variable costing) would you expect would show the least net income? Why?

Q11–15   You are trying to convince management to adopt a variable costing system, but it is concerned about treating fixed manufacturing costs as a period cost. What arguments can you make to justify treating fixed manufacturing costs as period costs?

Q11–16   "If we adopt variable costing we will have to keep two sets of books—one for external reporting purposes and one for internal use. We can't afford that!" How would you respond to this statement?

Q11–17   Is it possible for a cost that is direct under one level of segment reporting to be a common cost under another level of segment reporting? Explain.

Q11–18   What problem can be associated with cost-volume-profit analysis (such as breakeven) if a firm uses typical absorption costing?

Q11–19   A general manager is paid a bonus for the year based on net income and his firm uses full (absorption) costing. Is it possible for the general manager to increase his bonus without increasing sales? Explain.

Q11–20   How would the costs of a central corporate office located in Chicago be shown on the segment income statement for a segment located in Des Moines, Iowa?

Q11–21   "If we value the inventory using variable costing, the marketing people are going to start thinking there are no other costs to cover. We'll pay the piper sooner or later!" What is being referred to, and do you agree?

Exercises

E11–1   **Variable versus absorption costing: finished goods and income.** Selected information concerning the operations of Keith Company for the year ended December 31, 19X7 is available as follows:

Units produced	10,000
Units sold	9,000
Direct materials used	$40,000
Direct labor incurred	$20,000
Fixed manufacturing overhead	$25,000
Variable manufacturing overhead	$12,000
Fixed selling and administrative expenses	$30,000
Variable selling and administrative expenses	$ 4,500
Finished goods inventory, January 1, 19X7	None

Required:
1. What would Keith's finished goods inventory be at December 31, 19X7, if the company used variable costing? Show computations by cost elements.
2. Which costing method, variable or absorption costing, would show a higher operating income for 19X7 and by what amount?

(CPA Adapted)

E11–2   **Variable versus absorption costing; finished goods inventory and income.** Information from Patterson Company's records for the year ended December 31, 19X7, is available as follows:

Net sales	$1,400,000
Cost of goods manufactured:	
Variable	$ 630,000
Fixed	$ 315,000
Operating expenses:	
Variable	$ 98,000
Fixed	$ 140,000
Units manufactured	70,000
Units sold	60,000
Finished goods inventory, January 1, 19X7	None

There were no work in process inventories at the beginning or end of 19X7.

Required: 1. What would Patterson's finished goods inventory cost be at December 31, 19X7, if
         a. The variable costing method is used?
         b. The absorption costing method is used?
    2. Compute Patterson's operating income under both variable costing and absorption costing. Show your work.

(CPA Adapted)

E11–3   **Variable versus absorption costing: reconciliation of income difference.** Klondike Enterprises began operations on January 2, 19X7. The company sells a single product for $15 per unit. During 19X7, 120,000 units of product were produced and 100,000 units were sold. There was no work in process inventory at December 31, 19X7.

Klondike uses an absorption costing system. Manufacturing costs and selling and administrative expenses for 19X7 were as follows:

	Fixed Costs	Variable Costs
Direct materials	–0–	$3.00 per unit produced
Direct labor	–0–	1.50 per unit produced
Manufacturing overhead	$120,000	.85 per unit produced
Selling and administrative expenses	75,000	1.10 per unit sold

Required: 1. What is the finished goods inventory cost at December 31, 19X7, under both variable and absorption costing?
    2. Determine Klondike's operating income for 19X7 under both variable and absorption costing.
    3. Reconcile the difference between variable costing and absorption costing incomes.

E11–4   **Converting income statement from absorption to variable costing.** Sellers Manufacturing uses an absorption costing system. The company's income statement for 19X7 is presented below:

Sales (15,000 units @ $50)		$750,000
Cost of goods sold:		
Finished goods inventory, January 1	–0–	
Cost of goods manufactured (20,000 units @ $36)	$720,000	
Goods available for sale	$720,000	
Finished goods inventory, December 31 (5,000 @ $36)	180,000	
Cost of goods sold		540,000
Gross margin		$210,000
Operating expenses:		
Selling	$110,000	
Administrative	80,000	
Total selling and administrative		$190,000
Net income		$ 20,000

The following additional information is available:

Variable costs per unit:	
Direct materials	$12
Direct labor	12
Manufacturing overhead	4
Selling expense	2

Fixed costs for the period:
    Manufacturing overhead $160,000
    Selling   80,000
    Administrative   80,000

Required: 1. How much of the ending finished goods inventory of $180,000 consists of fixed manufacturing overhead that is being deferred to be charged against income generated from sales next period?
2. Recast the income statement using variable costing and the contribution format. Explain the difference in net income under the two costing methods.

E11–5   **Acceptable costing for external purposes.** Sendiri Company manufactures and sells a single product. The company has prepared the following income statement for the period just completed:

SENDIRI COMPANY
Income Statement
For the Period Ending December 31, 19X7

Sales (30,000 units @ $27)		$810,000
Less variable expenses:		
Cost of goods sold:		
Finished goods inventory, January 1	–0–	
Cost of goods manufactured:[a]		
(40,000 units @ $18)	$720,000	
Goods available for sale	$720,000	
Finished goods inventory, December 31	180,000	
Cost of goods sold	$540,000	
Selling expenses (30,000 × $3)	90,000	
Total variable expenses		630,000
Contribution margin		$180,000
Fixed expenses:		
Manufacturing overhead	$120,000	
Selling	20,000	
General and administrative	60,000	
Total fixed expenses		200,000
Net loss		$ 20,000

[a]There was no beginning or ending work in process inventories.

Required: 1. What method of costing is Sendiri Company using—absorption or variable? Justify your answer.
2. Is the ending finished goods inventory acceptable for external reporting purposes? If not, recast the income statement in a more traditional format and one that would show the finished goods inventory at an acceptable figure for statements prepared for external users.

E11–6   **Variable versus absorption costing: sales vary, production constant.** DRI Company began the year 19X7 with no inventories of work in process or finished goods. The company has projected the costs listed on page 396 for the year.

	Per Unit
Direct material	$10
Direct labor	12
Variable manufacturing overhead	6
Fixed manufacturing overhead ($80,000 per month with	
expected production of 20,000 units per month)	4
Total	$32

During the first three months of 19X7, the following unit production and sales were achieved:

	Production	**Sales**
January	20,000	10,000
February	20,000	20,000
March	20,000	25,000
Total	60,000	55,000

There were no variations from projected costs during the first three months. Work in process inventories are negligible and can be ignored.

Required:
1. Compute the ending finished goods inventory and the cost of goods sold for each month using absorption costing.
2. Compute the ending finished goods inventory and the cost of goods sold for each month using variable costing.
3. Determine the amount of difference that there will be in net income each month under the two costing methods. Reconcile or explain what causes the difference.

E11–7 **Conversion from absorption to variable costing income statement.** Danville Company uses an absorption costing system and has prepared the following income statement for the month of October 19X7:

DANVILLE COMPANY
Income Statement
For the Month Ending October 31, 19X7

Sales (10,000 units)		$500,000
Cost of goods sold:		
Finished goods inventory, October 1	$120,000	
Cost of goods manufactured (8,000 × $30)	240,000	
Goods available for sale	$360,000	
Finished goods inventory, October 31	60,000	
Cost of goods sold		300,000
Gross margin		$200,000
Operating expenses:		
Selling expenses	$ 75,000	
General and administrative expenses	85,000	
Total operating expenses		160,000
Net income		$ 40,000

The variable costs per unit have remained stable during the year. During September, 8,000 units were produced.

The fixed manufacturing costs have also remained stable at $48,000 per month. Variable selling expenses are $3 per unit. There was no significant beginning or ending work in process for October, and FIFO perpetual inventories are maintained.

Required:
1. How much fixed manufacturing overhead was deferred from September to October by using absorption costing?
2. Recast the income statement for October 19X7 using variable costing and the contribution format.
3. Reconcile the net income in your variable costing income statement with the net income shown above in the absorption costing income statement.

E11–8 **Variable versus absorption costing: production varies, sales constant.** RIB Company began the year 19X7 with no inventories of work in process or finished goods. The company projected the following costs for the year:

Variable costs:
Direct material	$4 per unit
Direct labor	5 per unit
Manufacturing overhead	3 per unit
Selling expenses	2 per unit

Fixed costs:
Manufacturing overhead	60,000 per month
Selling and administrative	20,000 per month

During the first three months of 19X7, the following unit production and sales were achieved:

	Production	*Sales*
January	12,000	12,000
February	15,000	12,000
March	9,000	12,000
Total	36,000	36,000

RIB sells its product for $20 per unit. There were no variations from the projected costs during the first three months. There were negligible work in process inventories at the end of each month, and the company uses FIFO perpetual inventory costing.

Required:
1. What is the unit cost of production each month under both variable and absorption costing?
2. Prepare income statements for the three months for both variable costing and absorption costing.
3. What can be said about the relationship of income under the two methods of costing when production equals sales, production exceeds sales, and production is less than sales (given that selling prices and costs do not change significantly from one period to the next)?

E11–9 **Segmented income statements by product.** Welton Industries manufactures and sells two products, Zays and Kays. Information relating to the products for 19X7 is shown on the next page.

	Zays	Kays
Units produced and sold	15,000	10,000
Selling price per unit	$10.00	$12.00
Variable expenses per unit	$3.50	$6.00
Direct fixed expenses	$30,000	$24,000

Fixed expenses that cannot be identified directly with either product but that are necessary for the operation of the company amounted to $64,000.

Required: Prepare contribution format income statements segmented by the two products. (If necessary, round percentages to three places, such as 76.4%.) Set up your statement with the following column headings:

	Total		Zays		Kays	
Item	Amount	Percent	Amount	Percent	Amount	Percent

E11–10   **Income statements segmented by type of service.** One-Stop Service is noted for providing clients with a first-class auto body shop, excellent automotive engine and transmission repair, and having an extensive inventory of auto parts. The company is using variable costing, and the income statement for the past year is shown below:

ONE-STOP SERVICE
Income Statement
For the Year Ended December 31, 19X7

Sales	$1,500,000
Less variable expenses	620,000
Contribution margin	$ 880,000
Less fixed expenses	610,000
Net income	$ 270,000

The management of One-Stop Service knows that it is "making money" but would like to see what each of the three services is contributing to the overall profitability of the company. Accordingly, it has asked if the income statement could be prepared so that it would show what each type of service "makes."

The sales, contribution margin ratios, and direct fixed expenses for each of the company's services are as follows:

	Parts	Auto Repair	Body Shop
Sales	$600,000	$500,000	$400,000
Contribution margin ratios	45%	70%	65%
Direct fixed expenses	$100,000	$200,000	$160,000

Required: Prepare an income statement for One-Stop Service segmented by type of service. Include a total column for the company along with the three service columns.

E11–11   **Examples and problems associated with common costs.** You own and operate a management consulting firm. One of your clients operates a large department store with a full range of consumer products, including a self-service grocery supermarket along with furniture, hardware, clothing, and so forth. The management has found it difficult to use accounting data as a basis for decisions regarding possible changes in departments operated, products handled, marketing methods, and so on.

Required: List several overhead costs, or costs not applicable to a particular department, and explain how these common or joint costs complicate and limit the use of accounting data in making decisions in such a store.

(CPA Adapted)

E11–12 **Income statements segmented by territory.** Diversified Manufacturing produces and sells snowmobiles and ski-jets (the water ski equivalent of the snowmobile). The company concentrates its marketing of the snowmobile in Minnesota and Wisconsin and the marketing of the ski-jet in Florida and Louisiana. The segmented income statements by product, using variable costing and the contribution format, for 19X7 are given below:

DIVERSIFIED MANUFACTURING
Product Line and Company Income Statements
For the Year Ended March 31, 19X7

	Snowmobiles	Ski-jets	Total
Sales	$1,500,000	$2,000,000	$3,500,000
Less variable expenses	1,050,000	1,000,000	2,050,000
Contribution margin	$ 450,000	$1,000,000	$1,450,000
Direct fixed expenses	125,000	500,000	625,000
Product segment margin	$ 325,000	$ 500,000	$ 825,000
Less common fixed expenses			200,000
Net income			$ 625,000

The following additional information is available regarding the snowmobiles:

	Minnesota	Wisconsin
Sales	$800,000	$700,000
Direct fixed expenses	75,000	25,000

Required: 1. Prepare a segmented income statement for snowmobiles by territory (Minnesota and Wisconsin). Include a column for snowmobile totals.
2. Why do the direct expenses related to snowmobiles on the product segmented income statements not agree with the direct expenses shown on your income statements for snowmobiles segmented by territories?

Problems

P11–13 **Absorption costing versus variable costing: income statements.** The following annual flexible budget has been prepared by Enthoven, Inc. for use in making decisions relating to its product Y:

	100,000 Units	150,000 Units	200,000 Units
Sales	$800,000	$1,200,000	$1,600,000
Manufacturing costs:			
Variable	$300,000	$ 450,000	$ 600,000
Fixed	200,000	200,000	200,000
Total manufacturing cost	$500,000	$ 650,000	$ 800,000
Marketing and other expenses:			
Variable	$200,000	$ 300,000	$ 400,000
Fixed	160,000	160,000	160,000
Total marketing and other expenses	$360,000	$ 460,000	$ 560,000
Operating income (loss)	$ (60,000)	$ 90,000	$ 240,000

The 200,000 unit budget has been adopted and will be used for applying the fixed manufacturing cost to units of product Y. At the end of the first six months, the following information is available:

Production completed   120,000 units
Sales @ $8 per unit   60,000 units

All fixed costs are budgeted and incurred uniformly throughout the year, and all costs incurred coincide with the budget. Assume that underapplied or overapplied fixed manufacturing overhead is closed to Cost of Goods Sold.

Required:

1. Compute the amount of fixed manufacturing overhead applied to production during the first six months under absorption costing.
2. Prepare income statements for the first six months showing
   a. the operating income or loss under absorption costing, and
   b. the operating income or loss under variable costing.
   Include a cost of goods sold section in each statement so that the amount of the ending inventory is shown.
3. Prepare computations explaining the difference in operating income or loss under the two methods.

(CPA Adapted)

P11–14   **Absorption versus variable costing: projected income statements.** Management of Centennial Company used the following unit costs for the one product it manufactures:

Direct material (all variable)	$30.00
Direct labor (all variable)	19.00
Manufacturing overhead:	
Variable cost	6.00
Fixed cost (based on 10,000 units per month)	5.00
Selling, general and administrative:	
Variable cost	4.00
Fixed cost (based on 10,000 units per month)	2.80

The projected selling price is $80 per unit. The fixed costs remain fixed within the relevant range of 4,000 to 16,000 units of production.

Management has also projected the following data for the month of June 19X7:

	Units
Beginning inventory	2,000
Production	9,000
Available	11,000
Sales	7,500
Ending inventory	3,500

Required:

1. Prepare a projected income statement for June 19X7 for management purposes using absorption costing. Assume all variances (if any) are charged to Cost of Goods Sold each month.

2. Prepare a projected income statement for June 19X7 for management purposes using variable (direct) costing. Be sure to show supporting computations of the inventoriable production costs per unit for each costing method.

(CPA Adapted)

P11–15 **Prepare variable costing income statement and reconcile with absorption costing statement.** Baker Corporation is a manufacturer of a synthetic element. Gary Moss, president of the company, has been eager to get the operating results for the just completed fiscal year. He was surprised when the income statement revealed that income before taxes has dropped to $885,000 from $900,000 even though sales volume had increased 100,000 kg. This drop in net income had occurred even though Moss had implemented the following changes during the past twelve months to improve the profitability of the company.

a. In response to a 10% increase in production costs, the sales price of the company's product was increased by 12%. This action took place December 1, 19X6.

b. The managements of the Selling and Administrative departments were given strict instructions to spend no more in fiscal 19X7 than in fiscal 19X6.

Baker's Accounting Department prepared and distributed to top management the comparative income statements presented below. The accounting staff also prepared related financial information that is presented in the schedule following the income statement to assist management in evaluating the company's performance. Baker uses the FIFO inventory method for finished goods.

BAKER CORPORATION
Statements of Operating Income
For the Years Ended November 30, 19X6 and 19X7
($000 omitted)

	19X6	19X7
Sales revenue	$9,000	$11,200
Cost of goods sold	$7,200	$ 8,320
Manufacturing volume variance	(600)	495
Adjusted cost of goods sold	$6,600	$ 8,815
Gross margin	$2,400	$ 2,385
Selling and administrative expenses	1,500	1,500
Income before taxes	$ 900	$ 885

BAKER CORPORATION
Selected Operating and Financial Data
For 19X6 and 19X7

	19X6	19X7
Sales price	$10.00/kg.	$11.20/kg.
Material cost	$1.50/kg.	$1.65/kg.
Direct labor cost	$2.50/kg.	$2.75/kg.
Variable overhead cost	$1.00/kg.	$1.10/kg.
Fixed overhead cost	$3.00/kg.	$3.30/kg.
Total fixed overhead costs	$3,000,000	$3,300,000
Selling and administrative (all fixed)	$1,500,000	$1,500,000
Sales volume	900,000 kg.	1,000,000 kg.
Beginning inventory	300,000 kg.	600,000 kg.

Required:

1. Explain to Gary Moss why Baker Corporation's net income decreased in the current fiscal year despite the sales price and sales volume increases.

2. A member of Baker's Accounting Department has suggested that the company adopt variable costing for internal reporting purposes.

   a. Prepare an operating income statement through income before taxes for the year ended November 30, 19X7, for Baker Corporation using the variable costing method.

   b. Present a numerical reconciliation of the difference in income before taxes using the absorption costing method as currently employed by Baker and the variable costing method as proposed.

   (CMA Adapted)

P11–16   Manipulating income by manipulating production. Jeff Manders is the general manager of Smith Gaskets. The company just started this year and makes engine gasket sets that are supplied to auto parts stores primarily in the midwest — although the company is hoping to expand.

Jeff earns a yearly guaranteed salary plus a bonus based on the profits of the company. The projections for the year made during the fourth quarter of 19X7 are as follows:

Sales (95,000 gasket sets @ $23)		$2,185,000
Cost of goods sold:		
Beginning inventory	–0–	
Cost of goods manufactured (100,000 × $15.50)	$1,550,000	
Available for sale	$1,550,000	
Ending inventory (5,000 @ $15.50)	77,500	
Cost of goods sold		1,472,500
Gross margin		$ 712,500
Operating expenses:		
Selling	$ 240,000	
General and administrative	200,000	
Total operating expenses		440,000
Net income		$ 272,500

Variable costs associated with Smith's operations are given on the next page.

Per Gasket Set

Direct materials	$6
Direct labor	2
Manufacturing overhead	3
Selling	2

Jeff has a daughter in the final year of dental school who also is marrying immediately after graduation. Jeff's bonus is structured such that if the net income of the company equals or exceeds $300,000 in 19X7, his bonus makes a significant jump (giving Jeff enough extra income to be able to pay tuition costs for the year *and* a lavish wedding reception). Smith Gaskets has excess capacity and Jeff still has time to produce a total of 112,500 gasket sets for the year. He doesn't feel that sales, however, can be pushed beyond the projected 95,000 units for the year.

Required: 1. If Jeff gives the "go-ahead" to produce up to 112,500 gasket sets for the year, and sales do not exceed the 95,000 gasket sets projected, what will be the effect on net income?
2. If Smith Gaskets had been using variable costing, what would be the effect on net income of producing the additional 12,500 gasket sets? (Show computations.)

P11-17 **Absorption costing versus variable costing using standards.** Reefer Corporation is considering changing its method of inventory costing from absorption to variable costing and wants to determine the effect of the proposed change on its financial statements. The firm manufactures Gunk, which is sold for $20 per unit. A raw material, Mush, is added before processing starts; labor and manufacturing overhead are added evenly during the manufacturing process. Production capacity is budgeted at 110,000 units of Gunk annually. The standard costs per unit of Gunk are:

Mush (2lbs @ $1.50)	$ 3.00
Direct labor	6.00
Variable manufacturing overhead	1.00
Fixed manufacturing overhead	1.10
Total unit cost	$11.10

Process costing is used with standard costs. Variances from standard cost are now debited or credited to Cost of Goods Sold. If variable costing were adopted, only variances resulting from variable costs would be debited or credited to Cost of Goods Sold. Inventory data for the year are as follows:

	January 1	December 31
Mush	50,000 lbs.	40,000 lbs.
Work in process		
2/5 processed	10,000 units	
1/3 processed		15,000 units
Finished goods	20,000 units	12,000 units

During the year, 220,000 lbs. of Mush were purchased, and 230,000 lbs. were transferred to work in process inventory. Also, 110,000 units of Gunk were transferred to finished goods inventory. Annual fixed manufacturing overhead, budgeted and actual, was $121,000. There were no variances between standard and actual variable costs during the year.

Required: 1. Compute the following:
  a. Equivalent units of production for materials, labor, and manufacturing overhead for the year.
  b. The number of units sold during the year.
  c. The standard unit costs under variable costing and absorption costing.
  d. Overapplied or underapplied fixed manufacturing overhead, if any, for the year.
2. Prepare a comparative cost of goods sold statement for the year using standard variable costing and standard absorption costing.

(CPA Adapted)

P11–18   **Income statements: standard variable costing versus standard absorption costing.** Heidi Company uses variable costing for its internal management purposes and absorption costing for external reporting. Thus, at the end of each year, financial data must be converted from variable costing to absorption costing in order to satisfy external requirements.

At the end of 19X6, the company anticipated that sales would increase 20% next year. Therefore, production was increased from 20,000 units to 24,000 units to meet this expected demand. However, economic conditions kept the sales level at 20,000 units for each year.

The following data pertain to 19X6 and 19X7:

	19X6	19X7
Sales price per unit	$30	$30
Sales (units)	20,000	20,000
Beginning inventory (units)	2,000	2,000
Production (units)	20,000	24,000
Ending inventory (units)	2,000	6,000
Total unfavorable materials, labor, and variable manufacturing overhead variances	$5,000	$4,000

Standard variable costs per unit for 19X6 and 19X7 are:

Materials	$ 4.50
Direct labor	7.50
Variable manufacturing overhead	3.00
Total	$15.00

Annual fixed costs for 19X6 and 19X7 (budgeted and actual) are:

Production	$ 90,000
Marketing and administrative	100,000
Total	$190,000

The manufacturing overhead rate under absorption costing is based on practical (rather than expected) plant capacity, which is 30,000 units per year. All variances and overapplied or underapplied manufacturing overhead are closed to Cost of Goods Sold.

Required: 1. Prepare income statements for 19X7, based on (a) variable costing and (b) absorption costing. (The beginning and ending inventories need not be shown on the income statements; that is, show cost of goods sold as one figure.)

2. Explain the difference, if any, in the operating income figures and make the entry, if necessary, to adjust the book figures to the financial statement figures.

(CMA Adapted)

P11–19 **Variable costing versus absorption costing: all fixed costs.** Ralph Richards, an independently wealthy maverick chemist, lived on the bank of a river rumored to have large amounts of nondetectable chemicals. He discovered a process to make liquid fertilizer by using the unusual water and food garbage. He was located near a large metropolitan area, so he decided to construct a plant to utilize his discovery. He contracted with the city to accept its food and burnable garbage if it were delivered to his plant in a separated and satisfactory manner and in quantities subject to his discretion — including none if he so desired. The city was happy to comply with his request because whatever Ralph accepted reduced its garbage processing costs.

Ralph also constructed a power plant that utilized the burnable garbage as its energy source for the production of electricity and heat for operating the plant. Ralph's plant was highly mechanized and required only a few salaried operating and management personnel. He started operations in January 19X8.

The first year of operations went well but Ralph was able to produce beyond customer demand. At the end of 19X8 he decided that from then on he would produce to meet demand only. The following data apply to Ralph's operations for the years 19X8 and 19X9:

	19X8	19X9
Sales	1,000,000 gal.	1,000,000 gal.
Production	2,000,000 gal.	–0–
Selling price	$2/gal.	$2/gal.
Costs (all fixed):		
Production	$2,000,000	$2,000,000
General and administrative	$ 200,000	$ 200,000

Required:
1. Using three columns for your numbers, prepare income statements for Ralph's company for 19X8, 19X9, and the two years together using:
   a. Variable costing.
   b. Absorption costing.
2. What inventory costs would Ralph show on his balance sheets at December 31, 19X8 and 19X9 under each method? Which inventory value do you think is correct and why?
3. Determine the break-even point in gallons of fertilizer under both variable costing and absorption costing. Why does your income statement according to absorption costing disagree with your break-even calculation?

P11–20 **Production and sales volume effects: variable versus absorption costing.** Satellite Company, a wholly owned subsidiary of Jupiter Inc., produces and sells three main product lines. The company employs an absorption cost accounting system for record-keeping purposes.

At the beginning of the year, the president of Satellite Company presented the budget to the parent company and accepted a commitment to contribute $15,800 to Jupiter's consolidated profit in 19X7. The president has been confident that the year's profit would exceed the budget target because the monthly sales reports have shown that sales for the year will exceed the budget by 10%. The president is both disturbed and confused when the controller presents an adjusted forecast as of November 30, indicating that profit will be 11% under budget. The two forecasts are as follows:

	Forecasts as of	
	January 1	November 30
Sales	$268,000	$294,800
Cost of goods sold	$212,000[a]	$233,200
Plus underapplied manufacturing overhead	–0–	6,000
Adjusted cost of goods sold	$212,000	$239,200
Gross profit	$ 56,000	$ 55,600
Operating expenses:		
Marketing expense	$ 13,400	$ 14,740
Administrative expense	26,800	26,800
Total operating expenses	$ 40,200	$ 41,540
Income from operations	$ 15,800	$ 14,060

[a]Includes fixed manufacturing overhead of $30,000.

There have been no sales price changes or product mix shifts since the January 1 forecast. The only cost variance on the income statement is the underapplied manufacturing overhead. This arose because the company used only 16,000 machine hours during the year (the manufacturing overhead rate had been determined on the basis of 20,000 machine hours) because of a shortage of raw materials. Fortunately, Satellite's finished goods inventory was large enough to fill all sales orders received.

Required:
1. Analyze and explain the forecast profit decline, in spite of increased sales and good cost control.
2. Explain and illustrate an alternative internal cost reporting procedure which would avoid the confusing effect of the present procedure.

(CMA Adapted)

P11–21 **Preparing and using segment reports.** The Hamline Corporation produces and sells three products. The three products A, B, and C, are sold in a local market and in a regional market. After the end of the first quarter of 19X7, the following income statement was prepared:

HAMLINE CORPORATION
Territory and Company Income Statements
For the First Quarter of 19X7

	Local	Regional	Total
Sales	$1,000,000	$300,000	$1,300,000
Cost of goods sold	775,000	235,000	1,010,000
Gross profit	$ 225,000	$ 65,000	$ 290,000
Selling expenses	$ 60,000	$ 45,000	$ 105,000
Administrative expenses	40,000	12,000	52,000
Total	$ 100,000	$ 57,000	$ 157,000
Net income	$ 125,000	$ 8,000	$ 133,000

Management has expressed special concern with the regional market because of the extremely poor return on sales. This market was entered a year ago because of excess capacity. It was originally believed that the return on sales would improve with time, but after a year no noticeable improvement can be seen from the results as reported in the above quarterly statement.

In attempting to decide whether to eliminate the regional market, the following information has been gathered:

| | Products | | |
	A	B	C
Sales	$500,000	$400,000	$400,000
Variable manufacturing expenses as a percentage of sales	60%	70%	60%
Variable selling expenses as a percentage of sales	3%	2%	2%

Sales by Markets

Product	Local	Regional
A	$400,000	$100,000
B	300,000	100,000
C	300,000	100,000

All administrative expenses and fixed manufacturing expenses are common to the three products and the two markets and are fixed for the period. The remaining selling expenses are fixed for the period and separable by market. All fixed expenses are based on a prorated yearly amount.

Required:

1. Prepare the quarterly segmented income statements showing contribution margins by markets (territories). Include a column for the company as a whole.
2. Prepare the quarterly segmented income statements showing contribution margins by products. Include a column for the company as a whole.
3. Assuming that there are no alternative uses for the Hamline Corporation's present capacity, would you recommend dropping the regional market? Why or why not?
4. It is believed that a new product can be ready for sale next year if the Hamline Corporation decides to go ahead with continued research. The new product can be produced by simply converting equipment now used in producing product C. This conversion will increase fixed costs by $10,000 per quarter. What must be the minimum contribution margin per quarter for the new product to make the changeover financially feasible?

(CMA Adapted)

P11–22 Segmented income by product. Caprice Company manufactures and sells two products—a small portable office file cabinet that it has made for over fifteen years and a home/travel file introduced in 19X6. The files are made in Caprice's only manufacturing plant. Budgeted variable production costs per unit of product are as follows:

	Office File	Home/Travel File
Sheet metal	$ 3.50	–0–
Plastic	–0–	$3.75
Direct labor (@ $8 per DLH)	4.00	2.00
Variable manufacturing overhead (@ $9 per DLH)	4.50	2.25
Total	$12.00	$8.00

Variable manufacturing overhead costs vary with direct labor hours. The annual fixed manufacturing overhead costs are budgeted at $120,000. A total of 50% of these costs are directly traceable to the Office File Department and 22% of the costs are traceable to the Home/Travel File Department. The remaining 28% of the costs are not traceable to either department.

Caprice employs two full-time salespersons — Pam Price and Robert Flint. Each salesperson receives an annual salary of $14,000 plus a sales commission of 10% of his or her total gross sales. Travel and entertainment expense is budgeted at $22,000 annually for each salesperson. Price is expected to sell 60% of the budgeted unit sales for each file and Flint the remaining 40%. Caprice's remaining selling and administrative expenses include fixed administrative costs of $80,000 that cannot be traced to either file plus the following traceable selling expenses:

	Office File	Home/Travel File
Packaging expenses per unit	$2.00	$1.50
Promotion	30,000	40,000

Data regarding Caprice's budgeted and actual sales for the fiscal year ended May 31, 19X7, are presented in the schedule below. There were no changes in the beginning and ending balances of either finished goods or work in process inventories.

	Office File	Home/Travel File
Budgeted sales volume in units	15,000	15,000
Budgeted and actual unit sales price	$29.50	$19.50
Actual unit sales:		
Pam Price	10,000	9,500
Robert Flint	5,000	10,500
Total units	15,000	20,000

Data regarding Caprice's operating expenses for the year ended May 31, 19X7, follow:

a. There were no increases or decreases in raw materials inventory for either sheet metal or plastic and there were no usage variances. However, sheet metal prices were 6% above budget and plastic prices were 4% below budget.

b. The actual direct labor hours worked and costs incurred were as follows:

	Hours	Amount
Office file	7,500	$ 57,000
Home/Travel file	6,000	45,600
	13,500	$102,600

c. Fixed manufacturing overhead costs attributable to the Office File Department were $8,000 above the budget. All other fixed manufacturing overhead costs were incurred at the same amounts as budgeted, and all variable manufacturing overhead costs were incurred at the budgeted hourly rates.

d. All selling and administrative expenses were incurred at budgeted rates or amounts except the following items:

Nontraceable administrative expenses		$ 34,000
Promotion:		
Office files	$32,000	
Home/travel files	58,000	90,000
Travel and entertainment:		
Pam Price	$24,000	
Robert Flint	28,000	52,000
		$176,000

Required: Prepare a segmented income statement of Caprice Company's actual operations for the fiscal year ended May 31, 19X7. The report should be prepared in a contribution margin format by product and should reflect total income (loss) for the company before income taxes.

(CMA Adapted)

 P11–23 **Levels of segmented income statements.** Gro-Max is a supplier of basic soil nutrients including nitrogen, phosphate, and potash. The company operates in the central region of the United States with two divisions. The Northern Division has its offices located in Minneapolis, Minnesota, and the Southern Division has its offices in Kansas City, Missouri. The corporate headquarters is also located in its own building at the Northern Division office site.

The Northern Division marketing area is broken into two territories. Northern-One covers the states of North and South Dakota, Minnesota, Wisconsin, and Michigan. Northern-Two covers the states of Nebraska, Iowa, Illinois, and Indiana. There are no separate territories as yet in the Southern Division.

The company uses variable costing for internal reporting and prepares its income statements for management using the contribution format. Information regarding sales and expenses by products within the divisions for the year 19X7 are given below:

	Nitrogen	*Phosphate*	*Potash*
Northern Division:			
Sales	$600,000	$400,000	$200,000
Direct fixed expenses	$50,000	$30,000	$10,000
Contribution margin ratio	35%	40%	20%
Southern Division:			
Sales	$300,000	$400,000	$100,000
Direct fixed expenses	$30,000	$40,000	$12,000
Contribution margin ratio	40%	45%	15%

The total fixed expenses by division and for the company as a whole during 19X7 were as follows:

Northern Division	$110,000
Southern Division	90,000
Gro-Max total	300,000

The percentage of total sales of each product in the Northern Division by each of the territories and the direct costs associated with each product by territory were:

	Nitrogen	Phosphate	Potash
Northern-One:			
Sales	40%	60%	70%
Direct fixed expenses	$20,000	$14,000	$6,000
Northern-Two:			
Sales	60%	40%	30%
Direct fixed expenses	$22,000	$10,000	$3,000

Required:

1. Prepare a Level 3 segmented income statement for the Northern Division for the sales of *nitrogen*. Include a column for the total associated with nitrogen in the Northern Division. Your other columns should show nitrogen sales in Northern-One and Northern-Two territories.

2. Prepare a Level 2 segmented income statement for the Northern Division segmented by *product*. You should have a total column for the Northern Division and separate columns for nitrogen, phosphate, and potash.

3. Prepare a Level 1 segmented income statement for Gro-Max segmented by *division*. You should now have a total column for Gro-Max and separate columns for Northern Division and Southern Division.

4. Indicate on your statements by labeling with letters (that is, A-A, B-B, and so forth) showing how the detail of the statements is summarized as you move up from level to level.

CHAPTER 12

Relevant Costs for Short-Run Decisions

Learning Objectives

After reading this chapter you should be able to:

1. Understand the general rule for determining which costs and revenues are applicable to a decision.

2. Understand the need to specify a situation correctly so that irrelevant or tangential issues do not interfere with the decision-making process.

3. Be familiar with the types of special or nonroutine decisions discussed in the chapter such as make or buy, dropping segments, special order pricing, sell or process further, joint and by-product decisions, and limited resource problems.

4. Appreciate the meaning and role of opportunity costs in special or nonroutine decisions.

5. Appreciate the need to keep qualitative factors in mind in special or nonroutine decisions.

6. Appreciate how linear programming can be used to solve problems when more than one constraint is present (Appendix 12-A).

An important function of the management accountant is to provide analysis for many short-run, nonroutine types of decisions. The term *short run* means that the results of these choices occur in less than a year. *Nonroutine* means that these decisions arise on an occasional and irregular basis as opposed to regularly recurring functions such as the budgetary process.

Although this chapter focuses on short-run decisions, the underlying concepts presented here are likewise applicable to long-run choices. Because the effects of long-run alternatives extend beyond a year, the time value of money must be considered in them: inflows and outflows of cash in the future must be "discounted" in order to make them comparable with dollars that are committed to these ventures at the time of the decision. Because long-run choices usually involve the potential investment of large sums of money, they are known as *capital budgeting* decisions. Thus the categories of nonroutine short-run decisions and investment selections rest on the same basic bedrock concepts, although the latter also is affected by the time value of money.

A representative number of short-run, nonroutine types of decisions will be examined in this chapter. These include the make or buy choice, dropping segments such as product lines, special order pricing, selling a product versus processing it further, joint product decisions, and maximizing usage of limited resources. Because all these problems entail the usage of the same basic concepts of decision making applied to slightly different problem situations, we examine the general role of costs and revenues in decision making prior to examining the specific decision situations mentioned above.

Basic Concepts of Decision Making

The basic concepts that guide decision making were discussed in Chapter 2. Decision making requires an understanding of ideas such as differential costs, sunk costs, and opportunity costs. You may wish to review them again at this time. In order to correctly and appropriately apply these concepts, a general rule can be formulated that is applicable to all of the decision categories discussed in this chapter as well as in capital budgeting. A **relevant cost** is

> a cost or revenue that is crucial to a particular decision if and only if (1) it differs between the alternatives being considered and (2) involves the actual receipt or expenditure of funds.

The first requirement should be self-evident. If a cost or revenue does not differ relative to the alternatives, it is not germane to the decision and can be disregarded. For example, if a firm is considering whether to make blenders or mixers, the potential revenues from each are relevant to the decision. On the other hand, if the production manager of the factory in which blenders or mixers will be manufactured receives the same salary no matter which product is manufactured, that cost is not relevant to the decision and can be omitted from the analysis.

The second requirement deals with the fact that many sunk or unavoidable costs are often reshuffled as a result of managerial decisions. However, the reallocation of costs resulting from a decision does not affect the cash flows or profits of the enterprise. A simple example will illustrate this point.

Assume that a production department within a firm performs finishing operations on two products, A and B. Overhead is charged to product on the basis of direct labor hours. The company is evaluating whether to replace product B with product C. The fixed manufacturing overhead of the department is $25,000. Assume that the fixed manufacturing overhead is assigned to products on the basis of direct labor hours. If A and B are produced, the budgeted direct labor hours are 2,500, with 1,500 applicable to A and 1,000 to B. If C replaces B, direct labor hours are expected to decline to 2,000, with 500 estimated for product C. The resulting allocations of the department foreman's salary under the two allocations follow:

Original Alternative

Assigned to A: $15,000 $\left(\$25,000 \times \dfrac{1,500}{2,500} \right)$

Assigned to B: $\underline{10,000}$ $\left(\$25,000 \times \dfrac{1,000}{2,500} \right)$

Total $\underline{\underline{\$25,000}}$

New Alternative

Assigned to A: $18,750 $\left(\$25,000 \times \dfrac{1,500}{2,000} \right)$

Assigned to C: $\underline{6,250}$ $\left(\$25,000 \times \dfrac{500}{2,000} \right)$

Total $\underline{\underline{\$25,000}}$

As a result of the decision, the fixed manufacturing overhead is "chopped up" differently. However, the total amount of $25,000 is unaffected by the decision, and no part of it should be considered relative to that decision. Of course this illustration implies that there would be a relevant direct labor cost saving for product C relative to B. Before examining the various types of nonroutine short-run decisions, two additional points must be made relative to this type of analysis.

Estimating Costs and Revenues

First of all, because decision making involves assessing the relevant cash inflows and outflows that are expected to occur in the future, they must be estimated. Obviously, estimates must be as realistic and accurate as possible. There is no place for unwarranted biases in the estimation of future costs and revenues. After decisions are made, the results should be audited in terms of comparing actual results against plan in order to assess both the profitability of the alternative selected as well as for evaluating the effectiveness of the planning process itself. Hence planning and control should be closely linked in the area of nonroutine decision making.

Defining Problems Appropriately

The second point is that problems must be appropriately defined if meaningful solutions are to result. An understanding of the relevant cost concepts discussed in Chapter 2 is to no avail if problems are incorrectly specified. The problem of appropriate definition can be understood by means of a hypothetical example.

Athletic Scholarships at Marion University

Marion University is a medium-size, private, comprehensive university located in a large city. The university has approximately 5,000 students and suffers from a large enrollment shortage: in the language of managerial accounting, the university has considerable **excess capacity.** The university has an extensive intercollegiate athletics program and is a member of the Mid-States Athletic Conference. Like other universities throughout the nation, Marion University awards scholarships to prospective athletes granting them room, board, and tuition in exchange for their athletic services. Most of the athletes are enrolled as physical education majors in Marion's College of Education.

Marion's football program is in considerable trouble because the team was constantly losing money as well as many games. As a result, faculty groups were continually attempting to scuttle the football program.

In presenting the annual budget for 19X8–X9 to the administration and the board of trustees of Marion, Buddy Ewell, the university's financial vice-president, showed a cost of $2,000,000 in scholarships, which in turn was subdivided into $600,000 for athletic scholarships and $1,400,000 for nonathletes. On seeing these numbers, many professors at Marion became incensed. They perceived two problems with the athletic scholarships: (1) athletic scholarships cost the university "real money," and (2) if athletic scholarships were transferred to regular academic areas, the number of real students at Marion could be increased.

Unfortunately, many professors at Marion (none of whom, by the way, were managerial accountants) were clearly incorrect on the first issue and were, at the least, misguided on the second one. However, the method of presentation of the budget by the financial vice-president misled not only the faculty but also numerous other involved individuals including members of the board of trustees. The real issue with scholarships was one of how to generate the most contribution margin for the university, not one of allocating a limited amount of resources between two groups of competing recipients. Hence the problem was poorly specified.

In order to understand the nature of the confusion caused by Marion's budget, let us examine the nature of athletic and academic scholarships. A scholarship is basically a discount or credit against tuition. If Marion's tuition were $6,000 per year and a student received a scholarship of $2,500, she would pay tuition of $3,500. If the university were at **full capacity** and our scholarship student "bumped" a prospective full-tuition-paying student, there is a real cost to the university of $2,500. The question then becomes one of whether the scholarship student's qualifications are attractive enough to the university to warrant displacement of an "ordinary" student. The question may be difficult to answer, but at least it has been correctly defined: is the "better" student worth the $2,500 cost to the school? This is a qualitative question, one that cannot be reduced to just looking at the relevant cost differences between the alternatives.

On the other hand, as was the case at Marion University, there was a severe shortage of students, and the scholarship recipient bumped no one. Consequently, the university was very definitely better off from the cash flow standpoint in the amount of the $3,500 tuition paid by the student less any direct variable costs incurred solely as a result of this student enrolling. Of course, when a fairly sizable group of potential scholarship students is being evaluated, from a purely cash flow standpoint, the differential costs of the decision must be evaluated. These might include, for example, the need to hire additional teaching faculty. Again, the point is being stressed that although all the relevant information may not be available, at least framing the question correctly facilitates making an appropriate decision.

Two more important observations should be made about this hypothetical illustration. Tuition aid at Marion and other U.S. universities is invariably called *scholarships* for both athletes and nonathletes. Because of the virtual professional nature of big-time sports at major U.S. colleges and universities, however, athletes are generally in a different category than other students and use different resources. Thus, professors at Marion felt that athletic scholarships were reducing aid for other students. Given Marion's ability to handle additional students without crowding resources such as size of faculty and dormitory space, the university might easily have improved its cash flows by *increasing* its scholarship awards for nonathletes above the $1,400,000 previously mentioned without disturbing the $600,000 designated for athletic scholarships. Additional scholarships at $2,500 would increase cash flows by $3,500 per student less any differential costs. For example, further analysis by the university's planning staff would have revealed that up to 500 additional students could be enrolled at Marion without any significant effect on fixed resources such as the number of teaching faculty. If 500 additional students could be recruited provided they could get scholarships of $2,500 each, the effect on cash flows from tuitions would be

Budgeted Tuitions for 5,000 Students	Budgeted Tuitions for 5,500 Students	Differential Cash Flows
$28,000,000	$29,750,000	$1,750,000

The original budget for 5,000 students at a tuition of $6,000 each less total scholarships of $2,000,000 is equal to $28,000,000. The differential cash flows are equal to 500 students times an average net tuition receipt of $3,500 each. Moreover, additional cash flows would be derived from room and board contracts because additional capacity was also available in the dormitories.

Of course, quality of students in the prospective addition of up to 500 students would also have to be carefully considered. This is a qualitative consideration. Nevertheless, the main point to stress is that the problem was neither well understood nor handled in an effective fashion because of the confusing way in which the problem was specified by lumping athletic and nonathletic scholarships and making it appear as if a pot with limited resources was being divided between the two categories when such was clearly not the case. Most faculty and trustees saw scholarships only in the light of being an outflow of resources. Instead, it was a means for adjusting tuition rates to tap markets that could not pay $6,000 per year with a resulting *increase* of cash flows.

A last point to make is that more confusion was added to this problem by including scholarship aid as a cost in the budget and countering this amount by showing tuition revenues gross (without deducting scholarship discounts). Although this information is quite important to users, the scholarships should, nevertheless, have been shown in a separate schedule because of their non–cash flow nature.

Thus appropriately defining and presenting problems is necessary not only from the standpoint of maximizing contribution margin but also to maintain organizational cohesiveness and morale.

Make or Buy

The **make or buy** decision arises on a fairly frequent basis. The essence of this decision centers around the question of whether a firm should manufacture a part, a subassembly, or even a product as opposed to acquiring it from another firm. In these problems it is generally assumed that the enterprise presently manufactures the item and is considering an offer to buy it from an outside supplier. However, the opposite situation may also hold: the firm may be considering whether to manufacture something that it is presently purchasing. If the "make" alternative requires the acquisition of machinery and equipment, then it is an investment type decision rather than a short-run–oriented one.

Qualitative Factors

Before considering the quantitative aspects of a make or buy situation with purely short-run aspects, mention should be made of several qualitative factors that should always be considered. First is the question of whether the quality of the supplier's part is better, equal, or poorer than what the firm is presently manufacturing. If equality does not exist, the possible consequences of the quality difference should be carefully evaluated. In some cases, the quality difference may be crucial to the decision.

The second important consideration involves reliability of supply from an outside manufacturer. At issue here is the reliability of the supplier in terms of providing the needed quantities of the part on a timely basis. Lack of reliability should virtually rule out a switch from making to buying. Let us now examine a hypothetical make or buy situation.

Illustration

The Lionette Company presently manufactures a subassembly for one of its products. It has been in contact with the Mazzone Company concerning the possible outside manufacture of the subassembly. Lionette needs 10,000 subassemblies per year. The cost accounting department has provided the following analysis of manufacturing costs per subassembly:

Direct materials	$15
Direct labor	20
Variable manufacturing overhead	10
Fixed manufacturing overhead	25
Total	$70

Further analysis showed that the three variable cost items were totally avoidable. Direct materials would not be required. Workers providing direct labor would either be let go or be used in other manufacturing operations. If the direct labor were reassigned to other products, the company would forgo the need to hire additional labor and thus avoid incremental costs. The variable overhead was either a function of direct labor (social security and payroll taxes, for example) or consisted of items such as power costs of operating machinery that would be avoided if the product were not manufactured. Total fixed manufacturing overhead assigned to the subassemblies was $250,000 (10,000 units × $25 each). Of this amount, $20,000 of indirect labor (inspection of finished units) could be avoided. The workers would either be let go or productively reassigned elsewhere in the plant. All other fixed overhead costs were either allocations of sunk costs (depreciation of machinery and equipment as well as factory buildings) or were unavoidable out-of-pocket costs (salaries of production department foremen, for example).

The relevant costs of the subassembly for purposes of a make or buy analysis consist of the avoidable costs only. Direct materials, direct labor, and variable overhead are all avoidable, so they would be the same as in the analysis provided by the cost accounting department. The avoidable fixed overhead would be $2 per unit consisting of the $20,000 of indirect labor that could be saved divided by 10,000 units of output. The avoidable costs are:

Direct materials	$15
Direct labor	20
Variable manufacturing overhead	10
Fixed manufacturing overhead	2
Total	$47

Therefore, assuming that no qualitative problems were present, the appropriate break-even point would be $47 per unit. If the total acquisition cost (including any transportation-in) exceeds $47 per unit, the firm is better off making. If Mazzone's price is under $47 per unit, the firm should buy the subassembly.

The essence of the differential analysis is that the real cost of making the unit is $47 per unit or a total of $470,000 because this is the amount that can be saved (avoided) by not manufacturing the subassembly. Therefore, Lionette cannot afford to pay more to an outside supplier than it saves. On the other hand, it is better off if it pays less than the amount that it saves. In a very real sense, $47 is the cost of making the product when considering the aspect of comparison with potential outside purchases of the subassembly. This is, of course, less than the cost accounting calculation of full cost, which is not correct for the particular decision at hand, whether to continue making or whether to buy from an outside source.

Other Uses of Capacity

Two additional aspects of make or buy analysis should be borne in mind. As presented thus far, the Lionette example assumed that there was no other use for the machinery and equipment used to manufacture the subassembly. Assume that if the subassembly were purchased, the machinery and equipment could be used to manufacture 5,000 units of a new product. The product would sell for $60 per unit and would have the following costs per unit as estimated by the cost accounting department:

Direct materials	$12
Direct labor	16
Variable manufacturing overhead	8
Fixed manufacturing overhead	20
Total	$56

Further analysis showed that all the fixed costs were unavoidable: the decision to make the new product would not lead to any incremental fixed manufacturing costs. In other words, the fixed manufacturing costs were simply an allocation of existing fixed costs. Such, of course, need not be the case. However, further analysis showed that the new product would have delivery costs of $4 per unit (delivery costs of the subassembly were not affected by the make or buy decision in this illustration). The contribution margin per unit would therefore be

Revenues		$60
Incremental costs:		
Direct materials	$12	
Direct labor	16	
Variable manufacturing overhead	8	
Delivery costs	4	40
Contribution margin		$20

The total contribution margin *lost* by not producing the new product is $100,000 (5,000 times the $20 contribution margin per unit).

The break-even point in terms of make versus buy would increase above the $47 previously calculated by the opportunity cost of making the subassembly, which is the $100,000 of lost contribution. margin on the new product:

$$\frac{\text{Contribution margin on new product}}{\text{Units of subassembly}} = \frac{\$100,000}{10,000 \text{ units}} = \$10$$

This total of $100,000 is distributed over 10,000 units of the subassembly, which then raises the break-even outside buying price to $57 per unit. Because the total expected contribution margin on the potential new product is an opportunity cost of the original item, the subassembly, it is added in to the subassembly's costs because it is income given up if the subassembly is produced. Notice that because it is an opportunity cost of *making* the subassembly, it *raises* the minimum acceptable purchase price.

Short-Run Analysis

The second point to be emphasized relative to make or buy is that the analysis used here is single year and short run in nature. As long as costs, revenues, and quantities are the same beyond a year, the present analysis suffices. However, if factors are expected to change, a more extensive multiyear analysis taking into account the time value of money should be used.

Another factor that introduces potential long-run elements arises if the enterprise can eliminate machinery and equipment as a result of switching from make to buy. The easiest way to handle this situation is to include the imputed interest that would arise if machinery and equipment were sold as an increase in the cost of manufacturing. Assume in the Lionette example that the machinery and equipment used to manufacture the subassembly has a book value of $150,000 and could be sold in the used equipment market for $120,000. The funds generated from the disposal could then be invested to produce a return of 10% per year after taxes. The total earnings from the proceeds of the sale would be $12,000 ($120,000 × .10), which would equal $1.20 per unit of output ($12,000/10,000). This would raise the break-even cost in the original example from $47 to $48.20 per unit.

Dropping Segments

Another problem of nonroutine decision making that arises fairly frequently concerns dropping or adding segments such as a department within a retailing operation, a product line, or a territory. The same concepts are used in evaluating either a drop or an add decision, but the latter will frequently require sizable capital investments. Additions of segments are thus highly likely to be long-run types of problems. In this section we will examine dropping a segment, the example being a department in a retailing operation. We will first assume that there is no other use for the facilities made available by the departmental elimination. This assumption is then changed to a situation where the space and other facilities of the department in question can be put to other productive uses.

Illustration

Arlen and Mercer's Department Store had the budgeted departmental income statement for the year 19X6 shown in Exhibit 12–1. Because the Appliance Department was expected to lose money, the question arose as to whether the department should be closed. A further investigation of the operations of the store and the department produced the following information:

1. All sales and administrative personnel in the department would be let go except for Martha Dietz and Henry Warren. Warren was a long-time employee to whom management felt a moral obligation. If the department were closed, he would be reassigned to Housewares. There was no particular need for him there, but at least he would not get in anyone's way. On the other hand, Ms. Dietz was the best salesperson in

EXHIBIT 12–1

ARLAN AND MERCER DEPARTMENT STORE
Budgeted Income Statement (by Department)
Year Ending December 31, 19X6

	Clothing	Housewares	Appliances	Total
Revenues	$800,000	$400,000	$300,000	$1,500,000
Cost of goods sold	320,000	220,000	200,000	740,000
Gross profit	$480,000	$180,000	$100,000	$ 760,000
Operating expenses				
Salaries and wages	$120,000	$ 65,000	$ 75,000	$ 260,000
Employment taxes	12,000	6,500	7,500	26,000
Utilities	8,000	4,000	3,000	15,000
Telephone	3,000	1,800	1,200	6,000
Building depreciation	10,000	8,000	7,000	25,000
Depreciation of cash				
registers & display cases	2,500	2,400	2,000	6,900
Insurance on machinery				
and equipment	2,000	1,750	1,450	5,200
Property taxes on machinery				
and equipment	1,500	1,250	800	3,550
General store expense	80,000	40,000	30,000	150,000
Total	$239,000	$130,700	$127,950	$ 497,650
Net operating income	$241,000	$ 49,300	$ (27,950)	$ 262,350

the Appliance Department. If Appliances were closed, she would be reassigned to Clothing. If Appliances were kept open, an additional salesperson would have to be hired for Clothing. Warren makes $12,500 per year and Dietz earns $15,000. A new salesperson would make $15,000 per year.

2. Employment taxes are equal to 10% of salaries.

3. Utility costs would not be affected by a departmental shutdown.

4. Telephone costs consisted of a fixed portion of $3,000, which was assigned in a 3:2:1 portion to Clothing, Housewares, and Appliances. The remainder is for long-distance, which mainly dealt with purchasing matters. The total fixed cost portion would be unaffected by the shutdown of Appliances.

5. Building depreciation is assigned on the basis of square footage.

6. Cash registers and display cases have a book value of $10,000 on December 31, 19X5. There is no other use for this equipment in other departments, but it could be sold for $6,000 with the proceeds invested at 12%.

7. Building insurance is unaffected by the shutdown decision.

8. Insurance and property taxes on machinery and equipment are completely avoidable.

9. General store expenses are allocated on the basis of sales. If Appliances is closed, one less clerk would be needed in gift wrapping. Her salary is $7,500 per year.

The budgeted income statement for 19X6 for the Appliances Department is now cast into a more useful relevant cost format that takes into account cost avoidability in Exhibit 12–2 (page 422). For comparative purposes, we show the original budget beside the relevant cost format. The difference between the two are the unavoidable or irrelevant costs. Before discussing the significance of the results, a few brief remarks about how the numbers were determined are in order.

All salaries are avoidable except for that of Mr. Warren. Though Ms. Dietz's salary will continue, her transference to Clothing if Appliances is shut down would avoid the need to hire an additional person at her salary if Appliances were kept open. The saving in employment taxes is proportionate to the saving in salaries. Utility costs are not avoided by the shutdown decision. The unavoidable portion of telephone costs is $500 ($1/6 \times \$3,000$). Building depreciation is unaffected by the decision, although it would have to be differently apportioned if the department were closed down. Depreciation of cash registers and display cases is also sunk, but interest on the disposal value of $720 ($.12 \times \$6,000$) is an imputed cost of keeping the department open. Building insurance is not relevant, but insurance and property taxes on machinery and equipment are a cost only if the department is maintained. Finally, the only relevant general store expense of keeping the department running is the salary of the gift wrapping clerk.

EXHIBIT 12–2

APPLIANCES DEPARTMENT
Relevant Costing Budgets
Year Ending December 31, 19X6

	Relevant Cost Budget	Original Budget	Difference (unavoidable costs)
Revenues	$300,000	$300,000	—
Cost of goods sold	200,000	200,000	—
Gross profit	$100,000	$100,000	—
Operating expenses			
Salaries and wages	$ 62,500	$ 75,000	$12,500
Employment taxes	6,250	7,500	1,250
Utilities	—	3,000	3,000
Telephone	700	1,200	500
Building depreciation	—	7,000	7,000
Depreciation of cash			
registers & display cases	720[a]	2,000	1,280
Insurance on machinery			
and equipment	1,450	1,450	—
Property taxes on machinery			
and equipment	800	800	—
General store expense	7,500	30,000	22,500
Total	$ 79,920	$127,950	$48,030
Net operating income	$ 20,080	$ (27,950)	$48,030

[a]Imputed interest ($6,000 × .12).

The relevant costing income statement tells a far different story than the original budgeted income statement. If the Appliances Department is closed down, the firm can expect to lose $20,080, the incremental profit contributed by the department if it were kept open. Moreover, analysis of this type should always take into account synergistic effects: the loss in sales of other units as a result of closing down a complementary one. Synergy is an important consideration for shopping malls, department stores, and many manufacturing firms. Malls attempt to have a good balance of stores in terms of products merchandised. Similarly, a good mix of departments is extremely important for a department store (the Arlan and Mercer example was restricted to three departments for the sake of simplicity). Finally, manufacturing firms in many industries have to offer a full line for synergistic reasons. It is difficult to envision a cracker manufacturer that does not make good old reliable saltines.

Opportunity Costs

In the Arlan and Mercer example, the Appliances Department should be kept open for the time being as long as no other alternative is present. However, assume that the Clothing Department is expanding rapidly and needs additional space. In this situation, a relevant costing analysis should be undertaken of the incremental cash flows that could be generated by the Clothing Department if it were to use Appliances space and facilities. If it appears that the differential income generated by Clothing will exceed the amount generated by Appliances, then Clothing should expand and Appliances should be closed, other things being equal.

Related Problems

There are several other short-run, nonroutine decisions that are quite similar to the departmental elimination problem. The temporary plant shutdown problem arises where the firm has excess productive capacity in the short-run in comparison with potential sales. The key measurement is to compare total avoidable costs against any potential lost sales revenues. If the former exceed the latter, the plant should be temporarily closed down until the situation turns around. Permanent plant closings or dispositions require a long-run type of analysis, although the relevant costing technique still applies.

Another similar problem is the question of whether to drop a product line. Once again, long-run considerations will probably apply to this situation.

Finally, dropping an unprofitable territory, where a firm's marketing organization is decentralized along geographical lines, requires the same type of analysis. However, the long-run considerations of this type of decision should also be very carefully analyzed.

Special Order Pricing

Pricing of an enterprise's products is one of the major components of the marketing mix. The other elements involve what the product itself is or should be, how the product should be promoted, and how it should be distributed to consumers in a fashion that will adequately minimize cost of distribution and maximize the availability of the product.

Regular Pricing

Pricing schedules should be reviewed annually as part of the budgetary process. *The ongoing array of product prices should be set so that they will cover all costs, both manufacturing and nonmanufacturing, as well as an acceptable return to invested capital* (owner's equity). In oligopolistic industries (relatively few competitors) there is more freedom to set prices so that a particular target *return on investment* (income divided by total assets) can be sought. However, in more competitive industries, the firm is much more susceptible to competitive pressures in the area of pricing. If all costs and an acceptable rate of return for capital cannot be attained in more competitive situations, then new product opportunities should be sought.

Pricing Formulas

Pricing is far from being an exact science. Where some degree of pricing latitude is present, firms often attempt to recover a markup on either total manufacturing cost or on total manufacturing and nonmanufacturing costs. Another possibility is to structure pricing so that a particular return on investment is earned. Let us examine these possibilities at the Grillo Company, a manufacturer of small electrical appliances. Budgetary data for the Grillo Company and its two product lines is shown in Exhibit 12–3.

If markup is based on total manufacturing costs, management might select a markup percentage of 100% with the following results:

	Toasters	Electric Coffee Pots
Total manufacturing costs	$200,000	$300,000
Markup (100%)	200,000	300,000
Total revenue	$400,000	$600,000
Divide by production	÷ 25,000	÷ 50,000
Price per unit	$ 16	$ 12

A similar approach can be used on a total cost basis. You should bear in mind that the indirect selling costs were divided up between the two products on a basis of 50% of all manufacturing costs. This may well be quite arbitrary. In this situation, shown below, we will presume that management has decided to add a 33 1/3% markup to total costs. The following pricing structure would therefore result:

	Toasters	Electric Coffee Pots
Total manufacturing costs	$200,000	$300,000
Selling and administrative costs	100,000	150,000
Total costs	$300,000	$450,000
Markup (33 1/3%)	100,000	150,000
Total revenue	$400,000	$600,000
Divide by production	÷ 25,000	÷ 50,000
Price per unit	$ 16	$ 12

EXHIBIT 12–3
Costs of Toasters and Electric Coffee Pots

	Toasters	Electric Coffee Pots
Quantity to be produced	25,000	50,000
Direct manufacturing costs	$150,000	$200,000
Indirect manufacturing costs	$50,000	$100,000
Selling and administrative costs	$100,000	$150,000
Total investment in assets is $5,000,000.		

Finally, on return on investment pricing, the desired income is calculated as a percentage of total assets. If, for example, a 5% return on investment were desired, we would multiply the total assets of $5,000,000 by 5% giving us a total markup of $250,000, which would then be assigned to the two products in order to determine selling price per unit.

Although these three methods are frequently used in business as a means of arriving at possible selling prices for products, we would add a strong cautionary note. These methods do not really take market conditions into mind. They are merely formulas to arrive at reasonable markups intended to generate reasonable profits. However, there is no necessary relationship between selling price and the quantity that the firm would like to be able to sell. We would strongly advocate the use of market research as a guide to help the firm set prices under its particular competitive and market situations. We next quickly examine two general pricing policies that are used when new products are introduced.

Pricing of New Products

When new products are first introduced, one of two pricing strategies is often adopted. The first policy, **skim pricing**, sets a relatively high initial price when a product is first introduced. The price will then be lowered as time passes and new competition enters the market for the product. This policy is one that attempts to maximize profits in the short run. The contribution margin ratio (as well as the gross margin ratio) will be quite high with this method of pricing. Of course, the easier it is for new competition to enter the market, the less successful this strategy is likely to be.

The second pricing strategy is called **penetration pricing.** As its name implies, the objective here is to go after a fairly large share of the market by having a relatively low price. Over time as the product becomes established and a strong degree of customer loyalty is built up, an attempt can be made to raise prices without adversely affecting the firm's share of the market. Let us next examine special order pricing.

Pricing of Special Orders

One pricing situation is of particular interest in terms of nonroutine, short-run decisions: the special order. Typically, the **special order** arises as a result of a buyer desiring a relatively large order of a product. The product will either be the same or quite similar to a regular product made by the firm. Special orders are often received from large retailing firms for their own private brand. Let us examine a special order pricing situation.

Illustration

Assume that the Bostrom Company manufactures one product, a small home appliance, which has the following cost structure:

Item	Cost
Direct materials	$ 3.00 per unit
Direct labor	5.00 per unit
Variable manufacturing overhead	2.00 per unit
Variable selling costs	2.50 per unit
Fixed manufacturing overhead	6,600,000 per year
Fixed period costs	3,000,000 per year

Assume that the regular selling price is $30 per unit and that sales are expected to be 1,000,000 units during the year. Suppose that a European firm desires to purchase a special order of 200,000 units at $15 each. The European firm will pay all transportation costs, and there are no sales commissions because negotiation is occurring directly with Bostrom's top marketing management rather than going through their sales force. Bostrom has enough productive capacity available to produce the units. Furthermore, analysis reveals that fixed costs will be unaffected by the decision.

By breaking down costs into their fixed and variable components, it can be determined that the firm would have a contribution margin of $1,000,000 on the special order:

Total revenues (200,000 × $15)	$3,000,000
Total variable costs (200,000 × $10)	2,000,000
Contribution margin	$1,000,000

Notice that a unitization of fixed manufacturing overhead costs would give an incorrect answer:

Total variable costs per unit	$10
Total fixed costs per unit $\left(\dfrac{\$6,600,000}{1,200,000}\right)$	5.50
Total manufacturing costs per unit	$15.50

A loss of $.50 per unit is apparently the case because selling price is $15 per unit. However, this would be incorrect because fixed costs are not affected by the decision. Nonmanufacturing period costs are traditionally not stated in per unit terms, so they have been left entirely out of the decision. However, the unitizing of fixed manufacturing overhead is frequently done, although as can be seen from this simple situation, incorrect decisions can result.

Our analysis revealed that the European special order had a positive contribution margin. Had there been a negative contribution margin, the order most certainly would have been rejected. The positive contribution margin is necessary to take on the order, but other considerations might also have to be taken into account. For example, if the market looks promising, should the firm immediately start developing the means of distributing its product at the regular price or close thereto and not sell in large lots at considerably lower prices to European firms that would perform the distribution function? Available capacity and market segmentation should also be carefully considered.

Availability of capacity   If excess capacity is present, the minimum pricing benchmark to keep in mind is that total revenues must cover differential costs: variable costs plus fixed out-of-pocket costs affected by the decision. On the other hand, if available capacity is not present and units of a product that would be sold through regular channels must be sacrificed, selling price on the special order must also cover the contribution margin on the units given up. This is, of course, an example of opportunity costs. Generally speaking, special orders are sought when excess capacity exists.

Market segmentation   The special order should not affect the firm's regular sales. This is particularly important because special orders almost always have a smaller contribution margin per unit than regular sales. Hence special orders apply to situations where **market segmentation** is present: they apply to markets that are outside the firm's regular markets.

Markets may be segmented on either a geographic or a socioeconomic basis. Geographic segmentation arises if the special order is for a region of the country or a foreign nation that is not presently served by the enterprise. Socioeconomic market segmentation concerns demographic characteristics of the final consumers who buy the firm's products. Two important socioeconomic characteristics are wealth and shopping habits of customers. An example of market segmentation of this type might involve a manufacturer of expensive watches that are sold in exclusive jewelry stores. If the manufacturer were evaluating a special order for a large retail discount chain, it would be relying on market segmentation. To some extent, new buying habits by the public have eroded socioeconomic class distinctions of this type.

Dangers of the Special Order

One of the dangers of the special order is that if the manufacturer gets too dependent on this form of sale, profit margins may tend to become badly compressed because of the price concessions given on these orders. There have even been examples of manufacturers becoming wholly reliant on these sales to large retailing chains. The better practice is to restrict special orders to occasional capacity filling situations and to concentrate marketing efforts on the regular customers served by the enterprise. Unfortunately, this practice is not always followed.

A second danger involves the potential violation of the Robinson-Patman Act if the firm is engaged in interstate commerce (which will virtually always be the case). The firm must be able to justify lower prices to different customers. Generally this can be done either on the basis of economies arising from larger shipments or lower costs due to longer production runs. The latter is a full costing concept. The fact that a full costing approach may be used to defend a differential costing decision is a complexity but not an insurmountable one.

Sell or Process Further

There are occasional manufacturing situations where a market may exist for a product prior to its completion in the normal course of production. These decisions are called **sell or process further** decisions.

In sell or process further situations, the guideline for short-run decision making is completely consistent with previous decisions: incremental revenues that would arise from further processing should exceed incremental processing costs. If this is not the case, the product should be sold in its intermediate stage. A simple example should clarify this rule.

Illustration

Assume that Bartnick Company has two production departments. Costs by department for 1,000 units are

	Department 1	Department 2
Variable manufacturing costs	$10,000	$20,000
Fixed manufacturing costs	25,000	30,000
	$35,000	$50,000

There are no variable selling costs involved. If other units of the final product are being produced and none of the fixed manufacturing costs in Department 2 are avoidable, the total revenues from the final product should exceed the total revenues that can be gained by selling the output at the end of Department 1 by at least $20,000. The $20,000 represents the variable costs in Department 2 that are avoidable if sale takes place at the intermediate stage. Notice that the variable costs in Department 1 are irrelevant because these costs will be incurred no matter which alternative is taken. Thus variable costs of Department 1 are sunk or unavoidable relative to this particular situation.

If, on the other hand, this is the entire productivity of the period and Department 2 would be closed down resulting in $5,000 of fixed out-of-pocket costs being avoided (in addition to the $20,000 of variable costs), then revenues from the final product should exceed those from the intermediate product by at least $25,000 in order to justify additional processing.

Again, it should be borne in mind that the analysis presented takes into account short-run factors only. Long-run considerations such as the firm's reputation as a reliable supplier may override short-run incremental income considerations.

Joint and By-product Decisions

Accounting for joint product costs was discussed in Chapter 8. The relevant costing problem that can arise is one of selling at the split-off point or processing further. Hence this problem is closely related to the sell or process further situation just discussed. The key point to remember is that any joint costs that have been assigned to a product are sunk and irrelevant from a decision-making standpoint. The relevant costs are the market value at the point of split-off compared with the revenues that would result from further processing minus the differential costs of the additional processing.

The Gage Corporation processes a raw material in Department 1 that is a joint process. Three products emerge at the end of the process. Data for the three products are shown in Exhibit 12–4.

Joint costs of the raw materials and the joint process are assumed to be $2,500,000. These costs are divided in proportion to market valuation at the split-off point but do not affect the decision. Products B and C should be processed further but not A, as shown by the last column. Differential contribution margin is the excess of market value after further processing less market value at split-off ($400,000 for A) less the avoidable costs of further processing ($700,000 for A). The unavoidable costs are irrelevant from the decision-making standpoint.

Usage of Limited Resources

If productive resources — materials, labor, capital equipment — are not capable of keeping up with needed orders in the short run, a problem arises in terms of the most effective way to utilize scarce factors. Obviously, if this is expected to be a recurring problem, the solution is to expand capacity by acquiring more machinery and equipment and, if necessary, more space. However, in the short run this may not be possible. Furthermore, if the problem is only temporary, acquisition of additional resources may not be warranted. We first examine a situation where one resource is in short supply relative to productive needs.

EXHIBIT 12–4
Joint and By-product Decisions

		Costs of Further Processing			
Product	Market Value at Split-off	Avoidable	Unavoidable	Market Value After Further Processing	Differential Contribution Margin from Further Processing
A	$2,000,000	$ 700,000	$300,000	$2,400,000	$(300,000)
B	1,000,000	200,000	100,000	1,250,000	50,000
C	3,000,000	400,000	200,000	4,000,000	600,000
	$6,000,000	$1,300,000	$600,000	$7,650,000	

One Scarce Resource

Carmichael Company manufactures two products, the A1 and the B2. The company's capacity is constrained because only 1,000 machine hours are available, demand for the products has taken a temporary jump, and inventory stocks are low. Contribution margin per unit for each product is

	A1	B2
Revenue	$20	$30
Variable costs	8	10
Contribution margin	$12	$20

Analyzing each product on the basis of contribution margin per unit indicates that B2 is more profitable. However, this ignores how much machine time — the scarce resource — is needed to produce a unit of output. An A1 requires one hour of machine time and a B2 needs two machine hours per unit.

Profitability per unit of the scarce resource is determined by dividing the contribution margin per unit of product by the amount of machine time necessary to turn out a unit. The result is the contribution margin per unit of the scarce resource:

	A1	B2
Contribution margin per unit	$12	$20
÷ Machine time required per unit	÷ 1	÷ 2
= Contribution margin per machine hour	$12	$10

The contribution margin per hour of machine time provides the critical analysis because machine hours is the scarce resource. The company should therefore produce all the A1s that it needs, up to the point of using all available machine time, before undertaking production of B2s. If the entire 1,000 machine hours were devoted to A1s, 1,000 units could be produced with a total contribution margin of $12,000 (1,000 units times $12). Only 500 units of B2 can be produced during the period leading to a total contribution margin of $10,000 (500 units times $20).

Several Constraints

If there is more than one resource that is in short supply, the analysis becomes more complex. A solution to production problems where more than one constraint is present is usually derived by the application of linear programming, which is introduced in Appendix 12–A.

Summary

Relevant costs for short-run decision-making purposes require an understanding of concepts such as differential costs, opportunity costs, and sunk costs. For a cost or revenue to be relevant to a particular decision, it must differ between the alternatives under consideration and involve the actual receipt or expenditure of funds. The concepts developed here are also applicable to long-run decisions. Long-run decisions necessitate the discounting of cash flows received or spent beyond a year.

Numerous decisions involving the applications of these principles were discussed in this chapter. They include make or buy, dropping segments such as departments or product lines, special order pricing, sell or process further, joint and by-product analysis, and usage of limited resources. Differential costs and revenues of the various alternatives were considered along with possible opportunity costs arising from other uses of the resources being analyzed.

Relevant costing analysis requires that estimations of differential variables such as costs and revenues should be as accurate as possible within the constraints of available time and money. Problems should also be defined in a clear and understandable manner to avoid misconceptions.

Appendix 12—A
Allocating Production
with More than One Constraint:
Linear Programming

We considered in the chapter the problem created when one of the resources needed to produce two products was in short supply. The limited resource, or constraint, was machine hours. A contribution margin per machine hour was computed to compare products with different demands on the scarce resource. What if in addition to a constraint on machine time, the number of direct labor hours were limited? When two or more constraints or scarce resources are present, a more powerful approach is needed. **Linear programming** is a mathematical technique that is useful in a wide range of business situations when allocation decisions must be made in the presence of two or more constraints.

Recognizing the Uses and Limitations
of Linear Programming

The manager needs to be aware of the types of problems that lend themselves to a linear programming solution. First, as the name implies, it is necessary that the relationships among the variables be linear. **Linearity** as we will use the term refers to any relationship between variables that can be represented by a straight line. For example, $y = a + bx$ is a linear equation, whereas $y = a + bx^2$ indicates a curvilinear relationship between the variables x and y. Strictly speaking, only when the relationships are linear is linear programming a valid tool.

Linear programming has been used successfully in many different settings. Its applications range from the blending of gasoline to the scheduling of production facilities. A special application of linear programming, called the *transportation method*, has proven useful in determining the most economical routing for a company's vehicles, such as a fleet of delivery trucks or rail cars.

Depending on the number of variables (for example, products) and the number of constraints present, the actual mathematical solution to a linear programming problem can be fairly complex. These problems require the solution of a set of simultaneous equations but are easily manageable with the help of a computer. Rather than being able to solve the equations, it is much more important for the manager to be able to identify problems that are suited to a linear programming solution and to formulate the equations for the problem, based on an understanding of the facts in each situation. Although we will concentrate on these aspects of the problem, we will also see how simpler linear programming problems can be solved with a graphical approach.

Graphical Solution to a Simple Problem

Four basic steps are necessary in the solution of a linear programming problem:

1. Determine the objective and state it in terms of an equation, called the *objective function*;
2. Identify all of the constraints, and express the relationship of each constraint to the variables in the form of an equation;
3. Determine the feasible alternatives, taking into account the various constraints;
4. Determine which of the feasible alternatives provides the optimal solution to the objective function.

We will now illustrate how these four basic steps are used to solve a simple problem, using the following information:

Two products, X and Y, share the same production facility. Machine time in the facility is limited to 1,000 hours and direct labor time available is 1,600 hours. Each unit of X uses two hours of machine time, and each unit of Y takes one machine hour. Product X requires two direct labor hours, and Y takes four hours of labor. Finally, each unit of X contributes $6 to profits, while the contribution margin on Y is $10 per unit.

Step 1   Determine the **objective function,** which in our problem involves the maximization of contribution margin (CM):

Maximize CM: $6X$ + $10Y$

where X and Y represent the number of units of products X and Y that should be manufactured to maximize contribution margin. In the chapter, we saw how contribution margins could be expressed in terms of the limited resource. In this example, because X takes two hours of machine time the contribution margin per machine hour is $6/2 or $3 per hour. The contribution margin for Y is $10/1 or $10 per hour. However, an additional constraint, direct labor time available, requires that a more powerful tool, linear programming, be used.

Step 2   Identify each of the **constraints** and express each in the form of an equation. The two obvious constraints in our problem are the limited availability of machine time and labor time. Algebraically, the two constraints are

Machine hour constraint: $2X + 1Y \leq 1,000$ hours

Labor hour constraint: $2X + 4Y \leq 1,600$ hours

because only 1,000 hours of machine time are available, and each unit of X takes two hours and each unit of Y one hour, and only 1,600 direct labor hours are available, and each unit of X requires two hours and each unit of Y four hours. Two other constraints, although less obvious, must be identified to recognize that the production of each of the two products must be greater than or equal to zero. These are necessary so that when the problem is solved only positive solutions are considered. The nonnegativity constraints, as they are called, are stated as

Nonnegativity constraints: $X \geq 0$ and $Y \geq 0$

Step 3   Determine the **feasible alternatives,** taking into account the constraints. With 1,000 machine hours available, for example, we could produce 200 units of X and 600 units of Y [(200 × 2) + (600 × 1) = 1,000]. Or we could produce 300 units of X and 400 units of Y. Either one of these combinations requires 1,000 machine hours. However, neither of these combinations is feasible, considering the limited availability of direct labor. For example, the production of 600 units of Y alone would take 2,400 hours of labor time and only 1,600 total labor hours are available. A convenient way to portray the large number of possible alternatives, based on the various constraints, is to construct a graph, as illustrated in Exhibit 12–5 (page 434).

First, note that the two axes on the graph represent the number of units of each product to be produced. The nonnegativity constraint is represented by the fact that both the X and Y axes start at zero and move only in a positive direction. The two constraint lines indicate the boundaries for produc-

EXHIBIT 12—5

LP Problem with Two Constraints: Graphical Solution

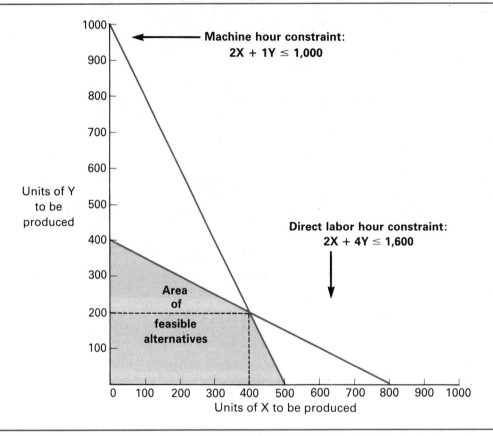

tion based on the two limited resources. The constraint lines can be drawn by determining the end points of each. For example, consider the machine hour constraint. If no units of X are produced and we assume that machine time is to be utilized to its capacity, according to the equation 1,000 units of Y could be produced:

$$2X + 1Y = 1,000$$

$$2(0) + 1Y = 1,000$$

$$Y = 1,000 \text{ units}$$

Thus, one end point of the machine hour constraint line is (0, 1,000), where the first number refers to the X axis and the second refers to the Y axis. The other end point for the machine constraint line is found by assuming no production of Y and solving for the equation:

$$2X + 1Y = 1,000$$

$$2X + 1(0) = 1,000$$

$$2X = 1,000$$

$$X = 500 \text{ units}$$

The other end point for the machine constraint line is therefore (500, 0).

Similar reasoning can be used to find the two end points for the direct labor time constraint. If no units of X are produced, the total 1,600 hours would be available to produce 400 units of Y. Or the entire 1,600 hours could be used to produce 800 units of X. Thus, the two sets of end points for the labor time constraint are (0, 400) and (800, 0).

Once the two constraint lines are drawn, the area of feasible alternatives becomes obvious, as indicated by the shaded area in Exhibit 12–5. Any mix of products X and Y within the shaded area is feasible because neither one of the two constraints is violated in this area.

Step 4 Determine which of the feasible alternatives provides the **optimal solution** to the objective function. Although any number of possible product mixes is feasible, only one represents the optimal solution, assuming our objective is to maximize contribution margin. We could find the optimal solution by computing the contribution margin for each of the different product mixes within the shaded area of the graph. But with the production of Y being any number from 0 to 400 units and the production of X ranging anywhere from 0 to 800 units, the number of tests that we would have to make would be staggering.

Fortunately, logic dictates that the optimal solution occurs at one of the *corners* of the feasible production area. At each of the corners, either one or both of the constraints is pushed to its limits. Because the objective is to maximize contribution margin, it makes sense to utilize the resources to the fullest extent possible in generating profits. However, would we be better off producing only Y and thus using all of the 1,600 direct labor hours available? Or would it be better to produce only X and fully utilize the 1,000 machine hours available? Or finally, what would be the contribution margin from producing a mix of the two products based on the point on the graph where the two constraint lines intersect (as indicated by the dotted lines in the exhibit)? We can find the optimal solution by simply comparing the contribution margins at each of the four corners:

Corner	Production of X	Y	Contribution Margin = $6X + $10Y	
0, 0	0	0	($6 × 0) + ($10 × 0)	= $0
0, 400	0	400	($6 × 0) + ($10 × 400)	= $4,000
400, 200	400	200	($6 × 400) + ($10 × 200)	= $4,400
500, 0	500	0	($6 × 500) + ($10 × 0)	= $3,000

Because the contribution margin of $4,400 from producing 400 units of X and 200 units of Y exceeds the margin at any one of the other corners on the graph, the objective function is satisfied by operating at this level.

Note that the best product mix occurs at the intersection of the two constraint lines on the graph. Because the solution is at the intersection, we can check on the accuracy of the hand-drawn graph by solving the equations simultaneously.

First, the two inequalities are changed to equalities:

(1) $2X + 1Y = 1,000$ machine time constraint

(2) $2X + 4Y = 1,600$ direct labor time constraint

Next, equation 1 is subtracted from equation 2:

$$
\begin{array}{rl}
(2) & 2X + 4Y = 1,600 \\
-(1) & \underline{2X + 1Y = 1,000} \\
& 0X + 3Y = 600 \\
& Y = 200 \text{ units}
\end{array}
$$

Finally, substituting Y = 200 into either one of the two equations:

(1) $2X + 1(200) = 1,000$

$2X = 1,000 - 200$

$2X = 800$

$X = 400$ units

Therefore, because the simultaneous solution to these two equations occurs at the point where X = 400 and Y = 200, this is in fact the exact intersection of the two constraint lines on the graph.

Extended Example: An Additional Constraint

Assume the same facts as before but with the addition of another constraint: the raw material needed to produce one of the two products, X, is in short supply. Only 3,000 pounds are available for product X, and each unit requires 10 pounds of the material. Therefore, production of X is limited to less than or equal to 300 units. Our solution to this problem proceeds as before, but with the addition of one more constraint equation:

Raw material constraint: $X \leq 300$

A graph of the feasible alternatives for this example is shown in Exhibit 12–6. The raw material constraint is indicated in the exhibit by the vertical line on the X axis at 300 units. Note the differences between the areas of feasible alternatives in Exhibits 12–5 and 12–6. The feasible alternatives in Exhibit 12–6 are fewer in number, with the addition of the raw material constraint. Note also that the machine hour constraint in Exhibit 12–6

EXHIBIT 12–6
LP Problem with Three Constraints: Graphical Solution

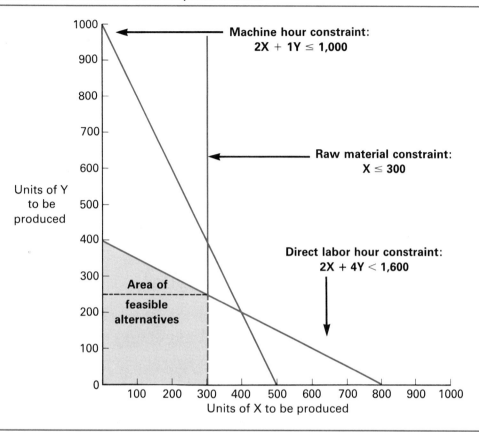

loses its significance because the line for it is totally outside the boundaries of the area of feasible alternatives. The only significant constraints in this example are the available direct labor for both products and raw material for product X.

Once the feasible alternatives have been determined (step 3), the best product mix can once again be found by comparing the contribution margins at each of the corners in the exhibit:

	Production of		
Corner	*X*	*Y*	*Contribution Margin = $6X + $10Y*
0, 0	0	0	($6 × 0) + ($10 × 0) = $0
0, 400	0	400	($6 × 0) + ($10 × 400) = $4,000
300, 250	300	250	($6 × 300) + ($10 × 250) = $4,300
300, 0	300	0	($6 × 300) + ($10 × 0) = $1,800

The profit maximizing product mix is now 300 units of X and 250 units of Y because this mix results in the highest contribution margin of any of the corner alternatives. As before, it is possible to check on the accuracy of the exact point of intersection in the solution by solving the constraint equations simultaneously. However, in this example, because the machine hour constraint is outside the area of feasible alternatives, this equation can be ignored, and we need solve only for the other two.

First, the two inequalities are changed to equalities:

(1) $2X + 4Y = 1,600$ direct labor hour constraint

(2) $X = 300$ raw material constraint

Next, X = 300 is substituted in the first equation and we solve for Y:

(1) $2(300) + 4Y = 1,600$

$$600 + 4Y = 1,600$$

$$4Y = 1,000$$

$$Y = 250 \text{ units}$$

Thus, the optimal solution in this example is to produce 300 units of X and 250 units of Y.

More Than Two Products: The Simplex Method

The graphical approach works as long as only two products are involved. The approach cannot be used, however, if more than two products, or variables, are present because this would require a three-dimensional (or more) graph. In addition, the equation technique that we used to check on the accuracy of the point of intersection becomes unwieldy if many more constraints are involved. The **simplex method** is a mathematical technique that is useful when a large number of variables and constraints are present in a linear programming problem. The technique involves an iterative approach in which the equations are solved simultaneously until an optimal solution is reached, with each solution being an improvement over the prior one. The actual mathematics of the solution can be carried out with the use of a computer. The manager's primary responsibilities are to identify those problems in which various techniques such as linear programming are useful and to aid in the formulation of the solution to the problems.

Key Terms

Constraints are limitations on factors such as resources or demand for the firm's products.

Feasible alternatives   are possible production alternatives given the particular constraints on resources.

Full capacity   occurs when no additional production can take place without eliminating something that is presently being produced.

Excess capacity   occurs when additional production can take place without eliminating any presently scheduled production.

Linear programming   is a mathematical technique that is useful in many business situations when allocation decisions must be made due to constraints being present.

Linearity   refers to any relationship between variables that can be represented by a straight line.

Make or buy   is a type of business decision concerning whether products, or parts thereof, should be made or bought.

Market segmentation   is the separation or splitting of markets so that sales in one market have little or no effect in the other market. The segmentation may be geographic or socioeconomic in nature.

Objective function   is the maximization of a revenue factor or a minimization of a cost factor in a linear programming problem.

Optimal solution   is the best of the feasible alternatives. It will be found at the corner of a production area in a linear programming problem.

Penetration pricing   is a pricing policy that attempts to capture a large market share by entering the market with a relatively low price.

Relevant cost   is one that is crucial to a decision. It must differ between alternatives and not merely be a reallocation of an existing cost.

Sell or process further   is a type of decision concerning whether incremental revenues or further processing exceed the incremental costs.

Simplex method   is a mathematical technique that is useful when a large number of variables and constraints are present in a linear programming problem.

Skim pricing   is a pricing policy that sets a relatively high initial price when a product is first introduced.

Special order   is a large order usually in a market that is not presently served. Buyers generally look for quantity type price discounts.

Questions

Q12–1   If increased output of a particular product were to result in a greater amount of overhead being charged to it (building depreciation, for example), would these costs be relevant to the decision of whether to increase output?

Q12–2   How do short-run and long-run decisions differ?

Q12–3   What are some of the qualitative factors underlying make or buy decisions?

Q12–4   From the standpoint of relevant cost analysis in make or buy and similar types of nonroutine decisions, what distinctions do we look for in fixed costs?

Q12–5   In a make or buy situation and other types of short-run nonroutine decisions, what is the significance of other uses of capacity that could become available as a result of the decision?

Q12–6   How does the concept of break-even enter into make or buy and other types of short-run nonroutine decisions?

Q12–7   If make or buy and other types of short-run nonroutine decisions involves selling fixed assets, how can this type of factor be plugged into the decision analysis?

Q12–8   Why is traditional income statement analysis often misleading in nonroutine decisions such as dropping departments or other segments?

Q12–9   What are synergistic effects in decisions involving dropping departments?

Q12–10   If a decision concerning the closing of a department involved the question of reassigning personnel from the department being closed to other departments, these costs would not be relevant to the decision because the costs of the personnel would be the same under either alternative. Comment on this statement.

Q12–11   What is usually involved in temporary plant shutdown situations?

Q12–12   What is return on investment pricing?

Q12–13   What is the potential weakness of the various formula pricing methods?

Q12–14   What are skim pricing and penetration pricing policies?

Q12–15   Why must the special order apply exclusively to situations where market segmentation is present?

Q12–16   What are some of the dangers of the special order?

Q12–17   How should joint costs be handled in situations involving a decision of whether to process one of the product lines further?

Q12–18   When deciding between production of different product lines when a scarce resource such as direct labor is present, why should one not use contribution margin of the product lines as a decision criterion?

Q12–19   What types of problems lend themselves to linear programming solutions?

Q12–20   Why do optimal solutions to linear programming problems invariably result in corners of the feasible production areas?

Q12–21   Briefly describe the four basic steps in the solution of a linear programming problem.

Q12–22   The use of LP in the solution of a production problem requires the recognition of the nonnegativity constraints. Explain what is meant by a *nonnegativity constraint*.

Q12–23   When is it necessary to abandon the use of the graphical method to solution of a linear programming problem in favor of the simplex method?

Exercises

E12–1   **Special order multiple choice.** Brike Company, which manufactures robes, has enough idle capacity available to accept a special order of 10,000 robes at $8 a robe. A predicted income statement for the year without this special order is as follows:

	Per Unit	Total
Sales	$12.50	$1,250,000
Manufacturing costs – variable	$ 6.25	$ 625,000
Manufacturing costs – fixed	1.75	175,000
Manufacturing costs – total	$ 8.00	$ 800,000
Gross profit	$ 4.50	$ 450,000
Selling expenses – variable	$ 1.80	$ 180,000
Selling expenses – fixed	1.45	145,000
Selling expenses – total	$ 3.25	$ 325,000
Operating income	$ 1.25	$ 125,000

Required:

1. Assuming no additional selling expenses, what would be the effect on operating income if the special order was accepted?
   a. $8,000 increase
   b. $17,500 increase
   c. $32,500 decrease
   d. $40,000 increase
2. Would the effect on contribution margin differ from your answer in 1? Explain briefly.

(CPA Adapted)

E12–2 **Make or buy, two departments.** A part used in the assembly of a final product is manufactured by the Watson Tool Company in two operations. Ordinarily 150,000 parts are manufactured each year with total manufacturing costs as follows:

Operation 1:

Direct materials	$ 84,000
Direct labor	78,000
Variable costs of supplies and indirect materials	18,000
Allocated costs of plant occupancy	40,000
	$220,000

Operation 2:

Direct labor	$23,000
Variable costs of supplies and indirect materials	11,000
Allocated costs of plant occupancy	30,000
	$64,000

Operation 1 can be eliminated if these parts are purchased from an outside supplier at a price of $1.10 per unit. The space used for operation 1 can be rented for $6,000 a year. The parts purchased from an outside supplier will still have to be put through operation 2. If the parts are purchased, Watson Tool Company must absorb the freight charges estimated at $15,000 a year.

Required: Should the parts be manufactured, or should they be purchased? Give computations to support your conclusion.

E12–3   **Special order, changing costs.** Corvina Company's variable costs for its anticipated output level of $800,000 sales consisting of 1,000 units of product are

Direct materials	$300,000
Direct labor	60,000
Variable overhead	40,000
Sales commissions	80,000

Corvina's fixed costs are $250,000. In addition, Corvina has the possibility of taking on a special order of 250 units that are very similar to their regular line. The nature of this special order is such that direct materials would increase by 10% per unit. However, there would be no sales commissions. Because of the fact that production went beyond their relevant range, fixed costs would increase by $7,500.

Required: What would the price per unit have to be on the special order to give Corvina a total profit equal to 10% of their regular sales?

E12–4   **Special order, multiple choice.** Bar Harbor Company manufactures a leisure boot. The boot regularly sells for $50 a pair. Variable manufacturing costs are $20 a pair, and fixed manufacturing costs are $8 a pair. Davart Shoe, a large wholesaler located in Brockton, Massachusetts, would be willing to pay $26 a pair for 3,000 pairs. The company has enough excess capacity to take the job on without incurring any extra fixed costs.

Required: Operating income for Bar Harbor would experience a(n)

a. $6,000 decrease.
b. $18,000 increase.
c. $6,000 increase.
d. None of the above.

E12–5   **Make or buy, avoidable costs and opportunity costs.** Rutland Company manufactures a part for use in its production cycle. Cost per unit for the part is

Direct materials	$ 8
Direct labor	15
Variable manufacturing overhead	6
Fixed manufacturing overhead	11
	$40

Fredonia Company manufactures a similar part and would sell Rutland its needed 5,000 parts for $38 per unit. If Fredonia gets the job, $3 of the fixed manufacturing overhead per unit could be avoided. In addition, the released facilities that would not be needed for the production could be leased for $20,000 per year.

Required: Based purely on relevant cost differences should Rutland make or buy?

E12–6   **Special order, producing at full capacity.** Annual productive capacity of Kaftan Company is 25,000 units a year. Budgeted operating results for 19X9 are:

Revenues (20,000 units @ $100)		$2,000,000
Variable costs		
Manufacturing	$800,000	
Selling	200,000	1,000,000
Contribution margin		$1,000,000
Fixed costs		
Manufacturing	$200,000	
Selling and administrative	350,000	550,000
Operating income		$ 450,000

A foreign wholesaler wants to buy 8,000 units at a price of $80 per unit. Production cannot exceed 25,000 units. Variable manufacturing costs would be the same per unit but variable selling costs would increase by $3 per unit on the special order only.

Required: 1. If Kaftan has to either take or reject the entire 8,000 units, what should it do in terms of maximizing its contribution margin? Show figures.
2. Suppose that Kaftan could take on the special order for as many units as it is willing to supply *up to* 8,000 units. What should it do?

E12–7 **Joint product, sell or process further.** Mullaney Company manufactures three joint products: A, B, and C. During 19X0, the anticipated production of C would be 10,000 units that have a selling price of $7 per unit at the split-off point. The joint costs assigned to it would be $30,000. If C is processed further, it would sell for $10 per unit. Additional processing costs (all variable) would be $20,000. Total joint costs assigned to C, if it is processed further, would be $42,000.

Required: Should the product be processed further or sold at split-off? Show figures.

E12–8 **Elimination of a division, multiple choice.** Rice Corporation currently operates two divisions, which had operating results for the year ended December 31, 19X2, as follows:

	West Division	Troy Division
Sales	$600,000	$300,000
Variable costs	310,000	200,000
Contribution margin	$290,000	$100,000
Fixed costs for the division	110,000	70,000
Margin over direct costs	$180,000	$ 30,000
Allocated corporate costs	90,000	45,000
Operating income (loss)	$ 90,000	$ (15,000)

Because the Troy division also sustained an operating loss during 19X1, Rice's president is considering the elimination of this division. Assume that the Troy Division fixed costs could be avoided if the division were eliminated. If the Troy Division had been eliminated on January 1, 19X2, Rice Corporation's 19X2 operating income would have been

a. $15,000 higher.
b. $30,000 lower.
c. $45,000 lower.
d. $60,000 higher.

(CPA Adapted)

E12–9   **Make or buy, multiple choice.** Motor Company manufactures 10,000 units of part M1 for use in its production annually. The following costs are reported:

Direct materials	$ 20,000
Direct labor	55,000
Variable overhead	45,000
Fixed overhead	70,000
	$190,000

Valve Company has offered to sell Motor 10,000 units of part M1 for $18 per unit. If Motor accepts the offer, some of the facilities presently used to manufacture part M1 could be rented to a third party at an annual rental of $15,000. Additionally, $4 per unit of the fixed overhead applied to part M1 would be totally eliminated. Should Motor accept Valve's offer, and why?

a. No, because it would be $5,000 cheaper to make the part.
b. Yes, because it would be $10,000 cheaper to buy the part.
c. No, because it would be $15,000 cheaper to make the part.
d. Yes, because it would be $25,000 cheaper to buy the part.

(CPA Adapted)

E12–10   **Usage of limited resources.** Dolich Company manufactures two products, P1 and P2. Contribution margin information for each product *per unit* is:

	P1	P2
Revenue	$50	$100
Variable costs	25	40
Contribution margin	$25	$ 60

Total demand for P1 is 7,000 units and for P2 is 12,000 units. Direct labor is a scarce resource. 10,000 total direct labor hours are available during the coming year. P1 requires 1 direct labor hour per unit and P2 requires 3 direct labor hours per unit.

Required: How many units of P1 and P2 should Dolich produce?

E12–11   **Pricing using return on investment.** Antheil Company has total assets of $2,000,000. Variable cost per unit is $50. Total fixed costs are $750,000.

Required: 1. Assume that the firm wants to determine the selling price for 10,000 units if it is desired to earn a 15% return on investment. Determine the selling price per unit.
2. What danger do you see in this form of pricing?

Problems

P12–12   **Make or buy.** Scoopa Company is investigating whether to continue manufacturing a part, called the *Faktron*, or to buy it from an outside supplier. Your investigation has revealed the following information:

When you had completed your audit of the Scoopa Company, the management staff asked for your assistance in arriving at a decision whether to continue manufacturing a part or to buy it from an outside supplier. The part is a component used in some of the finished products of the company.

From your audit working papers and from further investigation, you develop the following data as being typical of the company operations.

1. The annual requirement for Faktrons is 5,000 units. The lowest quotation from a supplier was $8 per unit.
2. Faktrons have been manufactured in the Precision Machinery Department. If Faktrons are purchased from an outside supplier, certain machinery will be sold, and the company would realize its book value.
3. Following are the total costs of the Precision Machinery Department during the year under audit when 5,000 Faktrons were made:

Materials	$67,500
Direct labor	50,000
Indirect labor	20,000
Light and heat	5,500
Power	3,000
Depreciation	10,000
Property taxes and insurance	8,000
Payroll taxes and other benefits	9,800
Other	5,000

4. The following Precision Machinery Department costs apply to the manufacture of Faktrons: material, $17,500; direct labor, $28,000; indirect labor, $6,000; power, $300; other, $500. The sale of equipment used for Faktrons would reduce the following costs by the amounts indicated: depreciation, $2,000; property taxes and insurance, $1,000.
5. The following additional Precision Machinery Department costs would be incurred if Faktrons were purchased from an outside supplier: freight, $.50 per unit; indirect labor for receiving, materials handling, inspection, etc., $5,000. The cost of the purchased Faktrons would be considered a Precision Machinery Department Cost.

Required:

1. Prepare a schedule showing a comparison of the relevant costs of making and buying Faktrons.
2. Discuss the considerations in addition to the cost factors that you would bring to the attention of the management team in assisting them to arrive at a decision whether to make or buy Faktrons. Include in your discussion the considerations that might be applied to the evaluation of the outside supplier.

(CPA Adapted)

P12–13   **Pricing formula for special order.** Framar Inc. manufactures automation machinery according to customer specifications. The company is relatively new and has grown each year. Framar operated at about 75% of capacity during the 19X7–X8 fiscal year. The operating results for the most recent fiscal year are presented below.

FRAMAR INC.
Income Statement
For the Year Ended September 30, 19X8
($000 omitted)

Sales		$25,000
Less: sales commissions		2,500
Net sales		$22,500
Expenses		
Direct material		$ 6,000
Direct labor		7,500
Manufacturing overhead – variable		
Supplies	$ 625	
Indirect labor	1,500	
Power	125	2,250
Manufacturing overhead – fixed		
Supervision	$ 500	
Depreciation	1,000	1,500
Corporate administration		750
Total expenses		$18,000
Net income before taxes		$ 4,500
Income taxes (40%)		1,800
Net income		$ 2,700

Most of the management personnel had worked for firms in this type of business before joining Framar, but none of the top management had been responsible for overall corporate operations or for final decisions on prices. Nevertheless, the company has been successful.

The top management of Framar wants to have a more organized and formal pricing system to prepare quotes for potential customers. Therefore, it has developed the pricing formula presented below. The formula is based on the company's operating results achieved during the 19X7–X8 fiscal year. The relationships used in the formula are expected to continue during the 19X8–X9 year. The company expects to operate at 75% of practical capacity during the current 19X8–X9 fiscal year.

APA Inc. has asked Framar to submit a bid on some custom-designed machinery. Framar used the new formula to develop a price and submitted a bid of $165,000 to APA Inc. The calculations to arrive at the bid price are given next to the pricing formula shown below.

Pricing Formula

Details of Formula	APA Bid Calculations
Estimated direct material cost	$ 29,200
Estimated direct labor cost	56,000
Estimated manufacturing overhead calculated at 50% of direct labor	28,000

Pricing Formula (continued)

Details of Formula	APA Bid Calculations
Estimated corporate overhead calculated at 10% of direct labor	5,600
Estimated total costs excluding sales commissions	$118,800
Add 25% for profits and taxes	29,700
Suggested price (with profits) before sales commissions	$148,500
Suggested total price equals suggested price divided by .9 to adjust for 10% sales commission	$165,000

Required: 1. Calculate the impact the order from APA Inc. would have on Framar Inc.'s net income after taxes if Framar's bid of $165,000 were accepted by APA.
2. Assume that APA Inc. has rejected Framar's price but has stated that it is willing to pay $127,000 for the machinery. Should Framar Inc. manufacture the machinery for the counter offer of $127,000? Explain your answer.
3. Calculate the lowest price that Framar Inc. can quote on this machinery without reducing its net income after taxes if it should manufacture the machinery.
4. Explain how the profit performance in 19X8–X9 would be affected if Framar Inc. accepted all of its work at prices similar to the $127,000 counter offer of APA Inc. described in 2 above.

(CMA Adapted)

P12–14   **Adding a product.**   Helene's, a high-fashion women's dress manufacturer, is planning to market a new cocktail dress for the coming season. Helene's supplies retailers in the east and mid-Atlantic states.

Four yards of material are required to lay out the dress pattern. Some material remains after cutting that can be sold as remnants.

The leftover material could also be used to manufacture matching cape and handbag. However, if the leftover material is to be used for the cape and handbag, more care will be required in the cutting, which will increase the cutting costs.

The company expected to sell 1,250 dresses if no matching cape or handbag were available. Helene's market research reveals that dress sales will be 20% higher if a matching cape and handbag are available. The market research indicates that the cape and/or handbag will not be sold individually but only as accessories with the dress. The various combinations of dresses, capes, and handbags that are expected to be sold by retailers are as follows.

	Percent of Total
Complete sets of dress, cape, and handbag	70%
Dress and cape	6
Dress and handbag	15
Dress only	9
Total	100%

The material used in the dress costs $12.50 a yard or $50.00 for each dress. The cost of cutting the dress if the cape and handbag are not manufactured is estimated at

$20.00 a dress, and the resulting remnants can be sold for $5.00 for each dress cut out. If the cape and handbag are to be manufactured, the cutting costs will be increased by $9.00 per dress. There will be no salable remnants if the capes and handbags are manufactured in the quantities estimated.

The selling prices and the costs to complete the three items once they are cut are presented below.

	Selling Price per Unit	Unit Cost to Complete (excludes cost of material and cutting operation)
Dress	$200.00	$80.00
Cape	27.50	19.50
Handbag	9.50	6.50

Required:

1. Calculate Helene's incremental profit or loss from manufacturing the capes and handbags in conjunction with the dresses.
2. Identify any nonquantitative factors that could influence Helene's management in its decision to manufacture the capes and handbags that match the dress.

(CMA Adapted)

P12–15 **Dropping a department.** Ace Publishing Company is in the business of publishing and printing guide books and directories. The board of directors has engaged you to make a cost study to determine whether the company is economically justified in continuing to print, as well as publish, its books and directories. You obtain the following information from the company's cost accounting records for the preceding fiscal year:

	Departments			
	Publishing	Printing	Shipping	Total
Salaries & wages	$275,000	$150,000	$25,000	$ 450,000
Telephone & telegraph	12,000	3,700	300	16,000
Materials & supplies	50,000	250,000	10,000	310,000
Occupancy costs	75,000	80,000	10,000	165,000
General & administrative	40,000	30,000	4,000	74,000
Depreciation	5,000	40,000	5,000	50,000
	$457,000	$553,700	$54,300	$1,065,000

Additional data:

1. A review of personnel requirements indicates that, if printing is discontinued, the Publishing Department will need one additional clerk at $4,000 per year to handle correspondence with the printer. Two layout people and a proofreader will be required at an aggregate annual cost of $17,000; other personnel in the Printing Department can be released. One mailing clerk, at $3,000, will be retained; others in the Shipping Department can be released. Employees whose employment was being terminated would immediately receive, on the average, three months' termination pay. The termination pay would be amortized over a five-year period.
2. Long distance telephone and telegraph charges are identified and distributed to the responsible department. The remainder of the telephone bill, representing basic service at a cost of $4,000, was allocated in the ratio of 10 to Publishing,

5 to Printing, and 1 to Shipping. The discontinuance of printing is not expected to have a material effect on the basic service cost.

3. Shipping supplies consist of cartons, envelopes, and stamps. It is estimated that the cost of envelopes and stamps for mailing material to an outside printer would be $5,000 per year.

4. If printing is discontinued, the company would retain its present building but would sublet a portion of the space at an annual rental of $50,000. Taxes, insurance, heat, light, and other occupancy costs would not be significantly affected.

5. One cost clerk would not be required ($5,000 per year) if printing is discontinued. Other general and administrative personnel would be retained.

6. Included in administrative expenses is interest expense on a 5% mortgage loan of $500,000.

7. Printing and shipping room machinery and equipment having a net book value of $300,000 can be sold without gain or loss. These funds in excess of termination pay would be invested in marketable securities earning 5%.

8. The company has received a proposal for a five-year contract from an outside printer, under which the volume of work done last year would be printed at a cost of $550,000 per year.

9. Assume continued volume and prices at last year's level.

Required: Prepare a statement setting forth in comparative form the costs of operation of the Printing and Shipping departments under the present arrangement and under an arrangement in which inside printing is discontinued. Summarize the net saving or extra cost in case printing is discontinued.

(CPA Adapted)

P12–16   **Make or buy.** Southwest Company is analyzing whether to make or buy mansers, a component of their major product. The annual requirement for mansers is 10,000 units and the part is available from an outside supplier in any quantity at $5 per unit. The following information is available:

1. The Machining Department starts and substantially completes mansers, and minor finishing is completed by the use of direct labor in the Finishing Department. The Assembly Department places mansers in the finished product.

2. Machinery used to produce mansers could be sold for its book value of $15,000 and the proceeds invested at 6% per year if the mansers were purchased. Property taxes and insurance would decrease $300 per year if the machinery were sold. The machinery has a remaining life of ten years with no estimated salvage value.

3. The Machining Department is about 25% devoted to the production of mansers, but labor and some other costs for mansers in this department could be reduced without affecting other operations. The costs of the Finishing Department include direct labor totaling $800, devoted to mansers. If mansers were not manufactured, one-half of the resulting available direct labor would be used as indirect labor and the remaining one-half would result in paid idle time of employees.

4. In 19X7 when 10,000 mansers were produced, pertinent Machining Department costs were as shown on the next page.

	Total Costs	Cost Charged to Mansers
Materials	$95,000	$24,200
Direct labor	39,400	12,200
Indirect labor	20,600	7,800
Heat and light	12,000	3,000
Depreciation	6,000	1,500
Property taxes and insurance	15,000	3,750
Production supplies	4,000	800

5. In addition, the Machining Department total costs include $18,300 payroll taxes and other benefits.
6. Overhead allocated on the basis of 200% of direct-labor cost was $40,000 for the Finishing Department and $20,000 for the Assembly Department in 19X7. Overhead in these departments is 25% fixed and 75% variable.
7. If mansers are purchased, Southwest will incur added costs of $.45 per unit for freight and $3,000 per year for receiving, handling, and inspection of product.

Required: Prepare a schedule comparing the total annual cost of mansers if the company manufactured them with the annual cost if purchased. (Ignore income taxes.)

(CPA Adapted)

P12–17 **Eliminating a product line, imputed costs.** The Scio Division of Georgetown Inc. manufactures and sells four related product lines. Each product is produced at one or more of the three manufacturing plants of the division. Presented below is a product line profitability statment for the year ended December 31, 19X7, which shows a loss for the baseball equipment line. A similar loss is projected for 19X8.

The baseball equipment is manufactured in the Evanston Plant. Some football equipment and all miscellaneous sports items also are processed through this plant. A few of the miscellaneous items are manufactured, and the remainder are purchased for resale. The item purchased for resale is recorded as materials in the records. A separate production line is used to produce the products of each product line.

A cost schedule presents the costs incurred at the Evanston Plant in 19X7. Inventories at the end of the year were substantially identical to those at the beginning of the year.

The management of Georgetown Inc. has requested a profitability study of the baseball equipment line to determine if the line should be discontinued. The Marketing Department of the Scio Division and the Accounting Department at the plant have developed the following additional data to be used in the study:

1. If the baseball equipment line is discontinued, the company will lose approximately 10% of its sales in each of the other lines.

Product Line Profitability — 19X7
($000 omitted)

	Football Equipment	Baseball Equipment	Hockey Equipment	Miscellaneous Sports Items	Total
Sales	$2,200	$1,000	$1,500	$500	$5,200
Cost of goods sold:					
Material	$ 400	$ 175	$ 300	$ 90	$ 965
Labor and variable overhead	800	400	600	60	1,860

	Football Equipment	Baseball Equipment	Hockey Equipment	Miscellaneous Sports Items	Total
Fixed overhead	350	275	100	50	775
Total	$1,550	$ 850	$1,000	$200	$3,600
Gross profit	$ 650	$ 150	$ 500	$300	$1,600
Selling expense:					
Variable	$ 440	$ 200	$ 300	$100	$1,040
Fixed	100	50	100	50	300
Corporate administration expenses	48	24	36	12	120
Total	$ 588	$ 274	$ 436	$162	$1,460
Contribution to corporation	$ 62	$ (124)	$ 64	$138	$ 140

2. The equipment now used in the manufacture of baseball equipment is quite specialized. It has a current salvage value of $105,000 and a remaining useful life of five years. This equipment cannot be used elsewhere in the company.
3. The plant space now occupied by the baseball equipment line could be closed off from the rest of the plant and rented for $175,000 per year.
4. If the line is discontinued, the supervisor of the baseball equipment line will be released. In keeping with company policy he would receive severance pay of $5,000.
5. The company has been able to invest excess funds at 10% per annum.

Evanston plant costs are shown below.

Evanston Plant Costs – 19X7
($000 omitted)

	Football Equipment	Baseball Equipment	Miscellaneous Sports Items	Total
Material	$100	$175	$ 90	$ 365
Labor	$100	$200	$ 30	$ 330
Variable overhead				
Supplies	$ 85	$ 60	$ 12	$ 157
Power	50	110	7	167
Other	15	30	11	56
Subtotal	$150	$200	$ 30	$ 380
Fixed overhead				
Supervision[a]	$ 25	$ 30	$ 21	$ 76
Depreciation[b]	40	115	14	169
Plant rentals[c]	35	105	10	150
Other[d]	20	25	5	50
Subtotal	$120	$275	$ 50	$ 445
Total costs	$470	$850	$200	$1,520

[a]The supervision costs represent salary and benefit costs of the supervisors in charge of each product line.
[b]Depreciation costs for machinery and equipment is charged to the product line on which the machinery is used.
[c]The plant is leased. The lease rentals are charged to the product lines on the basis of square feet occupied.
[d]Other fixed overhead costs are the cost of plant administration and are allocated arbitrarily by management decision.

(CMA Adapted)

Required: Should Georgetown Inc. discontinue the baseball equipment line? Support your answer with appropriate calculations and qualitative arguments.

P12–18 **Plant shutdown.** You have been engaged to assist the management of the Arcadia Corporation in arriving at certain decisions. Arcadia has its home office in Ohio and leases factory buildings in Texas, Montana, and Maine, all of which produce the same product. The management of Arcadia has provided you with a projection of operations for 19X6, the forthcoming year, as follows:

	Total	Texas	Montana	Maine
Sales	$4,400,000	$2,200,000	$1,400,000	$800,000
Fixed costs:				
Factory	$1,100,000	$ 560,000	$ 280,000	$260,000
Administrative	350,000	210,000	110,000	30,000
Variable costs	1,450,000	665,000	425,000	360,000
Allocated home office costs	500,000	225,000	175,000	100,000
Total	$3,400,000	$1,660,000	$ 990,000	$750,000
Net profit from operations	$1,000,000	$ 540,000	$ 410,000	$ 50,000

The sales price per unit is $25.

Due to the marginal results of operations of the factory in Maine, Arcadia has decided to cease operations and sell that factory's machinery and equipment by the end of 19X5. Arcadia expects that the proceeds from the sale of these assets would be greater than their book value and would cover all termination costs.

Arcadia, however, would like to continue serving its customers in that area if it is economically feasible and is considering one of the following three alternatives (total home office costs of $500,000 will remain the same under all conditions):

1. Expand the operations of the Montana factory by using space presently idle. This move would result in the following changes in that factory's operations:

	Increase over Factory's Current Operations
Sales	50%
Fixed costs:	
Factory	20%
Administrative	10%

Under this proposal, variable costs would be $8 per unit sold.

2. Enter into a long-term contract with a competitor who will serve that area's customers. This competitor would pay Arcadia a royalty of $4 per unit based on an estimate of 30,000 units being sold.

3. Close the Maine factory and not expand the operations of the Montana factory.

Required: In order to assist the management of Arcadia Corporation to determine which alternative is most economically feasible, prepare a schedule computing Arcadia's estimated net profit from total operations that would result from each of the following methods:

1. Expansion of the Montana factory.
2. Negotiation of long-term contract on a royalty basis.
3. Shutdown of Maine operations with no expansion at other locations.

(CPA Adapted)

P12–19   **Pricing a product already produced, sunk costs.** Auer Company had received an
order for a piece of special machinery from Jay Company. Just as Auer Company completed the machine, Jay Company declared bankruptcy and forfeited a downpayment
of $7,500 on the order. Auer's manufacturing manager identified the costs already
incurred in the production of the special machinery for Jay as follows:

Direct materials used		$16,600
Direct labor incurred		21,400
Overhead applied:		
Manufacturing:		
Variable	$10,700	
Fixed	5,350	16,050
Fixed selling and administrative		5,405
Total cost		$59,455

Another company, Kaytell Corp., would be interested in buying the special machinery
if it were reworked to Kaytell's specifications. Auer has offered to sell the reworked
special machinery to Kaytell as a special order for a net price of $68,400. Kaytell has
agreed to pay the net price when it takes delivery. The additional identifiable costs to
rework the machinery to Kaytell's specifications are as follows:

Direct materials	$ 6,200
Direct labor	4,200
	$10,400

A second alternative available to Auer is to convert the special machinery to the standard model. The standard model lists for $62,500. The additional identifiable costs to
convert the special machinery to the standard model are

Direct materials	$2,850
Direct labor	3,300
	$6,150

A third alternative for the Auer Company is to sell, as a special order, the
machine as is (without modification) for a net price of $52,000. The following addi-
tional information is available regarding Auer's operations:

Sales commission rate on sales of standard models is 2%, while on special orders
it is 3%. All sales commissions are calculated on net sales price (that is, list price less
cash discount, if any).

Normal credit terms for sales of standard models are 2/10, net/30. Customers
take the discounts except in rare instances. Credit terms for special orders are negotiated with the customer and usually do *not* include a discount.

The application rates for manufacturing overhead and the fixed selling and administrative costs are as follows:

Manufacturing:	
Variable	50% of direct labor cost
Fixed	25% of direct labor cost
Selling and administrative:	
Fixed	10% of the total of direct material, direct labor,
	and manufacturing overhead costs

Auer normally sells a sufficient number of standard models to allow it to operate
at a volume in excess of the break-even point.

Required:

1. Determine the dollar contribution margin that each of the three alternatives will add to the Auer Company's before-tax profits.
2. If Kaytell makes Auer a counteroffer, what is the lowest price that Auer should accept for the reworked machinery from Kaytell? Explain your answer.
3. Discuss the influence that fixed factory overhead cost should have on the sales prices quoted by Auer for special orders when:
   a. A firm is operating at or below the break-even point.
   b. A firm's special orders constitute efficient utilization of unused capacity above the break-even volume.

(CMA Adapted)

P12–20   **Special order, production in excess of capacity limits.** Jenco Inc. manufactures a combination fertilizer/weed-killer under the name Fertikil. This is the only product Jenco produces at the present time. Fertikil is sold nationwide through normal marketing channels to retail nurseries and garden stores.

Taylor Nursery plans to sell a similar fertilizer/weed-killer compound through its regional nursery chain under its own private label. Taylor has asked Jenco to submit a bid for a 25,000 pound order of the private brand compound. Although the chemical composition of the Taylor compound differs from Fertikil, the manufacturing process is very similar.

The Taylor compound would be produced in 1,000 pound lots. Each lot would require 60 direct labor hours and the following chemicals:

Chemicals	Quantity in Pounds
CW-3	400
JX-6	300
MZ-8	200
BE-7	100

The first three chemicals (CW-3, JX-6, MZ-8) are all used in the production of Fertikil. BE-7 was used in a compound that Jenco has discontinued. This chemical was not sold or discarded because it does not deteriorate, and there have been adequate storage facilities. Jenco could sell BE-7 at the prevailing market price less $.10 per pound selling/handling expenses.

Jenco also has on hand a chemical called CN-5, which was manufactured for use in another product that is no longer produced. CN-5, which cannot be used in Fertikil, can be substituted for CW-3 on a one-for-one basis without affecting the quality of the Taylor compound. The quantity of CN-5 in inventory has a salvage value of $500.

Inventory and cost data for the chemicals that can be used to produce the Taylor compound are as shown below.

Raw Material	Pounds Inventory	Actual Price per Pound When Purchased	Current Market Price per Pound
CW-3	22,000	$ .80	$ .90
JX-6	5,000	.55	.60
MZ-8	8,000	1.40	1.60
BE-7	4,000	.60	.65
CN-5	5,500	.75	(salvage)

The current direct labor rate is $7.00 per hour. The manufacturing overhead rate is established at the beginning of the year and is applied consistently throughout the year using direct labor hours (DLH) as the base. The predetermined overhead rate for the current year, based on a two-shift capacity of 400,000 total DLH with no overtime, is as follows:

Variable manufacturing overhead	$2.25 per DLH
Fixed manufacturing overhead	3.75 per DLH
Combined rate	$6.00 per DLH

Jenco's production manager reports that the present equipment and facilities are adequate to manufacture the Taylor compound. However, Jenco is within 800 hours of its two-shift capacity this month before it must schedule overtime. If need be, the Taylor compound could be produced on regular time by shifting a portion of Fertikil production to overtime. Jenco's rate for overtime hours is one-and-one-half the regular pay rate or $10.50 per hour. There is no allowance for any overtime premium in the manufacturing overhead rate.

Jenco's standard markup policy for new products is 25% of full manufacturing cost.

Required:

1. Assume Jenco Inc. has decided to submit a bid for a 25,000 pound order of Taylor's new compound. The order must be delivered by the end of the current month. Taylor has indicated that this is a one-time order that will not be repeated.

   Calculate the lowest price that Jenco should bid for the order and not reduce its net income.

2. Without prejudice to your answer to requirement 1, assume that Taylor Nursery plans to place regular orders for 25,000 pound lots of the new compound during the coming year. Jenco expects the demand for Fertikil to remain strong again in the coming year. Therefore, the recurring orders from Taylor will put Jenco over its two-shift capacity. However, production can be scheduled so that 60% of each Taylor order can be completed during regular hours or Fertikil production could be shifted temporarily to overtime so that the Taylor orders could be produced on regular time. Jenco's production manager has estimated that the prices of all chemicals will stabilize at the current market rates for the coming year and that all other manufacturing costs are expected to be maintained at the same rates or amounts.

   Calculate the price Jenco Inc. should quote Taylor Nursery for each 25,000 pound lot of the new compound assuming that there will be recurring orders during the coming year.

(CMA Adapted)

P12–21 **Usage of pricing formulas.** The Fiore Company manufactures office equipment for sale to retail stores. Tim Lucas, vice-president of marketing, has proposed that Fiore introduce two new products to its line — an electric stapler and an electric pencil sharpener.

Lucas has requested that Fiore's Profit Planning Department develop preliminary selling prices for the two new products for his review. Profit Planning is to follow the company's standard policy for developing potential selling prices using as much data as available for each product. Data accumulated by Profit Planning regarding these two new products are reproduced on the next page.

	Electric Stapler	Electric Pencil Sharpener
Estimated annual demand in units	12,000	10,000
Estimated unit manufacturing costs	$10.00	$12.00
Estimated unit selling and administrative expenses	$4.00	$8.00
Assets employed in manufacturing	$180,000	Not available

Fiore plans to employ an average of $2,400,000 of assets to support its operations in the current year. The condensed pro forma operating income statement presented below represents Fiore's planned goals with respect to cost relationships and return-on-assets employed for the entire company for all of its products.

FIORE COMPANY
Pro Forma Operating Income Statement
For the Year Ending May 31, 19X5
($000 omitted)

Revenue	$4,800
Cost of goods sold (manufacturing costs)	2,880
Gross profit	$1,920
Selling and administrative expenses	1,440
Operating profit	$ 480

Required:

1. Calculate a potential selling price using last year's rates for
   a. electric stapler using return-on-investment pricing.
   b. electric pencil sharpener with mark-up based on total costs.
2. Could a selling price for the electric pencil sharpener be calculated using return-on-assets pricing? Explain your answer.
3. Which of the two pricing methods — return-on-investment pricing or mark-up on total costs — is more appropriate for decision analysis? Explain your answer.
4. Discuss the additional steps that Tim Lucas is likely to take after he receives the potential selling prices for the two new products (as calculated in 1 above) to set an actual selling price for each of the two products.

(CMA Adapted)

P12–22 **Evaluating different opportunities.** Ruidoso Ski Lodge operates a ski shop, restaurant, and lodge during the 120-day ski season from November 15 to March 15. The proprietor is considering changing his operations and keeping the lodge open all year. Results of the operations for the year ended March 15, 19X1, were as follows:

	Ski Shop		Restaurant		Lodge	
	Amount	Percent	Amount	Percent	Amount	Percent
Revenue	$27,000	100%	$40,000	100%	$108,000	100%
Costs:						
Cost of goods sold	$14,850	55	$24,000	60		
Supplies	1,350	5	4,000	10	$ 7,560	7
Utilities	270	1	1,200	3	2,160	2

	Ski Shop		Restaurant		Lodge	
	Amount	Percent	Amount	Percent	Amount	Percent
Salaries	1,620	6	12,000	30	32,400	30
Insurance	810	3	800	2	9,720	9
Property taxes on building	540	2	1,600	4	6,480	6
Depreciation	1,080	4	2,000	5	28,080	26
Total costs	$20,520	76	$45,600	114	$ 86,400	80
Net income or (loss)	$ 6,480	24%	$ (5,600)	(14)%	$ 21,600	20%

1. The lodge has 100 rooms, and the rate from November 15 to March 15 is $10 per day for one or two persons. The occupancy rate from November 15 to March 15 is 90%.
2. Ski shop and restaurant sales vary in direct proportion to room occupancy.
3. For the ski shop and restaurant, cost of goods sold, supplies, and utilities vary in direct proportion to sales. For the lodge, supplies and utilities vary in direct proportion to room occupancy.
4. The ski shop, restaurant, and lodge are located in the same building. Depreciation on the building is charged to the lodge. The ski shop and restaurant are charged with depreciation only on equipment. The full cost of the restaurant equipment became fully depreciated on March 15, 19X1, but the equipment has a remaining useful life of 3 years. The equipment can be sold for $1,200 but will be worthless in 3 years. All depreciation is computed by the straight-line method.
5. Insurance premiums are for annual coverage for public liability and fire insurance on the building and equipment. All building insurance is charged to the lodge.
6. Salaries are the minimum necessary to keep each facility open and are for the ski season only except for the lodge security guard who is paid $5,400 per year.

Two alternatives are being considered for the future operation of Ruidoso Ski Lodge:

1. The proprietor believes that during the ski season the restaurant should be closed because "it does not have enough revenue to cover its out-of-pocket costs." It is estimated that lodge occupancy would drop to 80% of capacity if the restaurant were closed during the ski season. The space utilized by the restaurant would be used as a lounge for lodge guests.
2. The proprietor is considering keeping the lodge open from March 15 to November 15. The ski shop would be converted into a gift shop if the lodge should be operated during this period with conversion costs of $1,000 in March and $1,000 in November each year. It is estimated that revenues from the gift shop would be the same per room occupied as revenues from the ski shop, that variable costs would be in the same ratio to revenues, and that all other costs would be the same for the gift shop as for the ski shop. The occupancy rate of the lodge at a room rate of $7 per day is estimated at 50% during the period from March 15 to November 15 whether or not the restaurant is operated.

Required:

1. Prepare a projected income statement for the ski shop and lodge from November 15, 19X1, to March 15, 19X2, assuming the restaurant is closed during this period and all facilities are closed during the remainder of the year.

2. Assume that all facilities will continue to be operated during the 4-month period of November 15 to March 15 of each year.

   a. Assume that the lodge is operated during the 8 months from March 15 to November 15. Prepare an analysis that indicates the projected marginal income or loss of operating the gift shop and lodge during this 8-month period.

   b. Compute the minimum room rate that should be charged to allow the lodge to break even during the 8 months from March 15 to November 15 assuming the gift shop and restaurant are not operated during this period.

   Ignore income taxes and use 30 days per month for computational purposes.

   (CPA Adapted)

P12–23 **Linear programming.** A company markets two products, Alpha and Gamma. The marginal contributions per gallon are $5 for Alpha and $4 for Gamma. Both products consist of two ingredients, D and K. Alpha contains 80% D and 20% K, while the proportions of the same ingredients in Gamma are 40% and 60%, respectively. The current inventory is 16,000 gallons of D and 6,000 gallons of K. The only company producing D and K is on strike and will neither deliver nor produce them in the foreseeable future. The company wishes to know the numbers of gallons of Alpha and Gamma that it should produce with its present stock of raw materials in order to maximize its total revenue.

1. The objective function for this problem could be expressed as:
   a. $f_{max} = 0X_1 + 0X_2$
   b. $f_{min} = 5X_1 + 4X_2$
   c. $f_{max} = 5X_1 + 4X_2$
   d. $f_{max} = X_1 + X_2$
   e. $f_{max} = 4X_1 + 5X_2$

2. The constraint imposed by the quantity of D on hand could be expressed as:
   a. $X_1 + X_2 \geq 16,000$
   b. $X_1 + X_2 \leq 16,000$
   c. $.4X_1 + .6X_2 \leq 16,000$
   d. $.8X_1 + .4X_2 \geq 16,000$
   e. $.8X_1 + .4X_2 \leq 16,000$

3. The constraint imposed by the quantity of K on hand could be expressed as:
   a. $X_1 + X_2 \geq 6,000$
   b. $X_1 + X_2 \leq 6,000$
   c. $.8X_1 + .2X_2 \leq 6,000$
   d. $.8X_1 + .2X_2 \geq 6,000$
   e. $.2X_1 + .6X_2 \leq 6,000$

4. To maximize total revenue, the company should produce and market:
   a. 106,000 gallons of Alpha only.
   b. 90,000 gallons of Alpha and 16,000 gallons of Gamma.
   c. 16,000 gallons of Alpha and 90,000 gallons of Gamma.
   d. 18,000 gallons of Alpha and 4,000 gallons of Gamma.
   e. 4,000 gallons of Alpha and 18,000 gallons of Gamma.

5. Assuming that the marginal contributions per gallon are $7 for Alpha and $9 for Gamma, the company should produce and market:
   a. 106,000 gallons of Alpha only.
   b. 90,000 gallons of Alpha and 16,000 gallons of Gamma.
   c. 16,000 gallons of Alpha and 90,000 gallons of Gamma.
   d. 18,000 gallons of Alpha and 4,000 gallons of Gamma.
   e. 4,000 gallons of Alpha and 18,000 gallons of Gamma.

(CPA Adapted)

P12–24   **Basic linear programming.** The Elon Company manufactures two industrial products — X10, which sells for $90 a unit, and Y12, which sells for $85 a unit. Each product is processed through both of the company's manufacturing departments. The limited availability of labor, material, and equipment capacity has restricted the ability of the firm to meet the demand for its products. The Production Department believes that linear programming can be used to routinize the production schedule for the two products.

The following data are available to the Production Department:

	Amount Required per Unit	
	X10	Y12
Direct material: weekly supply limited to 1,800 pounds at $12 per pound	4 pounds	2 pounds
Direct labor:		
Department 1 — weekly supply limited to 10 people at 40 hours each at an hourly rate of $6	$\frac{2}{3}$ hours	1 hour
Department 2 — weekly supply limited to 15 people at 40 hours each at an hourly rate of $8	$1\frac{1}{4}$ hours	1 hour
Machine time:		
Department 1 — weekly capacity limited to 250 hours	$\frac{1}{2}$ hour	$\frac{1}{2}$ hour
Department 2 — weekly capacity limited to 300 hours	0 hours	1 hour

The overhead costs for Elon Company are accumulated on a plantwide basis. Overhead is assigned to products on the basis of the number of direct labor hours required to manufacture them. This base is appropriate for overhead assignment because most of the variable overhead costs vary as a function of labor time. The estimated overhead cost per direct labor hour is:

Variable overhead cost	$ 6
Fixed overhead cost	6
Total overhead cost per direct labor hour	$12

The company wants to produce the mix of the two products that will allow it to maximize total contribution margin. The Production Department formulated the equations on page 460 for the linear programming statement of the problem.

X = number of units of X10 to be produced

Y = number of units of Y12 to be produced

Objective function equation to minimize costs:

Minimize: $Z = \$85X + \$62Y$

Constraint equations:

Material: $4X + 2Y \leq 1{,}800$ pounds

Department 1 labor: $\frac{2}{3}X + Y \leq 400$ pounds

Department 2 labor: $1\frac{1}{4}X + Y \leq 600$ hours

Required:

1. The linear programming equations as formulated by the company's Production Department are incorrect. Examine these equations, and explain what errors and omissions have been made.
2. Prepare the proper equations for the linear programming statement of the company's problem.
3. Explain how linear programming could help Elon Company determine how large a change in the price of direct materials would have to be to change the optimum production mix of X10 and Y12.

(CMA Adapted)

P12–25   Formulation of linear programming problem. Jenlock Mill Company produces two grades of interior plywood from fir and pine lumber. The fir and pine lumber can be sold as saw lumber or used in the plywood.

To produce the plywood, thin layers of wood are peeled from the logs in panels, the panels are glued together to form plywood sheets, and then dried. The peeler can peel enough panels from logs to produce 300,000 sheets of plywood in a month. The dryer has a capacity of 1,200,000 minutes for the month. The amount of lumber used and the drying time required for each sheet of plywood by grade is shown below.

	Grade A Plywood Sheets	Grade B Plywood Sheets
Fir (in board feet)	18	15
Pine (in board feet)	12	15
Drying time (in minutes)	4	6

The only restriction on the production of fir and pine lumber is the capacity of the mill saws to cut the logs into boards. These saws have a capacity of 500,000 board feet per month regardless of species.

Jenlock has the following quantities of lumber available for July production.

Fir   2,700,000 board feet
Pine   3,000,000 board feet

The contribution margins for each type of output are as follows.

Fir lumber	$ .20 per board foot
Pine lumber	.10 per board foot
Grade A plywood	2.25 per sheet
Grade B plywood	1.80 per sheet

The demand in July for plywood is expected to be a maximum of 80,000 sheets for grade A and a maximum of 100,000 sheets for grade B. There are no demand restrictions on pine and fir lumber.

Required: Assume that Jenlock decides to use linear programming to determine the production quantities of each of the four products. Formulate the objective function and all necessary constraint equations to determine the optimal production mix.

(CMA Adapted)

P12–26 **Linear programming using graphical method.** The Cleo Company distributes two products, Tracks and Racks. Cleo buys the parts for the two products from various manufacturers and then assembles and packages them for sale to wholesalers. Tracks sell for $10 per unit, and Racks are sold for $20 each. Variable costs are $6 for Tracks and $15 for Racks. Time available to assemble the two products is limited to 1,200 hours per month; each Track takes 2 hours to assemble, and each Rack takes only 1 hour. Each Track requires 15 minutes to package, whereas a Rack requires 30 minutes. Total packaging time available per month is 250 hours.

Required:
1. Formulate the objective function and all necessary constraint equations to be able to solve for the optimal mix of the two products.
2. Find the optimal mix using the graphical method. It may be helpful to solve the constraint equations simultaneously to find the exact point of intersection for the optimal solution.

CHAPTER 13

Capital Budgeting

Learning Objectives

After reading this chapter you should be able to:

1. Understand what capital budgeting is.

2. Comprehend how payback works and that it is a measure of liquidity and not profitability.

3. Understand accounting rate of return and its weakness as a profitability measure.

4. Understand the two discounted cash flow methods (time adjusted rate of return and net present value) of capital budgeting.

5. Be familiar with what capital rationing is.

6. Understand how to deal with unequal lives in capital budgeting analysis.

7. Understand time value of money concepts (Appendix 13–A).

L ong-run planning involves assessing alternatives that affect the enterprise for many years into the future. Budgeting for long-term commitments is concerned with policy decisions such as acquiring new businesses, developing new product lines, and modernizing or expanding buildings, machinery, and equipment. Because transactions of this type involve very large amounts of capital and, in effect, lock the firm in over long periods of time, these decisions must be very carefully weighed and calculated. Major projects in many companies require the approval of the corporate board of directors.

Projects of the type being discussed here require sizable initial investments and benefits that are expected to be received beyond a year. The process of determining which of these projects will be accepted and which will be rejected is called *capital budgeting* (the term was introduced in Chapter 5). Capital budgeting requires two principal elements: (1) the relevant costing approach to differential costs and revenues (discussed previously in Chapter 12) and (2) an analytical means for handling the relevant costs and revenues of the various alternatives that will enable decision makers to rank or assess competing projects.

This chapter will concentrate on the analytical framework used for evaluating capital budgeting projects. We start by examining methods that do not take into account the time value of money: payback and the accounting rate of return. We then discuss the two discounted cash flow techniques: time adjusted rate of return and net present value. If you are not familiar with the time value of money concept, you should read Appendix 13–A prior to reading this part of the chapter. The remainder of the chapter is concerned with additional technical problems and issues when time value of money approaches to capital budgeting are employed.

The subject of how income tax considerations affect capital budgeting is covered in Chapter 14. Another issue that is not covered here concerns the problem of risk and uncertainty that underlies relevant costing estimates which may extend far into the future. This subject is discussed in Chapter 17.

Payback

Payback is a method for measuring how rapidly capital investments are recovered. Assume that a firm is evaluating a project requiring a $1,000,000 investment in plant and equipment for the purpose of manufacturing a new product. It is expected that the project will generate revenues of $500,000 per year and will have costs for direct materials, direct labor, and variable overhead of $300,000 per year for an indefinite period. The $200,000 difference between revenues and expenses (excluding depreciation) is the differential net cash inflows arising from the project.

To measure the projected payback, the amount of the investment is divided by the differential net cash inflows:

$$\frac{I}{C} = \text{Payback}$$

where

I = capital investment of the project

C = differential annual net cash inflows.

In our example, the results would be

$$\frac{\$1,000,000}{\$200,000} = 5 \text{ years}$$

Payback simply tells us how rapidly our investment is recovered. Under payback the period beyond the recovery of the capital investment is ignored. Whether the project were to last for 10 years or 20 years would be irrelevant. Its payback period is still 5 years. Payback is thus not really a measurement of profitability of investment projects. Instead, it is a measure of *liquidity* because it simply attempts to answer the question of how rapidly investment outlays are recovered.

Depreciation and Payback

Notice that depreciation was not considered in computing payback. Depreciation accounting is an assignment of the cost (investment) of an asset to operating periods in order to get a "fair and equitable" measurement of income. Because payback measures how rapidly capital recovery occurs, including depreciation would be totally inappropriate. It would, in fact, be a form of double counting. A similar consideration applies to other noncash flow items, as well as to depreciation, in both payback and the discounted cash flow methods.

Advantage of Payback

The great advantage of payback is that it is simple and easily understood. Because of its simplicity and the fact that it gives information other than profitability (liquidity), many firms use payback as a secondary measure for assessing investment projects along with profitability indicators. Unfortunately many firms use payback without accompanying measurements of profitability.

Payback and Nonuniform Cash Flows

In the example given above, an **annuity** — a uniform cash flow series — was used. Payback is easily adaptable to situations other than annuities. Assume that a project requires an initial capital outlay of $1,000,000. It has the following projected annual net cash inflows:

Year	Projected Net Cash Inflows
1	$ 200,000
2	250,000
3	350,000
4	300,000
5	275,000
6	225,000
7	150,000
8	74,000
	$1,824,000

In this situation, the individual net cash flows should be cumulated until they equal the investment outlay of $1,000,000. Assuming that cash flows occur evenly throughout the year, payback would occur in 3⅔ years:

Year	Projected Net Cash Inflows
1	$ 200,000
2	250,000
3	350,000
4	200,000 (⅔ × $300,000)
Total	$1,000,000

Disadvantages of Payback

As we have stressed, payback is not a measure of profitability. In addition, it ignores the time value of money, even within the payback period, as well as all cash flows after the payback period. Because payback is not a measure of profitability, we turn next to profitability approaches.

Accounting Rate of Return

This method can be best illustrated by comparing two investment projects. Information for two hypothetical investment projects is presented in Exhibit 13–1 (page 366).

The formula for determining **accounting rate of return** is

$$\frac{C - D}{I} = \text{Accounting rate of return}$$

where

C = Average annual net cash inflows

D = Average annual depreciation

I = Capital investment of the project.

EXHIBIT 13–1

Two Capital Investment Projects

		Annual Cash Inflows		
Project	Investment	1	2	3
A	$1,000	$500	$400	$300
B	1,000	300	400	500

In our example, for both projects A and B, the accounting rate of return is

$$\frac{\$400 - \$333}{\$1,000} = 6.67\%$$

Notice that depreciation is deducted from net average annual cash inflows from the project in the numerator of the formula. The result is an average annual income measure for the project. Dividing income by the investment outlay in the project gives a ratio or relative number: the amount of income generated on the average per year for each dollar of initial capital investment in the project.

Using Average Investment

A question may be raised as to why the average annual income is divided by the total investment in the project. After all, because depreciation is deducted from the average annual net cash inflows in determining income, it can be argued effectively that the amount of the investment is being "recovered" throughout its life. Therefore, it can be argued, a better approximation of the capital tied up in an investment project is measured by taking the investment and dividing by two ($\$1,000/2 = \$500$ in our example). Although we agree with this approach, as long as all projects are treated consistently, the rank order of projects by rate of return would generally not be affected by which of the two types of investment base is used.

Disadvantages of Accounting Rate of Return

Although accounting rate of return, unlike payback, is a measure of profitability, it has one extremely serious drawback. Notice in our example that projects A and B are equal to each other in terms of their accounting rate of return under either of the two approaches. However, a firm would not be indifferent between them. Although they have the same *average* annual cash flow, project A's cash flows are received more rapidly (it has a faster payback). Thus the excess amount of $200 that is received from A over B in year 1 could be invested for two years until the annual cash inflows are equalized in year 3. Hence the problem with the accounting rate of return as a means of evaluating the profitability of investment projects is that it cannot take into account time value of money differences between projects.

As we shall see in Chapter 15, the method does have utility as a control tool in terms of evaluating profitability of divisions of a firm for a past period. There is no time value of money problem when evaluating the results of a past period. However, as a planning tool where budgeted results of many future periods must be assessed, accounting rate of return ignores the time value of money problem. Thus discounted cash flow methods should be used for more beneficial planning decisions.

Discounted Cash Flow Methods

Discounted cash flow methods for assessing and ranking capital investment projects are superior to the previous methods because they are (1) measurements of profitability and (2) they take into account the time value of money. The two methods, time-adjusted rate of return (TARR) and net present value (NPV) differ only slightly in approach. Both methods will be discussed and compared.

Time-Adjusted Rate of Return (TARR)

Time-adjusted rate of return (also frequently called *internal rate of return*) is a discounted cash flow technique that finds the interest rate that will just equate the present value of the future cash flows with the investment outlay. Let us examine an extremely simple situation to see how TARR works. Assume a project requires an investment of $56,865 with 5 annual net cash inflows of $15,000 received at the end of each year. This is shown in the form of a time line where the expected cash flows are shown at the time when they are expected to occur:

0	1	2	3	4	5
−$56,865	$15,000	$15,000	$15,000	$15,000	$15,000

Zero indicates an immediate cash flow, and the other numbers represent the end of the respective years when each cash flow is expected to occur. The time line approach is used extensively in other examples in this chapter.

Because we are dealing with an annuity, the capital investment is divided by the annual cash flow amount to determine the appropriate present value factor of an annuity (this is similar to payback but used in an entirely different fashion). TARR involves finding that interest rate that just equates the present value of future cash inflows with the amount of the investment. Thus time-adjusted rate of return would be determined by the following formula:

$$I = CF \times PV$$

where

   I = Capital investment of the project

   CF = Annual cash flows

   PV = Present value factor

In our example, the present value factor is 3.791 ($56,865 ÷ $15,000) because $56,865 = $15,000 × 3.791.

We would now scan across the 5-year line in Table D (see page 492) in order to find the time-adjusted rate of return. The amount is 10% in our example. Where the present value factor does not equal a whole percent integer, interpolation must be used to determine the time-adjusted rate of return. This will be demonstrated shortly with a more complex example. First, however, let us see exactly what is meant by a project's time-adjusted rate of return.

The Meaning of Time-Adjusted Rate of Return

Suppose that a firm had the capital investment opportunity just discussed. Assume that the firm had to borrow the $56,865 from a bank. Further assume that the repayment terms called for equal annual amounts to be repaid to the lender at the end of each year for the next 5 years with an interest rate of 10%. The annual amount that would have to be repaid to the bank would be $15,000. The annual repayment schedule would be determined by dividing the $56,865 by the present value of a 5-year annuity at 10% (3.791). This is, of course, a variant on the calculation previously made when we arrived at the factor of 3.791. A 10% return on the project and a 10% borrowing cost implies a break-even situation. A further understanding of this relationship can be derived from Exhibit 13–2.

Exhibit 13–2 shows that each repayment is broken down into two portions: (1) interest on the unpaid balance (usually called the "unamortized" balance) and (2) the remainder, which is a repayment of principal. As can be seen, annual repayments of $15,000 just cover interest on the unpaid balance of the loan and repayment of the principal amount borrowed of $56,865. Therefore, the time-adjusted rate of return on a project is the rate that would just cover a similar borrowing on the capital investment itself. It can also be seen that time-adjusted rate of return is the rate that provides both a level return on the unamortized portion of the investment as well as amortization of the investment itself.

Comparison of Time-Adjusted Rate of Return with Cost of Capital

Once the time-adjusted rate of return on a project is determined, it is then compared with the cost of capital. **Cost of capital** refers to the weighted average cost of all long-term capital sources that the firm uses, which can include bonds and long-term notes payable as well as all forms of equity capital.

EXHIBIT 13–2
Repayment of Borrowing at 10%

End of Year	Principal[a] Balance	Total Cash Payment	Repayment of	
			Interest[b]	Principal[c]
0	$56,865.00			
1	47,551.50	$15,000	$ 5,686.50	$ 9,313.50
2	37,306.65	15,000	4,755.15	10,244.85
3	26,037.31	15,000	3,730.66	11,269.34
4	13,641.04	15,000	2,603.73	12,396.27
5	0[d]	15,000	1,364.10	13,635.90
		$75,000	$18,140.14	$56,859.86

[a]Previous balance minus repayment of principal.

[b]Interest is 10% of end of previous year balance of principal.

[c]Repayment of principal is equal to $15,000 total cash payment minus interest on unpaid principal balance.

[d]Rounding error of approximately $5 as shown by the difference of $13,641.04 and $13,635.90.

In addition, an element for risk of the particular project may also be included in the cost of capital. More will be said in Chapter 14 relative to determining the cost of capital.

If the time-adjusted rate of return of a project exceeds the cost of capital, investment in it is beneficial and should be made subject to certain qualifications to be noted later in this chapter. However, if time-adjusted rate of return is less than the cost of capital, the project is unattractive and should be rejected. The cost of capital is often referred to as a "hurdle rate": a rate that the project's time-adjusted rate of return must exceed if investment is to be considered.

Uneven Cash Flows

Let us now examine a more complicated situation. The Engels Toy Company is considering whether to manufacture a new product called a Hula Whirl. The Hula Whirl is a fad toy that is expected to have a market for 5 years. Cost analyses and market research showed the following relevant estimates for the project:

Cost of new equipment	$2,000,000
Expected annual sales:	
Year 1	$800,000
Year 2	$1,000,000
Year 3	$1,800,000
Year 4	$1,200,000
Year 5	$600,000

Total variable manufacturing and marketing costs (as a percentage of sales revenues)	25%
Annual fixed out of pocket costs for maintenance and insurance on the new equipment	$ 100,000

For the sake of simplicity in our computations, we will assume that all cash flows occur at year end. Our objective is to find the discount rate that will make the future cash flows just equal to the investment outlay. The total relevant cash flows for the Hula Whirl are shown in Exhibit 13–3.

Calculating Time-Adjusted Rate of Return

Time-adjusted rate of return is easily computed with a financial calculator or personal computer with appropriate software. In the absence of these, a trial and error method must be adopted because uneven cash flows must be individually discounted. One attempts to find the discount rate that comes closest to the correct rate. Assume that a careful "eyeballing" of the numbers leads us to try a discount rate of 22%. The present value of the future net cash flows is $2,025,850 as shown in Exhibit 13–4.

Because this slightly exceeds the investment outlay of $2,000,000, time-adjusted rate of return is slightly *above* 22% (had the Hula Whirl project required an initial investment of $2,025,850, time-adjusted rate of return would have been exactly 22%). Repeating the process at 23% shows a present value of $1,981,250, also shown in Exhibit 13–4 (again, time-adjusted rate of return would have been exactly 23% if the required initial investment were $1,981,250). Because the present value of the cash flows is just below the investment outlay of $2,000,000, time-adjusted rate of return is under 23%. The exact rate can be determined by **interpolation.**

Interpolation   We interpolate by relating the $2,000,000 investment outlay to the present value of the cash flows at 22% and 23%:

EXHIBIT 13–3
Relevant Cash Flows for the Hula Whirl

Item						
Time point	0	1	2	3	4	5
Investment	−$2,000,000					
Sales		$800,000	$1,000,000	$1,800,000	$1,200,000	$600,000
Variable costs		− 200,000	− 250,000	− 450,000	− 300,000	− 150,000
Maintenance and insurance		− 100,000	− 100,000	− 100,000	− 100,000	− 100,000
Net cash flows		$500,000	$ 650,000	$1,250,000	$ 800,000	$350,000

EXHIBIT 13—4

Discounting Hula Whirl Cash Flows

			22% Discounting			
Item						
Time point	0	1	2	3	4	5
Investment	$2,000,000					
Cash flows		$500,000	$650,000	$1,250,000	$800,000	$350,000
Present value factors (22%)		× .82	× .672	× .551	× .451	× .37
Sum of the present values	2,025,850	$410,000	$436,800	$ 688,750	$360,800	$129,500
Difference	$ 25,850					

			23% Discounting			
Time point	0	1	2	3	4	5
Investment	$2,000,000					
Cash flows		$500,000	$650,000	$1,250,000	$800,000	$350,000
Present value factors (23%)		× .813	× .661	× .537	× .437	× .355
Sum of the present values	1,981,250	$406,500	$429,650	$ 671,250	$349,600	$124,250
Difference	−$ 18,750					

Present value at 22%	$2,025,850	$2,025,850
Investment outlay	2,000,000	
Present value at 23%		1,981,250
Difference	$ 25,850	$ 44,600

Because the $2,000,000 is closer to the present value of the cash flows at 23% ($1,981,250) than it is to the present value at 22% ($2,025,850), the exact rate is closer to 23%. It is determined by the following calculation:

$$22\% + \left(1\% \times \frac{\$25,850}{\$44,600}\right) = 22.58\%$$

The 22.58% time-adjusted rate of return would then be compared with the cost of capital in the manner previously suggested. Suppose, however, that another project is competing with the Hula Whirl.

Competitive Investment Projects

Another Engels Toy Company project is Skateboards. Like the Hula Whirl, this is a fad project with a limited life. Furthermore, given limited factory space, the firm can produce either Hula Whirls or Skateboards but not both. When projects are directly competitive with each other and accepting one means rejecting the other, the projects are **mutually exclusive.** Relevant data for the Skateboard are as follows:

Cost of new equipment	$3,000,000
Expected annual sales:	
Year 1	$1,000,000
Year 2	$1,800,000
Year 3	$2,400,000
Year 4	$1,500,000
Year 5	$400,000
Total variable manufacturing and marketing costs (as a percentage of sales revenues)	20%
Annual fixed out of pocket costs for maintenance and insurance on the new equipment	$150,000

Relevant cash flows for the Skateboard are shown in Exhibit 13–5. As is shown in Exhibit 13–6, the time-adjusted rate of return for Skateboards is between 20% and 21%. Once again, using interpolation, we determine the difference between the appropriate present value factors:

Present value at 20%	$3,035,980	$3,035,980
Investment outlay	3,000,000	
Present value at 21%		2,972,220
Difference	$ 35,980	$ 63,760

The time-adjusted rate of return would then be

$$20\% + \left(1\% \times \frac{\$35,980}{\$63,760}\right) = 20.57\%$$

Selecting a project   Thus the time-adjusted rate of return for Hula Whirls is 22.58% and for Skateboards 20.57%. Neither project would be acceptable if the cost of capital is above 22.58%; between 20.57% and 22.58%, only

EXHIBIT 13–5
Relevant Cash Flows for the Skateboard

Item						
Time point	0	1	2	3	4	5
Investment	−$3,000,000					
Sales		$1,000,000	$1,800,000	$2,400,000	$1,500,000	$400,000
Variable costs		− 200,000	− 360,000	− 480,000	− 300,000	− 80,000
Maintenance and insurance		− 150,000	− 150,000	− 150,000	− 150,000	− 150,000
Net cash flows		$ 650,000	$1,290,000	$1,770,000	$1,050,000	$170,000

EXHIBIT 13–6

Discounting Skateboard Cash Flows

			20% Discounting			
Item						
Time point	0	1	2	3	4	5
Investment	−$3,000,000					
Cash flows		$650,000	$1,290,000	$1,770,000	$1,050,000	$170,000
Present value factors (20%)		× .833	× .694	× .579	× .482	× .402
Sum of the present values	3,035,980	$541,450	$ 895,260	$1,024,830	$ 506,100	$ 68,340
Difference	$ 35,980					

			21% Discounting			
Time point	0	1	2	3	4	5
Investment	−$3,000,000					
Cash flows		$650,000	$1,290,000	$1,770,000	$1,050,000	$170,000
Present value factors (21%)		× .826	× .683	× .564	× .467	× .386
Sum of the present values	2,972,220	$536,900	$ 881,070	$ 998,280	$ 490,350	$ 65,620
Difference	−$ 27,780					

the Hula Whirl would be acceptable. Finally, below 20.57%, both projects are acceptable though only one can be chosen. Because the Hula Whirl has the higher time-adjusted rate of return, we might conclude that Hula Whirls should be selected.

This is not necessarily the case, however. Until now, the Hula Whirl and Skateboard projects have been analyzed separately. The investments are similar to the extent that they both have 5-year lives. The Skateboard, however, requires an additional $1,000,000 "up front" in the investment commitment. We might view this $1,000,000 additional investment from the incremental standpoint and determine the differential cash flows by combining the two projects in Exhibit 13–7 (page 474). In this exhibit, the incremental amounts are arrived at by subtracting each Hula Whirl number in Exhibit 13–3 from its corresponding Skateboard number in Exhibit 13–5. Thus the incremental investment amount of $1,000,000 is determined by taking the investment requirement for Hula Whirls for $2,000,000 (Exhibit 13–3) from the corresponding investment outlay of $3,000,000 for Skateboards (Exhibit 13–5). All other numbers in Exhibit 13–7 were determined in a similar fashion.

The time-adjusted rate of return on the incremental investment of $1,000,000 is derived in Exhibit 13–8. As we can see in Exhibit 13–8, the

EXHIBIT 13—7
Incremental Approach to TARR:
Excess Investment in Skateboards over Hula Whirls

Item						
Time point	0	1	2	3	4	5
Investment	−$1,000,000					
Sales		$200,000	$800,000	$600,000	$300,000	−$200,000
Variable costs		0	− 110,000	− 30,000	0	70,000
Maintenance and insurance		− 50,000	− 50,000	− 50,000	− 50,000	− 50,000
Net cash flows		$150,000	$640,000	$520,000	$250,000	−$180,000

EXHIBIT 13—8
Discounting Cash Flows: Incremental Basis

	15% Discounting					
Item						
Time point	0	1	2 .	3	4	5
Investment	−$1,000,000					
Cash flows		$150,000	$640,000	$520,000	$250,000	−$180,000
Present value factors (15%)		× .87	× .756	× .658	× .572	× .497
Sum of the present values	1,010,040	$130,500	$483,840	$342,160	$143,000	−$ 89,460
Difference	$ 9,698					

	16% Discounting					
Time point	0	1	2	3	4	5
Investment	−$1,000,000					
Cash flows		$150,000	$640,000	$520,000	$250,000	−$180,000
Present value factors (16%)		× .862	× .743	× .641	× .552	× .476
Sum of the present values	990,460	$129,300	$475,520	$333,320	$138,000	−$ 85,680
Difference	−$ 9,540					

time-adjusted rate of return on the incremental investment is between 15% and 16%. Using interpolation, we get the following differentials:

Present value at 15%	$1,010,040	$1,010,040
Investment outlay	1,000,000	
Present value at 16%		990,460
Difference	$ 10,040	$ 19,580

The time-adjusted rate of return on the differential investment would be

$$15\% + \left(1\% \times \frac{\$10,040}{\$19,580}\right) = 15.51\%$$

What is the meaning of the incremental time-adjusted rate of return of 15.51%? If the investment differential of $1,000,000 can be invested above 15.51%, Engels should invest in Hula Whirls and the incremental project. On the other hand, if the $1,000,000 investment differential cannot be invested at a return of at least 15.51%, Skateboards is the better project.

TARR gives a valid measure of the profitability of investment projects. Clearly, however, computation of time-adjusted rate of return can be somewhat awkward unless one has a financial calculator or a personal computer with appropriate software to eliminate the "drudge work" from the calculations. Let us next, therefore, examine the other discounted cash flow approach.

Net Present Value (NPV)

NPV is less cumbersome to use than TARR because the time-adjusted rate of return is not directly calculated. Thus, the main difference between TARR and NPV involves how the cost of capital is introduced into the analysis. As we have seen, the pure rate of return is determined under TARR and then compared with the cost of capital to facilitate making the decision. With net present value, the cost of capital is introduced directly into the process by using it as the discount rate. The key factor becomes the difference between the investment outlay and the present value of the net cash flows of the project.

Our original annuity example had a 10% time-adjusted rate of return. If the discount rate is also 10%, the present value of the net cash flows equals the investment outlay. If the discount rate is below 10%, a positive net present value must result. The **net present value**—which is where the method gets its name—is the difference between the present value of the net cash flows and the investment outlay. Similarly, if the discount rate is above 10%, a negative net present value results. These relationships are illustrated in Exhibits 13–9 and 13–10 using 8% and 12% as the respective costs of capital.

EXHIBIT 13–9
Net Present Value with 8% Discounting

Investment	−$56,865
Annual cash flow times present value of a 5-year annuity at 8% ($15,000 × 3.993)	59,895
Net present value	$ 3,030

EXHIBIT 13—10

Net Present Value with 12% Discounting

Investment	−$56,865
Annual cash flow times present value of a	
5-year annuity at 12% ($15,000 × 3.605)	54,075
Net present value	−$ 2,790

An investment should be rejected outright if it has a negative net present value. If a positive net present value results, the investment should be beneficial to the firm. A comparison of decision rules under TARR and NPV is shown in Exhibit 13—11. Results will always be in the same row: if time-adjusted rate of return is greater than the cost of capital, then a positive net present value would also result. Similarly if time-adjusted rate of return is less than the cost of capital, a negative net present value must occur.

Hula Whirls and Skateboards

Let us next examine the NPV approach in the more complex examples of Hula Whirls and Skateboards used previously with TARR. Assume that the cost of capital is 16%. NPV analyses for Hula Whirls and Skateboards are shown in Exhibits 13—12 and 13—13.

Once again, as with TARR, NPV can be done on an incremental basis from the standpoint of differential investment in the projects and the resulting differential cash flows. This is shown in Exhibit 13—14. What is the meaning of the negative net present value of $9,540 shown in Exhibit 13—14? Notice first that this is the difference between the two net present values shown in Exhibit 13—12 and 13—13 with Hula Whirls exceeding Skateboards. Because the net present value in the incremental analysis is negative, investment should be made in Hula Whirls rather than Skateboards with the incremental investment of $1,000,000 being invested elsewhere. You might also note that Exhibit 13—14 is similar to the bottom portion of Exhibit 13—8

EXHIBIT 13—11

Comparison of Decision Rules Under TARR and NPV

Condition	TARR	NPV
Investment desirable	Time-adjusted rate of return exceeds cost of capital	Positive net present value
Investment not desirable	Cost of capital exceeds time-adjusted rate of return	Negative net present value

EXHIBIT 13–12
NPV Analysis of Hula Whirls (16%)

Item						
Time point	0	1	2	3	4	5
Investment	−$2,000,000					
Cash flows		$500,000	$650,000	$1,250,000	$800,000	$350,000
Present value factors (16%)		× .862	× .743	× .641	× .552	× .476
Sum of the present values	2,323,400	$431,000	$482,950	$ 801,250	$441,600	$166,600
Net present value	$ 323,400					

EXHIBIT 13–13
NPV Analysis of Skateboards (16%)

Item						
Time point	0	1	2	3	4	5
Investment	−$3,000,000					
Cash flows		$650,000	$1,290,000	$1,770,000	$1,050,000	$170,000
Present value factors (16%)		× .862	× .743	× .641	× .552	× .476
Sum of the present values	3,313,860	$560,300	$ 958,470	$1,134,570	$ 579,600	$ 80,920
Net present value	$ 313,860					

EXHIBIT 13–14
Incremental NPV Analysis (16%)

Item						
Time point	0	1	2	3	4	5
Investment	−$1,000,000					
Cash flows		$150,000	$640,000	$520,000	$250,000	−$180,000
Present value factors (16%)		× .862	× .743	× .641	× .552	× .476
Sum of the present values	990,460	$129,300	$475,520	$333,320	$138,000	−$ 85,680
Incremental NPV	−$ 9,540					

where 16% was used in determining time-adjusted rate of return. If the cost of capital is 15%, a positive net present value results indicating that the investment should be made in Skateboards. This is shown in Exhibit 13–15. (Exhibit 13–15 is, of course, similar to the top portion of Exhibit 13–8.) You

EXHIBIT 13–15

Incremental NPV Analysis (15%)

Item						
Time point	0	1	2	3	4	5
Investment	−$1,000,000					
Cash flows		$150,000	$640,000	$520,000	$250,000	−$180,000
Present value factors (15%)		× .87	× .756	× .658	× .572	× .497
Sum of the present values	1,010,040	$130,500	$483,840	$342,160	$143,000	−$ 89,460
Net present value	$ 10,040					

will recall that the break-even time-adjusted rate of return computed previously was 15.51%. The cost of capital is thus a surrogate for the reinvestment rate and provides beneficial decision-making information for competing projects where the size of the investment outlay differs. This brings us to the subject of "capital rationing."

Capital Rationing

Where available capital investment funds exceed the total capital outlay commitment for projects having positive net present values, it is beneficial for the firm to invest in all of these projects, assuming that none are mutually exclusive. Capital rationing must be employed in the opposite situation. **Capital rationing** refers to conditions where the funds available for capital investment are not adequate to cover those projects having positive net present values.

Although much has been written on this topic, it appears that the best way to proceed in a capital rationing situation is to select the group of projects that maximizes the total net present value of future cash flows over required investment outlays. Assume that at the beginning of 19X6 the Engels Toy Company decided to commit $7,500,000 to new investment projects. A total of seven projects had positive net present values:

Project	Required Investment	Net Present Value	Net Present Value per Dollar of Investment
A	$ 3,000,000	$ 360,000	12%
B	2,000,000	250,000	12½
C	2,500,000	500,000	20
D	1,500,000	120,000	8
E	500,000	50,000	10
F	500,000	80,000	16
G	2,000,000	220,000	11
Total	$12,000,000	$1,580,000	

The net present value per dollar of investment is determined by dividing the required investment by the net present value for each project. Assume that projects A and B are mutually exclusive.

In arriving at a decision as to which projects to choose, you should be attempting to maximize the total net present value of the projects selected. We would therefore start with project C with its 20% net present value per dollar of investment. Project F with its 16% net present value per dollar of investment would appear to be next. Because A and B are mutually exclusive, we would utilize a "cut and try" matching in which we would try to even out the investment alternatives. Thus A with its investment outlay of $3,000,000 would be paired against B, E, and F, which total to the same investment commitment. Because B, E, and F have a combined net present value of $380,000 ($250,000 for B, $50,000 for E, and $80,000 for F), this trio would be selected over A with its net present value of only $360,000. The last project to be selected, filling out the total budgetary commitment of $7,500,000, would be G. The optimal combination, therefore, consists of the following group of projects:

Project	Required Investment	Net Present Value
C	$2,500,000	$ 500,000
B	2,000,000	250,000
F	500,000	80,000
E	500,000	50,000
G	2,000,000	220,000
	$7,500,000	$1,100,000

This selection of projects has a higher total net present value than any other combination of Engels's projects having a total investment outlay of $7,500,000. The example used here, of course, was quite simple. More complicated situations can be quite cumbersome in terms of the "cut and try" approach, but the computer can easily handle complex capital rationing problems.

Unequal Lives

A problem somewhat similar to choosing between investments of different sizes concerns selection among projects having different lives. Assume that there are two competing projects requiring investments of $10,000 each. The first project has one cash inflow of $12,000 to be received in one year. The second project also has one cash inflow, $17,488, to be received in four years. The first project has a time-adjusted rate of return of 20% and the second one a return of 15%.

Selecting purely on the basis of the time-adjusted rate of return is not necessarily correct. The key point concerns the reinvestment rate of the $12,000 from the first project. NPV provides a better basis for selecting among projects provided that the cost of capital is a good surrogate for the reinvestment rate. Net present values of the two projects are equalized at a discount rate between 13% and 14% (approximately 13.7%). This means that for reinvestment rates above 13.7% the first project is preferable and for rates below 13.7% the second project would be preferable.

Where project lives differ, a reasonable solution is to attempt to carry both projects out to the same future time point, usually the expected life of the longer-lived project (which often includes a reinvestment in new equipment for the shorter-lived project). Even though one, if not both, projects may have further remaining life, salvage value of project assets is a fairly reasonable substitute for any remaining future cash flows beyond the common end point of the analysis. Salvage values will be illustrated in Chapter 14.

Summary

Capital budgeting is the general term used for methods that are employed as an aid in the selection of major capital investments having a life in excess of one year.

Payback is a method that attempts to measure how rapidly capital investment in a project is recovered. It is, therefore, concerned with the question of liquidity rather than profitability. Periods beyond the recovery of the investment are ignored. In the case of nonuniform cash flows, recovery of the investment should be calculated on a cumulative basis. Payback is still extensively used by business. It should not, however, be employed as the prime evaluator for project selection because it does not measure profitability.

Accounting rate of return is a method that attempts to evaluate project profitability. It is computed by dividing either the initial capital investment in a project or one-half of this amount into the average incremental income specifically generated by the project. The weakness of the method as a planning instrument is that it ignores the time value of money. As such, it is really inapplicable to capital budgeting. Its best usage is as a control tool for evaluating the results of a past period. In the control context, time value of money does not present a problem.

Only the discounted cash flow methods provide profitability measures of investment projects that take into account the time value of money. TARR involves finding the interest rate that just equates the present value of future cash flows with the investment outlay. The rate of return is then compared with the cost of capital. Cost of capital is a hurdle rate consisting of the weighted average cost of all long-term sources of capital as well as a risk factor for the particular project. If the cost of capital is less than the time-adjusted rate of return, the project is potentially beneficial to the firm. On the other hand, if the cost of capital is more than the time-adjusted rate of return, the project should be summarily rejected. In the case of mutually exclusive projects with different investment outlays, the incremental approach to TARR gives the time-adjusted rate of return on the incremental capital investment of the larger project.

NPV uses the cost of capital directly in the discounting process itself. The result is either a positive or negative net present value for the project. The decision rules are consistent between TARR and NPV. The advantage of NPV is that it is less awkward to use because TARR requires interpolation unless one is working with a financial calculator or an appropriate program on a personal computer. NPV also adapts more easily to the situation of capital rationing where the acceptable projects exceed the funds available for investment. Finally, where competing projects have different lives, the key point to bear in mind is the anticipated reinvestment rate applicable to the period from the end of the project with the shorter life until the end of the other project's life. An acceptable substitute for working with reinvestments is to carry both projects out to the same point in time (often the life of the shorter project) and then use the salvage value applicable to the two projects at that time.

Appendix 13–A
The Time Value of Money

The idea of the **time value of money** is extremely simple. A dollar in hand today is more valuable than a dollar to be received in a year because the dollar we have today can be put to work—gaining interest or a return on its investment—and will thus be worth more than a dollar in a year. This description of the time value of money also embraces one of the two main concepts to be covered here: the process of **compounding**. We shall discuss compounding first and then examine discounting and the relationship between the two concepts. The discussion will be at a nontechnical level, enabling you to gain a solid grasp of the concepts and allowing you to use the compounding and discounting tables at the end of this appendix to make rapid calculations.

Compounding

If $1 is invested today at a rate of 8% and the interest is added (compounded) once a year, the $1 will be worth $1.08 in a year. The formula for compounding is shown at the top of Table A (see pages 486–495 for the tables referred to in this appendix). It stands to reason that the longer the length of time for which the $1 is invested, the greater will be its growth. To use Table A, one merely multiplies the amount that is being invested times the compounding factor for the appropriate number of time periods at the particular rate of interest. Thus $5 invested for a year at 8% with annual compounding would be worth $5.40 ($5 × 1.08) in a year. Similarly, $5 invested for 2 years at

8% with annual compounding would grow to $5.83 ($5 × 1.166). It also stands to reason that for the same given number of investment periods, the lower the interest rate, the lower the compounding factor. Similarly, the higher the interest rate, the higher the compounding factor.

Annuities

Table C is also a compounding table. It is applicable to ordinary annuities. An **ordinary annuity** is a uniform series of amounts where the first cash flow is paid or received in a year. Thus as you look across the first-year row, the compounding factor is 1 for all interest rates. Looking across the second-year row it should also be evident that the dollar at the end of the first year has earned interest and the second dollar has been added but has not earned interest. As with Table A, one merely multiplies the amount in question by the compounding factor indicated for the particular rate and number of periods. Hence an ordinary annuity of $5 for 10 periods at 8% would be worth $72.435 ($5 × 14.487). Of course, the higher the interest rate, the higher the compounding factor for the same number of years and the converse for lower interest rates.

Table C can also be used to compute the future value of an annuity due. An **annuity due** is one where the first cash flow is received or paid immediately. Hence it earns a full year's interest at the end of a year. To find the appropriate compounding factor for an annuity due from an ordinary annuity table, you merely go 1 year *beyond* the number of years of the given annuity and subtract 1. For example, the compounding factor for a 3-year annuity due at 8% would be 3.506. The reason that the conversion is done in this manner can be seen from Exhibit 13–16.

In Exhibit 13–16, each X represents a dollar invested and each arrow represents the compounding of interest for a year. Notice that a 3-year annuity due and a 4-year ordinary annuity have a total of 6 compoundings. The only difference is that the 4-year ordinary annuity has one more dollar added in the fourth year (the circled X) that does not gain interest. Thus, the 3-year annuity due and the 4-year ordinary annuity will have the same future value when the $1 (for the circled X) is subtracted from the 4-year ordinary annuity factor.

Discounting

Compounding tables, for both a single amount, as well as annuities, determine valuation for a future time point. **Discounting** is the exact opposite of compounding. It takes a future amount or amounts and shows what they are worth today. The term describing this process is quite literal: **present value.**

Let us further examine this process and see the relationship between compounding (future value) and discounting (present value). If we invest $1 today at 10%, it will grow to a value of $1.10 in a year. On the other hand, $1 to be received in a year discounted at 10% would be worth $.909 today

EXHIBIT 13—16

Converting an Ordinary Annuity to an Annuity Due (Compounding)

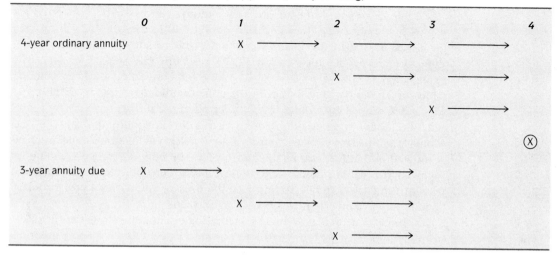

(see Table B). But if we had \$.909 today, it would grow to \$1 in a year (\$.909 × 1.1 from Table A). The processes of compounding and discounting do exactly the same thing, but they go in "opposite" directions as illustrated in this diagram using 10% ("0" means now and "1" means in a year):

	0	1
Compounding	\$1	\$1.10
Discounting	\$.909	\$1

To further highlight the reverse natures of compounding and discounting, note from Table A and Table B that all factors for the same interest rate and number of periods are reciprocals. Thus 1/.909 = 1.1 and, of course, 1/1.1 = .909.

There are several other noteworthy relationships in Table B. For any given interest rate, the further in the future the amount to be received, the smaller is its present value. This is the corollary to the fact that under compounding, the further in the future for which we compound, the larger the factor must be. This must be the case given the reciprocal relationship just mentioned between compounding and discounting. Similarly, as we view the same year across any row, the lower the discount rate the higher the present value and, of course, the converse. This is also linked with the reciprocal relationship between compounding and discounting.

Table D is a present value table for an ordinary annuity. As such, it consists of the sum of the factors for the corresponding number of years at the same interest rate as Table B. Hence from Table D, the present value factor for a 5-year annuity at 10% is 3.791. This equals the sum of the factors for the first 5 years at 10% listed in Table B. The value of Table D is that it can save time in calculating present value for an annuity series as opposed to using individual year calculations from Table B.

Table D, which is for an ordinary annuity, can easily be converted for use with annuities due. It is necessary only to go to the present value factor for 1 year less than the life of the annuity and to add 1. Thus the present value of a 5-year annuity due at a 10% discount rate would be 4.17. The explanation is similar to that given above for converting ordinary annuity tables to an annuity due format in the compounding process. In Exhibit 13–17, each X represents a dollar to be received in the future. Each arrow represents the discounting of a dollar for a year. A 5-year annuity due and a 4-year ordinary annuity have 10 discountings applicable to 4 dollar amounts received at the end of the first year to the fourth year. The only difference is the dollar received (or paid) immediately at time point zero (circled), which has a present value of 1. Hence adding 1 to the present value of a 4-year ordinary annuity factor converts it to a 5-year annuity due.

Table E is a present value table for single amounts. However, it differs from Table B. That table is geared to present value factors for single amounts at discrete year-end points. Table E has been constructed for amounts that are received uniformly throughout a year. It is thus extremely useful for revenues and expenses that arise on a relatively even basis throughout a year. Referring to Table E, we can see that the present value of $500,000 of sales at 11% received between 2 and 3 years in the future would be $380,000

EXHIBIT 13–17
Converting an Ordinary Annuity to an Annuity Due (Discounting)

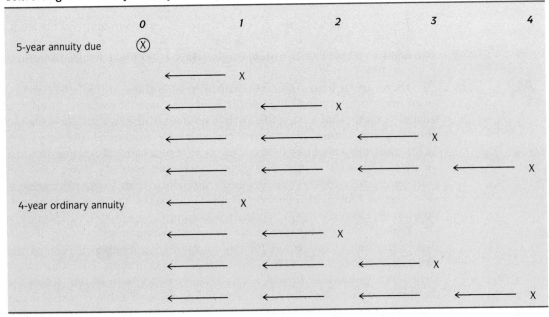

($500,000 × .76). Notice that the present value factors on Table E are slightly higher than the corresponding amounts on Table B. Hence the present value of a dollar received in 3 years and discounted at 11% is .731 as opposed to the .76 from Table E.

Use of the Tables

The above discussion provides the basic information that the user needs to employ the tables in capital budgeting analysis. Notice that all five tables, whether for compounding or discounting or for single amounts or annuities, have one important factor in common. They all give a single value either at the present time (Tables B, D, and E) or at some specified future time (Tables A and C). All of these tables take into account the time value of money. Although either group of tables, A and C or B, D, and E could be used for capital budgeting purposes, business almost always uses the present value approach. Hence the two most important capital budgeting methods, both of which are discussed in the chapter, are known as **discounted cash flow approaches.**

TABLE A
Future Value of $1 $F_n = P(1 + r)^n$

Year	1%	2%	3%	4%	5%	6%	7%	8%	9%	10%
1	1.010	1.020	1.030	1.040	1.050	1.060	1.070	1.080	1.090	1.100
2	1.020	1.040	1.061	1.082	1.102	1.124	1.145	1.166	1.188	1.200
3	1.030	1.061	1.093	1.125	1.158	1.191	1.225	1.260	1.295	1.331
4	1.041	1.082	1.126	1.170	1.216	1.262	1.311	1.360	1.412	1.464
5	1.051	1.104	1.159	1.217	1.276	1.338	1.403	1.469	1.539	1.611
6	1.062	1.126	1.194	1.265	1.340	1.419	1.501	1.587	1.677	1.772
7	1.072	1.149	1.230	1.316	1.407	1.504	1.606	1.714	1.828	1.949
8	1.083	1.172	1.267	1.369	1.477	1.594	1.718	1.851	1.993	2.144
9	1.094	1.195	1.305	1.423	1.551	1.689	1.838	1.999	2.172	2.358
10	1.105	1.219	1.344	1.480	1.629	1.791	1.967	2.159	2.367	2.594
11	1.116	1.243	1.384	1.539	1.710	1.898	2.105	2.332	2.580	2.853
12	1.127	1.268	1.426	1.601	1.796	2.012	2.252	2.518	2.813	3.138
13	1.138	1.294	1.469	1.665	1.886	2.133	2.410	2.720	3.066	3.452
14	1.149	1.319	1.513	1.732	1.980	2.261	2.579	2.937	3.342	3.797
15	1.161	1.346	1.558	1.801	2.079	2.397	2.759	3.172	3.642	4.177
16	1.173	1.373	1.605	1.873	2.183	2.540	2.952	3.426	3.970	4.595
17	1.184	1.400	1.653	1.948	2.292	2.693	3.159	3.700	4.328	5.054
18	1.196	1.428	1.702	2.026	2.407	2.854	3.380	3.996	4.717	5.560
19	1.208	1.457	1.754	2.107	2.527	3.026	3.617	4.316	5.142	6.116
20	1.220	1.486	1.806	2.191	2.653	3.207	3.870	4.661	5.604	6.727

Year	11%	12%	13%	14%	15%	16%	17%	18%	19%	20%
1	1.110	1.120	1.130	1.140	1.150	1.160	1.170	1.180	1.190	1.200
2	1.232	1.254	1.277	1.300	1.322	1.346	1.369	1.392	1.416	1.490
3	1.368	1.405	1.443	1.482	1.521	1.561	1.602	1.643	1.685	1.728
4	1.518	1.574	1.630	1.689	1.749	1.811	1.874	1.939	2.005	2.074
5	1.685	1.762	1.842	1.925	2.011	2.100	2.192	2.228	2.386	2.488
6	1.870	1.974	2.082	2.195	2.313	2.436	2.565	2.700	2.840	2.986
7	2.076	2.211	2.353	2.502	2.660	2.826	3.001	3.185	3.379	3.583
8	2.305	2.476	2.658	2.853	3.059	3.278	3.511	3.759	4.021	4.300
9	2.558	2.773	3.004	3.252	3.518	3.803	4.108	4.435	4.785	5.160
10	2.839	3.106	3.395	3.707	4.046	4.411	4.807	5.234	5.695	6.192
11	3.152	3.479	3.836	4.226	4.652	5.117	5.624	6.176	6.777	7.430
12	3.498	3.896	4.335	4.818	5.350	5.936	6.580	7.288	8.064	8.916
13	3.883	4.363	4.898	5.492	6.153	6.886	7.699	8.599	9.596	10.699
14	4.310	4.887	5.535	6.261	7.076	7.988	9.007	10.147	11.420	12.839
15	4.785	5.474	6.254	7.138	8.137	9.266	10.539	11.974	13.590	15.407
16	5.311	6.130	7.067	8.137	9.358	10.748	12.330	14.129	16.172	18.488
17	5.895	6.866	7.986	9.276	10.761	12.468	14.426	16.672	19.244	22.186
18	6.544	7.690	9.024	10.575	12.375	14.463	16.879	19.673	22.901	26.623
19	7.263	8.613	10.197	12.056	14.232	16.777	19.748	23.214	27.252	31.948
20	8.062	9.646	11.523	13.743	16.367	19.461	23.106	27.393	32.429	38.338

TABLE B

Present Value of $1 $P = \dfrac{1}{(1 + r)^n}$

Year	1%	2%	3%	4%	5%	6%	7%	8%	9%	10%	11%	12%	13%
1	0.990	0.980	0.971	0.962	0.952	0.943	0.935	0.926	0.917	0.909	0.901	0.893	0.885
2	0.980	0.961	0.943	0.925	0.907	0.890	0.873	0.857	0.842	0.826	0.812	0.797	0.783
3	0.971	0.942	0.915	0.889	0.864	0.840	0.816	0.794	0.772	0.751	0.731	0.712	0.693
4	0.961	0.924	0.888	0.855	0.823	0.792	0.763	0.735	0.708	0.683	0.659	0.636	0.613
5	0.951	0.906	0.863	0.822	0.784	0.747	0.713	0.681	0.650	0.621	0.593	0.567	0.543
6	0.942	0.888	0.837	0.790	0.746	0.705	0.666	0.630	0.596	0.564	0.535	0.507	0.480
7	0.933	0.871	0.813	0.760	0.711	0.665	0.623	0.583	0.547	0.513	0.482	0.452	0.425
8	0.923	0.853	0.789	0.731	0.677	0.627	0.582	0.540	0.502	0.467	0.434	0.404	0.376
9	0.914	0.837	0.766	0.703	0.645	0.592	0.544	0.500	0.460	0.424	0.391	0.361	0.333
10	0.905	0.820	0.744	0.676	0.614	0.558	0.508	0.463	0.422	0.386	0.352	0.322	0.295
11	0.896	0.804	0.722	0.650	0.585	0.527	0.475	0.429	0.388	0.350	0.317	0.287	0.261
12	0.887	0.788	0.701	0.625	0.557	0.497	0.444	0.397	0.356	0.319	0.286	0.257	0.231
13	0.879	0.773	0.681	0.601	0.530	0.469	0.415	0.368	0.326	0.290	0.258	0.229	0.204
14	0.870	0.758	0.661	0.577	0.505	0.442	0.388	0.340	0.299	0.263	0.232	0.205	0.181
15	0.861	0.743	0.642	0.555	0.481	0.417	0.362	0.315	0.275	0.239	0.209	0.183	0.160
16	0.853	0.728	0.623	0.534	0.458	0.394	0.339	0.292	0.252	0.218	0.188	0.163	0.141
17	0.844	0.714	0.605	0.513	0.436	0.371	0.317	0.270	0.231	0.198	0.170	0.146	0.125
18	0.836	0.700	0.587	0.494	0.416	0.350	0.296	0.250	0.212	0.180	0.153	0.130	0.111
19	0.828	0.686	0.570	0.475	0.396	0.331	0.277	0.232	0.194	0.164	0.138	0.116	0.098
20	0.820	0.673	0.554	0.456	0.377	0.312	0.258	0.215	0.178	0.149	0.124	0.104	0.087

Year	14%	15%	16%	17%	18%	19%	20%	21%	22%	23%	24%	25%
1	0.877	0.870	0.862	0.855	0.847	0.840	0.833	0.826	0.820	0.813	0.806	0.800
2	0.769	0.756	0.743	0.731	0.718	0.706	0.694	0.683	0.672	0.661	0.650	0.640
3	0.675	0.658	0.641	0.624	0.609	0.593	0.579	0.564	0.551	0.537	0.524	0.512
4	0.592	0.572	0.552	0.534	0.516	0.499	0.482	0.467	0.451	0.437	0.423	0.410
5	0.519	0.497	0.476	0.456	0.437	0.419	0.402	0.386	0.370	0.355	0.341	0.328
6	0.456	0.432	0.410	0.390	0.370	0.352	0.335	0.319	0.303	0.289	0.275	0.262
7	0.400	0.376	0.354	0.333	0.314	0.296	0.279	0.263	0.249	0.235	0.222	0.210
8	0.351	0.327	0.305	0.285	0.266	0.249	0.233	0.218	0.204	0.191	0.179	0.168
9	0.308	0.284	0.263	0.243	0.225	0.209	0.194	0.180	0.167	0.155	0.144	0.134
10	0.270	0.247	0.227	0.208	0.191	0.176	0.162	0.149	0.137	0.126	0.116	0.107
11	0.237	0.215	0.195	0.178	0.162	0.148	0.135	0.123	0.112	0.103	0.094	0.086
12	0.208	0.187	0.168	0.152	0.137	0.124	0.112	0.102	0.092	0.083	0.076	0.069
13	0.182	0.163	0.145	0.130	0.116	0.104	0.093	0.084	0.075	0.068	0.061	0.055
14	0.160	0.141	0.125	0.111	0.099	0.088	0.078	0.069	0.062	0.055	0.049	0.044
15	0.140	0.123	0.108	0.095	0.084	0.074	0.065	0.057	0.051	0.045	0.040	0.035
16	0.123	0.107	0.093	0.081	0.071	0.062	0.054	0.047	0.042	0.036	0.032	0.028
17	0.108	0.093	0.080	0.069	0.060	0.052	0.045	0.039	0.034	0.030	0.026	0.023
18	0.095	0.081	0.069	0.059	0.051	0.044	0.038	0.032	0.028	0.024	0.021	0.018
19	0.083	0.070	0.060	0.051	0.043	0.037	0.031	0.027	0.023	0.020	0.017	0.014
20	0.073	0.061	0.051	0.043	0.037	0.031	0.026	0.022	0.019	0.016	0.014	0.012

TABLE C

Future Value of an Ordinary Annuity of $1

$$F_n = \frac{(1 + r)^n - 1}{r}$$

Year	1%	2%	3%	4%	5%	6%	7%	8%	9%	10%
1	1.000	1.000	1.000	1.000	1.000	1.000	1.000	1.000	1.000	1.000
2	2.010	2.020	2.030	2.040	2.050	2.060	2.070	2.080	2.090	2.100
3	3.030	3.060	3.091	3.122	3.153	3.184	3.215	3.246	3.278	3.310
4	4.060	4.122	4.184	4.246	4.310	4.375	4.440	4.506	4.573	4.641
5	5.101	5.204	5.309	5.416	5.526	5.637	5.751	5.867	5.985	6.105
6	6.152	6.308	6.468	6.633	6.802	6.975	7.153	7.336	7.523	7.716
7	7.213	7.434	7.662	7.898	8.142	8.394	8.654	8.923	9.200	9.487
8	8.286	8.583	8.892	9.214	9.549	9.897	10.260	10.637	11.028	11.436
9	9.368	9.755	10.159	10.583	11.027	11.491	11.978	12.488	13.021	13.580
10	10.462	10.950	11.464	12.006	12.578	13.181	13.817	14.487	15.193	15.937
11	11.567	12.169	12.808	13.486	14.207	14.972	15.784	16.646	17.560	18.531
12	12.682	13.412	14.192	15.026	15.917	16.870	17.889	18.977	20.141	21.384
13	13.809	14.680	15.618	16.627	17.713	18.882	20.141	21.495	22.953	24.523
14	14.947	15.974	17.086	18.292	19.599	21.015	22.551	24.215	26.019	27.975
15	16.097	17.294	18.599	20.024	21.579	23.276	25.129	27.152	29.361	31.773
16	17.258	18.639	20.157	21.824	23.658	25.673	27.888	30.324	33.003	35.950
17	18.430	20.012	21.762	23.697	25.840	28.213	30.840	33.750	36.974	40.545
18	19.615	21.412	23.414	25.645	28.132	30.906	33.999	37.450	41.301	45.599
19	20.811	22.841	25.117	27.671	30.539	33.760	37.379	41.446	46.018	51.159
20	22.019	24.297	26.870	29.778	33.066	36.786	40.996	45.762	51.160	57.275

Year	11%	12%	13%	14%	15%	16%	17%	18%	19%	20%
1	1.000	1.000	1.000	1.000	1.000	1.000	1.000	1.000	1.000	1.000
2	2.110	2.120	2.130	2.140	2.150	2.160	2.170	2.180	2.190	2.200
3	3.342	3.374	3.407	3.440	3.473	3.506	3.539	3.572	3.606	3.640
4	4.710	4.779	4.850	4.921	4.993	5.066	5.141	5.215	5.291	5.368
5	6.228	6.353	6.480	6.610	6.742	6.877	7.014	7.154	7.297	7.442
6	7.913	8.115	8.323	8.536	8.754	8.977	9.207	9.442	9.683	9.930
7	9.783	10.089	10.405	10.731	11.067	11.414	11.772	12.142	12.523	12.916
8	11.859	12.300	12.757	13.233	13.727	14.240	14.773	15.327	15.902	16.499
9	14.164	14.776	15.416	16.085	16.786	17.518	18.285	19.086	19.923	20.799
10	16.722	17.549	18.420	19.337	20.304	21.321	22.393	23.521	24.709	25.959
11	19.561	20.655	21.814	23.045	24.349	25.733	27.200	28.755	30.404	32.150
12	22.713	24.133	25.650	27.271	29.002	30.850	32.824	34.931	37.180	39.581
13	26.212	28.029	29.985	32.088	34.352	36.786	39.404	42.219	45.245	48.497
14	30.095	32.393	34.883	37.581	40.505	43.672	47.103	50.818	54.841	59.196
15	34.405	37.280	40.417	43.842	47.580	51.659	56.110	60.965	66.261	72.035
16	39.190	42.753	46.672	50.980	55.718	60.925	66.649	72.939	79.850	87.442
17	44.501	48.884	53.739	59.117	65.075	71.673	78.979	87.068	96.022	105.931
18	50.396	55.750	61.725	68.394	75.836	84.141	93.405	103.740	115.266	128.117
19	56.940	63.440	70.749	78.969	88.212	98.603	110.284	123.414	138.166	154.740
20	64.203	72.052	80.947	91.025	102.444	115.379	130.033	146.628	165.418	186.688

TABLE D

Present Value of Annuity of $1

$$P_n = \frac{1}{r}\left[1 - \frac{1}{(1+r)^n}\right]$$

Year	1%	2%	3%	4%	5%	6%	7%	8%	9%	10%	11%	12%	13%
1	0.990	0.980	0.971	0.962	0.952	0.943	0.935	0.926	0.917	0.909	0.901	0.893	0.885
2	1.970	1.942	1.913	1.886	1.859	1.833	1.808	1.783	1.759	1.736	1.713	1.690	1.668
3	2.941	2.884	2.829	2.775	2.723	2.673	2.624	2.577	2.531	2.487	2.444	2.402	2.361
4	3.902	3.808	3.717	3.630	3.546	3.465	3.387	3.312	3.240	3.170	3.102	3.037	2.974
5	4.853	4.713	4.580	4.452	4.329	4.212	4.100	3.993	3.890	3.791	3.696	3.605	3.517
6	5.795	5.601	5.417	5.242	5.076	4.917	4.767	4.623	4.486	4.355	4.231	4.111	3.998
7	6.728	6.472	6.230	6.002	5.786	5.582	5.389	5.206	5.033	4.868	4.712	4.564	4.423
8	7.652	7.325	7.020	6.733	6.463	6.210	5.971	5.747	5.535	5.335	5.146	4.968	4.799
9	8.566	8.162	7.786	7.435	7.108	6.802	6.515	6.247	5.995	5.759	5.537	5.328	5.132
10	9.471	8.983	8.530	8.111	7.722	7.360	7.024	6.710	6.418	6.145	5.889	5.650	5.426
11	10.368	9.787	9.253	8.760	8.306	7.887	7.499	7.139	6.805	6.495	6.207	5.938	5.687
12	11.255	10.575	9.954	9.385	8.863	8.384	7.943	7.536	7.161	6.814	6.492	6.194	5.918
13	12.134	11.348	10.635	9.986	9.394	8.853	8.358	7.904	7.487	7.103	6.750	6.424	6.122
14	13.004	12.106	11.296	10.563	9.899	9.295	8.745	8.244	7.786	7.367	6.982	6.628	6.302
15	13.865	12.849	11.938	11.118	10.380	9.712	9.108	8.559	8.061	7.606	7.191	6.811	6.462
16	14.718	13.578	12.561	11.652	10.838	10.106	9.447	8.851	8.313	7.824	7.379	6.974	6.604
17	15.562	14.292	13.166	12.166	11.274	10.477	9.763	9.122	8.544	8.022	7.549	7.120	6.729
18	16.398	14.992	13.754	12.659	11.690	10.828	10.059	9.372	8.756	8.201	7.702	7.250	6.840
19	17.226	15.678	14.324	13.134	12.085	11.158	10.336	9.604	8.950	8.365	7.839	7.366	6.938
20	18.046	16.351	14.877	13.590	12.462	11.470	10.594	9.818	9.129	8.514	7.963	7.469	7.025

Year	14%	15%	16%	17%	18%	19%	20%	21%	22%	23%	24%	25%
1	0.877	0.870	0.862	0.855	0.847	0.840	0.833	0.826	0.820	0.813	0.806	0.800
2	1.647	1.626	1.605	1.585	1.566	1.547	1.528	1.509	1.492	1.474	1.457	1.440
3	2.322	2.283	2.246	2.210	2.174	2.140	2.106	2.074	2.042	2.011	1.981	1.952
4	2.914	2.855	2.798	2.743	2.690	2.639	2.589	2.540	2.494	2.448	2.404	2.362
5	3.433	3.352	3.274	3.199	3.127	3.058	2.991	2.926	2.864	2.803	2.745	2.689
6	3.889	3.784	3.685	3.589	3.498	3.410	3.326	3.245	3.167	3.092	3.020	2.951
7	4.288	4.160	4.039	3.922	3.812	3.706	3.605	3.508	3.416	3.327	3.242	3.161
8	4.639	4.487	4.344	4.207	4.078	3.954	3.837	3.726	3.619	3.518	3.421	3.329
9	4.946	4.772	4.607	4.451	4.303	4.163	4.031	3.905	3.786	3.673	3.566	3.463
10	5.216	5.019	4.833	4.659	4.494	4.339	4.192	4.054	3.923	3.799	3.682	3.571
11	5.453	5.234	5.029	4.836	4.656	4.486	4.327	4.177	4.035	3.902	3.776	3.656
12	5.660	5.421	5.197	4.988	4.793	4.611	4.439	4.278	4.127	3.985	3.851	3.725
13	5.842	5.583	5.342	5.118	4.910	4.715	4.533	4.362	4.203	4.053	3.912	3.780
14	6.002	5.724	5.468	5.229	5.008	4.802	4.611	4.432	4.265	4.108	3.962	3.824
15	6.142	5.847	5.575	5.324	5.092	4.876	4.675	4.489	4.315	4.153	4.001	3.859
16	6.265	5.954	5.668	5.405	5.162	4.938	4.730	4.536	4.357	4.189	4.033	3.887
17	6.373	6.047	5.749	5.475	5.222	4.990	4.775	4.576	4.391	4.219	4.059	3.910
18	6.467	6.128	5.818	5.534	5.273	5.033	4.812	4.608	4.419	4.243	4.080	3.928
19	6.550	6.198	5.877	5.584	5.316	5.070	4.843	4.635	4.442	4.263	4.097	3.942
20	6.623	6.259	5.929	5.628	5.353	5.101	4.870	4.657	4.460	4.279	4.110	3.954

TABLE E
Present Value of $1 Spread Uniformly Throughout the Time Period

Year Between		1%	2%	3%	4%	5%	6%	7%	8%	9%	10%	11%
0	1	0.9950	0.9901	0.9851	0.9803	0.9754	0.9706	0.9658	0.9610	0.9563	0.9516	0.9470
1	2	0.9851	0.9705	0.9560	0.9418	0.9278	0.9141	0.9005	0.8872	0.8740	0.8611	0.8483
2	3	0.9753	0.9512	0.9278	0.9049	0.8826	0.8608	0.8396	0.8189	0.7988	0.7791	0.7600
3	4	0.9656	0.9324	0.9004	0.8694	0.8395	0.8107	0.7829	0.7560	0.7300	0.7050	0.6808
4	5	0.9560	0.9139	0.8737	0.8353	0.7986	0.7635	0.7299	0.6979	0.6672	0.6379	0.6099
5	6	0.9465	0.8958	0.8479	0.8026	0.7597	0.7190	0.6806	0.6442	0.6098	0.5772	0.5463
6	7	0.9371	0.8781	0.8229	0.7711	0.7226	0.6772	0.6346	0.5947	0.5573	0.5223	0.4894
7	8	0.9277	0.8607	0.7985	0.7409	0.6874	0.6377	0.5917	0.5490	0.5093	0.4726	0.4385
8	9	0.9185	0.8437	0.7749	0.7118	0.6538	0.6006	0.5517	0.5068	0.4655	0.4276	0.3928
9	10	0.9094	0.8270	0.7520	0.6839	0.6219	0.5656	0.5144	0.4678	0.4254	0.3869	0.3519
10	11	0.9003	0.8106	0.7298	0.6571	0.5916	0.5327	0.4796	0.4318	0.3888	0.3501	0.3152
11	12	0.8914	0.7945	0.7082	0.6313	0.5628	0.5017	0.4472	0.3986	0.3553	0.3168	0.2824
12	13	0.8825	0.7788	0.6873	0.6066	0.5353	0.4724	0.4169	0.3680	0.3248	0.2866	0.2530
13	14	0.8737	0.7634	0.6670	0.5828	0.5092	0.4449	0.3888	0.3397	0.2968	0.2593	0.2266
14	15	0.8650	0.7483	0.6473	0.5599	0.4844	0.4190	0.3625	0.3136	0.2713	0.2347	0.2030
15	16	0.8564	0.7335	0.6282	0.5380	0.4608	0.3946	0.3380	0.2895	0.2479	0.2123	0.1819
16	17	0.8479	0.7189	0.6096	0.5169	0.4383	0.3716	0.3151	0.2672	0.2266	0.1921	0.1629
17	18	0.8395	0.7047	0.5916	0.4966	0.4169	0.3500	0.2938	0.2467	0.2071	0.1738	0.1459
18	19	0.8311	0.6907	0.5741	0.4771	0.3966	0.3296	0.2740	0.2277	0.1893	0.1573	0.1307
19	20	0.8228	0.6771	0.5571	0.4584	0.3772	0.3104	0.2554	0.2102	0.1730	0.1423	0.1171

Year Between		12%	13%	14%	15%	16%	17%	18%	19%	20%	21%	22%	23%	24%	25%
0	1	0.9423	0.9377	0.9332	0.9286	0.9241	0.9196	0.9152	0.9107	0.9063	0.9020	0.8976	0.8933	0.8891	0.8848
1	2	0.8358	0.8234	0.8112	0.7993	0.7875	0.7758	0.7644	0.7531	0.7421	0.7311	0.7204	0.7098	0.6994	0.6891
2	3	0.7413	0.7230	0.7053	0.6879	0.6710	0.6546	0.6385	0.6228	0.6075	0.5926	0.5781	0.5639	0.5501	0.5367
3	4	0.6574	0.6349	0.6131	0.5921	0.5718	0.5522	0.5333	0.5150	0.4974	0.4804	0.4639	0.4481	0.4327	0.4179
4	5	0.5831	0.5575	0.5330	0.5096	0.4873	0.4659	0.4455	0.4259	0.4072	0.3894	0.3723	0.3560	0.3404	0.3255
5	6	0.5172	0.4895	0.4634	0.4386	0.4152	0.3931	0.3721	0.3522	0.3334	0.3156	0.2988	0.2829	0.2678	0.2535
6	7	0.4587	0.4299	0.4029	0.3775	0.3538	0.3316	0.3108	0.2913	0.2730	0.2559	0.2398	0.2247	0.2106	0.1974
7	8	0.4068	0.3775	0.3502	0.3250	0.3015	0.2798	0.2596	0.2409	0.2235	0.2074	0.1924	0.1786	0.1657	0.1538
8	9	0.3608	0.3314	0.3045	0.2797	0.2569	0.2360	0.2168	0.1992	0.1830	0.1681	0.1544	0.1419	0.1303	0.1197
9	10	0.3200	0.2910	0.2647	0.2407	0.2189	0.1991	0.1811	0.1647	0.1498	0.1363	0.1239	0.1127	0.1025	0.0933
10	11	0.2838	0.2556	0.2301	0.2072	0.1866	0.1680	0.1513	0.1362	0.1227	0.1105	0.0995	0.0896	0.0807	0.0726
11	12	0.2517	0.2244	0.2001	0.1783	0.1590	0.1417	0.1264	0.1126	0.1004	0.0895	0.0798	0.0712	0.0634	0.0566
12	13	0.2233	0.1971	0.1739	0.1535	0.1355	0.1196	0.1055	0.0932	0.0822	0.0726	0.0641	0.0565	0.0499	0.0441
13	14	0.1980	0.1730	0.1512	0.1321	0.1154	0.1009	0.0882	0.0770	0.0673	0.0588	0.0514	0.0449	0.0393	0.0343
14	15	0.1756	0.1519	0.1314	0.1137	0.0984	0.0851	0.0736	0.0637	0.0551	0.0477	0.0413	0.0357	0.0309	0.0267
15	16	0.1558	0.1334	0.1143	0.0979	0.0838	0.0718	0.0615	0.0527	0.0451	0.0387	0.0331	0.0284	0.0243	0.0208
16	17	0.1382	0.1172	0.0993	0.0842	0.0714	0.0606	0.0514	0.0436	0.0369	0.0313	0.0266	0.0225	0.0191	0.0162
17	18	0.1225	0.1029	0.0864	0.0725	0.0609	0.0511	0.0429	0.0360	0.0302	0.0254	0.0213	0.0179	0.0150	0.0126
18	19	0.1087	0.0903	0.0751	0.0624	0.0519	0.0431	0.0358	0.0298	0.0248	0.0206	0.0171	0.0142	0.0118	0.0098
19	20	0.0964	0.0793	0.0653	0.0537	0.0442	0.0364	0.0299	0.0246	0.0203	0.0167	0.0137	0.0113	0.0093	0.0077

Key Terms

Accounting rate of return   provides a profitability measurement of capital investment projects that does not take into account the time value of money. It is determined by dividing the average annual incremental income for a project by the required capital investment (or one-half of the capital investment).

Annuity   refers to a uniform series of cash flows.

Annuity due   is a type of annuity in which the initial cash flow is received or paid immediately.

Capital rationing   refers to a situation in which there is a shortage of funds for investment relative to acceptable capital investment projects.

Compounding   refers to the process for determining the future value of a receipt or series of cash flows at a given interest rate.

Cost of capital   is the discount rate used in discounted cash flow analysis. In the approach advocated in this text, it would be measured by taking the weighted average cost of all long-term capital sources used by the enterprise.

Discounted cash flow approaches   to capital budgeting refers to the time-adjusted rate of return and net present value approaches, both of which discount future cash flows to present values.

Discounting   is the process of converting future cash flows to their present value.

Interpolation   is the process of calculating time-adjusted rate of return when the correct rate falls between whole integers (numbers).

Mutually exclusive   projects are those for which acceptance of one means automatic rejection of other projects. Two different uses (capital projects) for the same piece of land would be one example.

Net present value   is a discounted cash flow method of capital budgeting that discounts future cash flows by the cost of capital. The net investment outlay is then subtracted from the present value of the future cash flows resulting in a positive or negative net present value amount.

Ordinary annuity   is a type of annuity in which the initial cash flow is received or paid in one year.

Payback   is a method of evaluating capital investment projects that measures how rapidly net investment outlays are recovered. It does not measure profitability but rather liquidity of capital projects. It is not a time value of money adjusted method.

Present value   results from discounting future cash flows by a discount rate, which determines the valuation of the cash flows at the present time.

Time-adjusted rate of return   is a discounted cash flow method of capital budgeting that discounts future cash flows by the interest rate that will make them exactly equal to the net investment outlay.

Time value of money   is the concept that a dollar in hand today is worth more than a dollar to be received in a year. The question of how much is based on the interest rate in effect.

Questions

Q13–1   Why is payback ineffective in terms of providing a measure of profitability for capital investment projects?

Q13–2 Why is the question of the superiority of using the average investment rather than total investment when using the accounting rate of return a totally irrelevant issue?

Q13–3 Why is depreciation irrelevant when using discounted cash flow methods of analyzing capital investment projects?

Q13–4 What does the term *cost of capital* mean?

Q13–5 How does the usage of cost of capital differ between the TARR and the NPV methods?

Q13–6 Why are the results of using TARR and NPV consistent with each other?

Q13–7 When two capital investment projects are mutually exclusive, why does the incremental approach to NPV provide a particularly useful frame of analysis?

Q13–8 Given two mutually exclusive capital investment projects having the same useful economic life, the one with the higher time-adjusted rate of return is always superior. Is this statement correct? Explain.

Q13–9 In what ways is the concept of "break even" present in discounted cash flow analysis?

Q13–10 What is capital rationing?

Q13–11 In selecting capital budgeting projects in a capital rationing situation, projects should be ranked in terms of highest net present value per dollar of investment. Is this statement correct? Explain.

Q13–12 What problems do you see in terms of ranking projects in capital rationing situations?

Q13–13 If two mutually exclusive capital investment projects have the same initial investment but have unequal lives, why is TARR not a good method for selecting between them?

Q13–14 Where two mutually exclusive capital investment projects have the same initial investment but unequal lives, what is the crucial factor for selecting between them?

Q13–15 How may analysis of projects with unequal lives be effectively implemented?

Q13–16 Briefly explain the difference between compounding and discounting.

Q13–17 How can an ordinary annuity table of present values be used for annuity due types of projects?

Q13–18 Why do you think that discounting has proven to be much more popular in capital budgeting analysis than compounding?

Exercises

E13–1 **Annuity with payback, accounting rate of return and TARR.** A capital investment project requires an investment of $100,000. It has an expected life of 4 years with annual cash flows of $40,000 received at the end of each year.

Required:
1. Compute payback (assume for this part that the cash flows occur evenly throughout each year).
2. Determine the accounting rate of return (use the total investment base and straight-line depreciation with no salvage).
3. Compute the time-adjusted rate of return.

E13–2 **Payback, accounting rate of return, and TARR.** A capital investment project requires an investment of $100,000. It has an expected life of 4 years. Annual cash flows at the end of each year are

Year	Amount
1	$30,000
2	60,000
3	45,000
4	25,000

Required:
1. Compute payback (assume for this part that cash flows occur evenly throughout the year).
2. Determine the accounting rate of return (use the total investment base and straight-line depreciation with no salvage).
3. Compute the time-adjusted rate of return.

E13–3 **TARR and NPV.** A capital investment project requires an initial investment of $170,000. It has the following annual cash flows at the end of each year.

Year	Amount
1	$60,000
2	90,000
3	70,000
4	30,000

Required:
1. Determine the time-adjusted rate of return for the project.
2. Determine the net present value of the project if the cost of capital is 10%.

E13–4 **TARR and NPV.** A project requires an investment of $2,487. It is expected to have 3 cash inflows of $1,000 occurring at the end of each of the next 3 years.

Required:
1. Determine the time-adjusted rate of return for the project.
2. Determine the net present value of the project at discount rates of (a) 8%, (b) 10%, (c) 12%.

E13–5 **Compounding.** Refer to the data in Exercise 13–4.

Required:
1. Compound forward to the end of the *third* year both the initial investment and the cash flows at 8%. Discount back any difference at 8% and compare your answer with part (2a) of Exercise 13–4.
2. Compound forward to the end of the *third* year both the initial investment and the cash flows at 10%.
3. Compound forward to the end of the *third* year both the initial investment and the cash flows at 12%. Discount back any difference at 12% and compare your answer with part (2c) of Exercise 13–4.

E13–6 **Two projects, NPV.** Joachim Company is evaluating two mutually exclusive projects with 3-year lives. Each project requires an investment of $10,000. The projects have the following cash inflows received at the end of each year:

Year	Project 1	Project 2
1	$6,000	$ 4,000
2	6,000	4,000
3	5,000	10,000

Required:
1. Find the net present value of each project using an 18% discount rate.

2. Find the net present value of each project using a 10% discount rate.
3. What do you conclude?

E13–7 **Mutually exclusive projects, NPV, incremental approach.** Raymond Corporation is evaluating two mutually exclusive investment projects. Project A requires an investment of $12,000, and project B an investment of $11,000. Each project has a 3-year life and the following configuration of cash flows at the end of each year:

Year	Project A	Project B
1	$8,000	$ 4,000
2	6,000	4,000
3	5,000	11,000

Required: 1. Compute the net present value for each project separately at an 18% discount rate.
2. Compute the net present value at an 18% discount rate using the incremental approach.

E13–8 **Mutually exclusive projects, NPV, incremental approach.** Refer to the data in Exercise 13–7.

Required: 1. Compute the net present value for each project separately at a 6% discount rate.
2. Compute the net present value at a 6% discount rate using the incremental approach.

E13–9 **Multiple choice, determining capital acquisition cost.** Cause Company is planning to invest in a machine with a useful life of 5 years and no salvage value. The machine is expected to produce cash flow from operations, net of income taxes, of $20,000 in each of the 5 years. Cause's expected rate of return is 10%. Information on present value and future amount factors is as follows.

	Period				
	1	*2*	*3*	*4*	*5*
Present value of $1 at 10%	.909	.826	.751	.683	.621
Present value of annuity of $1 at 10%	.909	1.736	2.487	3.170	3.791
Future amount of $1 at 10%	1.100	1.210	1.331	1.464	1.611
Future amount of annuity of $1 at 10%	1.000	2.100	3.310	4.641	6.105

How much will the machine cost?
   a. $32,220
   b. $62,100
   c. $75,820
   d. $122,100

(CPA Adapted)

E13–10 **Finding TARR by interpolation.** A project with a 5-year life is expected to receive annual cash flows of $12,000 per year at the end of each year. The project has a required investment outlay of $40,000.

Required: Determine the project's time-adjusted rate of return.

E13–11   **Determining cash flows from the interest rate.** A project requires an investment of $20,000. The cash inflows are expected to be uniform for a 5-year period beginning at the end of the first year. The time-adjusted rate of return on the project is 12%.

Required: Determine the annual cash flows.

Problems

P13–12   **Minimizing cost of expansion.** The Paramount Bakery owns a bread slicing machine that was acquired 4 years ago at a cost of $200,000. It is expected to last for 6 more years. This machine has an annual capacity of 100,000 breads. It requires one employee to tend it when the breads are wrapped. Annual salary of the employee is $12,000. Variable manufacturing overhead is two and one-half cents per bread sliced and wrapped.

Paramount forecasts an increased demand for its breads. Over the next 10 years, the following demand is projected (in breads):

Year	Demand
1	75,000
2	80,000
3	120,000
4	150,000
5	175,000
6	180,000
7	180,000
8	180,000
9	190,000
10	200,000

Paramount could acquire a newer model of the bread slicing machine at a cost of $300,000. The old machine has a trade-in value of $60,000 now. The new machine has an annual capacity of 200,000 breads. It is fully automated and would not need an employee tending it when the bread is wrapped. Variable manufacturing overhead is one cent per bread sliced and wrapped. The new machine is expected to last for 10 years. Paramount is investigating the following investment proposals:

Plan 1: Buy a second machine at the beginning of year 3 and another one at the beginning of year 7 when the original machine wears out. Purchase prices are expected to remain constant. Salvage (residual) values at the end of the tenth year are expected to be $40,000 for the machine acquired at the beginning of year 3 and $120,000 for the machine acquired at the beginning of year 7.
Plan 2: Acquire the newer model immediately. It would have no trade-in value at the end of the tenth year.

Required: Determine a net present value for each plan separately. Cost of capital is 10% (assume that all cash flows occur at the end of the year).

P13–13   **Mutually exclusive revenue generating projects.** Bernie Cole has $100,000 that he wants to invest in a business. He is looking at two possible proposals, a bicycle shop and a gift shop. He would like to be in business for 4 years and then sell out. Shown below are the expected revenues, variable costs, and fixed costs requiring cash outlays for the two alternatives. All costs occur at year end.

Bicycle Shop

Year	1	2	3	4
Revenues	$80,000	$120,000	$150,000	$160,000
Variable costs	20,000	30,000	37,500	40,000
Fixed costs	10,000	10,000	12,000	15,000

Gift Shop

Year	1	2	3	4
Revenues	$120,000	$150,000	$102,000	$90,000
Variable costs	40,000	50,000	34,000	30,000
Fixed costs	15,000	15,000	15,000	20,000

Cole estimates that the bicycle shop could be sold for $125,000 and the gift shop could be sold for $60,000 at the end of the fourth year.

Required: Show the net resent value of each project assuming a cost of capital of 16%.

P13–14 **Incremental NPV, service firm.** Salem Transit, Inc., has decided to inaugurate express bus service between its headquarters city and a nearby suburb (one-way fare of $.70) and is considering the purchase of either 32- or 52-passenger buses, on which pertinent estimates are as follows:

	32-Passenger Bus	52-Passenger Bus
Number of each to be purchased	6	4
Useful life	8 years	8 years
Purchase price of each bus (paid on delivery)	$100,000	$130,000
Mileage per gallon	10	7.5
Salvage value per bus	$10,000	$12,500
Drivers' hourly wage	$6.00	$7.50
Price per gallon gasoline	$1.25	$1.25
Other annual cash expenses (total)	$22,500	$20,000

During the daily rush hour (which totals 4 hours), all buses would be in service and are expected to operate at full capacity (state law prohibits standees) in both directions of the route, each bus covering the route 12 times (6 round trips) during that period. During the remainder of the 16-hour daily service period, 500 passengers would be carried, and Salem would operate 4 buses on the route. Part-time drivers (paid at the regular rate) would be employed to drive during the rush hours. A bus traveling the route all day would go 480 miles, and one traveling only during rush hours would go 120 miles a day during the 260-day year.

Required:
1. Prepare a schedule showing the computation of estimated annual revenue of the new route for both alternatives.
2. Prepare a schedule showing the computation of estimated annual drivers' wages for both alternatives.

3. Prepare a schedule showing the computation of estimated annual cost of gasoline for both alternatives.

4. Assuming that a minimum rate of return of 12% before income taxes is desired and that all annual cash flows occur at the end of the year, prepare separate net present value analyses of the above.

(CPA Adapted)

13–15 **Equipment acquisition.** The Baxter Company manufactures toys and other short-lived fad-type items. The research and development department came up with an item that would make a good promotional gift for office equipment dealers. Aggressive and effective effort by Baxter's sales personnel has resulted in almost firm commitments for this product for the next 3 years. It is expected that the product's value will be exhausted by that time.

In order to produce the quantity demanded, Baxter will need to buy additional machinery and rent some additional space. It appears that about 25,000 square feet will be needed; currently available are 12,500 square feet of presently unused, but leased, space. (Baxter's present lease, with 10 years to run, costs $3.00 a foot.) There is another 12,500 square feet adjoining the Baxter facility that Baxter will rent for 3 years at $4.00 per square foot per year if it decides to make this product.

The equipment will be purchased for about $900,000. It will require $30,000 in modifications, $60,000 for installation, and $90,000 for testing; all of these activities will be handled by a firm of engineers hired by Baxter. All of the expenditures will be paid for on January 1, 19X3.

The equipment should have a salvage value of about $180,000 at the end of the third year. No additional general overhead costs are expected to be incurred.

The following estimates of revenues and expenses as they would be reported on the firm's external financial statements for this product for the 3 years have been developed.

	19X3	19X4	19X5
Sales	$1,000,000	$1,600,000	$800,000
Material, labor, and incurred overhead	400,000	750,000	350,000
Assigned general overhead	40,000	75,000	35,000
Rent	87,500	87,500	87,500
Depreciation	450,000	300,000	150,000
	$ 977,500	$1,212,500	$622,500
Net income	$ 22,500	$ 387,500	$177,500

Required:

1. If the company requires a 2-year payback period for its investment, would it undertake this project? Show your supporting calculations clearly.

2. A newly hired business school graduate recommends that the company consider the use of net present value analysis to study this project. If the company sets a required rate of return of 20%, will this project be accepted? Show your supporting calculations clearly. (Assume that all operating revenues and expenses occur at the end of the year.)

(CMA Adapted)

P13–16 **Make or buy, equipment replacement.** Shlager Company has been making a part for its industrial scooping machine. It is presently making the part using its CPE machine. Variable costs for the part are $3 for direct materials, $2 for direct labor, and $1 for variable manufacturing overhead.

The Gross Company has offered to sell the part to Shlager for $10 per part including shipping.

Another alternative is to replace the CPE machine with a newer model. The newer model would cost $50,000. It would cut direct labor cost to $1 per unit and variable costs to $.50 per part. If the newer model is acquired, the old machine would be sold for $20,000.

Shlager needs 20,000 parts per year for the next 3 years. At that point, any capital equipment would be sold. The CPE machine could be sold for $5,000 in 3 years. The newer model could be sold for $15,000.

All costs are assumed to occur evenly throughout the year (use Table E). Cost of capital is 12%.

Required: Use the net present value approach to analyze each of the three alternatives.

P13–17 **Capital rationing.** Figuroa Company is evaluating its capital investment projects for the forthcoming year. A total of eight projects have net present values exceeding the capital investment outlays. They are shown below:

Project	Capital Investment	Net Present Value
A	$2,000,000	$2,400,000
B	1,000,000	1,260,000
C	500,000	530,000
D	800,000	890,000
E	600,000	810,000
F	1,400,000	1,680,000
G	1,100,000	1,250,000
H	1,600,000	1,710,000

Figuroa will not invest more than $3,000,000. If project A is selected, neither E nor F can be selected. E and F can be selected together or separately.

Required: How should the $3,000,000 be invested to maximize the net present value? Assume an unlimited opportunity for investment exists at 8%.

P13–18 **Make or buy, NPV analysis.** Lamb Company manufactures several lines of machine products. One unique part, a valve stem, requires specialized tools that need to be replaced. Management has decided that the only alternative to replacing these tools is to acquire the valve stem from an outside source. A supplier is willing to provide the valve stem at a unit sales price of $20 if at least 70,000 units are ordered annually.

Lamb's average usage of valve stems over the past 3 years has been 80,000 units each year. Expectations are that this volume will remain constant over the next 5 years. Cost records indicate that unit manufacturing costs for the last several years have been as follows:

Direct material	$ 3.80
Direct labor	3.70
Variable factory overhead	1.70
Fixed factory overhead[a]	4.50
Total unit cost	$13.70

[a]Depreciation accounts for two-thirds of the fixed overhead. The balance is for other fixed overhead costs of the factory that require cash expenditures.

If the specialized tools are purchased, they will cost $2,500,000 and will have a disposal value of $100,000 after their expected economic life of 5 years. Cost of capital is 12%.

The sales representative for the manufacturer of the new tools stated, "The new tools will allow direct labor and variable factory overhead to be reduced by $1.60 per unit." Data from another manufacturer using identical tools and experiencing similar operating conditions, except that annual production generally averages 110,000 units, confirm the direct labor and variable factory overhead savings. However, the manufacturer indicates that it experienced an increase in raw material cost due to the higher quality of material that had to be used with the new tools. The manufacturer indicated that its costs have been as follows:

Direct material	$ 4.50
Direct labor	3.00
Variable factory overhead	.80
Fixed factory overhead	5.00
Total unit cost	$13.30

Required:

1. Present a net present value analysis covering the economic life of the new specialized tools to determine whether Lamb Company should replace the old tools or purchase the valve stem from an outside supplier.

2. Identify any additional factors Lamb Company should consider before deciding whether to replace the tools or purchase the valve stem from an outside supplier.

(CMA Adapted)

P13–19   Equipment replacement. The management of Essen Manufacturing Company is currently evaluating a proposal to purchase a new and innovative drill press as a replacement for a less efficient piece of similar equipment that would then be sold. The cost of the equipment including delivery and installation is $175,000. If the equipment is purchased, Essen will incur costs of $5,000 in removing the present equipment and revamping service facilities. The present equipment has a book value of $100,000 and a remaining useful life of 10 years. Due to new technical improvements that have made the equipment outmoded, it presently has a resale value of only $40,000.

Additional information:

a. Management has provided you with the following comparative manufacturing cost tabulation:

	Present Equipment	*New Equipment*
Annual production — units	400,000	500,000
Annual costs:		
Labor	$30,000	$25,000
Operating costs:		
Depreciation (10% of asset book value)	$10,000	$17,500
Other costs, one-quarter of which require cash	48,000	20,000
	$58,000	$37,500
Total	$88,000	$62,500

b. Management believes that if the present equipment is not replaced now, it will have to wait 7 years before replacement is justifiable.

c. Both pieces of equipment are expected to have a negligible salvage value at the end of 10 years.

d. Revenues would increase by $50,000 per year with the new equipment.

Required:

1. In order to assist the management of Essen in reaching a decision on the proposal, prepare a schedule showing the computation of the net present value of investment at a 6% discount rate using the incremental approach.

2. Would you recommend this investment? Why?

(CPA Adapted)

P13–20   **Different investment lives.** A capital investment project requiring an investment of $10,000 has a single cash inflow of $12,000 coming at the end of the first year. A second capital investment project also requiring an investment of $10,000 has a single cash inflow of $15,600 coming in at the end of the third year.

Required:

1. Determine the time-adjusted rate of return for each project.

2. Determine the net present value for each project at a discount rate of 18%.

3. Determine the net present value for each project at 6%.

P13–21   **Equipment replacement, uneven lives.** Oshry Company owns a drill press that was acquired 3 years ago at a cost of $80,000. The drill press is expected to last another 7 years with a salvage of $3,000. Annual variable operating costs are $55,000 and fixed out of pocket costs are $15,000 per year.

A newer model drill press could be acquired now at a cost of $100,000. If the new drill press is acquired, the old one would be sold now for $50,000. Annual variable operating costs are $30,000 and fixed out of pocket costs are $20,000 per year. Salvage value at the end of 7 years is expected to be $40,000 (it would decline to $8,000 at the end of 10 years).

All operating costs are expected to occur at the end of the year. Cost of capital is 10%.

Required: Prepare an incremental NPV analysis showing whether replacement should occur now.

CHAPTER 14

Advanced Topics in Capital Budgeting

Learning Objectives

After reading this chapter you should be able to:

1. Understand the various income tax factors that affect capital budgeting calculations.

2. Comprehend why working capital investments should be included in capital budgeting calculations.

3. Have knowledge of the weighted average cost of capital.

4. Appreciate how inflation can be handled in capital budgeting analysis (Appendix 14–A).

5. Comprehend how to analyze financing alternatives after the investment decision has been made (Appendix 14–B).

C apital budgeting methods were presented and discussed in Chapter 13. In this chapter, several additional issues pertaining to this subject will be considered.

Income taxes were not considered in capital budgeting calculations in Chapter 13. Profitable capital investments, of course, result in income taxes that must be paid. The situation is not that simple, however. Although tax benefits of capital investment have been extensively scaled back by the Tax Reform Act of 1986, they still remain considerable. The tax area will be the first topic covered.

Many projects require investments in working capital. Working capital investments represent incremental amounts tied up in inventories and accounts receivable resulting from specific capital projects. These investments are amounts that are subsequently recovered. Hence their net cash flow effect is zero, but they have a very real cost due to opportunity costs and the time value of money. Proper treatment of working capital will be briefly examined in this chapter.

Another topic to be considered is the cost of capital — a subject that has been surrounded by much controversy in the finance literature. We shall briefly examine the conceptual nature of the cost of capital.

An example involving taxes and working capital will be presented at the end of the chapter for the purpose of unifying and illustrating these complexities. This example is an extension of a previous illustration used in Chapter 13. Two other topics affecting capital budgeting are presented in Appendixes 14–A and 14–B. The first is a subject that is often ignored in capital budgeting analysis. At issue is the question of how the possibility of inflation should be considered as part of the capital budgeting process. A simple but effective method for taking inflation into account will be presented. The illustration used at the end of the chapter is further extended in Appendix 14–A to bring in inflation.

Finally, in the second appendix to the chapter, different financing alternatives for acceptable capital budgeting projects will be examined. Our emphasis will be on a discounted cash flow framework for comparing financing alternatives.

Capital Budgeting and Income Taxes

The discussion of capital budgeting in Chapter 13 omitted income taxes in order to focus on the basic elements of the discounted cash flow analysis. Nevertheless, income taxes are an extremely important aspect of capital budgeting. Income of corporations is presently taxed at a maximum rate of 34%.

The 34% rate begins at a level of $75,000 of taxable income. The first $50,000 of taxable income is taxed at 15%. Between $50,000 and $75,000 of taxable income, the rate is 25%.

The 1986 tax act decreased the benefits of accelerated depreciation that had existed since 1981. At the same time, the rules were made more complex. The act created six different classes of capital assets with stated lives for tax depreciation purposes. Some of the principal types of assets in the six classes are shown in Exhibit 14–1. In addition to the classes shown in Exhibit 14–1, there are two other classes. One is a 27½-year class for residential real estate and the other is a 31½-year class for nonresidential real estate. Both of these latter classes require straight-line depreciation.

Depreciation rates for the six classes are shown in Exhibit 14–2. You will be referring to this table several times as you analyze later exhibits. Several points are in order relative to Exhibit 14–2. First of all, the percentages are based on a complicated combination of declining balance depreciation combined with a straight-line switchback in later years. Secondly, salvage value is not deducted from the cost of the asset when calculating the tax depreciation. Finally, notice that each of the six classes is depreciated over one more year than is in the class itself. This is due to the complicated formula in the tax act that requires a half-year's depreciation beyond the class life to compensate for, in effect, one-half year's depreciation in the first year. Note that all columns total 100%.

Most gains or losses on the disposal of fixed assets are taxed at the rate of 34%. An example of taxation of gains or losses on fixed asset disposals will appear in the illustrative problem at the end of the chapter.

A last point to note about the 1986 tax act is that it eliminated the **investment tax credit.** This was an important benefit that reduced corporate taxes by 10% of the cost of eligible capital assets in the year of acquisition. In

EXHIBIT 14–1

Asset Depreciation Classes Created by the Tax Reform Act of 1986

Class (Years)	Types of Assets
3 years	Short-lived special manufacturing tools and handling devices in some industries. Examples include rubber manufacturing, glass products, fabricated metals, and manufacture of motor vehicles.
5 years	Cars, light trucks, and certain manufacturing equipment: oil drilling, construction, chemical manufacturing, and some clothing manufacturing. Also special tools for selected industries such as boat building.
7 years	Most heavy manufacturing equipment.
10 years	Includes railroad track, electrical generating and transmission equipment, cement manufacturing equipment as well as the food processing equipment for grain, sugar, and vegetable oil.
15 years	Includes gas pipelines and nuclear plants.
20 years	Includes sewer pipes and phone cables.

EXHIBIT 14–2
1986 Tax Reform Act Depreciation Allowances

Year	3-Year	5-Year	7-Year	10-Year	15-Year	20-Year
1	33.00	20.00	14.28	10.00	5.00	3.75
2	45.00	32.00	24.49	18.00	9.50	7.22
3	15.00[a]	19.20	17.49	14.40	8.55	6.68
4	7.00	11.52[a]	12.49	11.52	7.69	6.18
5		11.52	8.93[a]	9.22	6.93	5.71
6		5.76	8.93	7.37	6.23	5.28
7			8.93	6.55[a]	5.90[a]	4.89
8			4.46	6.55	5.90	4.52
9				6.55	5.90	4.46[a]
10				6.55	5.90	4.46
11				3.29	5.90	4.46
12					5.90	4.46
13					5.90	4.46
14					5.90	4.46
15					5.90	4.46
16					3.00	4.46
17						4.46
18						4.46
19						4.46
20						4.46
21						2.25
	100	100	100	100	100	100

[a]Indicates the year of switchback to straight-line depreciation.

summary, although the 1986 tax act lowered the maximum corporate income tax rate from 46% to 34%, it took away the important investment tax credit and slowed down tax depreciation benefits.

Working Capital Investment

Working capital of a firm equals its current assets minus its current liabilities. Capital investment projects often require sizable incremental **working capital investments** in inventories and accounts receivable. As incremental investments, of course, the implication is that the amounts differ between alternatives.

There are many reasons why working capital requirements differ between capital investment projects. For example, a larger project may require greater average investments in inventories and accounts receivable than would a smaller one. Another situation arises in cases where improved equipment comes on the market. If the new model produces more rapidly than the old equipment, the firm may be able to decrease its average inventory hold-ings because new orders can be filled faster with the new equipment.

Working capital investments are recovered at later points in the life of the capital project. As such, the effect of working capital investment differen-tials is that they have a zero undiscounted net cash flow effect. However, the important point to keep in mind is the *timing* effect. Because money has a time value, the cost to the firm is equal to the present value differential re-sulting from the timing difference. The timing difference entails an opportu-nity cost to the firm. The nature of working capital investments as an opportunity cost can be understood from the following example.

A Working Capital Example

Assume that a capital project requires a $5,000 working capital investment that is effective immediately and is recovered in 3 years. Cost of capital is 10%. Because the present value of $1 to be received in 3 years at 10% is .751, the present value of the recovered working capital is $3,755 ($5,000 × .751). The cost to the firm of the working capital investment, when viewed from the present value perspective, is $1,245 (the $5,000 that would be immediately tied up reduced by the present value of the recovery of $3,755).

Let us now see what is foregone by tying up funds in working capital re-quirements of projects. Assume that the $5,000 could be invested at 10% for 3 years with interest received annually at the end of each year. The resulting pattern of cash flows would be

	0	1	2	3
Investment	−$5,000			
Lost earnings		$500	$500	$500

The present value of the lost earnings would be equal to $500 × 2.487 (the present value of a 3-year ordinary annuity of $1 discounted at 10%), which equals $1,243.50. This is exactly the same amount as previously determined (save for a $1.50 rounding error) when the working capital investment and recovery were compared in present value terms. Hence, tying up funds in working capital requirements of capital projects is tantamount to losing the interest earnings on an alternative investment that would earn interest at the discount rate. Working capital investments are thus a classic example of an opportunity cost. Let us next consider the tax effects on working capital investment.

Working Capital Investments and Income Taxes

If working capital investments result in lost earnings, income taxes on the lost earnings are also avoided. Exhibit 14–3 takes the same example of a

EXHIBIT 14–3
Working Capital Investments and Income Taxes

	0	1	2	3
Working capital investment	−$ 5,000			
Recovery of working capital investment				$ 5,000
Times present value factor at 10%				× .751
Present value of working capital	3,755			$ 3,755
Net present value of working capital investment	−$ 1,245[a]			

Lost Earnings "Proof" of Equality

	0	1	2	3
Lost interest on investment at 16 ⅔%		−$833.33	−$833.33	−$ 833.33
Avoided income taxes on lost investment (40%)		333.33	333.33	333.33
Lost interest after taxes		−$500	−$500	−$ 500
Present value of lost interest after taxes (−$500 × 2.487)	−$1,243.50[a]			

[a]$1.50 rounding error.

$5,000 working capital investment with recovery in 3 years, a discount factor of 10% and a 40% income tax rate. For simplicity, the income tax effects are assumed to occur at the same time as each of the cash flow effects. The 10% discount factor is assumed to be the weighted average after-tax cost of capital, a topic to be discussed shortly. As long as the after-tax earnings rate on the foregone investment opportunity equals the after-tax cost of capital, income taxes should not be taken out of the working capital investment. In Exhibit 14–3, the before-tax earnings rate on the investment foregone is 16⅔%. This is determined by dividing the after-tax earnings rate of 10% by 1 minus the tax rate or 60% in our example. The before-tax earnings on the imputed investment would therefore be $833.33 ($5,000 × 16⅔%). Notice the equality between the present value of the working capital investment and the present value of the imputed earnings on the investment foregone on an after-tax basis in Exhibit 14–3 (save for a rounding error of $1.50).

Working capital requirements are easily "plugged" into the capital budgeting framework illustrated in Chapter 13. Investments in working capital are inserted as cash outflows when they are expected to occur and recoveries are shown as cash inflows at the time points when they are expected to materialize. Appropriate handling of working capital is shown in examples appearing later in this chapter.

Cost of Capital

Cost of capital has been referred to, up to this point, as a minimum required rate of return or "hurdle rate" that capital investment projects must clear by having a time-adjusted rate of return at least equal to the cost of capital. Similarly, if the net present value approach were being used, a project would have to have a positive net present value for investment to take place.

The conceptual nature as well as the actual measurement of a firm's cost of capital is an important subject that is discussed in depth in finance courses. It is also a subject that has engendered a great deal of controversy. A brief introduction to the subject for the purpose of gaining insight into its role in capital budgeting calculations should suffice for our purposes.

Conceptually, the cost of capital measurement is intended to provide a minimum required rate of return on capital projects that will at least maintain the current market value of the common stock of the enterprise. The measurement of cost of capital, however, takes into account all of the long-term sources of investment in the firm that are used by the firm as a means for financing capital budgeting projects. In measuring cost of capital, these sources are "weighted," based on their market value. In our brief discussion we will consider only common stock and long-term debt of a firm whose securities are publicly traded on a regional or national securities exchange. Extensive modifications would have to be made for firms that are privately owned.

Common Stock

From the theoretical standpoint, market values of stocks are determined by investors discounting expected future dividends at a rate that takes into account the risk inherent in the security. This is usually simplified and converted into a rate by dividing the current dividend of a security by its market price. In addition, a desired growth factor for future dividends is usually included in the calculation. The required rate of return on common stock thus becomes

$$\frac{\text{Current annual dividend per share}}{\text{Market value per share}} + \frac{\text{Expected rate of growth in dividends per share}}{\text{(expressed as a percentage)}} = \frac{\text{Required rate of return on common stock}}{}$$

If the common shares sell for \$62.50 each and the annual dividend rate is \$5 per share, the current annual dividend rate is 8% ($5 ÷ $62.50). Assuming an expected growth factor in dividends of 2% would therefore result in a 10% cost of equity capital.

Long-Term Debt

Cost of long-term debt such as bonds payable is easier to determine. Like the common stock, it will be based on the current market value of the firm's outstanding debt. When the market value of a bond is divided into the annual interest paid to a bondholder, the effective interest rate is determined. Thus if a $1,000 bond, with a stated rate of interest of 8%, presently sells for $960 in the market, the effective rate of interest would be 8 1/3% ($80 ÷ $960). However, bond interest, unlike dividends, is deductible by the firm for income tax purposes. Given a corporate tax rate of 34%, the after-tax interest cost would be $52.80. The $52.80 represents the before-tax interest of $80 reduced by the tax saving of $27.20 ($80 × .34).

Therefore, the effective after-tax rate for the bonds would be determined by

$$\frac{\text{After-tax interest}}{\text{Market value of the debt}} = \text{After-tax interest rate}$$

In our case this would be

$$\frac{\$52.80}{\$960} = 5.5\%$$

The Weighted Average Cost of Capital

The **weighted average cost of capital** is determined by multiplying the total proportion of capital from each source by its rate and summing the total. In the example developed above, assume that the total market value of outstanding common stock is $2,040,000 and the market value of the bonds is $960,000. Computation of the weighted average cost of capital of 8.56% is shown in Exhibit 14–4.

EXHIBIT 14–4
Weighted Average Cost of Capital

Source	(1) Market Value	(2) Proportion of Total Market Value		(3) Cost of Capital of Source	(4) (2) × (3) Weighted Average Cost of Capital
Common stock	$2,040,000	68%	×	10 %	6.8 %
Long-term debt	960,000	32	×	5.5	1.76
	$3,000,000	100%			8.56%

The Risk Factor

The 8.56% represents the minimum earnings necessary on new projects to maintain the market value of the common stock. Capital budgeting projects, however, may have differing degrees of risk. Risk in the capital budgeting context refers to the degree of possible variation of the future cash flows that can be expected for each capital investment project.

A widely used method for coping with risk where the weighted average cost of capital is used is to have an "add on" to the basic cost of capital rate based on the risk that is perceived in individual capital investment projects. For example, a firm may classify projects into three categories with the following "add on" factors to the weighted average cost of capital:

Risk Class	Add on Percentage
Least risk	2%
Average risk	4
Most risk	8

Additional coverage of the risk factor relative to capital budgeting appears in Chapter 17.

An Illustration

In order to illustrate tax elements and working capital investments applicable to capital budgeting analysis, we return to the Skateboard and Hula Whirl examples of Chapter 13. Project information, as originally developed, is shown in Exhibit 14–5.

EXHIBIT 14–5
Hula Whirl and Skateboard Project Information

	Hula Whirls	Skateboards
Cost of new equipment	$2,000,000	$3,000,000
Expected annual sales:		
Year 1	$800,000	$1,000,000
Year 2	$1,000,000	$1,800,000
Year 3	$1,800,000	$2,400,000
Year 4	$1,200,000	$1,500,000
Year 5	$600,000	$400,000
Total variable manufacturing and marketing costs (as a percentage of sales revenues)	25%	20%
Annual fixed out of pocket costs for maintenance and insurance on the new equipment	$100,000	$150,000

Additional assumptions to be considered here are the following:

1. Weighted average cost of capital is 10%;
2. Each project has a risk factor of 2%;
3. The income tax rate is 34%;
4. Investments in both Hula Whirls and Skateboards are in the 5-year tax depreciation class;
5. Hula Whirl and Skateboard investments have respective salvage values of $150,000 and $250,000 at the end of the fifth year;
6. Hula Whirl and Skateboards require immediate working capital investments of $200,000 and $300,000 respectively;
7. Working capital investments are recovered at the end of the fifth year.

Net present value analyses of the two projects are shown in Exhibits 14–6 and 14–7. A discount factor of 12% was used for each project (the sum of the weighted average cost of capital of 10% plus the risk factor of 2%). The incremental approach could also be used here because the hurdle rate is 12% for both projects. However, the incremental approach could not be used if the projects were subject to different discount rates due to differing amounts of risk assigned to each project.

Further Comments on the Analysis

Depreciation is not a cash flow. However, depreciation allowances reduce income taxes. Therefore, tax depreciation has a direct linkage to a cash flow item: income taxes. This effect is known as the **depreciation tax shield.** It is shown in Exhibits 14–6 and 14–7 (and later exhibits) by simply multiplying annual tax depreciation allowances by the 34% income tax rate. The annual depreciation allowance percentages come from the 5-year column in Exhibit 14–2.

Working capital investments, as noted in the assumptions, occur immediately and are recovered at the end of each project's life. Note that the salvage of both projects is taxed at the normal income tax of 34%. The book value of the asset for tax purposes is deducted from the salvage value to get the taxable gain or loss in Exhibits 14–6 and 14–7. Book value for tax purposes is determined by taking the cost of the asset times the tax depreciation not used at the time of the asset's disposition. See footnote g in Exhibits 14–6 and 14–7 for the calculations.

Our illustration has shown after-tax cash flows discounted at the after-tax weighted average cost of capital plus a risk factor. Many firms determine net present values and time-adjusted rate of return on a before-tax basis using a before-tax weighted average cost of capital in order to avoid some of the

EXHIBIT 14—6
Net Present Value Analysis of Hula Whirls

	0	1	2	3	4	5
Investment	−$2,000,000					
Working capital investment	− 200,000					
Revenues		$800,000	$1,000,000	$1,800,000	$1,200,000	$600,000
Variable costs		−$200,000	−$ 250,000	−$ 450,000	−$ 300,000	−$150,000
Maintenance and insurance		− 100,000	− 100,000	− 100,000	− 100,000	− 100,000
Total cash outflows		−$300,000	−$ 350,000	−$ 550,000	−$ 400,000	−$250,000
Net cash flows from operations before taxes		$500,000	$ 650,000	$1,250,000	$ 800,000	$350,000
Income taxes on net cash flows from operations (34% of net cash flows)		− 170,000[a]	− 221,000	− 425,000	− 272,000	− 119,000
Net cash flows from operations after taxes before depreciation tax shield		$330,000	$ 429,000	$ 825,000	$ 528,000	$231,000
Add: depreciation tax shield (depreciation allowances × .34)		136,000[b]	217,600[c]	130,560[d]	78,336[e]	78,336[f]
Net cash flows from operations after taxes		$466,000	$ 646,600	$ 955,560	$ 606,336	$309,336
Recovery of working capital investment						200,000
Net after-tax salvage						138,168[g]
Total cash flows		$534,000	$ 646,600	$ 955,560	$ 606,336	$647,504
Times present value factors at 12%		× .893	× .797	× .712	× .636	× .567
Sum of the present values	2,364,602	$416,138	$ 515,340	$ 680,359	$ 385,630	$367,135
Net present value	$ 164,602					

[a]Tax on net cash flows from operations of $170,000 ($500,000 × .34).

[b]$2,000,000 × .20 × .34.

[c]$2,000,000 × .32 × .34.

[d]$2,000,000 × .192 × .34.

[e]$2,000,000 × .1152 × .34.

[f]$2,000,000 × .1152 × .34.

[g]$150,000 of anticipated salvage is reduced by the unused tax depreciation of $115,200 which is $2,000,000 times 5.76% (the depreciation applicable to the sixth year). The gain is $34,800 ($150,000 minus $115,200), which is taxed at 34% or $11,832. This amount is deducted from the $150,000 resulting in $138,168. This effect would be felt in the sixth year but is put in the fifth year for convenience.

EXHIBIT 14—7

Net Present Value Analysis of Skateboards

	0	1	2	3	4	5
Investment	−$3,000,000					
Working capital investment	− 300,000					
Revenues		$1,000,000	$1,800,000	$2,400,000	$1,500,000	$400,000
Variable costs		−$ 200,000	−$ 360,000	−$ 480,000	−$ 300,000	−$ 80,000
Maintenance and insurance		− 150,000	− 150,000	− 150,000	− 150,000	− 150,000
Total cash outflows		−$ 350,000	−$ 510,000	−$ 630,000	−$ 450,000	−$230,000
Net cash flows from operations before taxes		$ 650,000	$1,290,000	$1,770,000	$1,050,000	$170,000
Income taxes on net cash flows from operations (34% of net cash flows)		− 221,000[a]	− 438,600	− 601,800	357,000	57,800
Net cash flows from operations after taxes		$ 429,000	$ 851,400	$1,168,200	$ 693,000	$112,200
Add: depreciation tax shield (depreciation allowances × .34)		204,000[b]	326,400[c]	195,840[d]	117,504[e]	117,504[f]
Net cash flows from operations after taxes		$ 633,000	$1,177,800	$1,364,040	$ 810,504	$229,704
Recovery of working capital investment						300,000
Net after-tax salvage						223,752[g]
Total cash flows		$ 633,000	$1,177,800	$1,364,040	$ 810,504	$753,456
Times present value factors at 12%		× .893	× .797	× .712	× .636	× .567
Sum of the present values	3,417,863	$ 565,269	$ 938,707	$ 971,196	$ 515,481	$427,210
Net present value	$ 117,863					

[a]Tax on net cash flows from operations of $221,000 ($650,000 × .34).

[b]$3,000,000 × .20 × .34.

[c]$3,000,000 × .32 × .34.

[d]$3,000,000 × .192 × .34.

[e]$3,000,000 × .1152 × .34.

[f]$3,000,000 × .1152 × .34.

[g]The $250,000 of anticipated salvage is reduced by the unused tax depreciation of $172,800, which is $3,000,000 × 5.76% (the depreciation that is applicable to the sixth year). The gain is $77,200 ($250,000 − $172,800) which is taxed at 34% or $26,248. This amount is deducted from the $250,000 resulting in $223,572. This effect would be felt in the sixth year but is put in the fifth year for convenience.

complexities of the income tax issue. The after-tax basis provides better information for management. The authors believe that its benefits outweigh its costs.

Summary

Income taxes are an important consideration relative to capital budgeting analysis because income from capital investment projects is presently taxed at the rate of 34%. A system of depreciation allowances for tax purposes was passed in the Tax Reform Act of 1986 and illustrated in the chapter.

A very important consideration that is often overlooked in capital budgeting analysis is investments in working capital. Working capital investments typically consist of inventories and accounts receivable tied up in particular capital investment projects. The nature of a working capital investment is that it represents an amount that will be fully recovered at a later point in time. Hence it has an imputed cost to the firm: a time value of money cost created by funds being tied up in working capital investments that could have been used for other productive purposes. Working capital investments are dealt with in the capital budgeting format by including the amounts of the investments and recoveries at the time points when they occur. On an undiscounted basis working capital investments and recoveries must always net out to zero.

The cost of capital is a "hurdle rate" that must be cleared by capital investment projects. Although much controversy surrounds the nature and computation of cost of capital, its most popular conception appears to be as a weighted-average after-tax calculation for the major sources on long-term funds. For common stock this is determined by the current annual dividend rate divided by the market value per share. In addition, a growth factor may be added in based on the expected annual rate of growth in dividends per share. For bonds the rate would be the annual interest cost reduced by the tax savings from the interest divided by the current market value per bond. A risk factor can be added in to the weighted average cost of capital based on the perceived risk of the individual project.

The problem of inflation and capital budgeting is discussed in the first appendix. The solution adopted here was to adjust the cash inflows and outflows by the specific rate of inflation expected to affect these various items.

In the second appendix, different financing alternatives for capital budgeting are examined. The first thing to bear in mind is to keep investment and financing decisions separate. Thus an investment project, no matter how it might be financed, must first be acceptable as a capital investment using a discounted cash flow approach. The net present value of each financing alternative, including tax effects that are specific to that form of financing, are then calculated. Although qualitative factors should always be kept in mind, this form of analysis provides a number that is equal to the difference in the present value of the costs, including relevant tax effects, of the financing alternatives.

Appendix 14—A
Inflation and Capital Budgeting

In the recent past, inflation has wracked the world economy. Although it has abated in the past few years, it could easily return, bringing with it extensive problems for individuals and families, as well as for business. One of the areas where business would be affected by inflation is capital investment. This is because future cash flows, in the face of inflation, can be expected to be higher than the cash flows anticipated at the time when capital budgeting estimations were made. Despite this fairly obvious fact, capital budgeting estimations of future cash flows have generally not taken into account expected price changes. Omitting expected price changes can seriously affect managerial investment policies, even if the level of inflation is not expected to be serious.

Several methods for coping with price changes have been proposed for capital budgeting calculations. The most reasonable method appears to be adjusting the future cash flows. An important point to remember about inflation is that it affects different items at different rates. Thus revenues might be expected to increase at a rate of 10%, whereas direct material costs might be expected to increase at only 6%. Hence the effect of inflation on individual cash flows should be separately calculated. At least one calculation, however, is unaffected by inflation: depreciation of fixed assets for tax purposes must be made in terms of the actual (historical) costs expended for these items.

As long as cost of capital is determined by current rates for both debt and equity capital, no adjustment for inflation needs to be made. The reason for no inflation adjustment is that market determined interest rates are assumed to reflect expected levels of inflation.

In order to illustrate inflation adjustments for capital budgeting, we will continue to use the Hula Whirl and Skateboard examples that were used at the end of this chapter. To the assumptions that were previously made, we add two additional ones relative to inflation:

1. Revenues of Hula Whirls and Skateboards are expected to increase at the rate of 6% per year above the amounts predicted under the constant price assumption used previously (compound amounts for 6% carried beyond three places were used in Exhibits 14—8 and 14—9; the student should use Table A);

2. Inflation is not expected to affect any of the costs of either the Hula Whirls or the Skateboards due to long-term contractual "lock-ins" on labor contracts and purchase contracts for materials.

Net present value analyses of the two projects are shown in Exhibits 14—8 and 14—9. Cost of capital remains at 12% because that rate is presumed to

EXHIBIT 14—8
Net Present Value Analysis of Hula Whirls Under Inflation

	0	1	2	3	4	5
Investment	-$2,000,000					
Working capital investment	- 200,000					
Revenues		$848,000[a]	$1,123,600[b]	$2,143,800[c]	$1,515,000[d]	$802,920[e]
Variable costs		-$200,000	- 250,000	- 450,000	- 300,000	-$150,000
Maintenance and insurance		- 100,000	- 100,000	- 100,000	- 100,000	- 100,000
Total cash outflows		-$300,000	-$ 350,000	-$ 550,000	-$ 400,000	-$250,000
Net cash flows from operations before taxes		$548,000	$ 773,600	$1,593,800	$1,115,000	$552,920
Income taxes on net cash flows from operations (34% of net cash flows)		- 186,320[f]	- 263,024	- 541,892	- 379,100	- 187,993
Net cash flows from operations after taxes		$361,680	510,576	$1,051,908	$ 735,900	$364,927
Add: depreciation tax shield (see Table 14—6)		136,000	217,600	130,560	78,336	78,336
Net cash flows from operations after taxes		$497,680	$ 728,176	$1,182,468	$ 814,236	$443,263
Recovery of working capital investment						200,000
Net after-tax salvage						138,168[g]
Total cash flows		$497,680	$ 728,176	$1,182,468	$ 814,236	$781,431
Times present value factors at 12%		× .893	× .797	× .712	× .636	× .567
Sum of the present values	2,827,626	$444,428	$ 580,356	$ 841,917	$ 517,854	$443,071
Net present value	$ 627,626					

a $800,000 × 1.06.
b $1,000,000 × 1.1236.
c $1,800,000 × 1.1910.
d $1,200,000 × 1.2625.
e $600,000 × 1.3382.
f Tax on net cash flow from operations of $186,320 (548,000 × .34).
g See note g in Exhibit 14—6. Inflation was not expected to affect the salvage value.

EXHIBIT 14—9
Net Present Value Analysis of Skateboards Under Inflation

	0	1	2	3	4	5
Investment	-$3,000,000					
Working capital investment	- 300,000					
Revenues		$1,060,000[a]	$2,022,480[b]	$2,858,400[c]	$1,893,750[d]	$535,280[e]
Variable costs		-$ 200,000	-$ 360,000	-$ 480,000	-$ 300,000	-$ 80,000
Maintenance and insurance		- 150,000	- 150,000	- 150,000	- 150,000	- 150,000
Total cash outflows		-$ 350,000	-$ 510,000	-$ 630,000	-$ 450,000	-$ 230,000
Net cash flows from operations before taxes		$ 710,000	$1,512,480	$2,228,400	$1,443,750	$305,280
Income taxes on net cash flows from operations (34% of net cash flows)		- 241,400[f]	- 514,243	- 757,656	- 490,875	- 103,795
Net cash flows from operations after tax before depreciation tax shield		$ 468,600	$ 998,237	$1,470,744	$ 952,875	$201,485
Add: depreciation tax shield (see Exhibit 14—7)		204,000	326,400	195,840	117,504	117,504
Net cash flows from operations after taxes		$ 672,600	$1,324,637	$1,666,584	$1,070,379	$318,989
Recovery of working capital investment						300,000
Net after-tax salvage						223,752[g]
Total cash flows		$ 672,600	$1,324,637	$1,666,584	$1,070,379	$842,741
Times present value factors at 12%		× .893	× .797	× .712	× .636	× .567
Sum of the present values	4,001,571	$ 600,632	$1,055,736	$1,186,608	$ 680,761	$477,834
Net present value	$ 701,571					

[a]$1,000,000 × 1.06.
[b]$1,800,000 × 1.1236.
[c]$2,400,000 × 1.1910.
[d]$1,500,000 × 1.2625.
[e]$400,000 × 1.338.
[f]Tax on net cash flows from operations of $241,400 ($710,000 × .34).
[g]See note g in Exhibit 14—7. Inflation was not expected to affect the salvage value.

include inflationary expectations. The annual unadjusted revenues were multiplied by the appropriate future value of $1 at 6%.

When the inflation factor is expected to be significant, it should be included in the capital budgeting analysis. It is enlightening to compare Exhibits 14–8 and 14–9 with Exhibits 14–6 and 14–7, which exclude the expected effects of inflation. It can be seen that Skateboards have a significantly higher net present value when inflation is taken into account. Hula Whirls, however, had a higher NPV without inflation. Even though inflationary expectations are not 100% accurate, their inclusion should be helpful for managerial decision-making purposes.

Appendix 14–B
Financing Capital Investment Projects

Throughout Chapters 13 and 14 the capital investment decision has been treated as a purchase with money immediately being expended to acquire the asset or assets involved. Purchase of the investment with cash being immediately spent, however, is only one possible financing alternative. A method of financing that has received an extensive amount of attention is leasing. Under one form of lease, called an **operating lease,** the user firm, called the **lessee,** does not record the asset on its books. At the end of the lease period the asset reverts back to the owning firm, called the **lessor.** Let us examine some of the possibilities.

Assume that a firm can acquire an asset with a 5-year economic life. It expects to use the asset for 3 years. For simplicity, we will ignore taxes. The asset has a cost of $2,500 with 3 annual net cash flows of $1,000 received at the end of each year and an expected salvage value of $300. The firm's cost of capital is 16%. An NPV analysis is shown in Exhibit 14–10.

EXHIBIT 14–10
Net Present Value Analysis

	0	1	2	3
Investment	−$2,500			
Annual cash inflows		$1,000	$1,000	$1,000
Salvage value		−	−	300
Total cash inflows		$1,000	$1,000	$1,300
× Present value factors at 16%		× .862	× .743	× .641
Present value of cash flows	2,438	$ 862	$ 743	$ 833
Net present value	−$ 62			

The project has a negative NPV of $62 so it is clear that the TARR is just under 16%. The project would thus be rejected. Suppose, however, that instead of buying the asset, the firm can lease it paying $50 "down" (immediately) and $950 at the end of each of the next three years. At the end of the third year the asset would revert back to the seller-lessor. An NPV analysis at the firm's 16% cost of capital is shown in Exhibit 14–11.

As can be seen, the project now has a positive NPV of $62, which is more than the "investment" of the $50 initial lease payment. With this structure of cash flows, the TARR is well in excess of 16%. It would appear that the lease has performed "magic" by taking a project with a TARR slightly under 16% and converting it into a project with an excellent TARR. This conclusion, however, must be viewed very suspiciously for two reasons.

First, the revenues, which would generally be estimated, have a great deal more risk attached to them than the lease payments that are clearly stipulated in the lease contract. At the very least, therefore, the revenue stream should be discounted at a higher rate than the lease repayment amounts.

Second, the capital budgeting analysis in Exhibit 14–11 takes into account the debt form of financing that the lease provides in arriving at the very beneficial capital budgeting results shown in Exhibit 14–11. Debt financing is almost always less expensive than equity financing because creditors assume less risk than owners. Because weighted average capital is a "pool" of funds made up of both debt and equity with the debt being less expensive, it is totally incorrect to assign debt funds to particular projects as part of the capital budgeting analysis because virtually all investments could qualify for some form of debt financing.

The solution to the problem is relatively simple: investment and financing decisions should be separated. The investment decision would be handled exactly as has been done in Chapters 13 and 14 by treating each project as an investment that would require immediate cash payment. Selection would then be made on the basis discussed in Chapter 13. Analysis of possible financing alternatives, however, requires a more extensive look.

EXHIBIT 14–11
Net Present Value with Lease

	0	1	2	3
Investment	−$ 50			
Annual cash inflows		$1,000	$1,000	$1,000
Lease payments		− 950	− 950	− 950
Net cash inflows		$ 50	$ 50	$ 50
× present value factors at 16%		× .862	× .743	× .641
Present value of cash flows	112	$ 43	$ 37	$ 32
Net present value	$ 62			

Analyzing Financing Alternatives

If a capital investment project is not acceptable as an investment, using a discounted cash flow approach, the project should be summarily rejected. Should the project pass the investment test, financing alternatives such as borrowing versus obtaining an operating lease can then be directly compared. The technique that will be suggested here is one that minimizes the present value of the borrowing costs. Taxes are also affected by a borrowing as opposed to an operating lease because the firm owns the asset in the former case but does not if an operating lease is used. Let us examine a situation involving these alternatives (we use a 40% tax rate for simplicity).

Borrowing versus Operating Lease Alternatives

Assume that an asset with a six-year life and a cost of $60,000 has successfully passed the investment hurdle. The firm is considering either borrowing from a bank on a 4-year note with annual repayments at the end of each year and a rate of 10% or leasing for 5 years with a cost of $17,000 payable at the end of each year. The asset is expected to be used for 5 years. It is expected to have a salvage of $4,000 at the end of the fifth year. If financed by means of a loan, the investment would fall into the 5-year tax depreciation class.

First, we determine the interest on the loan. If the firm borrows, the interest is fully deductible for tax purposes. In order to determine the interest, we start by determining the annual repayment to the bank. We do this by dividing the amount borrowed, $60,000, by the present value of an ordinary annuity for 5 years at 10%, 3.791. The result of $15,827 ($60,000 ÷ 3.791) is the annual loan repayment amount.

Next we determine the annual interest cost by separating the $15,827 into the interest and principal repayment portions. This is shown in Exhibit 14–12.

The net cash flows from the borrowing are computed next. In Exhibit 14–13, there are several noteworthy features. Depreciation allowances are based on the cost of the investment of $60,000. Notice that depreciation and interest, which are both deductible for tax purposes, have been added together in order to compute the income tax savings. The salvage of $4,000 is taxable. The salvage is a relevant cost because it is not received if the asset is leased. The entire $4,000 of anticipated salvage would be taxed at the ordinary rate of 40%. This amount is reduced by the undepreciated portion of the asset's cost, which is $3,456 ($60,000 × .0576), the sixth year's depreciation shown in Exhibit 14–2, resulting in a gain of $544. The gain is then taxed at the ordinary rate of 40% resulting in a tax of $218 on the disposition of the asset. The total tax benefits and net salvage are then deducted from the annual loan repayments to determine the after-tax costs of borrowing.

The after-tax cost of leasing is next calculated. Leasing costs are fully deductible for tax purposes. The after-tax cost of leasing is shown in Exhibit 14–14.

EXHIBIT 14–12
Repayment of Borrowing at 10%

End of Year	Principal Balance[a]	Total Cash Payment	Interest[b]	Repayment of Principal[c]
0	$60,000			
1	50,173	$15,827	$6,000	$ 9,827
2	39,363	15,827	5,017	10,810
3	27,472	15,827	3,936	11,891
4	14,392	15,827	2,747	13,080
5	0[d]	15,827	1,439	14,388

[a]Previous balance minus repayment of principal.
[b]Interest is 10% of end of previous year balance of principal.
[c]Repayment of principal is equal to $15,827 total cash payment minus interest on unpaid principal balance.
[d]Rounding error of $4.

EXHIBIT 14–13
After-Tax Costs of Borrowing

	1	2	3	4	5
Annual loan repayment	−$15,827	−$15,827	−$15,827	−$15,827	$15,827
Less: deductible expenses					
Depreciation allowances	$12,000[a]	$19,200[b]	$11,520[c]	$ 6,912[d]	$ 6,912[e]
Interest	6,000[f]	5,017	3,936	2,747	1,439
Total	$18,000	$24,217	$15,456	$ 9,659	$ 8,351
Income tax savings (40% of total expenses)	$ 7,200	$ 9,687	$ 6,182	$ 3,864	$ 3,340
Net salvage					3,782[g]
Total tax and net salvage benefits	$ 7,200	$ 9,687	$ 6,182	$ 3,864	$ 7,122
After-tax costs of borrowing	−$ 8,627	−$ 6,140	−$ 9,645	−$11,963	−$ 8,705

[a]$60,000 × .20.
[b]$60,000 × .32.
[c]$60,000 × .192.
[d]$60,000 × .1152.
[e]$60,000 × .1152.
[f]Interest expense is from Exhibit 14–12.
[g]Gain is taxed at the rate of 40%. Deducted from the salvage is the undepreciated amount of $3,456 ($60,000 × .0576) giving a gain of $544. Tax on the gain is $218 ($544 × .40), which is deducted from the salvage to give net salvage of $3,782.

The last step is to compare the present value of the after-tax costs of borrowing and leasing. The discount rate used is the after-tax borrowing rate of 6% rather than the cost of capital because we are concerned with a financing

EXHIBIT 14–14
After-tax Costs of Leasing

	1	2	3	4	5
Leasing cost	−$17,000	−$17,000	−$17,000	−$17,000	−$17,000
Less tax savings at 40%	6,800	6,800	6,800	6,800	6,800
After-tax cost of leasing	−$10,200	−$10,200	−$10,200	−$10,200	−$10,200

EXHIBIT 14–15
Present Value of the Two Financing Alternatives

	0	1	2	3	4	5
After-tax cost of borrowing (from Exhibit 14–13)		−$ 8,627	−$ 6,140	−$ 9,645	−$11,963	−$ 8,705
× present value factors at 6%		× .943	× .89	× .84	× .792	× .747
Sum of the present value factors	−$37,680	−$ 8,135	−$ 5,465	−$ 8,102	−$ 9,475	−$ 6,503
After-tax cost of leasing (from Exhibit 14–14)		−$10,200	−$10,200	−$10,200	−$10,200	−$10,200
× present value factors at 6%		× .943	× .89	× .84	× .792	× .747
Sum of the present value factors	− 42,962[a]	−$ 9,619	−$ 9,078	−$ 8,568	−$ 8,078	−$ 7,619
Net present value in favor of borrowing	$ 5,282					

[a]This amount could also be determined by multiplying the annuity of $10,200 by the present value of a five-year annuity at 6% of 4.212.

decision, the favorable investment decision having previously been made. The after-tax cost of debt is determined by taking 10% × (1 − .40), which equals 6%. Present values of the two financing alternatives are shown in Exhibit 14–15.

The results show that the borrowing alternative is less expensive, in present value terms, by $5,282. There are, however, qualitative factors to consider. If the asset is leased under an operating lease, the lease liability does not appear on the balance sheet. This can sometimes be an important factor for firms having a large total debt. The lower cost of the borrowing would have to be considered against the possibility of the "off the balance sheet" financing by means of the lease.

The financing alternative is a complex question. The comparison of present values of the financing alternatives presented here provides a useful tool of analysis for evaluating this situation.

Key Terms

Depreciation tax shield refers to the savings in income taxes stemming from tax depreciation allowances.

Investment tax credit refers to a reduction in income taxes equal to a maximum of 10% of the cost of eligible capital acquisitions. This benefit was eliminated in the Tax Reform Act of 1986.

Lessee is the party acquiring usage of an asset in a leasing transaction.

Lessor is the party owning the asset in a leasing transaction.

Operating lease is one in which an asset reverts back to the lessor at the end of the lease period. As such, it never appears as either an asset or liability on the books of the lessee.

Weighted average cost of capital takes the cost of each source of cost of capital and multiplies it by its proportionate weight relative to all sources of capital. These amounts are then summed in order to arrive at the weighted average cost of capital.

Working capital investments refers to amounts of inventories and accounts receivable in capital budgeting projects that will be fully recovered at some future point in time. They have an opportunity cost because the money tied up in these investments could have been used for other income-generating purposes.

Questions

Q14–1 Why must income taxes be considered in capital budgeting situations?

Q14–2 What effect would a liberalizing of depreciation allowances for tax purposes have on TARR and NPV?

Q14–3 What are working capital investments?

Q14–4 Why do working capital investments have to be considered in capital budgeting decisions?

Q14–5 Why should income taxes be considered relative to working capital investments in capital budgeting decisions?

Q14–6 How should working capital investments be handled in discounted cash flow approaches to capital budgeting decisions?

Q14–7 What is the role of the cost of capital in discounted cash flow approaches to capital budgeting?

Q14–8 Why are taxes deducted from interest in measuring the cost of debt?

Q14–9 Why is inflation ignored when market value approaches to measuring cost of capital are used?

Q14–10 Why is retained earnings ignored when computing the cost of capital when market value approaches to measuring cost of capital are used?

Q14–11   What is risk in the context of capital budgeting and how might it be handled in terms of the discount factor used in capital budgeting analyses?

Q14–12   If two mutually exclusive capital budgeting projects have different risks, can the incremental NPV approach be used?

Q14–13   If a capital investment project has an estimated life of 10 years and it falls in the 7-year class for tax depreciation allowances, over how many years will tax depreciation deductions apply?

Q14–14   "Future cash flows in capital budgeting analysis should be adjusted by the expected change in the general purchasing power of the monetary unit." Comment on this statement.

Q14–15   "The TARR of a project can be increased by financing the asset by means of leasing." Comment on this statement.

Q14–16   Are there any advantages to acquiring an asset by means of an operating lease even if the costs of this alternative are higher than other forms of financing?

Q14–17   Why are alternative financing costs discounted by a debt rate rather than the cost of capital?

Q14–18   Why are leasing costs generally slightly higher than borrowing costs?

Exercises

E14–1   **Simple NPV with taxes.** Hubbard Company can acquire an asset at a cost of $100,000. The project is expected to generate cash flows of $40,000 per year for 5 years. Cash flows are receivable at the end of each year. The asset falls into the 3-year class for depreciation allowances. The asset has no salvage value. Cost of capital is 12% and the income tax rate is 34%.

Required: Determine the net present value of the asset.

E14–2   **Keep or sell rental property.** A piece of rental property (not subject to depreciation) was acquired 3 years ago at a cost of $10,000. It can be sold today for $15,000. The gain would be taxed at 34% (the tax effect would be felt now). If the asset is kept, it would generate annual cash flows of $3,000 per year for 3 years subject to a 34% income tax effect, which would occur at the end of each year. The asset would be sold for $14,000 at the end of the third year (assume that the tax on the gain is felt at the end of the third year). Cost of capital is 8%.

Required: Prepare an NPV analysis showing the present value of each alternative.

E14–3   **Weighted average cost of capital.** Sloane Company's common stock has a cost of 16% and its debt has an after-tax cost of 6%. Seventy percent of the total market value of its capital is in the form of common stock and the other 30% consists of its debt.

Required: What is the after-tax cost of capital?

E14–4   **Benefit of depreciation allowances.** What is the present value of the depreciation benefits of an asset costing $100,000 that is in the 7-year depreciation class if the cost of capital is 12% and the income tax rate is 34%?

E14–5   **Cost of alternative working capital investments.** Two investments have different working capital requirements. Investment A requires an immediate working capital investment of $80,000 and investment B one of $50,000 now. The working capital investments are recovered in 5 years. Tax effects at 34% are felt immediately and in 5 years. Cost of capital is 10%.

Required: What is the present value differential (after taxes) between the working capital investments?

E14–6   **Essay on alternative forms of financing.** Discuss in detail why investment and financing decisions should be separated. What is the role of taxes in the financing decision?

E14–7   **Leasing versus financing alternatives, no income taxes.** Welch Company has decided to acquire a fixed asset costing $25,000 (it has passed a discounted cash flow investment criterion).

If purchased, the asset would be financed by means of a bank loan. Three annual payments of $9,137 would be made *with the first payment occurring immediately.* The asset would be sold at the end of the third year for $5,000.

If the asset is leased, 3 annual payments—beginning immediately—of $9,294 would be made.

Required: 1. Determine the relevant annual cash flows for each of the financing alternatives.
2. Discount these two cash flow streams from 1 above at the borrowing rate.
3. Which alternative would you select based on the numbers from 2 above?

E14–8   **Working capital.** Assume that $20,000 is tied up in an investment that earns 10% after taxes at the end of each of the next 3 years.

Assume as a second alternative that the $20,000 is tied up in working capital with recovery at the end of the third year.

Required: Using a 10% discount rate, determine the present value of each of the two above alternatives.

E14–9   **Inflation adjustments.** The Clemens Company manufactures a product that presently sells for $50 per unit with variable costs of $20 per unit. Sales, in units, at the end of each of the next 3 years are 1,000, 1,200, and 1,500 units (all revenues and costs are assumed to occur at the end of the year).

Inflation for the revenues is expected to increase at the rate of 8% per year and variable costs at the rate of 6% per year. Cost of capital is 12% (which includes expected inflation).

Required: 1. Determine the revenues, variable costs, and contribution margin in each of the three years *without* the effects of inflation.
2. Discount the contribution margin in 1 above to its present value.
3. Redo 1 above. Now include the expected effect of inflation.
4. Discount the contribution margin in 3 above to its present value.
5. Briefly comment on the above results.

E14–10   **Operating cash flows occur evenly throughout the year.** Project A requires an investment of $10,000 and project B requires an $8,000 investment. Project A has 4 annual cash inflows of $6,000 each, and project B has 4 annual cash flows of $5,000 each. These cash flows occur evenly throughout the year (use Table E for appropriate discount factors).

        Projects A and B both fall in the 3-year depreciation allowance category. The tax rate is 40%. Tax effects are expected to occur evenly throughout the year. Cost of capital is 10%. Neither project asset has any salvage value.

Required: Prepare an incremental NPV analysis of the above.

Problems

P14–11   **Weighted average cost of capital determination.** Vetter Company is attempting to determine its weighted average cost of capital based on market valuations. Common shares presently sell for $75 per share, and the current annual dividend rate is $12 per share. 100,000 shares are issued and outstanding. It has been estimated that stockholders expect a 2% rate of growth in dividends per share.

        Vetter has also issued $5,000,000 of 10% debenture bonds. The bonds are presently selling at $1,010 per bond.

Required: 1. Determine the weighted average cost of capital. The income tax rate is 40%.
        2. Why is inflation ignored when measuring the cost of capital using market valuation?

P14–12   **Equipment replacement with working capital investments.** Andante Company presently owns two X300 machines. These machines have an 8-year life, and each is capable of manufacturing 10,000 units of product per year. The oldest machine was acquired 4 years ago at a cost of $100,000 and has a scrap value of $10,000 today. The newest machine was bought 2 years ago at a cost of $110,000 and has a scrap value of $25,000 today. Each of these falls into the 7-year depreciation allowance class.

        A new model called the Q500 has a cost of $250,000. If it is acquired, the newest X300 would be sold and the oldest would be kept on a standby basis. The Q500 has a 10-year life and would have a scrap value of $100,000 in 6 years. It too falls into the 7-year depreciation allowance class.

        If the X300s are kept, a replacement would be made in 4 years at an estimated price of $125,000. Its scrap value 2 years after that would be $60,000. At the end of their 8-year life all X300s have a nominal scrap value of $5,000.

        X300s have a variable production cost of $10 a unit. The Q500 has a variable production cost of $6 a unit. Fixed out-of-pocket costs are $10,000 per year for each X300 and $27,500 per year for the Q500.

        After 6 years the product is expected to be phased out. Expected productivity per year is:

Year	1	2	3	4	5	6
Production	18,000	16,000	15,000	12,000	10,000	10,000

The X300s have a combined working capital investment of $60,000, which will be recovered in 6 years. If the Q500 is acquired, the working capital investment would be decreased to $30,000 at the end of a year. Full recovery will occur in 6 years.

Required: Prepare an incremental net present value analysis showing whether Andante should invest in the Q500. Cost of capital is 12% and the tax rate is 34%. All cash flows occur at year end.

P14–13 **Leasing versus financing alternative.** Heaston Company has examined the possible acquisition of an asset costing $200,000. The asset has successfully passed the investment test consisting of a net present value analysis.

The asset can either be leased for 7 years or acquired by means of a bank loan for the same period.

If acquired by means of a loan, the terms of the loan call for 7 annual repayments, the first one beginning in a year, of $38,415. The interest is fully deductible for tax purposes. The asset falls in the 5-year depreciation allowance category. The asset is expected to have a salvage value of $20,000 at the end of the seventh year. The gain is fully taxable at the 50% rate.

If the asset is leased, 7 annual payments of $41,084 will be made beginning in a year. These payments are fully deductible for tax purposes. At the end of the seventh year, the asset reverts back to the lessor.

Required:
1. Determine the annual after-tax costs that are relevant to the financing decision for each of the alternatives.
2. Discount the two cash flow streams in 1 above at the borrowing rate.
3. Determine the present value differential of the two alternatives from 2 above.
4. Are there any qualitative reasons for selecting the more expensive alternative? Discuss.

P14–14 **Equipment replacement with salvage on old equipment.** Wyle Co. is considering a proposal to acquire new manufacturing equipment. The new equipment has the same capacity as the current equipment but will provide operating efficiencies in direct and indirect labor, direct material usage, indirect supplies, and power. Consequently, the savings in operating costs are estimated at $150,000 annually.

The new equipment will cost $300,000 and will be purchased at the beginning of the year when the project is started. The equipment dealer is certain that the equipment will be operational during the second quarter of the year it is installed. Therefore, 60% of the estimated annual savings can be obtained in the first year. Wyle will incur a one-time expense of $30,000 to transfer the production activities from the old equipment to the new equipment. No loss of sales will occur, however, because the plant is large enough to install the new equipment without interfering with the operations of the current equipment. The equipment dealer states that most companies use a 5-year life when depreciating this equipment.

The current equipment has been fully depreciated and is carried in the accounts at zero book value. Management has reviewed the condition of the current equipment and has concluded that it can be used an additional 5 years. Wyle Co. would receive $5,000 net of removal costs if it elected to buy the new equipment and dispose of its current equipment at this time.

Wyle currently leases its manufacturing plant. The annual lease payments are $60,000. The lease, which will have 4 years remaining when the equipment installation would begin, is not renewable. Wyle Company would be required to remove any equipment in the plant at the end of the lease. The cost of equipment removal is expected to equal the salvage value of either the old or new equipment at the time of removal.

The equipment falls into the 5-year depreciation allowance class.

The company is subject to a 40% income tax rate and requires an after-tax return of at least 12% on any investment.

Required:

1. Calculate the annual incremental after-tax cash flows for Wyle Co.'s proposal to acquire the new manufacturing equipment.
2. Calculate the net present value of Wyle Co.'s proposal to acquire the new manufacturing equipment using the cash flows calculated in 1 and indicate what action Wyle Co.'s management should take.

(CMA Adapted)

P14–15 Keep or replace equipment. The WRL Company makes cookies for its chain of snack food stores. On January 2, 19X7, WRL Company purchased a special cookie cutting machine; this machine has been utilized for 3 years. WRL Company is considering the purchase of a newer, more efficient machine. If purchased, the new machine would be acquired on January 2, 19X0. WRL Company expects to sell 300,000 dozen cookies in each of the next 4 years. The selling price of the cookies is expected to average $.50 per dozen.

WRL Company has two options: (1) continue to operate the old machine or (2) sell the old machine and purchase the new machine. No trade-in was offered by the seller of the new machine. The following information has been assembled to help decide which option is more desirable.

	Old Machine	New Machine
Original cost of machine at acquisition	$80,000	$120,000
Salvage value at the end of useful life for depreciation purposes	$10,000	$20,000
Useful life from date of acquisition	7 years	4 years
Expected annual cash operating expenses:		
Variable cost per dozen	$.20	$.14
Total fixed costs	$15,000	$14,000
Depreciation method used for tax purposes	Straight-line	5-year depreciation class
Estimated cash value of machines:		
January 2, 19X0	$40,000	$120,000
December 31, 19X3	$7,000	$20,000

WRL Company is subject to an overall income tax rate of 40%. Assume that all operating revenues and expenses occur at the end of the year. Assume that any gain or loss on the sale of machinery is treated as an ordinary tax item and will affect the taxes paid by WRL Company at the end of the year in which it occurred.

Required:

1. Use the net present value method to determine whether WRL Company should retain the old machine or acquire the new machine. WRL requires an after-tax return of 16%.

2. Without prejudice to your answer to 1 above, assume that the quantitative differences are so slight between the two alternatives that WRL Company is indifferent to the two proposals. Identify and discuss the nonquantitative factors that are important to this decision that WRL Company should consider.

3. Identify and discuss the advantages and disadvantages of using discounted cash flow techniques (such as the net present value method) for capital investment decisions.

(CMA Adapted)

P14–16 **Critique of incorrect analysis.** Wisconsin Products Company manufactures several different products. One of the firm's principal products sells for $20 per unit. The sales manager of Wisconsin Products has stated repeatedly that he could sell more units of this product if they were available. In an attempt to substantiate his claim the sales manager conducted a market research study last year at a cost of $44,000 to determine potential demand for this product. The study indicated that Wisconsin Products could sell 18,000 units of this product annually for the next 5 years.

The equipment currently in use has the capacity to produce 11,000 units annually. The variable production costs are $9 per unit. The equipment has a book value of $60,000 and a remaining useful life of 5 years. The salvage value of the equipment is negligible now and will be zero in 5 years.

A maximum of 20,000 units could be produced annually on the new machinery that can be purchased. The new equipment costs $300,000 and has an estimated useful life of 5 years with no salvage value at the end of 5 years. Wisconsin Product's production manager has estimated that the new equipment would provide increased production efficiencies that would reduce the variable production costs to $7 per unit.

Wisconsin Products Company uses straight-line depreciation on all of its equipment for tax purposes. The firm is subject to a 40% tax rate, and its after-tax cost of capital is 15%.

The sales manager felt so strongly about the need for additional capacity that he attempted to prepare an economic justification for the equipment, although this was not one of his responsibilities. His analysis, presented below, disappointed him because it did not justify acquiring the equipment.

Required Investment

Purchase price of new equipment		$300,000
Disposal of existing equipment:		
Loss on disposal	$60,000	
Less tax benefit (40%)	24,000	36,000
Cost of market research study		44,000
Total investment		$380,000

Annual Returns

Contribution margin from product:	
Using the new equipment	
[18,000 × ($20 − 7)]	$234,000
Using the existing equipment	
[11,000 × ($20 − 9)]	121,000
Increase in contribution margin	$113,000
Less depreciation	60,000

Increase in before-tax income	$ 53,000
Income tax (40%)	21,200
Increase in income	$ 31,800
Less 15% cost of capital on the additional investment required (.15 × $380,000)	57,000
Net annual return of proposed investment in new equipment	($ 25,200)

Required:

1. The controller of Wisconsin Products Company plans to prepare a discounted cash flow analysis for this investment proposal. The controller has asked you to prepare corrected calculations of
   a. the required investment in the new equipment, and
   b. the recurring annual cash flows.
   Explain the treatment of each item of your corrected calculations that is treated differently from the original analysis prepared by the sales manager.
2. Calculate the net present value of the proposed investment in the new equipment.

(CMA Adapted)

P14–17   Capital budgeting and inflation. Catix Corporation is a divisionalized company, and each division has the authority to make capital expenditures up to $200,000 without approval of the corporate headquarters. The corporate controller has determined that the cost of capital for Catix Corporation is 12%. This rate does not include an allowance for inflation, which is expected to occur at an average rate of 8% over the next 5 years. Catix pays income taxes at the rate of 40%.

The Electronics Division of Catix is considering the purchase of an automated assembly and soldering machine for use in the manufacture of its printed circuit boards. The machine would be placed in service in early 19X1. The divisional controller estimates that if the machine is purchased, two positions will be eliminated yielding a cost savings for wages and employee benefits. However, the machine would require additional supplies and more power would be required to operate the machine. The cost savings and additional costs in current 19X0 prices are as follows:

Wages and employee benefits of the two positions eliminated ($25,000 each)	$50,000
Cost of additional supplies	3,000
Cost of additional power	10,000

The new machine would be purchased and installed at the end of 19X0 at a net cost of $80,000. If purchased, the machine would be depreciated on a straight-line basis for both book and tax purposes. The machine will become technologically obsolete in 4 years and will have no salvage value at that time.

The Electronics Division compensates for inflation in capital expenditure analyses by adjusting the expected cash flows by an estimated price level index. The adjusted after-tax cash flows are then discounted using the appropriate discount rate. The estimated year-end index values for each of the next 5 years are presented below.

Year	Year-end Price Index	Year	Year-end Price Index
19X0	1.00	19X3	1.26
19X1	1.08	19X4	1.36
19X2	1.17	19X5	1.47

The Plastics Division of Catix compensates for inflation in capital expenditure analyses by adding the anticipated inflation rate to the cost of capital and then using the inflation adjusted cost of capital to discount the project cash flows. The Plastics Division recently rejected a project with cash flows and economic life similar to those associated with the machine under consideration by the Electronics Division. The Plastics Division's analysis of the rejected project was as follows:

Net pretax cost savings	$37,000
Less incremental depreciation expenses	20,000
Increase in taxable income	$17,000
Increase in income taxes (40%)	6,800
Increase in after-tax income	$10,200
Add back noncash expense (depreciation)	20,000
Net after-tax annual cash inflow (unadjusted for inflation)	$30,200
Present value of net cash inflows using the sum of the cost of capital (12%) and the inflation rate (8%) or a minimum required return of 20%	$77,916
Investment required	(80,000)
Net present value	($ 2,084)

All operating revenues and expenditures occur at the end of the year.

Required:

1. Using the price index provided, prepare a schedule showing the net after-tax annual cash flows adjusted for inflation for the automated assembly and soldering machine under consideration by the Electronics Division.
2. Without prejudice to your answer to 1 above, assume that the net after-tax annual cash flows adjusted for inflation for the project being considered by the Electronics Division are as follows

	19X1	19X2	19X3	19X4
Net after-tax annual cash flow adjusted for inflation	$30,000	$35,000	$37,000	$40,000

Calculate the net present value for Electronic Division's project that will be meaningful to management.
3. Evaluate the methods used by the Plastics Division and the Electronics Division to compensate for expected inflation in capital expenditure analyses.

(CMA Adapted)

P14–18 Capital budgeting, working capital, and income taxes. Henry Company presently owns a punch press that was acquired two years ago at a cost of $110,000. It is being depreciated for tax purposes over a 5-year period by the straight-line depreciation method. Tax salvage is $10,000. It is estimated that it will last another 4 years.

If Henry gets rid of the old punch press, it would acquire a newer model at this time. The new machine would have a 5-year life for depreciation tax purposes. The machine costs $200,000. It would be depreciated for tax purposes according to the 1986 tax law. The new equipment is both faster and more efficient than the presently owned machinery. Variable costs per unit of output would be $16 per unit with the newer equipment and $20 per unit with the old. Annual fixed out-of-pocket costs for items like insurance, maintenance, and property taxes are $20,000 per year with the new equipment. Total fixed costs associated with the old technology are $25,000 per year. Of this amount, it is estimated that $8,000 is for unavoidable fixed costs which would not be affected by the decision to keep or dispose of the old technology.

Total output over the next 4 years is expected to be

Year	Output
1	18,000
2	22,000
3	14,000
4	8,000

Variable costs included in average inventory balances are $20,000 with the old equipment. By the end of the first year, average working capital investment would be $12,000 with the new technology (the old technology would be constant). All inventories would be used up at the end of the fourth year.

If the old machinery is disposed of now, it would be sold for $35,000. The tax effect in the gain or loss would be taxed at the normal rate of 34%. Tax effects of the sale would be felt at the end of the first year. If the old machine is kept it would have an estimated salvage value of $7,500 at the end of the fourth year. The new technology would have an estimated salvage of $55,000 at the end of the fourth year. Tax effects on salvage can be put in the fourth year for convenience.

Cost of capital is 10% and the tax rate is 34%.

Required: 1. Prepare an incremental net present value analysis of the above.

P14–19   **Make or buy.** Wardl Industries is a manufacturer of standard and custom-designed bottling equipment. Early in December 19X3 Lyan Company asked Wardl to quote a price for a custom-designed bottling machine to be delivered on April 1, 19X4. Lyan intends to make a decision on the purchase of such a machine by January 1 so that Wardl would have the entire first quarter of 19X4 to build the equipment.

Wardl's standard pricing policy for custom-designed equipment is 50% markup on full cost. Lyan's specifications for the equipment have been reviewed by Wardl's Engineering and Cost Accounting departments, and they made the following estimates for raw materials and direct labor:

Raw materials	$256,000
Direct labor (11,000 DLH @ $15)	165,000

Manufacturing overhead is applied on the basis of direct labor hours. Wardl normally plans to run its plant 15,000 direct labor hours per month and assigns overhead on the basis of 180,000 direct labor hours per year. The overhead application rate for 19X4 of $9.00 DLH is based on the following budgeted manufacturing overhead costs for 19X4:

Variable manufacturing overhead	$ 972,000
Fixed manufacturing overhead	648,000
Total manufacturing overhead	$1,620,000

The Wardl production schedule calls for 12,000 direct labor hours per month during the first quarter. If Wardl is awarded the contract for the Lyan equipment, production of one of its standard products would have to be reduced. This is necessary because production levels can be increased only to 15,000 direct labor hours each month on short notice. Furthermore, Wardl's employees are unwilling to work overtime.

Sales of the standard product equal to the reduced production would be lost, but there would be no permanent loss of future sales or customers. The standard product whose production schedule would be reduced has a unit sales price of $12,000 and the following cost structure:

Raw materials	$2,500
Direct labor (250 DLH @ $15)	3,750
Overhead (250 DLH @ $9)	2,250
Total cost	$8,500

Lyan needs the custom-designed equipment to increase its bottle-making capacity so that it will not have to buy bottles from an outside supplier. Lyan Company requires 5,000,000 bottles annually. Its present equipment has a maximum capacity of 4,500,000 bottles with a directly traceable cash outlay cost of $.15 per bottle. Thus, Lyan has had to purchase 500,000 from a supplier at $.40 each. The new equipment would allow Lyan to manufacture its entire annual demand for bottles and experience a raw material cost savings of $.01 for each bottle manufactured.

Wardl estimates that Lyan's annual bottle demand will continue to be 5,000,000 bottles over the next 5 years, the estimated economic life of the special purpose equipment. Wardl further estimates that Lyan has an after-tax cost of capital of 15% and is subject to a 40% marginal income tax rate, the same rates as Wardl.

Required:

1. Wardl Industries plans to submit a bid to Lyan Company for the manufacture of the special purpose bottling equipment.
   a. Calculate the bid Wardl would submit if it follows its standard pricing policy for special purpose equipment.
   b. Calculate the minimum bid Wardl would be willing to submit on the Lyan equipment that would result in the same profits as planned for the first quarter of 19X4.
2. Wardl Industries wants to estimate the maximum price Lyan Company would be willing to pay for the special purpose bottling equipment.
   a. Calculate the present value of the after-tax savings in directly traceable cash outlays that Lyan could expect to realize from the new special purpose bottling equipment.
   b. Identify the other factors Wardl would have to incorporate in its estimate of the maximum price Lyan would be willing to pay for the equipment.
   c. Describe how the cost savings (2a above) and the other factors (2b above) would be combined to calculate the estimate of the maximum price that Lyan would be willing to pay for the equipment.

(CMA Adapted)

P14–20 **Lease or buy.** LeToy Company produces a wide variety of children's toys, most of which are manufactured from stamped parts. The Production Department recommended that a new stamping machine be acquired. The Production Department further recommended that the company consider using the new stamping machine for only 5 years. Top management has concurred with the recommendation and has assigned Ann Mitchum of the Budget and Planning Department to supervise the acquisition and to analyze the alternative financing available.

After careful analysis and review Mitchum has narrowed the financing of the project to two alternatives. The first alternative is a lease agreement with the manufacturer of the stamping machine. The manufacturer is willing to lease the equipment to LeToy for 5 years even though it has an economic useful life of 10 years. The lease agreement calls for LeToy to make annual payments of $62,000 at the beginning of each year. The manufacturer (lessor) retains the title to the machine, and there is no purchase option at the end of 5 years. This agreement would be considered a lease by the Internal Revenue Service.

The second alternative would be for LeToy to purchase the equipment outright from the manufacturer for $240,000. Preliminary discussions with LeToy's bank indicate that the firm would be able to finance the asset acquisition with a 15% term loan with equal annual amounts paid once a year starting immediately.

LeToy would depreciate the equipment over 5 years using the 1986 depreciation allowances for the 5-year class. The market value of the equipment at the end of 5 years would be $45,000.

All nonfinancing costs are the same under both alternatives and are paid by LeToy. LeToy requires an after-tax cut-off return of 18% for investment decisions and is subject to a 40% corporate income tax rate on both operating income and capital gains and losses. Tax effects occur at year end with cash flows.

Required:

1. Calculate the relevant present value cost of the leasing alternative for LeToy Company.
2. Calculate the relevant present value cost of the purchase alternative for LeToy Company.
3. Which would you choose based on your analysis?

(CMA Adapted)

CHAPTER 15

Controlling Decentralized Operations

Learning Objectives

After reading this chapter you should be able to:

1. Understand why decentralization is so prevalent in U.S. business.

2. Understand the three different types of organizational units and how they are controlled.

3. Understand how information can be recast to highlight the performance of different types of profit or investment centers (modularization).

4. Understand how return on investment is calculated and its weaknesses.

5. Understand how residual income is calculated and its weaknesses.

6. Understand how compound interest depreciation can overcome some of the weaknesses of both return on investment and residual income (Appendix 15–A).

Business and industry in the United States has been characterized over the last several decades by an increasing concentration of economic power. This concentration has resulted from a steady torrent of acquisitions of large businesses by other major enterprises. The economic phenomenon of large firms controlling other large firms has given rise to a new use for the word *conglomerate* in our language. A **conglomerate** enterprise is one consisting of many semi-independent and diverse companies that have been brought together under one organizational umbrella by virtue of a single firm acquiring a majority of the common stock of other corporate entities.

Conglomerates often consist of enterprises in the same industry. General Foods, for example, is composed of such well-known companies as Oscar Mayer (meat packing), Maxwell House (coffee), Log Cabin (syrups), Jell-O (gelatins), and Bird's Eye (frozen foods). General Foods was itself acquired in 1985 by Philip Morris, a tobacco-based conglomerate. A conglomerate consisting of firms in the same industry acquires advantages such as economies of scale relative to distributing its products to consumers. It can also acquire a depth and breadth of managerial expertise if it concentrates within the same industry. A good example of a conglomerate that has concentrated in the publishing and media industries is Meredith Corporation. Its holdings are shown in Exhibit 15–1.

Conglomerates may also consist of firms in totally separate industries because the acquiring entity desires to minimize risks of its primary industry. USX (formerly United States Steel), a firm subject to heavy competition from imports, acquired Marathon Oil, a company with large proven petroleum reserves. Philip Morris diversified out of tobacco, an industry subject to pressures because of the health issue, and acquired a major brewer before securing control of General Foods.

Another important type of growth occurs as a result of vertical integration. **Vertical integration** arises when a firm goes downward to secure sources of supply or goes upward to secure outlets for reaching its customers. Campbell's Soup, for example, has bought farms as a means of growing some of the raw materials that go into its final product. Going upward toward the consumer, Goodyear developed a retail chain for selling tires, as well as providing automobile repair service.

All of these examples have important implications from the standpoint of management accounting. It is essential for the financial health of the entire organization that the performance of the various components of the conglomerate enterprise be continually monitored and evaluated. This, of course, embodies the managerial function of control.

All of the examples mentioned previously embody the managerial principle of decentralization. Because decentralization is so prevalent in U.S. business and industry, we begin by defining it and discussing its advantages. The type of managerial accounting controls employed are dependent on the scope of operations of the decentralized unit. A unit may be responsible only for meeting budgets and controlling costs; or it may also be responsible for generating revenues; finally, in addition to being held accountable for both

EXHIBIT 15–1

Meredith Corporation Holdings

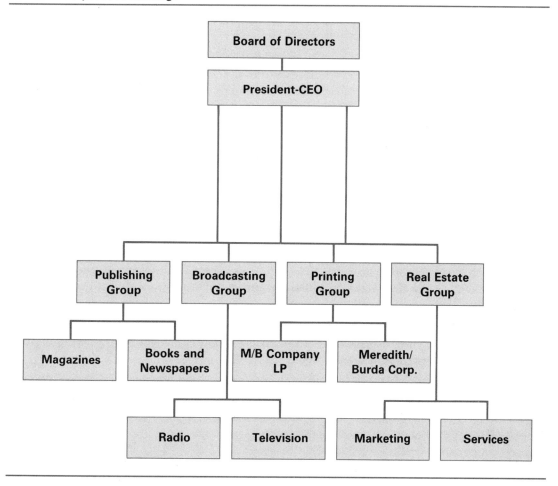

costs and revenues, a unit may also be answerable for the investment committed to it. The characteristics of these three types of organizational units are then discussed relative to the issue of decentralization. Finally, in the last sections of the chapter, some of the managerial accounting mechanisms for controlling the various decentralized entities are examined and analyzed.

Decentralization

Decentralization can be defined as a situation in which a large amount of authority is extended to subentities of the organization in terms of making important decisions. For a large division of a firm, some of these decisions would include what products should be made, how they should be manufactured, what **channels of distribution** should be utilized (the network used to get the product from the manufacturer to the ultimate consumer), and how the goods should be priced. Because decentralization is an extremely important managerial concept, let us examine the reasons that authority is frequently delegated to subentities of firms.

Advantages of Decentralization

The advantages of decentralization are so important that, for virtually all large organizations, the question is not one of centralization versus decentralization but rather one of how much decentralization should occur in each situation. There are several important reasons underlying the preponderance of decentralization:

1. Greater knowledgeability of those closest to the scene of action and ability to respond to changing conditions;

2. Top management can better concentrate on firmwide problems, long-range planning and evaluation of performance of subentities;

3. Greater motivation of management at the subentity level;

4. Management at the subentity level forms a better pool for promotion to top management of the organization than would be the case in more centralized situations.

Let us examine each of these reasons in greater depth. We will use the term divisional management in reference to management of decentralized organizational units.

Greater Knowledgeability of Decentralized Management

By virtue of operating in the field, divisional management will be more knowledgeable and aware of operating conditions such as dependability and capability of productive equipment and what is happening relative to customers and competition. For example, if a competitor cuts prices, divisional management will know about it more rapidly than top management. Top management, in fact, would probably learn about it from divisional management. As a result of being concerned with operations in the field, divisional management would not only learn of changing conditions more rapidly, they would also undoubtedly be more knowledgeable about the circumstances. Therefore, divisional management should be able to more rapidly and effectively respond to changing market conditions than would top management.

For example, in the case of a competitor's cutting prices, divisional management should be able to more effectively assess possible actions such as (1) lowering prices to meet a competitor or (2) minimizing price reductions due to factors such as quality differences between the competitor's product and that of the division or brand loyalty of customers. Thus, divisional management should be both more knowledgeable and able to react more rapidly to changing market and operating conditions than would top management.

Top Management Can More Effectively Concentrate on Firmwide Problems

With divisional management better able to respond to factors of concern at their level, top management can concentrate its efforts more effectively on firmwide problems and evaluation of divisional management performance.

Without decentralization, top management would require a huge expansion of staff to aid it in responding to lower-level problems. With decentralization, it can concentrate on firmwide and industry-level problems. For example, lobbying efforts either to open up foreign markets or to restrict imports would usually be the concern of top rather than divisional management.

Top management would also be more concerned with long-range planning efforts involving questions and issues such as development of new product lines and new markets. Of course, expertise from the field might well be involved with these areas.

Obviously by virtue of decentralization, top management has the task of constantly monitoring the efforts of divisional management and the performance of their entities.

Decentralization of decision-making authority to divisional management can be seen as an important application of the broader concept of the separation and division of labor. Without decentralization, it would be virtually impossible to have the type of modern economic structure that is present in the developed nations of the Western world.

Greater Motivation of Divisional Management

It is quite clear that motivation in terms of managerial performance will be greatly affected by decentralization. Having the authority to make important decisions, particularly when it is clear that evaluation of how well the job is being done goes along with that authority, is an important catalyst to divisional management in terms of encouraging it to perform well.

Divisional Management as a Source of Promotion to Top Management Positions

A decentralized form of organization where divisional management's performance is carefully monitored provides a better training ground for top management positions than a more centralized managerial structure where divisional management is carrying out top management's orders. Cronyism would more likely surface as a criterion for promotion to upper levels of management in centralized types of organizations.

Decentralization, then, is a management concept that "pushes down" the authority for making important decisions to those who are closest to and most knowledgeable relative to local operating conditions. Let us next examine organizational units and see how they may be classified in terms of the decentralization concept.

Organizational Units and Decentralization

In order to make decentralization work effectively, actual results of operations must be evaluated in relation to a plan or budget. This is, of course, the essence of control. However, what is to be evaluated depends on the type of organizational unit that is being appraised. Based on the functions being performed, organizational units fall into one of the following categories:

1. Cost centers,
2. Profit centers,
3. Investment centers.

Let us examine each of these.

Cost Centers

A **cost center** is basically responsible for the direct costs incurred in its operations and for meeting production budgets or quotas assigned to it. Production and service departments in manufacturing firms are a classic example of the cost center. Entire factories could also be considered as cost centers that are made up of numerous smaller cost centers. Authority and responsibility for cost centers must be clearly delineated under the leadership of a department head, often called a *foreman* (heads of plants are usually called *plant managers*). There should be no overlapping of authority relative to the operation of cost centers. Cost center operations can best be evaluated and controlled by means of a system of budgets and standard costs.

Profit Centers

The **profit center** unit is responsible not only for costs coming under its control but also for the generation of revenues. Profit centers usually do not contain large amounts of invested capital. Regional sales offices of large national enterprises would fall in this category. Some units within service organizations, such as consumer loan departments of banks, would also fall into the profit center category.

Book publishing provides another good example of the profit center concept. Large textbook publishers often decentralize by academic area served such as business administration, social sciences, and computer science. This type of decentralization occurs because of specialized marketing approaches for the various academic fields as well as particular personnel needs. Often these publishing company profit centers are responsible for generating new manuscripts, turning them into textbooks, and selling them to academic users. These are labor-intensive operations requiring considerable expertise. The books themselves are often manufactured—printed and bound—by outside firms or other divisions of the enterprise. Capital investment, therefore, is fairly minimal in specialized publishing divisions.

Profit centers are best evaluated by means of standard variable costing income statements. Standard costs and the variable costing approach have been previously covered in Chapters 9 through 11. However, some additional applications relative to major enterprises consisting of numerous product lines and profit centers will be further explored later in this chapter.

Investment Centers

Investment centers go a step beyond profit centers. The **investment center** is not only responsible for its costs and revenues, it also has accountability for investments in property, plant, and equipment assigned to it. Investment centers include units such as supermarkets, branches of banks, and department stores within a chain as well as previously independent firms that have become parts of conglomerates. The presumption in investment centers is that these organizations have at least some responsibility for major capital investments that are made for their benefit. This control may be virtually complete by the investment center if it is a large corporation that has been acquired by another large corporation, such as those examples cited at the beginning of this chapter. In other cases, major divisions (investment centers) of large enterprises may submit capital expenditure proposals to corporate headquarters for the entire firm with final selection of capital investment projects for all investment centers being made at the firmwide level. Even in these cases, there is considerable control by the investment centers because they submit the projects to top management for eventual selection. It is, of course, advocated that the capital investment process use the discounted cash flow techniques discussed in Chapters 13 and 14. The problem here, however, is one of assessment of investment center operations including capital investments.

Evaluation of investment center operations is accomplished by techniques that relate the investment in the division to the income generated from its operations. Two frequently employed methods will be discussed later in this chapter: return on investment and residual income.

An important situation that often surfaces relative to evaluating investment centers is called the *goal congruence problem*. Lack of **goal congruence** refers to a situation in which the goals of investment centers do not totally mesh with objectives of the entire firm. The control device should attempt to keep both sets of goals in harmony with each other. As will be seen, this can present a great deal of difficulty.

The three types of organizational units, their responsibilities, and methods for evaluating them are shown in Exhibit 15–2. Evaluation of cost centers was discussed in Chapters 5, 9, and 10. Profit center evaluation and how standard variable costing is employed will be examined next.

EXHIBIT 15–2
Summary of Decentralized Units

Type of Unit	Main Responsibilities	Principal Methods of Evaluation
Cost center	Carry out assigned production quotas as efficiently as possible	System of budgets and standard costs
Profit center	Generate revenues as effectively and efficiently as possible	Standard variable costing income statement
Investment center	Maximize income relative to asset investment	Return on investment; residual income

Evaluating Profit Centers

The primary tool for evaluating operating results of profit centers should be, we believe, standard variable costing income statements. Actual results should be compared against a revised budget, the latter being in the form of a standard variable costing income statement for the output level that should have been attained.

At the profit center level, an additional problem arises that is not present at the firmwide level: costs that are direct at the corporate (firmwide) level should not be allocated to profit centers. Examples of these costs include legal costs and interest expense as well as salaries and overhead pertaining to firmwide headquarters itself. These costs should not be charged against profit centers because allocation methods — in the absence of an ability to directly trace benefits to the profit centers — are generally quite arbitrary. In the past these costs were often assigned to profit centers on the basis of either revenues or income of the profit centers themselves. Hence, the more successful a profit center was relative to the firm's other profit centers, the more costs from corporate headquarters that would be charged to it. Bickering frequently arose among profit centers and also with corporate headquarters. As a result, assignment of these indirect costs to profit centers occurs much less frequently today than in years past.

Occasionally there are some activities that are concentrated at corporate headquarters in which services are directly performed for segmental units. An example would be a centralized computer facility. In these cases, assignment of operating costs to segments should attempt to measure, as carefully as possible, benefits received by the various organizational units for which services are provided.

Another feature that will be introduced is the possible need for modularizing the income statements. **Modularization** means that information can be regrouped and presented for different types of profit centers. For example, in the illustration that follows the profit centers will be, in one case, the sales territories and, in the other, the products lines themselves.

Illustration

The D-W Company is a small appliance manufacturer having two product lines: blenders and mixers. The organization chart for the company is shown in Exhibit 15–3. Within the two sales territories, the products are distributed through large retailers and wholesalers. Each territory is headed by a sales manager who supervises several salespersons. Budgets for blenders and mixers in the East territory are shown in Exhibit 15–4 (page 548). Several points require comment in this budget.

Revision of Budgets

The budget itself is labeled as a revised budget rather than the actual budget, which was forged at the beginning of the fiscal year. The reason for the revision is that conditions have changed during the year since the original budget was drafted. Consequently, the budget that is being used for comparison with actual results should likewise be revised in order to get a more meaningful comparison of actual results against budget or plan.

For example, assume that total industrywide sales for each product by territory can be determined. During the original budgetary process, management and marketing executives as well as territorial sales persons agreed that D-W should secure 20% of the blender market in the East territory. Budgeted total industry sales were expected to be 300,000 units. However, total actual sales for blenders in the East were much softer than anticipated. Actual total sales of blenders were only 250,000 units. There was no reason, however, to

EXHIBIT 15–3
Organization Chart of D-W Company

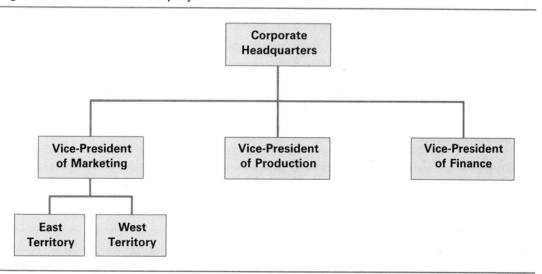

EXHIBIT 15–4

REVISED BUDGET
East Territory
19X5

	Blenders	Mixers	Total for Territory
Revenues ($30 per unit for blenders and $25 for mixers)	$1,500,000	$1,000,000	$2,500,000
Variable costs:			
Standard variable manufacturing costs	$ 750,000	$ 560,000	$1,310,000
Variable selling costs	150,000	100,000	250,000
Total	$ 900,000	$ 660,000	$1,560,000
Contribution margin	$ 600,000	$ 340,000	$ 940,000
Discretionary fixed costs:			
Advertising	120,000	100,000	220,000
Controllable margin	$ 480,000	$ 240,000	$ 720,000
Direct fixed costs of territory:			
Administrative salaries			$ 180,000
Depreciation			50,000
Utilities and communications			25,000
Indirect marketing costs of products			60,000
Total			$ 315,000
Territorial income			$ 405,000

revise D-W's market share of 20%. This caused the original budget for blenders in the East to be revised in the following fashion:

Original Budget		Revised Budget	
Total Market Size (units)	D-W's Target Share	Total Market Size (units)	D-W's Target Share
300,000	60,000	250,000	50,000

D-W's revised budget share was determined by taking actual total blender sales for the East (250,000) times D-W's target market share of 20% resulting in 50,000 units in the revised budget for 19X5. Although it was assumed that it was not necessary to change the target market share, intervening factors could have arisen here also. These would include entry or exit of competitors in the market and significant price changes of blenders manufactured by other firms.

Discretionary Fixed Costs

In the revised budget shown in Exhibit 15–4, advertising costs of the territory, which are a discretionary or programmed fixed cost (Chapter 3), are shown above the committed fixed costs of the territory. Those costs that are direct to the territory but are indirect relative to the product lines are not allocated to the product lines. These would include the territorial sales manager's salary and other expenses of running the territory. The principle involved here is the same as the one mentioned previously relative to not allocating costs of corporate headquarters to divisional segments when there is no fair basis of apportionment. For example, indirect marketing costs of products included sponsorship of television programming in the East in the name of the D-W Company without mentioning individual product lines. Allocation of these costs to the individual products would be arbitrary. As a result, the costs are not allocated to individual product lines.

Quite frequently, costs of corporate headquarters and other indirect costs such as production, finance, and marketing are allocated to the territories. This practice is not harmful as long as territorial management is not held accountable for them. These costs are indirect to the two territories and are not controllable by territorial management. This practice can be useful to the extent that it shows the territories other costs that must be covered in order for the firm to be profitable.

Comparison of Actual Results with Revised Budget

Actual results for 19X5 for the East territory are compared with the revised budget in Exhibit 15–5 (page 550). Variances by product line and in total provide information that is useful to both territorial management itself as well as the vice-president of marketing and possibly the executive vice-president.

Selling price and quantity variances can be determined for sales in a manner that is completely consistent with the columnar approach to standard cost variance analysis previously developed in Chapters 9 and 10. These are shown in Exhibit 15–6. It can be seen that there appears to be a price/quantity trade-off for blenders because a larger market share was secured but at a sacrifice in terms of selling price. The same strategy of lowering selling price did not produce substantial gains for mixers. A slight gain in units sold above budget — 42,000 actual versus 40,000 budget — led to unfavorable effects on contribution margin. New entrances into the market for mixers or increased competition from other suppliers may underlie the mixer situation. In any event, the variance analysis provides a useful starting point for analyzing operations of the territory. The other variances between actual results and budget would likewise provide a starting point for analysis of the respective items. Two other points should be stressed here.

Variable manufacturing costs are not controllable by territorial management Standard variable manufacturing costs for actual sales are used in both the actual operating results and revised budget. These costs are controllable by production management rather than territorial sales management; hence, any production variances should not be on a statement reporting on operating results of sales territories.

Meaning of profit categories on the standard variable costing income statement Three profit categories appear in Exhibit 15–5: contribution margin,

EXHIBIT 15–5

INCOME STATEMENT
East Territory
19X5

	Blenders			Mixers			Total for Territory		
	Budget	Actual	Variance	Budget	Actual	Variance	Budget	Actual	Variance
Revenues ($28 per unit for blenders and $22.50 for mixers)	$1,500,000	$1,820,000	$320,000 F	$1,000,000	$945,000	$55,000 U	$2,500,000	$2,765,000	$265,000 F
Variable costs:									
Standard variable manufacturing costs	$ 750,000	$ 975,000	$225,000 U	$ 560,000	$588,000	$28,000 U	$1,310,000	$1,563,000	$253,000 U
Variable selling costs	150,000	182,000	32,000 U	100,000	94,500	5,500 F	250,000	276,500	26,500 U
Total	$ 900,000	$1,157,000	$257,000 U	$ 660,000	$682,500	$22,500 U	$1,560,000	$1,839,500	$279,500 U
Contribution margin	$ 600,000	$ 663,000	$ 63,000 F	$ 340,000	$262,500	$77,500 U	$ 940,000	$ 925,500	$ 14,500 U
Discretionary fixed costs:									
Advertising	120,000	125,000	5,000 U	100,000	108,000	8,000 U	220,000	233,000	13,000 U
Controllable margin	$ 480,000	$ 538,000	$ 58,000 F	$ 240,000	$154,500	$85,500 U	$ 720,000	$ 692,500	$ 27,500 U
Direct fixed costs of territory:									
Administrative salaries							$ 180,000	$ 186,000	$ 6,000 U
Depreciation							50,000	50,000	—
Utilities and communications							25,000	27,000	2,000 U
Indirect marketing costs of products							60,000	57,000	3,000 F
Total							$ 315,000	$ 320,000	$ 5,000 U
Territorial income							$ 405,000	$ 372,500	$ 32,500 U

F = Favorable.
U = Unfavorable.

EXHIBIT 15–6

Sale Price and Quantity Variances for Blenders and Mixers in 19X5

	Actual Selling Price × Actual Units Sold	Budgeted Selling Price × Actual Units Sold	Budgeted Selling Price × Budgeted Unit Sales
Blenders	$28 × 65,000 = $1,820,000	$30 × 65,000 = $1,950,000	$30 × 50,000 = $1,500,000
Mixers	22.50 × 42,000 = 945,000	25 × 42,000 = 1,050,000	25 × 40,000 = 1,000,000
Total	$2,765,000	$3,000,000	$2,500,000

$235,000[a]
Sales price variance

$500,000 F[b]
Sales quantity variance

[a]$130,000 U for blenders
$105,000 U for mixers
[b]$450,000 F for blenders
$50,000 F for mixers

controllable margin, and segment margin. Each of these has importance relative to evaluating the segment and its management, in this case a sales territory. Contribution margin and segment margin were previously discussed in Chapter 11.

Contribution margin focuses directly on the attainment of management goals in the short run because its efforts are presumed to have an important influence on the level of sales. In addition, selling price per unit of product would be under the control of territorial management in a highly decentralized organizational situation.

Controllable margin likewise is an important measure for assessing managerial performance where programmed fixed costs such as advertising are under territorial management's control. However, the influence or benefits of advertising and other discretionary fixed costs such as training costs may take place over a longer period of time than a year. Also it is extremely difficult to measure how the benefits of these programs influence revenues.

At the level of territorial income, which is the income of the segment, direct committed fixed costs of the segment—such as depreciation—appear. These are not easily controllable by segment management in the short run. Previous territorial managements may have incurred them or these decisions may even be under control of a higher administrative level of the firm. Consequently, territorial income provides more of a long-run rather than a short-run orientation; in addition, it is keyed more to an assessment of the territory as opposed to the territorial management.

Modularization of Financial Data

Modularization is accomplished by recombining data to highlight different aspects of firm or profit center operations. In order to illustrate this idea, a standard variable costing income statement for the West territory in 19X5 is shown in Exhibit 15–7 (page 552). Modularization occurs when the information is recombined to show primary results by product line. This is shown for blenders as the primary segment with secondary emphasis placed on territories in Exhibit 15–8. Notice that in the segmental income statements presented in Chapter 11, the approach was one of breaking segments down into smaller units: from divisions to product lines within divisions to plants producing particular products. The modularization approach being illustrated here is one where recombination occurs at the same level: territories can be broken into product lines and products can be broken down into territorial components.

Recombination would be particularly important if blenders and mixers had different product managers. Modularization is accomplished as part of the management information system when data is captured and classified by different possible categories.

Evaluating Investment Centers

Investment centers have the additional cornerstone, beyond profit centers, of significant amounts of capital investment controllable by investment center management. This control is usually not total in nature because firmwide management usually reviews major capital budgeting proposals of investment centers. In other cases, firmwide management controls the total amount of capital funds to be invested and selects those projects for investment based

EXHIBIT 15–7

	WEST TERRITORY Income Statement 19X5		
	Blenders	*Mixers*	*Total*
Revenues	$1,600,000	$1,000,000	$2,600,000
Variable costs:			
Standard variable manufacturing costs	$ 820,000	$ 580,000	$1,400,000
Variable selling costs	160,000	100,000	260,000
Total	$ 980,000	$ 680,000	$1,660,000
Contribution margin	$ 620,000	$ 320,000	$ 940,000
Discretionary fixed costs:			
Advertising	140,000	125,000	265,000
Controllable margin	$ 480,000	$ 195,000	$ 675,000
Direct fixed costs of territory:			
Administrative salaries			$ 200,000
Depreciation			55,000
Utilities and communications			27,000
Indirect marketing costs of products			66,000
Total			$ 348,000
Territorial income			$ 327,000

EXHIBIT 15–8

BLENDERS
Income Statement
19X5

	East	West	Total
Revenues	$1,820,000	$1,600,000	$3,420,000
Variable costs:			
Standard variable manufacturing costs	$ 975,000	$ 820,000	$1,795,000
Variable selling costs	182,000	160,000	342,000
Total	$1,157,000	$ 980,000	$2,137,000
Contribution margin	$ 663,000	$ 620,000	$1,283,000
Discretionary fixed costs:			
Advertising	125,000	140,000	265,000
Controllable margin	$ 538,000	$ 480,000	$1,018,000
Direct fixed costs:			
Fixed manufacturing costs[a]			400,000
Product income			$ 618,000

[a]Indirect to territories.

on the proposals forthcoming from the investment centers themselves. In both cases, capital investment is major in size, and investment center management has, at the least, considerable input into the evaluation and selection process.

Standard variable costing income statements should be a major tool for evaluating investment center operations as well as those of profit centers. Unlike profit centers, manufacturing variances should be included in the computation of variable costing income if the production function is part of investment center operations. The problem of investment centers is to relate this income amount to divisional investment. Two basic methods have been used: return on investment (ROI) and residual income (RI).

Before discussing each of these methods, one important point must be made. Because investment in a division's assets represents a long-term commitment, ROI and RI are usually computed only on an annual basis. For interim periods of less than a year, standard variable costing income statements should be relied on.

Return on Investment

Methods for evaluating investment centers must relate investment to the income that they generate. In **return on investment** this is accomplished by dividing income by investment:

$$ROI = \frac{Income}{Investment}$$

This leads to two important questions: What income measurement should be used, and what type of investment base is appropriate?

Income Used in ROI

The income question is the easier of the two to analyze. The income that is most often recommended is earnings before interest and taxes (frequently referred to as *EBIT*). The purpose of using this number is to give as undiluted an analysis of operations of investment center management as possible. Consequently, interest costs, which arise from financing decisions, and income tax expense, which concerns questions of tax policy, are not included in ROI using EBIT. The profit measure that most closely corresponds to EBIT from the standard variable costing income statement previously discussed would be segment income. This number excludes items that are not related to operating performance such as interest and gains and losses on fixed asset disposals (disposals are likewise left out of the ROI calculation). Under this more restrictive approach, it takes this form:

$$\text{ROI} = \frac{\text{Segment income}}{\text{Investment}}$$

Investment Base Used in ROI

The asset base problem is more complex than the question of which income measurement to use. Four bases are frequently mentioned:

1. Total gross assets,
2. Total net assets,
3. Total net assets less presently nonproductive assets, and
4. Total net assets (with or without presently nonproductive assets) less current liabilities controllable by the investment center.

Total gross assets   Total gross assets are equal to the cost of all assets controlled by the investment center not reduced by accumulated depreciation and amortization. This base is sometimes recommended in situations where assets are maintained in top running order by means of extensive maintenance and repair policies. Using gross assets appears to be a dubious investment base for two reasons.

First, the investment center may be "punished" twice under this approach relative to calculating ROI. The extensive maintenance policy could result in lower income in any given year due to high maintenance expenses. The higher investment base also lowers ROI. Whether the investment center's operations are improved over the long run by maintaining greater efficiency of plant and equipment may be a difficult question to answer. It is clear, however, that ROI will be lowered as a result of the higher gross assets base. Hence, optimum maintenance policies may actually lower ROI, a factor that could create friction between top management and divisional management.

Second, even if plant and equipment are maintained at peak operating efficiency, technological obsolescence may occur: in terms of operating cost minimization, newer machinery and equipment may be more efficient than older equipment. Consequently, the total gross assets base will not result in a meaningful measure of ROI.

Sometimes the total gross assets base is advocated as a substitute for an inflation adjustment to the cost of plant and equipment charged to a division. Newer equipment often costs more than older equipment simply as a result of inflationary price rises. It has therefore been advocated that by not reducing the costs of assets assigned to a division, accumulated depreciation could be viewed as a substitute for an inflation adjustment to the net cost of the division's assets. Unquestionably, inflation presents great difficulties in terms of evaluating performance accurately (see below). However, using total gross assets as the investment base in ROI calculations is not the answer to the problem of rising prices. There is no necessary relationship between the total gross assets amount and inflationary adjustments to historical costs. Total gross assets is simply not appropriate as a substitute for an inflation adjustment.

Total net assets   The net assets base is equal to the gross assets base minus accumulated depreciation and amortization. It is probably the most frequently used investment base for ROI calculation purposes. Due to the weaknesses of the gross assets base mentioned above, the net asset base appears to be preferable.

Total net assets less presently nonproductive assets   This base is a natural extension of the total net assets base concept. Where an investment center has assets that are presently nonproductive, such as land being held for future development or assets under construction, it appears to be reasonable to leave them out of the investment base because they do not presently contribute to the generation of revenues and income. Thus, only productive assets should appear in the investment base, and the amounts of nonproductive assets should be monitored to make sure they do not get too extensive. This is generally not a serious problem.

Total net assets less current liabilities controllable by the investment center   Where the investment center controls the incurrence of short-term liabilities such as accounts payable, these may be deducted from total assets (presumably total net assets) to arrive at long-term invested capital. This approach provides a measurement of capital provided by long-term creditors and owners. However, this measurement should *not* deduct long-term liabilities such as bonds payable because this would measure the return to owners' equity only and not to all long-term providers of capital. The return to owners' equity thus intertwines operating issues with financing questions. This is the case because the return to owners is affected by whether a "profit" or "loss" is made on long-term debt. The results are favorable if the return on all assets exceeds the interest rate applicable to long-term creditors. If the return on all assets is less than the interest rate, the owners are adversely affected. Although return on owners' equity is a legitimate measure of return, it involves questions of both operations and finance. ROI is conceived as being a measure purely concerned with how well operations have been conducted by investment center management.

In conclusion, either total net assets, or total net assets less nonproductive assets, or total net assets less current liabilities controllable by the investment center provide viable investment base measurements for evaluating operations of investment centers.

Other investment base problems   Three other problems should be mentioned relative to measuring the investment base. First, assuming that one of the three recommended bases is being used, the question is whether the beginning-of-year asset balance or an average for the year should be employed (assets at the beginning of year plus assets at the end of the year divided by 2). Both measurements are used in practice. Conceptually, the average for the year is better because it would take into account the fact that additional investment does create additional income. Similarly, reductions of assets for purposes such as dividends eliminates their ability to generate revenues and income. However, from the practical standpoint this is not a serious problem because it is not generally material: increases or decreases in assets are generally relatively minor compared to the stock of assets existing at the beginning of the year. The main point here is one of consistency. The same type of base should be used from period to period to enhance comparability to see how the same investment center performs over time.

A second problem concerns situations where some assets used by investment centers are controlled at corporate headquarters. These would mainly be cash and accounts receivable. Where cash is centrally controlled, investment centers would maintain relatively small amounts of cash with disbursements for accounts payable and payrolls as well as major expenditures for noncurrent assets going through corporate headquarters. In these cases, an equitable allocation of cash to investment centers for purposes of inclusion in the investment base should be made. Sometimes the cash allocation is made on the basis of how large investments in cash would have to be if the investment center were operating as a totally independent entity. Accounts receivable is easier to handle. Relatively accurate assessments of receivables for each investment center can usually be made because sales can be traced directly to investment centers.

The third problem concerns an even more substantive issue: all of the previous investment bases were measured in historical cost terms. The question then is whether some form of current valuation of the firm's assets would provide a more meaningful economic measurement than historical costs. We would agree that it does. However, until current valuations of assets become more prevalent, historical costing—despite its weaknesses—will continue to be used. It might also be added that if current valuation of assets were used, current value measurements of income should also be used in the numerator of the ROI measurement for purposes of consistency. Many firms have been using current value income numbers that were provided in the annual report to shareholders of publicly traded firms. As time goes by, ROI measurements may become more contemporary in terms of both income and assets. In line with the current state of the art, we will assume that historical costs are being used throughout the balance of this chapter.

Measuring ROI

Assume that the W-G-P Division of the ABC Company is an investment center responsible for generating income and having responsibility for capital expenditures. The following figures pertained to the year 19X5:

Segment income	$ 750,000
Total net assets, Jan. 1, 19X5	4,800,000
Total net assets, Dec. 31, 19X5	5,200,000
Net sales	2,000,000

ROI using average total net assets would be

$$ROI = \frac{\$750,000}{\$5,000,000} = 15\%$$

Like many measurements, the figure is most meaningful when compared with the budgeted (target) ROI for the division as well as with performance of W-G-P for past periods. It may also be meaningful to compare W-G-P's ROI for 19X5 with competitors and with any standards of industry performance, if these figures are available for the current year.

Furthermore, it is possible to decompose ROI into two major subcomponents that provide more information than the aggregated measure standing by itself. ROI is broken into its two components in the following fashion:

$$\frac{\text{Segment income}}{\text{Net sales}} \times \frac{\text{Net sales}}{\text{Investment}} = ROI$$

The term on the left is called **profit margin.** It shows the relative profitability per dollar of net sales. The right-hand term is known as *capital turnover.* **Capitol turnover** shows the relationship between a balance sheet element, shown in the denominator, and an income statement factor to which it is related in the numerator. Capital turnover is thus related to other turnover measures such as accounts receivable turnover and inventory turnover (Chapter 19). Capital turnover is the broadest of all turnover measures. It shows the relationship between the division's investment in assets and the ability of those assets to generate revenues.

In our example the ROI for W-G-P during 19X5 using profit margin and capital turnover would be

$$\frac{\$750,000}{\$2,000,000} \times \frac{\$2,000,000}{\$5,000,000} = 15\%$$

$$37.5\% \times 40\% = 15\%$$

Net sales cancels out of the profit margin and capital turnover calculations leaving us with income over investment, which is the basic ROI formula. However, decomposing ROI into its two main component parts gives us more information than we would receive by just examining ROI. For example, profit margin is a measure of efficiency because it tells us how much of each sales dollar is left over as segment income after covering variable and fixed costs. As such, it gives us a view of the "forest" of operating efficiency. It should be backed up by a system of budgets and standard costs that are more at the "tree" level in terms of providing detailed insights into any perceived changes or trends that are emerging in terms of the investment center's operating efficiency.

Capital turnover, likewise, helps us to focus on other operating problems. Are sales lagging relative to the amount of investment maintained by the division? On the other hand, is investment growing without generating additional sales? Insights into this last point may be gained by examining whether accounts receivable turnover and inventory turnover (Chapter 19) are slowing down. Unquestionably, decomposing ROI into its two main components can provide considerable information relative to operations of the investment center. However, ROI measurements can lead to problems of goal congruence.

ROI and Goal Congruence

Goal congruence was defined earlier in terms of how well the goals of the individual investment center mesh with overall corporate goals. Let us, first of all, establish a basic assumption relative to the behavior of individuals in managerial positions: administrators will attempt to maximize their performance as perceived from the standpoint of the control measures that are used to evaluate that performance. Thus managers who are being evaluated by ROI will attempt to maximize the amount of their ROI.

It might be assumed that maximizing investment center ROI should automatically lead to maximizing the overall corporate ROI. However, this is not necessarily the case. One of the problems is that ROI is a *relative measure.* That is, the resulting measurement expresses the relationship between the numerator and the denominator. This can lead an investment center manager to reject profitable projects that are perceived to lower ROI.

Assume that during the forthcoming year a manager expects an ROI of 25% expressed by the following budgeted segment income and investment base:

$$\frac{\$125,000}{\$500,000} = 25\%$$

Suppose that the division is evaluating a capital investment project with the following annuity cash flow configuration:

Year	0	1 ---------- 25
Investment	−$100,000	
Net cash inflows		$20,000 $20,000

Time adjusted rate of return on this project would be just under 20% ($20,000 times 4.9476—present value of $1 at 20% for 25 years—is equal to $98,952). If the division's cost of capital were 15%, it would appear to make the project attractive for investment. This is not the case, however, in terms of the effect of the capital investment on ROI. Assume that annual depreciation on the project would be $4,000 per year (straight-line depreciation over 25 years with no salvage value). This would pull the net income of the project down to $16,000 ($20,000 minus $4,000) with a capital investment of $100,000. The perceived effect of accepting the project would *decrease* ROI:

Original   Incremental ROI
projection of ROI + from new project = Revised projection of ROI

$$\frac{\$125,000 + \$16,000}{\$500,000 + \$100,000} \qquad = \frac{\$141,000}{\$600,000} = 23.5\%$$

The new projection of ROI by divisional management would be 23.5%. Management would thus be strongly tempted to reject a project having a time-adjusted rate of return in excess of the cost of capital because its projection on ROI would show a decrease: from 25% down to 23.5%. Hence ROI, as an evaluation tool, can lead to poor decisions as long as managers are guided by the perceived effect of new investment decisions on ROI. We can, of course, expect this to be the case. As a result of the potential weakness of ROI, a second measure of the overall effectiveness of operating performance of investment centers has arisen. This measurement is called *residual income* and is discussed next.

Residual Income

The second method for evaluating investment center operations and how it relates to investment is the RI approach. **Residual income** is calculated by deducting from segment income a cost of capital charge for the applicable investment center. The capital charge against segment income is determined by taking the net assets at the beginning of the period times an appropriate cost of capital charge for the division. The cost of capital used in residual income analysis should be an interest rate based on the perceived long-run required earnings rate of the investment center. Among other factors, this rate will take into account a risk factor applicable to the division because some investment centers may be in more volatile types of operations than other divisions. Assume in the example just used that divisional cost of capital is 15%. Residual income with and without the incremental investment is shown in Exhibit 15–9.

Notice that the investment, which was sound when analyzed by means of TARR, is now attractive to the division when viewed from the perspective of residual income. Thus in this example, the planning tool — TARR — gives results that are consistent with the control tool: residual income. This is, in fact, one of the advantages cited by adherents of RI over ROI: more goal congruence between investment center and the firm as a whole, which is brought about by a greater consistency between planning tool and control instrument used at the investment center level.

RI, however, has its own weaknesses. Unlike ROI, RI is an absolute measure. It should therefore not be used as an evaluative tool for comparing different divisions because the investment center with the larger asset base will generally be favored. If comparison among divisions is to be made — something that is not wholeheartedly recommended — then ROI is the better tool for comparability purposes because it is a relative measure.

Other Goal Congruence Problems of ROI and RI

Furthermore, it should not be assumed that RI is totally free of problems of lack of goal congruence. The door is opened to goal congruence problems for both ROI and RI simply because of the fact that most investment centers use straight-line depreciation for profit reporting purposes.

The problem brought about from using straight-line depreciation can be illustrated by means of a simple example. Assume that an investment center is examining a capital budgeting project with the following cash flow configuration:

Year	0	1	2	3
Investment	−$2,487			
Net cash inflows		$1,000	$1,000	$1,000

EXHIBIT 15–9
Residual Income with and without Incremental Project

	Without	With
Projected segment income	$125,000	$141,000
Cost of capital charge	75,000[a]	90,000[b]
Residual income	$ 50,000	$ 51,000

[a].15 × $500,000.
[b].15 × $600,000.

The project has a 10% time-adjusted rate of return ($1,000 times the present value of a three-year annuity factor at 10% of 2.487 equals $2,487). The ROI on the project itself using straight-line depreciation, with no salvage, is shown in Exhibit 15–10.

Notice that the ROI in year 1 is only 6.87%, even though the project has a time-adjusted rate of return of 10%. If the investment center's cost of capital were, say, 8%, the tendency would be to reject the project even though it is profitable. Although the time-adjusted rate of return is 10% with a divisional cost of capital of only 8%, marginal ROI of under 7% makes the project look unattractive from the control standpoint even though it is profitable.

Furthermore, there is an additional unfavorable bias that also can be illustrated with this example. Notice that as this asset ages, its ROI increases. This is due to the diminishing book value (investment base) of the asset. There may well be a tendency to keep many assets that should be replaced because of higher ROIs as assets age. A possible means for improving ROI is discussed in Appendix 15–A.

The goal congruence problem relative to investment center actions stimulated by the possible effect of evaluation of the division is serious. Nevertheless, both ROI and RI will continue to have wide usage until better methods are developed. All that can be said is that both investment center management and corporate headquarters should be aware of these factors and should attempt, together, to work around them as they arise.

EXHIBIT 15–10
Projected ROI of Incremental Project with Straight-line Depreciation

Year	1	2	3
Revenues	$1,000	$1,000	$1,000
Depreciation	829	829	829
Net income	$ 171	$ 171	$ 171
Asset value at beginning of period	$2,487	$1,658[b]	$ 829[d]
Projected ROI	6.87%[a]	10.31%[c]	20.62%[e]

[a] $\dfrac{\$171}{\$2,487} = 6.87\%$

[b] $\$2,487 - \$829 = \$1,658$

[c] $\dfrac{\$171}{\$1,658} = 10.31\%$

[d] $\$1,658 - \$829 = \$829$

[e] $\dfrac{\$171}{\$829} = 20.62\%$

Summary

Our economy is characterized by the presence of many large firms that comprise numerous divisions and other entities that operate on a decentralized basis. The advantages of decentralization are numerous. Those who are closest to the action can ordinarily respond more rapidly and effectively than top management. In addition, decentralization avoids the need for huge staff and expanded communication that would be needed in its absence. Decentralization also provides greater motivation for divisional management and also can serve as a pool for promotion to top management levels. However, going along with decentralization is the need to monitor and evaluate the operations of decentralized units.

Three types of decentralized units were identified. Control of the cost center should be achieved by means of a system of budgets and standard costs. Profit centers are best controlled by means of standard variable costing income statements that can be modularized so that different types of profit centers can be evaluated. These profit centers could include both product lines and sales territories. A key point to remember is that these income statements should only include costs that are controllable by the particular level of management being evaluated. That is, indirect costs should not be arbitrarily assigned to cost centers.

The investment center is evaluated on both the income it generates and the asset investment committed to it. ROI is a relative measure that divides segment income by an asset base such as average total net assets. This measure can lead to a lack of goal congruence because ROI is a relative measure: ROI can be decreased by taking on projects that have a lower incremental ROI than the expected ROI without them, even though these projects are profitable to the total firm.

A second method for evaluating investment centers is to use RI. By building a cost of capital charge directly into segmental income, some of the goal congruency problems of ROI can be avoided. However, both methods are subject to goal congruency problems stemming from the use of straight-line depreciation. These problems can be avoided by using compound interest method depreciation. However, this is not likely to be done by management because compound interest method depreciation is not well understood and can lead to confusion. Confusion can arise because accelerated depreciation is used for tax purposes and straight-line depreciation is employed for published financial statements. The goal congruency problem is not one that will be easily solved.

Appendix 15–A
Improving ROI and RI by Using
Compound Interest Depreciation

In the discussion of ROI and RI in the body of the chapter, goal congruence problems stemming from the usage of straight-line depreciation were discussed. One possible solution would be to use **compound interest depreciation,** which evens out the ROI on an asset over its life. This approach is illustrated in Exhibit 15–11 with the capital investment project previously introduced.

Although compound interest method depreciation smooths out the projected ROI on capital investment projects, it has several drawbacks. The method itself is not well understood by management. The increasing charge pattern, which would occur quite frequently, would undoubtedly be looked at suspiciously by management. Increasing charges generally result from this method because the decreasing asset base requires *increasing* depreciation charges in order to keep the ROI percentage constant. Another serious problem is that three different types of depreciation would be kept for most assets:

Purpose	*Type of Depreciation*
Income taxes	Accelerated depreciation
Financial reporting	Straight-line
Investment center evaluation	Compound interest method

This expansion of depreciation methods for different purposes might well create "information overload" problems for management personnel.

EXHIBIT 15–11

Compound Interest Depreciation

Year	*1*	*2*	*3*
Revenues	$1,000	$1,000	$1,000
Depreciation[a]	751	826	909
Net income	$ 249	$ 174	$ 91
Asset value at beginning of period	$2,487	$1,736	$ 910
Projected ROI	10%	10%	10%

[a]Annual depreciation is intended to make ROI equal to time-adjusted rate of return. Start with the present value of the last year's cash flows ($1,000 × .751 = $751 for the *third* year's $1,000 cash flow). In later years, the depreciation is equal to $751 plus interest on accumulated depreciation:

Year 2: $751 + (.10 × $751) = $826

Year 3: $751 + .10($751 + $826) = $909

Another way to understand compound interest depreciation is to view it as a "plug" number that would result in a projected annual ROI that equals the same time-adjusted rate of return on a project, provided that actual annual cash flows of a project were the same as in the capital budget.

EXHIBIT 15–12
Residual Income with Straight-line Depreciation

Year	1	2	3
Revenues	$1,000	$1,000	$1,000
Depreciation	$ 829	$ 829	$ 829
Cost of capital charge	224[a]	149[b]	75[c]
Residual income	$ −53	$ 22	$ 96

[a].09 × $2,487
[b].09 × ($2,487 − $829)
[c].09 × ($2,487 − $1,658)

RI is also susceptible to goal congruence problems stemming from the use of straight-line depreciation. Continuing with our example, if cost of capital for the investment center is 9%, RI for this asset, on a projected basis, is illustrated in Exhibit 15–12. The resulting RI pattern is similar to the problem illustrated previously with ROI. In the case of RI, projected residual income is negative in the first year and dramatically increases as the asset ages. The underlying reason is the same as in the ROI case: diminishing book value decreases the cost of capital charge as the asset ages. Once again, it is very doubtful that divisional management always will desire to bite the bullet of negative residual income in the early years of an asset's life. Thus, lack of goal congruence once again occurs.

The solution in the RI case is similar to what was proposed in the ROI situation: the use of compound interest method depreciation. This is illustrated in Exhibit 15–13. Notice in Exhibit 15–13 that the residual income is

EXHIBIT 15–13
Residual Income with Compound Interest Depreciation

Year	1	2	3
Revenues	$1,000	$1,000	$1,000
Depreciation	$ 751	$ 826	$ 909
Cost of capital charges	224[a]	156[b]	82[c]
Total expenses	$ 975	$ 982	$ 991
Residual income	$ 25	$ 18	$ 9
Beginning of year asset value	$2,487	$1,736	$ 909
Residual income ÷ beginning of year asset value	$\frac{\$25}{\$2,487} = 1\%$	$\frac{\$18}{\$1,736} = 1\%$	$\frac{\$9}{\$909} = 1\%$

[a].09 × $2,487
[b].09 × ($2,487 − $751)
[c].09 × ($2,487 − $1,577)

equal to 1% of the book value of the asset. This is completely consistent with the fact that the asset has a projected 10% time-adjusted rate of return with a 9% divisional cost of capital. Unfortunately, the same reservations previously mentioned relative to compound interest method depreciation in regard to ROI also would hold relative to RI.

Key Terms

Capital turnover is a component of return on investment. It is measured by dividing net sales for the year by the investment base.

Channels of distribution refers to the means by which the product gets to the ultimate consumer from the manufacturer.

Compound interest depreciation results in equalizing annual ROI on assets assuming that actual annual cash flows for an investment project were the same as the capital budget.

Conglomerate refers to situations where many semi-independent and diverse companies are brought together under the control of a single firm.

Controllable margin refers to the contribution margin of a segment less its direct discretionary fixed costs.

Cost center is responsible for the direct costs incurred in its operations and for meeting production budgets or quotas assigned to it. Authority and responsibility for a cost center must be clearly delineated under the leadership of a department head.

Decentralization is a situation in which authority for important decisions is pushed down from the top to lower segments of the enterprise.

Goal congruence refers to situations in which goals of investment centers mesh with the objectives of the entire firm. Lack of goal congruence is present if investment center objectives do not harmonize with goals of the firm.

Investment center refers to organizational units that are responsible for generating income as well as the invested capital that has helped to generate the income.

Modularization means that information can be "reshuffled" and thus presented for different types of profit centers such as product lines and territories.

Profit center refers to an organizational unit that is responsible for generating income.

Profit margin is a component of return on investment. It is determined by dividing segment income by sales.

Residual income is an investment center performance measurement that deducts a cost of capital charge from segment income.

Return on investment is an investment center performance measurement in which segment income is divided by investment. It can also be determined by multiplying profit margin times capital turnover.

Vertical integration arises when a firm buys additional firms to either get "closer" to the consumer or to sources of supply (or both).

Questions

Q15–1   If a firm is expanding by acquiring other companies, what are the advantages of acquiring enterprises in the same general industry?

Q15–2   Why would a firm desire to acquire companies in totally different industries?

Q15–3   What is *decentralization?*

Q15–4   What are the advantages of decentralization?

Q15–5   How are the operations of cost centers best controlled?

Q15–6   Do you think that the traditional absorption costing income statement provides a good means of control relative to the operations of profit centers?

Q15–7   What does the term *goal congruence* mean?

Q15–8   It used to be the practice in decentralized enterprises that all costs, whether direct or indirect, had to be assigned to profit or investment centers. Why do you think that this philosophy has been sharply challenged?

Q15–9   What does *modularization* of information for financial statements mean?

Q15–10   What is *controllable margin* on a segmental income statement?

Q15–11   How do investment centers and profit centers differ?

Q15–12   In measuring ROI, why is earnings before interest and taxes (EBIT) used rather than earnings after interest and taxes?

Q15–13   Why is gross assets a dubious base to use for calculating ROI?

Q15–14   When might total net assets less current liabilities be a meaningful base to use for calculating ROI?

Q15–15   Why is total net assets less *all* liabilities not a useful base to use when calculating ROI?

Q15–16   Why is it the case that current value of assets is conceptually superior to all cost-based measures of assets when computing ROI?

Q15–17   Why does ROI resemble time-adjusted rate of return (TARR) and RI resemble net present value (NPV)?

Q15–18   Why is an absolute measure of profits such as RI better than a relative measure of profits such as ROI from the standpoint of goal congruence?

Q15–19   Why does straight-line depreciation present a problem from the standpoint of goal congruence regardless of whether ROI or RI is employed?

Q15–20   Why does compound interest depreciation improve both ROI and RI measurements of investment center performance?

Q15–21   Why is compound interest depreciation not popular for use in assessing investment center performance despite its superiority to straight-line and other depreciation methods?

Exercises

E15–1 **ROI: fill in the blanks.** Fill in the missing numbers in the following cases:

Division	A	B	C
Sales	$ 500,000	$2,000,000	$1,000,000
Segment income	80,000	400,000	?
Total assets of division	1,000,000	?	?
Profit margin	?	?	5%
Capital turnover	?	?	200%
Return on investment (ROI)	?	5%	10%

E15–2 **RI and ROI: fill in the blanks.** Fill in the missing numbers in the following cases:

Division	A	B	C
Segment income	$ 100,000	$150,000	$ 500,000
Total assets of division	1,000,000	?	1,000,000
Cost of capital charge	8%	10%	?
Residual income (RI)	?	100,000	400,000
Return on investment (ROI)	?	?	?

E15–3 **Basic ROI and RI calculations.** Hackenslay Company's D Division expects the following results during 19X4:

Revenues	$2,000,000
Variable costs	600,000
Contribution margin	$1,400,000
Fixed expenses	600,000
Segment income	$ 800,000

Total assets are $5,000,000.

Required:
1. Determine the ROI breaking it down into profit margin and capital turnover.
2. Present a residual income type income statement on the assumption that divisional cost of capital is 8%.

E15–4 **ROI and RI calculations with and without an incremental investment.** Lewis Company is a division of the Clark Corporation. During 19X7 it expects a net operating income of $200,000. It has an investment base of $1,000,000. Its sales are expected to be $2,000,000.

Lewis is appraising a capital investment project with a cost of $100,000 and annual cash flows of $15,000. The project has an expected life of 25 years and a TARR of just under 15%. Straight-line depreciation with no salvage would be used.

Required:
1. Lewis's profit margin without the investment.
2. Lewis's capital turnover without the investment.
3. Lewis's ROI without the investment.
4. Lewis's ROI with the investment.
5. Lewis's residual income without the investment (divisional cost of capital is 10%).
6. Lewis's residual income with the investment.

7. Would you expect Lewis's decision under ROI to conflict with the profit maximization of the Clark Corporation? Explain.

8. Would you expect Lewis's decision under residual income to conflict with the profit maximization of the Clark Corporation? Explain.

E15–5 **Multiple-choice definitions.**

1. A segment of an organization is referred to as a *profit center* if it has
   a. authority to make decisions affecting the major determinants of profit including the power to choose its markets and sources of supply.
   b. authority to make decisions affecting the major determinants of profit including the power to choose its markets and sources of supply and significant control over the amount of invested capital.
   c. authority to make decisions over the most significant costs of operations including the power to choose the sources of supply.
   d. authority to provide specialized support to other units within the organization.
   e. responsibility for combining the raw materials, direct labor, and other factors of production into a final output.

2. A segment of an organization is referred to as an *investment center* if it has
   a. authority to make decisions affecting the major determinants of profit including the power to choose its markets and sources of supply.
   b. authority to make decisions affecting the major determinants of profit including the power to choose its markets and sources of supply and significant control over the amount of invested capital.
   c. authority to make decisions over the most significant costs of operations including the power to choose the sources of supply.
   d. authority to provide specialized support to other units within the organization.
   e. responsibility for developing markets for and selling the output of the organization.

(CMA Adapted)

E15–6 **Analysis of performance of profit centers, revision of budgets.** Two products of the Junetag Appliance Company were sold in national markets. The budgets on these two products and Junetag's share in units are

Product A		Product B	
Total Market	Junetag's Share	Total Market	Junetag's Share
100,000	12,000	50,000	8,000

The actual sales for the total market were 120,000 for A and 45,000 for B. Junetag sold 13,000 As and 7,500 Bs.

Required: Which of these products did better in terms of its actual market share relative to plan? Show figures.

E15–7 **Decentralization.** Edwin Hall, chairman of the board and president of Arrow Works Products Company, founded the company in the mid-19X0s. He is a talented and creative engineer. Arrow Works was started with one of his inventions, an intricate diecast item that required a minimum of finish work. The item was manufactured for Arrow Works by a Gary, Indiana, foundry. The product sold well in a wide market.

The company issued common stock in 19X2 to finance the purchase of the Gary foundry. Additional shares were issued in 19X5, when Arrow purchased a fabricating plant in Cleveland to meet the capacity requirement of a defense contract.

The company now consists of five divisions. Each division is headed by a manager who reports to Hall. The Chicago division contains the Product Development and Engineering Department and the finishing (assembly) operation for the basic products. The Gary plant and Cleveland plant are the other two divisions engaged in manufacturing operations. All products manufactured are sold through two selling divisions. The eastern sales division is located in Pittsburgh and covers the country from Chicago to the east coast. The western sales division, which covers the rest of the country, is located in Denver. The western sales division is the newest operation and was established just eight months ago.

Hall, who still owns 53% of the outstanding stock, actively participates in the management of the company. He travels frequently and regularly to all of the company's plants and offices. He says, "Having a business with locations in five different cities spread over half the country requires all my time." Despite his regular and frequent visits he believes that the company is decentralized and that the managers have complete autonomy. "They make all the decisions and run their own shops. Of course, they don't understand the total business as I do, so I have to straighten them out once in a while. My managers are all good men, but they can't be expected to handle everything alone. I try to help all I can."

The last two months have been a period of considerable stress for Hall. During this period, John Staple, manager of the fabricating plant, was advised by his physician to request a six-month sick leave to relieve the work pressures that had made him nervous and tense. This request had followed by three days a phone call in which Hall had directly and bluntly blamed Staple for the lagging production output and increased rework and scrap of the fabricating plant. Hall made no allowances for the pressures created by the operation of the plant at volumes in excess of normal and close to its maximum-rated capacity for the previous nine months.

Hall thought that he and Staple had had a long and good relationship prior to this event. Hall attributed his loss of temper in this case to his frustration with several other management problems that had arisen in the past two months. The sales manager of the Denver office had resigned shortly after a visit from Hall. The letter of resignation stated that he was seeking a position with greater responsibility. The sales manager in Pittsburgh asked to be reassigned to a sales position in the field; he did not feel that he could cope with the pressure of management.

Required:

1. How do centralized and decentralized management differ?
2. Is Arrow Works Products Company as decentralized as Hall believes? Explain your answer.
3. Advise Mr. Hall, on the basis of the facts presented in the problem, whether the events that have occurred over the past two months in Arrow Works Products Company should have been expected. Carefully explain your answer.

(CMA Adapted)

E15–8 **ROI and goal congruence.** The Notewon Corporation is a highly diversified company that grants its divisional executives a significant amount of authority in operating the divisions. Each division is responsible for its own sales, pricing, production, costs of operations, and the management of accounts receivable, inventories, accounts payable, and use of existing facilities. Cash is managed by corporate headquarters; all cash in excess of normal operating needs of the divisions is transferred periodically to corporate headquarters for redistribution or investment.

Divisional executives are responsible for presenting requests to corporate management for investment projects. Proposals are analyzed and documented at corporate headquarters. The final decision to commit funds to acquire equipment, to expand existing facilities, or for other investment purposes rests with corporate management. This procedure for investment projects is necessitated by Notewon's capital allocation policy.

Notewon evaluates the performance of division executives by ROI. The asset base is composed of fixed assets employed plus working capital exclusive of cash.

The ROI performance of a divisional executive is the most important appraisal factor for salary changes. In addition, the annual performance bonus is based on the ROI results with increases in ROI having a significant impact on the amount of the bonus.

Notewon Corporation adopted the ROI performance measure and related compensation procedures about ten years ago. The corporation did so to increase the awareness of divisional management of the importance of the profit/asset relationship and to provide additional incentive to the divisional executives to seek investment opportunities.

The corporation seems to have benefited from the program. The ROI for the corporation, as a whole, increased during the first years of the program. Although the ROI has continued to grow in each division, the corporate ROI has declined in recent years. The corporation has accumulated a sizable amount of cash and short-term marketable securities in the past three years.

The corporation management is concerned about the increase in the short-term marketable securities. A recent article in a financial publication suggested that the use of ROI was overemphasized by some companies with results similar to those experienced by Notewon.

Required:
1. Describe the specific actions that division managers might have taken to cause the ROI to grow in each division but decline for the corporation. Illustrate your explanation with appropriate examples.
2. Explain, using the concepts of goal congruence and motivation of divisional executives, how Notewon Corporation's overemphasis on the use of ROI might result in the recent decline in the corporation's return on investment and the increase in cash and short-term marketable securities.
3. What changes could be made in Notewon Corporation's compensation policy to avoid this problem? Explain your answer.

(CMA Adapted)

E15–9   **ROI and suboptimization.** Peterdonn Corporation made a capital investment of $100,000 in new equipment two years ago. The analysis made at that time indicated that the equipment would save $36,400 in operating expenses per year over a 5-year period, or a 24% return on capital before taxes per year based on the time-adjusted rate of return analysis.

The department manager believed that the equipment had lived up to its expectations. However, the departmental report showing the overall return on investment

(ROI) rate for the first year in which this equipment was used did not reflect as much improvement as had been expected. The department manager asked the accounting section to break out the figures related to this investment to find out why it did not contribute more to the department's ROI.

The accounting section was able to identify the equipment and its contribution to the department's operations. The report presented to the department manager at the end of the first year is shown below:

Reduced operating expenses due to new equipment	$ 36,400
Less: depreciation — 20% of cost	20,000
Contribution before taxes	$ 16,400
Investment — beginning of year	$100,000
Investment — end of year	$ 80,000
Average investment for the year	$ 90,000

$$\text{ROI} = \frac{16,400}{90,000} = 18.2\%$$

The department manager was surprised that the ROI was less than 24% because the new equipment performed as expected. The staff analyst in the accounting section replied that the company ROI for performance evaluation differed from that used for capital investment analysis. The analyst commented that the discrepancy could be solved if the company used the compound interest method of depreciation for its performance evaluation reports.

Required:

1. Discuss the reasons why the return on investment of 18.2% for the new equipment as calculated in the department's report by the accounting section differs from the 24% internal rate of return calculated at the time that the machine was approved for purchase.
2. Will the use of the compound interest method of depreciation solve the discrepancy as the analyst claims? Explain your answer.

(CMA Adapted)

E15–10 **Compound interest depreciation.** An investment project has a cost of $46,862. It is expected to generate cash flows of $13,000 over the forthcoming 5-year period. The cash flows are received at the end of the period. There is no salvage value at the end of the fifth year.

Required:

1. Determine the time-adjusted rate of return for the project (no interpolation is necessary).
2. Compute the depreciation for each year using the compound interest approach.
3. Compute the ROI for each year using straight-line depreciation.
4. Compute the RI for each year using straight-line depreciation and a cost of capital of 10%.
5. Compute the ROI for each year using compound interest depreciation.
6. Compute RI for each year using compound interest depreciation and a cost of capital of 10%.

Problems

P15–11   **Analysis of performance of a profit center, revision of budget.** Hulbert and Tay Publishing Company has a leading psychology text authored by Anton and Brief. The 19X0 budget saw a total market demand of 500,000 copies. As a result of the budgetary process, it was agreed that Anton and Brief should get 15% of the total market.

Actual results showed that the size of the market during 19X0 was 550,000 copies. Furthermore, it was not foreseen that Houston and Macklin Publishing Company would enter into the market with a new text. It was felt that the new text should have cost Anton and Brief no more than 3% of their market share.

The budgeted wholesale price for the Anton and Brief text was $30 per book. There was a price decline in the industry on psychology texts. Hulbert and Tay decided to hold their price at $30. Hulbert and Tay's Planning Department felt that holding the price should have cost another 2% of Anton and Brief's market share. A price decline to $27.50 would have been necessary to avoid losing the 2%.

Actual sales of the Anton and Brief text during 19X0 was 58,000.

Required: 1. Under the circumstances, do you think that the performance of the text, from the standpoint of its sales, was better or worse than it should have been? Show figures.
2. Do you think that the decision not to lower the price of the text was a good one?
3. What other issues should be raised relative to this analysis? Discuss.

P15–12   **Computing various return on investment amounts.** Shown below is segment income for two divisions of Hectorious Company that are followed by two balance sheets at the beginning of the year.

HECTORIOUS COMPANY
Division Income Statements
For Year Ended December 31, 19X0

	Division 1	Division 2
Sales	$500,000	$800,000
Variable costs	150,000	200,000
Contribution margin	$350,000	$600,000
Discretionary fixed costs	50,000	160,000
Controllable margin	$300,000	$440,000
Direct fixed costs	100,000	180,000
Territorial income	$200,000	$260,000

HECTORIOUS COMPANY
Division Balance Sheets
January 1, 19X0

	Division 1	Division 2
Current assets	$600,000	$ 900,000
Fixed assets (cost)	200,000	600,000
Accumulated depreciation	(50,000)	(400,000)
Total assets	$750,000	$1,100,000

	Division 1	Division 2
Current liabilities	$ 80,000	$ 210,000
Long-term debt **8%**	100,000	300,000
Owners' equity	570,000	590,000
Total liabilities and owners' equity	$750,000	$1,100,000

Required:

1. For each of the two divisions compute return on investment on the following bases:
   a. Total gross assets
   b. Total net assets
   c. Total net assets less current liabilities
   d. Owners' equity
2. Comment on each of the four methods used.
3. Compute residual income for each division assuming that both are subject to a 10% cost of capital.
4. What comparisons would you make of the two divisions?

P15–13 **Product line and territorial income statements.** Beck and Buzby Corporation's income statement for 19X0 showed the following:

Sales	$2,000,000
Cost of goods sold	1,200,000
Gross profit	$ 800,000
Selling, general, and administrative costs	300,000
Net income before taxes	$ 500,000

The company manufactures two products that are sold in two territories. Tony Soich, the corporate controller, felt that segmental income statements would provide important information. The following segmental information was developed:

	Product		Territory	
	A	**B**	**East**	**West**
Sales[a]	40%	60%		
Variable manufacturing costs[b]	40%	50%		
Variable selling costs[c]	5%	5%	5%	5%
Product A			65%	35%
Product B			45%	55%
Fixed manufacturing costs	$60,000	$100,000		
Fixed selling, general and administrative costs			$50,000	$75,000

[a]As a percentage of total sales.

[b]As a percentage of product line sales.

[c]The 5% represents selling commissions, which are direct to *both* product line and territory. Any costs unaccounted for are indirect to *both* product and territory.

Required:

1. Prepare variable costing income statements by product line showing results for the entire firm in the third column.

2. Prepare variable costing income statements by territory showing results for the entire firm in the third column.
3. Comment on the information provided by the segmented income statements.

P15–14   **Segmental income statements, profitability of a territory.** The Justa Corporation produces and sells three products in two profit centers (by territory). The three products, A, B, and C, are sold in a local market and in a regional market. At the end of the first quarter of the current year, the following income statement has been prepared:

		Profit Centers	
	Total	Local	Regional
Sales	$1,300,000	$1,000,000	$300,000
Cost of goods sold	1,010,000	775,000	235,000
Gross margin	$ 290,000	$ 225,000	$ 65,000
Selling expenses	$ 105,000	$ 60,000	$ 45,000
Administrative expenses	52,000	40,000	12,000
	$ 157,000	$ 100,000	$ 57,000
Net income	$ 133,000	$ 125,000	$ 8,000

Management has expressed special concern with the regional market because of the extremely poor return on sales. This market was entered a year ago because of excess capacity. It was originally believed that the return on sales would improve with time, but after a year no noticeable improvement can be seen from the results as reported in the above quarterly statement.

In attempting to decide whether to eliminate the regional market, the following information has been gathered:

	Products		
	A	B	C
Sales	$500,000	$400,000	$400,000
Variable manufacturing expenses as a percentage of sales	60%	70%	60%
Variable selling expenses as a percentage of sales	3%	2%	2%

	Sales by Markets	
Product	Local	Regional
A	$400,000	$100,000
B	300,000	100,000
C	300,000	100,000

Administrative expenses and fixed manufacturing expenses are not controllable by the two profit center managers.

Remaining selling expenses are fixed for the period, but they are controllable by profit center managers. All fixed expenses are based on a prorated yearly amount.

Required: 1. Prepare revised income statements for the territories. Use a contribution margin format showing contribution margin, controllable margin, and segment margin.
2. If there are no other uses of present capacity, would you recommend dropping the regional market? Use the statement in 1 above to support your analysis.

3. Prepare contribution margin statements by product line. Assume that direct fixed manufacturing overhead by product line is $60,000 for A, $60,000 for B, and $50,000 for C. The balance is indirect to all product lines.

(CMA Adapted)

P15–15 **Evaluation of control system.** The ATCO Co. purchased the Dexter Co. three years ago. Prior to the acquisition, Dexter manufactured and sold plastic products to a wide variety of customers. Dexter has since become a division of ATCO and now manufactures only plastic components for products made by ATCO's Macon Division. Macon sells its products to hardware wholesalers.

ATCO's corporate management gives the Dexter Division managers a considerable amount of authority in running the division's operations. However, corporate management staff members retain authority for decisions regarding capital investments, price setting of all products, and the quantity of each product to be produced.

ATCO has a formal performance evaluation program for the management employees of all of its divisions. The performance evaluation program relies heavily on each division's return on investment. The income statement of the Dexter Division provides the basis for the evaluation of Dexter's divisional management employees.

The financial statements for the divisions are prepared by the corporate accounting staff. The corporate general services costs are allocated on the basis of sales dollars and the computer department's actual costs are apportioned among the divisions on the basis of use. The net division investment includes division fixed assets at net book value (cost less depreciation), division inventory, and corporate working capital apportioned to the divisions on the basis of sales dollars.

DEXTER DIVISION OF ATCO CO.
Income Statement
For the Year Ended October 31, 19X0
($000 omitted)

Sales		$4,000
Costs and expenses:		
Product costs:		
Direct materials	$ 500	
Direct labor	1,100	
Factory overhead	1,300	
Total	$2,900	
Less: increase in inventory	350	$2,550
Engineering and research		120
Shipping and receiving		240
Division administration:		
Manager's office	$ 210	
Cost accounting	40	
Personnel	82	332
Corporate costs:		
Computer	$ 48	
General services	230	278
Total costs and expenses		$3,520
Divisional operating income		$ 480
Net plant investment		$1,600
Return on investment		30%

Required: 1. Discuss the financial reporting and performance evaluation program of ATCO Co. as it relates to the responsibilities of the Dexter Division.

2. Based on your response to 1 above, recommend appropriate revisions of the financial information and reports used to evaluate the performance of Dexter's divisional managers. If revisions are not necessary, explain why revisions are not needed.

(CMA Adapted)

P15–16   **Residual income and performance evaluation.** Bio-grade Products is a multi-product company manufacturing animal feeds and feed supplements. The need for a widely based manufacturing and distribution system has led to a highly decentralized management structure. Each divisional manager is responsible for production and distribution of corporate products in one of eight geographical areas of the country.

Residual income is used to evaluate divisional managers. The residual income for each division equals each division's contribution to corporate profits before taxes less a 20% investment charge on a division's investment base. The investment base for each division is the sum of its year-end balances of accounts receivable, inventories, and net plant fixed assets (cost less accumulated depreciation). Corporate policies dictate that divisions minimize their investments in receivables and inventories. Investments in plant fixed assets are a joint division/corporate decision based on proposals made by divisional plant managers, available corporate funds, and general corporate policy.

Alex Williams, divisional manager for the southeastern sector, prepared the 19X9 and preliminary 19X0 budgets in late 19X8 for her division. Final approval of the 19X0 budget took place in late 19X9 after adjustments for trends and other information developed during 19X9. Preliminary work on the 19X1 budget also took place at that time. In early October 19X0, Williams asked the divisional controller to prepare a report that presents performance for the first nine months of 19X0. The report is presented below.

BIO-GRADE PRODUCTS – SOUTHEASTERN SECTOR
($000 omitted)

	19X0			19X9	
	Annual Budget	Nine-Month Budget[a]	Nine-Month Actual	Annual Budget	Actual Results
Sales	$2,800	$2,100	$2,200	$2,500	$2,430
Divisional costs and expenses:					
Direct materials and labor	$1,064	$ 798	$ 995	$ 900	$ 890
Supplies	44	33	35	35	43
Maintenance and repairs	200	150	60	175	160
Plant depreciation	120	90	90	110	110
Administration	120	90	90	90	100
Total divisional costs and expenses	$1,548	$1,161	$1,270	$1,310	$1,303
Divisional margin	$1,252	$ 939	$ 930	$1,190	$1,127
Allocated corporate fixed costs	360	270	240	340	320

	19X0			19X9	
	Annual Budget	Nine-Month Budget[a]	Nine-Month Actual	Annual Budget	Actual Results
Divisional contribution to corporate profits	$ 892	$ 669	$ 690	$ 850	$ 807
Imputed interest on divisional investment (20%)	420	321[b]	300[b]	370	365
Divisional residual income	$ 472	$ 348	$ 390	$ 480	$ 442
	Budgeted Balance 12/31/X0	Budgeted Balance 9/30/X0	Actual Balance 9/30/X0	Budgeted Balance 12/31/X9	Actual Balance 12/31/X9
Division investment:					
Accounts receivable	$ 280	$ 290	$ 250	$ 250	$ 250
Inventories	500	500	650	450	475
Plant fixed assets (net)	1,320	1,350	1,100	1,150	1,100
Total	$2,100	$2,140	$2,000	$1,850	$1,825
Imputed interest (20%)	$ 420	$ 321[b]	$ 300[b]	$ 370	$ 365

[a]Bio-grade's sales occur uniformly throughout the year.

[b]Imputed interest is calculated at only 15% to reflect that only nine months or three-fourths of the fiscal year has passed.

Required:

1. Evaluate the performance of Alex Williams for the nine months ending September 19X0. Support your evaluation with pertinent facts from the problem.
2. Identify the features of Bio-grade Products divisional performance-measurement reporting and evaluating system that need to be revised if it is to reflect effectively the responsibilities of the divisional managers.

(CMA Adapted)

P15–17   **Product-line profitability.** Valmar Products is a plumbing supply distributing company that carries the products of several manufacturers. Valmar sells its products to retail plumbing stores and to contractors over the counter. In addition, Valmar places orders for plumbing supplies and related materials for specific building and plumbing contractors directly with the manufacturers' factories. These special orders are sent directly to the contractors from the factories. Valmar bills the contractors for the direct orders and pays the manufacturer after the contractor has paid for the order. All customer orders except the direct shipment orders are filled from Valmar's inventories in its warehouse.

The income statement shown on page 578 presents the operating results for the past two fiscal years. In addition, the operating results by product line for the most recent fiscal year are presented on page 579. For internal reporting purposes, the selling expenses, warehouse costs, and other operating expenses are allocated to the product lines on the basis of sales.

VALMAR PRODUCTS
Income Statement
For the Fiscal Years Ended May 31
($000 omitted)

	19X9	19X0
Revenue from sales	$12,000	$10,000
Cost of goods sold	9,810	8,300
Gross margin	$ 2,190	$ 1,700
Operating expenses:		
Selling expenses	$ 250	$ 200
Warehouse costs	150	150
Other operating expenses	100	100
Total operating expenses	$ 500	$ 450
Net income from operations	$ 1,690	$ 1,250
Interest expense	250	300
Income before taxes	$ 1,440	$ 950
Income taxes (40%)	576	380
Net income	$ 864	$ 570

Jeremy Lypor, president of Valmar, is concerned because the current year's operating results are not up to expectations and have deteriorated from the prior year's results. The operating results by product line indicate that the cash counter sales are marginally profitable and the direct shipment business may not be worth the effort. However, Lypor does not have adequate information with which to make decisions concerning the separate product lines, nor does he have enough information to enable him to decide which lines should be promoted in order to improve the total results.

Statistics regarding the number of orders handled and the average book value of inventory carried in the warehouse were developed at the request of Lypor and are presented in the schedule shown below. In addition, the following information has been developed regarding Valmar's operations.

  a. Fifty percent of the selling expenses are commissions paid to salespersons on the basis of a flat percentage of sales billed; this same percentage is also paid on all cash counter sales.

  b. The other operating expenses and the balance of the selling expenses are related directly to the number of orders handled.

  c. Warehouse expenses are related to the value of inventory in the warehouse.

  d. Money is borrowed to carry inventory in the warehouse.

	Number of Orders Handled		Average Value of Inventory	
	Quantity	Percentage	Amount ($000 omitted)	Percentage
Trims and accessories	1,008	12%	$ 160	10%
Valve and pipe fittings	6,048	72	1,248	78
Fixtures	756	9	160	10
Cash counter sales	—	—	32	2
Direct shipments	588	7	—	—
Totals	8,400	100%	$1,600	100%

VALMAR PRODUCTS
Product-line Operating Results
For the Fiscal Year Ended May 31, 19X0
($000 omitted)

	Trims and Accessories	Valve and Pipe Fittings	Fixtures	Cash Counter Sales	Direct Shipments	Total
Sales	$2,000	$3,000	$1,000	$1,000	$3,000	$10,000
Cost of sales	1,480	2,445	705	865	2,805	8,300
Gross margin	$ 520	$ 555	$ 295	$ 135	$ 195	$ 1,700
Allocated operating expenses	90	135	45	45	135	450
Operating income	$ 430	$ 420	$ 250	$ 90	$ 60	$ 1,250
Return on sales	21.5%	14.0%	25.0%	9.0%	2.0%	12.5%

Required:

1. President Lypor has requested that the present product-line statement be reviewed to determine whether it can be revised to make it more useful in managing Valmar's business. Prepare a revised product-line statement for Valmar Products and explain all changes that were made in the revised statement.
2. Based on your revised product-line statement for Valmar Products and the other facts presented in the problem, what advice would you give to President Lypor regarding
   a. the direct shipment business?
   b. the cash counter sales business?
   c. the other three product lines?
   Explain your response in each case.

(CMA Adapted)

P15–18 ROI for performance measurement. The Texon Co. is organized into autonomous divisions along regional market lines. Each division manager is responsible for sales, cost of operations, acquisition and financing of divisional assets, and working capital management.

The vice-president of general operations for the company will retire in September 19X5. A review of the performance, attitudes, and skills of several management employees has been undertaken to find a replacement. Interviews with qualified outside candidates also have been held. The selection committee has narrowed the choice to the managers of Divisions A and F.

Both candidates were appointed division managers in late 19X1. The manager of Division A had been the assistant manager of that divsion for the prior 5 years. The manager of Division F had served as assistant division manager of Division B before being appointed to her present post. She took over Division F, a division newly formed in 19X0, when its first manager left to join a competitor. The financial results of their performance in the past 3 years is reported in the schedule on page 580.

	Division A			Division F		
	19X2	*19X3*	*19X4*	*19X2*	*19X3*	*19X4*
			($000 omitted)			
Estimated industry sales — market area	$10,000	$12,000	$13,000	$5,000	$6,000	$6,500
Division sales	$ 1,000	$ 1,100	$ 1,210	$ 450	$ 600	$ 750
Variable costs	$ 300	$ 320	$ 345	$ 135	$ 175	$ 210
Managed costs	400	405	420	170	200	230
Committed costs	275	325	350	140	200	250
Total costs	$ 975	$ 1,050	$ 1,115	$ 445	$ 575	$ 690
Net income	$ 25	$ 50	$ 95	$ 5	$ 25	$ 60
Assets employed	$ 330	$ 340	$ 360	$ 170	$ 240	$ 300
Liabilities incurred	103	105	115	47	100	130
Net investment	227	235	245	123	140	170
Return on investment	11%	21%	39%	4%	18%	35%

Required:

1. Texon Co. measures the performance of the divisions and the division managers on the basis of their return on investment (ROI). Is this an appropriate measurement for the division managers? Explain.
2. Many believe that a single measure, such as ROI, is inadequate to fully evaluate performance. What additional measure(s) could be used for performance evaluation? Give reasons for each measure listed.
3. On the basis of the information given, which manager would you recommend for vice-president of general operations? Present reasons to support your answer.

(CMA Adapted)

P15–19 **Evaluating profitability of operating division, cost accounting standards.** Callum Corporation is a diversified manufacturing company with corporate headquarters in St. Louis. The three operating divisions are the Aerospace Division, the Ceramic Products Division, and the Glass Products Division.

Much of the manufacturing activity of the Aerospace Division is related to work performed for the National Aeronautics and Space Administration (NASA) under negotiated contracts. The contracts provide that cost shall be allocated to the contracts in accordance with the federal government's Cost Accounting Standards (as promulgated by the Cost Accounting Standards Board and administered by the General Accounting Office).

Callum Corporation headquarters provide general administrative support and computer services to each of the three operating divisions. The computer services are provided through a computer time-sharing arrangement whereby the central processing unit (CPU) is located in St. Louis and the divisions have remote terminals that are connected to the CPU by telephone lines. The Cost Accounting Standards provide that the cost of general administration may be allocated to negotiated defense contracts. Further, the Standards provide that, in situations in which computer services are provided by corporate headquarters, the actual costs (fixed and variable) of operating the computer department may be allocated to the defense division based on a reasonable measure of computer usage.

Another provision of the Cost Accounting Standards deals with the situation in which a defense division acquires noncommercial components from a sister division. The Standards provide that when there is no established market price for the component, the component must be transferred to the defense division at cost without a mark-up for profit. This provision of the Standards applies to Callum Corporation because the Aerospace Division purchases custom-designed ceramic components from the Ceramic Products Division. There is no established market price for these custom components.

The general managers of the three divisions are evaluated as profit center managers based on the before-tax profit of the division. The November 19X2 performance evaluation reports (in millions of dollars) for each of the divisions are shown below.

	Aerospace Division	Ceramic Products Division	Glass Products Division
Sales	$23.0	$15.0[a]	$55.0
Cost of goods sold	13.0	7.0	38.0
Gross profit	$10.0	$ 8.0	$17.0
Selling and administration:			
Division selling and administration	$ 5.0	$ 5.0	$ 8.0
Corporate-general administration	1.0	–	–
Corporate-computing	1.0	–	–
Total selling and administration	$ 7.0	$ 5.0	$ 8.0
Profit before taxes	$ 3.0	$ 3.0	$ 9.0

[a]Includes $3,000,000 of custom ceramic products sold to the Aerospace Division at cost and the remainder ($12,000,000) sold to the Glass Products Division and outside customers at established market prices.

Required:

1. Review the November performance evaluation reports for the three operating divisions of Callum Corporation.
   a. Identify specific instances where the federal government's Cost Accounting Standards have influenced Callum's divisional performance reporting.
   b. For each specific instance identified, discuss whether the use of accounting practices based on Cost Accounting Standards is desirable for internal reporting and performance evaluation.
2. Considering the accounting practices and reporting methods currently employed by Callum Corporation, describe the suboptimal decision making that could result for the company as a whole if the demand for commercial (nondefense related) ceramic products is equal to or greater than the productive capacity of the Ceramic Products Division.
3. Without a charge for computing services, the operating divisions may not make the most cost-effective use of the resources of the Computer Systems Department of Callum Corporation. Why would this be the case and what (in general terms) should be done to overcome this problem?

(CMA Adapted)

P15–20 **Compound interest depreciation with ROI and RI.** Walker Company is investing in a capital project that is expected to produce annual net cash inflows at the end of each of the next 3 years of $5,000. Capital investment in the project is $10,870. It has no salvage value at the end of the third year.

Required: 1. Determine the time-adjusted rate of return on the project (hint: no interpolation is necessary).

2. Determine the annual return on investment using straight-line depreciation.

3. Determine the annual return on investment using compound interest depreciation.

4. Determine residual income using straight-line depreciation and a cost of capital of 10%.

5. Determine residual income using compound interest depreciation and a cost of capital of 10%.

6. Comment on the results in 2 through 5 above.

7. Why do you think that compound interest depreciation is seldom used for performance evaluation purposes?

P15–21 **Modularized variable costing income statements.** Dunaway Appliance Company manufactures two products, blenders and mixers. The marketing function is organized by territory, East and West, in which the products are sold. Within each territory the products are sold to two customer types: wholesalers and large retailers. The corporate income statement for 19X0 is shown in Exhibit 1.

Exhibit 1

Budgeted Income Statement
Corporate Level, 19X0

Revenues	$2,984,000	
Variable costs, total	2,205,695	
Contribution margin	$ 778,305	(26.1%)
Fixed costs, total	787,000	
Net loss	$ (8,695)	(0.3%)

Percentages shown are based on revenues.

Cost and revenue information by product line and territory is shown in Exhibit 2.

Exhibit 2

Dunaway Appliance Company
Master Cost Data Sheet for 19X0

	East		West	
	Blenders	**Mixers**	**Blenders**	**Mixers**
Revenue (per unit)	$ 42.00	$ 26.00	$ 38.00	$ 24.00
Variable manufacturing costs	$ 20.00	$ 15.00	$ 20.00	$ 15.00
Variable selling costs (10% of revenue)	4.20	2.60	3.80	2.40
Total	$ 24.20	$ 17.60	$ 23.80	$ 17.40
Contribution margin per unit before channel costs	$ 17.80	$ 8.40	$ 14.20	$ 6.60
Programmed advertising costs[a]	$20,000	$12,000	$15,000	$10,000
Sales (units)	15,000	28,000	15,000	44,000

	Blenders	Mixers	East	West	Unallocated
Fixed direct manufacturing costs	$200,000	$100,000			
Territorial fixed costs (joint to products)			$50,000	$30,000	
Joint fixed manufacturing costs					$100,000
Corporate headquarters costs					$250,000

ªProgrammed advertising costs are fixed costs that are reviewed each year through the budget process. (Therefore, they are not in a direct relationship with sales revenue or units sold. This could result from having a particular ad aimed at only one channel member or group of channel members. An example would be a trade magazine ad in a conference program for a Wholesalers Convention. Such an ad would not reach the retailer.)

In addition to the variable manufacturing and selling costs (Exhibit 2), there were variable distribution costs that were direct to the two channels of distribution (wholesalers and large retailers) within the two territories. These costs in total were $227,295. They were composed of $94,044 in the East and $133,251 in the West.

In the West territory, 17,000 mixers were sold to wholesalers and 27,000 mixers to large retailers. The variable distribution costs in total were $47,900 to wholesalers and $40,800 to large retailers for mixers. Of West's distribution costs, $69,446 are direct to the wholesaler channel and $63,805 are direct to the large retailer channel. Programmed advertising costs are indirect to channels and should not be assigned to products within channels.

Required:

1. Prepare the following variable costing income statements showing controllable margin and territorial income or product line income:

   a. Income statements for both territories showing product line segments within the territories. You need not break the variable channel distribution costs between the product lines.

   b. Income statements for both product lines showing territorial segments for each product line.

   c. Income statements for mixers in the West territory broken down by the two channels of distribution (wholesalers and large retailers). Channel totals and product lines within channels should be taken down to contribution margin. Indirect costs to products and channels should be charged directly to the territory.

2. What general comments would you make relative to the above analyses?

(American Marketing Association Adapted)

CHAPTER 16

Transfer Pricing in Decentralized Operations

Learning Objectives

After reading this chapter you should be able to:

1. Understand the nature of transfer pricing.

2. Appreciate why transfer pricing works best in terms of coordinating firmwide and divisional goals in situations of pure competition.

3. Understand how situations of excess capacity can be utilized to the advantage of both selling and buying divisions.

4. Understand the shortcomings of cost-based transfer pricing systems.

5. Understand how transfer pricing can be utilized in imperfect competition situations to benefit the selling and buying divisions as well as the entire corporation (Appendix 16–A).

One extremely important facet of decentralization and the resultant problem of lack of goal congruence was not discussed in Chapter 15. **Transfer pricing** refers to the setting of prices when products or services are sold by one decentralized division to another decentralized division within the same firm. Because profit and investment centers are decentralized, we can expect pricing decisions to be made from the standpoint of the selling division's own best interests. However, there can be complexities present that easily lead to problems of lack of goal congruence. Furthermore, the transfer pricing situation has become extremely important because of the rise of the conglomerate enterprise mentioned in Chapter 15.

A typical example of transfer pricing occurs in the automobile industry. An investment center of one of the nation's big three auto firms manufactures hardware for the motor car divisions of the enterprise. The hardware consists of items such as door handles, glove compartment locks, and cigarette lighters. As a decentralized investment center, the hardware manufacturer has the authority to sell to other automobile manufacturers as well as to divisions inside the firm. Goal congruence problems stemming from transfer pricing become particularly difficult when both buying and selling divisions are free to deal with outside firms, as in the automobile hardware case.

The nature of transfer pricing and its intricacies deserves careful scrutiny. It should be noted that transfer pricing per se does not affect total firm profits. The selling price of one division becomes the purchase price of the acquiring division. Purchase price and selling price thus cancel out when viewed from the perspective of the total firm. Hence, it is not the transfer price, as such, that is the important element. The significant point is the effect of the transfer pricing system on profit or investment center attempts to maximize how they are being evaluated (standard variable costing income, return on investment, or residual income). Transfer pricing arrangements between divisions may conflict with the broader firmwide goal of maximizing total corporate profits. Inconsistencies between maximizing divisional performance measures and firmwide profits can easily arise. This is the great danger of transfer pricing occurring within a decentralized organizational environment.

An important point to bear in mind is that transfer pricing is a relatively new topic of study in the managerial accounting area. Although some guidelines have been formulated, the state of the art in terms of understanding and applying concepts is still primitive. As a result, much diversity exists in practice, and suboptimization relative to total corporate goals is prevalent.

Most authorities agree that transfer pricing works best where market-based transfer prices are used under the economic condition of pure competition. Under pure competition where transfer prices are based on prices set in the marketplace, divisions will attempt to maximize their performance in the short-run in a manner that is consistent with maximizing profits of the entire firm. However, as economic conditions become imperfect, actions that divisions can take often conflict with firmwide goals. In this chapter, a series of transfer pricing situations will be developed starting with the relatively uncomplicated situation of pure competition and proceeding to more complex economic circumstances, with situations of imperfect competition being covered in Appendix 16–A. Transfer pricing approaches that attempt to eliminate inconsistencies between firmwide and divisional goals will be illustrated. In the second part of the chapter, cost-based transfer pricing approaches will be discussed. The weaknesses of cost-based transfer pricing systems will be discussed along with some possible attempts to improve this approach.

Market-Based Transfer Pricing

In order to understand how market-based transfer pricing works in terms of maintaining goal congruence between the divisions and the entire firm, a simple illustration will be utilized. However, a series of scenarios will be developed that will add increasing complexity to the problem. As will be seen, **market-based transfer pricing** systems use market prices as the basis for setting transfer prices. *The general rule for establishing the market-based transfer price for decision-making purposes is that the transfer price must at least equal the selling division's incremental costs plus any lost contribution margin.* Several examples of this principle will be illustrated here and in Appendix 16–A.

Assume, for our example, that W-G-P Company is a large conglomerate made up of twenty decentralized investment centers. The investment centers have a large degree of autonomy including setting prices for their products and being free to sell both within and outside W-G-P. Divisions are evaluated on the basis of residual income (RI).

Division A of W-G-P manufactures a part that is sold both to outside firms as well as to Division B of W-G-P. Division B, in turn, uses the part in the manufacture of a major industrial product. In the illustration that will be developed, we make the following assumptions:

1. The analysis is short-run only; long-run implications are ignored;
2. Total fixed costs are unaffected by transfer pricing decisions in the short run;
3. Divisions are autonomous and are attempting to maximize their own contribution margin and RI;
4. Divisional managements are "rational" in that they deal with other divisions of W-G-P as long as divisional contribution margin is at least equal to what would have been gained by dealing with outside firms;
5. Estimates of demand, costs, and pricing are assumed to be accurate.

Pure Competition

Pure competition is a model that is frequently employed in economic analysis even though its applications are quite limited. For our purposes, **pure competition** means that the manufacturing division can sell all of its product at one price that is determined by market forces beyond the division's control. In addition, all buyers and sellers are assumed to have complete information about prices. Finally, no quality differences exist relative to the product made by Division A and that made by competitors.

Division A manufactures a part that it can sell for $25 per unit with total variable costs of $10 each. Its total productive capacity is 2,000 units of the part during the period. Division B needs the part, which becomes a sub-assembly of a product that it manufactures. After further processing by B, the product sells for $50 per unit. B's variable costs to manufacture the product (exclusive of the cost of the part from Division A) are $15. B's capacity is 300 units during the period.

In pure competition, it would not matter whether the 300 units were sold internally to B or externally to A's customers as long as B can buy the part for $25 from outside sources. Total contribution margin on the 300 units for the firm of $7,500 and the individual contribution margins for Divisions A and B are shown in Exhibit 16–1 (page 588). It should be noted in terms of the general rule of transfer pricing that in pure competition, market price automatically includes the lost contribution margin that the selling division would have received from outside enterprises.

Negotiated Market Prices

Very often when divisions deal with each other, marketing cost savings in areas such as commissions, advertising, and possibly shipping costs can be made. Also, there may be minor modifications in cost where product specifications differ slightly. In these cases, the cost savings are factored into the transfer price. **Negotiated market prices** thus result. Assume that $1.50 per unit of A's variable costs represents commissions and shipping costs that can be avoided if Divisions A and B deal with each other rather than with external entities. Because there is a saving of $1.50 per unit in variable costs, the entire firm as well as the two divisions are better off dealing with each other rather than selling to outside firms. W-G-P's total contribution margin on both A and B's sales of the two products if A and B deal with each other is shown in Exhibit 16–2.

The increase in W-G-P's total contribution margin resulting from A and B dealing with each other is $450 (300 units times the $1.50 variable manufacturing cost saving). This difference can be seen when comparing W-G-P's incremental contribution margin from Exhibit 16–2 with the same category in Exhibit 16–1 where these savings were not present.

The increase in contribution margin that W-G-P would gain resulting from the internal sales would also be shared by the two divisions. At a price of $25, the increase in W-G-P's contribution margin would be totally absorbed by A. At a price of $23.50 ($25 − $1.50), the entire gain goes to B. If the two division managements are rational, which we have assumed, then a **natural bargaining range** exists between $23.50 and $25 where the divisions would be able to "dicker" without any interference from the management of W-G-P. Goal congruence exists within this range or core because the two divisions,

EXHIBIT 16–1
Transfer Pricing in Pure Competition

	Selling Division				Buying Division				
(1)	(2)	(3)	(4)	(5)	(6)	(7)	(8)	(9)	(10)
			(2) – (3)				(6) + (7)	(5) – (8)	(4) + (9)
			Contribution		Transfer	Buying	Total	Buying	Incremental
		Total	Margin of		Price or	Division's	Variable	Division's	Firm
Number	Total	Variable	Selling	Total	Outside	Own Variable	Costs of Buying	Contribution	Contribution
of Units	Revenues	Costs	Division	Revenues	Purchase Price	Costs	Division	Margin	Margin
300	$7,500[a]	$3,000[b]	$4,500	$15,000[c]	$7,500[a]	$4,500[d]	$12,000	$3,000	$7,500

[a] 300 × $25.
[b] 300 × $10.
[c] 300 × $50.
[d] 300 × $15.

EXHIBIT 16–2

Transfer Pricing at Negotiated Market Prices

	Selling Division					Buying Division			
(1)	(2)	(3)	(4)	(5)	(6)	(7)	(8)	(9)	(10)
		Total Variable Costs	(2) – (3) Contribution Margin of Selling Division	Total Revenues	Negotiated Transfer Price	Buying Division's Own Variable Costs	(6) + (7) Total Variable Costs of Buying Division	(5) – (8) Buying Division's Contribution Margin	(4) + (9) Incremental Firm Contribution Margin
Number of Units	Total Revenues								
300	$7,275[a]	$2,550[b]	$4,725	$15,000[c]	$7,275[a]	$4,500[d]	$11,775	$3,225	$7,950

[a]300 × $24.25.
[b]300 × $8.50.
[c]300 × $50.
[d]300 × $15.

as well as W-G-P, are better off as a result of the internal bargaining. Of course, the less that B is aware of how much A is saving, the more likely it is that A will garner the lion's share of the incremental contribution margin. In Exhibit 16–2, Divisions A and B split the additional profit because the transfer price is $24.25.

Different Market Prices

In a modification of pure competition, there may be occasional differences in price that exist. For example, a firm may think that by dropping its price it can increase market share. If this policy succeeds in the short run, it is liable to make other firms also drop their price. If the policy does not succeed, the firm will probably raise its price back to the previous level. Hence, temporary price aberrations can occur from pure competition as firms respond to the market with pricing and production decisions that attempt to maximize profits.

Still assuming that A can sell all of its output for $25, if B can purchase outside at a lower price, then the firm is better off if both A and B deal outside. If the outside price that B can negotiate is $23, incremental contribution margin for W-G-P and the two divisions would be as shown in the top row of Exhibit 16–3. Notice that both W-G-P and Division B's incremental contribution margin is $600 higher than in the original example. This is the result of B's acquiring outside at $23 rather than from A at $25, for a $2 saving on each of the 300 units.

Similarly, if the outside acquisition price for B were higher than $25, it should acquire from Division A. Both W-G-P and the divisions are better off if B acquires internally. If, for example, B were to acquire outside at $28, both Division B and W-G-P are worse off by $900 (300 units times $3 per unit), as shown in the bottom row of Exhibit 16–3. In this situation, incremental contribution margin of both W-G-P and Division B are $900 less than the respective contribution margins shown in Exhibit 16–1 where Division B acquired from A at $25 per unit. In all of these situations, decisions made by Division B and—where applicable—Division A are in harmony with the interests of W-G-P.

Excess Capacity

In this case we will assume that Division A still faces a market price of $25 per unit. However, it has overexpanded and expects to be able to sell only 2,750 units to outside buyers despite its capacity of 3,000 units. This is a situation of excess capacity.

If Division A were able to hide its excess capacity situation, they could sell B the 300 units at $25 each. However, if B is aware of the problem, a price should be negotiated between them for the 250 units for which A has no outside market. The natural bargaining range on these is between A's variable costs of $10 per unit and the outside selling price of $25. Both of the divisions, as well as W-G-P, are better off as a result of utilizing the excess capacity. The benefit to W-G-P of transferring the 250 units for which excess

EXHIBIT 16–3

Transfer Pricing with Different Outside Prices for the Buying Division

	Selling Division					Buying Division			
(1)	(2)	(3)	(4)	(5)	(6)	(7)	(8)	(9)	(10)
Number of Units	Total Revenues	Total Variable Costs	(2) − (3) Contribution Margin of Selling Division	Total Revenues	Negotiated Transfer Price	Buying Division's Own Variable Costs	(6) + (7) Total Variable Costs of Buying Division	(5) − (8) Buying Division's Contribution Margin	(4) + (9) Incremental Firm Contribution Margin
300	$7,500[a]	$3,000[b]	$4,500	$15,000[c]	$6,900[d]	$4,500[f]	$11,400	$3,600	$8,100
300	$7,500[a]	$3,000[b]	$4,500	$15,000[c]	$8,400[e]	$4,500[f]	$12,900	$2,100	$6,600

[a] 300 × $25.
[b] 300 × $10.
[c] 300 × $50.
[d] 300 × $23.
[e] 300 × $28.
[f] 300 × $15.

EXHIBIT 16—4

**Benefit to W-G-P of Transferring Excess Capacity Units
from Division A to Division B**

(1)	(2)	(3)	(4)	(5) (2) − (3 + 4)	(6) (1) × (5)
Number of Units	Selling Price per Unit	Variable Cost per Unit for Division A	Variable Cost per Unit for Division B	Contribution Margin per Unit	Total Contribution Margin
250	$50	$15	$10	$25	$6,250

capacity exists is shown in Exhibit 16—4. Assume, as before, that Division B sells its completed product for $50 per unit.

For the 50 additional units above the excess capacity usage B should pay the market price of $25. A will make the same profit on these units whether they are sold externally or to B. However, the total firm contribution is increased by $10 per unit if B acquires them. This is shown in Exhibit 16—5. Had B been able to acquire the additional 50 units outside at $25, it would not matter whether B acquired them from A or an outside firm.

In these situations, attempts to maximize contribution margin have been shown to be consistent with maximizing total corporate profits. The imperfect competition situation is far more complex. It is illustrated in Appendix 16—A. Although they are considerably less effective in decentralized profit and investment center situations than market-based transfer prices, let us next examine cost-based transfer pricing methods.

Cost-Based Transfer Pricing

Several forms of cost-based transfer pricing systems are used in practice. Some basis of cost is frequently used as a transfer price in the absence of market-oriented prices because the intermediate product is unique to the buying division's needs. These **cost-based transfer prices** include:

EXHIBIT 16—5

W-G-P Contribution Margin Alternatives

(1) Alternative	(2) Total Quantity	(3) Outside Selling Price per Unit	(4) Total Variable Costs per Unit	(5) (3) − (4) Contribution Margin per Unit	(6) (2) × (5) Total W-G-P Contribution Margin
A transfers to B, which sells outside at $50	50	$50	$25	$25	$1,250
A sells outside at $25	50	25	10	15	750
Differential	—	$25	$15	$10	$ 500

1. Actual variable costs;
2. Standard variable costs;
3. Actual full absorption costs;
4. Standard full absorption costs;
5. Actual full absorption costs plus a profit margin determined by formula (10% add-on to actual full cost, for example);
6. Standard full absorption costs plus profit margin determined by formula.

Actual-Cost Transfer Pricing

Any transfer pricing system that is based on actual costs does not encourage manufacturing (selling) divisions to be efficient in their production operations because actual costs—including inefficiencies—are passed on to the buying division. As a consequence of encouraging inefficiency by the selling division, a concurrent problem also arises. Actual-cost transfer pricing systems—because they encourage inefficiency, which is passed on to acquiring divisions—often generate frictions and antagonisms among divisions, which can drastically hamper their cohesiveness and cooperation. Consequently, actual-cost transfer pricing systems (items 1, 3, and 5 in the list above) should be summarily rejected for transfer pricing purposes even if the manufacturing division is construed as being a cost center.

Other Problems of Cost-Based Transfer Pricing

However, there are other concerns with cost-based transfer pricing systems, even where standard costs are used as the basis for the transfer price. One problem involves evaluating results of profit and investment center operations. The second problem is one of faulty resource allocation: contribution margin on a firmwide basis is not maximized.

If an organizational unit is designated as a profit or investment center, it should be evaluated on bases such as standard variable costing income, ROI, or RI. However, if the transfer price of some of that division's output is transferred at either standard variable cost or standard full cost, the selling unit would not be getting proper credit for its contribution to the total firm effort or for its own effectiveness as a profit generating center. Consequently, it becomes virtually impossible to assess the profit-generating effectiveness of the division by any of the measures previously mentioned. Even if a profit factor is added to standard full absorption costs, evaluation of profits becomes hollow because the profit element has not been determined by market conditions but has merely been added on by a formula. Furthermore, usage of a formula may create friction relative to the buying unit because there has been an arbitrary add-on to its costs.

Cost-based transfer prices, in addition to creating problems of evaluating at least one of the divisions of the firm, also can lead to suboptimization rela-

EXHIBIT 16–6

Transfer Pricing at Standard Absorption Cost: Divisional Analysis

	Selling Division				Buying Division					
(1)	(2)	(3)	(4)	(5)	(6)	(7)	(8)	(9)	(10)
							Buying		
						Transfer	Division's		
	Total	Total	(2) + (3)			Price	Own	(7) + (8)	(6) – (9)
Number	Variable	Fixed	Total	Number	Total	at Full	Variable	Total	Contribution
of Units	Costs	Costs	Costs	of Units	Revenues	Cost	Costs	Costs	Margin
100	$200[a]	$ 400[b]	$ 600	100	$ 800[c]	$ 600	$100[d]	$ 700	$100
200	400[e]	800[f]	1,200	200	$1,400[g]	1,200	200[h]	1,400	0
300	600[i]	1,200[j]	1,800	300	$1,800[k]	1,800	300[l]	2,100	–300

[a] 100 × $2.   [e] 200 × $2.   [i] 300 × $2.
[b] 100 × $4.   [f] 200 × $4.   [j] 300 × $4.
[c] 100 × $8.   [g] 200 × $7.   [k] 300 × $6.
[d] 100 × $1.   [h] 200 × $1.   [l] 300 × $1.

tive to resource allocation from the perspective of the firm. This problem of not maximizing the firm's contribution margin is illustrated in Exhibit 16–6.

In this illustration we assume that the selling division transfers at standard full absorption costs. These costs are $2 of standard variable cost and $4 of fixed overhead per unit. The buying division faces a downward sloping demand curve for its product. One hundred units can be sold for $8 per unit; 200 units at $7 per unit; and 300 units at $6 each. As can be seen in the exhibit, the buying division maximizes its profit by manufacturing and selling only 100 units.

However, when evaluated from the standpoint of the entire firm, the fixed costs should not be included because they are sunk costs, which do not affect operations in the short run as long as output remains within the relevant range. Consequently, when analyzing the transfer from the standpoint of W-G-P, the fixed costs should not be included. This is shown in Exhibit 16–7. As can be seen in this exhibit, the optimal transference from the standpoint of the entire firm would be 300 units.

These same considerations apply to standard full absorption cost plus a profit margin determined by formula. The profit margin plays exactly the same role as the fixed overhead: it will tend to make buying divisions acquire less than the firmwide contribution margin maximizing quantity of units.

Coping with the Limitations of Cost-Based Transfer Pricing

Transfer prices that include a markup based on a formula rather than real market prices can lead to both suboptimization relative to resource allocation and ineffective evaluation of cost and investment centers. Other arrange-

EXHIBIT 16–7

Transfer Pricing at Standard Absorption Cost: Total Firm Analysis

(1)	(2)	(3)	(4)	(5)	(6)
				(3) + (4)	(2) − (5)
		Variable Costs	Variable Costs	Total	Contribution
Number	Total	of Selling	of Buying	Variable	Margin
of Units	Revenues	Division	Division	Costs	
100	$ 800[a]	$200[b]	$100[c]	$300	$500
200	1,400[d]	400[e]	200[f]	600	800
300	1,800[g]	600[h]	300[i]	900	900

[a]100 × $8.   [d]200 × $7.   [g]300 × $6.
[b]100 × $2.   [e]200 × $2.   [h]300 × $2.
[c]100 × $1.   [f]200 × $1.   [i]300 × $1.

ments should therefore be employed. If the great bulk of the selling division's output is transferred internally, the organizational unit is really not a true profit or investment center. Two possibilities, therefore, are present for coping with this situation. One approach would be to combine the selling and buying units into one profit or investment center. The other possibility is to evaluate the selling division as a cost center, rather than as a profit or investment center, with product being transferred at standard variable cost.

From an organizational standpoint, it would probably be easier to take the alternative of converting the selling unit into a cost center. Over the long-run, however, it would probably be more effective to combine the buying and selling units into one profit or investment center. Profit would probably be maximized by placing the complementary functions of marketing and manufacturing under one management. One possible example of the need to combine is that the selling unit has no particular incentive to minimize its long-run costs through appropriate capital budgeting practices as long as it is meeting budgets and standard variable costs on presently utilized productive facilities.

A different problem exists if only a relatively small part of the selling unit's output does not have an outside market. In this case the selling unit should continue as a profit or investment center. If no excess capacity exists relative to product that might be transferred to other divisions, then a meaningful transfer price can be calculated based on the approach mentioned previously: variable costs plus lost contribution margin on whatever alternatives have been forgone by the selling division. Where excess capacity does exist, one possible approach might be to have the buying and selling divisions work together on an open basis. They would negotiate as to how to divide the prospective contribution margin at the profit-maximizing level of output of the buying division's product when viewed from the firmwide perspective.

These problems are not easy to solve. Much work still remains in terms of coping with transfer pricing situations and problems.

Summary

Transfer pricing describes the situation where one decentralized unit of an organization sells product to another unit. From the firmwide perspective the transfer price "washes out" because selling price of one unit is the purchase price of the other unit. The danger, however, is that the decentralized entities—which are acting in their own best interests in terms of how they are being evaluated—may take actions that are suboptimal relative to maximizing contribution margin for the entire firm.

Transfer pricing works best in situations of pure competition where the selling unit can sell in the outside market all that it produces at the established market price.

In situations of pure competition where minor product modifications are necessary or savings in marketing costs can be made, an appropriate market price can usually be negotiated by the two divisions. Another situation that can be solved by negotiation exists when the selling division has excess capacity. There is a natural bargaining range that exists in these situations. The floor of the range is the selling division's variable costs. The ceiling will be the lower of either the buying division's outside purchase price of the goods or the transfer price that would leave the buying division with a zero contribution margin on the goods.

A very difficult situation arises if the selling division is in an imperfectly competitive situation (this is covered in Appendix 16–A). In these situations, the higher the price that is set, the fewer the units it sells. Similarly, the lower that it sets prices, the more units that it can expect to sell. If the selling unit would have to modify its external selling price to accommodate the buying unit, the potential lost contribution margin is added to the variable costs in determining the floor price of the natural bargaining range. This may, of course, affect whether the buying division will acquire the product. Although this mechanism is somewhat awkward, it does maintain goal congruence between contribution margin maximizing actions of the entire firm and decisions that the decentralized units make for their own benefit in terms of how they are evaluated.

Cost-based transfer prices are often used in situations where there is a complete absence of market-based prices for the product. Actual costs should never be used because they promote inefficiencies on the part of the selling division, which would merely pass them on to the buying division. Friction between the divisions will usually arise as a by-product of actual costs being passed on to the acquiring division.

Standard costs are definitely preferable to actual costs as a transfer price. Standard full cost and standard full cost plus a profit margin determined by formula can easily lead to decisions that are not in the best interests of the entire firm. These methods also tend to make the evaluation of the divisions less meaningful and valid. In attempting to find a solution, if the selling division provides the great bulk of its product to other divisions of the firm, it should either be treated as a cost center or combined with its major profit or investment center with which it does the bulk of its business.

If the selling division does a relatively small portion of its business with other divisions of the firm, transfer prices might be set so that they include lost contribution margin from other business forgone in the event of full capacity. Another possibility is to deal with buying divisions on an open basis where the maximum contribution margin that pertains to the entire firm is split between them.

Transfer pricing is a difficult problem where pat solutions to all situations have simply not as yet been determined. As such, it presents an excellent opportunity for improving existing transfer pricing systems by those people who are at least familiar with the difficulties and intricacies presented by the problem.

Appendix 16–A
Imperfect Competition

The imperfect competition situation is more complex than the cases examined under pure competition and its offshoots. In the case of **imperfect competition,** at least one of the profit or investment centers involved faces a downward sloping demand curve: within the same time period, more units of a product can be sold if the price is lowered or fewer units will be sold if price is increased. We will assume that Division A is faced by the following demand curve.

Sales (units)	Price	Variable Cost	Contribution Margin
2,000	$25	$10	$30,000
1,800	$30	$10	$36,000

Given this situation, A would set their selling price at $30 per unit. Once again, if B were aware of A's excess capacity and needed 300 units, the first 200 units—which take up A's excess capacity—would have the following natural bargaining range:

Floor: A's variable costs;

Ceiling: the lower of (1) the outside price that B can acquire the part for, or (2) A's regular outside price, or (3) a transfer price that would give B a zero contribution margin on the sale of its final product.

The floor would be A's variable costs of $10 per unit. The ceiling transfer price is more complicated. The absolute upper bound would be $35, the transfer price that would result in a zero contribution margin for B, the $50 selling price minus B's variable cost of $15. Thus, if B's outside acquisition price were $28, this price would be the ceiling. If it were the case that B's best outside price was above A's selling price of $30, say $31, it is unlikely that A could "con" B into a transfer price above its regular outside selling price of $30.

Let us now examine a slightly more complex situation. Division A faces the following demand curve from outside buyers for its part:

Sales (units)	Price	Variable Cost	Contribution Margin
2,000	$25	$10	$30,000
1,800	$30	$10	$36,000
1,700	$31	$10	$35,700

If there were no transfer pricing situation to consider, Division A would set its price at $30 per unit, thereby maximizing its contribution margin (and income). With Division B still desiring up to 300 units from A, the transfer pricing problem should be broken down into two parts: (1) the first 200 units for which there is excess capacity and (2) the additional 100 units, which would require "bumping" some of A's outside customers.

A, if left to its own devices, would price at $30 per unit, the contribution margin maximizing price that leaves 200 units of excess capacity. As above, on these units there would be a bargained transfer price in the natural bargaining range between A's variable costs of $10 per unit and A's outside price of $30 unless B can come up with an outside purchase price that is less than this amount.

The third 100 units create an interesting situation in determining the floor of the natural bargaining range. If B did not desire the third 100 units, A would price at $30 selling 1,800 units and maximizing its contribution margin for the period at $36,000. However, if B were to desire a third 100 units, A would maximize contribution margin on the remaining 1,700 units available for external sale by raising the selling price to $31. If A were to do this, it would give up $300 in contribution margin: $36,000 to $35,700 (remember, the first 200 units that B desires are irrelevant at this point because they would be taking up excess capacity).

Because A is being asked to take a suboptimal position, A's floor in the calculation of its minimum acceptable transfer price would include both its own variable costs and the lost contribution margin from abandoning its outside selling price. In computing a cost per unit, the "lost" contribution margin of $300 is divided by the 100 units at issue. The floor transfer price per unit would be computed in this fashion, in accordance with the general rule of transfer pricing:

$$\begin{matrix} \text{Variable costs} \\ \text{per unit} \end{matrix} + \begin{matrix} \text{Lost contribution} \\ \text{margin per unit} \end{matrix} = \begin{matrix} \text{Minimum transfer} \\ \text{price per unit} \end{matrix}$$

$$\$10 \quad + \quad \frac{\$300}{100} \quad = \quad \$13$$

In this particular situation, the natural bargaining range would be between $13 and $31 unless B has a legitimate outside purchase price below $31 per unit. The adjustment of the floor in the natural bargaining range both protects A by assuring that it will not lose any contribution margin from dealing with B and also results in W-G-P's maximizing its contribution margin. The $13 floor to "protect" Division A provides it with a contribution margin of $300 on the transfer price (100 units times the excess of the $13 transfer price minus Division A's variable costs of $10). This contribution margin of $300 plus the contribution margin of $35,700 from selling 1,700 units to out-side firms at $31 per unit equals Division A's optimum contribution margin on outside sales of 1,800 units at $30 shown above.

Moreover, Division A's floor of $13 is an important marker for the two divisions and also for W-G-P. As long as Division B's best outside purchase price of the parts is above $13, both the divisions and the entire firm maxi-mize by A and B's dealing with each other. If the outside price to B were *below* $13, A should sell 1,800 units outside at $30 each and transfer only 200 units to B at a price between A's variable costs of $10 per unit and B's outside purchase price. B should then obtain its additional 100 units outside the firm at its purchase price below the $13 floor of Division A. These rela-tionships are shown in a break-even format in Exhibit 16–8 by using an out-side purchase price of $13 for the 100 key units in question. The figures used

EXHIBIT 16–8
Goal Congruence Analysis of "Floor" Transfer Price

Alternative 1 (A sells 1,700 units outside and transfers 100 units from A to B)					
(1)	*(2)*	*(3)*	*(4)*	*(5)*	*(6)*
				(3) + (4)	*(2) − (5)*
		Variable Costs	*Variable Costs*	*Total Variable*	*Contribution*
Units	*Revenues*	*of Division A*	*of Division B*	*Costs*	*Margin*
1,700 (outside sales)	$52,700[a]	$17,000[b]	–	$17,000	$35,700
100 (transferred to B)	5,000[c]	1,000[d]	$1,500[e]	2,500	2,500
	$57,700	$18,000	$1,500	$19,500	$38,200
Alternative 2 (A sells 1,800 units outside and B buys 100 units outside at $13)					
1,800 (outside sales)	$54,000[f]	$18,000[g]	–	$18,000	$36,000
100 (acquired outside by B)	5,000	1,300[h]	$1,500	2,800	2,200
	$59,000	$19,300	$1,500	$20,800	$38,200

[a] 1,700 × $31.   [e] 100 × $15.
[b] 1,700 × $10.   [f] 1,800 × $30.
[c] 100 × $50.   [g] 1,800 × $10.
[d] 100 × $10.   [h] 100 × $13.

in this exhibit are from the standpoint of W-G-P in order to show the goal congruence aspect provided by the floor of $13.

Of course the units in question should not always be transferred from A to B. In the case just analyzed, assume that Division B sells its finished product for only $26. The first 200 units should be transferred to it because there is a corporate profit of $200 on them which consists of the 200 units for which A has excess capacity at a corporate contribution margin of $1 per unit:

Revenue		$26
Variable costs:		
A's variable costs	$10	
B's variable costs	15	25
Contribution margin per unit		$ 1

The bargaining range on these units would be between a floor of $10 per unit and a ceiling of $11 per unit. B breaks even at the transfer price of $11 plus its own variable costs of $15 per unit, which equals B's selling price.

B will not buy the third 100 units because at the floor price of $13 per unit, as determined previously, it would lose $2 per unit:

Revenue		$ 26
Variable costs:		
Transfer price from A	$13	
B's variable costs	15	28
Contribution loss per unit		$ -2

EXHIBIT 16–9
W-G-P Loss on Transfer of Last 100 Units to Division B

(1) Units	(2) Revenues	(3) Variable Costs of Division A	(4) Variable Costs of Division B	(5) (3) + (4) Total Variable Costs	(6) (2) – (5) Contribution Margin
Alternative 1 (1,800 units sold externally by A)					
1,800 (outside sales)	$54,000[a]	$18,000[b]	—	$18,000	$36,000
Alternative 2 (1,700 units sold externally by A and 100 units transferred to B and sold for $26 each)					
1,700 (outside sales)	$52,700[c]	$17,000[d]	—	$17,000	$35,700
100 (transferred to B)	2,600[e]	1,000[f]	$1,500[g]	2,500	100
	$55,300	$18,000	$1,500	$19,500	$35,800

[a] 1,800 × $30.   [e] 100 × $26.
[b] 1,800 × $10.   [f] 100 × $10.
[c] 1,700 × $31.   [g] 100 × $15.
[d] 1,700 × $10.

Notice that under these conditions, W-G-P would lose $200 if the third 100 units were transferred to B, which is exactly what B loses. This is illustrated in Exhibit 16–9. Thus B will acquire only 200 units and A will sell 1,800 units outside of W-G-P at a price of $30 per unit.

Once again, it can be seen from these examples that transfer pricing is a mechanism that enables profit and investment centers to maximize their own contribution margins while acting in a manner that is consistent with contribution margin maximization for the entire firm. Nevertheless, the method can be cumbersome to employ in imperfect competition and will break down if divisional managements are not rational and cooperative relative to each other.

Key Terms

Cost-based transfer pricing refers to situations where the transfer pricing system is based on a measurement of cost. These systems encourage either inefficiency or suboptimization or both.

Imperfect competition refers to situations where a division can increase its unit sales during a period by lowering its selling price (or decrease unit sales by raising prices). The division thus faces a downward sloping demand curve.

Market-based transfer pricing refers to situations where market prices are used as the basis for setting transfer prices.

Natural bargaining range arises in negotiated market pricing situations where a profit is divided between a buying and selling division. The profit can be construed as a range. At the bottom or floor of the range, the entire profit goes to the buying division. At the top or ceiling of the range, the entire profit goes to the selling division.

Negotiated market prices arise when cost savings are "factored" into the transfer price by negotiation between the buying and selling division.

Pure competition refers to situations where the selling division can sell all of its products at only one price, which is determined by market forces beyond the division's control. In addition, all buyers and sellers are assumed to have complete information about prices. Finally, no quality differences are presumed to exist relative to different firms that produce a similar product (product homogeneity).

Transfer pricing is the general term used to cover the setting of prices when goods (or services) are sold by one decentralized division to another decentralized division within the same firm.

Questions

Q16–1 What is transfer pricing?

Q16–2 Why do transactions involving transfer pricing have no effect on the total profits of the entire firm?

Q16–3 Why does transfer pricing often ignore the long run?

Q16–4   Why is the outside price of a part or product sold in pure competition the ideal transfer price?

Q16–5   What does the term *natural bargaining range* mean?

Q16–6   What is the lower limit of the natural bargaining range in a situation where the selling division has excess capacity?

Q16–7   What is the upper limit of the natural bargaining range in a situation where the selling division has excess capacity?

Q16–8   Why do actual cost-based transfer pricing systems encourage inefficiency and friction between divisions?

Q16–9   If fixed costs are included in cost-based transfer pricing situations where imperfect competition exists, why will the buying division's acquisition decision be non–goal congruent?

Q16–10   If a division of a firm sells almost all its output to another division of the firm, do you think that it is a true profit or investment center?

Q16–11   What are negotiated market prices?

Q16–12   What are the opportunity costs to the selling division in pure competition?

Q16–13   What are the opportunity costs to the selling division in imperfect competition?

Q16–14   What are the buying division's opportunity costs?

Q16–15   What practical difficulties do you see in implementing the opportunity cost approach to transfer pricing in imperfect competition?

Q16–16   Why does the opportunity cost approach to transfer pricing in imperfect competition avoid problems of goal congruence?

Q16–17   What alternatives to opportunity cost pricing in situations of imperfect competition do you see?

Q16–18   Are the possibilities mentioned by you in Q16–17 above goal congruent? Explain.

Exercises

E16–1   **Pure competition.** Whelpley Company, a division of Leach Industries, produces an item that is sold under conditions of pure competition. The product sells for $50 each and has total manufacturing costs of $20 per unit. Of the total manufacturing costs of $20, $5 is applicable to fixed manufacturing overhead.

     Whelpley's productive capacity is 2,000 units per year. Another division of Leach Industries, Perry, Incorporated, needs 200 units of the product.

Required: 1. What is the correct transfer price?

     2. What is the difference in total profits to Leach Industries if Whelpley sells the 200 units to an outside entity at $50 each and Perry buys the units from an outside firm at $50 each? Discuss.

E16–2   **Negotiated market price.** Refer to the data in E16–1. Assume, in addition, that buying firms are responsible for paying freight charges on the product. Assume that if Perry acquires from Whelpley, it can save $3 per unit in transportation costs.

Required: 1. What is the natural bargaining range for the product, given the $3 saving per unit?
2. If Whelpley and Perry deal with each other, instead of buying and selling outside of Leach Industries, how much better off *in total* is Leach Industries as a result of the internal transfer?

E16–3 **Excess capacity.** Refer to the data in E16–1. Assume that Whelpley can sell only 1,900 units, leaving it with excess capacity of 100 units for the period. Whelpley has no other usage for the capacity. (Assume that no differences exist in freight charges as in E16–2.)

Required: 1. Is Leach Industries better off if Whelpley sells the units to Perry or if Perry acquires them outside? Show figures.
2. What is the natural bargaining range for the 100 units in question?

E16–4 **Opportunity cost and negotiated transfer price, multiple choice.** Ajax Division of Carlyle Corporation produces electric motors, 20% of which are sold to Bradley Division of Carlyle and the remainder to outside customers. Carlyle treats its divisions as profit centers and allows division managers to choose their sources of sale and supply. Corporate policy requires that all interdivisional sales and purchases be recorded at variable cost as a transfer price. Ajax Division's estimated sales and standard cost data for the year ending December 31, 19X2, based on the full capacity of 100,000 units, are as follows:

	Bradley	Outsiders
Sales	$ 900,000	$8,000,000
Variable costs	(900,000)	(3,600,000)
Fixed costs	(300,000)	(1,200,000)
Gross margin	$(300,000)	$3,200,000
Unit sales	20,000	80,000

Ajax has an opportunity to sell the above 20,000 units to an outside customer at a price of $75 per unit during 19X2 on a continuing basis. Bradley can purchase its requirements from an outside supplier at a price of $85 per unit.

Required: 1. Assuming that Ajax Division desires to maximize its gross margin, should Ajax take on the new customer and drop its sales to Bradley for 19X2 and why?
   a. No, because the gross margin of the corporation as a whole would decrease by $200,000.
   b. Yes, because Ajax Division's gross margin would increase by $300,000.
   c. Yes, because Ajax Division's gross margin would increase by $600,000.
   d. No, because Bradley Division's gross margin would decrease by $800,000.
2. Assume, instead, that Carlyle permits the division managers to negotiate the transfer price for 19X2. The managers agreed on a tentative transfer price of $75 per unit, to be reduced based on an equal sharing of the additional gross margin to Ajax resulting from the sale to Bradley of 20,000 motors at $75 per unit. The actual transfer price for 19X2 would be
   a. $52.50.
   b. $55.00.
   c. $60.00.
   d. $67.50.

(CPA Adapted)

E16–5   Optimizing profits, multiple choice. The Blade Division of Dana Company produces hardened steel blades. One-third of the Blade Division's output is sold to the Lawn Products Division of Dana; the remainder is sold to outside customers. The Blade Division's estimated sales and standard cost data for the fiscal year ending June 30, 19X1, are as follows:

	Lawn Products	Outsiders
Sales	$15,000	$40,000
Variable costs	(10,000)	(20,000)
Fixed costs	(3,000)	(6,000)
Gross margin	$ 2,000	$14,000
Unit sales	10,000	20,000

The Lawn Products Division has an opportunity to purchase 10,000 identical quality blades from an outside supplier at a cost of $1.25 per unit on a continuing basis. Assume that the Blade Division cannot sell any additional products to outside customers. Should Dana allow its Lawn Products Division to purchase the blades from the outside supplier, and why?

  a. Yes, because buying the blades would save Dana Company $500.
  b. No, because making the blades would save Dana Company $1,500.
  c. Yes, because buying the blades would save Dana Company $2,500.
  d. No, because making the blades would save Dana Company $2,500.

(CPA Adapted)

E16–6   Transfer pricing scenarios. Walker Company is a decentralized firm comprised of many divisions that are decentralized and evaluated on ROI.

Division A has capacity to make 5,000 units of a product. Division A's variable costs are $120. Division B can utilize the same product as an assembly in the manufacture of one of its products. Division B would require $80 of variable costs to convert the assembly into its own product, which sells for $325.

Required: Answer the following questions, which are independent of each other.

  1. Division A can sell all that it produces at a price of $200 each. Division B needs 500 units. What is the correct transfer price, and how many units will B buy?
  2. Division A can sell 4,000 units at $275. There is no market for the other 1,000 units of capacity except for B. B needs up to 1,000 units. What is the natural bargaining range for transfer pricing purposes?
  3. Would your answer to 2 above have changed if B could buy a substitute assembly for $175 with additional conversion costs of $25 (in addition to the $80 of variable costs)?

E16–7   Continuation of E16–6 with imperfect competition. Assume the same basic facts as in E16–6 except that Division A can either sell 4,500 units at $260 or 4,800 units at $253. Division B needs up to 500 units.

Required: Determine the appropriate transfer pricing schedule.

E16–8   Transfer pricing scenarios. Porter Company consists of many decentralized investment centers. Two of these centers are Divisions A and B. Division A sells a subassembly that B needs. The following data are available for each division:

Estimated selling price for final product	$250
Long-run average selling price for intermediate product (sold by Division A)	100
Outlay cost for completion in Division B (variable costs)	175
Outlay cost in Division A (variable costs)	40

Division A has the productive capacity to manufacture 2,000 units during the forthcoming period. Division B needs up to 300 units of the subassembly. Each of the following parts of the problem is independent of the others unless otherwise specified.

Required:

1. If Division A can sell all it produces at the price of $100, what is the correct transfer price?
2. Assume that Division A has some excess capacity: it can sell 1,900 units at $100, but there is no market at all for the last 100 units. Should these units be transferred to B (show figures)? If so, what is the natural bargaining range?
3. Division A faces a downward sloping demand curve. It can either sell 1,900 units at $95 per unit or 1,800 units at $100 (there is no market for 100 units). Determine a transfer pricing schedule for 300 units (assume that Division A would be willing to go to a less desirable point on its demand curve).

E16–9 **Continuation of E16–8 with imperfect competition.** Assume the same basic facts as in E16–8 except that Division A can either sell 1,800 units at $95 per unit or 1,600 units at $100. Division B needs up to 300 units.

Required: Determine the appropriate transfer pricing schedule.

E16–10 **Imperfect competition.** What difficulties do you see in establishing transfer pricing arrangements in situations of imperfect competition? Discuss.

Problems

P16–11 **Market versus cost-based transfer prices.** DePaolo Industries manufactures carpets, furniture, and foam in three separate divisions. DePaolo's operating statement for 19X3 is reproduced below. Additional information regarding DePaolo's operations follows:

a. Included in Foam's sales revenue is $500,000 in revenue that represents sales made to the Furniture Division that were transferred at manufacturing cost.
b. The cost of goods sold is comprised of the following costs:

	Carpet	Furniture	Foam
Direct material	$ 500,000	$1,000,000	$1,000,000
Direct labor	500,000	200,000	1,000,000
Variable overhead	750,000	50,000	1,000,000
Fixed overhead	250,000	50,000	–0–
Total cost of goods sold	$2,000,000	$1,300,000	$3,000,000

c. Administrative expenses include the following costs:

	Carpet	Furniture	Foam
Segment expenses:			
Variable	$ 85,000	$140,000	$ 40,000
Fixed	85,000	210,000	120,000
Home office expenses (all fixed):			
Directly traceable	100,000	120,000	200,000
General (allocated on sales dollars)	30,000	30,000	40,000
Total	$300,000	$500,000	$400,000

d. Selling expense is all incurred at the segment level and is 80% variable for all segments.

John Sprint, manager of the Foam Division, is not pleased with DePaolo's presentation of operating performance. Sprint claimed, "The Foam Division makes a greater contribution to the company's profits than what is shown. I sell foam to the Furniture Division at cost, and it gets our share of the profit. I can sell that foam on the outside at my regular markup, but I sell to Furniture for the well-being of the company. I think my division should get credit for those internal sales at market. I think we should also revise our operating statements for internal purposes. Why don't we consider preparing these internal statements on a contribution approach reporting format showing internal transfers at market?"

DEPAOLO INDUSTRIES
Operating Statement
For the Year Ended December 31, 19X3

	Carpet Division	Furniture Division	Foam Division	Total
Sales revenue	$3,000,000	$3,000,000	$4,000,000	$10,000,000
Cost of goods sold	2,000,000	1,300,000	3,000,000	6,300,000
Gross profit	$1,000,000	$1,700,000	$1,000,000	$ 3,700,000
Operating expenses:				
Administrative	$ 300,000	$ 500,000	$ 400,000	$ 1,200,000
Selling	600,000	600,000	500,000	1,700,000
Total operating expenses	$ 900,000	$1,100,000	$ 900,000	$ 2,900,000
Income from operations before taxes	$ 100,000	$ 600,000	$ 100,000	$ 800,000

Required:

1. John Sprint believes that the intracompany transfers from the Foam Division to the Furniture Division should be at market rather than manufacturing cost for divisional performance measurement. Explain why Sprint is correct.
2. Using the contribution approach and market-based transfer prices, prepare a revised operating statement by division for DePaolo Industries for 19X3 that will promote the evaluation of divisional performance.
3. Discuss the advantages of the contribution reporting approach for internal reporting purposes.

(CMA Adapted)

P16–12   **Variable cost plus opportunity cost transfer price.** PortCo Products is a divisional furniture manufacturer. The divisions are autonomous segments with each division being responsible for its own sales, costs of operations, working capital management, and equipment acquisition. Each division serves a different market in the furniture industry. Because the markets and products of the divisions are so different, there have never been any transfers between divisions.

The Commercial Division manufactures equipment and furniture that is purchased by the restaurant industry. The division plans to introduce a new line of counter and chair units that feature a cushioned seat for the counter chairs. John Kline, the division manager, has discussed the manufacturing of the cushioned seat with Russ Fiegel of the Office Division. They both believe a cushioned seat currently made by the Office Division for use on its deluxe office stool could be modified for use on the new counter chair. Consequently, Kline has asked Russ Fiegel for a price for 100 unit lots of the cushioned seat. The following conversation took place about the price to be charged for the cushioned seats:

Fiegel: "John, we can make the necessary modifications to the cushioned seat easily. The raw materials used in your seat are slightly different and should cost about 10% more than those used in our deluxe office stool. However, the labor time should be the same because the seat fabrication operation basically is the same. I would price the seat at our regular rate—full cost plus 30% markup."

Kline: "That's higher than I expected, Russ. I was thinking that a good price would be your variable manufacturing costs. After all, your capacity costs will be incurred regardless of this job."

Fiegel: "John, I'm at capacity. By making the cushion seats for you, I'll have to cut my production of deluxe office stools. Of course, I can increase my production of economy office stools. The labor time freed by not having to fabricate the frame or assemble the deluxe stool can be shifted to the frame fabrication and assembly of the economy office stool. Fortunately, I can switch my labor force between these two models of stools without any loss of efficiency. As you know, overtime is not a feasible alternative in our community. I'd like to sell it to you at variable cost, but I have excess demand for both products. I don't mind changing my product mix to the economy model if I get a good return on the seats I make for you. Here are my standard costs for the two stools and a schedule of my manufacturing overhead." (See below for standard costs and for overhead schedule.)

Kline: "I guess I see your point, Russ, but I don't want to price myself out of the market. Maybe we should talk to corporate to see if they can give us any guidance." Appropriate schedules for the Office Division are shown below.

OFFICE DIVISION
Standard Costs and Prices

	Deluxe Office Stool	Economy Office Stool
Raw materials:		
Framing	$ 8.15	$ 9.76
Cushioned seat:		
Padding	2.40	—
Vinyl	4.00	—
Molded seat (purchased)	—	6.00

	Deluxe Office Stool		Economy Office Stool	
Direct labor:				
Frame fabrication				
(.5 × $7.50/DLH)		3.75	(.5 × $7.50/DLH)	3.75
Cushion fabrication				
(.5 × $7.50/DLH)		3.75		—
Assembly[a] (.5 × $7.50/DLH)		3.75	(.3 × $7.50/DLH)	2.25
Manufacturing:				
Overhead				
(1.5DLH × $12.80/DLH)		19.20	(.8DLH × $12.80/DLH)	10.24
Total standard cost		$45.00		$32.00
Selling price (30% markup)		$58.50		$41.60

[a]Attaching seats to frames and attaching rubber feet.

OFFICE DIVISION
Manufacturing Overhead Budget

Overhead Item	Nature	Amount
Supplies	Variable — at current market prices	$ 420,000
Indirect labor	Variable	375,000
Supervision	Nonvariable	250,000
Power	Use varies with activity; rates are fixed	180,000
Heat and light	Nonvariable — light is fixed regardless of production, while heat/air conditioning varies with fuel charges	140,000
Property taxes and insurance	Nonvariable — any change in amounts/ rates is independent of production	200,000
Depreciation	Fixed dollar total	1,700,000
Employee benefits	20% of supervision, direct and indirect labor	575,000
	Total overhead	$3,840,000
	Capacity in DLH	300,000
	Overhead rate/DLH	$ 12.80

Required:

1. John Kline and Russ Fiegel did ask PortCo corporate management for guidance on an appropriate transfer price. Corporate management suggested that they consider using a transfer price based on variable manufacturing cost plus opportunity cost. Calculate a transfer price for the cushioned seat based on variable manufacturing cost plus opportunity cost.

2. Which alternative transfer price system — full cost, variable manufacturing cost, or variable manufacturing cost plus opportunity cost — would be better as the underlying concept for an intracompany transfer price policy? Explain your answer.

(CMA Adapted)

P16–13 **Transfer pricing and tie-in contracts with other divisions.*** "If I were to price these boxes any lower than $40 a thousand," said Mr. Brunner, manager of Birch Paper Company's Thompson Division, "I'd be countermanding my order of last month for our salespeople to stop shaving their bids and to bid full-cost quotations. I've been trying for weeks to improve the quality of our business, and if I turn around now and accept this job at $430 or $450 or something less than $480 I'll be tearing down this program I've been working so hard to build up. The division can't very well show a profit by putting in bids that don't even cover a fair share of overhead costs, let alone give us a profit."

Birch Paper Company was a medium-size, partly integrated paper company, producing white and kraft papers and paperboard. A portion of its paperboard output was converted into corrugated boxes by the Thompson Division, which also printed and colored the outside surface of the boxes. Including Thompson, the company had four producing divisions and a timberland division that supplied part of the company's pulp requirements.

For several years each division had been judged independently on the basis of its profit and return on investment. Top management had been working to gain effective results from a policy of decentralizing responsibility and authority for all decisions but those relating to overall company policy. The company's top officials felt that in the past few years the concept of decentralization had been successfully applied and that the company's profits and competitive position had definitely improved.

In early 19X7 the Northern Division designed a special display box for one of its papers in conjunction with the Thompson Division, which was equipped to make the box. Thompson's package design and development staff spent several months perfecting the design, production methods, and materials that were to be used. Because of the unusual color and shape these were far from standard. According to an agreement between the two divisions, the Thompson Division was reimbursed by the Northern Division for the cost of its design and development work.

When the specifications were all prepared, the Northern Division asked for bids on the box from the Thompson Division and from two outside companies. All division managers were normally free to buy from whichever supplier that they wished, and even on sales within the company, divisions were expected to meet the going market price if they wanted the business.

In early 19X7 the profit margins of converters such as the Thompson Division were being squeezed. Thompson, as did many other similar converters, bought its board, liner, or paper, and its function was to print, cut, and shape it into boxes. Although it bought most of its materials from other Birch divisions, most of Thompson's sales were to outside customers. If Thompson got the business, it would probably buy the linerboard and corrugating medium from the Southern Division of Birch. The walls of a corrugated box consist of outside and inside sheets of linerboard sandwiching the fluted corrugating medium. About 70% of Thompson's out-of-pocket cost of $400 represented the cost of linerboard and corrugating medium. Though Southern

---

*Copyright © 1957 by the President and Fellows of Harvard College. This case was prepared by William Rotch under the direction of Neil Harlan as a basis for class discussion rather than to illustrate either effective or ineffective handling of an administrative situation. Reprinted by permission of the Harvard Business School.

had been running below capacity and had excess inventory, it quoted the market price, which had not noticeably weakened as a result of the oversupply. Its out-of-pocket costs on both liner and corrugating medium were about 60% of the selling price.

The Northern Division received bids on the boxes of $480 per 1,000 from the Thompson division, $430 per 1,000 from West Paper Company, and $432 per 1,000 from Erie Papers, Ltd. Erie Papers offered to buy from Birch the outside linerboard with the special printing already on it but would supply its own inside liner and corrugating medium. The outside liner would be supplied by the Southern Division at a price equivalent of $90 per 1,000 boxes and would be printed for $30 per 1,000 by the Thompson Division. Of the $30, about $25 would be out-of-pocket costs.

Because this situation appeared a little unusual, William Kenton, manager of the Northern Division, discussed the wide discrepancy of bids with Birch's commercial vice-president. He told the vice-president: "We sell in a very competitive market, where higher costs cannot be passed on. How can we be expected to show a decent profit and return on investment if we have to buy our supplies at more than 10% over the going market?"

Knowing that Mr. Brunner had on occasion in the past few months been unable to operate the Thompson Division at capacity, the vice-president found it odd that Mr. Brunner would add the full 20% overhead and profit charge to his out-of-pocket costs. When asked about this, Mr. Brunner's answer was the statement that appears at the beginning of the case. He went on to say that having done the developmental work on the box and having received no profit on that, he felt entitled to a good markup on the production of the box itself.

The vice-president explored further the cost structures of the various divisions. He remembered a comment that the controller had made at a meeting the week before to the effect that costs that were variable for one division could be largely fixed for the company as a whole. He knew that in the absence of specific orders from top management, Mr. Kenton would accept the lowest bid, which was that of the West Paper Company for $430. However, it would be possible for top management to order the acceptance of another bid if the situation warranted such action. And though the volume represented by the transactions in question was less than 5% of the volume of any of the divisions involved, other transactions could conceivably raise similar problems later.

Required:

1. In the controversy described, how, if at all, is the transfer price system dysfunctional? Prepare an analysis of the cash flows under each alternative.

2. As the commercial vice-president, what action would you take?

P16–14   **Transfer pricing and tie-in contracts.** Bench Company is an integrated engine manufacturer. It has three divisions: Top, Middle, and Bottom. Middle and Bottom presently have excess capacity. Top needs an engine that can be manufactured by Middle and Bottom. Middle acquires the main components from Bottom at $10,000 (variable cost to Bottom is $6,000). Middle's own variable costs are $2,000. Top can buy the engine from Vancouver Company for $13,000. If Vancouver gets the job, it will buy some parts from Bottom at $3,500 (variable cost to Bottom is $2,000).

Required:

1. If Top accepts the price of $13,000, is Bench Corporation better off? Show figures.

2. Assume that all facts are the same except that Vancouver is selling the engine at $11,000. Is the Bench Corporation better off if Vancouver sells the engine to Top? If not, what would you recommend as Bench's controller? Show figures.

Assume that Middle now has no excess capacity. Vancouver is selling the engine at the original $13,000. Middle can either produce the engine for Top or make a somewhat similar engine for Victoria Company. Victoria would pay $14,000. Middle would buy parts from Bottom at $10,500, which have a variable cost of $6,300 to Bottom. Middle's variable costs on the Victoria job would be $2,800.

Required:

3. If Top and Middle work with each other, would you expect them to make a deal with each other? If so, give the natural bargaining range.

4. Is this decision good for the firm? Show figures.

P16–15 **Transfer pricing and tie-in contracts.** Bower Company has many divisions in a corporation that is largely decentralized. The divisions are evaluated on the basis of residual income. Bower's Top Division needs 100 units of a subassembly. The basic parts of the subassembly are manufactured by Bower's metal fabricating division, the Bottom Division. Bower's Middle Division assembles the basic parts and adds the motor. Middle's variable costs are $100 per unit. Bottom's variable costs of parts are $50 and the regular price—which is also the transfer price—is $75 per unit. Middle desires to sell the subassembly to Top for $300 per unit.

Adams, an outside supplier, is also willing to sell Top the subassembly. If Adams gets the contract, it would buy parts from Bottom at a price of $120. These parts have a variable cost to Bottom of $80. Both Middle and Bottom have excess capacity. Each of the following questions is independent unless otherwise stated.

Required:

1. If Adams's price is $250, is Middle better off from the standpoint of short-run contribution margin maximization if it meets this price? Is the Bower Corporation better off? Show figures and explain.

2. If Adams's price is $160, is the Bower Corporation better or worse off if the subassembly is manufactured internally or acquired from Adams? Show figures.

3. If the subassembly is internally produced in 2 above, what is the natural bargaining range for the materials transferred from Bottom to Middle? Show figures.

P16–16 **Continuation of previous problem, no excess capacity.** This problem continues P16–15 but with several changes. Middle is now operating without excess capacity. It can either take on the Top job or another order but not both in terms of required delivery dates. The other job is with the Morse Company. That company wants an order for 90 subassemblies that are similar to the ones that Top wants. Morse would pay $275 for each engine. Middle would buy parts from Bottom at a cost of $60.

These parts have a variable cost of $40 each. Middle's own variable costs on these units would be $100 each. Top can still acquire from Adams at $250 each.

Required:

1. Under the circumstances would you expect Top and Middle to make a deal with each other? Show figures.

2. Is the decision in 1 above in the best interest of the entire firm? Show figures.

P16–17   **Both divisions in imperfect competition.** Division A of the Friedan Company produces a subassembly that is needed by Division B. There is also a market for the subassembly when A completes it. Pertinent data follow:

A's productive capacity	10,000 units
A's variable costs	$320
A's fixed costs assigned to the product	$100
Additional costs (variable) of processing by B	$80
B's fixed costs assigned to the product	$50

Assume that each division faces the following demand curve:

A		B	
Units	Price	Units	Price
8,000	$490	2,000	$800
9,000	475	1,000	900
10,000	450		

Required:
1. What combination of units maximizes profits in the short run for the entire company?
2. Would A, acting in its own best interests, be likely to sell the profit-maximizing units to B?
3. How might the transfer price of the units be set up so that firm and division goals are congruent with each other? Show figures.

P16–18   **Complex problem with tie-in contracts.** Corporation X has many divisions. It is essentially decentralized in its operations with divisions being free to buy and sell either within or outside the corporation. Divisions are evaluated on the basis of residual income.

     In October of 19X0 Division A of Corporation X needed 100 subassemblies. Corporation Q is willing to sell them to A at a price of $120 each. If Q is given the job, one component of the subassembly would be manufactured by X's H Division. Q would pay H $50 per component, and H would have variable costs of $20.

     Division B of X Corporation could also manufacture the subassembly for A. If it did, it could do the whole job itself (without H's aid). Its variable costs would be $55 per subassembly.

     B also has the opportunity of manufacturing a subassembly for Corporation T. T would need 80 subassemblies. The selling price would be $100, and B would have $50 of variable costs. B is presently short of capacity and could take on either the A or T jobs but not both given the required delivery dates.

Required:
1. A and B are in communication with each other. Do you think that they will tend to make a deal with each other if they act in their best immediate short-run interests? If so, what do you think the minimum and maximum potential selling price would be if they negotiate the selling price? Show figures.
2. Is the decision arrived at in 1 above best for the firm as a whole? Show figures.
3. Assuming B had the capability to do both the A and T jobs, should they do both?
4. Assume all factors as originally given except that the number of subassemblies that T needs is not specified. How many units for T would constitute the break-even point — the point of indifference between an internal and an external transaction from (a) Division B's standpoint and (b) Corporation X's standpoint?

P16–19   **Transfer pricing and goal congruence.** National Industries is a diversified corporation with separate and distinct operating divisions. Each division's performance is evaluated on the basis of total dollar profits and return on division investment.

The WindAir Division manufactures and sells air conditioner units. The coming year's budgeted income statement, based on a sales volume of 15,000 units, appears below.

WINDAIR DIVISION
Budgeted Income Statement
For the 19X9–19X0 Fiscal Year

	Per Unit	Total ($000 omitted)
Sales revenue	$400	$6,000
Manufacturing costs:		
Compressor	$ 70	$1,050
Other raw materials	37	555
Direct labor	30	450
Variable overhead	45	675
Fixed overhead	32	480
Total manufacturing costs	$214	$3,210
Gross margin	$186	$2,790
Operating expenses:		
Variable selling	$ 18	$ 270
Fixed selling	19	285
Fixed administrative	38	570
Total operating expenses	$ 75	$1,125
Net income before taxes	$111	$1,665

WindAir's division manager believes that sales can be increased if the unit selling price of the air conditioners is reduced. A market research study conducted by an independent firm at the request of the manager indicates that a 5% reduction in the selling price ($20) would increase sales volume 16% or 2,400 units. WindAir has sufficient production capacity to manage this increased volume with no increase in fixed costs.

At the present time WindAir uses a compressor in its units that it purchases from an outside supplier at a cost of $70 per compressor. The division manager of WindAir has approached the manager of the Compressor Division regarding the sale of a compressor unit to WindAir. The Compressor Division currently manufactures and sells a unit exclusively to outside firms that is similar to the unit used by WindAir. The specifications of the WindAir compressor are slightly different, which would reduce the Compressor Division's raw material cost by $1.50 per unit. In addition, the Compressor Division would not incur any variable selling costs in the units sold to WindAir. The manager of WindAir wants all of the compressors it uses to come from one supplier and has offered to pay $50 for each compressor unit.

The Compressor Division has the capacity to produce 75,000 units. The coming year's budgeted income statement for the Compressor Division is shown on page 614 and is based on a sales volume of 64,000 units without considering WindAir's proposal.

COMPRESSOR DIVISION
Budgeted Income Statement
For the 19X9–19X0 Fiscal Year

	Per Unit	Total (000 omitted)
Sales revenue	$100	$6,400
Manufacturing costs:		
Raw materials	$ 12	$ 768
Direct labor	8	512
Variable overhead	10	640
Fixed overhead	11	704
Total manufacturing costs	$ 41	$2,624
Gross margin	$ 59	$3,776
Operating expenses:		
Variable selling	$ 6	$ 384
Fixed selling	4	256
Fixed administrative	7	448
Total operating expenses	$ 17	$1,088
Net income before taxes	$ 42	$2,688

Required:

1. Should WindAir Division institute the 5% price reduction in its air conditioner units even if it cannot acquire the compressors internally for $50 each? Support your conclusion with appropriate calculations.

2. Without prejudice to your answer to 1 above, assume that WindAir needs 17,400 units. Should the Compressor Division be willing to supply the compressor units for $50 each? Support your conclusions with appropriate calculations.

3. Without prejudice to your answer to 1 above, assume that WindAir needs 17,400 units. Would it be in the best interest of National Industries for the Compressor Division to supply the compressor units at $50 each to the WindAir Division? Support your conclusions with appropriate calculations.

(CMA Adapted)

P16–20 **Profit center operations.** A. R. Oma, Inc., manufactures a line of men's colognes and after-shave lotions. The manufacturing process is basically a series of mixing operations, with the addition of certain aromatic and coloring ingredients; the finished product is packaged in a company-produced glass bottle and packed in cases containing six bottles.

A. R. Oma feels that the sale of its product is heavily influenced by the appearance and appeal of the bottle and has therefore devoted considerable managerial effort to the bottle production process. This has resulted in the development of certain unique bottle production processes in which management takes considerable pride.

The two areas (perfume production and bottle manufacture) have evolved over the years in an almost independent manner; in fact, a rivalry has developed between management personnel as to "which division is the more important" to the company. This attitude is probably intensified because the bottle manufacturing plant was purchased intact ten years ago and no real interchange of management personnel or ideas (except at the top corporate level) has taken place.

Since the acquisition, all bottle production has been absorbed by the perfume manufacturing plant. Each area is considered a separate profit center and evaluated as such. As the new corporate controller you are responsible for the definition of a proper transfer value to use in crediting the bottle production profit center and in debiting the packaging profit center.

At your request, the Bottle Division's general manager has asked certain other bottle manufacturers to quote a price for the quantity and sizes demanded by the Perfume Division. These competitive prices are as follows:

Volume (equivalent cases)[a]	Total Price	Price per Case
2,000,000	$ 4,000,000	$2.00
4,000,000	7,000,000	1.75
6,000,000	10,000,000	1.67

[a]An "equivalent case" represents 6 bottles.

A cost analysis of the internal bottle plant indicates that they can produce bottles at the following costs:

Volume (equivalent cases)	Total Price	Cost per Case[b]
2,000,000	$3,200,000	$1.60
4,000,000	5,200,000	1.30
6,000,000	7,200,000	1.20

[b]The cost analysts point out that these costs represent fixed costs of $1,200,000 and variable costs of $1.00 per equivalent case.

These figures have given rise to considerable corporate discussion as to the proper value to use in the transfer of bottles to the Perfume Division. This interest is heightened because a significant portion of a division manager's income is an incentive bonus based on profit center results.

The Perfume Division has the following costs in addition to the bottle costs:

Volume (cases)	Total Cost	Cost per Case
2,000,000	$16,400,000	$8.20
4,000,000	32,400,000	8.10
6,000,000	48,400,000	8.07

After considerable analysis, the Marketing Research Department has furnished you with the following price-demand relationship for the finished product:

Sales Volume (cases)	Total Sales Revenue	Sales Price per Case
2,000,000	$25,000,000	$12.50
4,000,000	45,600,000	11.40
6,000,000	63,900,000	10.65

Required: 1. A. R. Oma, Inc. has used market-based transfer prices in the past. Using the current market prices and costs, and assuming a volume of 6,000,000 cases, calculate the income for (1) the Bottle Division, (2) the Perfume Division, and (3) the corporation.

2. Is this production and sales level the most profitable volume for (1) the Bottle Division, (2) the Perfume Division, and (3) the corporation? Explain your answer.

3. The company uses the profit center concept for divisional operation. (1) Define *profit center*. (2) What conditions should exist for a profit center to be established? (3) Should the two divisions of A. R. Oma, Inc. be organized as profit centers?

(CMA Adapted)

CHAPTER 17

Quantitative Techniques for Decision Making

Learning Objectives

After reading this chapter you should be able to:

1. Identify the types of managerial problems to which quantitative techniques are applicable.

2. Have knowledge of the key characteristics of decision theory problems.

3. Be able to construct a payoff table, using expected values.

4. Be able to construct a decision tree to aid in solving problems.

5. Understand the concept of the expected value of perfect information.

6. Appreciate the role of risk in competing projects and know how to measure risk.

7. Distinguish between joint and linked probabilities.

Throughout this book we have emphasized the importance of planning and control to a business. Decision making is the culmination of the planning process. The importance of decision making in a business cannot be overestimated. Although the correct decision may not always be made, the planning and controlling functions will be rendered ineffective if the role of decision making is not emphasized.

We consider in this chapter various quantitative techniques that can aid the manager in the decision making process. First, we consider the role of decision making in business and illustrate the basic principles of decision theory with the use of a simple example. The principles are then illustrated for four different managerial tools discussed in this book: cost-volume-profit analysis, investigation of variances, capital budgeting, and budgeting for short-run goals. We will see how payoff tables and decision trees aid in the modeling of various types of decision theory problems. The quantitative techniques we will examine add further depth to the decision-making aspect of the planning process. In other words, decision making can be greatly facilitated and improved by these techniques.

Basic Principles of Decision Theory

Decision making is, by its very nature, future oriented. Managers are concerned with what has happened in the past, but only as it pertains to the future. What happens in the future is dependent to a large extent on the choices made today. Managers must often choose among competing alternatives in making their decisions. Should a new plant be built to handle increased business, or should the company buy the needed inventory from an outside source? How many units of a perishable product should be ordered this week? The alternative that a manager chooses will not only affect the current profitability of the company but may set a precedent for future decisions.

In making decisions, the manager must learn to accept and deal with uncertainty. A body of knowledge has developed over recent years to attempt to formalize the decision process. **Decision theory** applies various concepts from statistics, economics, and other related fields to the decision-making tasks of business and other disciplines. In particular, statistical tools, such as probabilities, have been used to aid in the process. Traditionally, managers have been wary of using quantitative techniques in arriving at decisions. This reluctance often stems from a lack of understanding of the role of quantitative methods in decision making. We are not suggesting that statistics replace the use of good business judgment in making decisions. However, managers should at least consider the use of these techniques as one possible aid in their thought process. None of the techniques to be discussed will *solve* problems. Professional judgment is still the most important ingredient in the decision-making process.

The Characteristics of Decision Theory Problems

Five key elements are characteristic of all decision theory problems:

1. A choice exists among **alternatives.** More than one choice can be made in response to a problem. The alternatives are sometimes called the *actions.*

2. Various **events** or states are possible. That is, what will actually happen in the future?

3. A certain **outcome** is identified with each of the various possible events. In business applications, the outcomes are normally stated in financial terms. For example, what will income be in the future, given a particular event?

4. A **probability** is attached to each of the various possible events. A probability is the likelihood that a particular event will take place.

5. Finally, an **objective** is identified. In business applications, the objective may be to minimize costs or to maximize revenues. Although the objective may seem obvious, is should always be stated so that everyone in the organization understands the company's goals.

Simple Example

Before turning to a business application of decision theory, consider the following proposition. A friend will allow you to draw one card from a standard deck of playing cards. If you draw a heart, the friend pays you $100. If you draw anything other than a heart, you pay the friend $25. Should you play? Your *alternatives* are to play or not play the game. The possible *events* are that you will either draw a heart or not draw a heart. The *outcomes* are that you win $100 if you draw a heart or lose $25 if you draw one of the other three suits. Assuming that the deck is well shuffled and the cards have not been tampered with in any way, the *probabilities* are 25% that you will draw a heart and 75% that you will not draw a heart. Of course, your *objective* in playing the game is to maximize your profit.

A common approach to a problem of this type is to calculate an **expected value** for each of the possible alternatives or actions. An expected value for any one alternative is simply a weighted average of the outcomes of each event, with the probabilities as the weights. The expected value (EV) for the choice to play the game is

$$\text{EV (play game)} = .25(\$100) + .75(-\$25)$$
$$= \quad \$25 \quad - \quad \$18.75 = \underline{\underline{\$6.25}}$$

Alternatively, if you choose not to play the game, the expected value is $0 because you will neither win nor lose any money.

Using the expected value concept as the sole criterion in making a decision, you would choose to play the game because that choice has a higher expected value. However, note that you would *never* win $6.25 on any one draw. You either win $100 or lose $25. Expected values do not occur themselves—they are merely an indication of what the expected outcome will be over the *long run.* For example, what would happen if you played the game 1,000 times? You would expect to win $100 one-fourth of the times you drew a card, or 250 times in total. Your winnings would be 250 times $100, or $25,000. The other 750 times you played you would expect to lose $25, or a total of $18,750. You could expect to net $6,250 from playing 1,000 times, for an average winning of $6.25.

Should expected values always be used in making decisions? What if you cannot afford to lose $25? If this is the case, you are implying that the loss of $25 would be more detrimental than the benefit derived from a gain of $100. **Utilities** are values assigned to the various outcomes to compensate for the user's feelings toward risk. We will return to a discussion of their use and the assessment of risk in decision theory later in the chapter.

Applications of Decision Theory in Management Accounting

Many of the topics discussed in earlier chapters of this book lend themselves to decision theory analysis. Although we will limit discussion to the application of the concepts to four topics, any business problem where there are choices among alternatives is a candidate for decision theory techniques.

Cost-Volume-Profit Application

Daily Distributors sells daily newspapers to the various hotels in a large city. The company is faced with the decision as to how many papers to buy from the publisher each day. We will assume that the company must buy from the publisher in lots of 1,000 papers, and we will limit our alternatives to the purchase of either 1,000, 2,000, 3,000, or 4,000 papers. Demand at the hotels for the newspapers can range anywhere from 0 to 4,000 newspapers, although again we will assume demand in even lots of 1,000. Based on past experience, the company estimates the probabilities of the various levels of demand to be

Event (Demand)	Probability
0	.10
1,000	.20
2,000	.40
3,000	.20
4,000	.10

Keep in mind that the selection of only four possible alternatives and five levels of demand (the events) may be unrealistically restrictive. In real-world applications, the use of the computer allows a company to consider an almost unlimited number of alternatives and events.

Payoff Tables

The outcome of each event is a function of four variables: the selling price per paper, the cost per paper, the number bought, and the number demanded. Daily buys the papers for $.15 each and sells them to the hotels for $.20 each. A **payoff table** can be constructed to identify all of the various outcomes, given different levels of demand and different numbers of papers bought from the publisher. The outcomes or payoffs are stated in terms of contribution margin because Daily's objective is to maximize profits from the sale of the papers. The cost per paper is assumed to be the only variable cost. No other costs are assumed to be relevant to the decision, and therefore profit is maximized by maximizing contribution margin. A payoff table for the problem is shown in Exhibit 17–1.

First consider the calculation of the payoffs if there is no demand for the papers. Due to the timely nature of the product, the papers have no resale value, and the company will lose $.15 for every paper bought for which there is no demand. Thus, the entries in the first row of the table are found by multiplying each of the purchase lots by $.15. For example, if it buys 3,000 papers and cannot sell any, it will lose 3,000 × $.15 or $450.

If the hotels demand 1,000 papers and 1,000 papers are bought, the company will earn 1,000 times the contribution margin of $.05 per paper or $50. If *only* 1,000 papers are purchased, the contribution margin is the same $50 regardless of whether demand is for 1,000, 2,000, 3,000, or 4,000 papers. Similar logic is used to arrive at the other numbers in the payoff table. To summarize, the payoff for each cell in the table is calculated by multiplying the demand times the selling price of $.20 (unless the number bought is less

EXHIBIT 17–1

Daily Distributors
Payoff Table[a]

Events (Demand)	Alternatives: Number of Papers to Buy			
	1,000	*2,000*	*3,000*	*4,000*
0	$(150)	$(300)	$(450)	$(600)
1,000	50	(100)	(250)	(400)
2,000	50	100	(50)	(200)
3,000	50	100	150	0
4,000	50	100	150	200

[a]The amount in each cell is determined by multiplying the demand by the selling price of $.20 (unless the number bought is less than the demand, in which case the number bought is used) and subtracting from this the purchase quantity times the cost of $.15. For example, if 3,000 papers are purchased and only 2,000 are demanded, the payoff would be the revenue of $400 (2,000 times $.20) less the cost of $450 (3,000 times $.15), which equals $(50).

than the demand, in which case the number bought is used) and subtracting from this the corresponding purchase quantity times the cost of $.15 per paper. Before proceeding, you should verify for yourself the accuracy of each of the numbers in Exhibit 17–1.

Alternative Solutions to Problem

How many papers should the company buy each day? The answer depends on the company's choice of a criterion in solving the problem. The expected value criterion is only one of a number of different approaches to the problem. For example, if the company wants to minimize the risk of loss, they would choose the alternative that has the largest minimum profit. Referring to Exhibit 17–1, the minimum profit for each of the alternatives is shown in the first row, corresponding to zero demand. The company would always buy 1,000 papers because this would minimize the risk of loss. This criterion is referred to as a **maximin approach** and would be used by a manager that is risk averse.

Alternatively, the **maximax approach** would be used by a manager that is a risk taker. With this approach, the manager selects the alternative that has the largest maximum profit. This criterion would cause the manager to buy 4,000 papers because there is the potential for $200 of profit, whereas if only 3,000 papers are ordered there is the potential for only $150 of profit.

The weakness inherent in both of these approaches is that they do not take into account the probability or likelihood of the various levels of demand. Another alternative would be to buy 2,000 papers because this is the most likely demand. In fact, the probability of demand being for 2,000 papers is 40% or twice as high as the 20% probability of either 1,000 or 3,000 papers. However, this approach considers only the probabilities and does not take into account the consequences — that is, the payoffs associated with each of the different outcomes.

The expected value criterion considers both the probabilities and financial consequences of each alternative. Recall the concept: the outcomes of each event are weighted by the likelihood of their occurrence. For example, the expected value for the alternative of buying 2,000 papers is

$$\text{EV (buy 2,000 papers)} = .10(-\$300) + .20(-\$100) + .40(\$100)$$
$$+ .20(\$100) + .10(\$100)$$
$$= -\$30 - \$20 + \$40 + \$20 + \$10 = \underline{\underline{\$20}}$$

Exhibit 17–2 is similar to Exhibit 17–1 except that a column for the probabilities has been added and each of the payoffs in the cells of the table has been replaced with expected values. Using the expected value criterion, the company should buy only 1,000 papers daily because this alternative has a higher expected value than either of the other three.

The Value of Additional Information

Ideally, Daily Distributors would like to know in advance what demand will be on any one day. Although it is impossible to know this, the company could

EXHIBIT 17–2
Daily Distributors
Calculation of Expected Values[a]

Events (Demand)	Probability of Each Event	Alternatives: Number of Papers to Buy			
		1,000	2,000	3,000	4,000
0	.10	$(15)	$(30)	$(45)	$(60)
1,000	.20	10	(20)	(50)	(80)
2,000	.40	20	40	(20)	(80)
3,000	.20	10	20	30	0
4,000	.10	5	10	15	20
Expected values		$30	$20	$(70)	$(200)

[a]Each individual expected value is the product of the probability for that particular alternative and the payoff from the corresponding cell in Exhibit 17–1. For example, if 3,000 papers are bought and the demand is for only 2,000, the expected value is 40% times $(50), which equals $(20).

hire someone to do a study of the demand for papers. How much should the company be willing to pay for the results of this market research? One approach to the problem is to calculate the **expected value of perfect information** (EVPI). The concept involves calculation of the difference between the expected value of the best alternative with no additional information and the expected value of the best alternative if the company always knew in advance what demand would be each day.

The expected value of the best alternative—buying 1,000 papers—with no additional information is, of course, $30, as calculated earlier. If the company knew in advance the demand each day, it would buy exactly that many papers. Referring to Exhibit 17–1, if the company knew demand would be for 1,000 papers, it would buy 1,000 papers and its contribution margin would be $50. Because this demand is expected 20% of the time, Exhibit 17–2 indicates an expected value of $10. Summarizing, the expected value of perfect information is

EVPI = Expected value with advance knowledge of demand

Less: Expected value of best alternative without advance knowledge of demand

= ($10 + $40 + $30 + $20) less $30

= $100 less $30 = $70

Notice that perfect information unites the corresponding demand and buying cells (the boldfaced cells in Exhibit 17–2).

Should Daily Distributors pay someone $70 to conduct a study of demand? The company would be foolish to pay this amount because it is impossible for anyone to predict the future with complete accuracy. The EVPI simply puts an *upper* limit on the amount to spend to obtain additional information. Any market research study, whether contracted on the outside or performed internally, will yield only imperfect information. With the use of sampling techniques it is possible to at least add to the information available to reach decisions. Statistics textbooks include discussion of these sampling techniques and the calculation of the expected value of sample information.

Investigation of Variances

In Chapter 9 we discussed the criteria that management should use in deciding whether to spend the money to investigate variances from standards. One of the criteria discussed was the probability of occurrence associated with cost alternatives. If probabilities can be assigned realistically to the various states or events, a payoff table can be a useful aid in deciding whether to investigate a variance.

For example, assume that management is trying to decide whether or not to investigate a particular variance that suggests that a production process is out of adjustment (control). It has been determined that there is a .70 probability that the process is in adjustment and, therefore, a .30 probability that the process is out of adjustment. The costs associated with the possible alternatives have been determined to be the following:

Cost to investigate	$ 400
Cost to adjust, if necessary	500
Excess operating costs that will be incurred if production process is out of adjustment and not corrected	2,500

The payoff table illustrating the costs associated with the two alternative courses of action is shown in Exhibit 17–3. The object, of course, is to minimize costs. The payoff table in Exhibit 17–3 indicates that the expected value

EXHIBIT 17–3
Payoff Table for Variance Investigation

			Alternatives (Actions)	
Production State (Event)	**Probability of Each Event**		**Investigate**	**Do Not Investigate**
In adjustment	.70		$400	$ 0
Out of adjustment	.30		900[a]	2,500
Expected cost of action			550[b]	750[c]

[a]Investigation costs of $400 plus cost of adjusting of $500.
[b].7(400) + .3(900).
[c].7(0) + .3(2,500).

of the costs associated with the first course of action (investigate) is $550 and that the expected value of the costs associated with the second course of action (do not investigate) is $750. The table, therefore, tells management that it should investigate the variance. The value of this approach to deciding whether further investigation is warranted depends on the accuracy with which the probabilities and the associated costs can be estimated. If reliable estimates are possible, the method can be a valuable management tool.

Capital Budgeting Applications

Capital budgeting, with its emphasis on the long run, is an excellent area to apply the concepts of decision theory and expected values. The capital budgeting examples in Chapters 13 and 14 all had one element in common: a single point estimate was used for the yearly cash inflows. Although not explicitly stated, the single point approach takes that event with the highest expected probability of occurrence.

Calculating the Expected Value of Cash Flows

Consider Project A, which requires a $10,000 initial outlay today and a salvage value of $10,000 at the end of two years.[1] Rather than a single estimate, the yearly cash inflows are estimated according to the following probability distribution:

Yearly Cash Inflows	Probability of Occurrence
$1,700	.10
2,000	.80
2,100	.10

The three possible cash flows represent management's pessimistic, most likely, and optimistic estimates. Using the net present value technique discussed in Chapter 13, we will evaluate the project using two different criteria: (1) the most likely cash inflow per year of $2,000 and (2) the expected value for the yearly cash inflow, calculated as follows:

Yearly Cash Inflows	× Probability	= Expected Value
$1,700	.10	$ 170
2,000	.80	1,600
2,100	.10	210
Total expected value		$1,980

The net present values for Project A, using first the most likely estimate for the cash flows of $2,000 and then the expected value of $1,980, are shown

---

[1]A two-year life and a return of the entire amount invested at the end of the two years may be somewhat unrealistic. However, both are used to simplify the illustration and allow us to concentrate on the application of decision theory techniques to capital budgeting.

EXHIBIT 17–4

NPV Analysis of Project A (16%)

Cash Flow Estimate		End of Year		
		0	1	2
Most likely	Investment	−$10,000		
	Cash flows		$2,000	$ 2,000
	Salvage value			10,000
	Total inflows		$2,000	$12,000
	Present value factors (16%)		×.8621	× .7432
	Sum of the present values	10,642	$1,724	$ 8,918
	Net present value	$ 642		
Expected value	Investment	−$10,000		
	Cash flows		$1,980	$ 1,980
	Salvage value			10,000
	Total inflows		$1,980	$11,980
	Present value factors (16%)		×.8621	× .7432
	Sum of the present values	10,611	$1,707	$ 8,904
	Net present value	$ 611		

in Exhibit 17–4. A discount rate of 16% is used to approximate the firm's cost of capital.

Although the net present value using the expected value for the cash flows is $31 less than if the most likely cash flow value is used, the project still meets the company's cutoff, assuming a 16% cost of capital.

Consider Project B, with the same investment as Project A, the same salvage value after two years, but the following expected distribution for the cash inflows:

Yearly Cash Inflows	× Probability	= Expected Value
$ 500	.30	$ 150
1,000	.30	300
2,500	.40	1,000
Total expected value		$1,450

Project B is analyzed in Exhibit 17–5 using the net present value technique, with both the most likely value for the cash inflows of $2,500 and the expected value of $1,450.

Project B is acceptable if the company uses the most likely value for the cash flows of $2,500 but unacceptable if the expected value of $1,450 is used. Comparison of Projects A and B reveals some interesting observations. The most likely cash flow on Project A is lower than on Project B ($2,000 compared to $2,500), but Project A has the higher expected value ($1,980

EXHIBIT 17–5
NPV Analysis of Project B (16%)

Cash Flow Estimate		End of Year		
		0	1	2
Most likely	Investment	−$10,000		
	Cash flows		$2,500	$ 2,500
	Salvage value			10,000
	Total inflows		$2,500	$12,500
	Present value factors (16%)		×.8621	× .7432
	Sum of the present values	11,445	$2,155	$ 9,290
	Net present value	$ 1,445		
Expected value	Investment	−$10,000		
	Cash flows		$1,450	$ 1,450
	Salvage value			10,000
	Total inflows		$1,450	$11,450
	Present value factors (16%)		×.8621	× .7432
	Sum of the present values	9,760	$1,250	$ 8,510
	Net present value	$ (240)		

compared to $1,450). Given the higher expected value, the net present value for Project A is higher than for Project B. In fact, the lower expected value for Project B results in its rejection, assuming 16% as the cost of capital.

Measuring the Relative Risks of Competing Projects

Can we conclude from the previous example that two competing projects are equally acceptable as long as the expected values of the cash flows are the same? The answer, as we will see, depends on the *dispersion* of the possible cash flows around the expected value. What caused Project A in the earlier example to be so attractive compared to Project B was the high likelihood (an 80% probability) of the cash flows being $2,000 per year.

Consider two competing capital projects that have the same expected value, as shown below, but different distributions around the expected value:

Project	Cash Flows	Probability	Expected Value
High risk	$1,000	.30	$ 300
	1,500	.40	600
	2,000	.30	600
	Total expected value		$1,500
Low risk	$1,000	.10	$ 100
	1,500	.80	1,200
	2,000	.10	200
	Total expected value		$1,500

Should a company be indifferent between the two investments? Comparison of the two probability distributions indicates that the low risk project ia a "safer" investment because there is a higher likelihood that the most likely cash flow of $1,500 will be achieved. But how much "safer" or less risky is the project? The **standard deviation** is a statistical measure of the risk of a probability distribution around the expected value. The steps to be followed in calculating a standard deviation are

1. Compute the difference between each of the possible values (cash flows) and the *total* expected value;
2. Square each of the differences (deviations) and multiply each by its corresponding probability;
3. Sum the amounts found in 2 above and take the square root of the sum.

In equation form, the standard deviation is

$$\text{Standard deviation (SD)} = \left[\sum_{i=1}^{N} (X_i - EV)^2 P_i \right]^{1/2}$$

where:

X_i is each of the possible values
EV is the total expected value
P_i is the probability of each value
and Σ is the Greek symbol for summation

The standard deviations for the two projects are:

$$\text{High} = [.30(1,000 - 1,500)^2 + .40(1,500 - 1,500)^2$$
$$+.30(2,000 - 1,500)^2]^{1/2}$$
$$= [75,000 + 0 + 75,000]^{1/2} = \underline{\underline{387}}$$

$$\text{Low} = [.10(1,000 - 1,500)^2 + .80(1,500 - 1,500)^2$$
$$+.10(2,000 - 1,500)^2]^{1/2}$$
$$= [25,000 + 0 + 25,000]^{1/2} = \underline{\underline{224}}$$

The standard deviation is a sufficient measure of the relative riskiness of these two projects because their expected values are the same. However, another measure is useful in comparing the riskiness of projects where the expected values are not the same:

$$\textbf{Coefficient of Variation (CV)} = \frac{\text{Standard deviation}}{\text{Expected value}}$$

To illustrate the calculation of this measure and its usefulness, we return to Projects A and B. The standard deviations of the two projects and their respective coefficients of variation are

Project A:

$$SD = [.10(1,700 - 1,980)^2 + .80(2,000 - 1,980)^2$$
$$+.10(2,100 - 1,980)^2]^{1/2}$$
$$= [7840 + 320 + 1440]^{1/2} = \underline{98}$$

$$CV = 98/1980 = .049 \quad \text{or} \quad \underline{4.9\%}$$

Project B:

$$SD = [.30(500 - 1,450)^2 + .30(1,000 - 1,450)^2$$
$$+.40(2,500 - 1,450)^2]^{1/2}$$
$$= [270,750 + 60,750 + 441,000]^{1/2} = \underline{879}$$

$$CV = 879/1450 = .606 \quad \text{or} \quad \underline{60.6\%}$$

The calculations show that Project B not only has a higher amount of absolute risk than Project A but also is relatively riskier, as indicated by the higher coefficient of variation. In summary, even though Project B has a higher most likely annual cash flow, Project A appears to be a more rational investment choice because it has less risk as indicated by the coefficient of variation and it is the only one of the two projects that meets the 16% cost of capital criterion, assuming use of the expected value.

Two Probabilistic Estimates: Cash Flows and Salvage Value

We now consider one final capital budgeting project. Project C requires the same investment of $10,000 as Projects A and B and has the following probability distribution for the annual cash flows:

Yearly Cash Inflows	× Probability	= Expected Value
$1,000	.40	$ 400
9,000	.60	5,400
Total expected value		$5,800

The project also differs from the previous two in that there is uncertainty with regard to the salvage value at the end of the two years. Rather than a single point estimate, salvage value is also subject to a probability distribution:

Salvage Value	× Probability	= Expected Value
$ 2,000	.40	$ 800
10,000	.60	6,000
Total expected value		$6,800

The most likely annual cash flow for Project C of $9,000 is much higher than the cash flow for either Projects A or B. The most likely salvage value is the same as the single point estimate on the other two. Although the expected value of the annual flows of $5,800 is also much higher than on Projects A and B, the expected value for the salvage value of $6,800 is lower than the single point estimate of $10,000 on the other two projects. To compare Project C with the other two as an investment alternative, Exhibit 17–6 presents the relevant net present value analysis for the project.

On the basis of either the most likely values or the expected values, Project C appears to be a better investment alternative than either of the other two projects. However, using the expected value criterion, it is necessary, as discussed earlier, to consider the riskiness of the project. Because both the cash flows and the salvage value are subject to uncertainty, standard deviations and coefficients of variation are computed for both:

For the cash flows:

$$SD = [.40(1,000 - 5,800)^2 + .60(9,000 - 5,800)^2]^{1/2}$$
$$= [9,216,000 + 6,144,000]^{1/2} = \underline{3,919}$$

$$CV = 3,919/5,800 = .676 \quad \text{or} \quad \underline{67.6\%}$$

For the salvage value:

$$SD = [.40(2,000 - 6,800)^2 + .60(10,000 - 6,800)^2]^{1/2}$$
$$= [9,216,000 + 6,144,000]^{1/2} = \underline{3,919}$$

$$CV = 3,919/6,800 = .576 \quad \text{or} \quad \underline{57.6\%}$$

EXHIBIT 17–6
NPV Analysis of Project C (16%)

Cash Flow Estimate		*End of Year*		
		0	*1*	*2*
Most likely	Investment	−$10,000		
	Cash flows		$9,000	$ 9,000
	Salvage value			10,000
	Total inflows		$9,000	$19,000
	Present value factors (16%)		×.8621	× .7432
	Sum of the present values	21,880	$7,759	$14,121
	Net present value	$11,880		
Expected value	Investment	−$10,000		
	Cash flows		$5,800	$ 5,800
	Salvage value			6,800
	Total inflows		$5,800	$12,600
	Present value factors (16%)		×.8621	× .7432
	Sum of the present values	14,364	$5,000	$ 9,364
	Net present value	$ 4,364		

EXHIBIT 17-7

Comparison of Capital Budgeting Projects

	Cash Flows		Net Present Value (16%)			
Project	Most Likely	Expected Value	Most Likely	Expected Value	Stand. Dev.	Coef. Var.
A	$ 2,000	$1,980	$ 642	$ 611	$ 98	4.9%
B	2,500	1,450	1,445	(240)	879	60.6
C	9,000	5,800	11,880	4,364	3,919	67.6
C	Salvage value:					
	10,000	6,800			3,919	57.6

The three projects are compared, in summary form, in Exhibit 17-7. Note the two standard deviations and two coefficients of variation for Project C, one for the cash flows and one for the salvage values.

Assuming limited resources, which of the three projects is the best? If expected values are used for an estimate of cash flows, Project B would be rejected on a net present value basis because it would not provide the desired 16% return. Project C unquestionably provides the highest net present value of the three, but with considerably more risk than either of the other two. The situation with Project C is typical of the dilemma companies must constantly face: higher overall returns are possible, but only if the company is willing to take on more risk.

Joint probabilities We have assumed for Project C that either of the two cash flows is possible in combination with either of the two salvage values. That is, the two sets of events, cash flows and salvage values, are assumed to be independent. By combining the two sets of probabilities, **joint probabilities** can be determined for each of the following possibilities:

		Probabilities		
				Joint
Cash Flows	Salvage Value	Cash Flows	× Salvage Value	= Probability
$1,000	$ 2,000	.40	.40	.16
1,000	10,000	.40	.60	.24
9,000	2,000	.60	.40	.24
9,000	10,000	.60	.60	.36

The joint probabilities give a good indication of the risk involved with Project C. There is a 16% chance that the cash flows will be $1,000 and the salvage $2,000. A company must decide whether or not it can afford to take this type of risk. If this particular sequence of events would have disastrous consequences for the company, then the project may not be acceptable, even with its high expected return. Alternatively, if a company is in a position to take some risk, there is a 36% chance of doing extremely well, as indicated by the earlier net present value analysis.

Utilities, as mentioned earlier in the chapter, are subjective values assigned to the various outcomes to adjust for the decision maker's feelings toward risk. Utilities can be helpful when a manager feels that any one particular outcome should be given more consideration than is warranted by the probability assigned to its occurrence. The problem in attaching utilities to the various outcomes is the subjective nature of the assignment process. The judgment involved in assigning utilities adds one more element of subjectivity to a process that already requires estimates in the assignment of the probabilities.

Linked probabilities   Finally, assume instead for Project C that the probabilities for particular cash flows and salvage values are related rather than independent. Dependent or **linked probabilities** for Project C means that if the lower cash flows of $1,000 occur, then the lower salvage value of $2,000 must occur. The probability of this occurrence is 40%. Similarly, the higher salvage value of $10,000 would be linked to the higher cash flows of $9,000 and would be expected to occur 60% of the time. Although the net present value for Project C of $4,364 is the same whether linked or joint probabilities are assumed, the risk with the two differs. For example, assuming linked probabilities, there is a 40% chance that the worst possible case will occur: the cash flows of $1,000 and the salvage value of $2,000. A decision based on the circumstances in each situation must be made as to whether the probabilities are independent or linked.

Short-Run Budgeting Application

A fourth and final application of quantitative techniques that we will consider is short-run budgeting or profit planning. The discussion of budgeting in Chapter 5 was limited to situations in which a single point estimate of each of the budget inputs was made. Sales volume, selling price, and all of the various costs were estimated as a single amount. Rather than a point estimate, we will consider the preparation of a budget for operating income in which certain key elements are estimated according to a probability distribution. Although all inputs in a budget could be assumed to be probabilistic, we will limit consideration to an example in which two elements, sales volume and variable manufacturing costs per unit, are estimated as follows:

Item	Amount	Probability
Sales volume	8,000 units	.20
	10,000 units	.50
	12,000 units	.30
Variable manufacturing costs	$2.50 per unit	.60
	$3.00 per unit	.40

Assuming a selling price of $5 per unit, the three possible levels of sales revenue are $40,000, $50,000, and $60,000. Total variable manufacturing costs will depend on two factors: sales volume and the cost per unit. In situations such as this, a **decision tree** is useful. The name comes from the fact that each of the possible outcomes is represented by a separate level on a diagram that resembles branches on a tree. A decision tree for this budget is illustrated in Exhibit 17–8. Variable selling, general, and administrative costs are assumed to be $.50 per unit, and fixed costs $8,000 per period.

EXHIBIT 17–8
Probabilistic Budget of Operating Income: Decision Tree

Units sold	Sales revenue	Var. mfg. costs[a]	Var. S, G & A costs	Fixed costs	Operating income	× Joint prob.	Expected value
	$40,000 / p = .40	$24,000	$4,000	$8,000	$4,000	.08	$320
8,000 / p = .20							
	$40,000 / p = .60	$20,000	$4,000	$8,000	$8,000	.12	$960
	$50,000 / p = .40	$30,000	$5,000	$8,000	$7,000	.20	$1,400
10,000 / p = .50							
	$50,000 / p = .60	$25,000	$5,000	$8,000	$12,000	.30	$3,600
	$60,000 / p = .40	$36,000	$6,000	$8,000	$10,000	.12	$1,200
12,000 / p = .30							
	$60,000 / p = .60	$30,000	$6,000	$8,000	$16,000	.18	$2,880

Expected value – Operating income $10,360

Assuming independent events, the joint probabilities are the product of one of the three probabilities for sales volume and one of the two probabilities for variable manufacturing costs. For example, the probability that operating income will be $4,000 is 20% times 40%, which equals 8% because this is the joint probability of 8,000 units being sold at a variable manufacturing cost of $3 per unit. With three sales levels and two unit manufacturing costs, there are a total of six possible outcomes for operating income. Keep in mind that any of the other costs in the budget could have been treated as probabilistic rather than as a single amount. This would result in a magnification of the number of possible outcomes but would be easily manageable with the aid of the computer.

Use of the expected value approach to budget operating income results in an estimate of $10,360. However, what amount of risk or uncertainty is there in this estimate? The uncertainty is measured, of course, by calculation of the standard deviation and coefficient of variation. Similarly, expected values and measures of variation can be calculated for each of the items on the budgeted income statement. For example, the expected value for sales revenue is

$$.20(\$40,000) + .50(\$50,000) + .30(\$60,000) = \$51,000$$

A budgeted income statement for our illustration, with the expected value for each item and the corresponding standard deviation and coefficient of variation, is shown in Exhibit 17–9. You should verify for yourself the accuracy of each of the numbers in the exhibit.

Note the agreement between the operating income in Exhibits 17–8 and 17–9. In Exhibit 17–8, operating income was found by adding the expected values for the six possible income levels. In Exhibit 17–9, the same amount was found by computing the expected value for each of the items on the income statement. Also note from Exhibit 17–9 that the expected value for

EXHIBIT 17–9

Probabilistic Budget of Operating Income: Expected Values and Measures of Variation

Item	Expected Value	Standard Deviation	Coefficient of Variation
Sales revenue	$51,000	$7,000	13.7%
Variable manufacturing costs	$27,540	4,544	16.5
Variable S, G & A costs	5,100	700	13.7
Total variable costs	$32,640[a]		
Contribution margin	$18,360	3,565	19.4
Fixed costs	8,000	0	0
Operating income	$10,360	3,565	34.4

[a]Standard deviation and coefficient of variation could be calculated for total variable costs but are unnecessary here because this has been done for variable manufacturing costs and variable selling, general, and administrative costs.

fixed costs is $8,000 with no standard deviation and thus a zero coefficient of variation. Because fixed costs were assumed to be nonprobabilistic and they do not vary with sales volume, the point estimate is the expected value and there is no variation from this amount. Although variable selling, general, and administrative costs were also assumed to be nonprobabilistic, they do depend on sales volume, and, thus, there is variation from the expected value of $5,100.

Summary

The ability to make sound business decisions is one of the most important qualities in a good manager. The manager should use all available information in making key decisions, as well as whatever tools and techniques are available. We introduced in this chapter the principles of decision theory and showed how they can be used in conjunction with various planning and control techniques to aid in the solution of typical problems faced by the manager.

Payoff tables are a useful means of organizing the information in a problem in which there are multiple events that can take place and a number of alternatives in reacting to the problem. We illustrated the use of a payoff table for a cost-volume-profit problem involving uncertain demand for a perishable product. The expected value of perfect information indicated the maximum amount that would be paid for additional information to aid in reaching a decision. Payoff tables were also illustrated for the investigation of variances from standard.

The principles of decision theory were illustrated for both capital budgeting and short-run budgeting. If a problem involves more than one set of probabilistic events, then a decision must be made as to whether the events are independent or related. Joint probabilities were developed for situations in which the events were assumed to be independent. A decision tree was found to be useful in identifying all of the possible combinations of events that could take place. Dependent or linked probabilities involve a different degree of risk, and the manager must decide whether events are more appropriately treated as independent or linked.

Expected values, standard deviations, and coefficients of variation are useful summary measures in decision theory problems. The expected value is a weighted average of the various possible outcomes in a problem. The standard deviation is a measure of the dispersion around the expected value and is an important measure of the risk in a specific probability distribution. The coefficient of variation is a measure of relative risk and thus allows for comparisons to be made among alternatives.

It is worth repeating that none of the techniques discussed in this chapter solve a manager's problems. Decision theory simply provides a framework to aid the manager in the identification, organization, and analysis of business problems. The solution to all problems will always remain a matter of professional judgment.

Key Terms

Alternatives   are choices or actions available in response to a problem requiring a decision.

Coefficient of variation   is a statistical measure useful in comparing the relative risk of competing projects. It is computed by dividing the standard deviation by the expected value.

Decision theory   is a body of knowledge that applies concepts from statistics, economics, and related fields to the decision making tasks of business and other disciplines.

Decision tree   is a diagram used to indicate each of the possible outcomes in a decision problem. Each of the outcomes is represented by a separate level on the diagram with the levels resembling branches on a tree.

Events   are the possible states in a decision problem—what could happen in the future.

Expected value   for any one alternative in a decision problem is the weighted average of the outcomes of each event, with the probabilities of the outcomes as the weights.

Expected value of perfect information   is the mathematical difference between the expected value of the best alternative if the future were known with certainty and the expected value of the best alternative with no additional information.

Joint probability   is the mathematical product of two independent probabilities.

Linked probability   is the mathematical product of two dependent probabilities.

Maximax approach   is an approach to solution of a problem in which the alternative with the largest maximum value (such as profit) is selected and used by a risk taker.

Maximin approach   is an approach to solution of a problem in which the alternative with the largest minimum value (such as profit) is selected and used by someone that is risk averse.

Objective   is the stated goal to be attained in a decision problem, such as the minimization of costs.

Outcome   is the result or consequence of a particular event, usually stated in decision problems in terms of dollars.

Payoff table   is a table in which the cells represent the possible outcomes given certain events on one axis and certain alternatives on the other axis.

Probability   is the likelihood, stated as a percentage, of a particular event occurring.

Standard deviation   is a statistical measure of the risk of a probability distribution around the expected value.

Utility   is a value assigned to an outcome in a decision problem to compensate for the user's feelings toward risk.

Questions

Q17–1   Define *decision theory*. What are the five key elements of decision theory?

Q17–2   What is an expected value? Do expected values themselves necessarily occur in a particular problem? Explain.

Q17–3   What are utilities? What is the relationship between utilities and expected values?

Q17–4   What is a payoff table?

Q17–5   Evaluate the following statement: "The use of probabilities to make business decisions is fine in theory but will not work in practice. The only way to make sound business decisions is with good sound business judgment."

Q17–6   An investor is risk averse. Would it be better for the investor to use a maximin approach or a maximax approach to making decisions? Explain.

Q17–7   Explain what is meant by the *expected value of perfect information?* Is it ever possible to obtain perfect information?

Q17–8   Two competing capital budgeting projects have the same expected value for their cash flows. Would a company always be indifferent between the two projects? Explain.

Q17–9   What is wrong with using the standard deviation alone to compare two competing projects? How does the use of the coefficient of variation improve the comparison?

Q17–10   Define the term *probability.* What is a joint probability?

Q17–11   What is a linked probability? How does it differ from a joint probability?

Q17–12   What is the inherent weakness in using single point estimates in either capital budgeting or in short-run budgeting?

Q17–13   What is a decision tree? How can the construction of one be useful in a decision theory problem?

Q17–14   A recent college graduate made the following statement: "Decision theory is a useful technique to solve managerial problems. Professional judgment is less necessary when a manager learns to take advantage of this technique." Evaluate this statement.

Q17–15   The budget manager tells you that the expected value of net income for the coming year is $150,000 with a standard deviation of $25,000. What is the coefficient of variation for net income, and what is its meaning?

Q17–16   Explain how the expected value of perfect information can be found by examining a payoff table.

Q17–17   Why might you expect the management of a firm to be skeptical of decision theory techniques? What can be done to alleviate this skepticism?

Q17–18   Planning and control are the two key elements in the success of a business. How does decision making relate to each of these two elements?

Q17–19   Explain why the expected value of perfect information places an *upper* limit on the amount that one would spend to obtain additional information before making a decision.

Q17–20   Should an individual or a company always make decisions using the expected value criterion? How might a company's aversion to risk affect the use of the expected value criterion?

Exercises

E17–1   **Variance investigation with expected values.** Recent analysis of the variances from standards suggests that there is a 40% probability that a setting on a machine is out of adjustment. The cost to investigate the variance to determine if this is the case is $1,000. The cost to adjust the machine, if necessary, is $750. Excess operating costs of $2,500 will be incurred if the process is out of adjustment and not corrected.

Required:

1. Construct a payoff table to determine whether or not the variance should be investigated. Should you investigate?
2. Assume that your answer in 1 above was not to investigate. Also assume that the cost to investigate the variance and the cost to adjust the machine are the same as stated above. How much would the excess operating costs have to be before you would change your mind about whether to investigate?

E17–2   **Expected values and point of indifference.** A friend offers you the following proposition. You roll a die one time. If you roll a six, the friend pays you $4. If you roll anything other than a six, you pay the friend $1.

Required:

1. Using the expected value criterion, should you play the game?
2. Assume that the answer in 1 above is that you should not play the game. Assuming that you still pay the friend $1 if you don't roll a six, how much would you have to get for rolling a six before you would be indifferent about the game?

E17–3   **Cost-volume-profit analysis.** A wholesaler of fresh fruits and vegetables must decide how many bushels of apples to order from the grower for the coming week. Based on past experience, the probabilities associated with the various levels of demand are estimated to be

Demand (bushels)	Probability
0	.05
200	.20
400	.50
600	.20
800	.05

The wholesaler buys a bushel of apples for $10 and sells each bushel for $15. Any apples remaining at the end of the week are thrown out.

Required:

1. Construct a payoff table to determine the contribution margin associated with the alternatives of ordering 200, 400, 600, or 800 bushels of apples. Assume that these are the only possible order sizes.
2. Calculate the expected values for each of the alternatives in 1 above. How many bushels of apples should be ordered?

E17–4   **Expected value of perfect information.** Refer to the facts in E17–3. Assume that the wholesaler is interested in hiring a market researcher to investigate the weekly demand for apples. The researcher charges $500 for the service.

Required:

1. Calculate the expected value of perfect information for the data in E17–3. Explain the meaning of this number.
2. Should the wholesaler hire the market researcher? Justify your recommendation and also indicate any other information that you would want to have before deciding whether to hire the researcher.

E17–5   **Competing projects.** A company is considering an investment in one of two competing projects. The estimated cash flows for the first year for each of the two projects and the corresponding probabilities are

Project	Annual Cash Inflows	Probability
A	$10,000	.2
	25,000	.5
	30,000	.3
B	$ 5,000	.1
	20,000	.5
	40,000	.4

Required:
1. Which of the two projects should be chosen using the most likely criterion?
2. Which of the two projects should be chosen using the expected value criterion?
3. Assume the company is risk averse (that is, use the maximin approach). Which project should be chosen?
4. Assume the company is a risk taker (that is, use the maximax approach). Which project should be chosen?

E17–6   **Expected values for alternative investments.** A friend has come to you for your advice about an investment in a security that is currently free from federal income tax. She has heard that Congress is considering doing away with the tax-free status of this type of investment.

The security promises an effective yield of 6%. Your friend is in the 40% tax bracket and would therefore have to find a taxable investment with a yield of 10% to give her the same return as the nontaxable investment. For example, if she invested $100 in a taxable security yielding 10%, her annual return would be $10, of which 40% or $4 would go to the government. This would leave her with $6 or an after-tax yield of 6% —the same as the yield on the tax-free security. Unfortunately, the best taxable investment available (with similar risk to that of the tax-free security) yields a before-tax return of only 9%.

Your subjective estimate is that there is a 40% chance that Congress will repeal the tax-free status of this type of security during the next legislative session.

Required: Using the expected value criterion, what advice would you give to the friend: should she invest in the tax-free security, not knowing whether it will retain its tax-free status, or in the taxable security?

E17–7   **Improvement decision.** The Badger Company is considering what it should do with a piece of unimproved property it holds. It paid $100,000 for the land ten years ago and estimates that it could sell the land "as is" for $250,000.

The alternative would be to make the necessary improvements to the land to make it attractive to a builder. The improvements would cost the company $150,000 to make. However, the value of the land will ultimately depend on whether the zoning ordinance is changed to allow commercial construction in this particular area. Badger estimates the selling price and the associated probabilities for the two possible outcomes as follows:

Outcome	Probability	Estimated Selling Price
Ordinance changed	.25	$500,000
Ordinance not changed	.75	$300,000

Required: 1. Assuming that Badger is conservative and wants to minimize the risk of loss, should it sell the land today "as is," or should it make the improvements? Explain.
2. Using the expected value criterion, should it sell "as is" or make the improvements? Use either a payoff table or a decision tree to help you arrive at the correct decision.

E17–8   **Capital project proposal.** A company is currently evaluating capital investment proposals. One proposal being considered appears attractive, but there is a lot of uncertainty as to the cash flows associated with it.

The project requires an investment today of $250,000 and an estimated salvage value at the end of five years of $20,000. The annual cash flows associated with the project are subject to considerable uncertainty as indicated by the following probability distribution (cash flows are assumed to occur at the end of each of the next five years):

Annual Cash Inflows	Probability of Occurrence
$ 60,000	.40
75,000	.30
92,500	.20
100,000	.10

The company has established a hurdle rate for all capital projects of 16%.

Required: 1. Using the most likely criterion for an estimate of annual cash inflows, compute the net present value for the project. Should the project be accepted?
2. Using the expected value criterion for an estimate of annual cash inflows, compute the net present value for the project. Should the project be accepted?

E17–9   **Relative risk of competing projects.** Two capital projects are being considered. The annual cash flows and the probabilities associated with each of the cash flows were used to calculate their expected values:

Project	Cash Flows	Probability	Expected Value
A	$ 5,000	.25	$1,250
	7,500	.50	3,750
	10,000	.25	2,500
	Total expected value		$7,500
B	$ 4,000	.20	$ 800
	8,000	.60	4,800
	12,000	.20	2,400
	Total expected value		$8,000

Assuming that the two projects have equal lives, Project B appears to be slightly more attractive based on its higher expected value. However, the company is concerned with the relative risk of the two projects.

Required: 1. Compute the standard deviation for each of the projects. What is wrong with using the standard deviation in comparing relative risk of the two projects?
2. Compute the coefficient of variation for each of the projects. Which of the two projects would you select if you want to avoid risk as much as possible?

E17–10 **Sales forecast using expected value.** The Arthur Company is trying to forecast sales for the coming year. The entire forecast is dependent on the introduction of a new product. If the new product is highly successful, the product manager feels that sales of it could reach as high as 8 million units. If only moderately successful, sales would peak at about 5 million units. If the product is a dud, sales are expected to be no higher than 500,000 units. The manager feels that there is a 30% chance that the product will be highly successful, a 50% chance that it will be moderately successful, and a 20% chance that it will be a dud. The product will sell for $2 per unit.

Required: 1. Compute the expected value for sales dollars for the new product. Hint: To keep the calculations manageable, use *$16 million* for the highly successful case, not *$16,000,000* — and the same idea for the other two cases.
2. Compute the standard deviation and the coefficient of variation for the new product.
3, As a manager, would you feel comfortable using the expected value arrived at in 1 above as a point estimate of sales in a budget?

Problems

P17–11 **Capital budgeting for an airline.** The Wildwings Airlines is considering adding a new route to its system. Addition of a new route would require the purchase of a new airplane at a cost of $20 million. The airplane would have a useful life of 10 years and a salvage value at the end of that time of $2 million.

Wildwings would charge $400 for a first-class round-trip ticket and $250 for a coach seat. The company estimates the demand for each flight on the new route on the basis of the following probability distribution:

Seat Type	Number Sold	Probability
First class	0	.10
	5	.20
	10	.40
	15	.20
	20	.10
Coach	20	.10
	40	.15
	80	.30
	120	.30
	150	.10
	180	.05

The Accounting Department estimates the operating costs, such as salaries, fuel, and insurance, for each flight of the proposed route to be $15,000. The company estimates that the new route would be flown 300 times per year.

Required: 1. Compute the expected value for the number of tickets sold per flight, for both first-class and coach seats.
2. Using your answer to 1 above, compute the annual net cash inflow from the new route.
3. Compute the payback period for the acquisition of the new airplane.

4. Compute the net present value for the new airplane, assuming a cost of capital of 12%. For simplicity, assume that the annual net cash inflow computed in 2 above occurs at the end of each year. Should the new plane be purchased?

P17–12 **Alternative distribution channels.** George Eaton, a financial analyst with the Marketing Division of Ajax Industries, has been asked to evaluate the distribution alternatives for a new product. Eaton obtains the aid of two knowledgeable market analysts in the division to estimate the possible net present value of the cash flows from the alternatives and to assess the probabilities of each possibility.

The alternatives being considered are immediate national distribution or regional distribution with national distribution to follow if it is economically feasible. The possible cash flows and the probabilities associated with each alternative are presented below.

	Net Present Value of Cash Flows (in millions of dollars)	Probability of Cash Flow
Immediate national distribution only:		
High national results	$+10.0	.30
Medium national results	+ 2.0	.40
Low national results	− 3.0	.30
		1.00
Regional distribution only:		
Excellent regional results	+ 2.0	.40
Moderate regional results	+ .5	.40
Poor regional results	− 1.0	.20
		1.00
National Distribution Following Regional Distribution:		
National distribution as a consequence of excellent regional results:		
High national results	$+ 9.0	.70
Medium national results	+ 2.0	.20
Low national results	− 2.7	.10
		1.00
National distribution as a consequence of moderate regional results:		
High national results	$+ 8.0	.30
Medium national results	+ 1.8	.40
Low national results	− 3.0	.30
		1.00
National distribution as a consequence of poor regional results:		
High national results	$+ 7.0	.10
Medium national results	+ 1.5	.30
Low national results	− 4.0	.60
		1.00

Required:

1. Formulate the decision tree framework for analyzing whether Ajax Industries should use national distribution or regional distribution with national to follow. Identify the probabilities and expected cash flows for each branch in the tree.

2. Using a maximum expected value criterion for decision-making purposes, indicate whether Ajax Industries should select national distribution or regional distribution with national distribution to follow. Support your decision with appropriate calculations.

3. Suppose Ajax Industries is conservative (risk averse) and wishes to minimize the expected value of taking any loss in making its decision. Determine whether Ajax Industries should select national distribution or regional distribution with national distribution to follow. Support your decision with appropriate calculations.

(CMA Adapted)

P17–13 **Alternatives for idle plant.** Kravel Corporation is a diversified manufacturing company with several manufacturing plants. Kravel's Dayton plant has been supplying parts to midwestern truck manufacturers for over thirty years. The last shipment of truck parts from the Dayton plant will be made in December 19X8. Kravel's management is currently studying three alternatives relating to its soon-to-be-idle plant and equipment in Dayton.

1. Wasson Industries has offered to buy the Dayton plant for $3,000,000 cash on January 1, 19X9.

2. Harr Enterprises has offered to lease the Dayton facility for four years beginning on January 1, 19X9. Harr's annual lease payments would be $500,000 plus 10% of the gross dollar sales of all items produced in the Dayton plant. Probabilities of Harr's annual gross dollar sales from the Dayton plant are estimated as follows:

Annual Gross Dollar Sales	Estimated Probability
$2,000,000	.1
4,000,000	.4
6,000,000	.3
8,000,000	.2

3. Kravel is considering the production of souvenir items to be sold in connection with a world's fair in 19X0 and the 19X2 Olympic Games. The Dayton plant would be used to produce 70,000 items per month at an annual cash outlay of $2,250,000 during 19X9, 19X0, and 19X1. Linda Yetter, vice-president of marketing, has recommended a selling price of $5 per item and believes that the items will sell uniformly throughout 19X0, 19X1, and 19X2.

The adjusted basis of the Dayton plant as of the close of business on December 31, 19X8, will be $4,200,000. Kravel has used straight-line depreciation for all capital assets at the Dayton plant: if the Dayton plant is not sold, the annual straight-line depreciation charge for the plant and equipment will be $900,000 each year for the next four years. The market value of the plant and equipment on December 31, 19X2, is estimated to be $600,000.

Kravel requires an after-tax rate of return of 15% for capital investment decisions. Assume that Kravel is subject to a corporate income tax rate of 40% on operating income as well as on any capital gains. Assume that all recurring cash flows take place at the end of the year.

Required: 1. Calculate the present value (at December 31, 19X8) of the expected after-tax cash flows for each of the three alternatives available to Kravel Corporation regarding the Dayton plant.
2. Discuss the additional factors, both quantitative and qualitative, that Kravel Corporation should consider before a decision is made regarding the disposition or use of the idle plant and equipment at the Dayton plant.

(CMA Adapted)

P17–14   **Valuation of materials.** Pribram Company is attempting to value materials for the purpose of quoting a price on a contract. The material involved is 5,000 pounds of X. Each pound of X has a cost, computed on a FIFO basis, of $2. Replacement cost is $2.50 per pound.

If Pribram does not get this contract, there is a 40% probability of it getting another contract at this time. Another alternative available at the present time is to dispose of the materials at a price of $2.10.

Pribram could hold on to the goods for a year. There is a 60% chance that it could get a contract with the Leskovar Company at that time. If it got the Leskovar contract, there is an 80% probability that it would need X for the job. Otherwise, it would sell X at a price of $2.15. The replacement cost of X is estimated to be $2.75 one year from now. Assume that the relevant interest rate is 20%.

Required: What should be the value of material X for the current contract? Show all computations.

P17–15   **Probabilistic operating budget.** The Roberts Company is putting together its budgets for 19X9. John Jones, vice-president of the western region, is responsible for submitting an operating budget for his region. In the past Jones has not felt comfortable with the figures that he has submitted and thus has come to you for advice. You suggest to him that he consider the use of a probabilistic approach rather than the use of a single point estimate for all line items on the budget.

Jones feels that if the region has an exceptionally good year sales volume could reach 500,000 units. An average year would result in sales of 400,000 units, and a poor year of sales would yield only 250,000 units of sales. After some thought, Jones gives the probabilities of these three sales levels to be 15%, 60%, and 25% respectively. Roberts plans to increase the selling price of its single product by 20% over the current selling price of $2 per unit.

Variable manufacturing costs during 19X8 were

Direct materials	$ .65
Direct labor	.50
Variable overhead	.25
Total	$1.40 per unit

The cost of direct materials is expected to increase to $.75 per unit in 19X9. Variable manufacturing costs in 19X9 are dependent on the outcome of the current negotiations with the union. If the union gets the 20% cost of living raise it wants, direct labor cost per unit will increase by 20% over last year. Otherwise direct labor will go up by 10% per unit. Jones thinks that there is a 40% chance that the union will get the higher 20% raise. Variable overhead is based on direct labor hours worked and is not expected to increase over this past year's rate of $.25 per unit.

Variable selling, general, and administrative costs are expected to be $.10 per unit in 19X9, and fixed costs are estimated at $50,000 for the year.

Required:

1. Using a decision tree approach, prepare a probabilistic budget of operating income for the western region of the Roberts Company for 19X9. Combine variable manufacturing and selling, general, and administrative costs in your budget.

2. Jones wants some feel for the possible variation in the budgeted amounts. Prepare a report indicating for each of the items on the budget prepared in 1 above, the expected value, standard deviation, and coefficient of variation. Also, provide Jones with a sufficient explanation of each of these three statistics.

P17–16 **Probabilistic operating budget for a public utility.** The Midwest Public Utility Company is engaged in the generation and sale of electricity and the production and sale of natural gas in a large metropolitan area. Sales of electricity, stated in kilowatt hours (KWH), and natural gas, stated in million cubic feet (MCF), account for all of the company's revenues.

Because Midwest is a utility, it is subject to strict regulation by a federal commission, and revenues are closely tied to the approval, or denial, of rate increases by the commission. The current rates for the company's two products result in average revenue per kilowatt hour of electricity of $4 and average revenue per million cubic feet of natural gas of $1.20 (these are averages of the rates for sales to residential, commercial, and industrial customers). The company has requested a 20% increase in both rates for 19X2. Management feels that the probability of the rate increases being approved is 70%.

Total revenues for each product are found by multiplying the average rate times the units of each product sold. Usage of electricity and natural gas by the utility's customers depends on a number of factors, particularly population trends and weather. Census statistics show a leveling off of the population in the area in the last few years. The weather, however, is the variable that presents the company with more of a problem in forecasting revenues. If the area experiences a particularly cold winter season, usage of natural gas for heating purposes increases over the normal usage. Similarly, if the summer is particularly hot, electric revenues rise due to increased use of air conditioners and other cooling devices.

Faced with the difficulty of forecasting the weather, Midwest decided to hire a meteorologist. His predictions for 19X2 are summarized below:

Season	Outcome	Probability
Winter	Normal	.60
	Unusually cold	.40
Summer	Normal	.80
	Unusually hot	.20

Management forecasts the following levels of usage for the four possible combinations of weather during 19X2:

Weather Conditions	Gas (MCF) (in thousands of units)	Electric (KWH) (in thousands of units)
Normal winter and summer	50,000	20,000
Normal winter and hot summer	50,000	25,000
Cold winter and normal summer	60,000	20,000
Cold winter and hot summer	60,000	25,000

Midwest has two major variable costs: fuel (primarily coal) used in the generation of electricity and natural gas purchased for resale. The cost last year of each kilowatt hour of electricity generated was $1. The cost of gas for resale was $.70 per MCF. The company estimates a 10% increase in each of these variable costs in 19X2. Other variable expenses are estimated to be 5% of gross revenues in 19X2, and total fixed costs are budgeted at $30 million.

Required:

1. Prepare a decision tree to identify the different possible outcomes for Midwest's operating income and the expected value for operating income for the year 19X2.
   (Hint: Your decision tree should have 8 branches in total.)
2. Prepare an operating profit budget for Midwest for 19X2, indicating the expected value for each line item on the budget. The operating income should agree with the amount on your decision tree in 1 above.
3. Management of Midwest is concerned about the potential for variation from the budgeted operating income. Compute the standard deviation and coefficient of variation for operating income and explain the significance of both numbers.

P17–17 **Order size for a perishable product.** The Jessica Co. has been searching for more formal ways to analyze its alternative courses of action. The expected value decision model was among those considered. In order to test the effectiveness of the expected value model, a one-year trial in a small department was authorized.

This department buys and resells a perishable product. A large purchase at the beginning of each month provides a lower cost than more frequent purchases and also assures that Jessica Co. can buy all of the item that it wants. Unfortunately, if too much is purchased, the product unsold at the end of the month is worthless and must be discarded.

If an inadequate quantity is purchased, additional quantities probably cannot be purchased. If any should be available, they would probably be of poor quality and be overpriced. Jessica chooses to lose the potential sales rather than furnish poor quality product. The standard purchase arrangement is $50,000 plus $.50 for each unit purchased for orders of 100,000 units or more. Jessica is paid $1.25 per unit by its customers.

The needs of Jessica's customers limit the possible sales volumes to only four quantities per month—100,000, 120,000, 140,000, or 180,000 units. However, the total quantity needed for a given month cannot be determined prior to the date that Jessica must make its purchases. The sales managers are willing to place a probability estimate on each of the four possible sales volumes each month. They noted that the probabilities for the four sales volumes change from month to month because of the seasonal nature of the customers' business. Their probability estimates for December 19X8 sales units are 10% for 100,000, 30% for 120,000, 40% for 140,000, and 20% for 180,000.

Required:

1. What quantity should be ordered for December 19X8 if the expected value decision model is used?
2. Suppose that Jessica could ascertain its customers' needs prior to placing its purchase order rather than relying on the expected value decision model. How much would it pay to obtain this information for December?

(CMA Adapted)

P17–18 **Capital budgeting for an oil company.** Texas Gold is a large oil and gas exploration company with primary interests in off-shore drilling. This form of drilling is extremely costly and also subject to a high degree of risk. One of the newer members of the corporate staff, John Wells, has suggested that the company use probability analysis in making decisions on drilling at certain locations. The staff has asked Wells to illustrate how the technique could be used for a proposed drilling site — Site 101 — that the company is considering.

Wells consults with the company's geologists to determine the likelihood of finding oil at Site 101. The geologists attach the following probabilities to each of three possible outcomes:

Outcome of Drilling	Probability
Dry well	.40
Moderately successful	.30
Highly successful	.30

A dry well is defined as one that contains no oil or so little oil that it is not economically feasible to go beyond the initial drilling. The geologists estimate that a moderately successful well will result in the availability of 250,000 barrels of oil from the hole in each of the next three years. The company would be able to pump 400,000 barrels of oil for each of the next three years from a highly successful well.

The initial cost to drill a well is currently $1,800,000. Any oil from this year's drilling at Site 101 could be sold for $10 per barrel. Wells estimates that the selling price will go up by 10% in each of the following two years. Variable production costs are currently $6 per barrel and are also expected to increase by 10% in each of the next two years.

Texas Gold has a hurdle rate of 16% for all capital projects. Assume that all cash flows, other than the initial investment in the well, occur at year end. Finally, assume that Texas Gold is able to sell all of the output of the well in each of the three years.

Required:

1. Determine the net present value of the capital project assuming Texas Gold uses the expected value criterion.
2. Assume the company uses the most likely criterion in deciding whether to drill the hole. Should the hole be drilled? Explain.

P17–19 Decision tree for marketing strategy. Tastee-Cola produces and sells nationally a popular soft drink and has enjoyed good profits for many years. However, in recent years its sales volume has not grown with the general market. This lack of growth is due to the increasing popularity of diet soft drinks and the fact that Tastee-Cola has not entered the diet soft drink market.

Tastee-Cola is now developing its own diet drink and is considering potential marketing strategies. Introducing the new diet drink nationally would require a large commitment of resources for a full nationwide promotion and distribution campaign. In addition, there is some risk in a nationwide introduction because Tastee-Cola is a late entry in the diet soft drink market. Tastee-Cola's advertising agency has helped assess the market risk and convinced the Tastee-Cola management that there are only two reasonable alternative strategies to pursue:

Strategy 1.

Perform a test advertising and sales campaign in a limited number of states for a six-month period. Tastee-Cola would decide whether to introduce the diet drink nationally on the basis of the results of the test campaign.

Strategy 2.

Conduct a nationwide promotion campaign and make the new diet drink available in all fifty states immediately without conducting any test campaign. The nationwide promotion and distribution campaign would be allowed to run for a full two years before a decision would be made to continue the diet drink nationally.

Tastee-Cola management believes that if Strategy 2 is selected there is only a 50% chance of its being successful. The introduction of the diet drink nationally will be considered a success if $40 million of revenue is generated while $30 million of variable costs are being incurred during the two-year period that the nationwide promotion and distribution campaign is in effect. If the two-year nationwide campaign is unsuccessful, revenues are expected to be $16 million and variable costs will be $12 million. Total fixed costs for the two-year period will amount to $6 million regardless of the result.

The advertising agency consultants recognize that if Strategy 1 is selected there is a chance that the test will indicate Tastee-Cola should conduct a nationwide promotion and distribution campaign when, in fact, a nationwide campaign would be unsuccessful. Also, the consultants recognize that there is a chance that the test results will indicate that Tastee-Cola should not conduct a nationwide promotion and distribution campaign when, in fact, a nationwide campaign would be successful.

Required:

1. Represent Tastee-Cola's decision problem through the use of a tree diagram. The tree diagram should identify all decision alternatives and possible outcomes.
2. Calculate the expected monetary value (EMV) of Strategy 2 for Tastee-Cola.
3. Assume that Strategy 1, the test campaign, could predict perfectly whether or not a nationwide campaign would be successful. Using EMV as the decision criterion, calculate the maximum dollar amount that Tastee-Cola should be willing to pay for the perfect information.

(CMA Adapted)

P17–20   Decision table for shipping alternatives. The Jon Co. has just agreed to supply Arom Chemical Inc. with a substance critical to one of Arom's manufacturing processes. Due to the critical nature of this substance, Jon Co. has agreed to pay Arom $1,000 for any shipment that is not received by Arom on the day that it is required.

Arom establishes a production schedule that enables it to notify Jon Co. of the necessary quantity 15 days in advance of the required date. Jon can produce the substance in 5 days. However, capacity is not always readily available, which means that Jon may not be able to produce the substance for several days. Therefore, there may be occasions when only one or two days are available to deliver the substance. When the substance is completed by Jon Co.'s Manufacturing Department and released to its Shipping Department, the number of days remaining before Arom Chemical Inc. needs the substance will be known.

Jon Co. has undertaken a review of delivery reliability and costs of alternative shipping methods. The results are presented in the following table:

		Probability That the Shipment Will Take X Days					
Shipping Method	Costs per Shipment	1	2	3	4	5	6
Motor freight	$100	—	—	.10	.20	.40	.30
Air freight	$200	—	.30	.60	.10	—	—
Air express	$400	.80	.20	—	—	—	—

Required:

1. Prepare a payoff matrix to indicate the expected value (in terms of shipping cost) for each mode of transportation.
2. Based on the table prepared in 1 above, prepare a decision table that can be used by Jon Co.'s shipping clerk to decide which delivery alternative to select, given the number of days until a shipment is needed by Arom.

(CMA Adapted)

P17–21 **Variance investigation; payoff table.** The Dilco Company sells three grades of gasoline: regular, premium, and "regular plus," which is a mixture of regular and premium. Regular plus is advertised as being "at least 50% premium." Although any mixture containing 50% or more premium gas could be sold as "regular plus," it is less costly to use exactly 50%. The amount of premium gas in the mixture is determined by one small valve in the blending machine. If the valve is properly adjusted, the machine provides a mixture that is 50% premium and 50% regular. Assume that if the valve is out of adjustment, the machine provides a mixture that is 60% premium and 40% regular. Once the machine is started, it must continue until 100,000 gallons of "regular plus" have been mixed.

Available cost data are as follows:

Cost per gallon:	
Premium	$.64
Regular	$.60
Cost of checking the valve	$80.00
Cost of adjusting the valve	$40.00

Subjective estimates of the probabilities of the valve's condition are estimated to be:

Condition	Probability
Valve in adjustment	.70
Valve out of adjustment	.30

Required: With the aid of a payoff table, determine whether the valve should be checked and adjusted, if necessary, before each batch of 100,000 gallons of "regular plus" is mixed.

(CMA Adapted)

CHAPTER 18

Funds Flow Statements: Cash and Working Capital

Learning Objectives

After reading this chapter you should be able to:

1. Appreciate the importance of the funds statement to management in analyzing operations.

2. Identify the major sources and uses of funds.

3. Be able to prepare a funds statement on the working capital basis.

4. Be able to prepare a cash basis funds statement using the indirect approach.

5. Be able to prepare a cash basis funds statement using the direct approach.

The **statement of changes in financial position** is an important statement for external users, such as stockholders and creditors, as well as for the managers of a company. In fact, in 1971 the accounting profession elevated the statement to the status of the balance sheet and the income statement by requiring it in published annual reports. Although the "Statement of Changes in Financial Position" is the most descriptive title for the statement, other names are often used in practice, such as: statement of sources and uses, statement of funds flow, or simply the **funds statement.** Because of the popularity and simplicity of the title "Funds Statement," it will be used throughout the remainder of the chapter.

We begin with a simple example to illustrate the purpose of the funds statement. Next, we identify the most common types of sources and uses of funds. The T-account approach to preparation of the statement on a working capital basis is then illustrated. Finally, we will see how we can extend this approach to prepare the statement on a cash basis.

Purpose of the Statement

The purpose of the funds statement is to summarize the financing and investing activities of a business for a period of time, normally a year, although a shorter time period is possible. The important point to note is that the funds statement is a flow statement rather than a position statement. In this respect, the funds statement is similar to the other basic flow statement, the income statement. A logical question at this point might be: why are two flow statements necessary? Doesn't the income statement tell us everything that we need to know about the activity of the business for the period? A simple example will help to answer these questions and to underscore the importance of the funds statement.

A Simple Example

Consider the following possible discussion between the owner of a small service-oriented business and the owner's accountant. After a successful first year in business in which he earned a profit of $100,000, the owner is reviewing the income statement for the second year, as presented in Exhibit 18–1 (page 652).

The owner is pleased with the results and asks to see the balance sheet. Comparative balance sheets for the first two years are presented in Exhibit 18–2.

Where Did the Cash Go?

At first glance, the owner is surprised to see the significant decline in the cash account. He immediately presses the accountant for answers. With

EXHIBIT 18–1

Income Statement – Year Two	
Revenues	$400,000
Depreciation expense	$ 50,000
All other expenses	100,000
Total expenses	$150,000
Net income	$250,000

EXHIBIT 18–2

Comparative Balance Sheets		
	End of	
	Year One	Year Two
Cash	$150,000	$ 50,000
Plant and equipment	350,000	600,000
Accumulated depreciation	(100,000)	(150,000)
Total assets	$400,000	$500,000
Notes payable	$150,000	$100,000
Common stock	200,000	250,000
Retained earnings	50,000	150,000
Total equities	$400,000	$500,000

such a profitable year, where has the cash gone? Specifically, why has cash decreased by 300% while income rose by 250%?

The accountant begins his explanation to the owner by pointing out that income on a strict cash basis is even *higher* than the reported $250,000. Because depreciation expense is not an expense that uses cash (cash was used when the plant and equipment was purchased, not when it is depreciated), cash provided from operations is calculated as follows:

Net income	$250,000
Add back: depreciation expense	50,000
Cash provided from operations	$300,000

Further, the accountant reminds the owner of the additional $50,000 that he invested in the business during the year and carries the analysis one step further:

Net income	$250,000
Add back: depreciation expense	50,000
Cash provided from operations	$300,000
Other sources of funds:	
Additional investment by owner	50,000
Total sources of funds	$350,000

Now the owner is even more bewildered: with cash from operations of $300,000 and his own infusion of $50,000, why did the cash *decrease* by $100,000? The accountant refreshes the owner's memory on three major uses of cash during the year: first, even though the business earned $250,000, the owner withdrew $150,000 in dividends during the year; second, the comparative balance sheets indicate that notes payable with the bank were reduced from $150,000 to $100,000, requiring the use of $50,000 in cash; and finally, the comparative balance sheets show an increase in plant and equipment for the year from $350,000 to $600,000—a sizable investment of $250,000 in new operating assets.

Simple Funds Statement

To summarize what happened to the cash, the accountant prepares a funds statement as displayed in Exhibit 18–3.

Although the owner is not particularly happy with the decrease in cash for the year, he is at least satisfied with the funds statement as an explanation of where the cash came from and how it was used. The statement summarizes for him the important sources or inflows of cash and the uses or outflows of cash. In essence, the funds statement fills a void created with the presentation of just an income statement and a balance sheet.

EXHIBIT 18–3

Simple Funds Statement	
Sources:	
Net income	$ 250,000
Add back: depreciation expense	50,000
Cash provided from operations	$ 300,000
Other sources:	
Additional investment by owner	50,000
Total sources	$ 350,000
Uses:	
Cash dividends paid to owner	$ 150,000
Repayment of notes payable to bank	50,000
Purchase of new plant and equipment	250,000
Total uses	$ 450,000
Net decrease in cash	$(100,000)

Sources and Uses of Funds

Note in the example above the use of the word *funds* to refer to the cash in the business. Further note that in the absence of any accounts receivables or accounts payables, the business is operated on a strict cash basis. Therefore, the funds statement was prepared with cash as the definition of funds and with a "bottom line" equal to the increase or decrease in cash for the period.

Alternatively, the funds statement could be prepared on a **working capital basis** — that is, with funds defined as current assets minus current liabilities. The important point in preparing a funds statement is that *funds* must be defined. The selection of the most appropriate basis for preparation of the statement will depend on the uses to which the statement is to be put. For years the working capital basis was favored in annual reports to stockholders. A recent shift in popularity to the **cash basis** has resulted in a change in the rules to require the cash basis in the annual report. However, for the purpose of developing certain key ideas, we will first look at the procedures for preparation of a funds statement on a working capital basis and then learn how the statement can be altered to reflect a cash basis.

Funds Defined as Working Capital

Consider the basic accounting equation:

$$\text{Assets} = \text{Liabilities} + \text{Owners' equity}$$

Next, the equation can be expanded to distinguish between current and noncurrent items:

$$\text{Current assets} + \text{Noncurrent assets} = \text{Current liabilities} \\ + \text{Noncurrent liabilities} \\ + \text{Owners' equity}$$

Finally, the equation can be rearranged to group current items together and noncurrent items together:

$$\text{Current assets} - \text{Current liabilities} = \text{Noncurrent liabilities} \\ + \text{Owners' equity} \\ - \text{Noncurrent assets}$$

The rationale for this last step should be evident: funds, defined as working capital or current assets less current liabilities, are now isolated on the left side of the equation, and all other accounts are on the right side. *Logic would dictate that for there to be a change in the left side of the equation, that is, a change in working capital, there must be a change in the right side, that is, a change in the noncurrent or long-term accounts.* For example, when an account receivable is collected, cash is increased, but there is no change in funds defined as working capital. The importance of this idea cannot be overemphasized. The explanations as to why working capital changed during the year are found by analyzing the changes in the noncur-rent accounts.

Three Types of Transactions

Although a business may enter into thousands of different types of transac-tions during any given year, these transactions could be categorized into three basic types:

1. *Transactions affecting only current or working capital accounts:* A business records many of these transactions every day. Inventory is purchased on credit — the journal entry would be

Debit: Inventory
    Credit: Accounts Payable

Consider the follow-up to this transaction. The account payable is paid:

Debit: Accounts Payable
    Credit: Cash

The important point to note about both of these transactions is that only working capital accounts are involved. From an informational point of view, this type of transaction is of no value. Stated another way, if a transaction does not result in a net change in the amount of working capital, then it is of no value in explaining why funds, or working capital, went up or down during the year.

2. *Transactions affecting both current and noncurrent accounts:* This type of transaction is probably not as common as the first type, but still many examples exist. A five-year note is signed at the bank:

Debit: Cash
    Credit: Long-Term Notes Payable

Or new plant and equipment is purchased for cash:

Debit: Plant and Equipment
    Credit: Cash

Each of these transactions results in either a net increase (the borrowing at the bank) or a net decrease (the purchase of equipment) in working capital. These are the types of transactions that are important in preparing the funds statement on a working capital basis. Recall the accounting equation presented earlier:

Current assets − Current liabilities = Noncurrent liabilities
                                    + Owners' equity
                                    − Noncurrent assets

Each of these transactions affects both sides of the equation and therefore tells us about either a net inflow or source of funds (the borrowing) or a net outflow or use of funds (the purchase of equipment).

3. *Transactions affecting only noncurrent accounts:* There are probably even fewer of these transactions. Consider a variation of the transaction earlier in which plant and equipment was purchased for cash. Assume that the plant and equipment was acquired by signing a five-year note at the bank. In fact, the transaction is a combination of the two transactions in 2 above:

Debit: Plant and Equipment
    Credit: Notes Payable

At first glance, this entry does not appear to have a place on the funds statement—no current accounts are affected, and there is no change in the amount of working capital. However, consider the *substance* of the transaction rather than just its *form*. How does the result of this transaction differ in substance from the two earlier transactions? It does not. The transactions in 2 above resulted in the recognition of a source of funds (from the borrowing) and a use of funds (from the acquisition). Even though no working capital was directly involved in the single transaction in 3, it contains the same informational value as the two individual transactions and should be reflected on the funds statement. In other words, the exchange was *both* an important source of funds and a use of funds, even though the net effect on working capital is zero.

One final word of caution regarding the third category of transaction: not all of these are important financing and investing activities that should be reflected on the funds statement. For example, consider the entry to record a stock dividend:

Debit: Retained Earnings
    Credit: Common Stock

Even though this qualifies as a transaction affecting only noncurrent accounts, it does not result in any important information to be shown on the funds statement. No significant financing or investing activities took place. The transaction would, of course, be reflected on a statement of retained earnings.

Common Sources and Uses

We have concluded that we are primarily interested in transactions affecting *both* current and noncurrent accounts. Three major categories of noncurrent accounts make up the right side of our equation: (1) noncurrent or long-term liabilities; (2) owners' equity, which consists of capital stock accounts and retained earnings; and (3) noncurrent or long-term assets. Logically, increases in the left and right side of the equation tell us about sources or inflows of funds, and decreases in the left and right side indicate uses or outflows of funds:

$$\text{Working capital (WC)} = \text{Long-term liabilities (LTL)}$$
$$+ \text{ Capital stock (CS)}$$
$$+ \text{ Retained earnings (RE)}$$
$$- \text{ Long-term assets (LTA)}$$

Abbreviating, WC = LTL + CS + RE − LTA. Therefore, increases in WC (or *sources* of WC) result from

1. Increases in LTL,
2. Increases in CS,
3. Increases in RE, or
4. Decreases in LTA.

Decreases in WC (or *uses* of WC) result from

1. Decreases in LTL,
2. Decreases in CS,
3. Decreases in RE, or
4. Increases in LTA.

Each of the four categories of sources of funds and four categories of uses of funds will now be explored in detail.

Major Sources of Funds

1. *Increases in long-term liabilities:* A source of funds for most businesses is long-term borrowings. Management is confronted with the decision as to the most appropriate (and available) source of financing for operations at the time that a new business is started, as well as during the life of the entity. The two primary choices are debt financing and equity financing. The former involves borrowing to finance operations, whereas equity financing involves the sale of stock in the entity. Certainly all businesses must start with a certain amount of equity financing, regardless of whether they are organized as a proprietorship, a partnership, or a corporation.

   Determining the proper mix of debt and equity financing is one of the most critical tasks for the managers of any business — no matter how big or small it may be. The ratio of existing debt to equity is a crucial ingredient in any banker's decision about whether to loan money to a business. Bankers must attempt to evaluate the likelihood that their loan will be repaid, and an unusually high debt to equity ratio could have an adverse impact on their decision to make the loan.

   Various sources of long-term borrowings are available to businesses, depending to some degree on the size of the business. For example, only large companies are able to issue bonds to raise funds. For large companies, the sale or issuance of bonds can represent a significant source of funds. Smaller companies rely more on direct borrowings from banks and other financial institutions for funds.

2. *Increases in capital stock:* As mentioned earlier, all companies rely on the owners to provide some of the funds. Assuming the corporate form of organization, common stock is issued to provide the initial financing. At a later point in time this may be supplemented with the sale of additional common stock or possibly with the issuance of preferred stock. Just as management must be constantly concerned with the proper mix of debt and equity, it also must attempt to find the best mix of common and preferred stock. The company is not bound to pay any dividends on common stock but must pay dividends to preferred stockholders before any dividends can be paid to common stockholders. Also, the preferred stockholder has priority over the common stockholder in the event of liquidation of the business. These are just two of the more important concerns of management in trying to find the best mix of common and preferred stock.

3. *Increases in retained earnings:* Retained earnings increase as a result of the profitable operation of the company. Through the closing process at the end of the period, net income is transferred to the retained earnings account. Although debt and additional equity financing *may be* sources of funds, it is absolutely *necessary* that operations, or the earning of net income, be a source of funds for a business to continue in existence. Stated differently, a company may look to outsiders for some of their funds, or to the stockholders for additional investments, but eventually it is imperative that funds be generated *internally* through profitable operations.

4. *Decreases in long-term assets:* Sales of long-term assets, such as plant and equipment, are not generally a significant source of funds. The distinctive feature of all long-term assets is their use in the operations of the business. They are acquired with the intention of using them to successfully operate the business, not with the intent of resale, as is true for inventory. Occasionally, however, plant and equipment may no longer be needed and are offered for sale.

Major Uses of Funds

1. *Decreases in long-term liabilities:* A principal use of funds for most companies is the repayment of existing liabilities. Management must be constantly aware of the maturity dates of all outstanding debt and make the necessary plans for their retirement. Some companies establish sinking funds so that sufficient funds will be available to retire bonds. Another technique is to issue serial bonds. For example, $10 million of

bonds might be sold by issuing five separate series of $2 million, each series with a different maturity date. In this way, it is not necessary to come up with $10 million all at once—the repayment is spread out over a series of years.

2. *Decreases in capital stock:* Investments by the owners are intended to be permanent. Once in a while, funds will be used to return the investment of some owners. In fact, recently, corporations have issued *redeemable* preferred stock. Such stock is normally redeemable at the option of the owner and in this respect is a hybrid instrument somewhere between debt and stock. Neither the redemption of preferred stock nor the reacquisition of common stock is a major use of funds for most companies.

3. *Decreases in retained earnings:* Just as profitable operations represent a source of funds, unprofitable operations, resulting in a net loss for the period, represent a use of funds. An excess of expenses requiring the use of working capital (depreciation does *not* require the use of working capital) over the revenues of the period will result in a drain on the company's funds and can be tolerated for only a limited period of time. The history of U.S. business is replete with examples of companies that went bankrupt because operations did not generate sufficient funds to pay the creditors.

A decrease in retained earnings may result from a use of funds other than unprofitable operations. Some businesses use a significant amount of their funds to pay dividends to stockholders. Cash dividends paid to both common and preferred stockholders are an important use of funds and must be properly planned and controlled by management. Many companies have established dividend policies and are proud of their uninterrupted record of dividend payments to stockholders. Normally, a dividend will be paid only in years in which the company is profitable, and even then, management must make a decision whether to reward the owners with a dividend or to retain the funds in the business. Management may decide that reinvesting the funds in additional inventory and plant and equipment is more in the long-range interests of the stockholders than paying dividends is.

4. *Increases in long-term assets:* The acquisition of plant and equipment is a major use of funds for almost all types of businesses. At the least, old plant and equipment must be replaced as they wear out. More likely, companies will not only replace existing assets but acquire additional operational assets during their growth years. Growth is, in fact, a primary objective of most corporations in this country. The acquisition of long-term assets includes not only individual assets, but often the purchase of entire businesses. Such acquisitions represent a significant use of funds for growth-oriented companies.

Summary of Major Sources and Uses

The following list is a summary of the most common sources and uses of funds:

Sources	Uses
Issuance of bonds	Retirement of bonds
Borrowing on long-term notes	Repayment of notes
Issuance of stock	Retirement of stock
Profitable operations	Unprofitable operations
Sale of plant and equipment	Acquisition of plant and equipment
	Payment of cash dividends

Preparation of a Funds Statement — Working Capital Basis

The procedures for preparation of a funds statement on a working capital basis follow logically from the expanded equation as developed earlier:

$$\text{Current assets} - \text{Current liabilities} = \text{Noncurrent liabilities} \\ + \text{Owners' equity} \\ - \text{Noncurrent assets}$$

T-accounts will be used to analyze the changes in the accounts on the right side of the equation (the noncurrent accounts). Additionally, a single T-account will be used to analyze *all* of the changes in the current accounts (working capital). At the same time, the single T-account for working capital will represent a rough draft of the funds statement itself. By analyzing, and accounting for, the changes in the noncurrent accounts we will also be explaining the increases (sources) and the decreases (uses) in working capital.

Exhibit 18–4 shows a combined statement of income and retained earnings for the Dixon Company for the year ended December 31, 19X6.

Comparative balance sheets are the key to the preparation of the funds statement. Beginning and ending balance sheets for Dixon Company are presented in Exhibit 18–5 (page 662).

Analysis of Changes in Working Capital

Before analyzing the noncurrent accounts and preparing a rough draft of the funds statement, a preliminary step is in order. An **analysis of working capital** simply involves computing the change in each of the working capital accounts to find the net increase or decrease in funds for the period. This number is a proof or check on the net increase or decrease in funds as shown on the funds statement. In fact, unlike the balance sheet or the income statement, the "bottom line" or answer to a funds statement (that is, the amount of sources less uses, or change in working capital) is known before the statement is ever prepared—simply by doing an analysis of changes in the working capital accounts. An analysis of changes in working capital for Dixon Company is presented in Exhibit 18–6.

EXHIBIT 18–4

DIXON COMPANY
Combined Statement of Income and Retained Earnings
For the Year Ended December 31, 19X6
(all amounts in thousands of dollars)

Sales revenue	$1,500
Cost of goods sold	1,000
Gross profit	$ 500
Selling, general, and administrative expense	$ 100
Depreciation expense	50
Total operating expense	$ 150
Operating income	$ 350
Interest expense	50
Net income before tax	$ 300
Income tax expense	120
Net income	$ 180
Add: Beginning retained earnings	150
Less: Cash dividends declared	80
Ending retained earnings	$ 250

T-Account Approach

The T-account approach to preparing the funds statement will now be demonstrated using the information for the Dixon Company. Each noncurrent account on the comparative balance sheets is analyzed to find the various explanations for the net increase in working capital for the year of $50,000. The T-account approach involves recreating entries for the events of the period. The key point throughout the process is that *increases in the right side of the equation result in sources of funds and decreases in the right side of the equation result in uses of funds.*

Analysis of Noncurrent Accounts

1. *Retained earnings:* The starting point in the process is normally the retained earnings account. Entry 1 involves taking the net income of $180 and crediting it to the retained earnings account and debiting it to the summary account for working capital (this summary account represents a rough draft of the funds statement):

Working Capital			**Retained Earnings**	
(1) +180			150	Beg.
			+180	(1)
			250	End

EXHIBIT 18—5

DIXON COMPANY
Comparative Balance Sheets
December 31, 19X5 and 19X6
(all amounts in thousands of dollars)

	12/31/X5	12/31/X6
Cash	$ 100	$ 65
Accounts receivable	50	25
Inventory	175	275
Prepaid insurance	25	15
Total current assets	$ 350	$ 380
Land	$ 150	$ 50
Plant and equipment	600	850
Less: accumulated depreciation	(100)	(150)
Total long-term assets	$ 650	$ 750
Total assets	$1,000	$1,130
Accounts payable	$ 100	$ 50
Income taxes payable	50	80
Total current liabilities	$ 150	$ 130
Bonds payable	$ 400	$ 250
Common stock	$ 300	$ 500
Retained earnings	150	250
Total stockholders' equity	$ 450	$ 750
Total equities	$1,000	$1,130

EXHIBIT 18—6

DIXON COMPANY
Analysis of Changes in Working Capital
For the Year Ended December 31, 19X6

Account	12/31/X5	12/31/X6	Change
Cash	$100	$ 65	$ (35)
Accounts receivable	50	25	(25)
Inventory	175	275	100
Prepaid insurance	25	15	(10)
Total current assets	$350	$380	$ 30
Accounts payable	$100	$ 50	$ (50)
Income taxes payable	50	80	30
Total current liabilities	$150	$130	$ (20)
Working capital	$200	$250	
Net increase in working capital			$ 50

2. Thus far we have accounted for a $180 increase in the retained earnings account. However, the account increased by only a *net* amount of $100 for the year. The most likely explanation for the debit to the account for $80 (the difference between the $180 net income and the net increase in the account of $100) is the payment of a cash dividend. Exhibit 18–4 confirms this suspicion — cash dividends of $80 were in fact declared. We can now complete our analysis of the retained earnings account and its effect on working capital:

	Working Capital				Retained Earnings		
(1)	+180					150	Beg.
						+180	(1)
		−80	(2)	(2)	−80		
						250	End

3. *Accumulated depreciation:* Recall the earlier discussion of depreciation. We have made a very broad generalization when we state that the net income of $180 resulted in the same amount of increase in working capital for the period. The assumption that we are making can be stated succinctly as follows: *all revenues result in an increase in working capital and all expenses result in a decrease in working capital.* If this assumption were always 100% accurate, no adjustments would ever have to be made to net income to arrive at funds generated from operations. Most revenues do result in an increase in working capital, or source of funds, as evidenced by either a cash sale or a credit sale. The journal entry for a cash sale is

Debit: Cash
    Credit: Sales Revenue

And the journal entry for a sale on credit is

Debit: Accounts Receivable
    Credit: Sales Revenue

In both cases, there is an increase in working capital equal to the amount of sales revenue. Situations in which revenues do not increase the amount of working capital are not very common and will not be considered any further.

Similarly, most expenses result in a decrease in working capital. Consider the entry to accrue wages:

Debit: Wage Expense
    Credit: Wages Payable

Or the entry to record the cost of inventory sold:

Debit: Cost of Goods Sold Expense
    Credit: Inventory

In both cases, there is a decrease in working capital equal to the expense. Because expenses are deducted in arriving at the net income of the period, and we have shown net income as a source of funds, expenses are appropriately reflected on the funds statement. The alternative would be to list each expense requiring the use of working capital as a separate use on the funds statement. Instead, the "indirect" method of listing net income as a source of funds saves both time and space on the funds statement.

However, now consider the entry to record depreciation:

Debit: Depreciation Expense
    Credit: Accumulated Depreciation

Unlike the two earlier entries, the credit in this entry to record an expense is *not* to a working capital account. Therefore, depreciation expense must be added back to net income to arrive at the amount of funds generated from operations. The erroneous conclusion is sometimes made that depreciation is a source of funds because it appears on the sources side of the funds statement. This is totally inaccurate. The *only* reason that depreciation appears at all on the statement is because the indirect approach to the statement is used. Remember the assumption being made with the indirect approach: all expenses use funds and are therefore properly reflected on the funds statement because they are deducted in computing net income. Because depreciation is an exception to the assumption, it must be added back. Returning now to the T-account analysis:

	Working Capital				*Accumulated Depreciation*	
(1)	+180	−80	(2)		100	Beg.
(3)	**+50**				**+50**	**(3)**
					150	End

4. *Land*: The land account decreased by $100 during the year. Recall that the sale of a noncurrent or long-term asset is a source of funds:

	Working Capital				*Land*		
(1)	+180	−80	(2)	Beg.	150		
(3)	+50					−100	**(4)**
(4)	**+100**			End	50		

5. *Common stock*. This account increased by $200. Recall that the issuance of stock is a source of funds:

	Working Capital				*Common Stock*	
(1)	+180	−80	(2)		300	Beg.
(3)	+50				**+200**	**(5)**
(4)	+100				500	End
(5)	**+200**					

6. *Plant and equipment*: The increase in this account for the year of $250 represents the acquisition of plant and equipment—an important use of funds:

	Working Capital				*Plant and Equipment*	
(1)	+180	−80	(2)	Beg.	600	
(3)	+50	**−250**	**(6)**	**(6)**	**+250**	
(4)	+100			End	850	
(5)	+200					

7. *Bonds payable*: Finally, the bonds payable account decreased by $150, indicating a use of funds for the retirement of the bonds:

	Working Capital				*Bonds Payable*	
(1)	+180	−80	(2)		400	Beg.
(3)	+50	−250	(6)	**(7)**	**−150**	
(4)	+100	**−150**	**(7)**		250	End
(5)	+200					

All of the noncurrent accounts for the Dixon Company have been analyzed. Likewise, the changes in working capital have been explained. A summary of the T-accounts is presented in Exhibit 18–7 (page 666). All that remains to be done is to take the information in the working capital account and prepare a more formal funds statement. The funds statement for Dixon Company is presented in Exhibit 18–8.

Cash Basis for the Funds Statement

Recall the importance of the definition of funds in preparing the statement. Thus far we have concentrated on a working capital definition. Many companies, however, find it more useful to prepare a cash basis funds statement. The management of cash is one of management's most critical duties and is aided by the use of a cash funds statement.

The procedures in the preparation of a funds statement are similar, regardless of whether a working capital or a cash basis is used. First, recall the funds statement for the Dixon Company in Exhibit 18–8. Two questions must be asked: are the various sources of working capital also sources of cash, and are the various uses of working capital also uses of cash? For reasons that will be evident later, we will first look at other sources and uses and then conclude by looking at cash provided from operations.

Two other sources of working capital appear on Dixon Company's funds statement: $100 from the sale of land and $200 from the sale of common stock. A reasonable assumption is that both sales were for cash and therefore belong on a cash basis funds statement as well as on the earlier working capital basis statement.

EXHIBIT 18—7

Dixon Company
Summary of T-Accounts

Working Capital					Retained Earnings		
(1)	+180	−80	(2)			150	Beg.
(3)	+50	−250	(6)	(2)	−80	+180	(1)
(4)	+100	−150	(7)			250	End
(5)	+200						
Net change:	+50						

Accumulated Depreciation				Land		
	100	Beg.	Beg.	150		
	+50	(3)			−100	(4)
	150	End	End	50		

Common Stock				Plant and Equipment		
	300	Beg.	Beg.	600		
	+200	(5)	(6)	+250		
	500	End	End	850		

Bonds Payable			
	400	Beg.	
(7)	−150		
	250	End	

Key to Entries
(1) Record net income.
(2) Declaration of cash dividends.
(3) Record depreciation expense.
(4) Sale of land.
(5) Issuance of common stock.
(6) Acquisition of plant and equipment.
(7) Retirement of bonds.

The same basic idea holds for the three uses of funds in Exhibit 18–8. Not only were these working capital uses of funds, more specifically they were cash uses of funds. All three items will appear on the cash funds statement as well.

Are there ever any differences between the other sources and uses on a working capital basis and a cash basis? Sometimes a difference exists between the effect of dividends on working capital and on cash. Recall the journal entry for the declaration of a cash dividend:

Debit: Retained Earnings
    Credit: Dividends Payable

EXHIBIT 18–8

DIXON COMPANY
Statement of Changes in Financial Position
Working Capital Basis
For the Year Ended December 31, 19X6
(all amounts in thousands of dollars)

Sources:		Uses:	
Working capital from operations:		Declaration of cash dividends	$ 80
Net income	$180	Acquisition of plant and equipment	250
Add back: expenses not requiring the use of		Retirement of bonds	150
working capital:		Total uses of funds	$480
Depreciation expense	50	Net increase in working capital	$ 50
Working capital provided from operations	$230		
Other sources:			
Sale of land	100		
Issuance of common stock	200		
Total sources of funds	$530		

It is the amount of dividends *declared* for the period that is a use on a *working capital* basis. On the other hand, consider the entry for the payment of that same dividend:

Debit: Dividends Payable
    Credit: Cash

This entry, of course, indicates the amount of cash used for dividends. Therefore, it is the amount of dividends *paid* for the period that is a use on a *cash* basis. Because the balance sheet for the Dixon Company does not include a dividends payable account, we can conclude that the amount of dividends declared and paid are the same.

Cash Provided from Operations

Recall the indirect method of computing working capital provided from operations. We started with net income and made adjustments for any revenues or expenses included in income that did not have a corresponding effect on working capital. The same basic approach is used on a cash basis. Just as it was necessary to analyze all non–working capital accounts to explain why working capital changed, it is now necessary to analyze all noncash accounts to explain why cash changed. This requires that all the working capital accounts *except cash* be analyzed.

Accounts Receivable

Accounts receivable for the Dixon Company decreased by $25. This is an indication that it collected more from customers than it sold (assuming that all sales are on credit). A T-account analysis of accounts receivable reveals the following:

Accounts Receivable

Beg. bal.	50		
Add: sales	1,500	Deduct: cash	
End. bal.	25	collected	X

Because we know the amount of sales from the income statement ($1,500), we can now figure out the amount of cash collected: Algebraically, $50 + $1500 − X = $25. Solving for X, we get $1,525 as the cash collections.

Which of the two amounts, sales, or cash collections, is reflected in the net income? Which of the two amounts is relevant for a cash basis funds statement? The answer to the first question is, of course, the sales of $1,500, whereas the relevant amount on a cash basis is $1,525. Therefore, in adjusting the net income number to arrive at cash provided from operations, we must *add* the *decrease* in accounts receivable. Logically, if there had been an increase in accounts receivable, the amount of the increase would be deducted from net income — because this would be an indication we sold more than we actually collected in cash.

Adjustment to net income
 Add back: decrease in accounts receivable + $25

Inventory and Accounts Payable

These two accounts are interrelated, as evidenced by an analysis of the two T-accounts:

Inventory

Beg. bal.	175		
		Deduct: cost of	
Add: purchases	X	goods sold	1,000
End. bal.	275		

Accounts Payable

		Beg. bal.	100
Deduct: cash			
payments	Y	Add: purchases	X
		End. bal.	50

Three amounts are relevant: (1) purchases, (2) cost of goods sold, and (3) cash payments. First, we know the cost of goods sold — from the income statement we see that it is $1,000. If cost of goods sold is $1,000, and we know that inventory increased by $100, then we can compute the amount of purchases to be $1,100. (Algebraically: $175 + X − $1,000 = $275; solving, $X = $1,100.$) Now that we know purchases, the last step is to plug the amount of cash payments: $1,150. (Algebraically: $100 + $1,100 − Y = $50; solving, $Y = $1,150.$)

Recall the two questions that we asked earlier regarding sales and cash collections. The same two questions are now relevant here. First, which of the three numbers has been deducted on the income statement? The answer, of course, is the cost of goods sold of $1,000. And which of the three is relevant on a cash basis funds statement? The answer here is the cash payments of $1,150. We know now that the difference of $150 must be deducted from net income to arrive at cash provided from operations and consists of the interrelated effect of the changes in the two accounts:

Deduct: increase in inventory	$(100)
decrease in accounts payable	(50)
Adjustment to net income	$(150)

Prepaid Insurance

An analysis of the prepaid insurance reveals the following:

Prepaid Insurance

Beg.bal.	25			
Add: cash payments		Deduct: expiration of		
for insurance	X	insurance	10	
End. bal.	15			

The expiration of insurance represents the amount of insurance charged to expense for the year. Unfortunately, the income statement in Exhibit 18–4 does not show a separate line item for insurance. We will assume, for simplicity, that insurance expense is $10 and is included in "selling, general, and administrative expense." Therefore, no additional cash was paid for insurance during the year. Because $10 was deducted from net income but no cash was expended, we must add back the decrease in prepaid insurance:

Adjustment to net income:
  Add back: decrease in prepaid insurance + $10

Income Taxes Payable

Finally, consider the income taxes payable account:

Income Taxes Payable

		Beg. bal.	50
Deduct: cash payments	X	Add: taxes accrued	120
		End. bal.	80

The amount of taxes accrued is the same amount as appears on the income statement for income tax expense: $120. Algebraically, $50 + $120 − X = $80. Solving for X, we get $90 as the cash payment for taxes.

Although the amount deducted on the income statement was the tax expense of $120, the relevant amount on a cash basis is only $90 — the amount paid. Therefore, we add back to net income the increase in income taxes payable:

Adjustment to net income:
  Add back: increase in income taxes payable + $30

Cash Basis Funds Statement for Dixon Company

A completed funds statement for Dixon Company is presented in Exhibit 18–9. Particular attention should be given to the section titled "cash from operations." Note that this is the only section of the statement that differs from the working capital basis statement in Exhibit 18–8. Also note that the net decrease in funds in Exhibit 18–9 — that is, the decrease in cash — agrees with the comparative balance sheets, which also show cash decreased by $35, from $100 down to $65.

EXHIBIT 18–9

DIXON COMPANY
Statement of Changes in Financial Position
Cash Basis
For the Year Ended December 31, 19X6
(all amounts in thousands of dollars)

Sources		Uses	
Cash from operations:		Payment of cash dividends	$ 80
Net income	$180	Acquisition of plant and equipment	250
Add back: depreciation expense	50	Retirement of bonds	150
decrease in accounts receivable	25	Total uses of funds	$480
decrease in prepaid insurance	10		
increase in income taxes payable[a]	30		
Deduct: increase in inventory	(100)		
decrease in accounts payable	(50)		
Cash provided from operations	$145		
Other sources:			
Sale of land	100		
Issuance of common stock	200		
Total sources of funds	$445	Net decrease in cash	$ (35)

[a]Note the logic in the adjustments to net income. A *decrease* in a *current asset* (accounts receivable) is added back. Therefore, an *increase* in a *current liability* (income taxes payable) is also added back. To summarize: increases in cash result from either decreases in current assets or increases in current liabilities, and decreases in cash result from either increases in current assets or decreases in current liabilities.

Direct Approach to Cash from Operations

We have emphasized thus far the **indirect approach** to calculating cash provided from operations: start with the net income for the year and make the necessary adjustments to transform this amount to a cash basis. However, it may be more informative, particularly for use by management, to compute cash provided from operations using a **direct approach.**

The direct approach requires looking at each item on the income statement and making the necessary adjustment to put it on a cash basis. In fact, what we are doing is simply unraveling the accrual basis—that is, returning the income statement to a cash basis. In the last section we made the necessary calculations to put each of the items on a cash basis. For example, our analysis of accounts receivable indicated that if sales were $1,500, and the accounts receivable account decreased by $25, then cash collections must have been $1,500 + $25 or $1,525. A format, using Dixon Company as an example, for converting the income statement to a cash basis is presented in Exhibit 18–10.

EXHIBIT 18–10

Dixon Company
Conversion from Accrual to Cash Basis

Accrual Item	Adjustment	Amount
Sales revenue	Amount reported on income statement:	$1,500
Add:	Decreases in accounts receivable	+25
Deduct:	Increases in accounts receivable	(0)
Equals:	Cash collected from customers	$1,525
Cost of goods sold	Amount reported on income statement:	$1,000
Add:	Increases in inventory	+100
Deduct:	Decreases in inventory	(0)
Add:	Decreases in accounts payable	+50
Deduct:	Increases in accounts payable	(0)
Equals:	Cash paid for inventory	$1,150
Selling, gen., and admin.	Amount reported on income statement:	$ 100
Add:	Increases in prepaid assets (insurance)	+0
Deduct:	Decreases in prepaid assets (insurance)	(10)
Add:	Decreases in accrued liabilities (none)	+0
Deduct:	Increases in accrued liabilities (none)	(0)
Equals:	Cash paid for S, G, & A activities	$ 90
Interest expense	Amount reported on income statement:	$ 50
Add:	Decreases in interest payable (none)	+0
Deduct:	Increases in interest payable (none)	(0)
Equals:	Cash paid for interest	$ 50
Income tax expense	Amount reported on income statement:	$ 120
Add:	Decreases in taxes payable	+0
Deduct:	Increases in taxes payable	(30)
Equals:	Cash paid for taxes	$ 90

EXHIBIT 18–11
Dixon Company
Cash Provided from Operations – Direct Approach

Cash collected from customers	$1,525
Cash payments for:	
Inventory	$1,150
Selling, general, and administrative activities	90
Interest	50
Income taxes	90
Total cash payments	$1,380
Cash provided from operations	$ 145

Using the numbers from Exhibit 18–10, the cash provided from operations with a direct approach is summarized in Exhibit 18–11. Two important observations are made: first, note the absence of depreciation from both exhibits—even though it appears on the income statement, no cash is involved; second, note that the amount of cash provided from operations is the same, $145, whether computed on an indirect basis or a direct basis.

Summary

The statement of changes in financial position, or funds statement, summarizes the financing and investing activities of a business for a period of time. Funds are normally defined as either working capital or cash, although variations are used in practice. The statement supplements the traditional income statement by providing important information on how funds were provided and how they were used during the period.

Preparation of a funds statement on a working capital basis requires the analysis of all noncurrent accounts. An analysis of the long-term accounts reveals the major sources of funds to be from profitable operations, borrowings, the sale of stocks and bonds, and the sale of used plant and equipment. Similarly, major uses of funds are unprofitable operations, cash dividends, repayment of borrowings, retirement of stocks and bonds, and the acquisition of new plant and equipment.

Preparation of a funds statement on a cash basis requires the addition of the noncash working capital accounts to the analysis. As an alternative to the indirect approach, however, cash from operations may be computed directly by computing the cash collected from customers and cash paid for such items as inventory, interest, and taxes.

T-accounts were used throughout the chapter to aid in the preparation of the statement. A variation of the T-account approach involves taking the beginning and ending balances in the accounts and entering them on a worksheet rather than in T-accounts. The worksheet approach is often used in practice when a large number of accounts must be analyzed.

As mentioned at the beginning of the chapter, the funds statement must be included in the annual report to stockholders. Recently, the Financial Accounting Standards Board changed the rules for inclusion of the statement in the annual report. The statement must now be prepared on a cash basis with major sections devoted to the operating, investing, and financing activities of the business. Our emphasis throughout the chapter has been on the use of the statement for internal decision-making purposes. Management, of course, has more flexibility in preparing the statement for its own use. For example, a different definition of *funds,* as well as an alternative format, might be used in the statement prepared for internal use as opposed to the version prepared for outsiders.

A properly prepared funds statement can be an invaluable aid to management. Emphasis on the income statement alone has the potential to lead management into making incorrect decisions. A large amount of income, for example, should not always result in the payment of a dividend. Analysis of the funds statement may indicate a deficiency of funds available for such uses. Management must consider all tools at their disposal. The funds statement is one of the most important of these tools.

Key Terms

Analysis of working capital is a mathematical check on the accuracy of the "bottom line" of a funds statement, involving the addition of increases in current assets and decreases in current liabilities and the deduction of decreases in current assets and increases in current liabilities, resulting in the net change in working capital.

Cash basis is the preparation of a funds statement that emphasizes the sources and uses of cash.

Direct approach is an approach to the computation of funds from operations in which each source and each use is identified separately — as opposed to the indirect approach in which net income is adjusted.

Funds statement is a popular alternative title for the statement of changes in financial position.

Indirect approach is an approach to the computation of funds from operations in which adjustments are made to net income for revenues and gains not resulting in an inflow of funds (deducted) and expenses and losses not resulting in an outflow of funds (added back).

Statement of changes in financial position is the financial statement summarizing the financing (sources) and investing (uses) activities of a business for a period of time.

Working capital basis is the preparation of a funds statement in which the emphasis is on the sources and uses of working capital — that is, current assets less current liabilities.

Questions

Q18–1 What is the purpose of the funds statement? Explain why the statement is a flow statement rather than a position statement.

Q18–2 Why is it important to define *funds* in preparing the funds statement? What are the two most common definitions of *funds?*

Q18–3 Why are explanations as to why working capital changed during the year (that is, the sources and uses) found by analyzing the changes in the noncurrent accounts?

Q18–4 Using the distinction between current and noncurrent accounts, identify the three basic types of transactions.

Q18–5 Assume that a company purchases a piece of real estate in exchange for shares of its common stock. Should this transaction be reflected on a funds statement? Explain.

Q18–6 Identify the major sources of funds for most companies. Which one of these sources is necessary for a company to stay in business?

Q18–7 Identify the major uses of funds for most companies.

Q18–8 The bottom line or solution to a funds statement can be found before the statement is prepared. Assuming the working capital basis, explain how this can be done.

Q18–9 Explain why depreciation expense must be added back to arrive at the amount of funds generated from operations. Is it because depreciation is a source of funds?

Q18–10 What does it mean to prepare the funds statement using an indirect approach? How does this differ from the direct approach?

Q18–11 Which basis, the working capital or the cash basis, is most appropriate for management's use? What factors should be considered in choosing between the two bases for internal use?

Q18–12 When determining the effect of dividends on funds, why is *declaration* of a cash dividend the critical event if the working capital basis is used? What event is crucial if a cash basis statement is prepared?

Q18–13 Assume that a cash basis funds statement is prepared using the indirect approach. Why is any decrease in accounts receivable for the period added back to net income to arrive at funds generated from operations?

Q18–14 Explain the relationship between inventory and accounts payable relative to the preparation of a cash basis funds statement assuming the use of the indirect approach.

Q18–15 What effect does a decrease in income taxes payable for the period have on cash generated from operations?

Q18–16 Which approach to the preparation of a funds statement is most useful to management—the indirect or the direct approach? Include in your response an explanation of each.

Q18–17 Explain the meaning of the following statement: "preparation of a cash basis funds statement using the direct approach involves an unraveling of the accrual basis—that is, returning the income statement to a cash basis."

Q18–18 Cash generated from operations consists of two elements: cash collections and cash payments. Identify some of the common cash payments that companies must make.

Q18–19 A company has a very profitable year. What explanations might there be for a decrease in the cash account?

Q18–20 A company has a very unprofitable year. What explanations might there be for an increase in the cash account?

Exercises

E18–1 **Effect of transactions on working capital.** The Allen Company has asked for your assistance in preparing a working capital basis funds statement. They are specifically interested in determining the effect of each of the following transactions on working capital. In the blank to the left of each transaction indicate whether the *net* effect of the transaction is to increase (I), decrease (D), or have no effect (NE) on working capital.

    1. Cash collections from customers' open accounts are $10,000 for the period.

    2. Inventory is purchased on account for $2,000.

    3. One of the company's suppliers of inventory is paid $500 in settlement of an open account.

    4. A new office copier is purchased for $6,000. A 90-day note payable is signed.

    5. An empty lot adjacent to the company's factory is purchased for $50,000. The seller of the land agrees to accept a 5-year promissory note as consideration.

    6. Sales on credit for the period are $20,000.

    7. The company's insurance policy is renewed for another 6 months. Cash of $1,000 is paid for the renewal.

    8. Cash dividends of $2,500 are declared, to be paid at a later date.

    9. A long-term note payable of $5,000 is due within the next year and is therefore reclassified as short-term.

    10. Depreciation expense on machinery and equipment for the period is estimated at $15,000.

E18–2 **Common sources and uses.** Listed below are some of the most common sources and uses of funds. A few of the transactions are neither a source nor a use of funds. Indicate for each numbered item whether it is a source (S), a use (U), both (B) a source and a use of funds, or neither (N) a source nor a use of funds. Assume that *funds* is defined as working capital.

    1. A company's own common stock is purchased in the open market and immediately retired.

    2. A company issues preferred stock in exchange for land.

    3. A 60-day loan is obtained at the bank.

    4. Ten-year bonds are issued in exchange for cash.

    5. A company reports a net loss for the year.

    6. A piece of machinery is no longer needed and is sold for cash.

    7. Cash dividends are declared and paid.

    8. A stock dividend is declared and paid.

    9. A 5-year loan is obtained at the bank.

    10. A company reports a net profit for the year.

    11. A creditor is given shares of common stock in the company in return for cancellation of a long-term loan.

    12. New plant and equipment are purchased for cash.

E18–3   **Analysis of changes in working capital.** The Ray Company is in the process of preparing a funds statement. Before proceeding any further, it decides to analyze the changes in working capital. The beginning and ending balances in each of the balance sheet accounts are as follows:

Account	12/31/X8	12/31/X9
Cash	$ 10,000	$ 8,000
Accounts receivable	15,000	20,000
Inventory	25,000	15,000
Prepaid rent	6,000	9,000
Land	75,000	75,000
Plant and equipment	300,000	400,000
Accumulated depreciation	(30,000)	(65,000)
Total assets	$401,000	$462,000
Accounts payable	$ 10,000	$ 12,000
Income taxes payable	5,000	3,000
Short-term notes payable	25,000	35,000
Bonds payable	100,000	75,000
Common stock	150,000	200,000
Retained earnings	111,000	137,000
Total equities	$401,000	$462,000

Required: Prepare, in good form, an analysis of the changes in working capital for the year 19X9.

E18–4   **Funds statement—working capital basis.** Assume the same facts as in E18–3. In addition, assume plant and equipment was acquired for cash during the year and common stock was issued for cash. The income statement for Ray Company for 19X9 is presented below:

Sales revenue	$500,000
Cost of goods sold expense	300,000
Gross profit	$200,000
Operating expenses	$111,000
Depreciation expense	35,000
Total expenses	$146,000
Net income before interest and taxes	$ 54,000
Interest expense	10,000
Net income before taxes	$ 44,000
Income tax expense	18,000
Net income	$ 26,000

Required: Prepare, in good form, a funds statement for 19X9, using the working capital basis. You should not need to use T-accounts to be able to prepare this statement.

E18–5   **Transactions affecting only long-term accounts.** Listed below are five independent transactions. Each transaction is the third type of transaction as discussed in the chapter—a transaction that affects only the long-term accounts.

1. A company issues a 10-year note payable in exchange for an office building. The purchase price is $500,000.
2. One thousand shares of common stock are issued to an inventor in exchange for the rights to a patent held by the inventor. The patent has no ready market value. The market price of the stock is $25 per share.

3. A 5-year note payable in the amount of $30,000 is retired by issuing preferred stock to the holder of the note. The preferred stock has a par value of $10,000.

4. A company declares and issues a 10% stock dividend. The par value of the stock issued is $200,000. The total amount of retained earnings to be capitalized is $500,000.

5. Equipment with a cost of $80,000 is retired. The equipment is fully depreciated and has no salvage value.

Required: For each of the independent cases above, prepare the appropriate journal entry to record the transaction, indicate whether the transaction should be shown on a funds statement, and explain your rationale as to why it should or should not be reflected on the statement.

E18–6 **Effect of transactions on funds—working capital versus cash.** Certain transactions have the same effect on working capital as on cash. Other transactions differ in terms of their effect on the definitions of funds. Listed below are a series of transactions for the month for the Wayne Company.

Required: For each transaction, indicate the effect of the transaction on working capital and cash. Indicate an increase in funds with an I, a decrease with a D, and no effect with a NE.

Transaction	Effect on	
	Working Capital	Cash
1. Customers remit $10,000 in payment of their open accounts.	_____	_____
2. Suppliers are paid $5,000 to settle open accounts with them.	_____	_____
3. A 60-day, $20,000 note payable is signed at the bank.	_____	_____
4. A 5-year, $50,000 note payable is signed at the bank.	_____	_____
5. New equipment is purchased for $100,000 in cash.	_____	_____
6. New equipment is purchased for $75,000 by signing a 3-year note payable.	_____	_____
7. New equipment is purchased for $50,000 by signing a 6-month note payable.	_____	_____
8. Cash dividends of $25,000 are declared; payment will be in 30 days.	_____	_____
9. Cash dividends of $15,000 are declared and paid immediately.	_____	_____
10. Inventory with a cost of $5,000 is purchased on account.	_____	_____
11. Ten-year bonds are issued at face value of $500,000.	_____	_____
12. Credit sales for the month are $80,000.	_____	_____
13. Cash sales for the month are $50,000.	_____	_____
14. Fully depreciated equipment with a cost of $90,000 is retired.	_____	_____
15. Income taxes for the month in the amount of $6,000 are accrued.	_____	_____
16. Income taxes of $5,000 are paid.	_____	_____

E18–7 **Cash provided from operations—indirect approach.** The following current account balances are available from the records of Day Company:

	Account Balances at:	
	12/31/X0	*12/31/X1*
Cash	$ 20,000	$ 17,000
Accounts receivable	35,000	43,000
Inventory	40,000	30,000
Short-term prepayments	15,000	17,000
Total current assets	$110,000	$107,000
Accounts payable	$ 19,000	$ 26,000
Income taxes payable	10,000	6,000
Interest payable	12,000	15,000
Total current liabilities	$ 41,000	$ 47,000
Working capital	$ 69,000	60,000

Net income for the year 19X1 is $40,000. Depreciation expense is $20,000. Assume all sales and all purchases are on account.

Required: Compute cash provided from operations for 19X1. Do *not* attempt to prepare an entire funds statement but only the first section—cash provided from operations.

E18–8 **Cash provided from operations—direct approach.** The direct approach to preparing a cash basis funds statement requires an analysis of the noncash working capital accounts and the effect of the income statement items on these accounts. The Beagle Company reports the following amounts:

	Balance Sheet at:	
	12/31/X8	*12/31/X9*
Debit balances:		
Accounts receivable	$ 6,000	$ 4,000
Inventory	25,000	32,000
Prepaid rent	10,000	7,000
Credit balances:		
Accounts payable	4,500	7,500
Salaries and wages payable	2,500	1,500
Interest payable	1,000	500
Income taxes payable	3,000	4,500

In addition, the income statement for 19X9 is as follows:

Sales revenue	$100,000
Cost of goods sold expense	75,000
Gross profit	$ 25,000
Selling, general, and administrative expenses	$ 8,000
Depreciation expense	3,000
Total operating expenses	$ 11,000

Income before interest and taxes	$ 14,000
Interest expense	3,000
Income before taxes	$ 11,000
Income tax expense	5,000
Net income	$ 6,000

Required: Using T-accounts (for each of the working capital accounts), compute each of the following amounts:

1. Cash collected from customers
2. Cash paid for inventory
3. Cash paid for selling, general, and administrative activities
4. Cash paid for interest
5. Cash paid for taxes

E18–9 **Determine missing amounts — cash from operations.** The computation of cash provided from operations requires the analysis of the noncash working capital accounts. Using T-accounts, determine the missing amounts for each of the following independent cases:

Case One

Accounts receivable, beginning of year	$150,000
Accounts receivable, end of year	100,000
Credit sales for the year	175,000
Cash sales for the year	60,000
Write-offs of uncollectible accounts	35,000
Total cash collections for the year	?

Case Two

Inventory, beginning of year	$ 80,000
Inventory, end of year	55,000
Accounts payable, beginning of year	25,000
Accounts payable, end of year	15,000
Cost of goods sold expense	175,000
Cash payments for inventory (assume all purchases of inventory are on account)	?

Case Three

Prepaid insurance, beginning of year	$ 17,000
Prepaid insurance, end of year	20,000
Insurance expense	15,000
Cash paid for new insurance policies	?

Case Four

Income taxes payable, beginning of year	$ 95,000
Income taxes payable, end of year	115,000
Income tax expense	300,000
Cash payments on taxes	?

E18–10 **Determine missing amounts — working capital.** Preparation of a working capital basis funds statement requires a clear understanding of the relationships among current assets, current liabilities, and the various noncurrent accounts. For each of the following independent cases, determine the missing amounts.

Case One

Current assets	$ 45,000
Noncurrent liabilities	40,000
Capital stock	60,000
Total assets	140,000
Retained earnings	18,000
Current liabilities	?

Case Two

Capital stock	$100,000
Working capital	75,000
Noncurrent assets	150,000
Retained earnings	40,000
Noncurrent liabilities	?

Case Three

Current assets	$ 40,000
Noncurrent liabilities	90,000
Retained earnings	100,000
Capital stock	160,000
Current ratio (current assets/current liabilities)	1.6 to 1
Noncurrent assets	?

E18–11 **Dividends on the funds statement.** The following selected account balances are available from the records of the Smith Company for the two prior years:

	12/31/X7	12/31/X8
Dividends payable	$ 20,000	$ 30,000
Retained earnings	250,000	375,000
Common stock, no par	500,000	550,000

Other information available for the most recent year follows:

a. The company reported net income for the year ended December 31, 19X8, of $285,000.

b. A small stock dividend amounting to $50,000 was declared and distributed during 19X8.

c. Cash dividends are declared at the end of each quarter and paid within the next 30 days of the following quarter.

Required:

1. Using T-accounts, determine the amount of cash dividends *declared* during the year.

2. Based on your answer to 1 above, determine the amount of cash dividends *paid* during the year.

3. Explain which one of the two amounts in 1 and 2 above should be shown on the funds statement. Does it depend on which of the two bases (the working capital or the cash basis) for the statement is being used?

E18–12 **Long-term assets and the funds statement.** The following account balances are taken from the records of Master Company for the past two years (credit balances are in parentheses):

	12/31/X2	12/31/X3
Plant and equipment	$500,000	$750,000
Accumulated depreciation	(200,000)	(160,000)
Patents	80,000	92,000
Retained earnings	(675,000)	(825,000)

Other information available for the most recent year follows:

a. Net income for the year was reported as $200,000.

b. Cash dividends of $50,000 were declared and paid during the year.

c. Depreciation of plant and equipment was $50,000.

d. Plant and equipment with a book value of $60,000 was sold for the same amount during the year.

e. Amortization expense on patents was $8,000.

f. Both new plant and equipment and patents were purchased for cash during the year.

Required:

1. Compute working capital provided from operations.

2. Using T-accounts, determine the amount of plant and equipment and the amount of patents purchased during the year. Indicate where each of these would be shown on a funds statement.

Problems

P18–13   Funds statement—working capital basis. The George Company has just completed another very successful year as indicated by the following income statement:

	For the Year Ended December 31, 19X9
Sales revenue	$1,250,000
Cost of goods sold	700,000
Gross profit	$ 550,000
Operating expenses	150,000
Income before interest and taxes	$ 400,000
Interest expense	25,000
Income before taxes	$ 375,000
Income tax expense	150,000
Net income	$ 225,000

Presented below are the beginning and end-of-the-year balance sheets for George Company.

	12/31/X8	12/31/X9
Cash	$ 90,000	$ 52,000
Accounts receivable	130,000	180,000
Inventory	200,000	230,000
Prepayments	25,000	15,000
Total current assets	$ 445,000	$ 477,000

	12/31/X8	12/31/X9
Land	$ 600,000	$ 750,000
Plant and equipment	500,000	700,000
Accumulated depreciation	(200,000)	(250,000)
Total long-term assets	$ 900,000	$1,200,000
Total assets	$1,345,000	$1,677,000
Accounts payable	$ 148,000	$ 130,000
Other accrued liabilities	63,000	68,000
Income taxes payable	110,000	90,000
Total current liabilities	$ 321,000	$ 288,000
Long-term bank loan payable	300,000	350,000
Common stock	400,000	550,000
Retained earnings	324,000	489,000
Total equities	$1,345,000	$1,677,000

Required:

1. Prepare an analysis of the changes in working capital for the year ended December 31, 19X9.
2. Prepare a funds statement for the year ended December 31, 19X9, using the working capital basis. Dividends declared and paid during the year were $60,000. Operating expenses include $50,000 of depreciation for the year.

P18–14 **Funds statement — cash basis using the indirect approach.** Assume the same facts as in P18–13. The president has come to you and asked some questions about the year's results. He is very impressed with the profit margin of 18% (net income divided by sales revenue). However, he is bothered by the tenuous cash position of the company at the end of the year. One of the conditions of the existing bank loan is that the company always maintain a minimum cash balance of $50,000.

Required:

1. Compute cash provided from operations, starting with net income (that is, the indirect approach).
2. Prepare a funds statement on the cash basis.
3. On the basis of your statement as prepared in 2 above, provide a brief explanation to the president why the cash of the company decreased during such a profitable year. Include in your explanation any recommendations for improving the cash flow of the company in future years.

P18–15 **Funds statement — working capital basis.** The income statement for the Bay Company for the most recent year is as follows:

	For the Year Ended December 31, 19X9
Sales revenue	$ 500,000
Cost of goods sold	400,000
Gross profit	$ 100,000
Operating expenses	180,000
Loss before interest and taxes	$ (80,000)
Interest expense	20,000
Net loss	$(100,000)

Presented below are the beginning and end-of-the-year balance sheets for Bay Company.

	12/31/X8	12/31/X9
Cash	$ 80,000	$ 95,000
Accounts receivable	75,000	50,000
Inventory	150,000	100,000
Prepayments	45,000	55,000
Total current assets	$ 350,000	$ 300,000
Land	400,000	475,000
Plant and equipment	800,000	870,000
Accumulated depreciation	(300,000)	(370,000)
Total long-term assets	$ 900,000	$ 975,000
Total assets	$1,250,000	$1,275,000
Accounts payable	$ 100,000	$ 125,000
Other accrued liabilities	45,000	35,000
Interest payable	10,000	15,000
Total current liabilities	$ 155,000	$ 175,000
Long-term bank loan payable	250,000	340,000
Common stock	400,000	450,000
Retained earnings	445,000	310,000
Total equities	$1,250,000	$1,275,000

Required:

1. Prepare an analysis of the changes in working capital for the year ended December 31, 19X9.
2. Prepare a funds statement for the year ended December 31, 19X9, using the working capital basis. Dividends declared and paid during the year were $35,000. Operating expenses include $70,000 of depreciation for the year.

P18–16 **Funds statement—cash basis using the indirect approach.** Assume the same facts as in P18–15. The president has come to you and asked some questions about the year's results. He is disturbed with the net loss for the year of $100,000. However, he notes that the cash position of the company at the end of the year is improved. He is confused about what appeared to be conflicting signals. "How could we have possibly added to our bank accounts during such a terrible year of operations?" he asks you.

Required:

1. Compute cash provided from operations, by starting with the net loss of $100,000 (that is, the indirect approach).
2. Prepare a funds statement on the cash basis.
3. On the basis of your statement as prepared in 2 above, provide a brief explanation to the president why the cash of the company increased during a year in which the company incurred a loss. Include in your explanation any recommendations for improving the profits in future years.

P18–17 **End of year balance sheet and funds statement—working capital basis.** The balance sheet of the Bulldog Company at the end of the prior year is presented on the next page along with certain other financial information for the current year.

	12/31/X7
Current assets	$ 295,000
Land	300,000
Plant and equipment	500,000
Accumulated depreciation	(150,000)
Investments	100,000
Total long-term assets	$ 750,000
Total assets	$1,045,000

Current liabilities	$ 205,000
Bonds payable	$ 300,000
Common stock	$ 400,000
Retained earnings	140,000
Total stockholders' equity	$ 540,000
Total liabilities and stockholders' equity	$1,045,000

Other information

a. Net income for 19X8 was $70,000.

b. Cash dividends of $25,000 were declared and paid.

c. An additional $150,000 of bonds were issued for cash.

d. Common stock of $50,000 was purchased for cash and retired.

e. Cash purchases of plant and equipment during the year were $200,000.

f. Included in operating expenses was $20,000 in depreciation.

g. An additional $100,000 of bonds were issued in exchange for land.

h. Current assets increased by $15,000 during the year.

Required:

1. Prepare a funds statement for 19X8, using the working capital basis.

2. Prepare a balance sheet at 12/31/X8 for Bulldog Company. Only the *total* current assets and *total* current liabilities need appear on the balance sheet, not the composition of each.

P18–18   **Funds statement—working capital basis—retirement of plant assets.** The Geneva Company is in the process of preparing a working capital basis funds statement for the year ended June 30, 19X9. An income statement for the year and comparative balance sheets at the end of the last two years are shown below.

	For the Year Ended June 30, 19X9
Sales revenue	$550,000
Cost of goods sold	350,000
Gross profit	$200,000
Operating expenses	135,000
Income before interest and taxes	$ 65,000
Interest expense	15,000
Income before taxes	$ 50,000
Income tax expense	17,000
Net income	$ 33,000

	6/30/X8	6/30/X9
Cash	$ 40,000	$ 31,000
Accounts receivable	75,000	90,000
Inventory	95,000	80,000
Prepaid rent	16,000	12,000
Total current assets	$226,000	$213,000
Land	$170,000	$250,000
Plant and equipment	600,000	750,000
Accumulated depreciation	(250,000)	(310,000)
Total long-term assets	$520,000	$690,000
Total assets	$746,000	$903,000
Accounts payable	$148,000	$155,000
Other accrued liabilities	26,000	32,000
Income taxes payable	10,000	8,000
Total current liabilities	$184,000	$195,000
Long-term bank loan payable	130,000	100,000
Common stock	200,000	350,000
Retained earnings	232,000	258,000
Total equities	$746,000	$903,000

Dividends declared and paid during the year were $7,000. Operating expenses include $75,000 of depreciation for the year. Plant assets were sold at book value during the year for $30,000 in cash. New plant assets were purchased for cash during the year.

Required: 1. Prepare an analysis of the changes in working capital for the year ended June 30, 19X9.

2. Prepare a funds statement for the year ended June 30, 19X9, using the working capital basis.

P18–19   **Funds statement—cash basis—both approaches.** Assume the same facts as in P18–18. The president of the company has come to you with a request. She does not feel that a funds statement prepared on a working capital basis is as informative as a cash basis statement. She wants you to prepare a cash basis funds statement for the Geneva Company for this past year.

Required: 1. Compute cash provided from operations, starting with net income (that is, the indirect approach).

2. Prepare a funds statement on the cash basis, using the indirect approach.

3. Using the format in Exhibit 18–10 of the chapter, convert each of the income statement items from an accrual to a cash basis. Assume that all sales are on account and all purchases of inventory are on account.

4. Prepare a funds statement on the cash basis, using the direct approach.

5. Recommend to the president the approach (direct or indirect) that you feel is the most informative. Include in your recommendation the advantages and disadvantages of each approach.

P18–20 **Analysis of The Quaker Oats Company.** The Quaker Oats Company is a multinational company with principal interests in the production of grocery products and the manufacture of toys (through its Fisher-Price Division). The company reported net income for the fiscal year ended June 30, 1985 of approximately $157 million on sales in excess of $3.5 billion.

The Quaker Oats Company's Consolidated Statement of Changes in Financial Position for the two most recent years as reflected in its 1985 annual report is shown on page 687.

Note to students: Two items on Quaker's statement need further explanation. Deferred income taxes represent amounts that will be paid to the government in future periods. Certain items are treated differently in determining income tax expense and income taxes payable. The most common difference is depreciation. Many companies use straight-line depreciation in determining income tax expense and accelerated depreciation in figuring the amount to pay the government. This treatment results in a deferral of taxes that will be payable in later periods when the straight-line depreciation exceeds the accelerated depreciation. The line "Effect of exchange rate changes" involves adjustments that result from the need to translate amounts stated in foreign currency into U.S. dollars.

Required:

1. Income from continuing operations in 1985 was $156.6 million (the first line on the statement). However, the first two adjustments result in a line item "Total from continuing operations" that amounted to $253.3 million. Are these two adjustments *sources* of funds? Explain your answer in terms understandable to someone with a general business background but not familiar with the details of financial statement preparation.

2. Quaker does not use either a strict cash basis or a working capital basis in preparing the funds statement. What is the definition of *funds* used in its statement? What justification is there for using this particular definition of *funds?*

3. Net income for 1985 was $156.6 million. However, funds from operations was over 150% of that amount — $245 million. Explain as fully as possible the difference. Do not simply repeat the account titles shown on the statement. *Explain* the reasons for the difference to someone unfamiliar with a funds statement.

4. Note that rather than categories for sources and uses, Quaker has categories for investing activities and financing activities. Each includes sources and uses. Also note that cash dividends are separately disclosed rather than included in either category. Other than funds from operations, what were Quaker's two largest sources of funds in 1985? How much were each of these sources?

5. What were Quaker's two largest uses of funds in 1985? How much were each of these?

6. Briefly compare the company's funds flow for 1985 and 1986. Include in your comparison the significant differences in the funds flow between the two years.

P18–21 **Comprehensive cash basis funds statement — indirect approach — dividend decision.** The Snudden Company just completed the most profitable year in its twenty-five-year history. Reported earnings of $1,020,000 on sales of $8,000,000 re-

Consolidated Statement of Changes in Financial Position

Year Ended June 30	1985	1984	1983
Operations			
Income from continuing operations	$ 156.6	$ 138.7	$ 119.3
Depreciation and amortization	77.8	74.2	55.1
Deferred income taxes and other items	18.9	60.3	22.2
Total from continuing operations	253.3	273.2	196.6
(Loss) from discontinued operations	—	—	(54.7)
Reclassification of noncurrent assets to other current assets	—	—	45.1
(Increase) decrease in receivables	(20.2)	(123.6)	1.8
(Increase) decrease in inventories	(17.9)	(70.5)	58.5
(Increase) decrease in other current assets	(12.9)	55.7	(42.2)
(Decrease) increase in trade accounts payable	(17.0)	56.1	(7.4)
Increase in other current liabilities	55.8	39.6	6.7
Effect of exchange rate changes	(3.0)	(10.6)	(6.2)
Other—net	6.9	19.7	(1.7)
Funds from operations	245.0	239.6	196.5
Cash Dividends Declared	(54.1)	(48.3)	(43.6)
Investing Activities			
Additions to properties	(109.0)	(120.1)	(126.0)
Cost of acquisitions, excluding working capital	(14.9)	(94.1)	(32.1)
Decrease in long-term receivables and investments	11.4	2.9	4.4
Disposals of property, plant and equipment	47.5	13.4	9.5
	(65.0)	(197.9)	(144.2)
Financing Activities			
Net (decrease) increase in short-term debt	(49.1)	26.9	1.9
Proceeds from new long-term debt	1.9	119.4	9.3
Retirement of long-term debt	(33.8)	(112.9)	(15.4)
Issuance of common treasury stock	16.0	12.3	10.1
Repurchases of common stock	(38.3)	—	—
	(103.3)	45.7	5.9
Net Increase in Cash and Marketable Securities	$ 22.6	$ 39.1	$ 14.6

See accompanying notes to consolidated financial statements.

sulted in a very healthy profit margin of 12.75%. Each year before releasing the financial statements, the board of directors meets to decide on the amount of dividends to declare for the year. For each of the past nine years the company has declared a dividend of $1 per share of common stock. The dividend declared each year end is always paid on January 15 of the following year.

Presented below are the income statement for the year and comparative balance sheets as of the end of the last two years.

**For the Year Ended
December 31, 19X9**

Sales revenue	$8,000,000
Cost of goods sold	4,500,000
Gross profit	$3,500,000
Operating expenses	1,450,000
Income before interest and taxes	$2,050,000
Interest expense	350,000
Income before taxes	$1,700,000
Income tax expense 40%	680,000
Net income	$1,020,000

	12/31/X8	12/31/X9
Cash	$ 450,000	$ 480,000
Accounts receivable	200,000	250,000
Inventory	600,000	750,000
Prepayments	75,000	60,000
Total current assets	$1,325,000	$1,540,000
Land	$2,200,000	$3,255,000
Plant and equipment	2,500,000	4,200,000
Accumulated depreciation	(1,000,000)	(1,250,000)
Long-term investments	900,000	500,000
Patents	750,000	650,000
Total long-term assets	$5,350,000	$7,355,000
Total assets	$6,675,000	$8,895,000
Accounts payable	$ 280,000	$ 350,000
Other accrued liabilities	225,000	285,000
Income taxes payable	100,000	170,000
Dividends payable	200,000	0
Notes payable due within next year	150,000	350,000
Total current liabilities	$ 955,000	$1,155,000
Long-term notes payable	$ 500,000	$ 300,000
Bonds payable	1,500,000	2,200,000
Total long-term liabilities	$2,000,000	$2,500,000
Common stock, $10 par	$2,000,000	$2,500,000
Retained earnings	1,720,000	2,740,000
Total owners' equity	$3,720,000	$5,240,000
Total liabilities and owners' equity	$6,675,000	$8,895,000

Additional information available

a. All sales are on account as are all purchases.

b. Land was purchased through the issuance of bonds. Additional land (beyond the amount purchased through the issuance of bonds) was purchased for cash.

c. New plant and equipment was acquired during the year for cash. No plant assets were retired during the year. Depreciation expense is included in operating expenses.

d. Long-term investments were sold for cash during the year.

e. No new patents were acquired, and none were disposed of during the year. Amortization expense is included in operating expenses.

f. The increase in "notes payable due within next year" represents the amount reclassified from long-term to short-term.

g. Fifty thousand shares of common stock were issued during the year at par value.

As controller of Snudden, you have been asked to make a recommendation to the board as to whether or not to declare a dividend this year and, if so, whether the precedent of paying a $1 per share dividend can be maintained. The president is eager to keep the dividend at $1 in view of the successful year just completed. However, he is also concerned with the effect of a dividend on the company's cash position. He is particularly concerned with the large amount of notes payable that comes due next year. He further notes the aggressive growth pattern in recent years, as evidenced this year by large increases in land and plant and equipment.

Required:

1. Compute cash provided from operations, starting with net income (the indirect approach).

2. Prepare a funds statement on the cash basis.

3. What is your recommendation to the board of directors concerning the declaration of a cash dividend? Should the $1 per share dividend be maintained? Should a smaller amount be declared? Should no dividend be declared? Support your answer with any necessary computations. Include in your response your concerns, from a funds flow perspective, about the following year.

P18–22 **Comprehensive cash basis funds statement—direct approach—dividend decision.** Assume the same set of facts as in P18–21.

1. Using the format in Exhibit 18–10 of the chapter, convert the income statement from an accrual basis to a cash basis.

2. Compute cash provided from operations, using the direct approach.

3. Prepare a funds statement on the cash basis.

4. What is your recommendation to the board of directors concerning the declaration of a cash dividend? Should the $1 per share dividend be maintained? Should a smaller amount be declared? Should no dividend be declared? Support your answer with any necessary computations. Include in your response your concerns, from a funds flow perspective, about the following year.

P18–23 **Cash basis funds statement—direct approach.** Odon Company has not yet prepared a formal statement of changes in financial position for the 19X8 fiscal year. Comparative Statements of Financial Position as of December 31, 19X7 and 19X8 and a Statement of Income and Retained Earnings for the year ended December 31, 19X8, are presented below.

ODON COMPANY
Statement of Financial Position
December 31
($000 omitted)

Assets	19X7	19X8
Current assets:		
Cash	$ 100	$ 60
U. S. treasury notes	50	0
Accounts receivable	500	610
Inventory	600	720
Total current assets	$1,250	$1,390
Long-term assets:		
Land	$ 70	$ 80
Buildings & equipment	600	710
Accumulated depreciation	(120)	(180)
Patents (less amortization)	130	105
Total long-term assets	$ 680	$ 715
Total assets	$1,930	$2,105

Liabilities and Owners' Equity	19X7	19X8
Current liabilities:		
Accounts payable	$ 300	$ 360
Taxes payable	20	25
Notes payable	400	400
Total current liabilities	$ 720	$ 785
Term notes payable – due 19X3	200	200
Total liabilities	$ 920	$ 985
Owners' equity:		
Common stock outstanding	$ 700	$ 830
Retained earnings	310	290
Total owners' equity	$1,010	$1,120
Total liabilities and equity	$1,930	$2,105

ODON COMPANY
Statement of Income and Retained Earnings
Year Ended December 31, 19X8
($000 omitted)

Sales		$2,408
Less expenses and interest:		
Cost of goods sold	$1,100	
Salaries and benefits	850	
Heat, light, and power	75	
Depreciation	60	
Property taxes	18	
Patent amortization	25	
Miscellaneous expense	10	
Interest	55	2,193

Net income before income taxes	$ 215
Income taxes	105
Net income	$ 110
Retained earnings — January 1, 19X8	310
	$ 420
Stock dividend distributed	130
Retained earnings — December 31, 19X8	$ 290

Required:

1. Compute cash provided from operations, using the direct approach.
2. Prepare a funds statement on the cash basis. Assume that all sales and purchases are on account.

(CMA Adapted)

CHAPTER 19

Financial Statement Analysis

Learning Objectives

After reading this chapter you should be able to:

1. Appreciate the importance of financial statement analysis in controlling operations.

2. Distinguish between horizontal and vertical analysis.

3. Identify the various ratios useful in analyzing liquidity.

4. Identify the various ratios useful in analyzing solvency.

5. Identify the various ratios useful in analyzing profitability.

6. Be able to compute the ratios useful in liquidity, solvency, and profitability analysis.

7. Understand the limitations of ratios in the analysis of operations.

The emphasis throughout management accounting is on the planning and control of operations. An important ingredient in the efficient control of operations is timely feedback. Managers receive feedback, of course in a variety of ways. In this chapter we discuss an important managerial tool for obtaining feedback—financial statement analysis.

Various groups have different needs in analyzing the financial statements of a company. For example, a banker is primarily interested in the likelihood that a loan will be repaid. Certain ratios, as we will see, are most indicative of the ability of the company to repay principal and interest. A stockholder, on the other hand, is concerned with a fair return on the amount invested in the company. Again, certain ratios will be helpful in making an assessment of the return to the stockholder.

Two important reasons can be given for management's interest in the tools of financial statement analysis. First, timely analysis will allow management to more effectively control operations and plan for the future. Second, and just as important, management is often judged by the various outside groups on the basis of its performance as measured by certain key ratios. Most annual reports contain a section devoted to a review of the past year in which management comments on its performance during the year as measured by selected ratios.

We begin the study of statement analysis by discussing some of the important limitations in the analysis of any business. The common techniques used in financial statement analysis are then presented and evaluated.

Considerations in Statement Analysis

We will soon turn our attention to various techniques commonly used in the financial analysis of a company. But before doing so it is important to understand some of the limitations and other considerations in statement analysis. Users of financial statements often place too much emphasis on summary indicators and key ratios. No single ratio is capable of telling the user everything there is to know about a particular company.

Alternative Accounting Principles

Every set of financial statements is based on various assumptions. For example, a cost-flow method must be assumed in valuing inventory and recognizing cost of goods sold expense. The accountant chooses FIFO, LIFO, or one of the other acceptable methods. The selection of a particular method will have a significant effect on certain key ratios. Recognition of the acceptable alternatives is especially important in comparing two or more companies.

Comparisons

The calculation of various ratios for a company is only a starting point. One technique we will discuss is the comparison of a ratio over a period of time. Has it gone up or down from last year? What is the percentage increase or decrease in the ratio over the last five years? Recognition of the trends in the ratios is important in analyzing the company.

Management must also recognize the need to make comparisons with other companies in the same industry. For example, a particular measure of performance may cause the manager to conclude that the company is not operating efficiently. However, comparison with an industry standard might show that the particular ratio is normal for companies in that industry. Various organizations publish summaries of selected ratios for a sample of companies in the United States. The ratios are usually organized by industry. Dun & Bradstreet's "Industry Norms and Key Business Ratios," for example, is an annual review with companies organized into five major industries and approximately 800 specific lines of business.

Although industry comparisons are useful, caution is necessary in interpreting the results of such analyses. Few companies in today's economy operate in a single industry. Exceptions exist (General Motors is almost exclusively in the automotive industry), but the majority of companies cross over the boundaries of any single industry. Companies operating in more than one industry, known as *conglomerates* (Chapter 15), present the analyst with a special challenge. Keep in mind also the point made earlier about alternative accounting methods. It is not unusual to find companies in the same industry using different inventory valuation techniques or depreciation methods.

The Effects of Inflation

Inflation, or an increase in the level of prices, is another important consideration in analyzing financial statements. The statements, as prepared for use by outsiders, are based on historical costs, and are not adjusted for the effects of increasing prices. For example, consider the following trend in a company's sales for the past three years:

	19X7	19X8	19X9
Net sales	$100,000	$110,000	$121,000

As measured by the actual dollars of sales, it appears as if sales have increased by 10% each year. Caution is necessary in concluding that the company is better off in each succeeding year because of the increase in sales *dollars*. Assume, for example, that 19X7 sales of $100,000 are the result of selling 100,000 units at $1 each. Are 19X8 sales of $110,000 the result of selling 110,000 units at $1 each, or the result of selling another 100,000 units at $1.10 each? Although on the surface it may seem insignificant which result accounts for the sales increase, the answer can have important ramifications. If the company found it necessary to increase selling price to $1.10 in the face of increasing *costs,* the company may be no better off than it was in 19X7 in terms of contribution margin. The point to be made is one of caution: published financial statements are stated in historical costs and therefore have not been adjusted for the effects of inflation.

Responsibility Accounting and Statement Analysis

Responsibility accounting is a system of holding the personnel in a company accountable for operations under their control. Ratio analysis is one aspect of responsibility accounting. As discussed in Chapter 5, in responsibility accounting authority and responsibility for each operation are clearly delineated. Ratio analysis must follow lines of responsibility. For example, a production manager should not be held accountable for a ratio that measures the effectiveness of accounts receivable collection. Control over this type of ratio would likely rest with the manager of the credit department.

Analysis of Comparative and Common-Size Statements

We are now ready to analyze a set of financial statements. We will begin by looking at the comparative balance sheets and income statements of a hypothetical company for a two-year period. The analysis of the statements over a series of years is often called **horizontal analysis.** We will then see how the income statement and balance sheet can be recast in what are referred to as *common-size statements.* The analysis of common-size statements is called **vertical analysis.** Finally, we will consider the use of a variety of ratios to analyze a company.

Horizontal Analysis

Comparative balance sheets for Samuelson Company are presented in Exhibit 19–1 (page 696). The increase or decrease in each of the major accounts on the balance sheet is shown in both absolute dollars and as a percentage. The base year for computing the percentage increase or decrease in each account is the first year, 19X8. By reading across (thus the name *horizontal analysis*) the manager can quickly spot any unusual changes in accounts from the prior year. Three accounts stand out: cash decreased by 76%, inventory increased by 73%, and accounts payable increased by 70%. Each of these large changes will need to be investigated further with the use of selected ratios.

EXHIBIT 19—1

SAMUELSON COMPANY
Comparative Balance Sheets
December 31, 19X9 and 19X8
(all amounts in thousands of dollars)

			Increase (Decrease)	
	12/31/X9	*12/31/X8*	*Dollars*	*Percent*
Cash	$ 320	$ 1,350	$(1,030)	(76)%
Accounts receivable	5,500	4,500	1,000	22
Inventory	4,750	2,750	2,000	73
Prepaid insurance	150	200	(50)	(25)
Total current assets	$10,720	$ 8,800	$ 1,920	22
Land	2,000	2,000	0	0
Buildings and equipment, net	4,150	3,000	1,150	38
Total long-term assets	$ 6,150	$ 5,000	$ 1,150	23
Total assets	$16,870	$13,800	$ 3,070	22
Accounts payable	$ 4,250	$ 2,500	$ 1,750	70
Taxes payable	2,300	2,100	200	10
Loans payable	600	800	(200)	(25)
Total current liabilities	$ 7,150	$ 5,400	$ 1,750	32
Bonds payable (long-term)	800	900	(100)	(11)
Total liabilities	$ 7,950	$ 6,300	$ 1,650	26
Preferred stock, $5 par	500	500	0	0
Common stock, $1 par	1,000	1,000	0	0
Retained earnings	7,420	6,000	1,420	24
Total stockholders' equity	$ 8,920	$ 7,500	$ 1,420	19
Total equities	$16,870	$13,800	$ 3,070	22

Exhibit 19–2 shows comparative statements of income and retained earnings for Samuelson for 19X9 and 19X8. At first glance, the 20% increase in sales to $24 million appears promising. However, management was not able to limit the increase in either cost of goods sold expense or selling, general, and administrative expense to 20%. The analysis indicates that cost of sales increased by 29% and selling, general, and administrative expense increased by 50%. The effect of the increases in these two expenses more than offsets the increase in sales and resulted in a decrease in operating income of 25%.

Horizontal analysis can be extended to include more than two years of results. Many annual reports include, as supplementary information, financial summaries of operations for extended periods of time. The Quaker Oats Company, for example, includes an eleven-year summary of selected financial

EXHIBIT 19–2

SAMUELSON COMPANY
Comparative Statements of Income and Retained Earnings
For the Years Ended December 31, 19X9 and 19X8
(all amounts in thousands of dollars)

	19X9	19X8	Increase (Decrease) Dollars	Increase (Decrease) Percent
Net sales	$ 24,000	$ 20,000	$ 4,000	20%
Cost of goods sold expense	18,000	14,000	4,000	29
Gross margin	$ 6,000	$ 6,000	$ 0	0
Sell., gen., & admin. expense	3,000	2,000	1,000	50
Operating income	$ 3,000	$ 4,000	$(1,000)	(25)
Interest expense	140	160	(20)	(13)
Net income before tax	$ 2,860	$ 3,840	$ (980)	(26)
Income tax expense	1,140	1,540	(400)	(26)
Net income	$ 1,720	$ 2,300	$ (580)	(25)
Preferred dividends	50	50		
Income available to common	$ 1,670	$ 2,250		
Common dividends	250	250		
To retained earnings	$ 1,420	$ 2,000		
Beginning retained earnings	6,000	4,000		
Ending retained earnings	$ 7,420	$ 6,000		

data. The inclusion of eleven years allows the reader to compare the current year with the prior ten years. The first item in the summary, net sales, is extracted from the 1985 annual report and shown below for the current and five preceding years (all amounts are in millions of dollars and each accounting year ends on June 30):

	1985	1984	1983	1982	1981	1980
Net sales	$3,520.1	$3,344.1	$2,611.3	$2,576.2	$2,385.1	$2,193.6

One observation about Quaker's net sales is that they have increased each of the six years (in fact, the same can be said about the entire eleven-year period). The trend for the past six years can be examined more closely by looking at the percentage increase in net sales, using 1980 as the base year:

	1985	1984	1983	1982	1981
Percent increase in net sales (from 19X0)	60.5%	52.4%	19.0%	17.4%	8.7%

An analysis of this trend indicates that sales increased most dramatically in 1984 and to a lesser extent in each of the other years. More advanced statistical techniques are available for analyzing trends in financial data and, most important, for projecting those trends to future periods. Some of the techniques, such as time series analysis, have been used extensively in forecasting sales trends.

Vertical Analysis

Common-size comparative balance sheets for Samuelson Company are presented in Exhibit 19–3. Common-size statements recast all items on the statement as a percentage of a selected item on the statement. Note that all asset accounts are stated as a percentage of total assets. Similarly, all liability and stockholders' equity accounts are stated as a percentage of total equities.

EXHIBIT 19–3

SAMUELSON COMPANY
Common-size Comparative Balance Sheets
December 31, 19X9 and 19X8
(all amounts in thousands of dollars)

	12/31/X9		12/31/X8	
	Dollars	*Percent*	*Dollars*	*Percent*
Cash	$ 320	1.9%	$ 1,350	9.8%
Accounts receivable	5,500	32.6	4,500	32.6
Inventory	4,750	28.1	2,750	19.9
Prepaid insurance	150	.9	200	1.5
Total current assets	$10,720	63.5%	$ 8,800	63.8%
Land	2,000	11.9	2,000	14.5
Buildings and equipment, net	4,150	24.6	3,000	21.7
Total long-term assets	$ 6,150	36.5	$ 5,000	36.2
Total assets	$16,870	100.0%	$13,800	100.0%
Accounts payable	$ 4,250	25.2%	$ 2,500	18.1%
Taxes payable	2,300	13.6	2,100	15.2
Loans payable	600	3.6	800	5.8
Total current liabilities	$ 7,150	42.4%	$ 5,400	39.1%
Bonds payable (long-term)	800	4.7	900	6.5
Total liabilities	$ 7,950	47.1%	$ 6,300	45.6%
Preferred stock, $5 par	500	3.0	500	3.6
Common stock, $1 par	1,000	5.9	1,000	7.3
Retained earnings	7,420	44.0	6,000	43.5
Total stockholders' equity	$ 8,920	52.9%	$ 7,500	54.4%
Total equities	$16,870	100.0%	$13,800	100.0%

The combination of the comparative balance sheets for the two years with the common-size feature allows the manager to spot critical changes in the composition of the assets. We noted in Exhibit 19–1 that cash had decreased by 76% over the two years. The shortage of cash is further highlighted in Exhibit 19–3 by noting that it has decreased from 9.8% of the total assets to only 1.9%.

Another observation from the exhibit is that total current assets have continued to represent just under two-thirds (64%) of the total assets. If cash has decreased significantly in terms of the percentage of total assets, then what accounts have increased to maintain current assets at two-thirds of total assets? We can quickly see that although inventory represented 19.9% of total assets at the end of 19X8, the percentage is up to 28.1% at the end of 19X9. This change in the relative composition of current assets between cash and inventory may have important implications. The change, for instance, may be a signal that the company is having trouble selling inventory.

Total current liabilities represent a slightly higher percentage of total equities at the end of 19X9, compared to the end of 19X8. The increase is balanced by a slight decrease in the percentages of long-term debt (the bonds) and by stockholders' equity. We will return later to further analysis of the composition of both the current and noncurrent accounts.

Common-size comparative income statements for Samuelson Company are presented in Exhibit 19–4. The base, or benchmark, on which all other items in the income statement are compared is net sales. Again, observations from the comparative statements alone are further confirmed by examining the common-size statements. Although gross margin as a percentage of sales

EXHIBIT 19–4

SAMUELSON COMPANY
Common-size Comparative Income Statements
For the Years Ended December 31, 19X9 and 19X8
(all amounts in thousands of dollars)

	19X9		19X8	
	Dollars	*Percent*	*Dollars*	*Percent*
Net sales	$24,000	100.0%	$20,000	100.0%
Cost of goods sold expense	18,000	75.0	14,000	70.0
Gross margin	$ 6,000	25.0%	$ 6,000	30.0%
Sell., gen., & admin. expense	3,000	12.5	2,000	10.0
Operating income	$ 3,000	12.5%	$ 4,000	20.0%
Interest expense	140	.6	160	.8
Net income before tax	$ 2,860	11.9%	$ 3,840	19.2%
Income tax expense	1,140	4.8	1,540	7.7
Net income	$ 1,720	7.1%	$ 2,300	11.5%

was 30% in 19X8, the same ratio for 19X9 is only 25%. Recall the earlier observation that although sales had increased by 20% from one year to the next, cost of goods sold expense increased by 29%.

In addition to the gross margin ratio, another important relationship from Exhibit 19–4 is the ratio of net income to net sales. The ratio is an overall indicator of management's ability to control expenses and reflects the amount of income for each dollar of sales. Some managers prefer to look at income before tax, rather than final net income, because taxes are not typically an expense that they can control. Further, if the firm does not earn a profit before tax, then no tax expense will be incurred. The ratio of net income to net sales is called the **profit margin.** (For ease of reference, all of the ratios are summarized in Exhibit 19–7 at the end of the chapter.) Note the decrease in Samuelson's profit margin: from 11.5% in 19X8 to 7.1% in 19X9 (or from 19.2% to 11.9% on a before-tax basis).

Ratio Analysis

Two ratios were already discussed in the last section: the gross profit ratio and the profit margin ratio. A ratio is simply the relationship, normally stated as a percentage, between two financial statement amounts. In this section, we consider a wide range of ratios used by management for a variety of purposes. We will divide the ratios into three main categories. Ratios are categorized according to their use in performing (1) liquidity analysis, (2) solvency analysis, and (3) profitability analysis.

Liquidity Analysis and the Management of Working Capital

We saw in Chapter 13 liquidity relative to investment recovery used as a means for assessing capital investment projects (payback). In financial statement analysis, **liquidity** is a relative measure of the nearness to cash of the assets and liabilities of a company. Various ratios are used to measure liquidity, and they are basically concerned with the ability of the company to pay its debts as they come due. Recall the distinction between current and long-term classification on the balance sheet. Current assets are those assets that will either be converted into cash or consumed within one year or the operating cycle, if the cycle is longer than one year in length. The operating cycle for a manufacturing company is the length of time between the purchase of raw material and the eventual collection of any outstanding account receivable from the sale of the product. Current liabilities are those obligations of a company that will require the use of current assets or the creation of other current liabilities to satisfy them.

The nearness to cash of the current assets and liabilities is indicated by their placement on the balance sheet. Current assets are listed on the balance sheet in descending order of their nearness to cash. Liquidity is, of course, a matter of degree, with cash being the most liquid of all assets. With few exceptions, such as prepaid insurance, most assets are convertible into cash. However, accounts receivable is closer to being converted into cash than is inventory. An account receivable need only be collected to be converted to cash. An item of inventory must first be sold and then, assuming that sales of inventory are on account, the account must be collected before cash is realized.

Working Capital

Working capital is the excess of current assets over current liabilities at a point in time:

Working capital = Current assets − Current liabilities

Reference to Samuelson's comparative balance sheets in Exhibit 19−1 indicates the following:

	12/31/X9	12/31/X8
Current assets	$10,720,000	$8,800,000
Current liabilities	7,150,000	5,400,000
Working capital	$ 3,570,000	$3,400,000

The management of working capital is an extremely important task for any company. Management must always strive for the ideal balance of current assets and current liabilities. However, the amount of working capital is limited in its informational value. For example, it tells us nothing about the composition of the current accounts. A comparison of the working capital at the end of each of the two years does indicate a slight increase in the degree of protection for short-term creditors of the company. But the amounts are of no value in making comparisons with other companies of different sizes in the same industry. Working capital of $3,570,000 may be adequate for Samuelson Company, but it may be a signal of impending bankruptcy for a company much larger than Samuelson.

Current Ratio

The **current ratio** is one of the most widely used of all financial statement ratios and is calculated as follows:

Current ratio = Current assets/Current liabilities

For Samuelson Company, the ratio at each year end is

12/31/X9	12/31/X8
$\dfrac{\$10,720,000}{\$7,150,000} = 1.50 \text{ to } 1$	$\dfrac{\$8,800,000}{\$5,400,000} = 1.63 \text{ to } 1$

The decrease in the current ratio indicates a decline in the buffer of protection for short-term creditors from one year to the next. At the end of 19X9, there was $1.50 of current assets for every $1 of current liabilities. Is this current ratio adequate? Or is it a sign of impending financial difficulties? There is no definitive answer to either of these questions. Some analysts use a general rule of thumb of 2 to 1 for the current ratio as a sign of short-term financial health. The answer first depends on the industry. Companies in certain industries have historically operated with current ratios much less than 2 to 1.

A second concern in interpreting the current ratio has to do with the composition of the current assets. Cash is usually the only acceptable means of payment for most liabilities. Therefore, it is important to consider the make-up or composition of the current assets. Refer back to Exhibit 19–3 and Samuelson's common-size balance sheets. Not only has the current ratio declined during 19X9, but the proportion of the total current assets made up by inventory has increased, whereas the proportion made up by accounts receivable has remained the same. Recall the earlier observation that accounts receivable is only one step removed from cash, whereas inventory requires both sale as well as collection of the subsequent account.

Acid-Test Ratio

The **acid-test or quick ratio** is a stricter test of a company's ability to pay its current debts as they are due. Specifically, it is intended to deal with the composition problem because it *excludes* from the numerator of the fraction inventories and prepaid assets:

$$\text{Acid-test or quick ratio} = \frac{\text{Quick assets}}{\text{Current liabilities}}$$

where:

$$\text{Quick assets} = \text{Cash} + \text{Marketable securities} + \text{Current receivables}$$

Samuelson's quick assets consist of only cash and accounts receivable, and its quick ratios are as follows:

12/31/X9	12/31/X8
$\dfrac{\$320{,}000 + \$5{,}500{,}000}{\$7{,}150{,}000} = .81 \text{ to } 1$	$\dfrac{\$1{,}350{,}000 + \$4{,}500{,}000}{\$5{,}400{,}000} = 1.08 \text{ to } 1$

Does the quick ratio of less than 1 to 1 at the end of 19X9 mean that Samuelson will be unable to pay creditors on time? Not necessarily so. Although the quick ratio is a better indication of short-term debt-paying ability than the current ratio, it is still not perfect. For example, we would want to know the normal credit terms that Samuelson extends to its customers, as well as the credit terms that the company receives from its suppliers.

Assume that Samuelson requires its customers to pay their accounts within 30 days. On the other hand, assume that the normal credit terms extended by Samuelson's suppliers allows payment any time within 60 days. The relatively longer credit terms extended by Samuelson's suppliers gives it some cushion in meeting its obligations. The due date of the $2,300,000 in taxes payable could also have a significant effect on the company's ability to remain in business.

Although the current and quick ratios are of some value in measuring a company's liquidity, periodic cash budgets, as discussed in Chapter 5, are invaluable aids in this respect. The fact that budgets are forward looking, rather than based on historical amounts, make them an important management tool in assessing short-run liquidity. It is also important for management to be able to analyze its position in absolute dollars, something that is possible with budgets but not with ratios. Periodic budgets, prepared monthly or even weekly, are important tools for assessing liquidity.

Accounts Receivable Analysis

The analysis of accounts receivable is an important component in the management of working capital. A company must be willing to extend credit terms that are liberal enough to attract and maintain customers. But at the same time, management must continually monitor the accounts to ensure collection on a timely basis. One measure of the efficiency of the collection process is the **accounts receivable turnover** ratio:

$$\text{Accounts receivable turnover} = \frac{\text{Net credit sales}}{\text{Average accounts receivable}}$$

Note an important distinction between this ratio and either the current or quick ratio. Both of those ratios are a measure of liquidity at a point in time. All numbers come from the balance sheet. A turnover ratio, however, is an *activity* ratio and consists of an activity (sales in this case) divided by a base to which it is naturally related (accounts receivable). Because an activity such as sales is for a period of time (a year in this case), the base must be stated as an average for that same period of time. Because we want to calculate turnover ratios for both years, it is necessary to add the ending balance sheet for 19X7 to the analysis. The balance sheet for Samuelson Company on December 31, 19X7, is given in Exhibit 19–5 (page 704).

The accounts receivable turnover ratios for both years can now be calculated (we assume that all sales are on account):

19X9

$$\frac{\$24,000,000}{(\$5,500,000 + \$4,500,000)/2} = 4.8 \text{ times}$$

19X8

$$\frac{\$20,000,000}{(\$4,500,000 + \$2,500,000)/2} = 5.7 \text{ times}$$

Accounts turned over, on the average, 5.7 times in 19X8, compared to only 4.8 times in 19X9. Another way to measure the efficiency in the collection process is to calculate the **number of days sales in receivables:**

$$\text{Number of days sales in receivables} = \frac{\text{Number of days in the period}}{\text{Accounts receivable turnover}}$$

EXHIBIT 19–5

SAMUELSON COMPANY
Balance Sheet
December 31, 19X7
(all amounts in thousands of dollars)

Cash	$ 1,250
Accounts receivable	2,500
Inventory	3,750
Prepaid insurance	250
Total current assets	$ 7,750
Land	2,000
Buildings and equipment, net	2,750
Total long-term assets	$ 4,750
Total assets	$12,500
Accounts payable	$ 3,000
Taxes payable	2,000
Loans payable	1,000
Total current liabilities	$ 6,000
Bonds payable (long-term)	1,000
Total liabilities	$ 7,000
Preferred stock, $1 par	500
Common stock, $1 par	1,000
Retained earnings	4,000
Total stockholders' equity	$ 5,500
Total equities	$12,500

For simplicity, we will assume 360 days in a year:

19X9	19X8
$\dfrac{360 \text{ days}}{4.8 \text{ times}} = 75 \text{ days}$	$\dfrac{360 \text{ days}}{5.7 \text{ times}} = 63 \text{ days}$

The average number of days an account is outstanding is 75 days in 19X9. Is this acceptable? The answer depends on the company's credit policy. If Samuelson's normal credit terms require payment within 60 days, further investigation is needed. Even if the normal credit terms are 75 days, management would want to analyze further the increase of 12 days in the average age of an account.

Inventory Analysis

A similar set of ratios can be calculated to analyze the efficiency in managing inventory. We will assume that Samuelson is a retailer and therefore has only one form of inventory — merchandise inventory — as opposed to a manufacturer with raw materials, work-in-process, and finished goods. The **inventory turnover** ratio is

$$\text{Inventory turnover ratio} = \frac{\text{Cost of goods sold expense}}{\text{Average inventory}}$$

The ratio for each of the two years is:

19X9	19X8
$\dfrac{\$18,000,000}{(\$4,750,000 + \$2,750,000)/2} = 4.8$ times	$\dfrac{\$14,000,000}{(\$2,750,000 + \$3,750,000)/2} = 4.3$ times

Samuelson has been more efficient in 19X9 in moving its inventory. The number of times that inventory turns over each year will vary widely in different industries. For example, a wholesaler of perishable fruits and vegetables may turn over inventory at least 50 times per year. An airplane manufacturer, however, may turn over its inventory once or twice a year. The **number of days sales in inventory** is an alternative measure of the company's efficiency in managing inventory:

$$\text{Number of days sales in inventory} = \frac{\text{Number of days in the period}}{\text{Inventory turnover}}$$

The number of days sales in inventory for Samuelson is

19X9	19X8
$\dfrac{360 \text{ days}}{4.8 \text{ times}} = 75$ days	$\dfrac{360 \text{ days}}{4.3 \text{ times}} = 84$ days

This measure can reveal a great deal about inventory management. For example, an unusually low turnover (and, of course, high number of days in inventory) may be a warning of a large amount of obsolete inventory. Or it may signal problems in the sales department. Finally, it may indicate that the company is pricing its products too high and the market is reacting by reducing their demand for the company's products.

Cash Operating Cycle

The **cash to cash operating cycle** is the length of time between the purchase of merchandise for sale, assuming a retailer, and the eventual collection of the cash from the sale. One method of approximating the number of days in a company's operating cycle involves combining two measures:

$$\text{Cash to cash operating cycle} = \text{Number of days sales in inventory} + \text{Number of days sales in receivables}$$

Samuelson's operating cycle for 19X9 and 19X8 is

19X9	19X8
75 days + 75 days = 150 days	84 days + 63 days = 147 days

The length of time, on the average, between the purchase of inventory and the collection of cash from sale of the inventory was 150 days in 19X9. Note that although the length of the operating cycle did not change significantly from 19X8 to 19X9, the composition did change: the decrease in the average days in inventory was offset by the increase in the average days in receivables.

Finally, keep in mind that we have only considered the operating cycle for a retailer. The number of days sales in inventory for a manufacturer would be expanded to include the additional amount of time to transform raw material into a finished product.

Solvency Analysis

Solvency refers to the ability of a company to remain in business over the long run. It is related to liquidity but differs in the time horizon. Although liquidity relates to the firm's ability to pay next year's debts as they are due, solvency has to do with the ability of the firm to stay financially healthy over the period of time that existing debt (short- and long-term) will be outstanding.

Debt-to-Equity Ratio

Capital structure is the focal point in solvency analysis. This refers to the composition of the right side of the balance sheet and the mix between debt and stockholders' equity. The composition of debt and equity in the capital structure is an important determinant of the cost of capital, as discussed in Chapter 13. We will have more to say later about the effects on profitability of the mix of debt and equity. For now, consider the **debt-to-equity** ratio:

$$\text{Debt-to-equity ratio} = \frac{\text{Total liabilities}}{\text{Total stockholders' equity}}$$

Samuelson's debt-to-equity ratio at each year end is

19X9	19X8
$\dfrac{\$7,950,000}{\$8,920,000} = .89 \text{ to } 1$	$\dfrac{\$6,300,000}{\$7,500,000} = .84 \text{ to } 1$

The 19X9 ratio indicates that for every $1 of capital provided by stockholders, $.89 was provided by creditors. Variations of the debt-to-equity ratio are sometimes used in assessing solvency. For example, management might calculate the ratio of total liabilities to the sum of total liabilities and stockholders' equity. A different ratio will result than if the debt-to-equity ratio is computed, but the objective of the measure is the same — to determine how reliant the company is on outsiders for funds.

Times Interest Earned

The debt-to-equity ratio is a measure of the company's overall long-term financial health. Management must also be aware of its ability to meet current interest payments to creditors. The **times interest earned** ratio is an indication of the company's ability to meet the current year's interest payments out of the current year's earnings:

$$\text{Times interest earned} = \frac{\text{Income before interest and taxes}}{\text{Interest expense}}$$

The numerator is income before taxes because interest is a deduction in arriving at the amount of income subject to tax. Stated slightly differently, if a company had just enough income to cover the payment of interest, tax expense would be zero. The ratio for Samuelson for each of the two years is

19X9

$$\frac{\$3,000,000}{\$140,000} = 21.4 \text{ to } 1$$

19X8

$$\frac{\$4,000,000}{\$160,000} = 25 \text{ to } 1$$

Debt Service Coverage

Two problems exist with the times interest earned ratio as a measure of the ability to repay creditors. First, the denominator of the fraction takes into account only the repayment of *interest*. Management must also be concerned with the *principal* amount of loans maturing in the next year. The second problem with the times interest earned ratio is the fact that the numerator is not a measure of the *cash* available to repay loans. Keep in mind the various noncash adjustments, such as depreciation, which enter into the determination of net income. The **debt service coverage** ratio is a measure of the amount of cash generated in the year that is available to repay interest due and any maturing principal amounts (that is, the amount available to "service" the debt):

$$\frac{\text{Debt service}}{\text{coverage ratio}} = \frac{\text{Income before interest, taxes, and noncash adjustments}}{\text{Interest and principal payments}}$$

We will assume that depreciation is the only noncash adjustment and that the amount of depreciation included in selling, general, and administrative expense is $35,000 in 19X9 and $25,000 in 19X8. Reference to the comparative balance sheets indicates a decrease, or repayment, of $100,000 in bonds payable each year and a decrease of $200,000 in loans payable each year. The debt service coverage ratio for Samuelson for each of the two years is

19X9

$$\frac{\$3,000,000 + \$35,000}{\$140,000 + \$300,000} = 6.9 \text{ to } 1$$

19X8

$$\frac{\$4,000,000 + \$25,000}{\$160,000 + \$300,000} = 8.8 \text{ to } 1$$

Although the amount of cash available to service debt has decreased from 19X8 to 19X9, the coverage ratio of 6.9 for 19X9 would appear to still provide Samuelson's creditors with a buffer of protection.

Profitability Analysis

Liquidity analysis and solvency analysis deal with management's ability to repay short- and long-term creditors. Management must also be concerned with the stockholder. Various measures of **profitability** indicate how well management is using the resources at its disposal to earn a return on the funds invested by various groups.

Rate of Return on Assets

Before computing the rate of return, an important question must be answered: return to whom? Every return ratio is a measure of the relationship between the income earned by the company and the investment made in the company by various groups. The broadest rate of return ratio is the **return on assets** ratio because it takes into account the investment made by all providers of capital—from short-term creditors to bondholders to stockholders. Therefore, the denominator, or base, for the return on assets ratio is total assets—which of course is the same as total liabilities and stockholders' equity.

The numerator of a return ratio will be some measure of the income of the company for the period. The income selected for the numerator must match the investment or base in the denominator. For example, if total assets is the base in the denominator, it is necessary to use an income number that is applicable to all the providers of capital. Therefore, the income number used in the rate of return on assets is income *after* adding back interest expense. This adjustment takes into account that creditors are one of the groups that have provided funds to the company. In other words, we want the amount of income before either creditors or stockholders have been given any distributions (that is, interest to creditors or dividends to stockholders).

The rate of return on assets ratio is

$$\text{Rate of return on assets} = \frac{\text{Net income} + \text{Interest expense, net of tax}}{\text{Average total assets}}$$

Note the addition of interest expense on a net of tax basis. Because net income is on an after-tax basis, for consistency purposes, interest must also be placed on a net, or after-tax basis. If we assume a 40% tax rate (which *is* the actual ratio of income tax expense to income before tax for Samuelson) the rates of return for Samuelson are as follows:

	19X9		*19X8*	
Net income	$ 1,720,000		$ 2,300,000	
Add back:				
+Interest expense $140,000		160,000		
Times: 1 − tax rate: × .6	84,000	× .6	96,000	
Numerator	$ 1,804,000		$ 2,396,000	
Assets − beginning of year	$13,800,000		$12,500,000	
Assets − end of year	16,870,000		13,800,000	
Total	$30,670,000		$26,300,000	

	19X9	*19X8*
Divided by 2 = Average total assets	$15,335,000	$13,150,000
Rate of return on assets	$ 1,804,000	$ 2,396,000
	$15,335,000	$13,150,000
	=11.76%	=18.22%

You have probably noticed the similarity between rate of return on assets and return on investment (ROI) for investment centers and segments of firms discussed in Chapter 15. The two measurements are quite similar. ROI, however, is concerned with the effectiveness of regular operations relative to investment so net operating income, before both interest and taxes, was used in the numerator. Rate of return on assets, however, is a slightly broader and more encompassing measurement of how effectively assets have been utilized. Therefore, net income after tax but before interest (as calculated above) is used in computing return on assets.

Components of Return on Assets

What caused Samuelson's return on assets to decrease so dramatically from the prior year? The answer can be found by looking at the two individual components that make up the return on assets. The first of these components is the **return on sales** and is calculated as follows:

$$\text{Return on sales} = \frac{\text{Net income} + \text{Interest, net of tax}}{\text{Net sales}}$$

The return on sales for Samuelson for the two years is

19X9	19X8
$\dfrac{\$1,720,000 + \$84,000}{\$24,000,000} = 7.52\%$	$\dfrac{\$2,300,000 + \$96,000}{\$20,000,000} = 11.98\%$

The ratio for 19X9 indicates that for every $1 of sales, the company was able to earn a profit, before the payment of interest, of between 7 and 8 cents, as compared to a return of almost 12 cents on the dollar in 19X8.

The other component of the rate of return on assets is the **asset turnover** ratio. The ratio is similar to both the inventory turnover and the receivable turnover ratios in that it is a measure of the relationship between some activity (net sales in this case) and some investment base (average total assets):

$$\text{Asset turnover ratio} = \frac{\text{Net sales}}{\text{Average total assets}}$$

For Samuelson, the ratio for each of the two years is

19X9	19X8
$\dfrac{\$24,000,000}{\$15,335,000} = 1.57 \text{ times}$	$\dfrac{\$20,000,000}{\$13,150,000} = 1.52 \text{ times}$

It now becomes evident that the explanation for the decrease in Samuelson's return on assets lies in the drop in the return on sales because the turnover was almost the same. To summarize, note the relationship among the three ratios:

Return on assets = Return on sales × Asset turnover

For 19X9 Samuelson's return on assets consists of

$$\frac{\$1,804,000}{\$24,000,000} \times \frac{\$24,000,000}{\$15,335,000} = 7.52\% \times 1.57 = 11.8\%$$

Finally, notice that net sales cancels out of both ratios, leaving the net income adjusted for interest divided by average assets as the return on assets ratio.

Return on Common Stockholders' Equity

Similar reasoning can now be used to compute the return on the capital provided by the common stockholder. Because we are interested in the return to the common stockholder, our base is no longer average total assets but rather average common stockholders' equity. Similarly, the appropriate income figure for the numerator is net income *after* the deduction of taxes, interest, and preferred dividends because we are interested in the return to the common stockholder after all claims have been settled.

The **return on common stockholders' equity** ratio is computed as

$$\frac{\text{Return on common}}{\text{stockholders' equity}} = \frac{\text{Net income} - \text{Preferred dividends}}{\text{Average common stockholders' equity}}$$

The average common stockholders' equity is calculated using information from Exhibits 19–1 and 19–5:

	Account balances at:		
	12/31/X9	*12/31/X8*	*12/31/X7*
Common stock, $1 par	$1,000,000	$1,000,000	$1,000,000
Retained earnings	7,420,000	6,000,000	4,000,000
Total common equity	$8,420,000	$7,000,000	$5,000,000

Average common equity for:
19X9: ($8,420,000 + $7,000,000)/2 = $7,710,000

19X8: ($7,000,000 + $5,000,000)/2 = $6,000,000

The net income less preferred dividends, or income available to common as it is called, can be found on Exhibit 19–2. The return on equity for the two years is

19X9	19X8
$$\frac{\$1,720,000 - \$50,000}{\$7,710,000} = 21.66\%$$	$$\frac{\$2,300,000 - \$50,000}{\$6,000,000} = 37.50\%$$

Return on Assets, Return on Equity, and Leverage

The return on assets for 19X9 was 11.8%. But the return to the common stockholders was much higher: 21.7%. How do you explain this phenomenon? Why are the stockholders getting a higher return on their money than all of the providers of money combined are getting? A partial answer to these questions can be found by reviewing the cost to Samuelson of the various sources of capital.

Reference to Exhibit 19–1 indicates three primary sources of capital other than common stockholders (accounts payable and taxes payable are *not* included since these in fact represent interest-free loans to the company from suppliers and the government). The three sources and the average amount of each outstanding during 19X9 are:

		Account balances at:	
	12/31/X9	*12/31/X8*	*Average*
Loans payable	$ 600,000	$ 800,000	$ 700,000
Bonds payable	800,000	900,000	850,000
Total liabilities	$1,400,000	$1,700,000	$1 550,000
Preferred stock	$ 500,000	$ 500,000	$ 500,000

What was the cost to Samuelson of each of these sources? The cost of the money provided by the preferred stockholders is clearly the amount of dividends or $50,000. The cost as a percentage is $50,000/$500,000 or 10%. The average cost of the borrowed money can be approximated by dividing the interest expense for 19X9 of $140,000 by the average of the loans payable and bonds payable of $1,550,000. The result is an average cost for these two sources of approximately 9%.

The concept of **leverage** refers to the practice of using borrowed funds and amounts received from preferred stockholders in an attempt to earn an overall return that is higher than the cost of these funds. Recall the rate of return on assets for 19X9: 11.8%. Because this return is on an after-tax basis, it is necessary for comparative purposes to convert the average cost of borrowed funds to an after-tax basis. Although we computed an average cost for borrowed money of 9%, the actual cost of these funds is less than 9% because each dollar of interest results in a tax savings of 40 cents (assuming a tax rate of 40%). The after-tax cost of the borrowed money is 9% times: 1 minus the 40% tax rate, or 5.4%. Because dividends are *not* tax deductible, the cost of the money provided by preferred stockholders is the 10% as calculated earlier.

Has Samuelson successfully employed leverage? That is, have they been able to earn an overall rate of return on assets that is higher than the amounts that they must pay creditors and preferred stockholders? Samuelson has been successful in using outside money; neither of the sources must be paid a rate in excess of the overall rate on assets employed of 11.8%. Also keep in mind that Samuelson has been able to borrow some amounts on an interest-free basis. As mentioned earlier, the accounts payable and taxes payable represent interest-free loans from suppliers and the federal government—although the loans are typically for a short period of time, such as 30 days.

In summary, the excess of the return on equity of 21.7% over the return on assets of 11.8% is an indication that the management of Samuelson has been successful in employing leverage—that is, there is positive leverage. Is it possible to be unsuccessful in this pursuit—that is, can there be negative leverage? If the company must pay more for the amounts provided by creditors and preferred stockholders than they can earn overall, as indicated by the return on assets, there will, in fact, be negative leverage.

Quaker's Use of Leverage

An example from the 1985 annual report of The Quaker Oats Company should tie together the concepts of return on assets, return on equity, and leverage. Quaker has set an objective of maintaining return on equity at approximately 20%. The goal was reached in fiscal year 1985 when the return on equity was 20.3%, the first time that it was over 20%. Quaker explains the improvement in the return on page 3 of the 1985 annual report:

> Over the past six years, our return has advanced from about 17 percent to over 20 percent. That improvement has resulted from better asset turnover, a solid return on sales and a modest increase in financial leverage.

A table on the same page of the report is entitled "Return on Equity from Continuing Operations." The table separates out the elements of return on equity. The past six years are presented in the table and the two most recent of those years are excerpted and shown below:

	Fiscal Years	
	1984	*1985*
Asset turnover	2.04	1.93
Return on sales	×4.03%	×4.35%
Return on assets	=8.22%	=8.40%
Leverage factor	×2.41	×2.42
Return on equity	=19.8%	=20.3%

Exhibit 19–6 presents a model of the elements that went into Quaker's return on equity calculation for 1985. The model should serve as a good review of the relationships among the various elements.

The two formulas for asset turnover and return on sales are the same formulas as illustrated earlier for Samuelson, with one exception. The net income used in the return on sales formula, $153 million, is the net income available for common. Recall that when we computed the return on sales ratio for Samuelson we used the income adjusted for interest expense. Quaker uses net income available for common because its ultimate objective is to calculate return on equity—and, of course, this requires the income available for common in the numerator. In fact, referring to Exhibit 19–6,

EXHIBIT 19–6

Model for Analyzing Return on Equity
(amounts from The Quaker Oats Company 1985 annual report)

Return on Equity =	Return on Assets	× Leverage Factor
Return on equity = Asset turnover	× Return on sales	× Leverage factor
= Sales	× Net income	× Average total assets
Average total assets	Sales	Average common shareholders' equity
ROE for 19X5: $3,520.1	× $ 153.0	× $1,824.4
(amounts in millions of dollars) $1,824.4	$3,520.1	$ 753.5
= 1.93 times	× 4.35%	× 2.42
=	8.40%	× 2.42
= 20.3%		

note that sales and average total assets cancel out in the equation and we are left with the formula for return on equity: net income (more correctly, income available for common) divided by average common shareholders' equity.

Finally, note from the exhibit the **leverage factor** used by Quaker:

$$\text{Leverage factor} = \frac{\text{Average total assets}}{\text{Average common shareholders' equity}}$$

$$= \$1,824.4 / \$753.5 = 2.42$$

The leverage factor can be calculated many different ways. However, the factor is always a measure of the extent to which the company relies on internal versus external funds for its financing. For example, Quaker's leverage factor indicates that for every $2.42 of assets, $1 has come from the common shareholder. Or, stated slightly differently, for every $2.42 of assets, $1.42 has come from creditors and preferred shareholders.

Earnings Per Share

Earnings per share is probably the single most quoted statistic for publicly traded companies. Stockholders and potential investors want to know what their share of profits is, not just the total dollar amount. Presentation of profits on a per share basis also allows the stockholder to relate earnings to what he or she paid for a share of stock or to the current trading price of a share of stock.

In simple situations, such as our Samuelson Company example, earnings per share (EPS) is calculated as follows:

$$\text{Earnings per share} = \frac{\text{Net income} - \text{Preferred dividends}}{\text{Number of common shares outstanding}}$$

Samuelson's EPS for each of the two years is:

<u>19X9</u>

$$\frac{\$1,720,000 - \$50,000}{1,000,000 \text{ shares}} = \$1.67 \text{ per share}$$

<u>19X8</u>

$$\frac{\$2,300,000 - \$50,000}{1,000,000 \text{ shares}} = \$2.25 \text{ per share}$$

A number of complications can arise in the computation of EPS, and the calculations can become exceedingly complex for a company with many different types of securities in its capital structure. We will mention just a few of the more common problems in computing earnings per share.

First, the denominator of the fraction must be modified if there are a different number of shares outstanding at the beginning of the year as compared to the end of the year. Weighted average number of shares outstanding is used in the denominator to take this into account. Second, two EPS ratios are computed if the company has either an extraordinary gain or loss during the year. Most investors are more interested in the EPS *exclusive* of the effect of gains and losses that are the result of extraordinary events. For this reason, two ratios are computed: EPS before extraordinary items and EPS after such items have been taken into account.

The most significant complications arise when a company has outstanding what are known as **potentially dilutive securities.** These are outstanding securities, such as convertible bonds and preferred stock, which have the potential of becoming common stock and decreasing earnings per share. To be conservative in the presentation of the EPS number, these securities that are not in *form* shares of common stock are treated *as if* they were common shares.

We will modify the Samuelson Company example to illustrate the concept of dilutive securities. Assume that the 100,000 shares of preferred stock (see Exhibit 19–1) are convertible into common shares at the rate of two shares of common for every one share of preferred. If all of the preferred shareholders exercised their option to convert their preferred shares into common shares, the company would have to issue 2 × 100,000 or 200,000 new shares of common stock. However, because there would not be any preferred stock outstanding if this happened, the company would not have to pay the $50,000 in preferred dividends. Note the *hypothetical* nature of this reasoning. The intent is to present a conservative estimate of EPS in situations in which convertible securities have the *potential* to dilute EPS. Assuming that certain additional tests are met, the calculation of EPS in this example would proceed as follows:

$$\text{Primary EPS} = \frac{\$1,720,000 - \$50,000}{1,000,000 \text{ shares}} = \$1.67 \text{ per share}$$

$$\text{Fully diluted EPS} = \frac{\$1,720,000}{1,200,000 \text{ shares}} = \$1.43 \text{ per share}$$

The primary EPS of $1.67 per share is the same as we calculated earlier. The fully diluted EPS takes into account the combined effect on EPS of saving

$50,000 in preferred dividends and the increase in the number of common shares if the preferred stock was converted into common stock. In this situation, the two EPS numbers would both be presented on the face of the income statement.

Price/Earnings Ratio

Earnings per share is an important ratio for an investor but only because of its relationship to dividends and market price. Stockholders hope to earn a return through either the receipt of periodic dividends or the eventual sale of the stock for more than was paid for it or both. Although earnings are related to dividends and market price, it is the latter two that are of primary interest to the stockholder.

We mentioned earlier the desire by investors to relate the earnings of the company to the market price of the stock. Now that we have stated Samuelson's earnings on a per share basis we can calculate the **price/earnings** ratio. What market price is relevant? Should we use the market price that the investor paid for a share of stock, or should we use the current market price? Because earnings are based on the most recent evaluation of the company for accounting purposes, it seems logical to use current market price, which is based on the stock market's current assessment of the company. Therefore, the ratio is computed as follows:

$$\text{Price/earnings ratio} = \frac{\text{Current market price}}{\text{Earnings per share}}$$

Assume a current market price for Samuelson's common stock of $15 per share at the end of 19X9 and $18 per share at the end of 19X8. Also, assume that the preferred stock is *not* convertible so that we only have one EPS each year. The price/earnings ratio for each of the two years is

19X9	19X8
$\dfrac{\$15 \text{ per share}}{\$1.67 \text{ per share}} = 9 \text{ to } 1$	$\dfrac{\$18 \text{ per share}}{\$2.25 \text{ per share}} = 8 \text{ to } 1$

The P/E ratio is often thought to be an indicator of the "quality" of a company's earnings. That is, the ratio of earnings per share to market price per share is an indication of the market's assessment of the company's performance. For example, assume that two companies have identical EPS ratios of $2.00 per share. Why should investors be willing to pay $20 per share (or 10 times earnings) for the stock of one company but only $14 per share for the stock of the other company?

First, we must realize that market prices are affected by many other factors in addition to the reported earnings of the company. General economic conditions, the outlook for the particular industry, and pending lawsuits are just three examples of the various factors that can affect the trading price of a company's stock. However, the difference in P/E ratios for the two companies may be a reflection of the market's assessment of the accounting practices of the companies. Assume that the company with a market price of $20 per share uses LIFO in valuing inventory and that the company trading at $14 per share uses FIFO. The difference in prices may be an indication that investors feel that even though the two companies have the same EPS, the LIFO company is "better off" because it will have less taxes to pay. (Recall that in a period of inflation the use of LIFO results in more cost of goods sold expense, less income, and therefore less income taxes.) The relationship between market prices and earnings continues to be a topic of considerable research interest to accountants.

Dividend Ratios

Two ratios are used to evaluate the dividend policies of a company: the **dividend payout** ratio and the **dividend yield.** The dividend payout is the ratio of the common dividends per share to the earnings per share:

$$\text{Dividend payout ratio} = \frac{\text{Common dividends per share}}{\text{Earnings per share}}$$

Exhibit 19–2 indicates that Samuelson paid $250,000 in common dividends each year, or with one million shares outstanding, $.25 per share. The two payout ratios are

19X9	19X8
$\dfrac{\$.25}{\$1.67} = 15.0\%$	$\dfrac{\$.25}{\$2.25} = 11.1\%$

Management of Samuelson was faced with an important financial policy decision in 19X9. Should the company maintain the same dividend of $.25 per share, even though EPS dropped significantly? Many companies prefer to maintain a level dividend pattern, hoping that a drop in earnings is only temporary.

The second dividend ratio of interest to stockholders is the yield ratio and is calculated as

$$\text{Dividend yield ratio} = \frac{\text{Common dividends per share}}{\text{Market price per share}}$$

The yield to Samuelson's stockholders would be

19X9	19X8
$\dfrac{\$.25}{\$15} = 1.7\%$	$\dfrac{\$.25}{\$18} = 1.4\%$

Samuelson common stock does not provide a high yield to its investors. The relationship between the dividends and the market price is an indication that investors buy the stock for reasons other than the periodic dividend return.

Summary

Financial statement analysis is an important tool for management use in the efficient control of operations. Management must understand the limitations in the use of the various techniques discussed in this chapter. "Rules of thumb" for the current ratio or any of the other ratios can be more harmful than helpful if not used properly. The calculation of a ratio and comparison with some industry standard is only a starting point. The term *analysis* implies something more—it requires the use of logical thinking to understand *why* a ratio has increased or decreased from the prior year.

Statement analysis often starts with a review of the most recent income statement and balance sheet. Horizontal analysis involves the comparison of the statements with one or more prior years. Vertical analysis requires the analyst to recast the statements into common size form. One item on the statement—for example, sales on the income statement—is set equal to 100%, and all other items are stated as a percentage of this base amount.

Three categories of ratios were discussed in the chapter. Liquidity ratios indicate the ability of the company to pay its debts as they are due. Solvency ratios deal with the company's long-term financial health, that is, the ability to repay long-term creditors. Finally, profitability ratios measure how well management has used the assets at its disposal to earn a return for the stockholders. The ratios are summarized in Exhibit 19–7.

EXHIBIT 19–7
Summary of Selected Ratios

Liquidity Analysis		Discussed on Page
Working capital	Current assets − Current liabilities	701
Current ratio	$\dfrac{\text{Current assets}}{\text{Current liabilities}}$	701
Acid-test ratio	$\dfrac{\text{Cash + Mkt. securities + Cur. receivables}}{\text{Current liabilities}}$	702
Accounts receivable turnover	$\dfrac{\text{Net credit sales}}{\text{Average accounts receivable}}$	703
Number days sales in receivables	$\dfrac{\text{Number of days in the period}}{\text{Accounts receivable turnover}}$	703
Inventory turnover	$\dfrac{\text{Cost of goods sold expense}}{\text{Average inventory}}$	705
Number days sales in inventory	$\dfrac{\text{Number of days in the period}}{\text{Inventory turnover}}$	705
Cash operating cycle	Number of days sales in inventory + Number of days sales in receivables	705

(continued)

Exhibit 19—7 (continued)

Solvency Analysis		Discussed on Page
Debt-to-equity ratio	$\dfrac{\text{Total liabilities}}{\text{Total stockholders' equity}}$	706
Times interest earned	$\dfrac{\text{Income before interest and taxes}}{\text{Interest expense}}$	707
Debt service coverage	$\dfrac{\text{Income before interest, taxes, and noncash adjustments}}{\text{Interest and principal payments}}$	707

Profitability Analysis		
Profit margin	$\dfrac{\text{Net income}}{\text{Net sales}}$	700
Return on assets	$\dfrac{\text{Net income} + \text{Interest expense, net of tax}}{\text{Average total assets}}$	708
Return on sales	$\dfrac{\text{Net income} + \text{Interest expense, net of tax}}{\text{Net sales}}$	709
Asset turnover	$\dfrac{\text{Net sales}}{\text{Average total assets}}$	709
Return on common stockholders' equity	$\dfrac{\text{Net income} - \text{Preferred dividends}}{\text{Average common stockholders' equity}}$	710
Leverage factor	$\dfrac{\text{Average total assets}}{\text{Average common stockholders' equity}}$	713
Earnings per share (simple)	$\dfrac{\text{Net income} - \text{Preferred dividends}}{\text{Number of common shares outstanding}}$	713
Price/earnings ratio	$\dfrac{\text{Current market price}}{\text{Earnings per share}}$	715
Dividend payout ratio	$\dfrac{\text{Common dividends per share}}{\text{Earnings per share}}$	716
Dividend yield ratio	$\dfrac{\text{Common dividends per share}}{\text{Market price per share}}$	716

Some of the ratios discussed in the chapter are only useful in analyzing product-oriented companies. The inventory turnover ratio, for example, would not be relevant to a service-oriented company. Companies providing a service rather than a product find it useful to develop ratios specific to their business. For example, an airline might calculate the ratio of revenue to total miles flown. Although not a cure-all, ratio analysis can be a valuable tool for monitoring the performance of management. The techniques discussed in this chapter are an important aspect in the efficient control of operations.

Key Terms

Note: Refer to Exhibit 19–7 for a summary of the various ratios discussed in the chapter.

Horizontal analysis is a comparison of financial statement items over a series of years in order to detect trends in the data.

Leverage is the practice of using borrowed funds and amounts contributed by preferred stockholders in an attempt to earn an overall return that is higher than the cost of these funds.

Liquidity is a relative measure of the nearness to cash of the assets and liabilities.

Potentially dilutive securities are outstanding securities, such as convertible bonds and preferred stock, that have the potential of becoming common stock and decreasing earnings per share.

Profitability is a relative measure of how well management is using company resources to earn a return on the funds invested by the various groups.

Solvency is a relative measure of the ability of a company to remain in business over the long run.

Vertical analysis is a comparison of various financial statement items within a single period with the help of common-size statements.

Questions

Q19–1 Two companies are in the same industry. Company A uses the LIFO method of inventory valuation and company B uses FIFO. What difficulties will arise in comparing the two companies? Specifically, what financial statement ratios will need to be monitored in comparisons between the two companies?

Q19–2 You are told to compare the company's results for the year, as measured by various ratios, with one of the published surveys, arranged by industry classification. What are some of the difficulties that you need to be aware of when making comparisons with industry standards?

Q19–3 What types of problems does inflation cause in analyzing financial statements?

Q19–4 Explain the relationship between responsibility accounting and statement analysis. What department in an organization would normally have responsibility for the turnover of accounts receivable?

Q19–5 Distinguish between horizontal and vertical analysis. Why is the analysis of common-size statements called *vertical analysis?* Why is horizontal analysis sometimes called *trend analysis?*

Q19–6 A company experiences a 15% increase in sales over last year. However, the gross margin actually decreased by 5% from the prior year. What are some of the possible causes for an increase in sales but a decline in gross profit?

Q19–7 A company's total current assets have increased by 5% over last year. However, management is concerned over the composition of the current assets. Why is the composition of the current assets important?

Q19–8   Ratios were categorized in the chapter according to their use in performing three different types of analysis. What are the three types of ratios?

Q19–9   Describe the operating cycle for a manufacturing company. How would the cycle differ for a retailer?

Q19–10   What accounts for the *order* in which current assets are presented on a balance sheet?

Q19–11   A company has a current ratio at year end of 1.25 to 1 but an acid-test or quick ratio of only .65 to 1. How can this difference in the two ratios be explained? What are some of the concerns that you would have about this company?

Q19–12   Explain the basic concept underlying all turnover ratios. Why is it necessary in computing a turnover ratio to use an average in the denominator (for example, average inventory)?

Q19–13   Smith Company's accounts receivable turned over 9 times during the year. The credit department extends terms of 2/10, net 30 to all customers. Does the turnover ratio indicate any problems that management should investigate?

Q19–14   The turnover of inventory for the Ace Company has slowed down from 6 times per year to 4.5 times per year. What are some of the possible explanations for this decrease?

Q19–15   Explain the difference between the operating cycle of a retailer and a manufacturer? How do both of these differ from the operating cycle of a service company — for example, an airline?

Q19–16   According to the distinction made in the chapter, explain the difference between liquidity analysis and solvency analysis.

Q19–17   A friend tells you that the most appropriate way to assess solvency — that is, the ability of a company to stay in business over the long run — is by comparing total debt to total assets. Another friend says that solvency is measured by comparing total debt to total stockholders' equity. Which one is right?

Q19–18   The times interest earned ratio is computed by dividing income before interest and taxes by interest expense. Explain why the numerator is income *before* interest and taxes.

Q19–19   A company is in the process of negotiating with a bank for an additional long-term loan. Why will the bank be very interested in the company's debt service coverage ratio?

Q19–20   The rate of return on assets ratio is computed by dividing net income and interest expense, net of tax by average total assets. Why is the numerator net income and interest expense, net of tax, rather than just net income?

Q19–21   A company has a return on assets of 14% and a return on common stockholders' equity of 11%. The president of the company has asked you to explain the reason for this difference. Explain the cause of the difference and how the concept of financial leverage is involved.

Q19–22   Explain the concept of potentially dilutive securities as the term is used in the calculation of earnings per share.

Q19–23 What is meant by the "quality" of a company's earnings? Explain why the price/earn-
.ings ratio for a company may be an indication of the quality of earnings for that particular company.

Q19–24 Some ratios are more useful for management, whereas others are better suited to the
needs of outsiders, such as stockholders and bankers. Give an example of at least one
ratio primarily suited to management use and another more suited to use by outsiders.

Q19–25 Service-oriented companies have different needs in analyzing financial statements as
opposed to product-oriented companies. Explain why this is true. Give an example of
a ratio that is meaningless to a service business.

Exercises

 E19–1 **Common-size balance sheets.** Comparative balance sheets for the Bassett Company for the past two years are as follows:

	12/31/X2	12/31/X3
Cash	$ 20,000	$ 16,000
Accounts receivable	30,000	40,000
Inventory	50,000	30,000
Prepaid rent	12,000	18,000
Total current assets	$112,000	$104,000
Land	$150,000	$150,000
Plant and equipment	600,000	800,000
Accumulated depreciation	(60,000)	(130,000)
Total long-term assets	$690,000	$820,000
Total assets	$802,000	$924,000
Accounts payable	$ 20,000	$ 24,000
Income taxes payable	10,000	6,000
Short-term notes payable	50,000	70,000
Total current liabilities	$ 80,000	$100,000
Bonds payable	$200,000	$150,000
Common stock	$300,000	$400,000
Retained earnings	222,000	274,000
Total stockholders' equity	$522,000	$674,000
Total liabilities and stockholders' equity	$802,000	$924,000

Required: 1. Prepare common-size comparative balance sheets for the two years for the
Basset Company.
2. What observations can you make about the changes in the relative composition
of Bassett's accounts from the common-size balance sheets? Prepare a list of at
least five observations.

E19–2   Common-size comparative income statements. Income statements for the Astro Company for the past two years are presented below:

	(in thousands of dollars)	
	19X7	19X8
Sales revenue	$50,000	$60,000
Cost of goods sold	30,000	42,000
Gross profit	$20,000	$18,000
Selling, general, & administrative expense	5,000	9,000
Operating income	$15,000	$ 9,000
Interest expense	2,000	2,000
Net income before tax	$13,000	$ 7,000
Income tax expense	4,000	2,000
Net income	$ 9,000	$ 5,000

Required: 1. Prepare common-size comparative income statements for the two years for the Astro Company.
2. What observations can you make from the common-size statements? Prepare a list of at least four observations.

E19–3   Effect of transactions on working capital, current ratio, and quick ratio. The following account balances are taken from the records of the Connors Company:

Cash	$ 50,000
Marketable securities (short-term)	60,000
Accounts receivable	80,000
Inventory	100,000
Prepaid insurance	10,000
Accounts payable	75,000
Taxes payable	25,000
Salaries and wages payable	40,000
Short-term loans payable	60,000

Required: 1. Compute the following for the Connors Company:

a. Working capital
b. Current ratio
c. Acid-test or quick ratio

2. For each of the following transactions, indicate the effect each would have on working capital, the current ratio, and the quick ratio. Indicate an increase with an I, a decrease with a D, and no effect with a NE. Consider each transaction independently; that is, assume that it is the *only* transaction that takes place.

	Effect of transaction on:		
Transaction	**Working Capital**	**Current Ratio**	**Quick Ratio**
1. Purchased inventory on account for $20,000.			
2. Purchased inventory for cash, $15,000.			
3. Paid suppliers on account, $30,000.			
4. Received cash on account, $40,000.			
5. Paid insurance for next year, $20,000.			
6. Sales on account, $60,000.			
7. Repaid loans at bank, $25,000.			
8. Borrowed $40,000 at bank for 90 days.			
9. Declared and paid $45,000 cash dividend.			
10. Purchased $20,000 of marketable securities for cash.			
11. Paid $30,000 in salaries and wages.			
12. Accrued additional $15,000 in taxes.			

E19–4   **Accounts receivable analysis.** The following account balances are taken from the records of the Wings Travel Agency:

	12/31/X7	*12/31/X8*	*12/31/X9*
Accounts receivable	$80,000	$100,000	$150,000
		19X8	*19X9*
Credit sales		$540,000	$600,000

Wings extends credit terms requiring full payment in 60 days, with no discount for early payment.

Required: 1. Compute Wings' accounts receivable turnover ratio for 19X8 and 19X9.
2. Compute the number of days sales in receivables for 19X8 and 19X9. Assume 360 days in a year.
3. Comment on the efficiency of Wings' collection efforts over the two-year period.

E19–5   **Inventory analysis.** The following account balances are taken from the records of the Sunshine Company, a wholesaler of fresh fruits and vegetables:

	12/31/X7	*12/31/X8*	*12/31/X9*
Merchandise inventory	$120,000	$150,000	$200,000
		19X8	*19X9*
Cost of goods sold expense		$8,100,000	$7,000,000

Required: 1. Compute Sunshine's inventory turnover ratio for 19X8 and 19X9.
2. Compute the number of days sales in inventory for 19X8 and 19X9. Assume 360 days in a year.
3. Comment on your answers in 1 and 2 above relative to the company's management of inventory over the two years. What problems do you see in its management of inventory?

E19–6 **Solvency analysis.** The following information is available from the two most recent balance sheets and income statement of the White Company:

	12/31/X1	12/31/X2
Accounts payable	$ 50,000	$ 65,000
Accrued liabilities	35,000	25,000
Taxes payable	45,000	60,000
Short-term notes payable	75,000	0
Bonds payable due within next year	200,000	200,000
Total current liabilities	$ 405,000	$ 350,000
Bonds payable	$ 800,000	$ 600,000
Common stock, $10 par	$1,000,000	$1,000,000
Retained earnings	500,000	650,000
Total stockholders' equity	$1,500,000	$1,650,000
Total liabilities and stockholders' equity	$2,705,000	$2,600,000

	19X2
Sales revenue	$1,600,000
Cost of goods sold	950,000
Gross profit	$ 650,000
Selling, general, & administrative expenses	300,000
Operating income	$ 350,000
Interest expense	89,000
Net income before tax	$ 261,000
Income tax expense	111,000
Net income	$ 150,000

Other available information:

a. Short-term notes payable represent a 12-month loan that matured in November of 19X2. Interest of 12% was paid at maturity.

b. One million dollars of serial bonds were issued ten years earlier. The first series of $200,000 matures at the end of 19X2, with interest of 8% payable annually.

c. Included in selling, general, and administrative expense is $50,000 of depreciation expense.

Required: Compute the following for White Company.

1. The debt to equity ratio at 12/31/X1 and 12/31/X2.
2. The times interest earned ratio for 19X2.
3. The debt service coverage ratio for 19X2. Assume depreciation expense is the only noncash adjustment.
4. Comment on White's solvency at the end of 19X2. Do the times interest earned ratio and the debt service coverage ratio differ in terms of their indication of White's ability to pay its debts?

E19–7 **Return ratios and leverage.** The following selected data are taken from the financial statements of the Baxter Company:

Sales revenue	$ 650,000
Cost of goods sold	400,000
Gross profit	$ 250,000
Selling, general, & administrative expenses	100,000
Operating income	$ 150,000
Interest expense	50,000
Net income before tax	$ 100,000
Income tax expense 40%	40,000
Net income	$ 60,000

Accounts payable	$ 45,000
Accrued liabilities	70,000
Income taxes payable	10,000
Interest payable	25,000
Short-term loans payable	150,000
Total current liabilities	$ 300,000
Long-term bonds payable	$ 500,000
Preferred stock, 10%, $100 par	$ 250,000
Common stock, no par	600,000
Retained earnings	350,000
Total stockholders' equity	$1,200,000
Total liabilities and stockholders' equity	$2,000,000

Required:

1. Compute the following ratios for the Baxter Company:

   a. Return on sales

   b. Asset turnover (assume that total assets at the beginning of the year were $1,600,000)

   c. Return on assets

   d. Return on common stockholders' equity (assume that the only changes in stockholders' equity during the year were from the net income for the year and dividends on the preferred stock)

2. Comment on Baxter's use of leverage. Has it successfully employed leverage? Explain your answer.

E19–8 **Relationships among return on assets, return on sales, and asset turnover.** A company's return on assets is a function of its ability to turn over its investment (asset turnover) and earn a profit on each dollar of sales (return on sales). For each of the *independent* cases below, determine the missing amounts. Note: Assume in each case that the company has no interest expense; that is, net income is used as the definition of income in all calculations.

Case One:

Net income	$10,000
Net sales	80,000
Average total assets	60,000
Return on assets	?

Case Two:

Net income	$ 25,000
Average total assets	250,000
Return on sales	2%
Net sales	?

Case Three:

Average total assets	$80,000
Asset turnover	1.5 times
Return on sales	6%
Return on assets	?

Case Four:

Return on assets	10%
Net sales	$50,000
Asset turnover	1.25 times
Net income	?

Case Five:

Return on assets	15%
Net income	$20,000
Return on sales	5%
Average total assets	?

E19–9   **EPS, P/E ratio, and dividend ratios.** The stockholders' equity section of the balance sheet for Speedy Distributing Company at the end of 19X8 appears as follows:

8%, $100 par, Cumulative preferred stock, 200,000 shares authorized, 50,000 issued and outstanding	$ 5,000,000
Additional paid in capital on preferred stock	2,500,000
Common stock, $5 par, 500,000 shares authorized, 400,000 shares issued and outstanding	2,000,000
Additional paid-in capital on common stock	18,000,000
Retained earnings	37,500,000
Total stockholders' equity	$65,000,000

Net income for the year was $1,300,000. Dividends were declared and paid on the preferred shares during the year and a quarterly dividend of $.40 per share was declared and paid each quarter on the common shares. The closing market price for the common shares on 12/31/X8 was $24.75 per share.

Required: Compute the following ratios:

1. Earnings per share (common)
2. Price/earnings ratio
3. Dividend payout ratio
4. Dividend yield ratio

E19–10   **Earnings per share and extraordinary items.** The stockholders' equity section of the balance sheet for Sturdy Construction Company at the end of 19X2 follows:

9%, $10 par, Cumulative preferred stock, 500,000		
shares authorized, 200,000 issued and outstanding		$ 2,000,000
Additional paid in capital on preferred stock		7,500,000
Common stock, $1 par, 2,500,000 shares authorized,		
1,500,000 shares issued and outstanding		1,500,000
Additional paid in capital on common stock		21,000,000
Retained earnings		25,500,000
Total stockholders' equity		$57,500,000

The lower portion of the 19X2 income statement indicates:

Net income before tax		$9,750,000
Income tax expense (40%)		(3,900,000)
Net income before extraordinary items		$5,850,000
Extraordinary loss from flood	$(6,200,000)	
Less: related tax effect (40%)	2,480,000	(3,720,000)
Net income		$2,130,000

Required:
1. Compute earnings per share *before* extraordinary items. Assume dividends are declared and paid on the preferred shares.
2. Compute earnings per share (that is, after the extraordinary loss).
3. Which of the two EPS ratios is more useful to management? Explain your answer. Would your answer be different if the ratios were to be used by an outsider — for example, a potential stockholder? Why?

Problems

P19–11   **Goals for sales and return on assets.** The president of Dynamo Company is reviewing the operating results of the year just completed with his vice-presidents. Sales increased by 15% from the prior year to $60,000,000. Average total assets for the year were $40,000,000. Net income, after adding back interest expense, net of tax, was $5,000,000.

The president of the company is happy with the performance over the past year but is never satisfied with the status quo. He has set two specific goals for next year:

1. A 20% growth in sales and
2. A return on assets of 15%.

As evidence of his committment to these two goals, the president has stated his intention to increase the total asset base by 12.5% over the base for the year just completed.

Required:
1. For the year just completed, compute the following ratios:
   a. Return on sales
   b. Asset turnover
   c. Return on assets
2. Compute the necessary asset turnover for next year to achieve the president's goal of a 20% increase in sales.

3. Calculate the target income for next year in order to achieve the goal of a 15% return on total assets. Note: Assume that *income* is defined as net income plus interest, net of tax.

4. Based on your answers to 2 and 3 above, comment on the reasonableness of the president's goals. What must the company focus on to attain these goals?

P19–12   Trend analysis for The Quaker Oats Company. The Quaker Oats Company is a multinational company with principal interests in the production of grocery products and the manufacture of toys (through its Fisher-Price Division). Quaker's 1985 annual report includes financial statements for the years ended June 30, 1985, 1984, and 1983. The consolidated income statements and balance sheets from the report appear on pages 729–731. (The income statement goes beyond the "bottom line" to reflect per share information as well.)

Required: 1. Arrange on a piece of paper a worksheet with the following headings:

	Increase (Decrease) from:			
	1984 to 1985		1983 to 1984	
Income Statement Accounts	Dollars	Percent	Dollars	Percent

a. Complete the worksheet using each of the account titles on Quaker's income statement. Do not go any further on the statement than income from continuing operations.

b. What observations can you make from this horizontal analysis? What is your overall analysis of operations? Have they improved over the last three years?

2. Prepare a worksheet with the following headings:

	Increase (Decrease) from:			
	6/30/84 to 6/30/85		6/30/83 to 6/30/84	
Balance Sheet Accounts	Dollars	Percent	Dollars	Percent

a. Complete the worksheet using each of the account titles on Quaker's balance sheet.

b. What observations can you make from this horizontal analysis of Quaker's financial position over the last three years? Has the financial position of the company been improved? Are there any specific areas of concern?

P19–13   Common-size statements for The Quaker Oats Company. Refer to the financial statements for The Quaker Oats Company in P19–12.

Required: 1. Prepare common-size comparative income statements for the years ended June 30, 1985, and June 30, 1984.

2. What changes do you detect in the income statement relationships from 1984 to 1985?

3. Prepare common-size comparative balance sheets at June 30, 1984, and June 30, 1985.

4. What observations can you make about the changes in the relative composition of Quaker's assets from the common-size statements? What observations can be made about the changes in the relative composition of liabilities and owners' equity accounts?

Consolidated Statement of Income

Year Ended June 30	1985	1984	1983
Net Sales	**$3,520.1**	$3,344.1	$2,611.3
Cost of goods sold	**2,133.0**	2,073.1	1,576.3
Gross profit	**1,387.1**	1,271.0	1,035.0
Selling, general and administrative expenses	**1,038.3**	952.9	758.7
Interest expense—net	**52.5**	59.9	41.9
Other (income) expense	**3.6**	(1.9)	14.5
Income from Continuing Operations before Income Taxes	**292.7**	260.1	219.9
Provision for income taxes	**136.1**	121.4	100.6
Income from Continuing Operations	**156.6**	138.7	119.3
Discontinued Operations—			
(Loss) from operations—net of income taxes	**—**	—	(7.0)
(Loss) on disposal—net of income taxes	**—**	—	(55.5)
Total (Loss) from Discontinued Operations	**—**	—	(62.5)
Net Income	**156.6**	138.7	56.8
Preference dividends	**3.6**	3.9	4.1
Net Income Available for Common	**$ 153.0**	$ 134.8	$ 52.7
Per Common Share:			
Income from continuing operations	**$ 3.76**	$ 3.35	$ 2.91
(Loss) from discontinued operations	**—**	—	(.18)
(Loss) on disposal	**—**	—	(1.40)
Net Income	**$ 3.76**	$ 3.35	$ 1.33
Dividends declared	**$ 1.24**	$ 1.10	$ 1.00
Average Number of Common Shares Outstanding (in thousands)	**40,746**	40,206	39,504

See accompanying notes to consolidated financial statements.

Millions of Dollars

Consolidated Balance Sheet

Assets

June 30	1985	1984	1983
Current Assets:			
Cash and short-term bank deposits	$ 70.7	$ 60.1	$ 23.1
Marketable securities, at cost which approximates market value	17.0	5.0	2.9
Receivables—net of allowances	505.1	484.9	361.3
Inventories:			
Finished goods	251.6	232.7	176.1
Grain and materials	94.0	105.4	91.9
Supplies	28.9	18.5	18.1
Total inventories	374.5	356.6	286.1
Other current assets	45.2	32.3	88.0
Current assets	1,012.5	938.9	761.4
Other Receivables and Investments	10.8	22.2	23.1
Property, Plant and Equipment	1,082.4	1,073.3	906.2
Less accumulated depreciation	389.0	342.7	289.9
Properties—net	693.4	730.6	616.3
Intangible Assets, Net of Amortization	125.2	115.1	62.9
Total	$1,841.9	$1,806.8	$1,463.7

See accompanying notes to consolidated financial statements.

Millions of Dollars

Liabilities and Shareholders' Equity

June 30	1985	1984	1983
Current Liabilities:			
Short-term debt	$ 144.9	$ 214.3	$ 178.0
Current portion of long-term debt	23.1	2.8	12.2
Trade accounts payable	179.1	196.1	140.0
Accrued payrolls, pensions and bonuses	81.3	82.1	66.4
Accrued advertising and merchandising	50.6	48.8	30.6
Income taxes payable	50.0	11.9	18.4
Other current liabilities	82.8	66.1	53.9
Current liabilities	611.8	622.1	499.5
Long-Term Debt	168.2	200.1	152.8
Other Liabilities	59.9	62.1	21.0
Deferred Income Taxes	177.2	163.9	109.7
Redeemable Preference Stock,			
without par value. $100 stated value.			
$9.56 cumulative	37.9	38.5	41.3
Common Shareholders' Equity:			
Common stock, $5 par value, issued 41,994,698 shares;			
20,997,349 shares; and 20,997,349 shares, respectively	210.0	105.0	105.0
Additional paid-in capital	3.4	26.3	23.1
Reinvested earnings	728.4	703.2	612.8
Cumulative exchange adjustment	(103.2)	(89.9)	(68.2)
Treasury common stock, at cost	(51.7)	(24.5)	(33.3)
Common shareholders' equity	786.9	720.1	639.4
Total	$1,841.9	$1,806.8	$1,463.7

P19–14   **Ratio analysis for The Quaker Oats Company.** Refer to the financial statements for The Quaker Oats Company in P19–12.

Required: 1. Compute the following ratios and other amounts for each of the two years, 1984 and 1985. Wherever appropriate, use average balances in your calculations. Assume an average tax rate of 46% and 360 days to a year. Round all ratios to the nearest one-tenth of a percent.

    a. Working capital
    b. Current ratio
    c. Acid-test ratio
    d. Number days sales in receivables
    e. Number days sales in inventory
    f. Cash operating cycle (in days)
    g. Debt-to-equity ratio
    h. Times interest earned
    i. Asset turnover
    j. Return on sales (use net income available for common)
    k. Return on assets
    l. Leverage factor
    m. Return on common stockholders' equity

    2. What is your overall analysis of the financial health of The Quaker Oats Company? What do you feel are the strengths and weaknesses of the company?

P19–15   **Goals for sales and income growth.** The Riverside Corp. is a major regional retailer. The chief executive officer (CEO) is concerned with the slow growth of both sales and net income and the subsequent effect on the trading price of the common stock. Selected financial data for the past three years are presented below.

RIVERSIDE CORP.
(in millions of dollars)

	19X6	19X7	19X8
1. Sales	$187.0	$192.5	$200.0
2. Net income	5.6	5.8	6.0
3. Dividends declared and paid	2.5	2.5	2.5
December 31 balances:			
4. Owners' equity	63.2	66.5	70.0
5. Debt	30.3	29.8	30.0
Selected year-end financial ratios:			
Net income to sales	3.0%	3.0%	3.0%
Asset turnover	2 times	2 times	2 times
6. Return on owners' equity	8.9%	8.7%	8.6%
7. Debt to total assets	32.4%	30.9%	30.0%

The CEO believes that the price of the stock has been adversely affected by the downward trend of the return on equity, the relatively low dividend payout ratio, and the lack of dividend increases. In order to improve the price of the stock, he wants to improve the return on equity and dividends.

He believes that the company should be able to meet these objectives by

1. Increasing sales and net income at an annual rate of 10% a year and
2. Establishing a new dividend policy that calls for a dividend payout of 50% of earnings or $3,000,000, whichever is greater.

The 10% annual sales increase will be accomplished through a new promotional program. He believes that the present net income to sales ratio of 3% will be unchanged by the cost of this new program and any interest paid on new debt. He expects that the company can accomplish this sales and income growth while maintaining the current relationship of total assets to sales. Any capital needed to maintain this relationship that is not generated internally would be acquired through long-term debt financing. The CEO hopes that debt would not exceed 35% of total liabilities and owners' equity.

Required:

1. Using the CEO's program, prepare a schedule that shows the appropriate data for the years 19X9, 19X0, and 19X1 for the items numbered 1 through 7 on the schedule presented with the problem.
2. Can the CEO meet all his requirements if a 10% per year growth in income and sales is achieved? Explain your answer.
3. What alternative actions should the CEO consider in order to improve the return on equity and support increased dividend payments?
4. Explain the reasons that the CEO might have for wanting to limit debt to 35% of total liabilities and owners' equity.

(CMA Adapted)

P19–16 **Basic financial ratios.** The accounting staff of CCB Enterprises has completed the preparation of financial statements for the 19X3 calendar year. The Statement of Income for the current year and the Comparative Statement of Financial Position for 19X3 and 19X2 follow.

CCB ENTERPRISES
Statement of Income
Year Ended December 31, 19X3
($000 omitted)

Revenue:	
Net Sales	$800,000
Other	60,000
Total revenue	$860,000
Expenses:	
Cost of goods sold	$540,000
Research and development	25,000
Selling and administrative	155,000
Interest	20,000
Total expenses	$740,000
Income before income taxes	$120,000
Income taxes	48,000
Net income	$ 72,000

CCB ENTERPRISES
Comparative Statement of Financial Position
December 31, 19X3 and 19X2
($000 omitted)

Assets	19X3	19X2
Current assets:		
Cash and short-term investments	$ 26,000	$ 21,000
Receivables, less allowance for doubtful accounts		
($1,100 in 19X3 and $1,400 in 19X2)	48,000	50,000
Inventories, at lower of FIFO cost or market	65,000	62,000
Prepaid items and other current assets	5,000	3,000
Total current assets	$144,000	$136,000
Other assets:		
Investments, at cost	$106,000	$106,000
Deposits	10,000	8,000
Total other assets	$116,000	$114,000
Property, plant, and equipment:		
Land	$ 12,000	$ 12,000
Buildings and equipment, less accumulated		
depreciation ($126,000 in 19X3 and		
$122,000 in 19X2)	268,000	248,000
Total property, plant, and equipment	$280,000	$260,000
Total assets	$540,000	$510,000

Liabilities and Stockholders' Equity	19X3	19X2
Current liabilities:		
Short-term loans	$ 22,000	$ 24,000
Accounts payable	72,000	71,000
Salaries, wages, and other	26,000	27,000
Total current liabilities	$120,000	$122,000
Long-term debt:	160,000	171,000
Total liabilities	$280,000	$293,000
Stockholders' equity:		
Common stock, at par	$ 44,000	$ 42,000
Paid-in capital in excess of par	64,000	61,000
Total paid-in capital	$108,000	$103,000
Retained earnings	152,000	114,000
Total stockholders' equity	$260,000	$217,000
Total liabilities and stockholders' equity	$540,000	$510,000

Required: 1. Calculate the following financial ratios for 19X3 for CCB Enterprises:

a. Times interest earned

b. Return on total assets

c. Return on common stockholders' equity

d. Debt/equity ratio (at 12/31/X3)

e. Current ratio (at 12/31/X3)

f. Quick (acid test) ratio (at 12/31/X3)

g. Accounts receivable turnover ratio (assume that all sales are on credit)

h. Number of days sales in receivables
i. Inventory turnover ratio (assume all purchases are on credit)
j. Number of days sales in inventory
k. Number of days in cash operating cycle

2. Prepare a few brief comments on the overall financial health of CCB Enterprises. For each comment, indicate any other information not provided in the problem that you would need to fully evaluate the company's financial health.

(CMA Adapted)

P19–17 **Ratio analysis for acquisition decision.** Diversified Industries is a large conglomerate and is continually in the market for new acquisitions. The company has grown rapidly over the last ten years through buy outs of medium-size companies. Diversified does not limit itself to companies in any one industry, but rather looks for firms with a sound financial base and the ability to stand on their own financially.

The president of Diversified recently told a meeting of the officers of the company: "There are two points I want to impress on all of you. First, we are not in the business of looking for bargains. Diversified has achieved success in the past by acquiring companies with the ability to be a permanent member of the corporate family. We don't want companies that may appear to be a bargain on paper, but can't survive in the long run. Second, a new member of our family must be able to come in and make it on its own—the parent is not organized to be a funding agency for struggling subsidiaries."

Pete Jackson is vice-president of acquisitions for Diversified, a position that he has held for the past five years. Jackson relies heavily on basic financial statement analysis in making recommendations to the board of directors on potential acquisitions. One of his assistants, Ralph Williams, recently brought him a set of financial statements for a manufacturer, Heavy Duty Tractors. Williams feels that Heavy Duty is a "can't miss" opportunity for Diversified and asks Jackson to consider recommending that the company put in an offer for Heavy Duty. The most recent income statement and comparative balance sheets for the company follow.

HEAVY DUTY TRACTORS, INC.
Statement of Income and Retained Earnings
For the Year Ended December 31, 19X2
($000 omitted)

Sales revenue	$875,250
Cost of goods sold	542,750
Gross margin	$332,500
Selling, general, and administrative expenses	264,360
Operating income	$ 68,140
Interest expense	45,000
Net income before taxes and extraordinary items	$ 23,140
Income tax expense	9,250
Income before extraordinary items	$ 13,890
Extraordinary gain, less taxes of $6,000	9,000
Net income	$ 22,890
Retained earnings, January 1, 19X2	169,820
	$192,710
Dividends paid on common stock	10,000
Retained earnings, December 31, 19X2	$182,710

HEAVY DUTY TRACTORS, INC.
Comparative Statements of Financial Position
($000 omitted)

Assets	12/31/X2	12/31/X1
Current assets:		
Cash	$ 48,500	$ 24,980
Marketable securities, at lower of cost or market	3,750	0
Accounts receivable, net of allowances	128,420	84,120
Inventories	135,850	96,780
Prepaid items	7,600	9,300
Total current assets	$324,120	$215,180
Long-term investments	$ 55,890	$ 55,890
Property, plant, and equipment:		
Land	$ 45,000	$ 45,000
Buildings and equipment, less accumulated depreciation of $385,000 in 19X2 and $325,000 in 19X1	545,000	605,000
Total property, plant and equipment	$590,000	$650,000
Total assets	$970,010	$921,070

Liabilities and Stockholders' Equity	12/31/X2	12/31/X1
Current liabilities:		
Short-term notes	$ 80,000	$ 60,000
Accounts payable	65,350	48,760
Salaries and wages payable	14,360	13,840
Income taxes payable	2,590	3,650
Total current liabilities	$162,300	$126,250
Long-term bonds payable, due 19X9	$275,000	$275,000
Stockholders' equity:		
Common stock, no par	$350,000	$350,000
Retained earnings	182,710	169,820
Total stockholders' equity	$532,710	$519,820
Total liabilities and stockholders' equity	$970,010	$921,070

Required:

1. How liquid is Heavy Duty Tractors? Support your answer with any ratios that you feel are necessary to justify your conclusion. Also indicate any other information that you would want to have in making a final determination on its liquidity.

2. In light of the president's comments, should Jackson be concerned about the solvency of Heavy Duty Tractors? Support your answer with the necessary ratios. How does the maturity date of the outstanding debt affect your answer?

3. Has Heavy Duty demonstrated the ability to be a profitable member of the Diversified family? Support your answer.

P19–18   **Projected results to meet corporate objectives.** Tablon Inc. is a wholly owned subsidiary of Marbel Co. The philosophy of Marbel's management is to allow the subsidiaries to operate as independent units. Corporate control is exercised through the establishment of minimum objectives for each subsidiary accompanied by substantial rewards for success and penalties for failure. The time period for performance review is long enough for competent managers to display their abilities.

Each quarter the subsidiary is required to submit financial statements. The statements are accompanied by a letter from the subsidiary president explaining the results-to-date, a forecast for the remainder of the year, and the actions to be taken to achieve the objectives if the forecast indicates that the objectives will not be met.

The Marbel management in conjunction with Tablon management had set the objectives listed below for the year ending May 31, 19X0. These objectives are similar to those set in prior years.

Sales growth of 20%.
Return on stockholders' equity of 15%.
A long-term debt to equity ratio of not more than 1.00.
Payment of a cash dividend of 50% of net income, with a minimum payment of at least $400,000.

Tablon's controller has just completed preparing the financial statements for the six months ended November 30, 19X9, and the forecast for the year ending May 31, 19X0. The statements are presented below.

After a cursory glance at the financial statements Tablon's president concluded that all objectives would not be met. At a staff meeting of the Tablon management the president asked the controller to review the projected results and recommend possible actions that could be taken during the remainder of the year that would enable Tablon more nearly to meet the objectives.

TABLON INC.
Income Statement
($000 omitted)

	Year Ended May 31, 19X9	Six Months Ended Nov. 30, 19X9	Forecast for Year Ending May 31, 19X0
Sales	$25,000	$15,000	$30,000
Cost of goods sold	$13,000	$ 8,000	$16,000
Selling expenses	5,000	3,500	7,000
Administrative expenses and interest	4,000	2,500	5,000
Income taxes (40%)	1,200	400	800
Total expenses and taxes	$23,200	$14,400	$28,800
Net income	$ 1,800	$ 600	$ 1,200
Dividends declared and paid	600	0	600
Income retained	$ 1,200	$ 600	$ 600

TABLON INC.
Statement of Financial Position
($000 omitted)

Assets	May 31, 19X9	Nov. 30, 19X9	Forecast for May 31, 19X0
Cash	$ 400	$ 500	$ 500
Accounts receivable (net)	4,100	6,500	7,100
Inventory	7,000	8,500	8,600
Plant and equipment (net)	6,500	7,000	7,300
Total assets	$18,000	$22,500	$23,500
Liabilities and Equities			
Accounts payable	$ 3,000	$ 4,000	$ 4,000
Accrued taxes	300	200	200
Long-term borrowing	6,000	9,000	10,000
Common stock	5,000	5,000	5,000
Retained earnings	3,700	4,300	4,300
Total liabilities and equities	$18,000	$22,500	$23,500

Required:

1. Calculate the projected results for each of the four objectives established for Tablon Inc. State which results will not meet the objectives by year-end.
2. From the data presented, identify the factors that seem to contribute to the failure of Tablon Inc. to meet all of its objectives.
3. Explain the possible actions that the controller could recommend in response to the president's request.

(CMA Adapted)

P19–19 **Comparison with industry averages.** Hackney, Inc. is a medium-size company that has been in business for twenty years. The industry has become very competitive in the last few years, and Hackney has decided that it must grow if it is going to survive. It has approached the bank for a sizable five-year loan, and the bank has requested its most recent financial statements as part of the loan package.

The industry in which Hackney operates consists of approximately twenty companies relatively equal in size. The trade association to which all of the competitors belong publishes an annual survey of the industry, including industry averages for selected ratios for the competitors. All the companies voluntarily submit their statements to the association for this purpose.

The controller of Hackney is aware that the bank has access to this survey and is very concerned about how the company fared this past year compared with the rest of the industry. The ratios included in the publication, and the averages for the past year, are as follows:

Ratio	Industry average
Current ratio	1.23
Acid-test (quick) ratio	.75
Accounts receivable turnover	33 times
Inventory turnover	29 times
Debt-to-equity ratio	.53

Ratio	Industry average
Times interest earned	8.65 times
Return on sales	6.57%
Asset turnover	1.95 times
Return on assets	12.81%
Return on common stockholders' equity	17.67%

The financial statements to be submitted to the bank in connection with the loan follow.

HACKNEY, INC.
Statement of Income and Retained Earnings
For the Year Ended December 31, 19X2
($000 omitted)

Sales revenue	$542,750
Cost of goods sold	(435,650)
Gross margin	$107,100
Selling, general, and administrative expenses	$ (65,780)
Loss on sales of securities	(220)
Income before interest and taxes	$ 41,100
Interest expense	(9,275)
Net income before taxes	$ 31,825
Income tax expense	(12,730)
Net income	$ 19,095
Retained earning, January 1, 19X2	58,485
	$ 77,580
Dividends paid on common stock	(12,000)
Retained earnings, December 31, 19X2	$ 65,580

HACKNEY, INC.
Comparative Statements of Financial Position
($000 omitted)

Assets	12/31/X2	12/31/X1
Current assets:		
Cash	$ 1,135	$ 750
Marketable securities, at lower of cost or market	1,250	2,250
Accounts receivable, net of allowances	15,650	12,380
Inventories	12,680	15,870
Prepaid items	385	420
Total current assets	$ 31,100	$ 31,670
Long-term investments	$ 425	$ 425
Property, plant and equipment:		
Land	$ 32,000	$ 32,000
Buildings and equipment, net of accumulated depreciation	216,000	206,000
Total property, plant and equipment	$248,000	$238,000
Total assets	$279,525	$270,095

Liabilities and Stockholders' Equity	12/31/X2	12/31/X1
Current liabilities:		
Short-term notes	$ 8,750	$ 12,750
Accounts payable	20,090	14,380
Salaries and wages payable	1,975	2,430
Income taxes payable	3,130	2,050
Total current liabilities	$ 33,945	$ 31,610
Long-term bonds payable	$ 80,000	$ 80,000
Stockholders' equity:		
Common stock, no par	$100,000	$100,000
Retained earnings	65,580	58,485
Total stockholders' equity	$165,580	$158,485
Total liabilities and stockholders' equity	$279,525	$270,095

Required:

1. Prepare a columnar report for the controller of Hackney, Inc. comparing the industry averages for the ratios published by the trade association with the comparable ratios for Hackney. For Hackney, compute the ratios as of 12/31/X2 or for the year 12/31/X2, whichever is appropriate.
2. Briefly evaluate Hackney's ratios relative to the industry.
3. Do you think that the bank will approve the loan? Explain your answer.

P19-20   **Statement analysis for loan extension.** Warford Corporation was formed five years ago through a public subscription of common stock. Lucinda Street, who owns 15% of the common stock, was one of the organizers of Warford and is its current president. The company has been successful but currently is experiencing a shortage of funds. On June 10 Street approached the Bell National Bank, asking for a 24-month extension on two $30,000 notes, which are due on June 30, 19X0, and September 30, 19X0. Another note of $7,000 is due on December 31, 19X0, but she expects no difficulty in paying this note on its due date. Street explained that Warford's cash flow problems are due primarily to the company's desire to finance a $300,000 plant expansion over the next two fiscal years through internally generated funds.

The commercial loan officer of Bell National Bank requested financial reports for the last two fiscal years. These reports are reproduced below.

WARFORD CORPORATION
Income Statement
For the Fiscal Years Ended March 31

	19X9	19X0
Sales	$2,700,000	$3,000,000
Cost of goods sold[a]	1,720,000	1,902,500
Gross margin	$ 980,000	$1,097,500
Operating expenses	780,000	845,000
Net income before taxes	$ 200,000	$ 252,500
Income taxes (40%)	80,000	101,000
Income after taxes	$ 120,000	$ 151,500

[a]Depreciation charges on the plant and equipment of $100,000 and $102,500 for fiscal years ended March 31, 19X9, and 19X0, respectively, are included in cost of goods sold.

WARFORD CORPORATION
Statement of Financial Position
March 31

	19X9	19X0
Assets:		
Cash	$ 12,500	$ 16,400
Notes receivable	104,000	112,000
Accounts receivable (net)	68,500	81,600
Inventories (at cost)	50,000	80,000
Plant & equipment (net of depreciation)	646,000	680,000
Total assets	$881,000	$970,000

	19X9	19X0
Liabilities and owners' equity:		
Accounts payable	$ 72,000	$ 69,000
Notes payable	54,500	67,000
Accrued liabilities	6,000	9,000
Common stock (60,000 shares, $10 par)	600,000	600,000
Retained earnings[b]	148,500	225,000
Total liabilities and owners' equity	$881,000	$970,000

[b]Cash dividends were paid at the rate of $1.00 per share in fiscal year 19X9 and $1.25 per share in fiscal year 19X0.

Required:

1. Calculate the following items for Warford Corporation:
   a. Current ratio at March 31, 19X9, and 19X0.
   b. Acid-test (quick) ratio at March 31, 19X9, and 19X0.
   c. Inventory turnover for fiscal year 19X0.
   d. Return on assets for fiscal years 19X9 and 19X0.
   e. Percentage change in sales, cost of goods sold, gross margin, and net income after taxes from fiscal year 19X9 to 19X0.
2. Identify and explain what other financial reports and/or financial analyses might be helpful to the commercial loan officer of Bell National Bank in evaluating Street's request for a time extension on Warford's notes.
3. Assume that the percentage changes experienced in fiscal year 19X0 as compared with fiscal year 19X9 for sales, cost of goods sold, gross margin, and net income after taxes will be repeated in each of the next two years. Is Warford's desire to finance the plant expansion from internally generated funds realistic? Explain your answer.
4. Should Bell National Bank grant the extension on Warford's notes considering Street's statement about financing the plant expansion through internally generated funds? Explain your answer.

(CMA Adapted)

Index